The Encyclopedia of

GHOSTS
AND
SPIRITS

The Encyclopedia of
GHOSTS
AND
SPIRITS

Rosemary Ellen Guiley

Facts On File

The Encyclopedia of Ghosts and Spirits

Facts On File, Inc.
460 Park Avenue South
New York NY 10016
USA

Library of Congress Cataloging-in-Publication Data
Guiley, Rosemary.
The encyclopedia of ghosts and spirits / Rosemary Ellen Guiley.
p.   cm.
Includes bibliographical references and index.
ISBN 0-8160-2140-6 (alk. paper)
1. Ghosts.   2. Spirits.   3. Parapsychology.   I. Title.
BF1461.G85   1992
133.1'03—dc20   91-37427

ISBN (hardcover) 0-8160-2140-6

ISBN (paperbound) 0-8160-2846-X

A British CIP catalogue record for this book is available from the British Library.

Facts On File books are available at special discounts when purchased in bulk quantities for businesses, associations, institutions or sales promotions. Please call our Special Sales Department in New York at 212/683-2244 (dial 800/322-8755 except in NY, AK or HI) or in Oxford at 865/728399.

Jacket design by Elaine Tannenbaum
Composition and manufacturing by the Maple-Vail Book Manufacturing Group
Printed in the United States of America

10 9 8 7 6 5 4 3 2

This book is printed on acid-free paper.

For Joanne P. Austin

CONTENTS

ACKNOWLEDGMENTS

I am deeply indebted to the following persons for their contributions to the research and writing of this book: to Joanne P. Austin, to whom this volume is dedicated, an indefatigable researcher and author who has contributed to this and other books of mine; to James G. Matlock, who served as editorial advisor, and whose invaluable expertise in parapsychology and anthropology helped shape the contents and perspective; to Tom Perrott, chairman of the Ghost Club, London, who also served as editorial advisor on some U.K. material and opened doors to many resources; and to Margaret Lee Guiley, Linda Lee and Dorothy Kroll, who assisted in the research.

I would also like to thank others who gave interviews and/or provided research assistance: Dale Kaczmarek, president of the Ghost Research Society; Howard E. Heim, research director of the Ghost Research Society; Graham Wyley, "Britain's number one ghostbuster"; Maurice Schwalm, writer and psychic investigator; Michaeleen Maher, parapsychologist; Andrew M. Green, psychical researcher; Vincent Hillyer, investigator of the paranormal; and Jeanne K. Youngson, founder and president of the International Society for the Study of Ghosts and Apparitions.

Finally, and perhaps most important, I would like to thank Kate Kelly, who came up with the idea for this book and brought forces into motion to make it reality.

A

Academy of Religion and Psychical Research, The See SPIRITUAL FRONTIERS FELLOWSHIP.

acheri In Indian lore, the ghost of a little girl who brings disease, especially to children. The ghost lives on mountaintops and comes into valleys during the night for revelry and to spread disease by casting its shadow over victims. Children are protected from the *acheri* with amulets of red thread tied around their necks. Similarly, in European lore, red charms protect against bewitchment and harm from evil spirits and witches.

Adelphi Theatre London theater said to be haunted by the ghost of William Terriss, a popular Victorian actor who was murdered there by a jealous rival.

The murder occurred on December 16, 1897, during the run of *Secret Service*, a thriller starring Terriss and his mistress and leading lady, Jessie Milward. Also in the production in a minor role was actor Richard Arbor Prince, who apparently harbored a great jealousy and growing hatred of Terriss. Finally, Prince went out and bought a dagger, intending to kill Terriss.

Early in the evening of the fateful date, Prince ambushed Terriss as the leading man unlocked the Adelphi stage door in Maiden Lane. Terriss expired dramatically in Milward's arms, whispering, "I'll be back." Prince was tried and convicted of murder but was found insane. He spent the rest of his days at an institution for the criminally insane. He died in 1937 at age 71.

The presence of Terriss's ghost was not reported until 1928. A stranger in town, who did not know about Terriss's murder, saw a male figure dressed in gray Victorian clothes in Maiden Lane. The figure vanished suddenly, and the witness concluded he had seen a ghost. He later identified the figure as Terriss from a photograph.

Also in 1928, poltergeist phenomena manifested in the dressing room once used by Milward. A leading comedy actress known as June felt light blows on her arms, a sensation of being grasped, and the inexplicable shaking of her chaise longue. She also witnessed a greenish light above her mirror, and heard two taps that seemed to come from behind it. Later she learned that Terriss had been in the habit of tapping Milward's dressing room door twice with his cane whenever he passed it.

In 1956, Terriss's ghost was reportedly drifting around the Covent Garden Underground Station, dressed in a gray suit, old-fashioned collar and white gloves. The ghost frightened witnesses. A Spiritualist held a seance at the station and produced a sketch that bore a remarkable resemblance to a photograph of Terriss.

The greenish light was reported as late as 1962, when night workmen saw it take the shape of a man and float across the stage. The ghostly figure opened the stage curtains and then proceeded into the stalls, tipping the seats as it went.

See also THEATRE ROYAL.

Further reading:
Brooks, J.A. *Ghosts of London: The West End, South and West.* Norwich, England: Jarrold Colour Publications, 1982.
Underwood, Peter. *Haunted London.* London: George G. Harrup & Co., 1973.

afrit In Arabian mythology, a terrible and dangerous demon, the spirit of a murdered man who seeks to avenge his death. The demon is believed to rise up like smoke from the victim's blood that falls on the ground. Its formation can be prevented by driving a new nail into the blood-stained ground.

Compare to VAMPIRE.

afterlife Almost every society known has some belief in SURVIVAL AFTER DEATH and what happens to people when they die, although these beliefs vary enormously. The basic possibilities include a continuation of life with little change in the nature or quality of existence; a series of lives and deaths before ulti-

1

A soul being carried away by Death. Drawn by George Cruik-shank.

mate extinction; moral improvement through a series of stages, levels, or "planes"; and bodily resurrection at some future date. Alongside the idea of a future life one often finds beliefs in REINCARNATION, a return to earth life in successive bodies.

Christian ideas about the afterlife include a judgment upon death and an assignment to either Heaven or Hell, depending on one's merit leading to an indefinite period of existence in a discarnate state that is followed by a resurrection in the body at the time of the second coming of Christ, which is also to be the end of the world. Christian ideas heavily influenced 19th-century SPIRITUALISM, although Spiritualist authors, such as Andrew Jackson DAVIS, mainly elaborated what it was like during the intermediary state. According to Davis, who dictated his lectures in trance, after death human beings continue their spiritual progress through a series of celestial spheres, until they reach the seventh sphere and become one with "the Infinite Vortex of Love and Wisdom and the great Spiritual Sun of the Divine Mind."

Most "primitive" or tribal societies also have beliefs about what happens to people when they die, although the conception of an afterlife is not always formulated clearly. Sometimes there is a vague belief in continued existence, with little interest or concern in the nature of this existence. In other societies, the afterlife is believed to be structured very similarly to life on earth: there is the same type of social organization, and there is plenty. It was images like this that led to the portrayal of a "Happy Hunting Ground" as the idea of the Native American afterlife. In some societies, existence is believed to continue much in the way as on earth, but in reverse. In communicat-

ing with the dead, one says and does the opposite of what one means.

The Land of the Dead is not always located in the heavens. Perhaps even more often, it is located under the earth. The Zulus believe in an underworld, where mountains and rivers and all things are as above. The dead live in villages, and milk their cattle, which are the spirits of the cattle which have been killed on earth. Or again, the dead may live on the mountain or in the valley on the surface of the earth. One European in Borneo managed to get native guides to take him to the summit of the mountain said to be the region of the spirits. He was shown the moss on which the spirits fed and footprints of the ghostly buffaloes which followed them, but his guides refused to spend the night there (see also KACHINAS; MOON).

Typically, in tribal societies, knowledge of the afterlife is said to have been gained from the experiences of shamans, whose primary function is to act as an intermediary between the living and the dead. Shamans may travel to the Land of the Dead in search of souls that have had difficulty getting back to their bodies, either through accident or illness (see SOUL LOSS). Not infrequently, shamanic teachings are supplemented by accounts of NEAR-DEATH EXPERIENCES, in which regular people have their own visionary experiences of the afterlife.

Spiritualism and the animistic belief of tribal societies have in common the beliefs in the possibility of communication between the living and the dead. In animism, ideas about the soul are fairly complicated and vary a great deal from one place to another. Many societies distinguish between the ghost, or the spirit proper (which travels to the land of the dead), and a different part of the spirit, which reincarnates. The ghost part of the spirit is believed to be particularly strong before the main spirit has begun its trip to the Land of the Dead, which may not begin until three or four days after death, and therefore various things are done to faciliate the departure and to discourage the ghost from returning to plague the living (see FUNERAL RITES AND CUSTOMS).

The spirits of ancestors may return at special occasions such as after death, however, and on these occasions they are no longer so dangerous (see FEASTS AND FESTIVALS OF THE DEAD). The GHOST DANCE was a special type of Native American festival, in which it was believed that the spirits of the dead would return to lead the way back to the life they had led before the coming of the white man.

Further reading:
Brown, Slater. *The Heyday of Spiritualism*. New York: Hawthorn Books, 1970.

Eliade, Mircea. *Shamanism: Archaic Techniques of Ecstasy.* Princeton: Princeton University Press, 1964.

Kung, Hans. *Eternal Life? Life After Death as a Medical, Philosophical, and Theological Problem.* New York: Doubleday, 1984.

Tylor, Edward Burnett. *Religion in Primitive Culture.* New York: Harper and Row, 1956.

Alcatraz   The harshest, loneliest and most dismal of America's federal prisons, located on a damp rock of an island in San Francisco Bay, is said to be haunted by sounds that seem to be connected to inmates and violence of the past.

Alcatraz, originally named La Isla de Los Altraces (The Island of the Pelicans), was first an Army fort and prison. In 1934 it was turned into a federal penitentiary. The toughest convicts were interred there solely for punishment, not for rehabilitation. Conditions were brutal and escape virtually impossible. The prison was closed in 1963 and is now a tourist attraction.

Al Capone was one of the first famous inmates there. After five years at "the Rock," as Alcatraz was called, he went insane, due in part to his incarceration and in part to his condition of advanced syphilis.

Insanity was the kindest fate to befall a prisoner—others committed suicide, murdered one another, mutilated themselves (one chopped off the fingers of one hand with an axe), or died unpleasant deaths from illness and disease. Beatings by guards were routine, and the screams of the beaten reverberated throughout the cells. Prisoners were shot trying to scale the walls. In 1946, six inmates attempted to break out of the prison. In the ensuing bloodshed, three guards were killed and three of the six would-be escapees were shot to death; many others were wounded.

Little besides the sounds of violence was heard at Alcatraz, for prisoners were forbidden to talk, except for three minutes twice a day during recreation and two hours on weekends. Capone, whose life was constantly threatened by other inmates, kept largely to himself and spent his time playing his banjo in his cell or in the shower (showers were granted to inmates once a week). Capone joined a four-man band whose members included "Machine Gun" Kelly.

The most notorious cells were four solitary cells called "holes" in Block D, numbered 11, 12, 13 and 14. In solitary confinement, a prisoner was stripped of clothing, beaten, and shut up in complete darkness in one of the tiny cement cells with only a hole in the floor for a bathroom. He was fed bread and water twice a day, and given one full meal every third day. The holes were notorious for breaking men, either through insanity, illness or death. Capone was thrown into a hole on three occasions. Another inmate, Rufe McCain, was confined to 14-D for three years and two months as punishment for attempting to escape in 1939. Upon his release, he murdered another inmate who had been part of the escape plan.

No visual apparitions have been reported at Alcatraz since its closing, but guards and tour guides have reported hearing the sounds of clanging metal doors, men's voices, whistling, screams and the running of feet along corridors. Clanging sounds have been heard at night in the corridor where the three 1946 escapees were gunned down. Screams have been heard coming from the dungeon, near Block A, where the surviving three escapees were chained. Men's voices have been heard in the hospital ward. Various individuals have reported feeling "strange" in the vicinity of 14-D, although some acknowledge their reaction may be influenced by their knowledge of what went on there. The cell also reportedly remains very cold, even if the surrounding area has warmed on a hot day. Banjo music has been reported wafting from the shower room, where Capone once held forth with his only solace.

Further reading:
Winer, Richard, and Nancy Osborn. *Haunted Houses.* New York: Bantam Books, 1979.

All Hallows Eve (Halloween)   Originally, a pagan festival of the dead, which has survived to the present in popular culture as Halloween, a night of trick-or-treating by children and others dressed in costumes of fantasy and the supernatural. All Hallows Eve is observed the night of October 31, followed on November 1 by All Hallows Day, also called All Hallowmas, All Saints, All Saints' Day and All Souls' Day.

The ancient Celts called the festival Samhain (pronounced sow' an) and observed it to celebrate the onset of winter and the beginning of the Celtic New Year; "samhain" means "end of summer." In Ireland the festival was known as Samhein, or La Samon, for the Feast of the Sun. In Scotland, the celebration was known as Hallowe'en. Samhain was a solar festival marked by sacred fire and fire rituals. During the height of the Druids, the priestly caste of the Celts, all fires except those of the Druids were extinguished on Samhain. Householders were levied a fee for the holy fire which burned at their altars.

In ancient Ireland, the Druids sacrificed to the deities by burning victims in wickerwork cages. All other fires were to be extinguished and were relit from the sacrificial fire. Samhain marked the third and final harvest, and the storage of provisions for the winter. The veil between the worlds of the living and the dead was believed to be at its thinnest point in the year, making communication between the living and the dead much easier. On the eve of the holiday, the souls of the dead freely roamed the land of the living.

The Romans observed the holiday as Feralia, intended to give rest and peace to the departed. Participants made sacrifices in honor of the dead, offered up prayers for them, and made oblations to them. The festival was celebrated on February 21, the end of the Roman year. In the 7th century, Pope Boniface IV introduced All Saints' Day to replace the pagan festival of the dead. It was observed on May 13. Later, Gregory III changed the date to November 1. The Greek Orthodox Church observes it on the first Sunday after Pentecost.

Numerous folk customs connected with the pagan observances for the dead have survived to the present. In addition to the souls of the dead roaming about, the Devil, witches and numerous spirits are believed to be out and at the peak of their supernatural powers. In Ireland and Scotland, the custom of extinguishing one's home fire and relighting it from the festival bonfire has continued into modern times.

Samhain, as it is still called in some parts, is a time for getting rid of weaknesses, as pagans once slaughtered weak animals which were unlikely to survive the winter. A common ritual calls for writing down weaknesses on a piece of paper or parchment, and tossing it into the fire. Cakes are baked as offerings for the souls of the dead.

In some parts of modern Scotland, young people still celebrate by building bonfires on hilltops and high ground, and then dance around the flames. The fire is known as Hallowe'en bleeze, and custom once included digging a circular trench around the fire to symbolize the sun.

Modern celebrants still believe that the unseen worlds of the Devil and witches have a free hand to exercise their powers on this night. Another belief is that certain ceremonies can be used to foretell events, mostly about the identity of future marital partners and their qualities, such as if they will be good-looking, rich or sweet-tempered. For example, if a young person eats a raw or roasted salt herring before going to bed, the future husband or wife will appear in a dream offering a drink of water.

In another example, a blindfolded man or woman is led to three plates set on a table. One plate contains clean water, a second contains foul water and the third plate is empty. The left hand is used to make contact with one of the plates. If the hand touches the plate with clean water, the future mate will be young, handsome and never married. If the hand touches the plate with the foul water, the future spouse will be a widower or widow. If the empty plate is touched, the person will remain single. The ceremony must be repeated three times, each time with the plates arranged in a different order.

The custom of trick-or-treating probably has several origins. An old Irish peasant practice called for going door to door to collect money, breadcake, cheese, eggs, butter, nuts, apples, etc., in preparation for the festival of St. Columb Kill. Another was the begging for soul cakes, or offerings of food for the dead, which became popularized as begging for offerings for one's self—particularly in exchange for promises of prosperity or protection against bad luck.

See also FEASTS AND FESTIVALS OF THE DEAD.

Further reading:

Bannatyne, Lesley Pratt. *Halloween: An American Holiday, an American History*. New York: Facts On File, 1990.

Guiley, Rosemary Ellen. *The Encyclopedia of Witches and Witchcraft*. New York: Facts On File, 1989.

American Association-Electronic Voice Phenomena See ELECTRONIC VOICE PHENOMENON.

American Society for Psychical Research (ASPR) Organization dedicated to psychical research, a field now called parapsychology. The American Society for Psychical Research (ASPR) was founded in late 1884 in Boston under the auspices of the SOCIETY FOR PSYCHICAL RESEARCH (SPR) of London. It operated independently of the SPR and had similar committees to investigate thought transference (telepathy), hypnosis, apparitions, mediumship and other paranormal phenomena. It attracted eminent scientists and scholars, among them William BARRETT, James H. HYSLOP and William JAMES.

Early financial difficulties forced the ASPR to cease independent operation and become a branch of the SPR in 1889. In 1906, the ASPR reestablished itself as an independent organization. Many new members were not scientists, but lay persons interested in Spiritualism.

Controversy among members over a fraudulent medium, "Margery" (see CRANDON, MINA STINSON), caused a faction to split off in 1925 and become the BOSTON SOCIETY FOR PSYCHICAL RESEARCH. That effort lasted until 1941, when the Boston group rejoined the ASPR.

Under leadership provided by psychologist Gardner MURPHY, the ASPR turned away from sittings with mediums and devoted itself to scientific experiments, particularly the extra-sensory perception laboratory work being done by J.B. RHINE. In the mid-

1950s, Murphy directed ASPR attention to spontaneous psi (extrasensory perception [ESP] and psychokinesis [PK]), which he hoped would yield more information on the nature of psi than did laboratory experiments. Murphy encouraged research on creativity, altered states of consciousness, meditation, deathbed visions and survival after death (see also KIDD, JAMES).

The ASPR maintains a wide range of interests, from continued empirical laboratory experiments concerning ESP and psychokinesis (PK) to inquiries into such areas as psychical healing, out-of-body experiences, near-death experiences, reincarnation and ESP in dreams. Some attention is devoted to poltergeist cases, considered of interest because of the possible involvement of human PK and psychological factors, but scant attention is paid to apparitions and hauntings.

Scientific articles appear in a quarterly *Journal of the American Society for Psychical Research*, while informal articles appear in a quarterly *ASPR Newsletter*. The ASPR maintains one of the largest parapsychology libraries in the world and offers symposia and lectures. Membership is international.

Further reading:

Fodor, Nandor. *An Encyclopedia of Psychic Science.* Secaucus, N.J.: Citadel Press, 1966. First published 1933.

Matlock, James G. "The ASPR in 1888." *ASPR Newsletter* 14 (1988):23.

———. "The ASPR in 1913." *ASPR Newsletter,* 14 (1988):29.

———. "The ASPR in 1938." *ASPR Newsletter* 15 (1989):8.

Mauskopf, Seymour H. "The History of the American Society for Psychical Research: An Interpretation." *Journal of the American Society for Psychical Research* 83 (1989):7–32.

Amherst Haunting A classic case of a late 19th-century poltergeist in Amherst, Nova Scotia that was so mean-spirited that it directed its nasty activities not only toward its young victim, but to all other persons who tried to help her. Even the family cat did not go unscathed.

The troublesome spirit, which gave itself the name "Bob" when leaving written messages on walls, confounded observers with strange, frightening noises and happenings, and even started fires. The case began in 1878 and attracted the notice of the public; people often gathered at the house in such great numbers that the police had to be summoned.

The victims were the Teed family of Amherst, headed by Daniel Teed, a foreman in a shoe factory, and including his wife, Olive, and their two young sons; Olive's two sisters, Jennie, 22 years old, and Esther, 19 years old; Olive's brother, William; and Daniel's brother, John. They lived in a crowded two-story cottage.

The family's travails began one night when Esther jumped out of the bed she shared with Jennie and screamed that there was a mouse in it. Finding no such thing, the two went back to sleep. The next night, they heard rustling sounds in a band-box which was rising and falling in the air. An examination by the frightened women revealed an empty box.

On the following night, the spirit turned ugly, setting the tone for its future activities. Esther, who had gone to bed feeling ill, suddenly awoke and declared that she was dying. Her cries alarmed family members, who rushed into her room, whereupon they were greeted with a hideous sight. Esther's short hair was almost standing on end, her face was blood-red and her eyes popping. Two family members proclaimed her mad, but their accusations turned to concern as Esther's body swelled to nearly double its normal size. Esther's pitiful cries of pain were accompanied by booming sounds of rolling thunder—although there was not a cloud to be seen in the sky.

Esther's swelling subsided, but four nights later when she and Jennie were once again asleep, their bedclothes were suddenly torn away and thrown into a heap in the corner of the room. Again, frightened family members rushed into the girls' room, saw a swollen Esther and heard the rolling thunder. Jennie replaced the bedclothes, only to have a pillow fly off the bed and strike John Teed in the face. John fled the room, but the others remained, sitting on the bedclothes to hold them fast while Esther fell back to sleep.

The next day the family called the local physician, Dr. Carritte, to check Esther. He became the poltergeist's next victim. While examining Esther, the bolster beneath her head rose up and violently hit him on the head before returning to its former spot. The astonished doctor took a few moments to restore his equilibrium and sat down in a chair. He heard a metallic scratching sound coming from the wall behind him. Turning to see its source, he saw written upon the wall, "Esther Cox! You are mine to kill." At the same time, the doctor heard peals of thunder and saw pieces of plaster fall from the ceiling and swirl around the room.

To the terrified Dr. Carritte's credit, he returned the next day to examine his patient. As he was bending over Esther, he was hit with a barrage of potatoes which sent him flying across the room. Nevertheless, the doctor continued his ministrations by giving Esther a sedative. She fell fitfully asleep;

meanwhile, the doctor heard loud, pounding sounds coming from the ceiling.

The next day, Esther complained of feeling as though electricity was passing through her body. Dr. Carritte administered more sedatives in the evening. As he put her to bed, loud raps sounded, as though someone were pounding on the roof of the house. Dr. Carritte went outside, where strong moonlight enabled him to see that no one was upon the roof. Yet, when the returned inside, the family said that while he had been out, it had sounded as though someone were pounding on the roof with a sledge-hammer. The poundings repeated intermittently, but eventually they went on all day long and were heard by passersby. The noises were written up in the local *Gazette* newspaper and other papers throughout Canada.

About three weeks after Dr. Carritte's initial visit, Jennie stated that she thought the ghost could hear and see everything the family did. Immediately, three clear reports were heard in response. Further questions put to the spirit were answered with loud reports: one knock for a negative answer and three knocks for an affirmative one. The family began to converse with the unseen spirit.

Word had now begun to spread throughout the community about these happenings. The clergy became interested, but they attributed the phenomena to the newly commercialized electricity rather than to supernatural or diabolical agents. A well-known Baptist clergyman, Rev. Dr. Edwin Clay, began to visit regularly. Rev. Clay agreed with Dr. Carritte that Esther was not producing the noises herself. He opined that her nerves had received some sort of electric shock, thus turning her into a living battery. He believed that her body was emitting tiny flashes of lightning, and the noises were actually small claps of thunder. This theory proved to be popular, and Rev. Clay began to give numerous lectures on it, always defending Esther against any accusations of fraud. The publicity caused throngs of people to gather outside the Teed cottage daily.

Rev. Clay quit visiting Esther when she contracted diphtheria months later. When she recovered, she left the Teed home to stay temporarily with a married sister in New Brunswick. For the first time, peace and quiet descended on the cottage.

But when Esther returned home, so did the spirit, with an even greater desire for destruction and disruption. One night, Esther told Jennie that she could hear a voice saying that it would burn the house down. The voice also stated that it had once lived on earth, had died, and now was only a ghost.

The girls called in family members to relay the message, and while all were laughing at the prepos-

terousness of such a thing happening, lighted matches began falling from the ceiling onto Esther's bed. Communication with the spirit was then initiated, and when asked if it would really set the house afire, it answered in the affirmative. As apparent proof, one of Esther's dresses, hanging on a nail on the wall, was rolled up by invisible hands, stuffed beneath the bed and lighted afire. Daniel Teed pulled the dress out and snuffed the fire before it could do serious damage.

"Bob" set Olive Teed's skirts on fire and allegedly set several small fires in different parts of the house, which again caused more fright than damage. During one fire emanating from a bucket of cedar shavings in the basement, Esther ran into the street screaming for help and neighbors came to her aid. The local fire department, however, suspected arson, perhaps by Esther. However, she was within view of Olive when the fire started and could not have been responsible.

Members of the public suggested that Esther should be flogged in order to beat the evil out of her. Instead, Daniel Teed sent her to the house of a Mr. White for safety. But the spirit apparently was having too much fun and continued setting fires in her absence.

Around this time, Walter Hubbell, an actor in a strolling company based in Amherst, became interested in the case as a possible money-maker. He decided to exhibit Esther on a platform in the hopes that the ghost would thrill the audience with strange activities. Unfortunately, the spirit wasn't interested in working on cue and irate spectators hissed and booed the couple off the stage, demanding the return of their money.

Esther returned to live in the Teed home, accompanied by the undaunted Hubbell, who moved into the house to learn more about the spirit. His efforts were rewarded by assaults upon him by his umbrella and by a large carving knife that flew briskly through the air in his direction. Being young and nimble, he was able to duck in time, only to see a huge armchair come marching across the room toward him.

Hoping to put an end to the family's torment, the local clergyman, Rev. R.A. Temple, held a meeting of prayer and exorcism in the house. When the reverend asked the spirit to speak, it responded with loud trumpet-playing. The reverend fled the house, but the spirit became enamored of its own playing and continued to blast on the instrument. The musical finale was accompanied by a display of lighted matches.

Mischief continued to plague other members of the household. George Cox, Esther's brother, was humiliated when he was mysteriously undressed three times in public. One day Walter Hubbell observed that the cat was the only resident that had not been tormented. The cat instantly was levitated about five feet into the air and set down upon Esther's shoulders. The terrified animal ran out of the house, where it remained for the rest of the day.

The fire-starting also continued. Hubbell, who in 1888 wrote his account of the case, "The Great Amherst Mystery," described his first encounter with the spirit's fire tricks:

> . . . I say, candidly, that until I had had that experience I never fully realized what an awful calamity it was to have an invisible monster, somewhere within the atmosphere, going from place to place about the house, gathering up old newspapers into a bundle and hiding it in the basket of soiled linen or in a closet, then go and steal matches out of the match-box in the kitchen or somebody's pocket, as he did out of mine; and after kindling a fire in the bundle, tell Esther that he had started a fire, but would not tell where; or perhaps not tell her at all, in which case the first intimation we would have was the smell of smoke pouring through the house, and then the most intense excitement, everybody running with buckets of water. I say it was the most truly awful calamity that could possibly befall any family, infidel or Christian, that could be conceived in the mind of man or ghost. And how much more terrible did it seem in this little cottage, where we were all strict members of the church, prayed, sang hymns, and read the Bible. Poor Mrs. Teed!

Finally, the landlord of the Teed home, Mr. Bliss, distressed at the potential for damage to his cottage, requested that Esther leave his property. Reluctantly, the family agreed to let Esther go to the home of a Mr. Van Amburgh. The Teed home then once again returned to normal.

The hapless Esther was to be harassed by the spirit one last time. "Bob" followed her into a barn and set it afire. She was arrested for arson and sentenced to four months' imprisonment, but appeals from persons who knew her sad history led to her release. The story ended happily, however, as Esther ultimately married and was finally rid of the ghost.

Members of the Teed family were convinced that the events were indeed caused by the evil ghost of a man who had decided to torment Esther. Some of the local townsfolk believed Esther had perpetrated everything. Wrote Hubbell, "Dr. Nathan Tupper, who had never witnessed a single manifestation, suggested that if a strong raw-hide whip were laid across Esther's bare shoulders by a powerful arm, the tricks of the girl would cease at once." Dr. Carritte believed in the ghost, as did Hubbell. The case was never solved.

In considering the case in light of modern theories of the origin and nature of poltergeists, it is likely that Esther was the unwitting focus of psychokinetic energy, which caused the phenomena, due to repressed emotions. She was within the age range of common poltergeist disturbances believed to be caused by human agents. She may have suffered repressed hostility and tension, perhaps from living in very close quarters with a large family. She also may have suffered repressed sexual feelings. The fact that the disturbance stopped, first when she left the crowded Teed household for temporary stays elsewhere, and finally to marry and have her own household, support this explanation.

Further reading:

Canning, John, ed. *50 Great Ghost Stories*. New York: Bonanza Books, 1988. First published 1971.

Cohen, Daniel. *The Encyclopedia of Ghosts*. New York: Dodd, Mead & Co., 1984.

Sitwell, Sacheverell. *Poltergeists: Fact or Fancy*. New York: Dorset Press, 1988. First published 1959.

Amityville Horror One of the most sensational and controversial cases of an alleged diabolical presence took place not in a haunted European chateau but in suburban Long Island, New York. The "Amityville Horror," as the case became known, was later exposed as a hoax, and spawned a spate of lawsuits.

George and Kathleen Lutz, with Kathleen's three children—Daniel, Christopher and Melissa—moved into a large Dutch colonial house at 112 Ocean Avenue in Amityville on December 18, 1975. The house seemed a dream come true for the Lutzes: six bedrooms, a swimming pool, space for George's surveying business, a boathouse on the water, plenty of yard for the kids and their dog, Harry, and all in relatively good condition. Best of all, such a palace was—amazingly—available for only $80,000.

The broker explained that the house had been on the market for a year at such a bargain price because it was the DeFeo house, scene of a mass murder by 23-year-old Ronnie DeFeo of his father, mother and four younger siblings on November 13, 1974. Not superstitious, the Lutzes bought the house.

By January 14, 1976, when the Lutzes fled the house, never to return, they had been terrorized, they later said, for 28 days. Ghostly apparitions of hooded figures, clouds of flies in the sewing room and the children's playroom, windowpanes that broke simultaneously, bone-chilling cold alternating with suffocating heat, personality changes, nightly parades by spirit marching bands, levitations, green slime spilling downstairs, putrid smells, sickness, strange scratches on Kathleen's body, objects moving of their own accord, repeated disconnection of telephone service, and even communications between the youngest, Melissa (Missy), and a devilish spirit pig she called "Jodie" turned their dream home into a hell on earth. Kathleen often had dreams about the murder and Mrs. DeFeo's love affair; George grew his beard and hair long, beginning to closely resemble Ronnie DeFeo. The children were frightened and unable to go to school, and George couldn't work, seriously jeopardizing his business.

Even people who had only been in the house to visit were affected. Kathy's brother Jimmy and his new bride mysteriously lost $1,500 in cash. And "Father Mancuso" (his real name: Father Ralph Pecararo), the local priest who blessed the house after the Lutzes moved in, suffered debilitating sickness, rashes, anxiety and pain, causing his eventual transfer to a distant parish. He claims he heard a voice ordering him to get out when he sprinkled the house with holy water.

Besides the influence of the murder, the house also was supposedly situated over an abandoned well in an old Shinnecock area used for keeping the sick and insane until they died of exposure. No burials were done there because the Shinnecocks believed the place was infested with demons. And strangest of all, the Lutzes found a small secret room, painted entirely in a blood red, behind the basement stairs. No one knew what purpose the room served, but it boded ill.

The Lutzes' initial reaction was that these occurrences were just coincidence, that they were seeing things. But their annoyance turned to fear, anger, frustration and finally the decision to leave as fast as they could, leaving behind all their possessions and the house they thought was perfect.

In 1977, *The Amityville Horror* by Jay Anson was published by Prentice-Hall as a nonfiction book. Anson, who was suffering from poor health, never visited the house himself. The book became a bestseller and led to a top-grossing movie of the same name in 1979, spawning a host of other books and films with the same possessed-house theme. John G. Jones followed Anson's success with *Amityville II: The Possession* and *Amityville: The Final Chapter*, supposedly chronicling the Lutz family's attempts to escape the dark entities that plagued the house and followed them across country to California, even after an exorcism. However, by the time the second and third "true" accounts were written, the Lutz children in the story were no longer named Danny, Chris and Missy but Greg, Matt and Amy. And George, who ran a family surveying company, had been transformed into an air traffic controller.

Skeptics quickly claimed the haunting was a hoax, pointing out discrepancies in Anson's book, including: descriptions of terrible weather and moon con-

ditions during the Lutzes' 28 days that didn't match actual weather reports; calling the Psychical Research Foundation in North Carolina the Psychical Research Institute; and, perhaps most interesting, referring to historical records that show the Shinnecock never lived anywhere near Amityville.

Jerry Solfvin of the Psychical Research Foundation, who was contacted by George Lutz in early January 1976 about poltergeist activity in the house, found the whole matter questionable. He and others, including Karlis Osis and Alex Tanous of the AMERICAN SOCIETY FOR PSYCHICAL RESEARCH, visited the house but did not conduct investigations, believing that the incidents were not paranormal. All the evidence was subjective. Furthermore, "Father Mancuso" was declared to be a poor witness, as he visited the house only once. Anson wrote the book within three or four months, working largely from tapes of telephone interviews, and apparently making only a superficial effort to verify the Lutzes' account.

Perhaps most significant is an interview that Ronnie DeFeo's lawyer, William Weber, gave a local radio station in 1979, in which he claimed the whole "horror" was cooked up around the Lutzes' kitchen table over several bottles of wine. He asserted that after approaching them with the idea, the Lutzes went on their own, and he sued for a share of the book and movie profits. The Lutzes countersued to reaffirm the reality of their experience. Mrs. Lutz's story was analyzed on a Psychological Stress Evaluator; results showed that events happened as she believed them.

While it is possible that haunting phenomena may have occurred at the house, especially in light of the violent events that took place there, the Lutzes' account was far more dramatic than other cases of hauntings.

After the Lutzes moved out, the house became quiet. The owners who immediately followed the Lutzes, Jim and Barbara Cromarty, said they experienced no unusual phenomena. However, they were so annoyed from tourists and curiosity seekers that they sued the Lutzes, Prentice-Hall and Jay Anson for $1.1 million. They won a settlement for an unspecified lesser amount. Father Ralph Pecararo sued the Lutzes and Prentice-Hall for invasion of privacy and distortion of his involvement in the case, and he received an out-of-court settlement.

In Weber's suit against the Lutzes, Judge Jack Weinstein, who presided over the trial, stated for the record that "the evidence shows fairly clearly that the Lutzes during this entire period were considering and acting with the thought of having a book published."

Anson, who shared the book copyright with the Lutzes, retained sole film rights. He died at age 58 on March 12, 1980 in Palo Alto, California, following heart surgery.

Further reading:
Anson, Jay. *The Amityville Horror.* New York: Bantam Books, 1977.
Auerbach, Loyd. *ESP, Hauntings and Poltergeists: A Parapsychologist's Handbook.* New York: Warner Books, 1986.
Kurtz, Paul. "A Case Study of the West Pittson, 'Haunted' House." *The Skeptical Inquirer* 11 (Winter 1986–87):137–146.
Morris, Robert L. "The Case of The Amityville Horror." Review of *The Amityville Horror* appearing in Kendrick Frazier, ed., *Paranormal Borderlands of Science.* Buffalo: Prometheus Books, 1981.

amulet Any material or object believed to have supernatural or magical powers of protection against ghosts, evil spirits, witchcraft, the evil eye, illness, misfortune, calamities and any kind of disaster. Amulets have been used universally since ancient times. The term "amulet" comes from the old Latin term *amoletum*, which means "means of defense."

Most amulets are worn or carried on the person. Other amulets are placed in a house, building or ship, or among one's possessions. Still other amulets are painted on houses, buildings and ships.

Virtually any object can be an amulet. Personal items commonly include pieces of jewelry, semiprecious and precious stones, and common stones that have odd but natural shapes such as those with holes in them. Religious objects are amulets.

The supernatural power of an amulet is believed to occur naturally, bestowed by nature or the gods. In occult lore, amulets also can be fashioned and imbued with supernatural power through magical ritual.

See also CHARMS AGAINST GHOSTS.

ancestral spirit See ANCESTOR WORSHIP; ANIMISM; SHINTO; SOUL.

ancestor worship The worship of deceased relatives, or ancestors, as if they were deities.

Ancestor worship may take several forms. In its most generalized form, it is manifested simply in the laying out of food or drink for the deceased in the belief that this will encourage them to bring good to the community, and ward off evil. Ancestral spirits are widely believed to be able to influence the fertility of women and crops. Propitiation of ancestors is characteristic of ANIMISM, the world view to which the majority of tribal societies around the world ad-

An Inuit drawing of a ghost spirit.

here, but since the ancestors are not really thought of as gods, it may be going too far to describe this as "worship."

A more definite form of ancestor worship is found in China, where one part of the spirit of a deceased person is believed to pass into a special tablet after death. The tablets are placed in a ceremonial room and are bowed to, talked to and fed regularly by their living descendants, quite as if they were living persons. The purpose of these acts is, however, the same as in the tribal societies: to please the ancestors, thereby making sure that they continue to look out for the household and community.

An intermediary type of ancestor worship is found throughout West Africa. Here each family line, or lineage, has its own ancestral shrine, inhabited, it is believed, by the founder of the lineage. These shrines are usually carved wooden representations of the persons in question, and they may be fed, cared for and asked for favors, especially for children.

Further reading:
Radin, Paul. *Primitive Religion: Its Nature and Origin.* New York: Dover Publications, 1957.
Tylor, Edward Burnett. *Religion in Primitive Culture.* New York: Harper and Row, 1956.

angels In Judeo-Christian and Islamic mythologies, a class of beings both good and evil who are intermediaries between God and man. The term "angel" is derived from the Greek *angelos* and the Latin *angelus*, translations of the Hebrew *mal'akh*, which originally meant "the shadow side of God" and then came to mean "messenger."

Angelology, which is the study of angels, was developed in ancient Persia and absorbed into Judaism and Christianity. Angels also exist in Islamic mythology. The ancient Greeks had a comparable concept, the daimon (q.v.). There is no exact equivalent for angels in Eastern mythologies; the closest concepts are the avatars (incarnations of God) in Hinduism and the bodhisattvas (enlightened beings) and devas (shining ones) of Buddhism. Beings with many of the same characteristics ascribed angels, such as playing an intermediary role between humankind and the gods, protecting a person or site, or providing counsel, exist universally throughout the world.

The Bible provides uneven and sometimes contradictory information on angels, initially portraying them as beings created by God who carry God's messages to earth, and then as intervenors, acting on God's instructions. They were said to pass as human beings while on earth. Some angels supposedly aided and protected humankind, while others wrought God's punishments and brought illness and destruction. They cohabited with human women and bore a race of giants called the Nephilim ("fallen ones"), who were supposed to be eradicated in the Flood. Most details about Judeo-Christian angelic hierarchies and functions belong to scriptures that were declared heretical, such as the Book of Enoch.

The New Testament tells of the angel Lucifer (Satan), who defied God and was cast out of heaven, along with one-third of the angelic realm. These fallen angels became the demons of hell under the leadership of Satan.

In Catholicism, it is believed that every person is born with at least one personal guardian angel, a protective being that stays with a person for his or her entire life. Although Martin Luther, the founder of Protestantism, rejected the doctrine of angels, many modern Protestants believe in angels and in guardian angels.

Until about the 18th century, angels were believed by many to play roles in everyday life. People prayed to them and magicians conjured them in spells. Visions of angels were interpreted as omens. However, during the Age of Enlightenment, with its emphasis on science and intellectual thought, angels retreated to the realm of poetry and romantic fancy, and mystics such as Emanuel Swedenborg. Swedenborg called the souls of the dead "angels" and said he visited with them in the afterlife during his mystical trances.

Encounters with angels continue to be experienced in the modern world. Angels are most often sensed or heard by clairaudience; occasionally they manifest as apparitions in brilliant white robes or as balls of brilliant white light. Interpretations of what is an angel vary widely and are highly subjective. Some persons consider the appearance of a spirit of the dead, such as a family member, to be an angel if the

Angel appearing to Jesus during His Agony in the Garden.

manifestation serves to warn, comfort or protect them. In deathbed visions (q.v.), angels appear to be the souls of deceased friends and relatives who come to help the dying to the Other Side.

Some experts in philosophy, mythology, psychology and parapsychology believe that angels are created in part or in whole by projection from the depths of the human unconscious in response to a need. Other theories have linked angels to extraterrestrials.

See also NEAR-DEATH EXPERIENCE.

Further reading:

Burnham, Sophy. *A Book of Angels.* New York: Ballantine Books, 1990.

Downing, Barry H. *The Bible and Flying Saucers.* New York: Avon Books, 1970. First published 1986.

Evans, Hilary. *Gods-Spirits-Cosmic Guardians: Encounters with Non-Human Beings.* Wellingborough, Northamptonshire, England: The Aquarian Press, 1987.

Godwin, Michael. *Angels.* New York: Simon & Schuster, 1990.

Graham, Billy. *Angels: God's Secret Agents.* Garden City, N.Y.: Doubleday & Co., 1975.

angels of Mons Bogus but curious story of apparitions of angels who allegedly saved French and British soldiers from death during a battle at Mons, Belgium in World War I.

Between August 26 and 28, 1914, during the first engagements of the war, French and British troops set out near Mons to engage the Germans, expecting a quick victory. Instead, they were overpowered by the German artillery, and 15,000 French and British men were lost in the initial stages of fighting. The survivors were forced to retreat, all the while being shelled by the Germans.

Afterward, reports began to circulate that the retreating soldiers had seen phantom fighters on horseback who had prevented the Germans from slaughtering them all. After being moved by a radio report, British journalist Arthur Machen wrote a short story, "The Bowmen," telling about how the retreating men had seen ghostly bowmen and medieval soldiers from the battle of Agincourt (located near Mons), which took place in the 15th century. The story was published on September 14, 1914 in the *London Evening News*.

Immediately, confirmations were made. Others reported seeing winged and robed angels interposing themselves between the retreating soldiers and the Germans. French soldiers saw visions of the archangel Michael, or Joan of Arc, and some British claimed to have seen one of their legendary national heroes, Saint George. Nurses reported that men who were fatally wounded died in states of exaltation.

Similar reports from other battlefronts were made. Books were written and published, including one by Machen, *The Angels of Mons: The Bowmen & Other Legends of War* (1915) and one by Harold Begbie, *On the Side of the Angels* (1915).

Machen later confessed that he had made his story up. A few refused to believe him, however; those who reported seeing apparitions of saviors during battle insisted on the truth of their experiences.

To complicate the case, in 1930 the director of German espionage, Friedrich Herzenwirth, stated the Mons soldiers had indeed seen angels, but they were movie projections cast on clouds by German aviators to prove that God was on their side. No proof of this claim was ever made.

Most likely, the stories of the Mons angels and phantom armies are based on faulty memories and fabrication (albeit sincere) to buttress Machen's story. However, the possibility that the soldiers did see apparitions of some sort cannot be ruled out. Some may have been hallucinations due to stress, fear and pain, and an intense desire to be saved. It has been theorized that some of the apparitions may have been the souls of soldiers freshly killed in the battle.

Further reading:
Burnham, Sophy. *A Book of Angels*. New York: Ballantine, 1990.
Machen, Arthur. *The Angels of Mons: The Bowmen & Other Legends of War*. London, 1915.

animism The name given by E.B. Tylor, the founder of modern anthropology, to the system of beliefs about souls and spirits typically found in tribal societies, from the Americas to Africa to Asia and Australia. For Tylor, animism was the world's most primitive religion.

Tylor identified two major branches of Animism (which he spelled with a capital "A"): beliefs about souls and spirits connected with the human body, and beliefs about spirits which had an independent existence. He published his book *Primitive Culture* (1871) at a time when Darwin's ideas about evolution were very much in the air, and he believed that human psychology, together with human culture and society, had undergone evolution similar to that then being claimed for the physical body. This led him to arrange various soul and spirit concepts in a developmental sequence, beginning with souls connected with the human being, through independent spirits, to polytheism, and then to monotheism—the idea of a single high God, as one finds in modern Western religions.

Andrew LANG was the first to question Tylor's developmental sequence, in *The Making of Religion* (1898), by pointing out that some very primitive societies had high gods. Although later study showed that these gods were not the supreme moral beings found in the great Western religions, nevertheless Tylor's scheme had been successfully challenged. Questions about animism's claim to be the earliest form of religion were also heard. Sir James Frazer, in *The Golden Bough* (1890), argued for a prior stage of belief in magic, and others hypothesized that belief in a psychic substance called "mana" had existed before beliefs in souls and spirits. However, since no societies with magic and mana but without souls and spirits have ever been found, this position is hypothetical at best.

Anthropologists today reject Tylor's evolutionary orientation and developmental sequence, but recognize that the system of beliefs he described under the heading of Animism is widespread. Spelled with a lowercase "a," animism is an appropriate label for the worldview characteristic of tribal societies around the world. This worldview is built upon the acceptance of the human being's survival of death and of a nonphysical realm alongside the physical world, and to the extent that it helps to channel religious sentiment (and it certainly does), it deserves to be called a religion. The question of whether it was in fact humankind's first religion cannot be answered.

As Tylor showed with example after example, the fundamental animistic soul beliefs are based on direct apprehension and experience of such things as sleep and dreaming, visions and trances—what today we would call out-of-body experiences and near-death experiences and apparitions. Observation and experiences of such events would naturally have suggested that the human being was composed of both physical and spiritual parts, and that the spiritual part, being detachable from the body during life, survived death. But this is only the beginning of the animistic belief system. Having survived death, the spirit might do more than simply go to the Land of the Dead (see AFTERLIFE). It might, for instance, take control of living persons during feasts and festivals of the dead (also see POSSESSION), or it might seek to send messages to the living through specially trained persons, as in mediumship. Shamans specialize in out-of-body travel and the direct contact with the spirits of the dead.

A spirit after death need not possess only living persons. It might lodge itself in various features of the natural world (such as trees or rocks) or in man-made objects (such as statues or spears), thereby imbuing them with a special power. The collection of beliefs about objects so imbued has been called "fetishism." A special type of fetishism involves the spirit's association with a ritual object, which is then propitiated, if not worshipped outright. Such is the case with ancestral tablets in China. In West Africa, ancestral shrines (in many cases, carved representations of human figures) serve a similar function (see ANCESTOR WORSHIP). Similar carved figures may also serve for the temporary lodging of a shaman's spirit helpers. Fetish objects do not always gain their power through association with a spirit, however. In West Africa, where fetishism is particularly strong, the power may also come from smearing the object with a special substance (see FETISH).

Parts of the body and its exuviae such as hair, nails, and even excrement, are intimately connected with it, and remain in connection with the person after they have been cast off. The same may be true of the afterbirth or the prepuce removed in circumcision. All these items must be carefully buried or otherwise disposed of, lest they be found and used against one by witches or sorcerers. In many places, the soul is thought to perch on the crown of the head, and practices such as scalping and headhunting have as their intention the taking of the victim's soul. Cannibalism often was associated with the belief that by eating a person's flesh one ingested part of his spiritual essence, and for that reason cannibalistic practices (before they were outlawed) were sometimes part of funeral customs and rites. When cremation is practiced, the resulting ashes are sometimes mixed with water and drunk, with the same intent.

Beliefs that a person may have more than a single soul are not uncommon. The different souls may account for different body functions (one may be associated with the bones, another with the breath, a third with the intellect), they may reside in different places in the body (the crown of the head, the liver, the skin), and they may face different fates after death (one may rest in the grave with the corpse, another travel to the Land of the Dead, a third return to earth to be reborn in a child). Siberian Yakut men have as many as eight souls, whereas Yakut women have seven. In some societies, men and women have different souls, or souls may be passed to all offspring from each parent, so that each person has two souls. Because each of these souls is believed to be reincarnated in different family lines, the souls from the parents provide each person with two different heritages. A person's given name frequently has a spiritual power, and among many Eskimo groups, a name is even a type of soul.

It is not surprising to find that in societies which live so much closer in touch with nature than the modern West, not only persons, but also animals and even plants, may have souls. In some societies, all animals are held to have souls, whereas in others, only certain animals do, and these animal souls may reincarnate in members of the same species, as happens with human beings. Human spirits may also be reborn in animals before dying and being born once more as children (see REINCARNATION). In other cases, people may have a spiritual affinity to animals of certain species. The subset of animistic beliefs concerning this side of the human relationship to animals is known as TOTEMISM.

Totemic animals may sometimes act as guardian spirits (q.v.) for persons. Sometimes, also, a guardian spirit is a deceased person in the community or perhaps part of the same person reincarnated in one, but most often the guardian spirit is a distinct spirit entity.

For the animist, the world abounds with spirit entities of various sorts. Most have no direct connection with living or deceased persons, though they may transform themselves into animals or human beings, or make themselves felt in some other way. Prominent or dramatic natural features such as volcanos, whirlpools or giant rocks may be held to be possessed by spirits, who must be propitiated by leaving food or drink, lest they harm persons who come near them. Water spirits and forest spirits are especially common. The animistic world is also populated by myriad monsters, such as the *windigo* of the Algonquian Indians. It is doubtless from ideas of this sort that beliefs in elves, fairies, and other beings of Western folklore developed.

Animism is more than simply a collection of beliefs about souls and spirits. Animistic beliefs have their own logic and consistency, which justifies calling animism a system of belief. A fully developed animistic system is rare today, but parts of it exist in many places, suggesting both that it is a very ancient way of perceiving the world, and that it was at one time universal.

Andrew Lang disagreed with Tylor about his developmental sequence of beliefs, though not with his description of the beliefs themselves. On this point, in fact, Lang went farther than Tylor did, and argued that clairvoyant dreams and apparitions had suggested the concepts of souls and spirits partly because they were veridical. The investigations of psychical research leave little doubt that Lang was right on this score as well, which in turn suggests that animism has managed to survive for as long as it has in part because it is based on a realistic perception of the world.

Further reading:
Lowie, Robert. *Primitive Religion.* New York: Boni and Liveright, 1923.
Radin, Paul. *Primitive Religion: Its Nature and Origin.* New York: Dover Publications, 1957.
Tylor, Edward Burnett. *Religion in Primitive Culture.* New York: Harper and Row, 1956.

ankou In the Celtic folklore of Brittany, a death omen (q.v.) that comes to collect the souls of the dead. The *ankou*, or "King of the Dead," is the last person to die in a parish during a year. For the following year, he or she assumes the duty of calling for the dead. Every parish in Brittany has it own *ankou*s.

The *ankou* is personified as a tall, haggard figure with long white hair, or a skeleton with a revolving head capable of seeing everything everywhere. It drives a spectral cart, accompanied by two ghostly figures on foot, and stops at the house of one who is about to die. There, it either knocks on the door—making a sound sometimes heard by the living—or gives out a mournful wail like the Irish banshee.

Occasionally it is reported to be seen as an apparition entering the house. It takes away the dead, who are placed in the cart with the help of the two companion ghosts.

The *ankou* is a powerful figure that dominates Breton folklore.

Further reading:
Evans-Wentz, W.Y. *The Fairy Faith in Celtic Countries.* 1911. New York: Carol Publishing Group, 1990.

apparition The supernormal appearance of a dead person or animal or of a living person or animal too distant to be within the range of the normal perception of the observer. Apparitions are uncommon and usually are seen but once. Apparitions of the dead which are seen repeatedly over a period of time, apparently haunting the same location, are also called ghosts. Contrary to popular belief, the majority of cases on record concern apparitions of the living and not of the dead.

Few apparitional experiences are visual. Most instead involve the sensing of a presence, perhaps accompanied by touch; hearing thumps, rappings, moanings, animal sounds and other strange noises; and smelling unexplained odors.

A radiant ghost making a nocturnal visit.

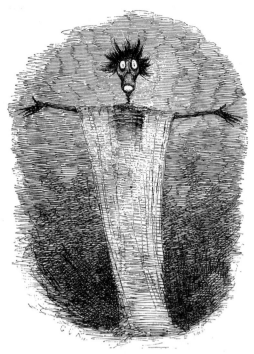

George Cruikshank's rendition of an apparition.

Apparitions have been studied extensively by psychical researchers, parapsychologists and others since the late 19th century. Tens of thousands of cases have been collected and analyzed. Various theories have been put forth, yet researchers still know very little about apparitions. In the discussion that follows, the term "agent" refers to the person (or animal) whose apparition is seen; the "percipient" is the person who sees the apparition.

CHARACTERISTICS OF APPARITIONS

According to a study of major features of apparitions published in 1956 by Hornell HART, an American sociologist and psychical researcher, and collaborators, there are no significant differences between apparitions of the living and of the dead. Some apparitions seem real and corporeal, with defineable form and features, and if, human, clothing. Other apparitions are fuzzy, luminous, transparent, wispy and ill-defined; some are little more than streaks, blobs or patches of light.

Apparitions appear and disappear suddenly, and sometimes just fade away. They both move through walls and objects and walk around them. They can cast shadows and be reflected in mirrors. Some have a marionette-like quality of limited gestures and movements, such as calling the attention of the percipient to a wound on the ghostly body, while others are more fluid and communicate verbally. Some are accompanied by sounds, smells, sensations of cold and movement of real objects in the percipient's environment.

In some cases, percipients attempt to touch apparitions; most find their hands go through them, but in a few cases, contact has been made with a substance that feels like a flimsy garment.

An overwhelming majority of apparitions—some 82% according to studies—seem to manifest themselves for a purpose: to communicate the agent's own crisis (usually grave danger or imminent death) to someone living; to comfort the grieving after the agent's death; to convey useful information to the living; or to warn the living of danger. Haunting apparitions appear to have emotional ties to a site, possibly resulting from violent or sudden death. Some haunting apparitions are believed to be earthbound spirits of the dead who are trapped by unfinished business (see RELEASEMENT).

Some ghost researchers do believe that certain apparitions, such as haunting earthbound spirits of the dead, do possess an intelligence that makes mediumistic communication possible. Some apparitions do not respond to attempts at communication, leading some researchers to conclude that they are merely some sort of psychic recording of an event.

HISTORICAL AND CULTURAL BELIEFS ABOUT APPARITIONS

Every civilization throughout history around the world has had, or has, beliefs about apparitions. Such beliefs usually are part of religion, myth or folklore. Among Asian peoples, belief in ancestral ghosts is strong, and rituals exist to honor and placate them (see ANCESTOR WORSHIP; FEASTS AND FESTIVALS OF THE DEAD). The spirits of the dead are believed to intervene regularly in the affairs of the living, and are credited for good luck and prosperity and blamed for illness and misfortune (see EXORCISM). The Chinese believe their ancestral ghosts can be dangerous, capable of even killing. Similar beliefs are held by tribal cultures around the world. The appearance of spirits of the dead plays a role in rituals and beliefs among Native North and South Americans. In some South American tribes, the dead appear as guardian spirits to medicine men and shamans.

The ancient Hebrews, Egyptians, Greeks and Romans believed that the souls of the dead could return to haunt the living. The Roman scholar Pliny the Younger recorded the case of a Greek philosopher who moved into a haunted house. An apparition appeared wearing chains and led the philosopher to a spot where an excavation later revealed a skeleton in chains (see ATHENODORUS, HAUNTING OF).

During the Dark Ages, people believed in all manner of apparitions, usually frightful: demons, vampires and spectral creatures such as devil dogs (see BLACK SHUCK; WHISHT HOUNDS) and wild huntsmen (see HERNE THE HUNTER; WILD HUNT). By the Middle Ages, beliefs in ghosts were manipulated by the Christian Church, which taught that ghosts were souls trapped in Purgatory until they expiated their sins. In 17th-century Europe, apparitions of the dead played an important social role as advisers to the living. When they appeared, they would counsel their wives and children, help solve crimes, and reproach wrongful executors. Such helpful ghosts have continued on into mdern times (see CHAFFIN WILL CASE; GREENBRIER GHOST). Belief in ghosts fell out of favor in educated circles during the Romantic Movement in the 18th century, then returned in the 19th century with Spiritualism, which espouses survival after death and mediumistic contact with the dead.

In Christian religion, apparitions of religious figures, such as angels, saints, the Virgin Mary and Jesus are holy and mystical manifestations permitted by God. (see MARIAN APPARITIONS). All other apparitions, including spirits of the dead, are delusions created by Satan or his demons for the purpose of tempting or confusing people, according to the Bible.

In folklore, apparitions are the spirits of the dead, who, through sin or tragedy, are condemned to haunt the realm of the living. Certain motifs exist in the folklore of diverse cultures, such as the ghostly ship (the FLYING DUTCHMAN is perhaps the most famous example), the ghostly hunter and the phantom traveler (q.v.) or phantom hitchhiker (q.v.). Except for religious visions, apparitions usually are feared in Western Christian culture.

SCIENCE AND APPARITIONS

Systematic studies of apparitions began with the founding of the SOCIETY FOR PSYCHICAL RESEARCH (SPR) in London in 1882. Three of the SPR's founders, Edmund GURNEY, Frederic W.H. MYERS and Frank PODMORE, questioned 5,700 persons about apparitions of the living and published their exhaustive findings in *Phantasms of the Living* (1886). This effort was followed in 1889 by a Census of Hallucinations, under the direction of Henry SIDGWICK, who was assisted by his wife, Eleanor SIDGWICK, Alice Johnson, Myers, A.T. Myers and Podmore. The census consisted of a single question: "Have you ever, when believing yourself to be completely awake, had a vivid impression of seeing or being touched by a living being or inanimate object, or of hearing a voice; which impression, so far as you could discover, was not due to any external physical cause?" The SPR collected 17,000 replies, of which 1,684, or 9.9%, answered "yes," reporting 352 apparitions of the living and 163 apparitions of the dead (some apparitions were witnessed by more than one person). A similar census carried out in France, Germany and the United States brought 27,329 replies, of which 11.96% were affirmative. By extrapolating the results to the population in general, the surveys showed that approximately 10% of the adult population experiences an apparition.

The actual figure is much higher, according to a more recent survey of Americans conducted by the University of Chicago's National Opinion Research Council (NORC), and published in 1987. Forty-two percent of the adult population—and 67% of widows—reported contact with the dead. Of those contacts, 78% said they saw an apparition, 50% heard one, 21% were touched by one, 32% merely felt a presence, and 18% talked with the dead. Forty-six percent experienced a combination of phenomena. The overall figures are higher than a similar survey taken by the NORC in 1973, in which 27% of adults and 51% of widows reported contact with the dead. The increasing incidence perhaps reflects changing attitudes which make paranormal experiences less frightening and easier to admit.

Before theories of apparitions can be considered, it is helpful to understand how researchers define various types of apparitions. Those apparitions that can be corroborated by circumstances and fact are called "veridical apparitions" and are of most value and interest to parapsychologists. Many ghost investigators have their own categories (see UNDERWOOD, PETER). The following are major categories defined by psychical research societies:

CRISIS APPARITIONS

These are apparitions which appear during an agent's moment of extreme crisis, particularly death. The apparition usually manifests to the agent's loved ones or others with whom the agent has close emotional ties. Most crisis apparitions seem to have the purpose of communicating to the living that the agent is dying or has just died. Some gesture to show their fatal wounds. Crisis apparitions appear both in waking visions and in dreams.

APPARITIONS OF THE DEAD

The majority of these cases also involve close emotional ties, in which the dead appear to comfort the grieving, or to communicate information pertaining to the estate or unfinished business of the deceased. After his death, Dante appeared to his son and guided him to where Dante had secreted the last cantos of his *Divine Comedy*. The son was not aware of their existence. Apparitions of the dead may appear years later to loved ones in times of crisis.

COLLECTIVE APPARITIONS

The majority of apparitions of both living and dead appear to individuals when they are alone; collective apparitions are those that are seen simultaneously by more than one person. Reported cases include hauntings and crisis apparitions. Approximately one-third of reported apparitions are witnessed collectively. Animals are sometimes among the multiple witnesses, and are gauged by their visible reactions to the apparition. For example, a dog may whimper and hide, or a cat may arch its back.

RECIPROCAL APPARITIONS

These are apparitions of the living in which both agent and percipient experience seeing each other. In most such cases, the agent has a powerful desire to be with the percipient, motivated by loneliness, longing, love or worry. The agent suddenly finds himself transported to the presence of the percipient, who in turn observes the agent. Reciprocal apparitions may also be collectively perceived. One possible explanation of reciprocal apparitions is that the agent may project himself in an out-of-body-experience (see WILMOT APPARITION).

DEATHBED APPARITIONS

The appearance of angelic beings, religious figures, luminosities and dead loved ones are sometimes reported by the dying shortly before death. Occasionally, deathbed apparitions also are perceived by the living who are in attendance to the dying (see DEATHBED VISIONS).

APPARITIONS IN CASES SUGGESTIVE OF REINCARNATION

Some cases of alleged reincarnation involve "announcing dreams," in which the deceased appears in a dream to a member of the family into which it will be born. Such dreams occur frequently among the Tlingit and other northwest Native American tribes, and in Turkey, Burma and Thailand. In some cases in Burma and Thailand, children who appear to have spontaneous memories of previous lives say they remember sending the announcing dream, or, in rare instances, manifesting as an apparition to their future mother (see REINCARNATION).

THEORIES ABOUT APPARITIONS

Of the early SPR researchers, Gurney and Myers had a profound impact upon apparition theories which continues to modern times. Both men believed apparitions were entirely hallucinations, a mental phenomenon that had no physical reality. Gurney believed they were the product of telepathy from the dead to the living, projected out of the percipient's mind in the form of an apparition. Furthermore, he believed that collective apparitions were also a product of telepathy among the living, projected by the primary percipient to others around him. However, telepathy among the living does not adequately explain collective sightings, in which apparitions are viewed from different angles, and different percipients notice different things. If the apparition were projected solely from a single percipient, then all percipients would see the same thing.

Myers, who believed strongly in survival after death, began to doubt the telepathic theory as early as 1885. In his own landmark book, *Human Personality and the Survival of Bodily Death* (1903), he postulated that apparitions consisted of a "phantasmogenic center," a locus of energies clairvoyantly expended by the agent and sufficiently strong enough to modify the space of the percipient. Apparitions, he theorized, appeared to the most psychically sensitive person or persons in a group, which could explain why an apparition might not be recognized by a percipient, but could be identified by another person, based on the percipient's description.

Other theories that have been advanced subsequently about apparitions suggest that:

- They are idea patterns or etheric images produced by the subconscious mind of the living, with or without the cooperation of the agent.
- They are the astral or etheric bodies of the agents.
- They are an amalgam of personality patterns, which in the case of hauntings are trapped tragic events in a psychic ether or psi field of a given site.
- They are personas, or vehicles through which the "I-thinking consciousness" can take on temporarily visible form, and experience and act. Personas may represent either the living or the dead, may or may not be "fully conscious," and may exhibit a personality structure, perhaps in part fictitious (as in the case of mediumistic control spirits).
- They are expressions of an individual's unconscious needs: externalized projections of unresolved feelings of guilt, or the embodiment of an unconscious wish. For example, at London's THEATRE ROYAL on Drury Lane, rehearsing actors glance

hopefully at the last seat of row D for the apparition of the "Man in Gray," allegedly an 18th-century theatergoer. Tradition has it that a sighting means a successful run for the play. The apparition is also believed to guide actors to better positions on stage, and make his approval known to them.

- They are projections of concentration that become thought-forms.
- Apparitions of the dead are truly the spirits of the dead, who possess an intelligence and ability to communicate with the living.

Investigation of out-of-body experiences (q.v.) and near-death experiences (q.v.) has led some modern researchers to the view that apparitions also have a physicality of their own and are not merely mental hallucinations, and furthermore, that they are directed by an intelligence or personality. Karlis Osis, an American parapsychologist, has suggested that consciousness can be an "autonomous unit capable of perception and action when localized away from the body."

Whether or not apparitions are animated by personalities has been controversial. Those who believe they are not propose various theories: that all apparitions are merely some sort of psychic "recording" picked up by sensitive individuals; or that the living create apparitions out of intense desire and to serve their own purposes. In Eastern mystical philosophy, the cosmos is permeated by a substance that absorbs and permanently records all actions, thoughts, emotions and desires. In Hinduism, this substance is called the Akasha; the term "Akashic records" refers to everything recorded since the beginning of time. Oxford philosopher H.H. Price called the substance "psychic ether," a term adopted by some psychical researchers. Thus, if all events are recorded forever on some invisible substance, then perhaps psychically tuned individuals can at times glimpse these records and get a "playback." Psychic ether also has been given as a possible explanation for the mysterious appearance of apparitions on photographic film (see SPIRIT PHOTOGRAPHY).

Other ghost researchers believe apparitions have personalities, and that apparitions are evidence in support of SURVIVAL AFTER DEATH. They cite cases in which apparitions communicate information unknown to the percipient, or adapt to their viewers.

It is unlikely that any single theory can explain all apparitions. It is possible that some apparitions are created by the living; that some have physicality and their own objective reality; that some are hallucinations; and that some are "psychic recordings."

Andrew MacKenzie, a modern psychical researcher, has theorized that the ability to have hallucinatory experiences might be a function of personality structure. In an examination of hallucinatory cases, he found that about one-third of the experiences occurred just before or after sleep, or when the witness was awakened at night. Other experiences took place when the witness was in a state of relaxation, doing routine work in the home, or concentrating on some activity such as reading a book. Thus, the external world was shut out and the person's guard was down, opening the way for impressions to rise from the subconscious. Occasionally, these impressions took the visual or auditory form of an apparition.

The linkage between this dream-like state and sightings of apparitions also was made by G.N.M. TYRRELL, an English physicist, mathematician and psychical researcher, who asserted that there were two stages in an apparitional experience. In stage one the witness unconsciously experiences the apparition, and in stage two the information from stage one is processed into consciousness through dreams and certain waking experiences which resemble ordinary cognition. Just as in a dream, apparitions appear fully clothed and are often accompanied by objects, such as a horse and carriage. The clothing and objects are as hallucinatory as the ghost itself, and are present because they are required by the "motif" of the apparitional drama, Tyrrell said.

Further reading:

Auerbach, Loyd. *ESP, Hauntings and Poltergeists: A Parapsychologist's Handbook.* New York: Warner Books, 1986.

Emmons, Charles. *Chinese Ghosts and ESP.* Metuchen, N.J.: Scarecrow Press, 1982.

Greeley, Andrew. "Mysticism Goes Mainstream." *American Health* (Jan./Feb. 1987):47–55.

Green, Celia and Charles McCreery. *Apparitions.* London: Hamish Hamilton, 1975.

Gurney, Edmund, F.W.H. Myers and Frank Podmore. *Phantasms of the Living,* vols. 1 and 2. London: The Society for Psychical Research and Trubner & Co., 1886.

Hart, Hornell. "Six Theories About Apparitions." *Proceedings of the Society for Psychical Research* 50 (1956):153–236.

———. *The Enigma of Survival.* Springfield, Ill.: Charles C Thomas, 1959.

Hart, Hornell and Ella B. Hart, "Visions and Apparitions Collectively and Reciprocally Perceived." *Proceedings of the Society for Psychical Research* 16 (1932–33):205–249.

Haynes, Renee. "What Do You Mean By A Ghost?" *Parapsychology Review,* 17 (1986):9–12.

Jaffé, Aniela. *Apparitions: An Archetypal Approach to Death Dreams and Ghosts.* Irving, Texas: Spring Publications, 1979.

MacKenzie, Andrew. *Hauntings and Apparitions.* London: Heinemann Ltd., 1982.

Myers, Frederic W.H. *Human Personality and Its Survival of Bodily Death Vols. I & II.* New ed. New York: Longmans, Green & Co., 1954. First published 1903.

Osis, Karlis. "Apparitions Old and New," in K. Ramakrishna Rao, *Case Studies in Parapsychology in Honor of Dr. Louisa E. Rhine.* Jefferson, N.C.: McFarland & Co., 1986.

Stevenson, Ian. "The Contribution of Apparitions to the Evidence for Survival." *The Journal of the American Society for Psychical Research* 76 (1982):341–356.

Thomas, Keith. *Religion and the Decline of Magic.* New York: Charles Scribner's Sons, 1971.

Tyrrell, G.N.M. *Apparitions.* London: The Society for Psychical Research, 1973. First published 1943, revised 1953.

apport Object that appears in the presence of a medium or spiritual adept, as though it has been formed from thin air or has passed through solid matter. This paranormal transportation is also known as teleportation. The word "apport" comes from the French *apporter,* meaning "to bring."

Apports once were a common phenomenon of Spiritualist seances, with mediums producing flowers, perfumes and the like, said to be gifts from the spirits present. Other apports have included vases, books, dishes of candy which moved about the seance table for the sampling of each sitter, and live birds, animals and sea life, including lions, hawks, buzzards, eels and lobsters. Some mediums were found to hide apports on their person before a seance and then produce them in the dark; others produced apports with no normal explanation. Apports also occur in POLTERGEIST cases.

Nineteenth-century mediums Agnes GUPPY and Eusapia PALLADINO were especially adept at apports, producing the customary flowers and fruit—even sea sand and ice. Palladino also produced disagreeable apports, such as dead rats.

Guppy was herself an apport at a seance conducted by mediums Frank Herne and Charles Williams, two of her protégés. In June 1871, at a seance at the mediums' home at 61 Lamb's Conduit Street, High Holborn, London, one of the sitters, a Mr. W.H. Harrison, jokingly asked controls John KING and Katie King if Guppy could be brought. She was an extremely large woman, and the sitters thought that such teleportation would surely test the powers of the spirits. According to all reports, within three minutes Guppy, clad only in her dressing gown, was sitting in a daze in the middle of the table, holding her pen and account book. Guppy claims that just as she was writing the word "onions" in her household ledger, she found herself transported from her home at Highbury about two miles away, whisked through the air at about 120 miles per hour.

More recently, American medium Arthur FORD reported the appearance of apports at a seance in England at the home of medium Catherine Barkel, which included Sir Arthur Conan DOYLE and Ford among the sitters. After Barkel went into a trance, her Native American spirit guide and control took over and announced that the "little people" had brought the sitters some valuable objects which had been lost on ships wrecked at sea or in other ways. Immediately, precious stones, one for each of the sitters, appeared in Barkel's hand in her lap. Doyle took them to a jeweler, who appraised them at several hundred pounds. Ford's stone was a garnet; others were diamonds, amethysts, emeralds and rubies. The sitters had them set in jewelry.

Perhaps the most unusual apports were produced by Charles Bailey, the pseudonym of an Australian medium who excited much interest on the part of psychical researchers. Born around 1870, Bailey enjoyed a 50-year career in mediumship until his death in 1947. He discovered his powers as a medium at age 18. Early on, his controls announced he had a gift for apports. He then produced his first, a stone dripping with sea water, said to be conveyed from the ocean by a spirit. Among the many apports Bailey produced were live birds in nests with eggs; live fish, crabs and turtles; a barely alive small shark; seedlings growing in pots of earth; an Arabic newspaper; rare coins and antiques (the values of which later were said to be grossly exaggerated); a human skull; a leopard skin; a huge piece of tapestry; precious stones; and clay tablets and cylinders said to bear ancient Babylonian inscriptions.

Bailey's modus operandi was to enclose himself in a double-sewn canvas bag with only his head and arms out, and with seals placed at the neck and wrists. Efforts to test Bailey were thwarted by his controls, who insisted on working in the dark. He was searched prior to donning the bag but was never undressed. Skeptics believed he hid apports on his person, or in hollow heels of his rather high-heeled boots (he was a short man), and then pushed them out through an undetected hole in the sack. Once, he was caught with his boots off. He also was exposed producing fake spirit materializations. Two exotic live birds he once produced as apports were taken to a local bird dealer for the purpose of identifying the species; the dealer recognized the birds as two he had recently sold to a man, and he later identified Bailey as the purchaser. Bailey retorted that the dealer was a "stooge" of the Catholic Church.

Several theories have been advanced to explain apports: that they are brought from other dimensions by spirits; that they are drawn from other dimensions by the will power and magnetic pull of the medium; or that they are objects already existing on the earth plane which are forcibly disintegrated by the medium, transported and reintegrated in another location.

According to apport medium John W. Bunker, in order for apports to appear the medium must put all his spiritual energy, or magnetic current, at the spirits' disposal. Bunker's technique called for deep breathing and relaxation. First, he inhaled in rhythm with the heartbeat for seven counts and mentally directed the magnetic energy in the air to the base of the spine, where he held it for three heartbeats. Next he drew this energy up the spine to the root of the neck and exhaled through the mouth for seven heartbeats. He paused for three heartbeats and repeated the process from the beginning. According to Bunker, this spiritual energy felt like a spot of heat about the size of a half dollar. He advised that mediums never attempt to do this procedure without first having full control of one's mind, emotions and passions. Bunker said he released his cosmic energy in the late evening, thereby converting apported objects to the vapor state, and rematerialized them at seances at 8:00 the next morning.

Certain mystical adepts, such as the Sufis of Islam and Hindu swamis, holy men and avatars (incarnations of God), claim to produce apports such as food, precious jewelry, religious objects and *vibuti* (holy ash). Like mediums, some adepts have been detected using sleight of hand, but others, such as Sai Baba of India, have never been exposed of fraud.

See also ASPORT; MATERIALIZATION; MEDIUMSHIP; SPIRITUALISM.

Further reading:
Brown, Slater. *The Heyday of Spiritualism*. New York: Hawthorn Books, 1970.

Chaney, Rev. Robert G. *Mediums and the Development of Mediumship*. Freeport, N.Y.: Books for Libraries Press, 1972.

Douglas, Alfred. *Extrasensory Powers: A Century of Psychical Research*. London: Victor Gollancz Ltd., 1976.

Fodor, Nandor. *Mind Over Space*. New York: The Citadel Press, 1962.

Haraldsson, Erlendur. *Modern Miracles: An Investigative Report on Psychic Phenomena Associated with Sathya Sai Baba*. New York: Fawcett Columbine, 1987.

Irwin, H.J. "Charley Bailey: A Biographical Study of the Australian Apport Medium." *Journal of the Society for Psychical Research* 54 (April 1987):97–118.

Mitchell, Edgar D. *Psychic Exploration: A Challenge for Science*. John White, ed. New York: Paragon Books, 1974.

Stevenson, Ian. "Are Poltergeists Living or Are They Dead?" *Journal of the American Society for Psychical Research* 66 (July 1972):232–52.

Wolman, Benjamin B., ed. *Handbook of Parapsychology*. New York: Van Nostrand Reinhold, 1977.

arrival cases The appearance of a person in advance of his actual arrival. The arriving phantom appears in the same clothing worn by the person at the time. Observers, believing the individual to be physically present, may speak to the phantom, and it may respond. The projecting individual usually is not aware of appearing in a distant location until he or she is told about it.

There are various theories to explain arrival cases. The most likely is that the individual somehow projects a double, which is perceived as his solid, real self. Another theory is that the individual projects himself out-of-body (see BILOCATION). Still another theory suggests that arrival cases occur in a quirk of time—a duplication of an event in time.

Mark Twain described his own arrival case experience. At a large reception, he spotted a woman whom he knew and liked. He lost sight of her in the crowd, but met her later at supper. She was dressed in the same clothes she had worn to the reception. However, the real woman was on board a train en route to the town where the party was being held—she hadn't yet physically arrived. Twain apparently had seen her double or a phantom duplicate of her.

Arrival cases were collected and studied by the early psychical researchers, the founders of the SOCIETY FOR PSYCHICAL RESEARCH (SPR) in London, in the late 19th and early 20th centuries. The key researchers—Edmund GURNEY, Frederic W.H. MYERS and Frank PODMORE—chronicled arrival cases in their exhaustive survey, *Phantasms of the Living* (1918). In some cases, intent and state of mind seem to be relevant factors—for example, a person is expected to arrive, and in transit is intent on getting there. Or, a person contemplates an activity in another location. *Phantasms* cites the case of a young girl whose arrival apparition was seen in a grove shortly before she actually arrived to commit suicide by hanging herself. The girl's intense emotional state may have contributed to the projection of her double in advance of her act.

In the Highlands of Scotland, the term for arrival cases is "spirits of the living." Highlanders believe arrival apparitions are visible only to those with second sight (CLAIRVOYANCE).

In Norway, the arrival case phenomenon is called Vardøger, which means "forerunner." One unusual Vardøger case occurred in Oslo to Erikson Gorique, an American importer, in 1955. For years, Gorique had wanted to go to Norway, a country he had never before visited, but was forced to keep postponing the trip. In July 1955, he was at last able to make the trip, to look for china and glassware.

He did not decide on his hotel accommodations until he arrived in Oslo, and inquired which hotel was the best. Much to his astonishment, he was greeted by name by the hotel clerk upon his arrival to check in. The clerk told him it was nice to have him return. When Gorique protested that he had never before been at the hotel or in Norway, the puzzled clerk insisted that he could not mistake Gorique's unusual name and American appearance. He said Gorique had stayed at the hotel several months earlier, and had made reservations to return in July.

Gorique was more astonished when he visited a wholesale dealer, who also greeted him familiarly, saying it was a pleasure to have him back to conclude business that had been initiated on his previous trip. Gorique expressed his confusion, whereupon the dealer nodded knowingly and explained the Vardøger phenomenon: it is not uncommon in Norway, he said.

Further reading:

Gurney, Edmund, Frederic W.H. Myers, and Frank Podmore. *Phantasms of the Living.* London: Kegan Paul, Trench, Trubner & Co. Ltd., 1918.

Knight, David C. *The Moving Coffins: Ghosts and Hauntings Around the World.* Englewood Cliffs, N.J.: Prentice-Hall, 1983.

Arundel Castle The ancestral home of the dukes of Norfolk in Sussex, England, haunted by several ghosts. The castle, of medieval style and dating mostly to the 19th century, stands on what is believed to be the remains of a 12th-century castle and an earlier castle. It has belonged to the Norfolk family since 1580, when the uncle of Catherine Howard, Henry VIII's fifth wife, took possession of it.

Best-known of the ghosts is the Blue Man, a Cavalier dressed in a blue silk suit, who is usually seen reading in the library as though searching for some bit of information. The Blue Man has been seen since the time of Charles II (1630–85, reigned 1660–85).

A second ghost is that of a kitchen boy said to have been so badly treated some 200 years ago that he died at a young age. His ghost has been both seen and heard returning to furiously clean pots and pans.

A third ghost is a girl dressed in white, who, according to legend, threw herself off Hiorne's Tower over an unrequited love. Her white form is sometimes seen near the tower on moonlit nights.

The castle has its own death omen, a phantom white bird that flutters against the windows to warn of the impending death of a member of the Howard family. The ghostly bird was said to have appeared just before the death of the Duke of Norfolk in 1917.

Phantom cannon sounds also have been reported booming in the vicinity of the castle. They are said to be from the guns of Sir William Waller, who fought under Oliver Cromwell in the English Civil War (1642–48) against Charles I. Waller's cannons battered Arundel Castle.

Further reading:

Underwood, Peter. *A Gazeteer of British Ghosts.* London: Pan Books Ltd., 1973.

Whitaker, Terence. *Haunted England.* Chicago: Contemporary Books, 1987.

Ash Manor Ghost A curious haunting which occurred in England in the 1930s and was solved by psychical researcher Nandor FODOR. The case demonstrated how underlying psychological factors of the living can create, or at least contribute to, an apparent ghostly manifestation. It also provided one explanation as to why some individuals are haunted at a particular site and others are not. The case was one of Fodor's most famous, and helped to establish his reputation and his theories of the psychological underpinnings of some hauntings. His detailed account of the case is included in his book *The Haunted Mind* (1959).

Ash Manor House, located in Sussex, was built in the 13th century during the time of Edward the Confessor. Over the centuries, much of it was destroyed and rebuilt, but a portion of the structure still survived when Mr. and Mrs. Keel (a pseudonym assigned them by Fodor) purchased the property and moved in on June 24, 1934. They were unaware that the house had a reputation for being "shady," or haunted, although two previous owners had lived there for thirteen and seven years respectively without disturbance.

Shortly after the Keels moved in with their 16-year-old daughter and their servants, they began to hear strange stamping noises in the attic, as though someone were walking on floor boards despite the fact that the attic had none. Then, at approximately 3:35 A.M. on November 18, 1934, Mr. Keel was awakened from a deep sleep by three heavy bangs upon his bedroom door. He got up and went down the hall to his wife's bedroom, and she confirmed that she also had heard the noises. They were at a loss to explain them.

The next night at the same time, Mr. Keel was awakened by two violent bangs upon his bedroom door. The third night at the same time, he was awakened by one bang. The Keels suspected something supernatural was afoot.

Mr. Keel went out of town and returned on November 25. Nothing happened in the house during his absence. On the night of his return, he had a feeling of ill boding. His room felt unnaturally cold. He tried to stay awake, but he fell asleep around 3:00. Shortly thereafter, he was awakened by a single violent bang on the door.

He sat up, and standing in the doorway was, as he described later, "a little oldish man, dressed in a green smock, very muddy breeches and gaiters, a slouch hat on his head and a hankerchief around his neck." At first Keel took the man for a servant; he questioned him but got no response. He jumped up and grabbed the man by the shoulder and was astonished to see his hand go straight through him. Mr. Keel evidently fainted at that point.

He then found himself at his wife's bedroom, babbling incoherently. Mrs. Keel raced out for brandy, and came upon the little man, still standing in the doorway of Mr. Keel's bedroom. At first she saw only his feet and leggings, then the whole figure. She observed a red kerchief around his neck and a pudding basin hat upon his head. His face was red, his eyes were "malevolent and horrid," and his mouth was open and dribbling. He stared at her stupidly. She thought he was a vagrant who had gotten in the house. She attempted to strike him, and her fist went through him. Mrs. Keel ran.

The green man, as the Keels called him, made more appearances, usually to Mr. Keel. The family also heard more knocks and footsteps, which they attributed to the ghost. The man frequently appeared in front of the chimney in Mr. Keel's room, which led Mrs. Keel to suspect that something was hidden inside the chimney wall. She also found that she had the power to make the ghost vanish by touching it, but that Mr. Keel could not do the same. Once, the specter raised his head, and Mrs. Keel could see that his neck had been cut all the way around. She concluded that the ghost was a murder victim, and speculated that it was his skeleton that was hidden in the chimney.

The manifestations were distressing to the Keels; their servants were so frightened that they quit their jobs. The Keels attempted to get help in "laying," or exorcising, the ghost by advertising in the newspaper. Two individuals claimed to be able to do the job but did not succeed, and a priest brought in to perform a formal exorcism only exacerbated the disturbances. Another two lay exorcists claimed the house had been built upon a Druid circle, and that the priest had riled up an evil force from it. In January 1936, an amateur photographer took a photograph of the landing at midnight, which showed a cocoon-like shape. However, the photograph was inconclusive as proof of a supernatural presence.

In July 1936, Fodor became involved in the case at the invitation of a writer who was including the Ash Manor haunting in a book about ghosts. Fodor arrived to find the Keels visibly strained and fearful of publicity that would harm their social reputations. He stayed at the house and took photographs, and slept in the haunted room. But no ghost manifested to him either visually or on film. Nor did he hear any phantom footsteps or bangs.

At that time, the medium Eileen J. GARRETT was living in England, and Fodor invited her to join him at Ash Manor. She arrived on July 25 with an American friend, Dr. Elmer Lindsay, and her daughter, also named Eileen. Garrett received the clairvoyant impression of a man who had been imprisoned and had suffered a great deal. He had a secret. He was a half-brother to either Edward IV or Edward V, and had started a rebellion. He was tortured because of some papers that had to do with the succession of one of the Edwards, and was left crippled as a result. The chimney may have been the hiding place of these papers.

That evening, the investigators entered the haunted room. Garrett went into a trance, and her control, Uvani, spoke. Uvani gave this explanation for the haunting: ghosts manifest when an atmosphere of unhappiness enables a spirit to draw energy and revive its own sufferings. "Haven't you discovered that these things only happen to you when you are in a bad emotional state, physically or mentally disturbed?" Uvani said. "Don't you realize that you yourself vivify this memory?" The control went on to say that in the early 15th century, a jail had existed near the house, where many unhappy souls had lost their lives and lingered about. Anyone living in the house who was "nervously depleted" would give out energy which would attract a ghost, who would use the energy to build itself up "like a picture on the stage." (See the apparitions theories of G.N.M. TYRRELL.)

Uvani announced that he would permit the ghost to possess Garrett. Her features changed; the Keels said her face looked like that of the ghost. In speaking through Garrett, the ghost identified himself in an apparent medieval English accent as "Charles Edward." He claimed to have been robbed of his lands by the "Earl of Huntingdon" and betrayed by a former friend, "Buckingham." He had been separated from his wife and son and left to rot in jail. His son, he said, was fighting for an "ungrateful king," but when pressed to identify the king he gave an evasive reply. He asked the witnesses to help him wreak vengeance upon his enemies.

Fodor and the others informed the ghost that he was dead, and pleaded with him to give up his desire for vengeance, which would enable him to join the spirits of his wife and son. The ghost reluctantly agreed to do so. He departed, unwillingly, and Garrett returned to normal consciousness.

The haunting was far from over, however. Twenty-four hours later, Fodor was informed by Mr. Keel that the ghost had reappeared in his doorway, only this time he was trying to speak. Mr. Keel seemed smug that the exorcism had failed. The ghost also manifested to another medium who knew nothing of the events; the medium's control advised Dr. Lindsay to conduct another seance at Ash Manor for purification.

Fodor then conducted another session with Garrett, but without the Keels. The ghost once again pleaded for help in getting vengeance. Uvani announced that the Keels had used "this poor, unhappy creature" in order to embarrass each other, and that they did not genuinely want the ghost to leave. The control also said that if the unhappiness in the house persisted, the house would become truly haunted and unhappy for future tenants.

Fodor at last felt he was closing in on the solution to the situation. Mrs. Keel confessed to him that her husband was homosexual, and that a great deal of tension existed between them. Fodor felt that the ghost provided distraction that prevented the tension from breaking out into the open.

Mr. Keel acknowledged that what Uvani had said was true. But now he felt the ghost was possessing him. Fodor suggested it might be identification with the ghost due to the shock of the exorcism. Whatever the cause, after Mr. Keel made the admission that he was hanging on to the ghost, the phantom departed and was not seen or heard again.

A scholarly investigation of the statements made by "Charles Edward," as well as handwriting he did through Garrett, was inconclusive. The ghost's apparent medieval English diction was deemed not authentic. Nor could any information be found to establish his historical identity.

In analyzing the case, Fodor considered the argument that the ghost was purely an invention of Mr. Keel's subconscious mind, which Garrett, as a psychic, had simply "borrowed" in the seances. However, some of the haunting phenomena at Ash Manor seemed truly paranormal, especially the fact that the ghost had been seen and heard independently by several persons, and had also been sensed by the family dog. Fodor concluded, "It may be that those who put themselves in an unguarded psychological position, in a place filled with historical memories and traditions, do, on rare occasions, come into contact with a force or an intelligence other than their own."

Further reading:
Fodor, Nandor. *The Haunted Mind.* New York: Helix Press, 1959.

asport   The opposite of APPORT: an object that allegedly is made to disappear or be transported through matter. During the height of physical mediumship, in the late 19th to early 20th centuries, apports produced at seances often became asports, mysteriously vanishing from the seance room, sometimes to be found in another room. This allegedly was accomplished with the help of the spirits of the dead present at the seance.

The Neopolitan medium Eusapia PALLADINO reportedly often asported her sitters' valuables, to their chagrin. Sometimes the items were recovered when the sitters returned home, but in many cases they remained forever with the spirits.

According to a story repeated by stage magician Harry HOUDINI in his book, *A Magician Among the Spirits,* the famous physical medium D.D. HOME, who had a fondness for jewels, asported an exquisite emerald necklace lent him by a member of the Russian Court to please the spirits. Unfortunately, the capricious spirits did not rematerialize the emeralds, and their owner appealed to the chief of police to urge the spirits to reconsider. After searching Home, the chief found that an evil spirit had apported the jewels in Home's pocket—without his knowledge, of course. The chief, not as sympathetic to the whims of spirits, suggested to Home that the climate of the Russian Court might be injurious to his health. He left the country soon thereafter.

Asports also occur in the alleged miracles of modern Eastern avatars, who are believed to be the incarnations of God. Sai Baba of India, famous for his apports of holy ash, food, precious jewelry, religious objects and other items, has been said to dematerialize apports if the recipients do not like them, and change them into something else.

Further reading:
Guiley, Rosemary Ellen. *Harper's Encyclopedia of Mystical and Paranormal Experience.* San Francisco: Harper San Francisco, 1991.
Haraldsson, Erlendur. *Modern Miracles: An Investigative Report on Psychic Phenomena Associated with Sathya Sai Baba.* New York: Fawcett Columbine, 1987.
Houdini, Harry. *Houdini: A Magician Among the Spirits.* New York: Arno Press, 1972.
Mysteries of the Unknown: Spirit Summonings. Alexandria, Va.: Time-Life Books, 1989.

Athenodorus, Haunting of (1st century A.D.)
Perhaps the first record of the classic chain-clanking

ghost is that of the haunting of the rented house of the philosopher, Athenodorus of Athens. The Roman philosopher Pliny the Younger relayed the story in a letter to his patron, Lucias Sura. It is not known how much of the story was embellishment, but it makes for an interesting tale. Wrote Pliny:

> There was formerly at Athens a large and handsome house which none the less had acquired a reputation of being badly haunted. The folk told how at the dead of night horrid noises were heard: the clanking of chains which grew louder and louder until there suddenly appeared the hideous phantom of an old man who seemed the very picture of abject filth and misery. His beard was long and matted, his white hair disheveled and unkempt. His thin legs were loaded with a weight of galling fetters that he dragged wearily along with a painful moaning; his wrists were shackled by long cruel links, while ever and anon he raised his arms and shook his shackles in a kind of impotent fury. Some few mocking skeptics who were once bold enough to watch all night in the house had been well-nigh scared from their senses at the sight of the apparition and what was worse, disease and even death itself proved the fate of those who after dusk had ventured within those accursed walls. The place was shunned. A placard ''To Let'' was posted but year succeeded year and the house fell almost to ruin and decay.

Even this state of affairs, however, did not deter Athenodorus, who had little money. When told the house was so cheap and in such deplorable condition because it was haunted, he rented it anyway.

His first night there, he sat up late working, as was his custom. Presently he heard a chain rattling. The sound grew closer, until suddenly the gruesome phantom of the old man stood before him. The ghost beckoned with his finger, but Athenodorus demurred, indicating he was preoccupied with his work. The ghost then shook the chains so angrily and persistently that the philosopher got up, took his lamp and followed it. The ghost led him outside to the garden, where he pointed to a spot and then vanished. Athenodorus marked the spot and then went inside and to bed. He slept undisturbed.

The next day, according to Pliny, he went to the local magistrates and told them what had happened. Digging commenced at the spot in the garden, and a human skeleton, with rusted chains still shackled to the bones, was uncovered lying close to the surface. The remains were given a proper burial, and the house was ritually purified. According to Pliny, the haunting and the bad luck of the house then came to an end.

Further reading:
Cohen, Daniel. *The Encyclopedia of Ghosts.* New York: Dodd, Mead & Co., 1984.

automatic writing   Writing done in a dissociated or altered state of consciousness that is attributed to spirits of the dead or other discarnate beings. It is believed by some that such spirits manipulate the writing utensil in order to communicate, especially since the writer often is unaware of what is being written, and the handwriting style is markedly different from his own. Most likely, however, the writer writes unconsciously, and messages are formed from material in the subconscious mind or from a secondary personality, or are obtained through extrasensory perception.

Various forms of automatic writing go back to ancient times (see PLANCHETTE). Automatic writing is the most common form of automatism. It has been known to occur involuntarily. Spiritualism made it popular as a deliberate means of attempting to communicate with the dead, and it replaced the much slower methods of spelling out messages with pointers such as the planchette, or counting out letters of the alphabet through rappings.

Through automatic writing, mediums have claimed to produce messages from famous persons in history. In the 1850s, Judge John Worth Edmonds, an American Spiritualist, incited a spate of automatic writing with his alleged messages from Francis Bacon and Emanuel Swedenborg; curiously, the latter always misspelled his name ''Sweedenborg.'' The material produced sounded nothing like the work of either famous man, but it nonetheless inspired others to communicate with more famous deceased persons, including Christ himself. Literary-minded spirits of the dead allegedly communicated entire books and novels and thousands of lines of poetry (see WORTH, PATIENCE). Pens were a common tool, but other Spiritualist methods included slate-writing and the use of typewriters.

Frederic W.H. MYERS, a founder of the SOCIETY FOR PSYCHICAL RESEARCH (SPR), found little evidence of survival after death in cases of automatic writing he investigated. After his death, numerous mediums claimed to receive automatic writing messages from him (see CROSS CORRESPONDENCES; PALM SUNDAY CASE.)

While late 19th-century psychical researchers pursued automatic writing in terms of the survival question, the budding field of psychology began to experiment with automatic writing in mental illness as a way for the unconscious mind to express thoughts and feelings that could not be verbalized. Automatic writing continues to be used as a therapeutic tool in present times.

Automatic writing also enjoys continuing popular appeal. Some individuals attempt to communicate with the alleged highly evolved discarnate beings made famous in channeling (q.v.). Jane Roberts, the American channeler of an entity known as Seth, said she produced automatic writing from Paul Cezanne and William JAMES as well.

Demonologists argue that automatic writing makes one vulnerable to obsession or possession by demons who masquerade as the dead. However, the real danger, if any, most likely comes from the expression of repressed material in the psyche, for which an individual may not be prepared.

Further reading:

Brown, Slater. *The Heyday of Spiritualism.* New York: Hawthorn Books, 1970.

Grattan-Guinness, Ivor. *Psychical Research: A Guide to Its History, Principles and Practices.* Wellingborough, Northamptonshire, England: The Aquarian Press, 1982.

Hyslop, James H. *Contact With the Other World.* New York: The Century Co., 1919.

James, William. "Notes on Automatic Writing" (1889), from *The Works of William James: Essays in Psychical Research.* Frederick Burkhardt, gen. ed. Cambridge: Harvard University Press, 1986.

Myers, Frederic W.H. *Human Personality and Its Survival of Bodily Death Vols. I & II.* New ed. New York: Longmans, Green & Co., 1954. First published 1903.

Pearsall, Ronald. *The Table-Rappers.* New York: St. Martin's Press, 1972.

Stevenson, Ian. "Some Comments on Automatic Writing." *The Journal of the American Society for Psychical Research* 72 (1978):315–32.

automatism   Unconscious muscular movement often attributed to supernatural guidance. Automatisms include virtually any physical activity, especially creative endeavors such as writing, drawing, painting, speaking, playing musical instruments, composing, dancing and singing.

Automatisms have been attributed to spirits and the divine since ancient times, when virtually any inspired activity was considered to be the gift of the gods.

During the rise of SPIRITUALISM, direct automatisms, which had no human medium, were sensational, and also were subject to extensive fraud. Many mediums purported to produce direct spirit automatic writings and drawings, but invariably these were done in the dark during seances.

Early psychical researchers investigated automatisms in search of proof of survival after death. Most evidence, however, was inconclusive at best. The prevailing modern view is that most automatisms are the products of secondary personalities that produce knowledge or information the person has learned and repressed or forgotten; in some cases extrasensory perception may come into play. Rarely is a case explainable only in terms of spirit guidance.

The most common forms of automatism are automatic writing followed by automatic painting. In the latter, individuals who have little or no artistic training suddenly feel overcome by the desire to draw or paint in distinctive, professional styles. They feel guided by a spirit, and may actually feel an invisible hand pushing theirs. In some cases, the style is recognizable as that of a deceased artist. Other types of motor automatisms include impulsive behavior, sudden inhibitions and sudden physical incapacities. Problems associated with automatisms include compulsions, obsession and a feeling of possession.

Sensory automatisms—those produced spontaneously by an inner voice or vision—can include apparitions of the living, inspirations, hallucinations and dreams. Hallucinations once were assumed to be caused by physical disorders, but Edmund GURNEY, an early psychical researcher and a founder of the SOCIETY FOR PSYCHICAL RESEARCH (SPR) in London, established that paranormal visions and sounds can occur without physical disorders.

See also BROWN, ROSEMARY; THOMPSON/GIFFORD CASE.

Further reading:

Douglas, Alfred. *Extrasensory Powers: A Century of Psychical Research.* London: Victor Gollancz Ltd., 1976.

Grattan-Guinness, Ivor. *Psychical Research: A Guide to Its History, Principles and Practices.* Wellingborough, Northamptonshire, England: The Aquarian Press, 1982.

Myers, Frederic W.H. *Human Personality and Its Survival of Bodily Death Vols. I & II.* New ed. New York: Longmans, Green & Co., 1954. First published 1903.

Rhine, J.B., and Robert Brier, eds. *Parapsychology Today.* New York: The Citadel Press, 1968.

The ba, *after an Egyptian wall painting, 13th century* B.C.

ba Egyptian concept of the soul. The *ba* is believed to be an invisible entity which does not permanently leave the body upon death, but remains with it in the tomb. It leaves the tomb at night and roams about the cemetery. It is fed cakes and is cared for by the goddess of the cemetery who lives in sycamore trees. The body must remain intact in order for the *ba* to return to it.

The ancient Egyptians believed the stars were *ba*s lit by their tomb lamps.

See also KA.

Bachelor's Grove Cemetery One of the Chicago area's most haunted sites, with more than 100 reports of numerous and different paranormal phenomena occurring there. The cemetery is a small, one-acre plot west of Crestwood near the Rubio Woods Forest Preserve and has been inactive since 1965. It is overgrown and unkempt and is subject to frequent vandalism, perhaps because of the popularity of the haunting legends. Graves and markers have been defaced and mutilated, and coffins have been disinterred and opened. Evidence of animal sacrifices near

a lagoon at one corner of the cemetery indicates that the cemetery is used by groups practicing Vodoun, Santería, Satanism or some sort of occult rites.

Bachelor's Grove Cemetery takes its name from the large numbers of unmarried men who once lived in the vicinity. The area was settled primarily by German immigrants, many of whom worked on the Illinois-Michigan Canal. The land for the cemetery was set aside in 1864 with the sale of a larger piece of land from one man to another. During the gangster era of the 1920s and 1930s, bodies of the victims of gang warfare were dumped in the lagoon.

Little of the strange phenomena reported at the cemetery seems connected to known historical fact or to specific individuals buried there. Legends have grown up around the hauntings. Similar stories are reported by a disparate cross-section of people, though it is difficult to determine how much the experiences might have been influenced by widely known lore.

Perhaps one of the cemetery's best-known legends is the Hooked Spirit. The story goes that a young man takes his date to the cemetery, where they sit in his parked car. He tells her about the Hooked Spirit, hoping she will be frightened into his arms. Instead, she asks to be taken home. The young man obliges her. When he reaches her home and gets out to open her door, he finds a hook swinging on the handle of the car door: the spirit had been attempting to open the door just as they had driven away.

Another legend tells the story of a young couple who park at the cemetery one night for necking and lovemaking. They are interrupted by a radio report that a mass murderer has escaped from a psychiatric hospital nearby and may be headed in their direction. They decide to leave, but, naturally, the car won't start. The young man gets out to go for help and instructs the girl to remain in the car. Presently she hears a strange scratching on the roof but thinks it is only the sound of tree branches. Her date does not return, but soon a police car comes. An officer tells her to get out, walk toward him and not look back.

She does. More police cars arrive. The girl's curiosity gets the better of her, and she looks behind her. She is horrified to see the body of her boyfriend hanging head down from a tree, his throat slit ear to ear. His fingernails are scratching the car's roof.

A number of ghosts of human beings have been reported, including repeated sightings of a hooded, monk-like figure and also a woman, called both the "White Lady" and the "Madonna of Bachelor's Grove." The latter, who sometimes carries a baby in her arms, is seen only on nights of the full moon. Apparitions are seen to emerge from the lagoon, including a two-headed man and, most commonly, a ghostly farmer and his horse and plow. Legend has it that in the 1870s, a farmer was plowing land near the lagoon when his horse inexplicably bolted into the water; both man and animal were drowned. Phantom vehicles have been reported. A phantom farmhouse mysteriously appears and disappears in different locations. There is no historical record of such a farmhouse, yet reports of the ghost date to the 1950s. Anyone who attempts to approach it sees it shrink and then vanish. Ghost lights (q.v.)—bobbing, elusive blobs of bluish light—weave about the cemetery, and red skyrocket-like lights streak through the air. In December 1971, a young woman said she succeeded in putting her hand through one of the ghost lights, but felt nothing. Other phenomena include sensations of unusual cold, the awareness of an invisible presence that causes discomfort, and the tactile sensation of sweaty but invisible hands upon the skin.

Numerous attempts have been made to capture the cemetery's ghostly occupants on film. Still photos reportedly reveal ghostly and demonic faces and forms. Most likely, these are effects known as "simulacra,"and are created out of random patterns in backgrounds. (See SPIRIT PHOTOGRAPHY.)

In 1982, Dale Kaczmarek, president of the GHOST RESEARCH SOCIETY, took a psychic to Bachelor's Grove in an attempt to learn more about the phenomena there. The psychic claimed to make contact with a number of ghosts of people buried there, who, she said, were frustrated because they were unable to leave the confines of the cemetery until a certain, but unspecified, amount of time had passed. No unusual images or sounds were recorded on their video camera and audio tape recorder. Infrared film shot was washed out, despite the fact that the second half of the roll, shot elsewhere, was normal.

Further reading:

Kaczmarek, Dale. "Bachelor's Grove: The Most Haunted Cemetery." In Sharon Jarvis, ed. *True Tales of the Unknown Vol. II.* New York: Bantam Books, 1989.

A tombstone rubbing.

Miller, Paul Richard. "Chicago: The World's Biggest Ghost Town." *Fate* (November 1990):53–68.

Balfour Family   Prominent Scottish family, several of whom were closely involved in the SOCIETY FOR PSYCHICAL RESEARCH (SPR).

Eleanor Balfour (1845–1936), the eldest of eight children, married Henry SIDGWICK in 1876 and devoted much of her life to the SPR. Her biography is given in a separate entry (see SIDGWICK, ELEANOR BALFOUR).

Arthur James Balfour (1848–1930), the First Earl of Balfour, was educated at Trinity College, Cambridge, where he was a student of Sidgwick and met other members of the group who were to form the SPR's inner circle. He devoted several years to metaphysical and philosophical studies, and he was vice president of the SPR from its inception in 1882 and its president in 1893. His political career gave him little time to devote to research, however. He first went to Parliament in 1876; he served as prime minister from 1902 to 1905 and as foreign minister from 1916 to 1922.

Arthur Balfour was the involuntary center of the important mediumistic PALM SUNDAY CASE, the details of which were made public only after his death.

Gerald William Balfour (1854–1945), the Second Earl of Balfour, also attended Trinity College, where he studied classics. He joined the SPR in 1883, the year after it was founded. He was elected to the House of Commons in 1885 but left politics after an electoral defeat in 1906, and he devoted himself to the study of the complex, interlocking set of mediumistic communications known as the CROSS CORRESPONDENCES. He contributed several important papers on mediumship to the SPR's *Proceedings* (including one on the famous EAR OF DIONYSIUS case), and served as president of the SPR in 1906 and 1907.

A sister, Evelyn, married Lord Rayleigh (John William Strutt), a Nobel Prize-winning physicist (1904) who also was active in psychical research (serving as president of the SPR in 1919).

A brother, Francis, an outstanding biologist, died in a mountaineering accident in the Swiss Alps in 1882. He appears in the psychical research literature as a communicator in the Palm Sunday Case and some other cross-correspondences.

Eleanor, Arthur, Evelyn and Lord Rayleigh took part in a group that included Henry Sidgwick, Frederic W.H. MYERS and Edmund GURNEY, formed in 1874 to investigate mediumistic phenomena. Although the SPR (founded in 1882) did not grow directly out of this group, it was an important forerunner of the SPR.

Further reading:

Gauld, Alan. *The Founders of Psychical Research*. London: Routledge & Kegan Paul, 1968.

Haynes, Renee. *The Society for Psychical Research, 1882–1892: A History*. London: Heinemann, 1982.

Oppenheim, Janet. *The Other World: Spiritualism and Psychical Research in England, 1850–1914*. Cambridge: Cambridge University Press, 1985.

Bailey, Charles See APPORT.

Ballechin House The bizarre haunting of this Highland mansion in Perthshire, Scotland allegedly came about because the wish of the house's owner to return to life in the body of one of his dogs was denied him. Hauntings were reported at the house for more than two decades, until they broke into public light in 1897.

Ballechin House was built in 1806 on property that since the 16th century had belonged to the Steuart family, descendants of King Robert II of Scotland. The mansion replaced an older manor house which was demolished. In 1834, the property was inherited by Major Robert Steuart upon the death of his father. Steuart, who was posted with the army of the East India Company and lived in India, let the house to tenants. In 1850, he retired after a service of 25 years and returned to the Scottish estate. He lived in a cottage for several years, until the main house was free of its tenants.

The Major, as he was called, had a pronounced limp and was known as a local character and eccentric. He kept many dogs. While in India, he had become a believer in reincarnation and transmigration, the ability of the soul to inhabit nonhuman bodies. His wish was that upon his death, his spirit would return to occupy the body of his favorite black spaniel.

The Major was unmarried and for 26 years lived alone at Ballechin House except for the company of his young housekeeper, Sarah, who died suddenly and mysteriously at the age of 27 in 1873. His only family consisted of two brothers and six sisters, one of whom, Isabella, became a nun. Isabella assumed the name of Frances Helen and lived in a nunnery until her death in 1880.

In a will made in 1853, the Major left the house to the five children of his married sister, Mary. The eldest son died without heirs, and the Major later excluded the three younger children in a codicil to the will. When the Major died in 1876, the estate was inherited by Mary's second son, John, who was married and had several children. The family abhorred the notion of the Major coming back to life in one of his dogs, no matter how preposterous, and ordered every one of them shot. Later, the theory was put forth that the Major was then forced to remain a disembodied spirit, and he haunted the house to protest.

The Major was buried next to young Sarah. Almost immediately after his death, strange happenings began, including rappings and knockings, sounds like explosions and the sound of people quarrelling. John's wife was in the Major's study one day when she experienced an overpowering smell of dogs. She also felt herself being pushed against by an invisible dog. These and other events were so frightening that servants and governesses would not stay in the house.

Speculation arose about the relationship between the Major and Sarah. She had died in the main bedroom, which became the most haunted room in the house, and it was said that the Major's ghost could often be heard limping around the bed.

Although the John Steuarts managed to live at the estate for 21 years, John was forced to build a new wing in 1883 for his children to live in, outside the haunted area. He allowed the cottage where the Major had lived to be used as a retreat by nuns.

One morning in 1895, John was talking on the telephone to his agent before leaving for London on family business. Their conversation was interrupted by three loud, violent knocks. Later that day, John was fatally struck by a cab on a busy London street. Believers in ghosts took the knocks to be a warning of doom.

By this time, Ballenchin House had gained the reputation of a haunted house, as frightening tales told by former guests circulated in the community. In 1892, Father Hayden, a Jesuit priest, slept there in two different rooms after hearing loud noises consisting of animal-like sounds, raps and shrieks. The next year, Hayden met a woman who had been a governess in the house for 12 years, but who had left because of the strange noises heard in the very same two rooms.

In 1896, a family rented the house for one year, but left after only 11 weeks. Family members reported being terrorized by poltergeist activity that included inexplicable rattles, knocks, thumps, footsteps, bedclothes pulled off beds by unseen hands, rustling sounds, groans, heavy breathing, an icy coldness and even two apparitions—one in the form of an indeterminate mist and one in the shape of a man.

Lord Bute, an avid ghost-hunter of the day, agreed to sponsor an investigation. He rented the house for two investigators, Colonel Lemesurier Taylor and Miss A. Goodrich-Freer. On their first morning, the researchers heard clanging sounds repeated at two-hour intervals, the sound of voices, footsteps, dragging and pattering, loud bangs, thumps and knockings.

The investigators invited 35 guests to stay at the house, all of whom were unaware of the house's reputation. The guests reported numerous supernatural activities, including strange rappings and knocks, the sound of someone reading aloud in the manner of a priest saying his office, a spectral hunchback seen walking up the stairs, the apparition of a black spaniel, and phantom dogs' tails heard striking doors and other objects. Goodrich-Freer, who had brought her own dog with her, was awakened one night by its whimpering. Following its gaze, she saw two disembodied dog's paws on the table beside the bed. A male guest reportedly saw a detached hand in the air at the foot of his bed, holding a crucifix. A maid saw the upper half of a woman's figure wearing a gray shawl, seemingly suspended in the air.

The investigators conducted sessions with a Ouija board and also received automatic writing messages. One message instructed the researchers to go to a nearby glen at dusk. Doing so, Goodrich-Freer saw a figure dressed as a nun move slowly up the glen and then disappear under a tree. She saw the same figure other times, either weeping or talking. Other reports described the figure as a young woman with a pale face, long hair and wearing a hood, and who disappeared quickly when people approached. Some people speculated that the figure was that of Isabella, who, for some unknown reason, was weeping in the snow-covered glen.

The entire account of the experiment was reported in *The Times* newspaper and was recorded in a book, *The Alleged Haunting of B-House,* published in 1899. The Steuart family raised so much opposition to the publicity, however, that all proper names had to be excluded from the story. The result was that hauntings had to be reported as "alleged," and the full story never gained credence as a true haunting.

Further reading:

Canning, John, ed. *50 Great Ghost Stories.* New York: Bonanza Books, 1988. First published 1971.

Harper, Charles G. *Haunted Houses: Tales of the Supernatural With Some Accounts of Hereditary Curses and Family Legends.* Rev. and enlarged ed. London: Cecil Palmer, 1924.

Baltimore Poltergeist.   A case of a modern-day poltergeist named for the city—Baltimore, Maryland—where it baffled its victims, citizens, public officials, the media and Nandor FODOR, a respected psychoanalyst and researcher of psychic phenomena. Between January 14 and February 8, 1960, this alleged spirit caused such havoc by making objects fly, break, crack and explode that its victims finally just threw everything that could possibly be undone or broken out of their house and into the backyard. At the end of a month of terror, the activity suddenly stopped, leaving numerous theories about the mystery but not one indisputable solution.

The head of the affected household was Edgar G. Jones, a former fireman who retired after 37 years of devoted service to Baltimore's fire department. Also involved were his wife, Mrs. Jones; the couple's son-in-law and daughter, Mr. and Mrs. Theodore Pauls; and the Pauls's 17-year old son, Ted Pauls.

Ted was a high school dropout, but he was highly intelligent, according to his family and former teachers. Shy and reclusive, Ted spent most of his time in solitary pursuits, such as reading science fiction and tales of the supernatural. In addition, he was a writer and editor of a newsletter, *Fanjack,* that he mimeographed in the basement and sent to a few selected friends. His parents and grandparents, however, were upset that he was devoting himself to these activities rather than attending school.

The first indication that something was amiss came on January 14, 1960, when 15 miniature pottery pitchers exploded on a dining room shelf. In the ensuing month of terror, objects jumped off shelves and crashed through windows, pictures fell to the floor, plants leapt out of their holders, and soda bottles burst open like firecrackers.

Initially, most of the happenings took place in the late morning and afternoon. On Sunday, January 17, the noisy ghost struck at night for the first time. Mr. Jones was the first victim, when he tried to pick up a can of corn that had fallen off a shelf and was rewarded with a bang on the head from a falling can of sauerkraut. This insult was followed by a small table moving from the living room to a stairway landing, where it threw itself down the stairs. At the other end of the house, a stack of kindling wood exploded in the basement.

The next day, January 18, came a respite. But the attacks resumed on the following day with various objects cracking and flying. On January 19, all hell broke loose, and family members were kept busy running from one room to another to assess the damage.

The next four days brought another much needed respite. But one again, as if the spirit had needed to regain its energy, it renewed its activities. The family was subjected to a nine-hour barrage of breaking and flying objects that forced Mrs. Jones to flee her house and find refuge in the home of her sister. Mr. Pauls and Mr. Jones took a more drastic step: they threw every breakable item and piece of furniture into the backyard so they could get some sleep.

Within the next week, there were a dozen more occurrences. But on February 9, the attacks suddenly and mysteriously stopped.

By then, word had spread and the Jones family had become local celebrities. Newspaper and broadcast reporters were a constant presence in the house as they pressed the family to make statements for a curious public.

Theories abounded. One theory held that young Ted was perpetrating a hoax on his family, an allegation that was vigorously denied by his parents and grandparents. Other theories had a more scientific basis, but each in its turn was found to be groundless. For example, radio signals, earth tremors or high-pitched sound waves were all considered. A high-frequency receiver, an investigation with a seismograph by city highway workers, an examination for explosives in objects that had exploded by the city policy department's crime lab, and a radio repair man looking for wind coming from a drainage pipe all failed to provide substantial proof.

One final theory, offered by a plumber visiting the house on the night of the last activities, suggested that the hot air furnace was the culprit. He advised the family to remove all storm windows and open a dining room window to equalize pressure. After the Joneses followed his instructions, the happenings ceased. The family thereafter credited the plumber as the problem-solver.

Before the happenings had stopped completely, Nandor Fodor visited the family to investigate. His conclusions were similar to those he had made in other cases involving a young household member: he concluded that Ted was an unconscious agent who used his mental power to create the disturbances.

Fodor theorized that Ted wanted to be esteemed for his writing talent, and being newsletter editor was one way he could raise himself above his readers. Ted's depressed ego might be hiding behind the poltergeist activity, and he might be releasing his creative energy into abnormal channels.

Fodor explained that the human body is capable of releasing energy that could produce such abnormal activities through brain activity. Ted's aggression was unconscious because he perceived himself to be a brilliant, misunderstood person, underappreciated by family, school and classmates. He could vent his frustrations by projecting them into aggressive poltergeist activities.

Fodor theorized that if Ted could feel appreciated and valued for his talents, his self-esteem would heighten and there would be no need for his expression in destructive poltergeist activities. Fodor explained this to Ted, who seemed relieved. However, Fodor instinctively knew that he had to do something more to prove what he was saying. He took an acknowledged risk by announcing during radio and television interviews that Ted was a gifted writer, and that recognition of his talent would seal a breach in his psyche and stop the poltergeist activity once and for all. Fodor suggested that, as therapy, Ted write his own account of what had happened, which also would have scientific value.

Fodor expected this statement to have a therapeutic effect on Ted, and it did. His parents and grandparents found a new respect for the boy, and Ted seemed to adopt a new attitude of acceptance about himself. Although the worst poltergeist outbreaks did continue for a short time after these statements and Fodor's departure (part of the psychological working-through process, Fodor explained), they gradually came to an end. The reason, said Fodor, was that Ted no longer needed to protest his frustrations through poltergeist activity.

In spite of this theory from an esteemed man of science, the Jones family remained convinced that it was the plumber's simple advice that produced the cessation of their torment. Skeptics contended it was merely a coincidence. The case was never solved conclusively.

In his writeup of the case in his book, *Between Two Worlds* (1964), Fodor concluded:

> The case is important because accidentally I tumbled on a novel cure of the Poltergeist psychosis. . . . It is as simple as the egg of Columbus. Find the frustrated creative gift, lift up a crushed ego, give love and confidence and the Poltergeist will cease to be. After that you can still proceed with psychoanalysis, release the unconscious conflicts, but whether you do it or not, a creative self-expression will result in a miraculous transformation.

Further reading:

Fodor, Nandor. *Between Two Worlds.* West Nyack, N.Y.: Parker Publishing, 1964.

Naver, Michael, and Travis Kidd. "The Baltimore Poltergeist." *Tomorrow* 8 (Spring 1960):9–16.

banshee   A female death omen spirit of Ireland and Scotland that attaches itself to families—especially those whose surnames begin with "Mac" and "O"—and manifests to herald an approaching death in the family. There are variations of the banshee in Irish and Scottish lore. An Irish variant, written as Bean Si, is said to be beautiful with long streaming hair, and wearing a gray cloak over a green dress. She also appears all in white or all in red. Her eyes are fiery red from continual crying for the about-to-be-departed. To warn a family of a coming death, the banshee most commonly is heard singing or crying, but is not seen. When seen, she appears as a woman singing, or as a shrouded woman wearing a veil, or as a flying figure in the moonlight, crying bitterly. The cry reportedly is so mournful that it is unmistakably the sound of doom. Contrary to some popular thought, banshees do not wail.

In both Ireland and the Scottish Highlands, the banshee is also known as Bean-Nighe or Little-Washer-By-The-Ford; the latter term comes from the lore that she signals a person's imminent and violent death by washing his blood-stained grave-cloths in a stream.

The Bean-Nighe or Little-Washer-By-The-Ford is lieved to be the spirit of a woman who died a mature death in childbirth, whose spirit must c tinue washing clothes until it is the time for natural destined death. Small and usually dresse green, this spirit is not beautiful like the Bean Si, is evil, mean and deformed. She has just one nos a large protruding front tooth, red webbed feet long pendulous breasts. The person who is co geous enough to suck a breast is believed to granted a wish by the spirit and become her fo child.

Banshee beliefs were taken to America with migrants, but only a few stories about them h entered into American folklore. One of those folk tales comes from the American South, se Revolutionary War days. According to the tal banshee haunted the muddy Tar River near Tarb in Edgecombe County, North Carolina. She arose misty nights when there was no moon, and fli from shore to shore crying like a loon, her yellow hair streaming behind her.

The Tar River mill was run by a large, rough named David Warner, a Whig who hated the Bri and aided the revolutionaries by giving them wl and corn ground at his mill. One hot August n day, Warner was warned that British soldiers w coming and was urged to flee, lest he be killed. stubbornly refused to leave.

Warner was grinding grain when five British diers arrived. He pretended not to see them loudly announced to his assistant, "Try to save ev precious ounce of it, my lad, and we'll deliver General Greene. I hate to think of those British h eating a single mouthful of gruel made from Am ca's corn."

With that, the enraged soldiers seized Warner, him and announced they were going to drown in the river. Warner told them to go ahead and so, but the banshee would get them in return.

The soldiers hesitated, but one who had evil and a cruel mouth egged them on. He and two oth tied Warner's hands behind his back, tied large st to his neck and feet, and cast him into the river. Warner sank beneath the water, a piercing, agoni woman's scream arose from somewhere along river banks. The frightened soldiers fled back to mill.

That night, the soldiers' commander and his cers arrived, and they all bedded down. A new m rose in the sky and a rain crow (cuckoo) called presaging rain. Suddenly the air was pierced by banshee's cry. The Commander and officers rus out of their tent and saw a cloud of mist over river take on the shape of a woman with long, flowing hair and a veil. She disappeared, and her cry could be heard farther downstream.

The three soldiers confessed their crime. The commander sentenced them to remain at the mill, grinding, for the rest of their lives. Every day, the men ground grain, and at night they were tormented by the banshee's cry. One night, she appeared in the doorway of the mill and drew aside her veil. She lured two of the men down to the river, where they fell in; they were never seen again. The soldier with the evil eyes went insane and began wandering through the woods calling out Warner's name. He was answered by the banshee. One day, his body was found floating in the river, at the spot where Warner had been drowned.

On August nights when the moon is new and the rain crow calls for rain, the banshee is still said to rise up out of the mist where Warner was drowned, and cry into the night.

Further reading:
Briggs, Katherine. *An Encyclopedia of Fairies: Hobgoblins, Brownies, Bogies, and Other Supernatural Creatures.* New York: Pantheon Books, 1976.

Leach, Maria and Jerome Fried, eds. *Funk & Wagnalls Standard Dictionary of Folklore, Mythology, and Legend.* San Francisco: Harper & Row, 1979.

Lysaght, Patricia. *The Banshee: The Irish Supernatural Death Messenger.* Dublin: The Glendale Press, 1986.

McNeil, W.K., comp. and ed. *Ghost Stories from the American South.* New York: Dell, 1985.

Barbanell, Maurice (1902–1981) English journalist and medium, widely known as "Mr. Spiritualism." The teachings of his spirit control, a Native American named "Silver Birch," continue to have a wide following.

Maurice Barbanell was born on May 3, 1902 in London. His father was a dentist. As a young man, Barbanell was an atheist and therefore was skeptical of Spiritualist claims. He heard a lecture on Spiritualism and challenged the speaker by saying that the subject should be addressed only by those with personal experience. He was challenged in return, and agreed to undertake a six-month personal investigation himself.

Barbanell began attending the home circle (q.v.) of a medium known as Mrs. Blaustein. Generally bored, he fell asleep at one sitting and awoke to hear that he had become a medium for a Native American spirit. Barbanell formed his own home circle, and the spirit, whose real name was kept confidential, began to dispense his wisdom. One member of the circle was the journalist Hannen Swaffer, an enthusiastic proponent both of Spiritualism and of the teachings of Barbanell's spirit guide. The circle became known as the Hannen Swaffer circle; for years, it was one of the best-kept secrets in British Spiritualism.

Barbanell preferred to remain anonymous. His mediumship was not widely publicized, even when he and others founded *Psychic News* in 1932. The idea for the Spiritualist newspaper came from Red Cloud, the Native American control of medium Estelle Roberts. Barbanell edited the paper from 1932 to 1946, and resumed it in 1962; he felt that it would not be proper to publicize his mediumship in it. Swaffer continually urged him to disseminate his spirit's messages to a wider audience than the home circles. Barbanell eventually agreed to publish them in the newspaper, but to keep himself anonymous as the medium. For publication, the spirit guide chose the pseudonym "Silver Birch."

Barbanell was active in the SPIRITUALISTS' NATIONAL UNION and also lectured widely during his career. He wrote numerous books and articles. He also edited another Spiritualist publication, *Two Worlds.*

Barbanell died at age 79 on July 17, 1981. At almost the moment of his passing, Tony Ortzen, then editor of *Psychic News*, received a two-word coded message that he and Barbanell had agreed upon while Barbanell was still living. Within days, medium Gordon Higginson, a friend of Barbanell, received spirit communications that were interpreted as evidential.

The teachings of Silver Birch have been edited and published by Barbanell's wife, Sylvia Abrahams Barbanell, and others. Barbanell had met Sylvia at Blaustein's home circle; they were married in 1932.

Barbanell steadfastly rejected the theory that controls are secondary personalities of mediums. Sitters in the circle attest to the difference in personalities between Silver Birch and Barbanell. Silver Birch taught reincarnation, a doctrine rejected by Barbanell.

According to Silver Birch, he had been reluctant to leave his own world and return to earth, a much more drab and depressing place, but had a mission to disseminate "old, old teachings" that humankind continually forgets. He chose Barbanell from "records" and watched the medium from birth. He led Barbanell into atheism, he said, apparently to make him more receptive to the material that was to come through in his own mediumship. Silver Birch's messages center on the oneness of all life; the importance of love, spiritual healing and service to others; and the immortality of the soul.

Further reading:
Bassett, Jean. *100 Years of National Spiritualism.* London: Spiritualists' National Union, 1990.

Storm, Stella, ed. *Philosophy of Silver Birch.* London: Psychic Press, 1969.

Bardo Thödol (The Tibetan Book of the Dead)

Nowhere is the art of dying more sophisticated than in the culture of Tibet, whose religion evolved from the shamanistic Bön into Tantric Buddhism beginning in the 8th century. In Tibetan thought, the process of right dying is as important as right living. A high form of yoga—a spiritual discipline of meditation—has developed over the centuries to speed the ghosts of the dead on their afterlife spiritual journey and enable them to be conscious of the experiences waiting to greet them.

The *Bardo Thödol*, the Tibetan handbook on dying, the afterlife and rebirth, is of remote antiquity. There is no known author or authors; more than likely, it was honed and refined over the course of history. It was first written down in the 8th century.

The central objective of Tibetan death rites is to extract the consciousness-principle from the gross physical body so that it can truly perceive the spiritual world. Following death, the spirit enters a transit that lasts exactly 49 days and is divided into three stages. At the end of the *Bardo,* one either enters nirvana, an ineffable state, or returns to earth for another reincarnation. Only the most enlightened avoid reincarnation.

It is of paramount importance that the dying person remain fully conscious for as long as possible, for the last thoughts of the dying influence the quality of the after-death experience and the subsequent reincarnation. He is laid on his right side, called the "Lion Posture," and his neck arteries are pressed to prevent loss of consciousness. The dying person is guided by a guru or lama, who advises him on what to prepare for. If the person is wealthy, many lamas assist; if he is poor, only one assists, and rites are terminated partway through the 49-day *Bardo.*

The first stage of the *Bardo* commences at the moment of death and lasts from a half day to four days; this is how long it takes for the deceased to realize he has been separated from his body. As soon as the individual expires, a white cloth is thrown over his face, and no one is allowed to touch the corpse. All doors and windows are sealed, and the "extractor of consciousness-principle" lama takes up his vigil by the corpse's head. No grieving is permitted. The lama takes up a mystical chant which provides directions for the deceased to find its way to the Western Paradise of Amitabha. If the person's karma is good enough, this will enable him to escape the ordeal of the intermediate period of the *Bardo.* The lama examines the top of the head to determine if the spirit has exited as it should through the "Aperture of Brahma"; if so, he pulls out three hairs, if the head is not bald. If circumstances are such that there is no corpse, the lama visualizes the body as though present, and proceeds with the rites. A setting-face-to-face with the Clear Light is repeated until a yellowish liquid exudes from body orifices. In some descriptions, it is a yellowish luminosity, like an aura. If the deceased led an evil life, this state lasts but a moment. If enlightened, it lasts for an hour or so.

An astrologer lama casts a death horoscope, based on the moment of death, to determine who may touch the corpse, how it will be disposed of, and what funeral rites should be performed.

At the end of the first stage, the corpse is seated upright in a corner of the death chamber. Care is taken not to use one of the corners assigned to the household demon. The relatives are summoned and a feast ensues, in which the corpse participates by being offered the invisible essences of all food and drink. The feast lasts for at least two days.

The corpse is then removed for disposal, and an effigy of the corpse is made of wood and dressed in the clothes of the deceased. For the remainder of the *Bardo,* it stays in the corner, attended by the lamas who chant by relays the various liturgies at the appropriate time. At the end of the *Bardo,* the effigy is hung with ornaments and dismantled, and the ghost of the dead is warned not to return to haunt the body.

The corpse, meanwhile, is given a funeral. Tibetans favor cremation, as they believe earth burial can cause the dead one to survive as a vampire. Another favored means is to dismember the corpse and leave it to the birds. (See BIRDS; VAMPIRE.)

At the moment of death, the spirit sees the primary Clear Light, an ecstasy. All persons get at least a glimpse of the Clear Light, but the more enlightened can see it longer and transcend to a higher reality. Most relapse into the Secondary Clear Light, a lesser ecstasy.

The second stage is like an awakening, in which the spirit is presented with hallucinations created by karmic reflexes of actions done while alive. Unless enlightened, the spirit is under the illusion that it still has a body like the one that died. There begins a series of apparitions, the Coming of the Peaceful and Wrathful Deities, or personifications of human sentiment, which must be faced without flinching. Most escape the second stage through rebirth, the third stage; the circumstances of rebirth are determined by past karma.

The most enlightened of yogis are said to bypass all of the *Bardo,* going directly to a paradise realm or else directly into another body in rebirth without any loss of consciousness. Yoga during life prepares one for the after-death experiences.

See also SURVIVAL AFTER DEATH.

Further reading:
Bromage, Bernard. *Tibetan Yoga*. Wellingborough, Northamptonshire, England: The Aquarian Press, 1979. First published 1952.

Evans-Wentz, W.Y., ed. *The Tibetan Book of the Dead*. 3rd ed. London: Oxford University Press, 1960.

barghest (also barguest) In English folklore, a spectral hound said to exist in Cornwall and northern England. As a DEATH OMEN, it manifests as a bear or large dog. Inhabitants of Lancashire call it the Shriker, after its shrieks emitted when it is invisible, and Trash, after the splashing sounds it sometimes makes when it walks. See also BLACK SHUCK; WHISHT HOUNDS.

Barrett, Elizabeth See BROWNING CIRCLE.

Barrett, Sir William Fletcher (1844–1925) Physicist and psychical researcher, a key figure in the founding of both the SOCIETY FOR PSYCHICAL RESEARCH (SPR) and the AMERICAN SOCIETY FOR PSYCHICAL RESEARCH (ASPR).

William Barrett was born on February 10, 1844 in Jamaica, British West Indies, the son of a clergyman. He attended a private boarding school in Manchester, England, where he distinguished himself by his aptitude for physics. At age 19, in 1862, he was hired as an assistant to physicist John Tyndall at the Royal Institution, in London. He left five years later to take up teaching positions, and in 1873 he was appointed to the chair in physics at the Royal College of Science, Dublin, where he stayed until his retirement in 1910.

Although he never attained the same stature as Sir William CROOKES and Sir Oliver LODGE, other physicists involved in psychical research, Barrett is credited with some important accomplishments. He was the first to notice the contraction of nickel when magnetized, and he invented a silicon-iron alloy called stalloy, important to the commercial development of the telephone and in the construction of transformers, dynamos and other equipment related to electrical engineering. He was knighted in 1912.

Barrett's first exposure to psychical research came while he was at the Royal Institution in the 1860s. Incredulous at what he heard about some ESP experiments conducted with subjects under hypnosis, he repeated the experiments with a different subject and found that "whatever sensations I felt, whether of touch, taste or smell, were transferred to the subject, and, moreover, ideas and words which I

thought of were produced more or less accurately by the hypnotized subject." A few years later, in 1874, he had his first experience with a medium and became convinced of physical phenomena as well.

In 1876 Barrett submitted a report of his hypnosis-ESP experiments to a meeting of the British Association for the Advancement of Science in Glasgow, Scotland. The Biology Section refused it, but it was accepted by the Anthropology subsection, thanks to the intercession of Alfred Russel Wallace, the chair for that year. The paper created a sensation at the conference and in the press, but it was denied the customary publication in the British Association *Proceedings*.

Whether it was Barrett or someone else who first suggested the idea of the SPR as an alliance of psychical researchers and Spiritualists has long been a matter of dispute, but it is probably true that only Barrett could have brought the two sides together. Barrett was acquainted with Frederick W.H. MYERS, Edmund GURNEY and Henry SIDGWICK, who from 1874 had been involved in systematic investigations of mediumship, and who were about to form the central force of the SPR, but he was also on good terms with the Spiritualist community.

The SPR's first organizational meeting was held at the offices of the BRITISH NATIONAL ASSOCIATION OF SPIRITUALISTS in 1881, and it was formally constituted the following year. Barrett was a member of the SPR's Council from the start, and he initiated publication of a *Journal* in 1884 (*Proceedings* had been issued from 1882).

Later in 1884 Barrett traveled to Montreal for that year's meeting of the British Association, and he was invited to Philadelphia to deliver before the American Association for the Advancement of Science the paper for which he had been snubbed two years earlier in Glasgow. A lively discussion followed the reading, and an American Society for Psychical Research was proposed. A few days later Barrett was in Boston talking about the SPR to a formation committee.

Although Barrett contributed important papers on dowsing to the SPR *Proceedings* in 1900 and 1901, and was elected to the SPR presidency in 1904, his Spiritualist tendencies placed him outside the ruling group that centered on Sidgwick and his colleagues. On the other hand, he was also interested in a broad range of psychical phenomena, and he was unhappy with the increasing emphasis on the cross correspondences (q.v.) after the turn of the century.

In 1916, when in his early 70s, Barrett married Florence Willey, an eminent gynecologist, and moved to London to be with her. He died there on May 26,

1925. The following year, Lady Barrett received communications through medium Gladys Osborne LEONARD that she believed to have come from her late husband; she published these in a book called *Personality Survives Death* (1937).

In the last years of his life, Barrett had been collecting accounts of apparitions seen by dying persons, and these were published posthumously as *Deathbed Visions* (1926). A book on dowsing was completed by SPR Librarian Theodore Besterman and also published posthumously (1926). Barrett's other books include *Thought-Transference* (1882); *On the Threshold of a New World of Thought* (1908); *On Creative Thought* (1910); *Psychical Research*, a volume in the Home University Library series (1911); *Swedenborg: The Savant and the Seer* (1912); and *On the Threshold of the Unseen* (1917).

See also DEATHBED VISIONS.

Further reading

Barrett, Sir William. "Some Reminiscences of Fifty Years in Psychical Research." *Proceedings of the Society for Psychical Research* 34 (1924):275–97.

Gauld, Alan. *The Founders of Psychical Research*. London: Routledge & Kegan Paul, 1968.

Haynes, Renee. *The Society for Psychical Research, 1882–1892: A History*. London: Heinemann, Ltd., 1982.

Oppenheim, Janet. *The Other World: Spiritualism and Psychical Research in England, 1850–1914*. Cambridge: Cambridge University Press, 1985.

Pleasants, Helene, ed. *Biographical Dictionary of Parapsychology*. New York: Helix Press, 1964.

Taylor, Eugene. "The American Society for Psychical Research, 1884–1889." In Debra H. Weiner and Dean I. Radin, eds., *Research in Parapsychology 1985*. Metuchen, N.J.: Scarecrow Press, 1986, pp. 187–96.

Battle Abbey A phantom fountain of blood is said to appear at this haunted abbey, constructed by William I (William the Conqueror) on the site of his victory over King Harold at the Battle of Hastings in 1066. Normans called the site Senlac, which means "Lake of Blood," and legend has it that the ground sweats blood after a rain. The presence of iron in the soil probably accounts for the reddish puddles of water, however.

William built the abbey to atone for the Normans' slaughter of the defending Anglo-Saxons, and perhaps to express his thanks to God for the victory. Within the church, he constructed a High Altar on the spot where Harold fell. Only a fir tree stands there now. According to legend, the phantom fountain of blood appears at this spot to commemorate the great amount of Christian blood that was shed in the battle.

Henry VIII began to dissolve the monasteries in 1536 in his break with the Catholic Church, and gave Battle Abbey to Sir Anthony Browne in 1538. But during a celebratory feast, Browne was cursed by an unhappy monk for taking church property. The monk said Browne's name would be wiped from the land by fire or water. Browne's inherited property, Cowdray Hall, which was passed down to Lord Montague, burned down in 1793. A week later, the surviving male in the family line, a viscount, was drowned in the Rhine, and Browne's lineage came to an end. to an end.

A phantom has been seen at Monk's Wall at Battle Abbey. Some believe it may be the monk who cursed Browne. Modern owners of the abbey believe it is the ghost of the Dutchess of Cleveland, who rented the abbey for a time. An unknown ghost of an old woman terrified residents in the 19th century.

Further reading:

Coxe, Anthony D. Hippisley. *Haunted Britain*. New York: McGraw-Hill, 1973.

Folklore, Myths and Legends of Britain. London: Reader's Digest Assn. Ltd., 1973.

Hole, Christina. *Haunted England*. London: B.T. Batsford Ltd., 1940.

Underwood, Peter. *A Gazeteer of British Ghosts*. London: Pan Books Ltd., 1973.

Bealings Bell-Ringer English poltergeist case. The ghostly bell-ringer that perplexed Major Edward Moore and his family in the early 19th century took its name from the Georgian house at Great Bealings, Suffolk. The mystery began on February 2, 1834 when the bells in the kitchen, attached by wires to various rooms to summon the servants, mysteriously began to jangle, apparently without any person pulling them. The bell-ringings continued until March 27, when they stopped just as abruptly as they had begun.

Moore, a retired officer from the Indian Army, Fellow of the Royal Society and author of a book on Hindu mythology, was as fascinated as he was mystified by the ringings, and he embarked on an investigation that culminated in a book. He began his research by writing to his local newspaper, explaining the occurrences, and asking for suggestions from readers.

He recounted that he had just returned from church on that Sunday in February when he was told by the servants that the dining-room bell had inexplicably rung three times between two and five o'clock. The next day, the same bell rang again three times around the same times in the afternoon. The last time it rang, it was actually heard by Moore.

The very next day, Moore returned just before five o'clock and learned that this time all the bells in the kitchen had been ringing violently. As this event was being related to him, he heard yet another bell-ringing coming from the kitchen.

He made a visit to the kitchen, where the cook told Moore that of nine bells hung in a row, the five bells on the right were the only ones ringing. These bells were attached to the dining-room, the drawing room over the dining room, an adjacent bedroom and two attics over the drawing room. As Moore stared at these five bells, they began to ring so violently that Moore thought they would disengage themselves from their moorings. The ringings also were witnessed by Moor's son, the cook and another servant. About ten minutes later, there was another ringing, followed by another fifteen minutes later.

While Moore and his son were dining in the break-fast room that evening at six o'clock, another peal was heard from the bell attached to that room. While eating, the men heard another five ringings at ten-minute intervals. While the servants were dining in the kitchen, the five bells rang but at longer intervals. At a quarter to eight, the ringing stopped.

The following day, the bells were heard at eleven o'clock in the morning when Moore and his son and grandson were having breakfast in the breakfast room. Moore went into the kitchen and five minutes later, the same five bells began to ring furiously. Four minutes later, one bell again rang so violently that it hit the ceiling. After that activity, the bells rang numerous times until March 27. Although skeptics believed the ringings to be the prank of someone in the household, no rational explanation was ever made. Moore and his family concluded that some super-natural activity was the cause.

Further reading:
Cohen, Daniel. *The Encyclopedia of Ghosts.* New York: Dodd, Mead & Co., 1984.
Underwood, Peter. *A Gazeteer of British Ghosts.* Rev. ed. London: Pan Books, Ltd., 1973.

Bean-Nighe   See BANSHEE.

Bean Si   See BANSHEE.

beans
Beans have numerous associations with ghosts, the souls of the dead, the powers of the dwellers of the underworld and various spirits. The early Aryans valued beans highly, along with honey, as a food offering to the dead. Ancient Greeks asso-ciated beans with the souls of the dead and trans-migration of the soul. The Pythagoreans would not eat beans, though the reasons may have been diverse. The Romans considered beans sacred and used them in various rituals for the dead, most notably during Lemuria, the May festival to propitiate and exorcise spirits of the dead, and during the Bean Calends on June 1, when beans were offered as food for the dead. (see LEMURIA.) A traditional Japanese New Year's ritual calls for using roasted beans to drive out of a house. The head of the household dons his best clothing and walks through the house at mid-night, scattering roasted beans and calling out, "Out demons! In luck!"

Native American traditions include rituals for beans, an important crop. The Iroquois performed dances for the bean spirit, one of the three key sister-spirits, along with corn and squash, which watched over crops and helped them grow. Similarly, the medicine men of the Papago, the Desert People of the Ameri-can Southwest, led an annual fertility circle dance to help the beans, squash and corn grow.

Among the Hopi Pueblos, one of the most elabo-rate festivals of the KACHINAS (supernatural beings) was the Powamu ("bean-planting"), a ceremony in February which honored the return of kachina clan-ancients and purified and renovated the earth for planting. Beans were planted and forced to grow in superheated kivas (subterranean cult chambers). On the final day, the beans were harvested, tied in small bundles and distributed by masked kachina dancers to children.

Further reading:
Hurwood, Bernhardt J. *Passport to the Supernatural: An Occult Compendium from All Ages and Many Lands.* New York: Taplinger, 1972.
Leach, Maria, and Jerome Fried, eds. *Funk & Wagnalls Standard Dictionary of Folklore, Mythology, and Legend.* San Francisco: Harper & Row, 1979.

Bell Witch
The famous pre–American Civil War haunting of the Bell Witch involved poltergeist phe-nomena and spectral creatures, and, according to legend, tormented one man to death. The haunting excited the curiosity of many people, including Gen-eral Andrew Jackson. The story exists in several versions, three of which are presented here. The first is probably closest to the true anecdote, as it allegedly is based on the diary of one of the Bell sons, Richard Williams Bell. The third version has a modern sequel. The different versions demonstrate how stories change in retelling.

LEGEND #1

John Bell was a prosperous farmer who owned 1,000 acres near Adams, Tennessee. He had a beautiful wife, Lucy, and eight children. They were all devout Baptists and model citizens. In 1817, their lives inexplicably were turned upside down. The first signs were spectral creatures witnessed by Bell. One was a large, dog-like thing that vanished when Bell fired upon it with his shotgun. The other was a large, turkey-like bird.

Following the appearances of the creatures, the home was plagued with knockings, rappings and scrapings on the outside doors and windows. Sounds that resembled giant rats gnawing the bedposts and giant dogs clawing the floor were heard. These phenomena went on for about a year, and then covers began to be pulled off beds and invisible hands slapped faces and pulled hair. Particularly tormented was the Bells' 12-year-old daughter, Betsy, who was slapped, pinched, bruised and stuck with pins. Betsy was so afflicted that at first the family suspected her of perpetrating a trick on everyone else.

At first Bell was determined to keep the haunting a secret, but it became intolerable for the family. Bell at last confided in a neighbor, James Johnson, who discovered the offending spirit seemed to be intelligent, for it would temporarily desist when beseeched in the name of the Lord. Johnson advised forming an investigatory committee. With that, word went out, and the Bell home became the object of great curiosity.

The spirit began to whistle and then to speak. It gave various identities. It said it was "a Spirit from everywhere, Heaven, Hell, the Earth. I'm in the air, in houses, any place at any time. I've been created millions of years. That is all I will tell you." On another occasion, it said it was the spirit of a person who had been buried in the woods nearby, and whose grave had been disturbed. The bones had been scattered about, and a tooth was under the Bells' house. The spirit was looking for the tooth. The Bells searched, but no tooth was found.

On yet another occasion, the spirit said it was the ghost of an immigrant who had died and left a hidden fortune; it had returned to reveal to Betsy the location of the money. The spirit gave a location, and the Bell boys dug for hours without finding a thing. That night, the spirit laughed over the joke.

The townspeople came to think of the spirit as a witch. The spirit agreed, saying, "I am nothing more nor less than old Kate Batts' witch, and I'm determined to haunt and torment old Jack Bell as long as he lives." Kate Batts was a hefty local woman married to an invalid. She had once been dissatisfied with business dealings with Bell and had threatened to get even. She was still alive. From then on, the spirit was called "Kate."

"Kate" made almost daily appearances at the Bell home and visited everyone else in Robertson County as well, abusing them with her caustic tongue. She made predictions about the future, including the Civil War and the two World Wars of the 20th century. But her primary purposes were to torment "Old Jack," as she called Bell, and to torment Betsy in order to dissuade her from marrying a young man named Josh Gardner. "Kate" did not disturb Lucy Bell, nor Betsy's favorite little brother, John Jr.

"Kate" grew so famous that General Andrew Jackson decided to visit and bring along a "witch layer," a professional exorcist. Just outside the Bell farm, however, the Jackson carriage suddenly stopped and the wheels refused to budge. "Kate's" voice then manifested, promising to appear that night in the home. The carriage became unstuck.

Later in the evening, "Kate" manifested with phantom footsteps and a voice. The witch layer attempted to shoot her with a silver bullet but was slapped about and frightened out of the house.

John Bell fell victim to repeated bouts of illness, for which "Kate" claimed responsibility. While he lay sick in bed, twitching and jerking, the spirit cursed him continuously. Finally, the ordeals wore him down and he told one son that the end was coming. He went to bed and never recovered.

His family found him in a stupor on the morning of December 19, 1920. A strange bottle was found in the medicine cabinet. When the liquid was administered to a cat, the animal went into convulsions and died. "Kate" exultantly declared that she had poisoned him with the liquid while he was a sleep. Bell died the next morning. "Kate" shrieked in triumph.

The torments of Betsy began to diminish, encouraging her to announce her engagement to Gardner. That brought on a renewed attack from "Kate." In despair, Betsy broke the engagement and married another man, Dick Powell.

"Kate" announced to the Bell family that she would leave for seven years and marked her pledge with a cannonball-like object that rolled down the chimney and burst like smoke. As promised, "Kate" returned seven years later and plagued Mrs. Bell and two sons with scratchings and the pulling off of bed covers. They kept the return a secret, and the torments stopped after two weeks.

Before "Kate" left a second time, she visited the home of John Jr. and pledged to return in 107 years—in 1935—when she would bring bad tidings for Tennessee and the entire country. The year came and went without incident, but the area around the Bell farm is said to be haunted still.

The Bells never understood why they were singled out for such an unearthly attack. It is not known what the real Kate Batts had to say about it. Theories have been advanced that Betsy may have been a poltergeist agent. She was the right age, around puberty, and her strict Baptist upbringing may have caused repressed sexual guilt. She also may have had subconscious resentment toward her father. However, there is no evidence that she was unhappy or repressed. And, while the spirit did plague Betsy the most, it roved all over Robertson County and meddled in everyone's affairs. Perhaps the intense resentment and hatred bottled up in the real Kate Batts created a thought-form which took on a life of its own.

LEGEND #2

John Bell was a wealthy planter in North Carolina who hired a foul-tempered overseer. The overseer abused the slaves and, some say, had an eye for Bell's oldest daughter, Mary. Bell and the overseer had many clashes, which escalated until Bell lost control and shot the overseer to death. At his trial, Bell pleaded self-defense and was acquitted.

After that, however, the Bell fortunes began to turn sour. The crops failed and he had to sell his slaves. Soon, he was broke. He sold his land and moved his family to Tennessee to start over again on a small piece of land near the home of Andrew Jackson.

Strange things began to happen in the Tennessee home. The children awoke in their beds each morning to find their hair tangled and their nightclothes snatched off. An old black woman told Bell his family was haunted by a witch, the "ha'nt," or ghost, of the dead supervisor. She offered to spend a night under the children's bed to find out for sure. In the middle of the night, the Bells were awakened by a horrible scream. They found the woman in a panic, claiming the ha'nt had pinched her, stuck her with pins, snatched the kinks out of her hair, and whipped her.

The terrified Bells told their neighbors, including Jackson, who did not believe in ha'nts. As soon as he said so, he was struck by an invisible force which knocked his hat off his head and sent it flying. Mary, meanwhile, began to suffer nightmares in which a cold and heavy weight pressed the breath and life out of her chest. (See OLD HAG.) The ha'nt appeared in her mirror and spoke to her.

These phenomena continued as Mary grew older. The ha'nt scared off all her boyfriends so that she received no marriage proposals. One night, the ha'nt spoke to the Bells from the andiron in the fireplace, telling them that he was in love with Mary and wanted to marry her. The Bells refused. The next day, Mary began to droop about, and her condition worsened over time until she was so ill she could not get out of bed. For a month she lay in bed, not responding to the ministrations of a doctor. One night, as her mother held her hand, she sat up suddenly and said she saw the ha'nt, and thought she was going to love him. Her face lit up with happiness and she died.

On the day of her burial, a great black bird with a bell tied around its neck appeared in the sky over the funeral procession. The bell tolled the most mournful note ever heard. The bird continued to circle over the mourners until Mary's grave was covered, and then flew away, the sad tolls of the bell lingering in the air.

LEGEND #3

In the early 1800s, John Bell of North Carolina became engaged to a widow, Kate Batts. He soon discovered she had a nasty temper. He tried to break the engagement, but she refused to allow it. One day, she fell on his farm, hit her head on a bucket and knocked herself unconscious. Bell thought she was dead, and he dragged her body into the root cellar and locked the door.

She awoke the next night, however, and began moaning and calling to John for food and help. He ignored her pleas, and two days later, she died. John surreptitiously took her body away and left it on her own farm, where it was found by a neighbor.

Happy to be rid of Batts, Bell married another woman and moved to a farm near Adams, Tennessee, north of Nashville. His happiness was short-lived, for soon after their arrival, horrible hauntings began. A huge black bird with fiery eyes and a terrible stench dive-bombed him while he was plowing his field. At home, strange noises were heard, and his three sons (presumably by a previous marriage) were awakened by what sounded like a giant rat gnawing at their bedposts.

The poltergeist phenomena were followed by a disembodied spirit, whom the family called "Kate Batts' witch," and who exhibited great hatred for Bell. One morning in 1820, the spirit announced that she had poisoned Bell during the night. He was, in fact, dead.

The family was haunted by the Bell Witch for one more year. Then, after a seven-year absence, the spirit returned again to torment the family with knockings, scratchings and the like. Once again, the spirit left and swore to return.

The Bell Witch was believed to make her appearance again in the late 1980s. An owner of part of what used to be the Bell farm claimed to see apparitions of a dark-haired woman floating across the fields, and to have mysterious knocks sound at his door. The Bell Witch is believed to haunt a nearby cave, called "the Bell Witch Cave," where unearthly screams, phantom footsteps and the sounds of chains dragging on the ground are reported heard.

Further reading:

American Folklore and Legend. Pleasantville, N.Y.: Reader's Digest Assn., 1978.

Guiley, Rosemary Ellen. The Encyclopedia of Witches and Witchcraft. New York: Facts On File, 1989.

benandanti See CAUL.

Bender, Hans (1907–   ) Distinguished German psychologist, director of the Institut für Grenzgebiete der Psychologie and Psychohygiene (Institute for Border Areas of Psychology and Mental Health) and editor of the journal Zeitschrift für Psychologie und Grenzgebiete der Psychologie und Psychohygiene. Hans Bender was born February 5, 1907 in Freiburg im Breisgau. His interest in the paranormal was triggered at the age of 17, when he was invited to participate in a Ouija-board session with a Spiritualist family in London. The evidently intelligent quality of the messages impressed him, but he was skeptical about their alleged provenance—they seemed more like products of the sitters' subconscious than communications from beyond the grave.

Bender studied at the College of France, in Paris, where he took courses from the renowned hypnotherapist Pierre Janet. Meanwhile, he began to experiment with automatic writing, which confirmed his hunch that these productions owed more to the subconscious than to discarnate entities, but also led him to the conclusion that ESP was sometimes involved. This work resulted in his Ph.D. dissertation, which linked the subconscious to ESP, the first study in the German academic world to have received positive results from ESP experiments. Bender was awarded his Ph.D. in 1936, two years after the publication of J.B. RHINE's seminal monograph Extra-Sensory Perception.

Bender decided to try to integrate parapsychological studies into the academic framework, to which end he took up the study of medicine. He received his M.D. from the University of Strasbourg in 1940. Following World War II, he began to teach at the University of Freiburg, but he then went into business for four years, in order to raise money to build an institute devoted to the study of paranormal psychology. In 1950, he founded the Institut für Grenzgebiete der Psychologie und Psychohygiene in Freiburg and began to edit and publish the journal.

After the establishment of his institute, Bender returned to teaching at the University of Freiburg, where he was given a chair in psychology and border areas of psychology. This chair was transformed into a full professorship in 1967, the first (and still the only) such position in Germany and one of the few anywhere in the world. Bender retired from teaching in 1975, but he continued as director of the Institut für Grenzgebiete and as editor of its journal.

Bender's approach to parapsychology combined laboratory and field research. He has written on a wide range of subjects, including spontaneous ESP, psychokinesis, poltergeists, mediumship, and spiritual healing. He has also translated into German books by William MCDOUGALL and G.N.M. TYRRELL. Among his investigations is the important ROSENHEIM POLTERGEIST case.

Further reading:

Pilkington, Rosemarie. Men and Women of Parapsychology: Personal Reflections. Jefferson, N.C.: McFarland, 1987.

Pleasants, Helene, ed. Biographical Dictionary of Parapsychology. New York: Helix Press, 1964.

Bentham, Jeremy (1748–1832) A founder of University College in London, Jeremy Bentham had his body mummified upon death and mounted on display in the college. His ghost is said to rise up at night, leave the cabinet and rattle about the halls.

Bentham was a law reformer, natural scientist and philosopher. He was greatly interested in mummification and proposed the idea of turning corpses into permanent memorials for display—"auto-icons" as he termed them. Not surprisingly, this idea failed to find a popular following.

However, Bentham pursued preserving his own corpse for generations to admire, and prior to his death discussed how his body should be handled. His will gave the following instructions:

> My body I give to my dear friend Doctor Southwood Smith to be disposed of in manner herinafter mentioned. And I direct that . . . he will take my body under his charge and take the requisite and appropriate measures for the disposal and preservation of several parts of my bodily frame in the manner expressed in the paper annexed to this my will and at the top of which I have written "Auto-Icon." The skeleton he will cause to be put together in such manner as that the whole figure may be seated in a Chair usually occupied by me when living in the

attitude in which I am sitting engaged in thought in the course of the time employed in writing. I direct that the body thus prepared shall be transferred to my executor. He will cause the skeleton to be clad in one of the suits of black occasionally worn by me. The Body so clothed together with the chair and the staff of my later years borne by me he will take charge of. And for containing the whole apparatus he will cause to be prepared in an appropriate box or case and will cause to be engraved in conspicuous characters on a plate to be offered hereon and also on the labels on the glass cases in which the preparations of the soft parts on my body shall be contained . . . my name at length with the letters ob. followed by the date of my decease. IF it should happen that my personal friends and other Disciples should be disposed to meet together on some day or days of the year for the purpose of commemorating the Founder of the greatest happiness system of morals and legislation my executor will from time to time cause to be conveyed to the room in which they meet the said Box or case with the contents there to be stationed in such part of the room as to the assembled company shall meet.

Bentham's preserved form is still on display in a moth-proof case with glass sides near the entrance hall of the college. He resembles Benjamin Franklin, and strikes an authoritative pose seated in one of his favorite chairs, one hand on "Dapple," his walking stick, which rests across one knee. He is dressed in tan breeches, a black coat, white shirt with jabot, white gloves and stockings and black shoes. He wears a straw hat. At his side is a small table that bears a pair of glasses and their case, and a cameo ring and pin. Apparently the mummification of Bentham's head was not successful, and it began to decompose. It was removed to a safe at the college and was replaced by a wax head modeled by French artist Jacques Talrich.

Bentham's ghost is said to be fond of walking about the halls especially during long winter nights. Sounds of his cane tapping on the floors can be heard. Some persons have reported seeing his ghost, dressed as the body is in the case and carrying Dapple. According to another story, unexplained nocturnal noises are made by Bentham's irate mummy, which raps Dapple upon the glass to demand a proper burial.

See also HAUNTING.

Further reading:
Underwood, Peter. *Haunted London.* London: George G. Harrup & Co., 1973.

Beraud, Marthe (c. 1886–?) French MATERIALIZATION medium, better known by her pseudonym

"Eva C." She was studied by Charles Richet, Baron Albert von SCHRENCK-NOTZING, and Gustave GELEY, among others.

The name "Eva C."—the "C." was supposed to stand for "Carriere"—was given to Marthe Beraud by Schrenck-Notzing in his book, *Phenomena of Materialisation* (1913; English-language edition 1920). Richet had used the medium's real name in reporting his earlier studies, but these met with so much ridicule that Schrenck-Notzing seems to have felt the need to disguise the identity of his subject by giving her a fictitious name.

Beraud was the daughter of a French army officer stationed in Algiers, the capital of Algeria, in northern Africa. Her date of birth is not known exactly. Her mediumistic talents were discovered by a General Noel and his wife, to whose son, Maurice, Beraud became engaged before the young man was killed on an expedition to the Congo. With a Ouija board, Madame Noel had been contacting a personality who called himself "Ben Boa," and who claimed to have known Beraud in a previous incarnation (see REINCARNATION). Beraud, in mediumistic trance, seemed to be able to materialize Boa's physical form. Richet responded to Madame Noel's invitation to visit Algiers and attended 20 seances with Beraud at the Noels' residence late in 1905. He observed Ben Boa on a number of occasions, and even took photographs of him. In these photographs, many of which he later published, the figure looks two-dimensional, almost like a cardboard cutout. This resemblance gave the inevitable critics a field day.

The skeptical position was strengthened when a former chauffeur of the family (who had been fired for stealing) came forward and claimed that he was responsible for the materializations, and when a family friend claimed that Beraud herself had confessed to fraud, an accomplice having sneaked into the seance room through a trapdoor in the corner. Investigation, however, showed there to be no such trapdoor, and the chauffeur was too tall and massive to have played the part of Ben Boa.

Whatever the genesis of Ben Boa, it is a curious fact that he did not manifest except at the Noels' residence. Richet held sittings with Beraud elsewhere in Algiers in 1906, at which he claimed to have seen a gooey substance, for which he coined the term "ectoplasm" (q.v.), emanating from various parts of Beraud's body—particularly from her mouth, ears, vagina and the nipples of her breasts. The ectoplasm would quickly organize itself into the shape of a hand or head, on which a face might appear, sometimes in miniature. It would then solidify into a sort of paste, dry to the touch, before retracting into the medium's body, or simply disappearing.

The materialized faces often had the same two-dimensional quality that characterized Ben Boa. Richet considered the behavior of ectoplasm (which he had seen sometimes at the Noels' as well) to be so outlandish that he held off publishing his notes until the phenomenon had been reported by others. Ben Boa he believed to be more acceptable, because so-called "full-form" materializations had been reported before, most notably by Sir William CROOKES, in reference to Katie King, the alleged spirit control of Florence COOK.

In 1908, when she was about 22, Beraud moved to Paris, where she met the playwright Alexandre Bisson and his wife, Juliette. The Bissons were interested in psychical research, and in 1910 they invited Beraud to live with them, the better to study the phenomena she produced. When Alexandre died in 1912, Juliette Bisson changed quarters, taking Beraud with her. Critics were quick to allege that Bisson was Beraud's helpmate as well as her patron, but Bisson worked closely with psychical researchers such as Richet and Schrenck-Notzing to design a careful research program, and published a detailed account of her work (Les Phenomenes de materialisation, not translated) in 1914.

Schrenck-Notzing's study of Beraud began in 1909, when he was introduced to her and to the Bissons by Richet, and was to last for more than four years. The sittings were held both in Paris and in the baron's personal laboratory in Munich, with Bisson absent. Schrenck-Notzing had spent 15 years studying physical mediums throughout Europe, and he was experienced in designing controls against fraud. Before each seance, Beraud was obliged to submit to a strip search, then was dressed in a tight-fitting costume. (When alone with Bisson, she was nude.) She was made to drink blueberry syrup before seances, so that if she had swallowed "ectoplasm" in order to regurgitate it during the sitting, it would be stained, and at the end of a sitting, she was given an emetic. These and other precautions never produced any reason to doubt the paranormal source of the ectoplasmic formations, which closely resembled those observed by Richet in Algiers. Schrenck-Notzing and Bisson between them took more than 200 photographs of the strange substance, many of them published in their books.

Although Schrenck-Notzing's work with Beraud was broken off by the outbreak of World War I, it was partially compensated by the addition of French researchers, including such figures as Camille Flam-

marion and Gustave Geley, connected with the INSTITUT METAPSYCHIQUE INTERNATIONAL (IMI). Geley's sittings with Beraud were conducted from 1916 to 1918, and the results were similar to those of his predecessors.

The phenomena were, however, becoming less strong, as occurs with many mediums as they age, especially those whose effects are primarily physical. Twenty of the forty sittings Beraud held at the SOCIETY FOR PSYCHICAL RESEARCH (SPR) in London in 1920 were "blank," and the investigating committee, even though they could come up with nothing better than the "regurgitation hypothesis" for the successful sittings, declined to rule in her favor. Two years later, the phenomena were weaker still. Three professors at the Sorbonne in Paris held 15 sittings with Beraud, at 13 of which nothing happened. These investigators, also, concluded that regurgitation was the mostly likely explanation for the phenomena they did witness, even though precautions which should have obviated this possibility had been taken.

In 1922, Beraud was only about 36, but she seems to have exhausted her talent. Her subsequent history is not known, but the research with her did have a sequel. Twenty-five years after Geley's death, skeptical psychical researcher Rudolf Lambert published an article in the Journal of the Society for Psychical Research in which he declared that Eugene OSTY, Geley's successor at the IMI (and recently deceased), had shown him a set of photographs that looked suspiciously like the two-dimensional ectoplasmic faces were pinned to Beraud's hair and body by wires.

The photographs in question were never published and are not now known to exist. Moreover, all the persons Lambert mentioned in his communication were deceased at the time he wrote. This is the type of hearsay evidence that would be heavily discounted if it were in favor of a medium's ability, and it would seem best to make a similar discounting in this instance. Many published photographs show signs similar to those described in Lambert's letter, but the discussion by those who were present and saw the ectoplasm in the process of formation, suggests that they should be understood as ectoplasmic threads, rather than wires.

Further reading:

Braude, Stephen. The Limits of Influence: Psychokinesis and the Philosophy of Science. London: Routledge and Kegan Paul, 1986.

Inglis, Brian. Science and Parascience: A History of the Paranormal from 1914–1939. London: Hodder and Stoughton, 1984.

Lambert, Rudolph. "Dr. Geley's Reports on the Medium 'Eva C.'" *Journal of the Society for Psychical Research* 37 (1954):380–86.

Salter, Helen. "The History of Marthe Beraud." *Proceedings of the Society for Psychical Research* 27 (1914):333–69.

Tabori, Paul. *Pioneers of the Unseen.* New York: Taplinger, 1972.

Berry Pomeroy Castle Haunted ruined castle in the wild countryside at Berry Pomeroy, Devon, England. The brooding ruins are said to be inhabited by a least three ghosts. A strange atmosphere pervades the grounds and leaves visitors with unexplained feelings of terror and foreboding.

According to legend, the hauntings are traced back to the original owners of the castle, the de la Pomerai (Pomeroy) family, which owned it from the time of the Norman Conquest (1066) until 1548, when they sold it. Stories of hauntings are said to have circulated for hundreds of years, but did not become widely known until they were publicized in the late 19th century in the memoirs of a well-known physician, Sir Walter Farquhar.

Farquhar related how he was once summoned to the castle to attend to the ill wife of the castle's steward. While he waited in a room, a beautiful young lady in white entered. She was in distress and was wringing her hands. She walked across the room, mounted a staircase, then looked directly at Farquhar and vanished.

The following day, Farquhar was once again attending the sick wife of the steward, when he remarked on the strange appearance of the woman in white. The steward became distressed, and explained that Farquhar had seen one of the family's death omens (q.v.): The ghost of a lady in white who preceded the death of someone closely associated with the castle. A few hours later, the steward's wife died.

According to family legend, the ghost is that of a daughter of a former owner of the castle. During life, she supposedly was cruel. As punishment for her sins, she is doomed to haunt the castle. The ghost also allegedly appears outside the castle, luring people into unsafe places where they might have accidents.

Another ghost said to haunt the ruins is that of Lady Margaret de Pomeroy, who loved the same man as her sister Eleanor. Out of jealousy, Eleanor imprisoned Margaret in the dungeon and starved her to death. Margaret's ghost, clothed in flowing white robes, is said to rise out of the dungeon on certain nights and walk the ramparts.

A third ghost is that of a woman in a hooded blue cape. By some accounts, she is another Pomeroy daughter, who murdered her baby by smothering it. The baby's ghostly cries are said to haunt the castle as well.

Further reading:

Loy, Sandra. "Go Ghosthunting," *Herald Express* (Torquay, Devon, England), July 27, 1991, n.p.

Underwood, Peter. *A Gazeteer of British Ghosts.* Rev. ed. London: Pan Books, Ltd., 1973.

Whitaker, Terence. *Haunted England.* Chicago: Contemporary Books, 1987.

Bettiscombe Skull See SCREAMING SKULLS.

bhut (also bhuta) In Indian lore, an evil ghost of the dead, especially a man who has died by execution, suicide or accident. *Bhuts* may be detected by their nasal twangs, their fear of burning turmeric, and the fact that they have no shadows. They never rest on the earth, so they may be avoided by lying on the ground.

The *airi* is a type of *bhut* of a man killed during a hunt. It lives in the hills and travels with a pack of spectral dogs. Its saliva is poisonous, and to see it usually results in death by fright. Those strong enough to survive are rewarded with treasures. The *airi* is worshipped, and temples to it are built in isolated regions.

bilocation An unusual phenomenon in which a person appears to be in two places simultaneously. Bilocation is thought to occur when a person's double is projected to another location and is visible to others, who perceive the double as the actual physical body. In some cases, the double appears to be an apparition, not a solid physical form. Persons witnessing a bilocation often notice that the double acts oddly or doesn't speak. Doubles of animals also have been reported in some cases.

Mystical and magical adepts are attributed with the ability to bilocate, sometimes at will. In Christianity, numerous saints and monks reportedly have bilocated, among them St. Anthony of Padua, St. Ambrose of Milan, St. Severus of Ravenna, and Padre Pio of Italy. Philip Neri, a 16th-century Florentine businessman who joined the Church and became known as "the Apostle of Rome," experienced bilocation following a transformational ecstatic experience during which he felt his heart enlarge. After that, he was subject to palpitations and sensations of great heat.

In 1774, St. Alphonsus Maria de'Ligouri, another ecstatic, created a stir by announcing one morning that during the night he had attended the dying Pope Clement XIV at his bedside in Rome, which was a four-day journey away. However, St. Ligouri had been confined to a cell for a fast, and had not left the premises. No one believed him until it was reported that Clement had just died, and that St. Ligouri had appeared at his bedside.

Reports of bilocation were collected in the late 19th century by Frederic W.H. MYERS, one of the founders of the SOCIETY FOR PSYCHICAL RESEARCH in London. Myers published them in *Human Personality and Its Survival of Bodily Death* (1903). One representative account, which occurred on February 5, 1887, concerned a father and two daughters who went hunting one afternoon. After a while, the daughters decided to return home with the coachman. Along the way, they spotted their father, astride his white horse on top of a small hill not far away, which was separated from the daughters by a dip in the land. The father waved his hat at them, and one daughter could clearly see the brand label inside the hatband, though it should have been impossible due to the distance. The horse looked dirty and shaken, as though it had been in an accident. The daughters were worried. They passed into the dip and the father and horse disappeared momentarily from view. When the girls rose out of the dip, father and horse were nowhere to be seen. The father arrived at home later and said he had not been in an accident, nor had he waved at them from the hilltop. The incident had no explanation.

Sometimes a spontaneous bilocation is in folklore a death omen (q.v.).

See also RODGERS, LOUIS; WRAITH.

Further reading:

Guiley, Rosemary Ellen. *Harper's Encyclopedia of Mystical and Paranormal Experience.* San Francisco: HarperSanFrancisco, 1991.

Hart, Hornell, and Ella B. Hart, "Visions and Apparitions Collectively and Reciprocally Perceived." *Proceedings of the Society for Psychical Research* 41 (1932–33):205–49.

Myers, Frederic W.H. *Human Personality and Its Survival of Bodily Death.* New York: Longmans, Green and Co., 1954. First published 1903.

birds   In mythology and folklore birds are messengers to the gods, death omens (q.v.), the souls of the dead and carriers of the souls of the dead.

The Greeks and Romans portrayed birds as messengers to the heavens in mythology. The Egyptians portrayed the *BA*, or soul as a bird with a human head. The souls of Horus and the pharaoh were represented by hawks. The Aztecs thought the dead

Birds, symbols of the soul, adorn many tombstones.

were reborn as colibris, the birds associated with the god Huitzilopochtli.

Among various tribal cultures, birds are seen as carriers of the souls of the dead. In parts of West Africa, it is traditional to tie a bird to a corpse and sacrifice it, so that it will carry the soul to the afterworld. In the South Sea Islands, the dead are buried in bird-shaped coffins for the same purpose.

In folklore, a wild bird flying into the house presages important news, especially death. Jackdaws and swallows which fly down chimneys are death omens, as is any bird which beats its wings against a window or flies into a window and kills itself on impact. It is considered bad luck in some parts to even bring an injured wild bird into the house. Black birds, such as crows and ravens, and nocturnal birds, such as owls, also are harbingers of death, especially if they gather, caw or hoot in the vicinity of a house.

In the lore of Irish fishermen, sea gulls embody the souls of drowning victims.

Birds appearing in dreams are said to represent spirits, angels, supernatural aid, and thoughts and flights of fancy.

Further reading:
Cirlot, J.E. *A Dictionary of Symbols*. New York: Philosophical Library, 1971.
Jung, Carl G., ed. *Man and His Symbols*. New York: Anchor Press/Doubleday, 1988. First published in the United States in 1964.
Leach, Maria, and Jerome Fried, eds. *Funk & Wagnalls Standard Dictionary of Folklore, Mythology, and Legend*. San Francisco: Harper & Row, 1979.

Black Shuck   A large spectral death omen (q.v.) demon dog in British folklore, especially in Norfolk and other parts of East Anglia, and in Devon, regions steeped in supernatural and witchcraft lore. Black Shuck, also called Old Shuck, derives its name from the Anglo-Saxon term *scucca* or *sceocca*, old Anglo-Saxon terms for "demon" or "Satan." The spectral dog descended from Norse mythology, for he is said to be the black Hound of Odin (Woden) brought by early Viking invaders.

Black Shuck is all black and is huge, about the size of a calf. He has large eyes that glow yellow, red or green as if on fire. Often, he is headless, yet his eyes—where eyes should be—glow in the dark.

Black Shuck haunts graveyards, lonely country roads, misty marshes, or the hills around villages. In certain areas, he frequents old straight roads; it has been theorized that these "old straight tracks" may be leys, thought to be ancient lines of invisible earth energy known to ancient peoples, and used to site villages and sacred places.

On stormy nights, Black Shuck's bone-chilling howls can be heard rising above the wind. His feet make no sound and leave no prints, but travelers feel his icy breath upon their necks. To meet Black Shuck means death within a year. In Suffolk, however, it is believed that Black Shuck is harmless as long as he is not bothered. In parts of Devon, it is bad luck to even speak of the Black Dog.

Sightings of Black Shuck are reported in modern times. Nocturnal travelers say they see his dark form leaping across the road in front of them, or racing along lonely country roads.

Black Shuck is known by various other names, such as the Galleytrot, Old Shuck, the Shug Monkey, the Hateful Thing, the Churchyard Beast, Hellbeast, Swooning Shadow and the Black Dog of Torrington.

The legends of both Black Shuck and the WHISHT HOUNDS are said to have inspired Sir Arthur Conan Doyle in his writing of *The Hound of the Baskervilles.*

Spectral black dogs in general haunt numerous locales and play a role in many haunting legends. They also are associated with the Devil, who is said to often assume the shape of a black dog, and with witches (see FAMILIAR).

A galleytrot, a spectral hound similar to Black Shuck.

Further reading:
Canning John, ed. *50 Great Ghost Stories*. New York: Bonanza Books, 1988.
Folklore, Myths and Legends of Britain. London: Reader's Digest Assoc., 1977.
Guiley, Rosemary Ellen. *The Encyclopedia of Witches and Witchcraft*. New York: Facts On File, 1989.
Hole, Christina. *Haunted England*. London: B.T. Batsford Ltd., 1940.

Blue-cap (also **Blue-bonnet**)   In the folklore of Britain, a mine spirit who assisted the miners and expected to be paid for his labors. Belief in the spirit began to die out in the mid-19th century.

Industrious like a brownie, Blue-cap was said to have enormous strength and was capable of toiling long hours. He was visible as a blue flame that floated about the shafts, moving whatever objects the flame settled on.

Blue-cap's wages were left in a corner of the mine every two weeks. If they were below what he felt he deserved, the spirit indignantly rejected the sum. If the wages were above what he felt he earned, he left the excess amount.

Further reading:
Briggs, Katherine. *An Encyclopedia of Fairies: Hobgoblins, Brownies, Bogies, and Other Supernatural Creatures*. New York: Pantheon Books, 1976.

Blue Man   See ARUNDEL CASTLE.

bogey   In British folklore, a class of horrible evil spirits or hobgoblins, traveling alone or in groups, that love to make mischief. Bogies go by various other names, the most common of which are Bogey-Man, Boogie-Man, Bug-a-boo, Boo, Bugbear, Bock, Boggart and Bogey-beast. Bogies are recognized in other cultures by still other names. They sometimes are synonymous with the Devil. In Wales, the bogey is called a bug (ghost), in Scotland a bogle and in Germany a Boggelmann. The Irish puca is similar. No matter where it is found, the bogey is usually big and black, typically does its work at night, and scares children. In past generations, the threat of calling upon bogies was used to frighten children into good behavior.

Further reading:

Briggs, Katherine. *An Encyclopedia of Fairies: Hobgoblins, Brownies, Bogies, and Other Supernatural Creatures.* New York: Pantheon Books, 1976.

Boggart   A type of BOGEY hobgoblin in English folklore that has poltergeist habits. Although it can be helpful and sociable with some people, the Boggart most often is mischievous, annoying and frightening. Without making a visual appearance, it makes itself known by playing tricks on people, such as pulling off their bedclothes. Sometimes Boggart acts are accompanied by terrible noises or laughter. Boggarts can also be nasty and mean, and have been known to scratch, punch and pinch people, and even snatch and carry them away. They inhabit a house, churchyard or field, or live in another body, such as that of a cat or dog. In some cases, exorcism successfully puts an end to their activities.

In parts of Lancashire and Yorkshire, threats of being thrown into a "boggart-hole" have been used to keep unruly children in line. Many old English houses reputedly have their resident Boggart, some of which are believed to be the ghosts of former residents.

Boggarts are said to be frightened of automobiles, thus accounting for their rare appearances in the modern world.

Further reading:

Haining, Peter. *Dictionary of Ghosts.* Englewood Cliffs, N.J.: Prentice-Hall, 1984.

Leach, Maria, and Jerome Fried, eds. *Funk & Wagnalls Standard Dictionary of Folklore, Mythology, and Legend.* San Francisco: Harper & Row, 1979.

Bond, Frederick Bligh (1864–1945)   Architect, archeologist, author and editor. He claimed to have psychic guidance from spirits of the dead in his excavations at Glastonbury Abbey, the earliest Christian church in England, connected by legend with King Arthur and the Knights of the Roundtable.

Frederick Bligh Bond was born on June 30, 1864 at Marlborough, Wiltshire, England, into the family of the Reverend Hookey Bond, Master of the Marlborough Royal Free Grammar School. The Bonds moved to Bath in 1876, where the Reverend Bond became headmaster of Bath College, a high school.

Bligh (the younger Frederick was called by his middle name) Bond's formal schooling ended with Bath College. From reading in his father's library, Bond developed a fascination for the Middle Ages and for church architecture. He showed a facility for drawing and apprenticed himself to an architect. In 1897, he passed the examination for certification by the Royal Institute of British Architects, and he established a private practice in Bristol.

In 1894, Bond entered into a fateful marriage with Mary Louise Mills. The couple had a single child, a daughter, born 18 months later. The marriage must have been unhappy almost from the start, because in 1898 Bond left home, taking his three-year-old daughter with him. His wife sued for legal separation, on the grounds of cruelty, based mainly on Bond's removal of their daughter. Bond granted the separation, although he denied the charge of cruelty. For a while thereafter the daughter lived alternately with each of her parents. Mary, meanwhile, began to spread malicious rumors about Frederick in conversation and in letters, apparently hoping to secure the divorce which he refused, for religious and moral reasons, to give her.

Bond joined the amateur Somerset Archaeological and Natural History Society in 1903. He was already fascinated with the history of Glastonbury, which tradition held was established in 166 A.D., perhaps as early as 47 A.D.. The monastery stood on an island which was said to be the Avalon of the Arthurian tales. Glastonbury had great prestige until the 16th century, when Henry VIII, determined to stamp out Catholicism in Britain, initiated moves which brought about its destruction. When the Somerset Archaeological and Natural History Society arranged for excavations at Glastonbury in 1907, Bond was quick to offer his services.

Bond had been drawn to the psychic from the age of 15, when he discovered Catherine Crowe's *The Night Side of Nature* in his father's library. Why he sought psychic aid in his excavations has not been recorded. He may have conceived of it as an experiment, the first practical attempt at psychic archeology. In any event, sessions of automatic writing with a retired navy captain, John Allen Bartlett ("John Alleyne"), began in Bond's architectural offices in Bristol in November 1907. Bartlett was the automatist, but Bond believed that his own presence was an essential part of Bartlett's mediumistic process.

At their first sitting, Bond and Bartlett received communications from a group calling themselves "the Watchers," purporting to be the spirits of monks who once had lived at Glastonbury. Two drawings of the abbey were produced, along with data relating to the famed Edgar Chapel, whose existence was then only indirectly known. More details about the Edgar Chapel and other structures came in later sessions. Bond was able to ask questions of the Watchers about buildings and events and receive sensible replies to them.

Following leads given by the Watchers, Bond uncovered the foundations of the north wall of the Edgar Chapel in 1908, and he eventually traced the building's perimeter. Over the next few years, guided at least in part by the Watchers, he found several more important structures, including the entire northern part of the Abbey, and what appeared to be the clock and bell tower, refectory, monks' kitchen, monks' dormitory, chapter house, a glass and pottery kiln, and a secret underground passage. He discovered no fewer than four previously unknown chapels, in addition to the Edgar Chapel. That he had indeed located the latter was established by an old set of plans he was sent, after his find became public.

As a result of his success, Bond was made Diocesan architect. He was quick to capitalize on this title, but it seemed to say more than it did, because his work remained unpaid. Bond's activities at Glastonbury were really a hobby. His income was derived from his architectural practice, the sale of his books, and the proceeds of lectures he was beginning to give. His wife's slanders, however, were affecting his ability to earn a living. Although he won every suit she brought against him, he was forced to declare bankruptcy in 1914.

Bond kept any mention of the psychic out of his annual reports to the Somerset Archaeological and Natural History Society. He hinted at the communications from the Watchers for the first time in his report for 1915, but it was not until three years later, in *The Gate of Remembrance* (1918), that he told the full story.

Bond did not believe that his monks were discarnate spirits. Rather, he held that there was a cosmic reservoir of human memory and experience, in which the personality was preserved and welded into a collective association extending through all time, and which could be tapped by sensitives appropriately attuned. He also believed in gematria, the idea that the measurements of buildings carry codes that reveal a secret interpretation of the Scriptures.

Bond was gradually pushed out of his work at Glastonbury, his great successes in locating unknown and little known structures notwithstanding. It would be easy to read this as a response to his psychic work and occult ideas, but according to his biographer,

William Kenawell, these provided more an excuse than a cause for his dismissal. A major contributing factor was his wife's slanders, but Bond himself was not an easy man to get along with. He was arrogant and vain, and tended to exaggerate the significance of whatever position he held. He was an amateur in archeology at a time when the field was becoming professionalized, and although his work was competent for its time, his refusal to follow the systematic plan of excavations laid down by the professionals were bound to create friction with them. By 1921, Bond was reduced to cleaning the artifacts he had found during earlier digs, and in 1922 he was relieved of all responsibility at Glastonbury.

For four years, beginning in 1922, Bond edited *Psychic Science*, the new monthly publication of the BRITISH COLLEGE OF PSYCHIC SCIENCE. This position accorded with his increasing public visibility, but once more it was unpaid. Meanwhile, his interest in Glastonbury continued. In 1925, he tried unsuccessfully to get the SOCIETY FOR PSYCHICAL RESEARCH (SPR), the Society of Antiquarians and the Royal Archeological Institute to form a joint committee for the purpose of overseeing additional excavations.

In about 1926, Bond became engaged in another major battle, this with the automatist Geraldine Cummins, over her claim of sole responsibility for the scripts later published by her as the Chronicles of Cleophas. Bond was present with Cummins at the early sittings in this series, and he argued that his presence was partly responsible for stimulating the communications, whereas Cummins believed that she alone was involved in their transmission. Their contention reached the courts, which found in Cummins' favor.

When a wealthy American offered to pay for his passage to the United States late in 1926, Bond seized the opportunity to get away. He found work with an architectural firm in New York, and in 1927 he had a successful lecture tour, arranged through the AMERICAN SOCIETY FOR PSYCHICAL RESEARCH (ASPR). Later that year, he was appointed "honorary" director of education at the ASPR, and in 1930 he succeeded J. Malcolm Bird as editor of the ASPR's *Journal*. He held this position for five years, until he quit over the ASPR's handling of the "Margery" affair (see CRANDON, MINA STINSON). When the president of the Board of Trustees refused to publish an explosive report on the identification of "Walter's" thumbprints, Bond published it anyway, submitting his resignation at the same time.

Bond was 72 when he left the ASPR, but he shortly became involved in yet another venture. This was the Survival Foundation, Inc., which was dedicated to the return of spirituality in America. Bond was to be editor of the Foundation's monthly magazine, *Survival*. He succeeded in getting out three consecutive issues, but then the enterprise folded, and Bond found himself once more out of a job.

At the end of 1935, again at his patron's expense, Bond returned to England for the last time. He was broke and homeless. His daughter was unable to take him in, and she warned that if he returned to England, his wife might once more make trouble for him (she did not die until 1938). There were also the Cummins lawsuits, aspects of which had been left unresolved when Bond left the country. Nevertheless, he returned to Britain. He found a home at Cottage Hospital in Dolgelly, Wales, where he spent the last 10 years of his life. Bond died in Dolgelly on March 8, 1945, at the age of 82.

His other books are *The Hill of Vision* (1919), *The Company of Avalon* (1924), *The Rose Miraculous* (1924), *The Gospel of Philip the Deacon* (1926), *The Wisdom of the Watchers* (1933), *The Secret of Immortality* (1934) and *The Mystery of Glaston* (1938). Most of these writings purported to come from the Watchers; as the titles indicate, Bond never lost his love for Glastonbury. At his death, Bond left an unpublished manuscript of a book written in 1935, comprising communications from Captain Bligh of the *Bounty* (Bond's great grand-uncle), received through an American sensitive.

The early communications from the Watchers contain many suggestions that have never been followed up. Bond's markings on the ground, outlining key parts of the abbey, were altered in 1939, obfuscating many of his gematria claims. His books are banned from the Glastonbury bookstore to this day.

Further reading:

Bond, F. Bligh. *The Gate of Remembrance*. Oxford: B.H. Blackwell, 1918.

Kenawell, William W. *The Quest at Glastonbury: A Biographical Study of Frederick Bligh Bond*. New York: Helix Press, 1965.

Schwartz, Stephen A. *The Secret Vaults of Time: Psychic Archaeology and the Quest for Man's Beginnings*. New York: Grosset and Dunlap, 1978.

book test See SURVIVAL TESTS.

Borley Rectory Called "the most haunted house in England," and the subject of one of the most intensive modern ghost hunting investigations. The investigation was conducted between 1929 and 1938 by Harry PRICE, founder and honorary director of the National Laboratory of Psychical Research of London, and renowned ghost hunter. Price claimed that Borley was "the best authenticated case in the annals of psychical research." His findings were controversial, and he was posthumously accused of fraud. The truth of what happened in the Borley case may remain unknown.

Compared to other English hauntings, Borley Rectory was fairly ordinary; it was only Price's investigation which made the case sensational. The structure, a gloomy and unattractive red brick building located about 60 miles northeast of London in Essex County, was built in 1863 by the Reverend Henry Bull, whose family occupied it for some 70 years. When Henry Bull died, he was succeeded by his son, Harry, as rector. After Harry died, there was no rector for a period of time. According to local lore, the rectory was haunted, and villagers avoided it after dark. In 1928, it was taken over by the Reverend G.E. Smith and his wife, both professed skeptics of the paranormal. Previously, 12 clergymen had turned down the post.

The house came to the attention of Price in June 1929, when articles in the *Daily Mail* talked of ghosts reported seen there, and revived legends about the place. A phantom nun (q.v.) drifted about the grounds, especially along a path dubbed "the nun's walk" by the Bulls. The nun was seen both in daylight and at night, but usually at dusk and always on July 28; once she was seen collectively by the four daughters of Henry Bull. There also was a phantom coach with horses; Harry Bull allegedly once had seen the coach driven by two headless horsemen.

According to legend, for which there is no historical documentation, the rectory was built on part of the site once occupied by a medieval monastery, where a tragedy had taken place. There are several variations of the story. One has it that a nun from a convent at nearby Bures tried to elope with a lay monk at Borley. The were aided by another lay brother and made their escape one night by coach. They were captured. The nun was interred alive in one of the monastery's walls and her lover was hanged. The fate of the accomplice was unknown. Another version has it that she was interred and both men were hanged. Another version says that the nun and her lover escaped but quarreled, and he strangled her on the monastery grounds. He was hanged. Still another version replaces the monks with grooms, with the same unlucky fates. There also was a "screaming girl" theory, though not widely believed (and not supported by any evidence), that held that shortly after the rectory was built, a young girl was seen one night clinging to the windowsill of the Blue Room on the second floor. She fell to her death.

The newspaper articles prompted Price to invite himself out to the rectory for investigation. He and his secretary, Lucie Kaye, arrived on June 12, 1929.

According to Price's account, as given in his book, *The Most Haunted House in England* (1940), the Smiths told him hauntings had begun shortly after they moved in. There were strange whispers, a woman's voice that moaned and then exclaimed, "Don't, Carlos, don't!," mysterious footsteps and the phantom nun, who reportedly was seen by two maids. There also were a strange light which appeared unaccountably in the windows of an unused wing, the ghost of Harry Bull and odd black shapes.

Price said he thoroughly examined the premises. While he was there, poltergeist phenomena occurred. He interviewed the staff and others and compiled a list of everything that had gone on in the rectory—some things allegedly for at least 50 years—including the telekinesis (spontaneous displacement) of objects; smashed pottery; voices; footsteps; banging of doors and other noises; spontaneous combustion of portions of the house; mysterious wall writings; paranormal bell rings; inexplicable and sudden thermal variations; touchings; choir singing; music; strange lights; coach-like rumblings outside the rectory; the sound of galloping horses; pleasant and unpleasant odors; fright of animals; mysterious smoke in the garden; unknown footsteps in the snow; rappings in response to questions; and accurate predictions given through communication with a planchette (q.v.).

Price himself heard the bells and saw strange rains of objects come tumbling down the stairs. A window pane broke and fell to the ground, and a candle was hurled. Price held a seance in the Blue Room with no medium. He and others heard a faint tapping in response to questions. The spirit identified itself as Harry Bull, and said it wished to attract attention.

Price returned several times to the rectory and got phenomena "on demand" by asking for them; he was answered, he said, by paranormal bellringing. The former gardener and his wife told him they had been haunted, as did three of Harry Bull's sisters.

On July 15, 1929 the Smiths moved out. They said they did not believe in spirits, but decided to leave because the rectory was an uncomfortable house with bad sanitation and water available only through a well. Price maintained his interest in the hauntings.

On October 16, 1930 the Reverend Lionel Algernon Foyster (a cousin of the Misses Bull) and his wife, Marianne, moved into Borley Rectory. Nearly a year later, two of the Misses Bull notified Price that the poltergeist activity had increased and the Foysters were much troubled, especially Marianne. Price secured an invitation to return and resume his investigations.

Upon his arrival, he said, he found the phenomena far more violent. Foyster was keeping a diary of the almost daily occurrences. The Foysters' daughter, Adelaide, age three-and-one-half, was once locked in a room with no key. Marianne, who had a bad heart, seemed particularly molested, and once received a severe blow to the eye from some invisible presence. Objects were broken. Many objects mysteriously disappeared. Some reappeared, but others seemed gone forever. At dinner the night of Price's arrival, wine poured into a glass turned to ink. The phenomena considered most significant by Price were the "Marianne messages," strange, barely legible notes to Marianne found scrawled on the rectory walls.

Marianne admitted hating the rectory and wanting to move. Since the poltergeist activity almost always occurred when Marianne was alone or absent, Price said later he suspected her of being the agent.

The Foysters left Borley Rectory in 1935. In 1937, Price leased it for a year. On June 2, he and an Oxford graduate friend, Ellic Howe, moved in and spent a couple of nights there. They drew chalk circles around some moveable objects. During their stay, they heard thumps and found objects moved out of their outlines.

Price then advertised in the newspaper for assistants. He received more than 200 replies and enrolled 40 persons, mostly men, and all amateurs, to assist him in his investigations. He drew up a "Blue Book" of procedures using equipment that included remote-control movie cameras, still cameras, fingerprinting paraphernalia, felt overshoes for quiet movement, steel tape measures to check the thicknesses of walls, and planchettes for communicating with spirits. Price documented haunting phenomena and discovered human remains buried in the cellar, which medical experts said might be those of a young woman. The assistants were dispatched throughout the house and told to draw chalk rings around every moveable object, note markings and messages on walls and record all paranormal phenomena. Initially, all assistants were enthusiastic, but some dropped out after obtaining no results.

Other results were less than conclusive, and some were highly speculative. A dark object taken to be the nun manifested in February 1938, but Price's description of the incident reveals a great deal of speculation about a nondescript shape. There were alleged apports, but again these were inconclusive.

Some of the enrolled assistants were mediums: S.H. Glanville and his son, Roger, and daughter, Helen, for example, produced some interesting but probably fabulous theories. In seances, a spirit claiming to be Harry Bull said the bodies of a nun and a monk named "Fadenoch" (perhaps Father Enoch) were buried in the garden. In planchette communications with Roger and Helen Glanville beginning in October 1937, another spirit claimed to be the dead nun, named "Marie Lairre." Supposedly, she had been a French Catholic nun who was enticed by one of the Waldengraves, an influential Roman Catholic family connected with Borley Church for about 300 years, to leave her convent at Le Havre, France, and come to Borley to marry him. He strangled her in a building on the site on May 17, 1667, and her body was buried beneath the cellar floor that existed at that time. She wanted Mass and proper burial to be put to rest.

On March 27, 1938, Helen Glanville received a planchette communiqué stating that "Sunex Amures and one of his men" would burn down the rectory that night at 9:00 to end the haunting, and that proof of the murder responsible for the haunting would be revealed. The fire would start over the hall. Nothing happened.

Price left the rectory on May 19, 1938. He concluded that no single theory could explain all the phenomena. He believed a poltergeist was present, but a poltergeist could not explain the apparitions of the nun. He claimed there were at least 100 witnesses to various phenomena, of which the "Marianne messages" were the most striking. No new messages had appeared since the Foysters' departure, however. Price continued to believe in the existence of a medieval monastery on the site, despite the fact that in 1938 it was proved that no ecclesiastical building other than a 12th-century church had ever existed on the site. There never was a Borley monastery.

Interestingly, the rectory did burn down, but not until February 27, 1939 at midnight. The house had been occupied since December 1938 by Captain W.H. Gregson, who renamed it Borley Priory. He was sorting books in the hall when a stack fell over and upset a paraffin lamp. The first part of the house to burn was the Blue Room upstairs over the hall. The rectory was never rebuilt.

Price's book, *The Most Haunted House in England,* was both hailed as extraordinary psychical research and criticized as fabulous. Psychical researchers tended to be skeptical, noting that Price had a reputation for showmanship.

After Price's death in 1948, allegations of fraud were made concerning Borley, and his research was reexamined by Eric Dingwall, Kathleen M. Goldney and Trevor H. Hall, all of whom were critics of Price. Dingwall and Goldney, both psychical researchers, had known Price for 30 and 20 years, respectively. Hall was a skeptic of the paranormal in general.

Charles Sutton, a reporter for the *Daily Mail,* said he had caught or suspected Price of faking phenomena on several occasions. One night at the rectory with Price and another colleague, a large pebble

had hit Sutton on the head. After much noisy "phenomena," Sutton had seized Price and found his pockets full of bricks and pebbles. Sutton had telephoned the newspaper, but after a conference with a lawyer the story had been killed. The editor had said it was Sutton's "bad luck," for it was his word against that of Price and another witness. The other witness was Lucie Kaye, who told Dingwall and the other researchers that she had no recollection of the incident. It was Kaye's theory that Price attracted poltergeist activity, as it did not happen in his absence.

Cynthia Ledsham, on the staff of *Time,* also accused Price posthumously of "hocus pocus." Perhaps the most persuasive evidence came from Mrs. Smith, who in 1949 signed a statement stating her suspicions, shared by her maid and others at the time, that Price himself had caused the poltergeist phenomena. Nothing had occurred in the house that she would consider paranormal, she stated. The strange light in the windows of the unused wing had been discovered to be the reflection of passing trains. "Don't, Carlos, don't" could have been the voices of passersby. The Smiths had reason to believe that tricks were played on them by the locals, many of whom did not want a new rector after having been without one for years. The Smiths had never sought help for hauntings, she said. They knew that many locals believed the rectory to be haunted and thus might avoid going there. So, they had written to the *Daily Mail* to ask for referral to a psychic research society which could help them dispel fears. The unfortunate result was a revival of the ghost legends and the unwanted publicity that attracted Price.

Mrs. Smith further stated that after Price arrived, she, her husband and others were "astonished" at the onset of poltergeist phenomena. They immediately suspected Price as the perpetrator. Concerning the wine-to-ink incident, Mrs. Smith said that it occurred during dinner when a guest remarked that the phenomena could be caused by a clever man. Her wine then turned to ink in the glass. Price blamed a poltergeist, but others suspected him of sleight of hand.

S.H. Glanville, the first assistant to be enrolled by Price in 1937, told Dingwall, Goldney and Hall he "deplored the laxity" of Price's organization. There was no common log book, and each observer was unaware of the work of others, most of whom, like Glanville himself, were not qualified investigators. Glanville had no faith in the planchette material, believing that the messages came from the subconscious of the operators. He did not believe in the existence of Marie Lairre, nor in the paranormal nature of the apports. He did experience auditory phenomena which could not be explained, but which may have been due to the acoustics of the courtyard.

Dingwall, Goldney and Hall concluded in their book, *The Haunting of Borley Rectory* (1956), that nothing much out of the ordinary had happened at Borley Rectory during Price's stay. They said that Price's data was vague and subjective, and he gave unsubstantiated accounts and theories. He magnified incidents which probably were commonplace into events of great paranormal import. He dismissed critics and the accounts of persons who had lived at the rectory and experienced nothing. He omitted information from his reports which considered normal causes of phenomena. For example, he did not include in his own accounts incidents which would throw doubt upon the phenomena, such as the time Mr. Smith mistook a column of smoke for a white clad apparition. All of the ghosts in his early investigation were seen out of doors, where it is easy to mistake natural phenomena for something paranormal. The *Daily Mail* articles helped to fuel speculation and brought hordes of curiosity seekers to the grounds. The poltergeist phenomena did not begin until after Price appeared on the scene. The authors concluded that:

> The influence of suggestion on the investigation of haunted houses cannot be exaggerated. In every ordinary house sounds are heard and trivial incidents occur which are unexplained or treated as of no importance. But once the suggestion of the abnormal is put forward—and tentatively accepted—then these incidents become imbued with sinister significance: in fact, they become part of the "haunt."

Borley Rectory, they said, was "absolutely ideal" for these psychological mechanisms to take hold and operate. However, these arguments may explain some but not all of the phenomena. The possibility that at least some of the phenomena may have been paranormal cannot be discounted.

The haunting of the rectory refused to go away in the public mind. In 1953 and 1954, newspaper accounts reported ghosts still appearing at the site and stated that bricks taken from the Borley ruins and buried under a school playing yard at Wellingborough were connected with the alleged appearance of a ghost, as reported by one of the boys. The burning of a Borley village chicken house also was connected to the rectory's haunted history.

Further reading:

Price, Harry. *The Most Haunted House in England*. London: Longmans, Green & Co., 1940.

Price, Harry. *The End of Borley Rectory*. London: George G. Harrapp & Co., Ltd., 1946.

Dingwall, E.J., Kathleen M. Goldney, and Trevor H. Hall. *Haunting of Borley Rectory*. London: Gerald Duckworth, 1956.

Boston Society for Psychic Research (1925–1941)

Important psychical research organization, now defunct.

The Boston Society for Psychic Research was brought into being as a result of internal strife at the AMERICAN SOCIETY FOR PSYCHICAL RESEARCH (ASPR). The ASPR had been established in Boston in 1885, under the management of William JAMES and Richard HODGSON, who modeled it on the prestigious SOCIETY FOR PSYCHICAL RESEARCH (SPR) in London. With the death of Hodgson in 1905, the ASPR had been reconstituted in New York by James H. HYSLOP, who sought to maintain the same high standards. Following Hyslop's death in 1920, however, liberal and conservative factions within the ASPR became evident.

The Spiritualist Frederick Edwards was elected to the presidency in December 1923 and introduced a series of populist policies that did not sit well with the Society's more academically-oriented members, including psychologists William McDougall and Gardner MURPHY and the Reverend Elwood Worcester. When Edwards was elected to a second term in January 1925, they stepped up their pressure on Walter Franklin PRINCE, the ASPR's renowned research officer, to leave and head up a rival society in Boston.

Prince at first was reluctant to give up on the ASPR, but his responsibilities were gradually reduced. Edwards took over editorship of the ASPR's *Journal* and then, in March 1925, hired J. Malcolm Bird to be research officer in charge of physical phenomena, leaving Prince in charge of mental phenomena only. With Bird's appointment, Prince submitted his resignation and moved to Boston. The Boston Society was officially organized in May 1925 "in order to conduct psychic research according to strictly scientific principles, thus maintaining the standards set by Hodgson and Hyslop."

Despite its name, the Boston Society aspired to be a national and international organization along the lines of the SPR and the old ASPR. However, because it did not actively seek members and eschewed quantity in favor of quality in research and publication, it never attained the public prominence of its sister societies. Within psychical research it was very well regarded, and it published an irregular series of bulletins and books, many of lasting interest.

Among the more important bulletins were a report in the 1920s by G.H. Estabrooks of ESP experiments conducted at Harvard University, a reanalysis by Prince of the drawing experiments reported by Upton Sinclair in his book *Mental Radio* (1932), and a paper entitled, "Towards a Method of Evaluating Mediumstic Material," by J.G. Pratt (1936). The bulletins also included the first exposures of the fraudulent thumbprints produced by the Boston medium "Margery" (see CRANDON, MINA STINSON). Up until their publication (1934), the Boston Society had kept up an official silence on this mediumship, which was being heavily promoted by the ASPR.

Besides Prince's books, the Boston Society published *Leonard and Soule Experiments in Psychical Research* by Lydia Allison (192?) and *Case Studies Bearing on Survival* (1929) and *Beyond Normal Cognition* (1937) by John F. Thomas. Thomas' books were groundbreaking studies of mediumship that applied the statistical method of evaluation introduced by Pratt. The Boston Society was also the original publisher of J.B. RHINE's seminal monograph *Extra-Sensory Perception* (1934), which described laboratory experiments carried out at Duke University.

Prince was the Boston Society's main worker, and with his death in 1934 its activities largely came to a halt. These were also the years of the Great Depression, and with its small membership base (the Society never had more than 200 members), it was not in good financial shape. Fortunately the situation at the ASPR changed in 1941, when the liberal faction was swept off the board in a "palace revolution." The Boston Society's leaders—including Gardner Murphy and Lydia Allison—became involved in the rejuvenated ASPR, and the two organizations were formally merged in June 1941.

Further reading:
Berger, Arthur S. *Lives and Letters in American Parapsychology: A Biographical History, 1850–1987.* Jefferson, N.C.: McFarland, 1988.
Matlock, J.G. "Cat's paw: Margery and the Rhines, 1926." *Journal of Parapsychology* 51 (1987):229–47.
Mauskopf, Seymour, and Michael McVaugh. *The Elusive Science.* Baltimore: Johns Hopkins, 1980.

bridge of souls A motif in folklore and mythology that is a heavenly path by which the souls of the dead travel to their afterlife.

The Milky Way is commonly called "The Road of the Gods" or "The Road of Souls," and has been regarded as a river of spirit light since ancient times. The Milky Way also is seen as milk from a woman's breast, or as sperm from a man, which tie into concepts of reincarnation. In German and Russian folklore, the Milky Way is the path taken by the spectral wild hunt.

The rainbow is another common bridge-of-souls motif in mythology and folklore. The ancient Norsemen believed that Odin built a heavenly palace that could be reached by the rainbow, which they called Bifrost. Its red center line symbolized fire, which would consume any unworthy souls who attempted to use the bridge. On runic gravestones in Denmark and Sweden, there are inscriptions stating that people built bridges for the good souls of their loved ones.

The rainbow also is recognized as a bridge to heaven among the natives of Hawaii and among many North American Native tribes, including the Iroquois in the northeastern United States, the Catawba in the southeastern United States and the Tlingit in British Columbia. Among the Hopis of the southwestern United States, the rainbow is the means by which the Cloud People and kachinas travel through the sky.

In parts of modern Austria and Germany, folklore still holds that children's souls are led up the rainbow to heaven. In some parts of England, it is considered a sin to point at the rainbow. When one appears, children will make a cross on the ground with a couple of twigs or straws, "to cross out the bow."

Among many tribes of North and South America, Australia and West Africa, the rainbow is associated with a snake and is called the rainbow serpent, a creator god, culture hero and fertility god who reaches up from the earth into the sky. Among Aborigines of northwestern Australia, the rainbow serpent is linked to rain, fertility and pools of water which are thought to contain the spirits of unborn children.

Further reading:
Leach, Maria, and Jerome Fried, eds. *Funk & Wagnalls Standard Dictionary of Folklore, Mythology, and Legend.* San Francisco: Harper & Row, 1979.

British College of Psychic Science (BCPS) A psychical research institute founded in 1920 in London by Hewat McKenzie and his wife. Modeled after the INSTITUT METAPSYCHIQUE INTERNATIONAL in Paris, the BCPS pursued the scientific study of mediums and mediumship, the collection of evidence of survival after death, and related paranormal phenomena. It also provided counseling and advice to the public concerning consulting mediums. It was somewhat competitive with the London Spiritual Alliance, which later became the COLLEGE OF PSYCHIC STUDIES. Both organizations provided facilities for numerous important studies done of mediums.

In 1938, the BCPS merged with the International Institute for Psychical Research; the new organization was known as the Institute for Experimental Metaphysics. Following a decline during World War II, it ceased to exist in 1947, and its library and records were destroyed or dispersed.

Britten, Emma Hardinge See SPIRITUALISTS' NATIONAL UNION.

broom In the folklore of Eastern Europe and northern Italy, placing a broom beneath one's pillow will keep away witches and evil spirits at night. In England, a broom laid across a threshhold will do the trick.

Stepping over a broomstick will prevent disturbances by ghosts. Evil spirits and ghosts also can be exorcised from a dwelling in rites that involve sweeping the floors or ceilings.

Brown, Rosemary British medium renowned for her automatisms, especially her musical compositions, which she says are dictated to her by the spirits of famous composers. Rosemary Brown also does automatic writing of poetry, plays, philosophy and psychology, and automatic painting.

Brown's mediumistic ability manifested in childhood, when she was aware of apparitional spirits of the dead. When she was seven years old, in 1924, the spirit of Franz Liszt, who died in 1886, appeared to her and told her that when she grew up, he would return and bring her music.

In 1952, she married Charles Philip Brown and became a housewife in London. Charles, a freelance journalist who suffered ill health, died of nonalcoholic cirrhosis of the liver in 1961, leaving Rosemary with two children.

In 1964, she suffered broken ribs in a minor accident and was forced to recuperate at home. To pass the time, she sat down at her piano, which she had not played in 12 years. She suddenly became aware of the spirit of Liszt beside her, guiding her hands to play unfamiliar music.

Beginning with his second visit, Liszt introduced Brown to a number of famous composers who wished to dictate to her: Bach, Berlioz, Brahms, Chopin, Debussy, Grieg, Mozart, Monteverdi, Rachmaninoff, Schubert and Schumann. Word of her mediumship led to public performances; she gave more than 400 of them by the late 1980s. Some critics say she does exhibit the style of the various dead masters; others contend she is drawing on subliminal knowledge that mimics their styles. Brown has been harassed as a "witch" by some persons.

Dictated writing allegedly comes from playwright George Bernard Shaw, psychiatrist Carl G. Jung, and

physicist Albert Einstein. Various artists allegedly draw and paint through Brown as well.

Further reading:
Brown, Rosemary. *Unfinished Symphonies: Voices from the Beyond.* New York: William Morrow, 1971.
May, Antoinette. *Haunted Ladies.* San Francisco: Chronicle Books, 1975.

Browning Circle One of the most celebrated HOME CIRCLES of the 19th century was organized by medium D.D. HOME for Robert and Elizabeth Barrett Browning. The seance convinced Elizabeth of the truth of Spiritualism, but it provoked Robert, a nonbeliever, to write a scathing poem ridiculing the practice.

In 1855, Home, then living in Connecticut, received word from the spirits that he should go to England for his health. After first living with a Spiritualist named Cox, Home took up residence with Mr. John S. Rymer, a wealthy solicitor, and his wife.

The Rymers lived in Ealing, a part of London that was considered less fashionable than other quarters, and to host the man Elizabeth Browning called the most interesting person in England that year was quite a coup. Home had already held several seances for the Rymers, putting them in touch with their son Wat, who had died three years previously.

Before the seance, Home mingled with the guests and unctuously flattered and kissed the Rymers, calling them "mama" and "papa." Browning found Home effeminate. Fourteen sitters then gathered around a large table in the darkened room, lighted only by an oil lamp placed in the center. Rymer admonished them to behave themselves, a barb directed at Robert Browning.

The table began to vibrate and tilt, and raps were heard announcing the child Wat Rymer. He "talked" to his grieving parents, then left. All manifestations stopped, and Home asked five sitters to leave because he felt they were annoying the spirits. Once the circle was smaller, table-tapping and tilting resumed, perilously threatening the oil lamp, which stayed on the table as if glued. Wat's spirit again touched the Rymers, then Elizabeth Browning's dress was lifted as if by hands or some foreign object pushing the fabric up from underneath. Browning found all hands on the table and admitted his mystification at the movements.

Next, by rapping, the spirit offered to play an accordion and show its hand to Browning. The lamp was extinguished, and the only light was dim moonlight through muslin curtains. Browning noted that one could distinguish objects directly against the curtained windows, but not on the table. Soon a ghostly hand clothed in flowing muslin-like fabric appeared at the edge of the table opposite Elizabeth, rising and sinking, but never leaving the table's edge. Then another hand, much larger, appeared above the table and began edging a clematis wreath toward Elizabeth, who had taken a chair next to Home. The hand picked up the wreath and placed it on her head, then, at her request, passed the wreath under the table to her husband.

Browning was touched several times under the table on his knees and hands, and he asked to touch the spirit hand. The spirit agreed, but reneged. Next, Home held an accordion under the table with one hand and the spirits played several melodies, then bells. Another hand appeared, again sticking close to the table edge. The sitters tried to learn the spirit's name through alphabet rapping, since Home speculated it was probably a relative of Elizabeth's, but with no success.

Finally, Home became entranced and began speaking to the Rymers in the childish tones of their son, Wat. After a while Home came to, and the seance ended.

Elizabeth was convinced that Home was a miraculous medium and she wrote to her sister Henrietta that the spirit hands were very beautiful. Robert was not only unimpressed, he found the whole performance clumsy and below par even for a moderately good medium. He noted that Home's loose clothing could conceal strings and tubes used to produce phenomena, and that operation of the hands was easy to fake.

Browning, in fact, so loathed Home, whom he described as "smarmy," that he used him as the model for his poem, "Mr. Sludge, the Medium," in 1864. Two thousand lines of verse scathingly indicted all mediums, but particularly attacked Home, whom Browning referred to publicly as "Dungball," a play on Home's middle name, Dunglas. He also called Home a toady, a fraud, a leech, a braggart and a sot.

The Brownings' disagreement over Spiritualism in general, and the Home seance in particular, was the only public quarrel between the two poets. Robert so detested any mention of the subject that Elizabeth dropped all discussion of it, even warning her sisters never to mention it in letters. *Punch* magazine took Robert's side, portraying Elizabeth as a goose receiving the clematis wreath from obviously mechanical hands.

What caused Robert Browning's hatred? Some speculated at the time that Robert sulked because Elizabeth, not he, received the clematis wreath, a poor argument given the poet's devotion to and admiration of his wife. More likely is Browning's low opinion of Home's effeminacy. Homosexuality,

whether proven or not, was much more scandalous in 1855, and rumors of Home's affairs with young men followed him even through his two marriages. In any case, the affair merely created more intrigue and publicity for Home.

See also MATERIALIZATION; PSEUDOPODS.

Further reading:
Brandon, Ruth. *The Spiritualists.* New York: Alfred A. Knopf, 1983.
Fodor, Nandor. *An Encyclopedia of Psychic Science.* Secaucus, N.J.: The Citadel Press, 1966. First published 1933.
Mysteries of the Unknown: Spirit Summonings. Alexandria, Va.: Time-Life Books, 1989.

Browning, Elizabeth See BROWNING CIRCLE.

Browning, Robert See BROWNING CIRCLE.

bucca (also **bucca-boo**) In Cornish folklore, a sea spirit that lives among fishermen, helping them, or plaguing them when not propitiated. The bucca may be compared to the puca of Ireland, pwca of Wales and Puck of England, and to various household and mine spirits (see KNOCKER; PUCA).

Originally, the bucca was a Celtic sea god who declined to the status of demon or hobgoblin (see GOBLIN). To stay in the good graces of buccas, fishermen traditionally leave a fish from their catch on the sand. They also toss a piece of bread over their left shoulder and spill a little bit of their beer on the ground.

Further reading:
Briggs, Katherine. *An Encyclopedia of Fairies: Hobgoblins, Brownies, Bogies, and Other Supernatural Creatures.* New York: Pantheon Books, 1976.

Bull, Titus (1871–1946) American physician and neurologist who believed spirit obsession and possession were at the root of many illnesses, and treated his patients accordingly.

Bull practiced neurology, psychiatry and general medicine during a time when little attention was paid to the workings of the mind, or how the mind influenced health. At some point shortly after the turn of the 20th century, he became acquainted with the obsession research of James H. HYSLOP; Hyslop consulted with him on the THOMPSON-GIFFORD CASE.

Like his predecessors Carl and Anna WICKLAND, Bull believed that the possessing spirits were not necessarily evil but merely confused. With help from either the doctor or other spirits, the entities could pass on to their proper plane, leaving the victim in peace and finding happiness themselves.

Based on his experiences, Bull concluded that spirits enter the victim through the base of the brain, the solar plexus or the reproductive organs. He also postulated that pains suffered by the living may be pains produced by the obsessing head spirit, especially if that spirit suffered in life.

In the 1920s and 1930s, Bull, working in New York City, treated many of his patients with Spiritualist therapy. With the assistance of a medium, Carolyn C. Duke (her real identity remains a mystery), Bull claimed to treat and sometimes cure schizophrenics, manic-depressives and alcoholics. However, he failed to explain his criteria for evaluating cures; consequently, his work is ignored by both medical and psychical research establishments.

In 1932, Bull published a booklet, *Analysis of Unusual Experiences in Healing Relative to Diseased Minds and Results of Materialism Foreshadowed*. In it he developed Hyslop's theory that spirit obsession rarely causes pathology, but is a complicating factor in it. Trauma, he said, could attract spirits to a person. Also, some illnesses might involve a host of spirits attached to a person.

Bull suffered a stroke in 1942 and was paralyzed and speechless for the rest of his life. He died in 1946.

See also RELEASEMENT.

Further reading:

Ebon, Martin. *The Devil's Bride, Exorcism: Past and Present.* New York: Harper & Row, 1974.

Rogo, D. Scott. *The Infinite Boundary.* New York: Dodd, Mead & Co., 1987.

Evelyn Byrd. Courtesy Colonial Williamsburg.

Burton Agnes Skull See SCREAMING SKULLS.

Byrd, Evelyn The oldest daughter of William Byrd II, an early American colonial father and the founder of the city of Richmond, Virginia. She reportedly has haunted the grounds of what was her childhood estate, Westover, located on the James River. Her erratic and infrequent appearances never threaten or frighten anyone; Evelyn, it seems, made a vow prior to death to return as a friendly ghost.

Evelyn was born at Westover in 1707. Her father was King George I's agent of the colony of Virginia, and surveyed the line dividing Virginia and North Carolina. His descendants include Admiral Richard E. Byrd, who explored Antarctica, and Senator Harry F. Byrd.

At age 10, Evelyn was sent to England to be educated. At age 16, she fell in love with a man her father deemed unsuitable for the Byrd family. The suitor's identity is not known for certain, but he may have been Lord Peterborough, who was four times older than Evelyn, or Charles Morduant, Peterborough's grandson.

Byrd forced the courtship to end. At age 19, Evelyn returned to Westover, broken in spirit. She withdrew from social contact, maintaining a relationship only with a neighboring friend, Anne Carter Harrison, whom she met almost daily in a poplar grove adjoining the two plantations. For 11 years Evelyn withered away, until finally she died.

Prior to her death, the two young women made a pact that the first to die would return as a benevolent ghost. After Evelyn's death, Anne was the first to see her ghost, strolling under tulip trees in the poplar grove. The ghost smiled at Anne and then disappeared.

Since then, Evelyn's ghost makes occasional appearances on the Westover grounds or in the plantation house. Usually she is dressed in white; sometimes she wears green velvet and lace. Evelyn always smiles. Sometimes she seems so real that she has been mistaken for a houseguest. She has been seen in the poplar grove walking with another figure, perhaps that of her friend, Anne.

Further reading:

Anderson, Jean. *The Haunting of America.* Boston: Houghton Mifflin, 1973.

C

cabinet A confined space, whether provided by an actual piece of furniture, a closet or merely an enclosed end of a seance room, that once served as a physical medium's working space. Its purpose was to attract and conserve spiritual forces, enabling the medium to produce manifestations. Psychical researcher Hereward CARRINGTON compared the cabinet to a spiritual storage battery, releasing psychic energy throughout the seance.

The use of a cabinet for paranormal revelations began with the DAVENPORT BROTHERS in the mid-1850s. Neither the FOX SISTERS nor any of the earlier mediums had used one. William and Ira Davenport, who never claimed to be Spiritualists, began their careers by performing with a table and chairs on a raised platform, most often in the dark. According to Harry HOUDINI, who attempted to expose mediums as frauds, a person in the audience asked if the Davenports could produce their manifestations in a closet to prevent collusion by confederates, and the Davenports, realizing the benefits of working in secret, agreed.

The wooden cabinet became an essential part of the Davenports' act. According to legend, the infamous spirit control John KING himself gave the Davenports the cabinet's specifications. Made of lightweight bird's-eye maple, it was seven feet high, six feet wide and two feet deep, and rested eighteen inches off the floor on three sawhorses. Three doors comprised the front side, which opened to fully show the interior. A diamond-shaped hole was cut in the middle door for air and to allow the spirits' hands to show. Behind the left and right doors were benches where the Davenports sat, bound hand and foot by members of the audience. Upon the center bench, supposedly out of reach, were piled musical instruments: tambourines, accordions, trumpets, guitars, violins, bells. Once the audience was convinced the Davenports were incapable of playing the instruments, the doors were closed.

Almost at once, spirit hands of men, women and children appeared in the aperture in the middle door, playing the instruments wildly and waving about. But upon opening the doors, the brothers were seen to be still bound with rope. Occasionally a brave soul from the audience volunteered to sit on the middle bench in the dark cabinet, tied to the Davenports, but the manifestations appeared regardless.

The act was an immediate sensation. Hardly any practicing medium anywhere could continue his or her performances without a cabinet to harness psychic energy. Many just hung black curtains in front of an alcove or corner of the seance room and retired behind them during the sitting. The full-form materializations of Florence COOK and Eva C. (see BERAUD, MARTHE) appeared from the cabinet curtains, with faces floating on the black surface. Critics found the cabinet a convenient prop for trickery.

Cabinets are rarely used in modern physical mediumship.

Further reading:

Brandon, Ruth. *The Spiritualists*. New York: Alfred A. Knopf, 1983.

Brown, Slater. *The Heyday of Spiritualism*. New York: Pocket Books, 1972.

Doyle, Sir Arthur Conan. *The Edge of the Unknown*. New York: Berkley Medallion Books, 1968. First published by G.P. Putnam's Sons, 1930.

———. *The History of Spiritualism, Vol. I & II*. New York: Arno Press, 1975.

Fodor, Nandor. *An Encyclopaedia of Psychic Science*. Secaucus, N.J.: The Citadel Press, 1966. First published 1933.

Houdini, Harry. *Houdini: A Magician Among the Spirits*. New York: Arno Press, 1972.

Mysteries of the Unknown: Spirit Summonings. Alexandria, Va.: Time-Life Books, 1989.

cairn Heaps of stones used as either memorials or grave markers. As memorials, cairns mark burial sites and protect both the living and the dead. In southern India, for example, they are believed to protect corpses against desecration and to protect the living from the spirits of the dead, who otherwise would rise out of the grave and wreak evil.

Calvados Castle   This Norman castle was subject to such a severe poltergeist haunting from October 12, 1875 to at least September 1876 that the owners were driven from the premises. The most plausible explanation advanced for the haunting was that it was caused by the previous owner, a woman who had died impenitent and was believed to have returned to her castle. In the written accounts given of the hauntings, individuals are identified only by initials.

Calvados Castle was a replacement of an earlier castle, belonging to the B. Family, which had fallen into a state of disrepair. In 1867, it was inherited by Monsieur and Madame de X. The new owners were subjected to strange noises and blows at night which eventually abated. Then, for unknown reasons, the noises resumed with greater fury in October 1875. At that time, the castle was occupied by M. and Mme. de X. and their son; the Abbe Y., who was the boy's tutor; and four domestic employees. The person who was plagued the most by the haunting was the Abbe.

The haunting resumed with the movement of furniture and with nightly thumps and great blows in various rooms, so loud and strong that the entire castle shook. The residents also heard some being going up and down the stairs with superhuman speed. One night, M. de X. wrote in his diary:

> At 2 A.M. some being rushed at top speed up the stairs from the entrance hall to the first floor, along the passage, and up to the second floor, with a loud noise of tread which had nothing human about it. Everybody heard it. It was like two legs deprived of their feet and walking on the stumps. Then we heard numerous loud blows on the stairs and the door of the green room.

In addition to the rushing and the blows, the residents heard cries or a long-drawn-out trumpet call, followed by shrieks that sounded like a woman in misery calling for help from outside the castle. As usual, an inspection was made and nothing was found.

By mid-November 1875, stifled cries and sounds of a woman sobbing were heard all over the house not only at night but during the day as well. The words "of demons or the damned" were discerned.

The Abbe, who always took great care to lock his room whenever he left it, invariably found upon his return that furniture had been moved, the closed window had been opened, and his possessions had

been strewn about. Once, about one hundred of his books were knocked to the floor, save for three books of the Holy Scriptures. On another occasion, the Abbe was reading at about five in the evening when a great quantity of water crashed down the chimney, put out the fire and spewed ashes in his face. The day had been sunny and clear, in the midst of a drought.

The poltergeist also played an organ which was closed and locked, turned keys in locks in front of eyewitnesses, and made sounds of bodies or cannonballs falling down the stairs and sticks jumping up and down on their ends. Galloping and stampeding noises went on nightly. Human-like cries continued to be heard, including that of a man who once was heard to cry, "Ha! Ha!"

M. de X. initially thought humans were responsible. He theorized that others who coveted the castle and grounds might be trying to scare him away and sell it for a fraction of its value. He bought two watchdogs which proved to be useless. Only once did they bark in the direction of a garden thicket. Their barks changed to whines and they ran away, refusing to return to the thicket. A search of the bushes revealed nothing. M. de X. then had to consider supernatural causes; the Abbe believed the haunting to be the work of the Devil. M. de X. appealed to ecclesiastical authorities for help.

On January 5, 1876 the Rev. Fr. H.L. arrived to investigate. An immediate calm set in, and nothing happened as long as he was in the house. On January 15, he performed a religious ceremony (the exact nature is not specified in the records). The noises began again, but in parts of the castle too remote for him to hear. The Rev. Fr. H.L. left on January 17, and the disturbances renewed with great intensity.

By January 28, the desperate family had a Novena of Masses said at Lourdes for them and had exorcisms performed. Church officials were of the opinion that the nature of the haunting was "diabolically supernatural." Following the exorcisms, calm reigned for two or three days. Then small noises and disturbances began once again, increasing to great frequency by August 1876. In September, following loud noises during the night, M. de X. opened the drawing room to find all the furniture rearranged in a horseshoe, as though a meeting had taken place. He sat down and played his harmonium for a long time. When he was finished, his playing was repeated for a long time in an opposite corner of the room.

Finally, M. and Mme. de X. could stand no more. They sold the castle and moved. The records do not indicate if the castle went cheaply, as M. de X. had feared. It is not known if subsequent occupants were haunted. The case remains unexplained.

Further reading:

Flammarion, Camille. *Haunted Houses.* London: T. Fisher Unwin, 1924.

Sitwell, Sacheverell. *Poltergeists: Fact or Fancy.* New York: Dorset Press, 1988. First published 1959.

Cambridge Ghost Club.   See GHOST CLUB.

candles   Candles have been used since ancient times in humankind's most important rituals and rites of passage, including those pertaining to the dead and ghosts of the dead.

The actual origin of candles is unknown, but they were in use as early as 3000 B.C. in Egypt and Crete, providing light to repel evil spirits in religious ceremonies. Old Jewish customs, adopted by Christians, call for lighting candles for the dying and dead: a lit candle by the bedside of a dying person frightens away demons, and it must remain lit for a week after death, perhaps to keep the air purified. Another custom calls for burning candles in all rooms of the house until the corpse is buried. A similar custom from Ireland calls for burning 12 candles in a circle around a corpse until it is buried, for the circle of fire will prevent evil spirits from carrying off the dead one's soul. Three candles are burned at Irish wakes, and the candle ends are then used to treat burns. Because of the association with wakes, three burning candles are considered an ill omen and harbinger of death; in the superstitions of the theater, three candles are never to be lit in dressing rooms.

In the Scottish Lowlands, a washed and laid out corpse is given a "saining" (blessing) by the oldest woman present, who lights a candle and passes it three times over the body. The candle is kept burning throughout the night. The candle must be obtained from an "unlucky" person (hence the opposite, or lucky) such as a witch, wizard, seer, or one who has flat feet or is "ringlet-eyed" or "lang-lipit" (probably hare-lipped).

A guttering candle generally presages a death in the family, while in American folklore, a candle left burning in an empty room will cause a death in the family. In Suffolk lore, a burning candle accidentally shut in a pantry is an omen of the same. A superstition common to the British Isles holds that candles whose wax drips not straight down but around the candle, thus giving the appearance of a winding sheet, is also a death omen; whoever is in the direction of the drip is the doomed one. In German lore, a candle wick that divides in two and burns in twin flames presages a death (interestingly, the same phe-

nomenon in Austrian lore merely foretells the arrival of a letter).

A candle that burns dim means that a ghost is nearby; so does a candle that burns blue. Shakespeare used this latter superstition in *Richard the Third*, in which the Ghost of Buckingham enters to blue candlelight at dead midnight. In some beliefs, the death omen can be nullified by extinguishing the candle under running water or by blowing it out. In the late 18th century, the concept of blue candle flames as ghost calling cards was "so universally acknowledged, that many eminent philosophers have busied themselves in accounting for it, without once doubting the truth of it," according to Francis Grose's *Provincial Glossary; with a Collection of Local Proverbs, and Popular Superstitions* (1787; 1790). However, in 1726, Daniel Defoe, writing in *History of the Devil*, maintained that blue candle flames were not supernatural but were merely produced by "any extraordinary emission of sulphurous or of nitrous particles" in close quarters.

Seventeenth-century lore advised treasure-hunters to carry lanterns containing consecrated candles in order to conjure the ghosts of dead men who were said to guard buried treasure. These ghostly guards were stationed by Captain Kidd and other pirates of the time, who reputedly killed a man at every site where they buried their loot. The spirits were to be summoned in the name of God and promised anything in order to help them find "a place of untroubled rest." According to lore, if the ghost caused a treasure-hunter to speak or scream—as they invariably did—the treasure vanished. In one Nova Scotia tale, four men who discovered the site of buried treasure were digging silently when one of them noticed that suddenly a fifth man had joined them. He shouted. The fifth man vanished, and the treasure sank beyond reach.

Further reading:

Guiley, Rosemary Ellen. *The Encyclopedia of Witches and Witchcraft.* New York: Facts On File, 1989.

Opie, Iona, and Moira Tatem. *A Dictionary of Superstitions.* Oxford: Oxford University Press, 1989.

Captain Kidd   See CANDLES; PHANTOM SHIPS.

Carrington, Hereward (1880–1958)   English-born journalist and psychic investigator, author of many popular books on psychic phenomena.

Hereward Carrington was born in Jersey, one of Britain's Channel Islands, on October 17, 1880. He received his early schooling in London and in Cranbook, Kent. His parents were agnostics; they raised their children with little or no religion, and encouraged them to think for themselves.

When he was eight, in 1888, Carrington's mother took him on a visit to the United States. On board ship they met three German men who were acquainted with psychical research and who talked with Mrs. Carrington about the book *Phantasms of the Living* (by Edmund GURNEY, Frederic W.H. MYERS and Frank PODMORE), which had then just been published. Carrington listened with rapt attention to the stories of crisis apparitions and the evidence for telepathy. He was fascinated as much by the stories as by their scientific standing: all the cases had been investigated by the authors and were well documented.

But however intrigued he was, the experience aboard the *Elbe* was not enough to draw Carrington into psychical research. He was skeptical about all things of a supernatural nature. He was more interested in conjuring; he read up on the history of magic, and gave a performance at age 13. When he read some books that described the tricks of some fraudulent mediums some years later, this only confirmed his skepticism about psychic phenomena. The book that finally changed his mind was Ada Goodrich Freer's *Essays in Psychical Research*, which he read when it appeared in 1899. He joined the SOCIETY FOR PSYCHICAL RESEARCH (SPR), and the following year, at age 20, he moved to the United States, where he was to spend the remainder of his life.

Carrington first went to Boston, where an older brother was already living. His early years in the United States were spent working as a journalist, but he had already decided to devote as must time as possible to psychical research, and he got in touch with Richard HODGSON at the AMERICAN SOCIETY FOR PSYCHICAL RESEARCH (at that time the SPR's American Branch). After Hodgson died in 1905, the ASPR was reestablished in New York by James H. HYSLOP, and Carrington joined the staff as an investigator.

His knowledge of conjuring now came in handy. In *Personal Experiences in Spiritualism* (1918) he tells of an investigation he made of a haunted town in Ontario, Nova Scotia in January 1907. The haunting turned out to be a practical joke by the entire town on their single Spiritualist neighbor: they used pulleys and ropes to open doors and threw things around the shops when he was not looking. Later in the year, Carrington spent two weeks at the Spiritualist camp at Lily Dale, New York. He discovered that all 17 of the mediums working there were frauds, with the result that all except one (who was able to persuade the authorities otherwise) were not invited back the next year.

Carrington thought better of the AMHERST HAUNTING, which he looked into on his way home from Nova Scotia, and in 1908 he had an impressive sitting with the famous mental medium Leonora PIPER. Piper was in trance, lying with her head on the table with her face turned away, engaged in automatic writing. Carrington's mother, who had recently died, was communicating; Carrington took a pair of small nail-scissors that had belonged to her out of his pocket and laid them silently on the table, behind the medium's head. Mrs. Piper immediately tried to draw a pair of scissors, and then "a little later a clearer attempt, coupled with the words, 'Those were mine; I used to use them.' "

In the summer of 1908 Carrington went to Naples, Italy to take part in an investigation of the physical medium Eusapia PALLADINO. His co-investigators, Everard Feilding and W.W. Baggally, were also knowledgeable about conjuring. In a series of seances they discovered that Palladino would cheat if given the chance, but that if she were restrained, she could produce genuine phenomena. In his book *Eusapia Palladino and her Phenomena* (1909), Carrington stated that he believed most of the attempts at cheating to be unconscious, due to the powerful urge to produce phenomena. If Palladino could cheat, she would; but if she were restrained, the results often were astonishing.

Palladino so impressed Carrington, in fact, that he arranged for her to visit the United States. She arrived in November 1909 and left in June 1910, having given 31 seances. The first 27 of these were under Carrington's supervision, and he restrained her when she tried to cheat. But the last four seances were held at Columbia University in Carrington's absence, and they were a disaster. Palladino was not restrained, and two detectives, hired for the purpose, were easily able to spot her tricks.

Carrington received a doctorate from William Penn College, in Iowa, in 1918. In 1921 he founded the American Psychical Institute and Laboratory in New York. The well-equipped laboratory was the only one of its day, preceding by a few years that of Harry PRICE and by several years the famous Parapsychology Laboratory established (in 1927) at Duke University by J.B. RHINE. Carrington's institute closed after only two years; but it was to reopen a decade later.

Carrington was one of two American delegates to the first International Congress on Psychical Research held in Copenhagen in 1921, as well as to later Congresses in Warsaw (1923), Paris (1927), Athens (1930) and Oslo (1935).

In 1924 he was named to the Scientific American committee investigating the controversial mediumship of Mina Stinson CRANDON ("Margery"). The committee sat with Crandon for two years, but eventually all except Carrington decided that she was a fraud. Carrington took a middle course; he acknowledged that there was some fraud, but thought that some part of the mediumship was genuine. Carrington, however, may have been having an affair with Crandon, who was a beautiful and vivacious woman some years younger than her husband. Carrington's friend Henry Gilroy later told his biographer Paul Tabori that they had met for several months "on the q.t."

When a young man named Sylvan Muldoon approached Carrington about his "astral projections" (see OUT-OF-BODY EXPERIENCE), Carrington helped him to write the well-known book, *The Projection of the Astral Body* (1929). It was followed several years later by *The Phenomena of Astral Projection* (1951).

In 1932 Carrington did some experiments with Eileen J. GARRETT at the ASPR offices in New York, but this was at the time that Mina Crandon's "Walter thumbprints," supposedly those of her deceased brother, were being shown to belong to her very much living dentist. When the ASPR persisted in supporting the mediumship, Carrington decided he could no longer be associated with the society; he reopened his American Psychical Institute, where experiments with Garrett were continued in 1933.

The Garrett experiments were described in the institute's first *Bulletin*. Garrett was given word association tests, both in and out of trance, and a galvanometer was used to record her brain waves. The results clearly showed a difference between Garrett in and out of trance, but because there were also differences between Garrett's normal personality and her trance personality from one session to the next, Carrington's conclusion was cautious.

In 1932 Carrington met Marie Sweet Smith, who became his wife. She also served as the institute's secretary from the time it reopened in 1933. After the Garrett experiments, the institute's main work involved the testing of a variety of instruments that had been used in research with mediums. Carrington described these tests in *Laboratory Investigations into Psychic Phenomena* (1939).

Carrington spent the last two decades of his life in southern California. There he revived his institute and expanded its activities, with the help of Henry Gilroy and his wife. The results of their investigations, however, were disappointing; they were unable to locate a single genuine medium or haunting. Carrington died on December 26, 1958 in Los Angeles, at the age of 78.

Carrington authored or coauthored more than 100 books and articles on psychical research and many other subjects, including bridge playing, nutrition, magic and yoga. His works on psychical research include, in addition to those already mentioned, *The Physical Phenomena of Spiritualism* (1907), *The Coming Science* (1908), *The Problems of Psychical Research* (1914), *Psychical Phenomena and the War* (1918), *Your Psychic Powers and How to Develop Them* (1920), *The Story of Psychic Science* (1930), *Houdini and Conan Doyle*, with Bernard M.L. Ernst (1932), *A Primer in Psychical Research* (1933), *Loaves and Fishes* (1935), *Psychic Science and Survival* (1947), *The American Seances of Eusapia Palladino* (1954) and *The Case for Psychic Survival* (1957). Two volumes of his essays were edited by Raymond Buckland and published under the title *Essays in the Occult* in 1958.

Further reading:

Pleasants, Helene, ed. *Biographical Dictionary of Parapsychology*. New York: Helix Press, 1964.

Tabori, Paul. *Pioneers of the Unseen*. New York: Taplinger, 1973.

caul A thin membrane of amniotic fluid which sometimes inexplicably remains covering the head of a newborn child at birth. Since the time of the Romans, to be born with a caul is to be blessed with luck, protection (especially against drowning) and supernatural powers, such as the ability to divine the future and see and converse with ghosts and spirits, even if the individual is deaf.

Traditionally, cauls were carefully preserved and kept as a sort of amulet and talisman; sometimes they were worn about the neck. It was not uncommon for midwives to take cauls and sell them as charms. They once commanded a good price among sailors, who valued them for protection against drowning at sea.

Cauls are said to indicate the health of the owner: if crisp and dry, health is good; if limp and wet, health is bad. Cauls become flaccid upon their owner's death. In the lore of parts of the American south, a person dies if his caul is torn.

The nearly universal good luck and magical power ascribed to cauls is contradicted in Greek folklore, which holds that anyone born with a caul will become a vampire.

Other terms for caul are "veil," "silly how" and "hallihoo" (holy or fortunate hood).

Cauls were of vital importance to a pagan agrarian cult of northern Italy called the *benandanti*, which was still active in the 17th century. The *benandanti* (which means "good walkers") was a corps of village men and women who had been born with the caul, and thus could see ghosts and true witches. They wore their cauls about their necks. They were compelled to serve their villages during the Ember Days, the seasonal transitions of the solstices and equinoxes. During the night, they claimed to be summoned by drums or angels to leave their bodies and assume animal shapes, and go out and do battle with an army of witches who also were in animal guise. The *benandanti* fought with stalks of fennel, while the witches fought with stalks of sorghum. If the *benandanti* won, the crops that year would be abundant, but if they lost, the harvest would be poor and the villagers would suffer famine. After the battle, the spirits of both sides would roam the countryside looking for clean water to drink. The *benandanti* were required to return to their bodies by the dawn crowing of the cock, lest they have difficulty re-entering them or be unable to re-enter them at all. If that happened, the bodies remained stiff and coma-like, and their disembodied spirits would be forced to wander the earth until the destined time of death arrived for their bodies.

The origins of the *benandanti* cult are not known. The leaving of the body is common to ancient shamanic practices. In 1575, the cult came to the attention of inquisitors of the Catholic Church, which began an investigation to determine whether the cult practiced witchcraft and worshipped the Devil. By then, the cult had absorbed Christian elements. By 1623, the Church had obtained "confessions" of diabolical activities from some *benandanti*, but authorities never meted out more than mild punishment, due to the increasing skepticism of the verity of so-called witches' sabbats, which were believed to be wild nights of drinking, dancing and copulating with devils. See also AMULET; VAMPIRE.

Further reading:
Ginzburg, Carl. *Night Battles, Witchcraft and Agrarian Cults in the Sixteenth and Seventeenth Centuries.* New York: Penguin Books, 1983.

Cauld Lad of Hilton

In English folklore, a helpful but mischievous spirit, half brownie and half ghost, who once haunted Hilton Castle in Northumbria.

According to legend, the Cauld once was a stable boy, Roger Skelton, who was killed in 1609 by Lord Robert Hilton in a state of passion. The lord ordered the boy to fetch his horse and became enraged when he failed to do so quickly enough. He stormed into the stable and struck the boy with a hay fork, killing him. He tossed the body in a pond.

The spirit, a naked boy, would make nighttime visits to the kitchen of the castle, in a wing built in 1735. He was seldom seen, but was often heard singing sadly. He made clean what was dirty, and if he found no work to do he made dirty what was clean, and mixed the salt, sugar and pepper and upset the utensils and dishes. He is said to have once given a terrible fright to a servant who liked to sneak drinks from the cream. Once while doing so she heard a voice over her shoulder say, "Ye sip, and ye sip, and ye sip; but you never give the Cauld Lad a sip." She fled in terror.

The servants eventually banished the spirit by laying out a cloak and hood of fairy green one night. At midnight the Cauld Lad appeared. He donned the clothes and gamboled about the kitchen all night. At the hour before dawn, he drew his clothes about him and said,

> Here's a cloak and here's a hood:
> The Cauld Lad of Hilton will do no more good.

With that, the spirit vanished forever. Hilton Castle is now in ruins.

Further reading:
Briggs, Katherine. *An Encyclopedia of Fairies: Hobgoblins, Brownies, Bogies, and Other Supernatural Creatures.* New York: Pantheon Books, 1976.
Harper, Charles G. *Haunted Houses: Tales of the Supernatural With Some Accounts of Hereditary Curses and Family Legends.* Rev. and enlarged ed. London: Cecil Palmer, 1924.

cemeteries

See BACHELOR'S GROVE CEMETERY; FUNERAL RITES AND CUSTOMS; GHOST; RESURRECTION MARY.

Chaffin Will Case

Unusual case in which the apparition of a deceased man appeared to one of his sons four years after his death to alert him to the existence of an unknown will. The case is seen by some as evidence in support of survival after death (q.v.), while others say it can be explained merely by clairvoyance.

James L. Chaffin was a farmer in North Carolina who had four sons. In November 1905, he made out a will leaving his farm and all assets to his third son, Marshall. He made no provision for his wife and three other sons, John, James P. and Abner.

Apparently Chaffin later had a change of heart, perhaps after reading the Bible. Genesis 27 tells how Jacob deceived his father, Isaac, into giving him the birthright intended for his older brother, Esau. In 1919, Chaffin executed a second will, written in his own hand, that stated:

> After reading the 27th Chapter of Genesis, I, James L. Chaffin, do make my last will and testament, and here it is. I want, after giving my body a decent burial, my little property to be equally divided between my four children, if they are living at my death, both personal and real estate, divided equal if not living, give share to their children. And if she is living, you must all take care of your mammy.

Now this is my last will and testament. Witness my hand and seal.

James L. Chaffin,
This *January* 16, 1919.

Though not witnessed, the will was valid under North Carolina law.

Chaffin then took the will and hid it in his father's old Bible. He secreted it in Genesis 27, folding pages to form a pocket to hold the paper. For reasons unknown, he said nothing to anyone of his new will. It is possible that he intended to do so at an appropriate moment but was unable to follow through. Chaffin did write a note, however, which said, "Read the 27th Chapter of Genesis in my daddie's old Bible." He rolled up the note, tied it with string and placed it in the inside pocket of his black overcoat. He stitched the pocket shut.

On September 7, 1921 Chaffin died of injuries sustained in a fall. His 1905 will was probated, and the estate went to Marshall Chaffin. No one contested.

Four years later, in 1925, son James P. Chaffin began having vivid dreams in which his father appeared at his bedside and stood in silence. In June 1925, the deceased Chaffin appeared by his bedside once again, dressed in his black overcoat. He took hold of his coat, pulled it back and said, "You will find my will in my overcoat pocket." He vanished.

It is not certain whether the apparition of the father was external or appeared as part of a dream. James was not certain that he was awake or asleep when the apparition appeared; he may have been dozing.

The next morning, James awoke convinced that his father had communicated with him for the purpose of clearing up some mistake. He went to his mother's home, where he found out that the overcoat was in the possession of his brother, John. On July 6, he visited John and found the coat. Upon examining it, James found the pocket that had been sewn shut. He opened it, found the note and read it.

James wisely found witnesses to accompany him back to his mother's to retrieve the Bible in question. They included Thomas Blackwelder, a neighbor, Blackwelder's daughter, and James's own daughter. They found the Bible and the will.

The second will was filed in court and offered for probate. Marshall had died, but his widow and son contested the new will. The case came for trial in December 1925. About a week before the trial, the deceased Chaffin appeared again to James in an agitated state, saying, "Where is my old will." James took this to be a sign that he would win the lawsuit.

Ten witnesses were prepared to testify at the trial that the handwriting on the second will was that of the deceased Chaffin. When shown the will, Marshall's widow and son acknowledged that the handwriting was Chaffin's, and they withdrew their opposition. The old will was annulled and the new will was probated.

Several explanations were considered for this case. The most obvious explanation is that James P. Chaffin, upset at being cut out of his father's will, forged a new and more favorable one and then concocted the ghost story. However, the handwriting of Chaffin in the second will was validated as genuine. And if son James P. Chaffin somehow did commit a forgery, there was no need for him to wait four years, or create a ghost story. He could have simply "found" the new will, which would have been much more plausible.

A second explanation is that surviving Chaffins knew of the existence of the second will. But a North Carolina attorney who was interested in parapsychology thoroughly interviewed James P. Chaffin, his wife, daughter and mother, and concluded that none of them had any prior knowledge of the second will. The lawyer said he was impressed with the Chaffins' honesty and sincerity.

A third explanation holds that James P. Chaffin had prior knowledge of the will, but had consciously forgotten it. The information may have been telepathically transmitted between father and son. The information was brought back to the son's attention by the apparition, which was a figment of his dreams. This is possible, but not likely, given the known facts concerning the case. It is doubtful that the father revealed the new will to anyone; otherwise, he would not have gone to such great lengths to hide it. The four-year lapse also cannot be adequately accounted for by this theory.

A fourth explanation is that during sleep, son James, through clairvoyance, obtained knowledge of the will, which was then projected onto an "apparition" to persuade himself that the information was true. This is possible, and if valid, it negates the case as evidence for survival after death.

Finally, it must be considered that a genuine apparition of the dead did appear to son James and deliver information, by telepathy, that was unknown to him. This theory supports survival after death. It also makes the case an unusual one, for it involves both sight and hearing on the part of James, the percipient. The four-year lapse gives added strength to the theory that the case is a genuine example of survival. It is unlikely that information telepathically transmitted just prior to Chaffin's death would not surface for four years. Nonetheless, the case remains inconclusive, as none of these theories can be proved.

The Chaffin Will case resembles a similar case that occurred near Ionia, Iowa in 1891. That case, too, involved a farmer, Michael Conley, who was found dead in an outhouse. Upon hearing of his death, Conley's daughter fell into a faint. Upon reviving, she said he had appeared to her and told her there was a large sum of money sewn inside a pocket inside the shirt he was wearing at the time of his death. She also described in detail his burial suit, including satin slippers that were of a new design, and which she could not have seen before. The clothes Conley had been wearing at the time of his death had been thrown away. They were recovered, and $35 were found sewn shut in an inside shirt pocket. This case could be evidence for survival after death. Or, the information could have been conveyed telepathically from father to daughter just before his death. Neither explanation can be ruled out.

See also CLAIRVOYANCE.

Further reading:

Berger, Arthur S. *Evidence of Life After Death: A Casebook for the Tough-Minded.* Springfield, Ill.: Charles C Thomas, 1988.

"Case of the Will of James L. Chaffin." *Proceedings of the Society for Psychical Research* 36 (1928):517–24.

Myers, Frederic W.H. *Human Personality and Its Survival of Bodily Death Vols. I & II.* New ed. New York: Longmans, Green & Co., 1954. First published 1903.

chalcedony A type of quartz used by the ancient Egyptians to drive away ghosts, night visions and sadness. Chalcedony is never crystalline, but translucent and waxy in appearance. It usually is a smoky blue, but it may also be yellow or a cloudy white. The Egyptians used it on their scarab seals.

See also AMULET.

channeling A form of mental mediumship that became popular in the United States and elsewhere as part of the so-called "New Age" movement. Channeling involves communication through automatic speech (see AUTOMATISMS) and automatic writing with various nonphysical beings, including angels, nature spirits, totem or guardian spirits, deities, demons and spirits of the dead; some channelers say they communicate with a Higher Self.

Channeling is done in a dissociated state of consciousness or trance. The channeler may allow the entity to take over control of his or her body and use the vocal chords. Or channelers receive information through clairaudience (paranormal hearing), visions, intuitions and inspirations.

While the mediumship of Spiritualism focuses on communication with the spirits of the dead, the proof of survival after death (q.v.), and spiritual healing, channeling focuses on delivery of sermons and teachings from supposedly highly evolved beings, or even Jesus Christ himself. Some of these beings, such as Lazaris, channeled by Jach Pursel, claim never to have incarnated on the earth.

Channeling came into vogue in the 1970s after the channeled writings of the entity Seth, speaking through Jane Roberts, became bestselling books. In a manner similar to the rush of popular interest in Spiritualist mediumship that occurred in the 19th century, channelers went into business, some charging exorbitant fees for sittings. Fad interest ended by the end of the 1980s, though the more prominent "channels," as some individuals prefer to be called, retained their followings.

The development and performance of channelers is comparable to mediums. Researchers who have studied channeling propose some of the same theories to explain it as they do mediumship: that the channeler does not literally communicate with another entity, but draws material from his or her own unconscious that takes on a secondary personality of an entity in order to be expressed. Some psychologists believe channeling is pathological in origin and is symptomatic of multiple personality disorder; however, channelers, like mediums, control access to their communicators, while mentally ill people typically do not have such control.

Other theories propose that everyone has multiple consciousnesses, but that only a few become aware of some of the layers and gain access to them; or, that channeling taps into a Universal Mind.

Further reading:

Anderson, Roger. "Channeling." *Parapsychology Review* 19 (1988):6–9.

Kautz, William H. "Channeling: Mediumship Comes of Age." *Applied Psi* (January/February 1987):3–8.

Kautz, William H., and Melanie Branon. *Channeling: The Intuitive Connection.* San Francisco: Harper & Row, 1987.

Klimo, Jon. *Channeling: Investigations on Receiving Information from Paranormal Sources.* Los Angeles: Jeremy P. Tarcher, 1987.

charms against ghosts Folklore the world over is replete with ways to ward off ghosts, prevent them from entering homes, or force them to depart from homes or sites. Some charms are simple and quick gestures, such as crossing one's self, while others are elaborate rituals. Ghosts generally are assigned the same category as evil spirits; thus, what works against demons usually is seen to be equally effective against ghosts.

Crossing one's self is a common charm to ward off ghosts, demons and the evil eye. Various gems and stones, such as chalcedony (q.v.) or obsidian (also called Apache's tears), carried or worn on the person, will protect one against ghosts. Salt, carried in the pocket or strewn across a threshhold, will keep ghosts, evil spirits and witches at bay; a pinch thrown over the left shoulder will bring good luck. Metals such as iron and silver also are effective. An iron rod placed on a grave will prevent a ghost from rising out of the ground, and an iron horseshoe hung over a doorway will prevent a ghost from entering a house, stable or building. Iron nails taken from a tomb and driven into the threshhold of a door will prevent nightmares (see OLD HAG). Pins should be stuck into gateposts where corpses have passed by in funeral processions; these will keep away evil and ghosts.

Silver amulets and jewelry also keep away evil and ghosts. Some ghost investigators wear crucifixes when checking out an alleged haunting. Any religious symbol or good luck piece may be substituted for a crucifix, as long as the individual believes in its protective powers. The advantage is most likely psychological, but, like the placebo effect, it seems to work.

In English lore, when a person dies, all door, cupboard and window locks must be undone, and doors and windows opened, so that the soul has free egress out of the house. If a person "dies hard" and has difficulty entering the afterworld, the spirit trapped in the house may haunt it.

Corpses must be carried out of a house feet first, otherwise the ghost of the dead person will return. Touching a corpse will prevent one from being haunted by dreams of the ghost of the dead. The knots in the corpse's shroud must be untied before the coffin lid is nailed shut, lest the ghost of the deceased wander about, visiting its former home. During the funeral, the furniture in the bedroom of the deceased should be rearranged, so that if the ghost comes back, it will not recognize the surroundings and will leave. Similarly, the funeral party should take a different route home than the route by which the body was transported. This will foil the ghost of the dead from following them home.

It is universally believed that one must not speak ill of the dead, lest the ghost come and haunt the living. Spoken references to the dead should be accompanied with phrases such as "God rest his (or her) soul" or "poor man!"

Further reading:
Guiley, Rosemary Ellen. *The Encyclopedia of Witches and Witchcraft.* New York: Facts On File, 1989.
Opie, Iona, and Moira Tatem. *A Dictionary of Superstitions.* Oxford: Oxford University Press, 1989.

Cheltenham Haunting Sometimes called the "Morton Case," after the family in whose home it occurred, this case is distinguished by an apparition of a woman that was seen over a period of years by at least 17 people, many of whom were not aware of the earlier sightings at the time. It is among the best attested cases of a haunting.

The house at Cheltenham, England was built in 1860. It is a frame house of three stories, with a large yard that included an orchard. It was purchased from the builders by Henry Swinhoe, its first owner and occupant.

Swinhoe's first wife died in 1866, and three years later he married a woman named Imogen Hutchins. This second marriage was unhappy, marred in part by Hutchins' insistence that she be given the first Mrs. Swinhoe's jewels, which her husband steadfastly refused to do. Instead, he hid them in a vault he had built below the floor in the living room. Shortly before Swinhoe's death in 1876, Hutchins left him, and she did not return to the house for his funeral or at any time thereafter. She died in 1878.

After Swinhoe's death, the house was leased by Mr. L., an elderly man who died suddenly six months after moving in. The house then remained vacant for about four years, before being taken, in March 1882, by a Captain Despard and his wife, their two sons, and three unmarried daughters. A fourth, married daughter visited occasionally, sometimes in the company of her husband.

It was during the Despards' stay in the house that the apparition made its most frequent appearances, although upon inquiry it was learned that there had been earlier appearances as well. The Despards' 19-year-old daughter Rosina (who became Rosina Morton) was the most frequent percipient, and it was she who eventually wrote an account for the *Proceedings of the Society for Psychical Research*, based on letters she wrote to a friend at the time.

Rosina's first experience occurred a few months after the Despards' arrival. She had gone up to her room one night, but was not yet in bed, when she heard a knock on the door. When she answered it, there was no one there, but when she advanced a few steps along the hall, she could see a tall woman, dressed in black, standing at the head of stairs. After a few minutes the woman descended the stairs, and Rosina followed until her candle burned out. She noticed that the woman's dress made a swishing sound as she moved, as if it were made of a soft woolen material.

Over the next three years, Rosina saw the woman a half dozen times, at first at long intervals, then shorter ones. She invariably followed the same route.

She would descend the stairs and go into the living room, where she would remain for awhile, generally standing to the right-hand side of the bay window. Then she would leave the living room and walk along the hall to the door to the garden, before which she disappeared. Rosina tried to speak to the woman, but she seemed unable to utter a word. She also tried, without success, to use sign language with her. The woman seemed aware of her surroundings and would move around persons and objects in her way. When she was cornered, however, she simply disappeared.

Although Rosina saw the woman more often than did other members of her family, she was not the only one to do so. One night her sister Edith was playing the piano in the living room when the woman appeared. She called Rosina. The sisters followed the woman along the hall until she disappeared in her usual place by the garden door. Another sister came in from the garden soon after, saying she had seen the figure there, and the married sister later reported that she had seen her from the window of her room. The sisters and one of their brothers, along with the Despards' cook and housemaid, who lived with them in the house, also heard footsteps and knocks at night and from time to time saw the woman. The Despards' dogs behaved oddly. Rosina's terrier once wagged his tail vigorously as if he expected to be petted, then suddenly shrank back, cowering in fear.

The haunting was brought to the attention of Frederic W.H. MYERS of the SOCIETY FOR PSYCHICAL RESEARCH (SPR) in December 1884. Myers visited the Despards early in 1885. At his suggestion, Rosina thereafter kept a camera ready to photograph the figure, but on the few occasions she tried, she got no results.

Sightings of the woman dropped off after 1887; she was not seen at all by members of the Despard household after 1889. Up until 1886 the figure appeared so solid that it was often mistaken for a real person, but in the later appearances it was much less substantial. The Despards were never able to determine whether it cast a shadow, although they noticed that it always blocked the light.

The apparition was taken to be that of Imogen Hutchins, the second Mrs. Swinhoe, on the basis of its stature and its mourning clothes, and the fact that when she was alive, she had often used the living room. However, because the woman habitually held a handkerchief over part of her face, the identification was never certain.

The Despards left the house in Cheltenham in 1893. It was vacant until 1898, when it became a preparatory school for boys. During this time, the apparition of a woman was repeatedly encountered on stairs, always leaving the house in broad daylight from the garden door and walking down the short drive. The school was soon closed, and the building again stood vacant until 1910, when it was converted into a nunnery. The nuns in turn stayed only two years . . . and so the history of occupancy of the house continues, empty for long periods between tenants who never stayed more than a few years. In 1973, the building was bought by a housing association for conversion into apartments.

Author Andrew MacKenzie, who investigated the later history of the house, learned of several other apparitions in Cheltenham, two of which were very similar in description to the figure seen by the Despards. Significantly, both of these appearances were in buildings which were in existence at the time the Despards lived in Cheltenham, and not in any of the newer structures that have gone up since. There have been no reported appearances at the Despards' old house since it was turned into apartments.

Further reading:

Collins, B. Abdy. *The Cheltenham Ghost*. London: Psychic Press, 1948.

MacKenzie, Andrew. *Hauntings and Apparitions*. London: Heinemann, 1982.

Morton, R.C. "Record of a Haunted House." *Proceedings of the Society for Psychical Research* 8 (1892):311–29.

Myers, Frederic W.H. *Human Personality and Its Survival of Bodily Death Vols. I & II*. New ed. New York: Longmans, Green & Co., 1954. First published 1903.

Ch'iang Shich   In Chinese folklore, a monster made of evil spirits and an unburied corpse, which comes to life and wreaks death and destruction. According to Chinese tradition, an unburied corpse is a great danger, because it invites inhabitation by the evil spirits believed to be present everywhere at all times.

The Ch'iang Shich story has various versions. According to one Ch'iang Shich folk tale, four travelers arrived late one night at an inn near Shangtung. No rooms were available, but the travelers persuaded the innkeeper to find them any space where they could sleep. They were placed out in a little shack, where, unbeknownst to them, lay the unburied corpse of the innkeeper's daughter-in-law, who had died earlier in the day. Her body was laid out on a plank behind a curtain.

Three of the travelers fell asleep immediately, but the fourth could not because he had a foreboding of danger. Presently, he saw a bony hand pull the curtain aside. The corpse, green and with glowing eyes, emerged and bent over the sleeping travelers, breathing the foul breath of death upon them. They died instantly. The fourth traveler managed to pretend to be asleep and held his breath while the Ch'iang Shich breathed on him, thus saving his life. When the monster returned to its plank, he ran out the door. The monster heard him and gave chase.

The man hid behind a willow tree, but the Ch'iang Shich found him. With a shriek, it lunged at him. He fainted from terror, an act which saved his life again, for the monster missed him and sank its claws so deep into the willow tree that it could not extricate itself. The next morning, others found the corpse, now no longer animated by spirits, and the man, who was still unconscious.

Further reading:
Hurwood, Bernhardt J. *Passport to the Supernatural: An Occult Compendium from All Ages and Many Lands.* New York: Taplinger, 1972.

Churchyard Beast   See BLACK SHUCK.

churel   In India, the evil ghost of a woman who dies in childbirth or ceremonial impurity. Originally, churels were ghosts of low-caste persons, whose corpses were buried face-down to prevent the ghosts from escaping. Churels typically have reversed feet and no mouths. They haunt squalid places. In the shape of a beautiful young woman, they ensnare young men and hold them captive until they are old. Areas believed to be haunted by churels are given exorcisms.

cipher test   See SURVIVAL TESTS.

clairvoyance   Paranormal vision of objects, events, places and people that are not visible through normal sight. Clairvoyance is an extrasensory perception (ESP) that overlaps with telepathy and precognition (knowledge of the future). It is a factor in mediumship and retrocognition, and may come into play in some cases of apparitions (see RETROCOGNITION).

The term "clairvoyance" comes from the French for "clear seeing." It is also popularly called "second sight," "ghost seeing" and "ghost vision." Individuals gifted with clairvoyance have, throughout history, been oracles, prophets, diviners, holy men and women, healers, wizards and witches. However, everyone possesses the capacity for clairvoyance and probably experiences at least one clairvoyant episode during life.

Clairvoyance can happen spontaneously, such as when a person has a vision of apparitions of the past (see VERSAILLES GHOSTS), or can perceive nonphysical forms in a place alleged to be haunted. Clairvoyance—and sensitivity to ESP in general—may account for the great disparity of experiences that occur

in an alleged haunting. For example, one person may be able to clairvoyantly perceive a ghost while another may not (and the other thus may not believe in the haunting). Virtually all stories of hauntings include testimony from individuals who claim they experience nothing. In a case where collective apparitions are seen, some psychical researchers speculate that one person may perceive the apparition and communicate it to others through telepathy.

In mediumship, clairvoyance may account for the ability of mediums to provide "unknown" information at seances. Information unknown to the medium (and perhaps the sitters) but that can be verified through other sources is considered "evidential" in support of survival after death. However, some psychical researchers say that a medium's unconscious clairvoyance of existing sources—anywhere in the world—cannot be ruled out (see SUPER ESP).

Clairvoyance may be induced through various techniques, such as fasting, ecstatic dancing, ingestion or inhalation of certain substances, and magical ritual. Such techniques have been employed whenever humankind has sought to commune with the spirits of the dead, the spirits of nature or the divine. Ancient Egyptian and Greek priests used herbal mixtures to induce temporary clairvoyance. The Pythia oracle at Delphi inhaled the smoke from burning laurel leaves to induce clairvoyant visions. Shamans induce clairvoyance through ecstatic dancing, chanting and drumming, and sometimes with the help of hallucinogens. Native Americans experience clairvoyance during vision quests and solitary spiritual pursuits in the wilderness.

Clairvoyance is experienced in different ways. Perhaps most common is a vision seen by the inner eye. Some clairvoyant visions seem to have an objective reality, temporarily replacing the present time and environment. Such is the case in shamanism, for shamans enter a "non-ordinary" reality in which they search for lost souls and heal the sick. Clairvoyance of distant places—called "traveling clairvoyance" by mesmerists and early psychical researchers—may involve an out-of-body experience (see also SWEDENBORG, EMANUEL). Clairvoyant visions also have been recorded of non-earthly places, such as the astral plane, the spirit world or "Other Side," and realms of heaven and hell. Descriptions of these places vary considerably. Clairvoyance can occur in dreams.

In his research with medium Eileen J. GARRETT, psychologist Lawrence LeShan conceived of two kinds of reality, sensory and clairvoyant. Sensory reality is everyday, real-time life, defined by the five senses. Clairvoyant reality, which is accessed by mediums, is a place where time is illusory (everything seems to exist in an ever-present "now"), judgments are impossible, and all things are perceived as interconnected.

Scientific study of clairvoyance began in the early 19th century with mesmerized subjects who exhibited paranormal, or "higher," phenomena. One of the subjects of Alphonse Cahagnet, a French magnetist, was a young woman named Adele Magnot. While entranced, Magnot had visions of the spirit world and could see and converse with the dead.

Tests for clairvoyance of concealed cards using hypnotized mediums began in the 1870s with French physiologist Charles Richet. Card testing reached its peak later in the 20th century in the laboratory experiments of J.B. RHINE.

Further reading:
Brown, Slater. *The Heyday of Spiritualism.* New York: Hawthorn Books, 1970.
Douglas, Alfred. *Extrasensory Powers: A Century of Psychical Research.* London: Victor Gollancz Ltd., 1976.
LeShan, Lawrence. *The Medium, the Mystic, and the Physicist: Toward a General Theory of the Paranormal.* New York: Viking Press, 1974.

Cock Lane Ghost   An 18th-century, London-area poltergeist that fascinated eyewitnesses and investigators because it was tainted with accusations of trickery and fraud. Sensational publicity caused curiosity-seekers to crowd Cock Lane, the street from which the ghost took its name. The veracity of the ghost was hotly debated by believers and detractors.

The excitement lasted for two years, from 1762 to 1764, culminating in a trial which found several persons guilty of fraud. The trial, however, did nothing to clarify how the deception was carried out, if indeed it was a deception. The full story was told in *Cock Lane & Common Sense*, a book written by Andrew Lang and published in 1894.

In 1760, a stockbroker named Kent rented a house on Cock Lane, in the London suburb of West Smithfield, from Mr. Parsons, a parish clerk in a nearby church. Kent's sister-in-law, Miss Fanny, was keeping house for him since his wife's death in childbirth the previous year. Fanny and Kent grew fond of one another and decided to make out a will, naming each other as beneficiary.

One day, Parsons borrowed money from Kent, but shortly thereafter, the two men argued. Not only did Kent move out of the house, but he began legal proceedings against Parsons for the return of his money. The suit was not contended for two years, and in the meantime, Fanny contracted smallpox. She died a few days later and was buried in a vault under St. John's Church.

This sad event gave the vengeful Parsons a chance to concoct a story that Fanny had not died of an illness, but instead was the victim of murder, most probably at the hands of Kent, who would benefit from the inheritance.

It wasn't until 1762, however, that Parsons began in earnest to blacken Kent's name. Parsons claimed that the house was now haunted by Fanny's ghost. Furthermore, his 12-year-old daughter, Elizabeth, had seen and spoken to the ghost, which asserted that she had been poisoned by Kent. Parsons added that the night following Fanny's demise, loud knockings could be heard in the house.

Not content with merely arousing suspicions among his neighbors, Parsons sought corroboration from a gentleman of high rank by inviting him to the house to witness the ghost. The gentleman saw the shaking, terrified Elizabeth shortly after she had been visited by the ghost, and he bore witness to the knockings and rappings that could be heard in the child's room. He promised to return the next evening with the local clergyman and others to further investigate the strange happenings.

The next night more than 20 people returned to the house, determined to stay up all night if necessary to wait for the ghost to appear. Parsons maintained that the ghost appeared only to Elizabeth, but that it would be willing to answer questions with a certain number of knocks signifying affirmative or negative answers.

Hours later, this committee of men was rewarded for its patience. Elizabeth saw the ghost, and the questions began. Once again, Fanny's ghost claimed that Fanny had been poisoned. And in response to a specific question, the ghost said that Fanny's soul would be at rest if Kent were hanged for his deed.

It did not take long for the news to spread in the neighborhood, and soon Cock Lane was full of the curious. Always with an eye toward commerce, Parsons even charged people a small fee to enter the house to listen to the ghost's knockings.

But the ghost was soon to cast a shadow upon itself when it made some promises it could not fulfill. The ghost asserted that it would follow Elizabeth everywhere, as well as anyone who entered Fanny's burial vault. The committee decided to take the ghost up on its suggestions and Elizabeth was taken to a clergyman's house where she underwent a search of her bedclothes by several ladies before being put to bed. In this unfamiliar house, the ghost would make only knockings and no appearance, fueling the committee's suspicions that some chicanery was afoot.

These suspicions were confirmed when the committee visited Fanny's vault, and the ghost failed to

THE
MYSTERY REVEALED;

Containing a SERIES of

TRANSACTIONS

AND

AUTHENTIC TESTIMONIALS,

Respecting the supposed

COCK-LANE GHOST;

Which have hitherto been concealed from the
P U B L I C.

—— *Since none the Living dare implead,*
Arraign him in the Person of the Dead.
DRYDEN.

LONDON:
Printed for W. BRISTOW, in St. Paul's Church-yard ;
and C. ETHRINGTON, York.
MDCCXLII.

Frontispiece of one account of the Cock Lane Ghost, written by Oliver Goldsmith.

either make an appearance or produce rappings. Some committee members suggested that Kent should be brought to the vault and have the ghost confront him. Kent complied, and while standing by the coffin, he was disappointed along with everyone else when there was no sight or sound from the ghost.

To quell these doubts, Parsons started a rumor that the ghost did not appear because Kent had removed Fanny's coffin. Kent finally fought back by taking several witnesses into the vault where he had the coffin opened to reveal the luckless Fanny. All present made depositions and when they were published, Kent indicted Parsons, along with his wife, daughter and several others whom he believed were conspirators.

The trial finally came up; all were found guilty and had to make monetary retribution to Kent for defa-

mation. Parsons also was sentenced to stand in the pillory before being imprisoned for two years.

Further reading:
Grant, Douglas. *The Cock Lane Ghost.* New York: St. Martin's Press, 1965.

Lang, Andrew. *Cock Lane & Common Sense.* London: Longmans, 1894.

Mackay, Charles. *Extraordinary Delusions and the Madness of Crowds.* New York: Farrar, Straus and Giroux, 1932. First published 1841.

collective apparitions   See APPARITIONS; WILMOT APPARITION.

College of Psychic Studies   British Spiritualist organization that evolved from the London Spiritualist Alliance, founded in 1884. In 1955 the organization changed its name to the College of Psychic Science, and in 1970 it became the College of Psychic Studies. It is not to be confused with the BRITISH COLLEGE OF PSYCHIC SCIENCE.

A non-profit organization based in South Kensington, London, the College of Psychic Studies offers programs and materials to the public and psychical researchers concerning mediumship, the evidence for survival after death, and spiritual healing and related topics. The college also offers training in mediumship. It maintains a large library.

combination lock test   See STEVENSON, IAN; SURVIVAL TESTS.

Committee for the Scientific Investigation of Claims of the Paranormal (CSICOP)   Organization based in Buffalo, New York, devoted to debunking claims of the paranormal. CSICOP members, many of whom are scientists, psychologists, philosophers or psychiatrists, investigate all types of paranormal phenomena, including hauntings, poltergeists, mediumship, psychic and faith healing, divination arts (such as astrology) and extrasensory perception. CSICOP has successfully debunked numerous claims of paranormal activity. The organization views itself as unbiased, but critics claim the group is hostile to the paranormal and goes too far in debunking—that it will debunk at all costs, regardless of evidence. Nonetheless CSICOP often provides a skeptical counterpoint to paranormal claims.

CSICOP originated as an offshoot of the American Humanist Association, following a controversy over claims made about astrology. At first an informal group, it incorporated in 1976 as a separate organization. The organization, under the direction of a founding member, Paul Kurtz, professor of philosophy at the State University of New York in Buffalo, found a dedicated following of skeptics.

CSICOP's stated objectives are "to establish a network of people interested in examining claims of the paranormal; to prepare bibliographies of published materials that carefully examine such claims; to encourage and commission research by objective and impartial inquirers in areas where it is needed; to convene conferences and meetings; to publish articles, monographs and books that examine claims of the paranormal; to not reject on *a priori* grounds, antecedent to inquiry, any or all of such claims, but rather to examine them openly, completely, objectively, and carefully."

A journal—originally named *The Zetetic* and renamed *The Skeptical Inquirer* after three issues—pursues scientific concerns about the perceived public credulity about the paranormal.

In 1988, five members of CSICOP's Executive Committee accepted an invitation from a Chinese scientific newspaper to visit and appraise the state of psychic research and paranormal belief in China, and to make scientific evaluations where possible. Preliminary tests of children, psychics and Qigong masters (an Eastern healing and martial art) produced negative results.

See also SMURL HAUNTING.

Further reading:

"CSICOP Defined." *Parapsychology Review* 19 (1988):5.

Guiley, Rosemary Ellen. *Harper's Encyclopedia of Mystical and Paranormal Experience*. San Francisco: HarperSanFrancisco, 1991.

Kurtz, Paul. "Testing Psi Claims in China: Visit by a CSICOP Delegation." *The Skeptical Inquirer* 12 (1988):364–75.

control An alleged spirit of the dead that acts as a medium's primary interface with the spirit world. The control allegedly takes over a medium's body for extended periods during altered states of consciousness. It communicates through the medium, either through mental impressions or through using the medium's vocal chords. In rare instances, controls allegedly communicate by direct voice, that is, speaking in a voice independent of the medium but in the same proximity. The role of the control is to look after the medium's interests, answer questions posed by the sitters, provide information from the Other Side, and orchestrate other spirits of the dead who wish to speak to the living and deliver messages.

Controls invariably assert that they are autonomous beings who are separate entities from the medium. They say they have bodies of a very subtle substance and that they can change shape and size, and can transport themselves through time and space. They explain that in order to communicate they must enter the "light" that surrounds the medium. This involves an energy transfer which controls do not explain exactly; but, they say that the transfer enables them to use the medium's sensory organisms to become aware of the physical surroundings. While the control has taken over the medium's consciousness and body, the medium's consciousness is either transported to the spirit world or is displaced out-of-body, according to various controls that have been questioned by psychical researchers.

Controls do have distinct personalities. Generally, they are childlike; some are mischievous and have a sense of humor. They may offer a great deal of information about themselves and their past and who they were in life, or they may say very little about themselves. In some cases they say they are ancestors of the medium. Their speech may be very fluid with the appropriate accents and intonations. Some, however, sound stilted and stylized, so that their personalities seem to be obviously fictitious.

The prevailing view among psychical researchers and parapsychologists who have studied mediums is that controls are secondary personalities of the medium which are drawn from the subconscious. Most controls do reflect some personality traits, interests and knowledge of the mediums they allege to serve. However, if controls are secondary personalities, they manage to stay out of a medium's normal waking life. Apart from the controlled circumstances of trance, controls do not intrude and disrupt as do secondary personalities in cases of schizophrenia and multiple personality.

Controls are capable of providing evidential information at seances, that is, information that the medium would be unlikely to know. Curiously, controls that are confronted with inaccurate information that they have given seldom own up to their errors but instead make excuses, usually rationalizing away the errors by blaming the allegedly complicated process of communicating through the medium's physical being.

Evidential information is taken by many as proof of survival after death, or at least as evidence in support of it. Some researchers argue that information that seems evidential actually can be obtained by the medium through SUPER-ESP, a theory that holds that clairvoyance and telepathy enable a medium to retrieve "unknown" information from sitters or an existing published source. Another theory proposes that information does indeed come from spirits of the dead, but that in order to be conveyed from a non-physical realm to a physical realm, it must go through the construct of a secondary personality of the medium, which then becomes the control.

Many prominent mediums have accepted their controls as spirits of the dead. Others, such as Eileen J. GARRETT, have believed that controls are indeed constructs from their own unconscious.

A medium may have more than one control. Controls may stay with the medium throughout a career, or come and go. Gladys Osborne LEONARD had one primary control, Feda, throughout her entire career. Leonora PIPER had a number of controls, but only had one center stage at a time. William Stainton MOSES had a bevy of controls who called themselves the Imperator Band. Many of the Imperator Band claimed to be famous personages from history. The ubiquitous pirate control, John KING, served a number of mediums.

Controls were accorded a great deal of attention and importance during the early days of Spiritualism and the early years of psychical research. They are less prominent in modern mediumship. Most modern mediums do not use the term "control" but prefer terms such as "spirit helpers," "helpers," "friends," and "spirit friends."

Controls are not the equivalent of the discarnate beings who communicate in the process known as channeling.

Further reading:

Gauld, Alan. *Mediumship and Survival: A Century of Investigations*. London: William Heinemann Ltd., 1982.

Grattan-Guinness, Ivor. *Psychical Research: A Guide to Its History, Principles and Practices*. Wellingborough, Northhamptonshire, England: The Aquarian Press, 1982.

Cook, Florence (1856–1904) The most famous medium known for spirit materializations, especially full-form, but who was exposed of fraud.

Florence Cook was born in 1856 in Hackney, then a suburb of London (now part of London's East End), a center of Spiritualism. Cook claimed that as a child she could hear the voices of angels, and had mediumistic gifts.

She began giving seances at home as an adolescent, and from the first she specialized in materialization. Initially, these were only "spirit faces." Cook's cabinet (q.v.) was a large cupboard in the family's breakfast room. Inside was a Windsor chair for her to sit upon. A hole was cut high in the cupboard door where the "spirit faces" would manifest.

Cook, who always dressed up for her seances, would enter the cupboard and sit down. A piece of cord would be placed on her lap. The door would be closed, and the sitters would sing hymns to establish the right "atmosphere." The cupboard would be opened, and sitters could see that Cook was tied to the back of her chair at the neck, waist and wrists. The door would be closed again, and then soon, in the dark, "spirit faces" would appear in the opening. When the faces vanished, the cupboard would be opened, and Cook would be found still tied to the chair, and giving the appearance of exhaustion from the energy allegedly expended to help the spirits manifest.

Critics observed that the faces looked like Cook draped in a white gauzy material, and that Cook probably slipped her knots, stood on the chair, and then retied herself. Audiences loved the performance, nonetheless.

Cook quickly attracted a following, in part because she charged no fee, and in part because she was a beautiful young woman. Her fame incited jealousy from other mediums, including Agnes GUPPY, who lost friends and supporters to Cook, and Mr. and Mrs. Nelson Holmes, the latter of whom claimed John KING and Katie King as their controls. In January 1873, Guppy tried to convince the Holmeses to help her ruin Cook by having someone throw vitriol in her "doll face" during a seance. The Holmeses refused and broke their relationship with Guppy.

By 1873, full-form materializations were the rage in Spiritualist circles, especially those of the control John King. It was probably no accident that Cook, to be competitive, began materializing the full form of King's alleged spirit daughter, Katie King. Cook still gave seances at home (but now in the drawing room), as well as in more fashionable parts of London, sometimes as the protégée of other mediums.

Like the spirit faces, Katie King bore a suspiciously strong resemblance to Cook. After the same preparations and singing of hymns, the cupboard would open and the alleged King, pale and white with fixed eyes, would emerge while Cook moaned and sobbed out of sight behind a curtain. These materializations began simply with King merely smiling and nodding and over time progressed to more elaborate entertainment, in which King walked among the sitters, offered her hand (suspiciously solid) to all and conversed with them. After King retired to the cabinet, Cook would be found, as usual, tied and drained. Cook gained fame for materializing King with lights on.

It was considered improper behavior for sitters to grab spirits or the medium (see MEDIUMSHIP), but some skeptics nevertheless did. In 1873, a Mr. Volckman grabbed Katie King by the wrist and announced his suspicion that she was Cook in disguise. The lights were put out and the "spirit" was rescued by Cook's fiancé, Edward Elgie Corner, and another sitter, and was taken back to Cook's cabinet. In her struggle with Volckman, the "spirit" had managed to scratch his nose and pull out some of his whiskers. When the cabinet was opened after the required wait of several minutes, Cook was found unusually disheveled, but tied up. This incident did not immediately harm Cook's budding career as a medium, though it did shake the faith of some.

The eminent British scientist Sir William CROOKES spoke out publicly in Cook's defense after the Volckman "outrage." Crookes subjected her to numerous tests in a series of private seances, but he did not eliminate all possibility of fraud. In 1874, he photographed Katie King. Cook lay down on a sofa behind a curtain and wrapped a shawl around her head. Soon, Katie appeared in front of the curtain. Crookes checked to see that a female form still lay on the sofa, but, incredibly, never lifted the shawl to verify its identity. In another experiment, he attached Cook to a galvanometer which passed a mild electrical current through her. Any movement on Cook's part would register on the meter. Katie appeared though the meter's needle never moved.

Crookes also walked arm in arm with King and noted that the form felt solid. However, he concluded that King was a true spirit. Historian Trevor H. Hall theorizes that Crookes's laxity was due to his romantic infatuation or involvement with Cook, and that he may have even collaborated in her fraud. Hall's views are considered controversial by many other historians.

In 1874, during the Crookes sittings, Katie announced her departure from Cook. The tearful farewell took place behind a curtain, with Crookes as an auditory witness. Another spirit named Marie then began to manifest. Marie sang and danced.

Cook was caught in outright fraud on at least one other occasion. At a seance in 1880, during which Marie materialized in full form, Sir George Sitwell noticed that the spirit's robes covered corset stays, and, like Volckman, he broke seance rules and grabbed her. Cook's curtain was pulled aside to reveal Cook's chair empty and the ropes slipped.

After that, Cook would perform only if someone was tied up in her cabinet with her. Florence Marryat participated on at least one occasion; Marie materialized, and she sang and danced while Marryat and Cook remained tied together in the cabinet.

These trials eventually caused Cook to retire from mediumship, save for tests in 1899 at the Sphinx Society in Berlin, where she materialized Marie.

D.D. HOME was among those who considered Cook a "skillful trickster" and "outright cheat." Nonetheless, Cook retained a core of supporters who denied

fraud and claimed she was somnabulistic and never intended to deceive.

Further reading:

Brandon, Ruth. *The Spiritualists.* New York: Alfred A. Knopf, 1983.

Douglas, Alfred. *Extrasensory Powers: A Century of Psychical Research.* London: Victor Gollancz Ltd., 1976.

Hall, Trevor H. *The Medium and the Scientist: The Story of Florence Cook and William Crookes.* Buffalo, N.Y.: Prometheus Books, 1984.

———. *The Spiritualists.* London: Gerald Duckworth & Co. Ltd., 1962.

Medhurst, R.G., and K.M. Goldney, "William Crookes and the Physical Phenomena of Mediumship." *Proceedings of the Society for Psychical Research* 54 (1964):25–156.

Oppenheim, Janet. *The Other World: Spiritualism and Psychical Research in England, 1850–1914.* Cambridge: Cambridge University Press, 1985.

Pearsall, Ronald. *The Table-Rappers.* New York: St. Martin's Press, 1972.

Corby Castle   See RADIANT BOYS.

corpse candles   Death omens in the folklore of Wales and elsewhere in the British Isles. Corpse candles, or *canwll corfe,* as they are called in Welsh, are mysterious lights which bob over the ground and stop at houses or other sites where a death is imminent. Similar lights are called fetch candles or fetch lights in Ireland and northern England. They seem to be similar to the corpse light (q.v.) phosphorescence, but differ in that they have the distinct appearance of candle flames.

Corpse candles are seen floating through the air at night. Beliefs about them vary according to locale. They are said to warn of the death of those who see them, or of someone beloved or someone else known to the party. They appear, it is said, halfway between the doomed person's home and his grave. In south Hampshire, England the lights are said to accompany the souls of the departed, and are extinguished when the souls leave the earth. Ghostly funerals are said to accompany some lights.

In Welsh lore, a small, pale or bluish corpse candle presages the death of an infant, while a big light presages the death of an adult. Multiple corpse candles reveal the number of persons soon to die. If the lights are approached, they vanish. Corpse candles are widely reported in Welsh coastal regions.

The English ghost-hunter, Elliott o'DONNELL, put corpse candles in the same category as a species of elementals (nature spirits) he called "Clanogrian," which he said included all kinds of family ghosts and national ghosts, and other harbingers of death, such as the banshee.

In his book, *Byways of Ghost-Land* (1911), O'Donnell recorded some accounts of witnesses to corpse candles. The following was attributed to a Reverend Mr. Davis, and was reported in *The Invisible World* by T. Charley:

> My sexton's wife, an aged, understanding woman, saw from her bed a little bluish candle upon her table: within two or three days after comes a fellow in, inquiring for her husband, and, taking something from under his cloak, clapt it down directly upon the table end where she had seen the candle; and what was it but a dead-born child? Another time, the same woman saw such another candle upon the other end of the same table: within a few day later, a weak child, by myself newly christened, was brought into the sexton's house, where presently he died; and when the sexton's wife, who was then abroad, came home, she found the women shrouding the child on the other end of the table where she had seen the candle. On a time, myself and a huntsman coming from our school in England, and being three or four hours benighted ere we could reach home, saw such a light, which, coming from a house we well knew, held its course (but not directly) in the highway to the church: shortly after, the eldest son in that house died, and steered the same course. . . .
>
> About thirty-four or thirty-five years since, one Jane Wyatt, my wife's sister, being nurse to Baronet Rud's three eldest children, and (the lady being deceased) the lady of the house going late into a chamber where the maid-servants lay, saw there no less than five of these lights together. It happened awhile after, the chamber being newly plastered, that five of the maid servants went there to bed as they were wont; but in the morning they were all dead, being suffocated in their sleep with the steam of newly tempered lime and coal. This was at Llangathen in Carmarthen [Wales].

Another O'Donnell account is taken from an unspecified issue of *Frazer's Journal* and concerns Welsh corpse candles whose flames were much larger:

> In a wild and retired district in North Wales, the following occurrence took place, to the great astonishment of the mountaineers. We can vouch for the truth of the statement, as many of our own teutu, or clan, were witnesses to the facts. On a dark evening a few weeks ago, some persons, with whom we are well acquainted, were returning to Barmouth or opposite side of the river. As they approached the ferryhouse at Penthryn, which is directly opposite Barmouth, they observed a light near the house, which they conjectured to be produced by a bonfire, and greatly puzzled they were to discover the reason why it should have been lighted. As they came nearer, however, it vanished; and when they inquired at the house respecting it, they were surprised to learn that not only had the people there displayed

no light, but they had not even seen one; nor could they perceive any signs of it on the sands. On reaching Barmouth, the circumstance was mentioned, and the fact corroborated by some of the people there, who had also plainly and distinctly seen the light. It was settled, therefore, by some of the old fishermen that this was a death-token; and, sure enough, the man who kept the ferry at that time was drowned at high water a few nights afterwards, on the very spot where the light was seen. He was landing from the boat, when he fell into the water, and so perished. The same winter the Barmouth people, as well as the inhabitants of the opposite bank, were struck by the appearance of a number of small lights, which were seen dancing in the air at a place called Borthwyn, about half a mile from the town. A great number of people came out to see these lights; and after awhile they all but one disappeared, and this one proceeded slowly towards the water's edge to a little bay where some boats were moored. The men in a sloop which was anchored near the spot saw the light advancing, they saw it also hover for a few seconds over one particular boat, and then totally disappear. Two or three days afterwards, the man to whom that particular boat belonged was drowned in the river, while he was sailing about Barmouth harbour in that very boat.

See also CANDLES; GHOST LIGHTS.

Further reading:

Leach, Maria, and Jerome Fried, eds. *Funk & Wagnalls Standard Dictionary of Folklore, Mythology, and Legend.* San Francisco: Harper & Row, 1979.
O'Donnell, Elliott. *Byways of Ghost-Land.* London: William Rider & Sons, 1911.

corpse lights   Phosphorescent lights seen floating about the air at night, which are believed to be harbingers of death. They are white, red or blue, and are seen both indoors and outdoors. They hug the ground, float in the air, hover over the roof of the doomed, or appear over the chest of the doomed. Corpse lights are called by various names, including corpse candles, jack-o'-lantern, ignis fatuus, corposant, fetch-candles and fetch-lights. Since they often appear in marshy areas, it is theorized that the lights are produced by marsh gas. Another theory holds that they may be produced by atmospheric conditions. Nonetheless, numerous accounts exist in folklore of their seemingly supernatural appearance.

See also DEATH OMENS; GHOST LIGHTS.

Further reading:

Leach, Maria, and Jerome Fried, *Funk & Wagnalls Standard Dictionary of Folklore, Mythology, and Legend.* San Francisco: Harper & Row, 1979.

Corpus Christi College   The ghost of a former college official is said to haunt the Old Lodge of Corpus Christi College in Cambridge, England.

Dr. Butts served as Master of the College from 1626 to 1632 and was Vice-Chancellor during a severe outbreak of plague in 1630. His correspondence at the time indicates that he seemed to be under great stress, describing himself as alone, destitute and forsaken by scholars within and outside the college.

On Easter Sunday in 1632, Butts was scheduled to preach before the college. He failed to appear, and was found hanging by his garters in his rooms. His ghost subsequently began to be reported on college grounds.

In 1904, a student who was living in the rooms opposite the rooms where Butts had died saw what later was believed to be Butts's ghost. One afternoon near Easter, the student suddenly became uneasy. He looked out of his window and saw a man with long hair leaning out of an upper window in the opposite rooms. Only the man's head and shoulders were visible. He stared at the student for several minutes. He seemed hostile.

The student ran upstairs to get a better view of the man, but when he reached the window, the man was gone. The student went across the court, but found the rooms locked. Later he found out that the resident of the rooms had been out all afternoon, and the room had remained locked.

The manifestations of the long-haired man continued. Some time later, a group of six undergraduates decided to attempt an exorcism. They entered the haunted rooms, recited the Lord's Prayer and summoned the ghost to appear. The rooms' occupant and an onlooker from another college, who was interested in Spiritualism, said they saw a mistiness in the air that gradually took on the form of a man in white with a gash across his neck. No one else saw an apparition, though everyone claimed to feel a sudden chill in the air.

The two men who saw the ghost held out a crucifix and approached it. An invisible force drove them back, they said, and they became so upset the exorcism was terminated.

The group tried another exorcism several days later. Again, the same two men saw the white figure and were repelled by an invisible force. The others still saw nothing, but felt an unexplained stiffness in their limbs. They were unable to banish the ghost.

At some later time, the rooms were closed off.

Further reading:
Hole, Christina. *Haunted England.* London: B.T. Batsford Ltd., 1940.

co-walker   See FETCH.

Crandon, Mina Stinson (1884–1941) Better known as "Margery," a Boston medium at the center of one of the most bitter controversies in the history of psychical research. Her supporters believed she was one of the greatest mediums who ever lived; her detractors called her a fraud and held her responsible for very nearly ending American psychical research as a scientific enterprise.

Mina Crandon, born in 1888 on a farm in Ontario, moved to Boston when she was 16, and a few years later she married a grocer named Earl P. Rand. She had a son by Rand and was happy with him until an operation brought her into contact with Le Roi Goddard Crandon, a prominent surgeon. She divorced Rand in 1918 and shortly thereafter married Crandon. It was her second marriage, his third.

There was no hint in Crandon's early life of what was to come, as there was with some other mediums (see GARRETT, EILEEN J.; PIPER, LEONORA). Her involvement in the psychic actually stemmed from her husband's interest, which was sparked by a meeting with Sir Oliver LODGE and a reading of the works of William Jackson CRAWFORD. Impressed by the home circle of the latter, Le Roi Crandon decided to set up one of his own. When the group he gathered in May 1923 succeeded in table-tilting, he suggested that they exit the room one at a time until they identified the person responsible. One by one the individuals left, but the table continued to tilt, until it was Mina Crandon's turn to leave. She returned to great applause.

Mina Crandon may not have been as surprised as were the others at the seance that night; a few days earlier, a psychic had told her she had mediumistic abilities. That same psychic had described seeing a "laughing young man" trying to contact her, a description Crandon recognized as corresponding to her brother Walter. She and Walter had been very close, but Walter had died five years earlier in a railway accident. Walter was to become Crandon's control as the home circle continued to meet, and his waggish personality was to become famous the world over.

The first of several investigations the Crandon mediumship was destined to endure was mounted by a team of Harvard graduate students and professors, including Gardner MURPHY and William McDougall, in July 1923. This concluded, rather ominously, with McDougall trying unsuccessfully to get Crandon to confess to fraud, and it would probably have spelled the end of serious interest in the mediumship had it not been for a contest sponsored by the *Scientific American.*

The contest was the brainchild of J. Malcolm Bird, who was then an associate editor at the magazine. Two prizes of $2,500 each were to be given, one for a psychic photograph, the other for a demonstration of physical mediumship. The judges were five persons well connected to psychical research—Walter Franklin PRINCE, considered by many to be America's foremost psychical researcher; Hereward CARRINGTON, a popular writer on the paranormal; Harry HOUDINI, the magician; Daniel F. Comstock, who brought technicolor to the movies; and McDougall. Bird made himself the committee's secretary.

The *Scientific American* investigation got a good deal of play in the press, but it turned into something of a fiasco. Houdini stormed off the committee after a year, claiming that the Crandons had been trying to make it seem that he had been framing them, and accusing his fellow committee members of being blind to obvious fakery. The rest of the committee continued attending seances for another six months, but eventually all except Carrington were satisfied that Houdini was right. The ruling went with the majority view, the contest was declared closed, and the prizes were never awarded.

The name "Margery," by which Crandon was to be known for the rest of her life, was given to her by Bird in his articles in the *Scientific American* and in his book, *"Margery" the Medium* (1925). This book was a popular account of the mediumship and was very favorable to the Crandons. Crandon had other supporters, many of them at the AMERICAN SOCIETY FOR PSYCHICAL RESEARCH (ASPR). Prince, the ASPR's research officer, however, was not a supporter, and when Bird was hired to share responsibilities with him, Prince left to head a rival society, the BOSTON SOCIETY FOR PSYCHIC RESEARCH.

The ASPR, with Bird as research officer, became a major promoter of the Margery mediumship. Bird and several members of the Board of Trustees were regular sitters at seances. Many hundreds of pages in the ASPR's *Journal* and *Proceedings* were devoted to the mediumship, first under Bird's editorship, later under the editorship of Frederick Bligh BOND.

But although the ASPR was always ready to defend Crandon, the suspicion of fraud never left her. Bird himself, in fact, resigned in 1930 after admitting that he had known of fraudulent activity from the start; he had nevertheless defended the mediumship, he said, because there were genuine aspects to it as well. Bond later also resigned in disillusionment; the clinching proof for him as for many others were thumbprints supposedly impressed in wax by Walter, but shown to be exact matches for the thumbprints of Crandon's dentist.

On her deathbed, Crandon is said to have been asked by Nandor FODOR to tell him what parts of her mediumship were fraudulent and how she had accomplished her tricks. She is said to have replied by telling him to go to hell, and then said, with a twinkle in her eye, "Why don't you guess? You'll all be guessing . . . for the rest of your lives."

The story may be apocryphal, but it captures the flavor of this strange case. Knowledgeable researchers today believe that there may have been some genuine psychic phenomena involved, but it is now impossible to disentangle this from the trickery that was certainly also present.

Mina Crandon and her husband seemed to revel in the cat-and-mouse game they played, and their only motive may have been to tweak the nose of psychical research. For all Walter's waggishness, Crandon herself was a vivacious personality who was not opposed to holding seances in the nude (the room was dark), and who was rumored to be having affairs with more than one of her would-be investigators.

The long-awaited amalgamation of the ASPR and the Boston Society occurred after the death of L.R.G. Crandon, and shortly before the death of Mina herself on November 1, 1941.

See also J.B. RHINE.

Further reading:

Bird, Malcolm. *"Margery" the Medium.* Boston: John Hamilton, 1925.

Matlock, J.G. "Cat's Paw: Margery and the Rhines, 1926." *Journal of Parapsychology* 51 (1987):229–47.

Tietze, Thomas R. *Margery.* New York: Harper and Row, 1973.

———. "The 'Margery' affair." *Journal of the American Society for Psychical Research* 79 (1985):339–79.

Cranshaw, Dorothy Stella (1900–?) British physical medium discovered and tested by Harry PRICE, known in research reports as "Stella C." An "e" is sometimes wrongly appended to her last name.

Stella Cranshaw was born on October 1, 1900 in North Woolwich, England. Little has been recorded about her early life, and what is known comes from Price, whose writings are of questionable reliability. According to Price, when Cranshaw was 11, she attended a service in a Spiritualist church, but she had to be removed when she became possessed by an uncontrollable fit of giggling. She is said to have been the center of poltergeist disturbances even into her twenties—small objects sometimes moved in her presence, rappings sounded around her, occasionally there were flashes of light. Two or three times a year, she would feel strong breezes in her room. These occurred even in the dead of winter, when the windows and doors were shut tight, but always when she had flowers close by. She was passionately fond of flowers.

Price reportedly met Cranshaw one evening early in 1923 on the train out of London, on his way home to Pulborough. She was at this time happily employed as a nurse in a hospital. She evinced little concern about her psychic experiences, about which she told Price she had never talked before. He explained his line of work, and had no trouble persuading her to let him test her in an experimental setting. In keeping with the style of the day, this meant a series of mediumistic seances, which were held at the London Spiritualist Association beginning on March 23 of that year. Cranshaw received a modest payment of a few pounds per week for her services, for which she had to take off work in the afternoon.

The first seance brought some surprises, most importantly the discovery that Cranshaw, who had never considered herself a medium, had a control—a personality, ostensibly a discarnate spirit, who was supposed to be responsible for all that took place. Cranshaw's control, "Palma," communicated with the sitters through raps, and would follow requests made of it, such as that it should move a heavy oak table in various directions around the room. At the same seance, thermometers recorded a rapid drop in temperature. Falls in temperature, in fact, were a hallmark of Cranshaw's mediumship.

Price introduced various devices into the seance room in an attempt to study the phenomena scientifically. One of the regular sitters built a special double table, the inner table actually being a sort of cage, into which various articles were put. The first time this was used it contained musical instruments such as a harmonica and a trumpet, which were sounded during the seance. A rattle somehow was thrown out of the cage. Price himself constructed a device called a "telekinetiscope," which would light up when two metallic contacts were joined. The contacts were in a cup covered by a strong soap bubble, making it impossible to press them together fraudulently without everyone present knowing about it. Nonetheless, the red light would occasionally go on during seances.

The first series ran to 11 sittings and was broken off by Cranshaw, who was exhausted by the weekly trials. She was often tired during seances, her pulse raced, and the drops in temperature would cause her to be overcome with shivers. She saw a doctor, who advised her to take a rest. Another unfortunate result of her work with Price was the loss of her hospital job.

Not only Cranshaw, but Price also, suffered from fallout from the sittings. Price had a background in conjuring (at this time, in fact, he still identified himself as a "conjurer"), and had only recently entered upon psychical research. His fellow conjurers criticized him for taking Cranshaw's phenomena seriously, whereas the SOCIETY FOR PSYCHICAL RESEARCH (SPR) was uncomfortable with Price's affiliation with the BRITISH COLLEGE OF PSYCHIC SCIENCE (BCPS), a Spiritualist organization, even though SPR research officers attended some of the sittings. These gentlemen convinced Price that it would be well to have additional sittings at the SPR headquarters.

Only with difficulty was Price able to persuade Cranshaw, who had found a secretarial position with a manufacturing firm, to continue the sittings. Two more seances were held at the SPR late in 1923, then Cranshaw again broke off the work. Her relations with Price, formerly warm, turned cool, then chilly, then momentarily icy, for reasons that are not altogether clear. Although she pleaded fatigue, a different motive is suggested by a letter she wrote to Price in February 1926, just before she began yet further work with him. In this letter, she says that she had come to the conclusion she had "badly misjudged" him before.

The 1926 sittings were held in Price's National Laboratory for Psychical Research, then newly established in rooms at the London Spiritualist Alliance (see COLLEGE OF PSYCHIC STUDIES). Cranshaw's phenomena were similar although weaker in the 1926 sittings. Fourteen sittings were held before Cranshaw once again broke off the proceedings, in August.

Cranshaw sat with Price again in 1927, so that he could study the nature of the temperature drops, and participated in a final series of nine sittings with him in 1928, shortly before her wedding.

Cranshaw married Leslie Deacon in August 1928 and ceased to give sittings. She never became a professional medium, and all of her scientific sittings were held with Price. The course of Cranshaw's later life is not known. She lived at least into her sixties, at which time she still resided in London.

Further reading:
Hall, Trevor. *Search for Harry Price*. London: Duckworth, 1978.
Tabori, Paul. *Companions of the Unseen*. New Hyde Park, N.Y.: University Press, 1978.
Turner, James T., ed. *Stella C: An Account of Some Original Experiments in Psychical Research*. London: Souvenir Press, 1973.

Crawford, William Jackson (1881–1920) Lecturer in mechanical engineering at Queens University, Belfast, Ireland, whose contribution to psychical research lies in his controversial studies of the "Goligher Circle."

W.J. Crawford was born on February 28, 1881 in Dunedin, New Zealand. He moved to Great Britain in 1899 at age 18, settling first in London and later in Glasgow. He received his bachelor's degree from the University of Glasgow in 1903 and began to teach at technical colleges. In 1907 he was appointed lecturer at the Technical Institute in Belfast, and in 1912 he became an extra-mural lecturer at Queens University. He received his doctorate in science from the University of Glasgow in 1911.

It is not known how Crawford became interested in psychical phenomena. He may have been the "Crawford" who attended a seance with "Eva C." (see BERAUD, MARTHE) in 1914. In any event, it was in that year that he persuaded a Spiritualist family in Belfast to let him attend their home circle, at which physical phenomena occurred. The Golighers were Spiritualists who held seances as part of their religious observance, but they had no objection to Crawford's studies. The "Goligher Circle," as the group came to be called, consisted of Goligher, a working man; his four daughters; his son; and his son-in-law. All four daughters were mediums, but one, Kathleen, was the most powerful (see GOLIGHER CIRCLE). In 1914, she was about 16 years old.

The phenomena produced by the Golighers were of the standard Spiritualist type. A table placed in the center of the circle would rise in the air (see LEVITATION), and a trumpet placed below it would fly about. The Golighers communicated with the spirits whom they believed to be responsible for these effects through rappings which sounded on the table or walls. Kathleen would sometimes go into trance and speak for them as well. The light was usually dim, although good enough to read by, and Crawford and other observers believed that it allowed them to see what was going on well enough to rule out trickery.

In his investigations, Crawford put his engineering expertise to good use. He put Kathleen's chair on a scale, in order to gauge her weight in relation to that of the levitated table, and found that both Kathleen and the chair increased in weight proportional to the table when it was lifted off the floor. He used an instrument designed to measure the elasticity of gases to track the psychokinetic force he hypothesized was emanating from her body and causing the table to rise. This revealed that the force operated on a "cantilever principle," angling downward as it left Kathleen's body (from the region of her lap), then making a right-angle with the floor, and rising to push up the table from below.

A Belfast woman with a reputation as a psychic claimed that she could see these "psychic rods," or "pseudopods" (q.v.), and they were at times visible to others. The psychic rods developed quickly, assuming various shapes and sizes. The similarity of Crawford's observations with Kathleen Goligher to those made of Marthe Beraud and Rudi Schneider (see SCHNEIDER BROTHERS) is striking. Crawford set up a battery of five cameras, with which he was able to record some of the psychic rods, which bear comparison with Beraud's ectoplasm. Some 25 photographs of these formations appear at the end of Crawford's *Psychic Structures of the Goligher Circle* (1921).

Although Crawford did not become a practicing Spiritualist, he believed "unseen operators" were responsible for producing the psychic rods. In this he differed from the investigators of Beraud and Rudi Schneider, who concluded the ectoplasm and psychokinetic effects were somehow produced by the medium, without the assistance of discarnate spirits.

A variety of outside observers attended Crawford's seances with the Golighers, including the president of the Glasgow Society of Conjurers, and concluded that the phenomena were genuine.

Sir William BARRETT, a physicist who lived in Belfast, looked into Crawford's work on behalf of the SOCIETY FOR PSYCHICAL RESEARCH (SPR) in 1915. He took with him a friend, a "Dr. W." At the seance they attended, knocks soon came and answered questions. Some knocks were very loud, and one, in response to a request by Dr. W. for an increase in volume, was so loud it caused the room to shake. Various imitative sounds, such as the sawing of wood, the boring of timber, and a bouncing ball, were also heard. The trumpet moved about, while Barrett and Dr. W. were encouraged to try to catch it. The table levitated to a height of 18 inches and stayed suspended in the air. They found that they could not push it down, no matter how hard they tried. Barrett then climbed onto the table and rode it, until he was thrown off.

When Barrett and Dr. W. returned the next day, they were informed by knocks that no phenomena would be forthcoming, due to "physical causes," evidently having to do with Kathleen. Indeed, when Dr. W. examined her after the seance was over, he found that she had begun her monthly period.

The only other SPR researcher to investigate the Golighers during Crawford's lifetime was W.W. Carington (who was then calling himself W.W. Smith). He had a series of sittings in 1916, with another in 1920. He later wrote that in 1916, he was persuaded that what he saw was genuine, but that by 1920, he believed the phenomena had turned fraudulent. If this is so, it may have been because Kathleen's mediumship was growing weaker, a frequent occurrence with physical mediums. It is interesting that by this date the Golighers had started to accept money from their investigators, something which they had not done earlier.

Crawford poisoned himself and died on July 30, 1920. Although he left a note saying his action had nothing to do with his "psychic work," which he believed was done well enough to stand, and in letters shortly before his suicide he complained of overwork, the suspicion that his action may have had something to do with a discovery about the Golighers is unavoidable. Carington's opinion that the family had turned to trickery by 1920 serves to strengthen this suggestion.

Another researcher who suspected the Golighers of fraud was E.E. Fournier d'Albe. He was acquainted with materialization phenomena through some sittings with Marthe Beraud, whom he considered to be genuine. Fournier d'Albe had a series of 20 sittings with the Golighers, at which little occurred. In his book, *The Goligher Circle* (1922), he used his largely negative findings to throw doubt on Crawford's claims and argued that the earlier phenomena must have been fraudulently produced.

Crawford's reputation has suffered greatly from Fournier d'Albe's verdict, all the more so because during his lifetime Crawford avoided association with the psychical research community, and published in the Spiritualist periodical *Light* and in popularly written books, rather than in the SPR's *Proceedings.* His affiliation may be due to no more than his preference for a spiritualistic explanation of the phenomena. But if he was indeed the "Crawford" who sat with Marthe Beraud, it may also be because he found objectionable the stringent measures against fraud practiced with that medium, who was obliged to submit to gynecological exams before seances and take emetics after them.

Crawford was not a medical man, as were many of Beraud's investigators, and he made no such requirement of Kathleen Goligher. Nor did he institute any of the other controls that by this time had become standard methodology in the study of physical mediumship. Having persuaded himself of the reality of the phenomena, he simply set about learning as much as he could about their physical characteristics.

The official jury will probably always be out on Crawford's work. Nonetheless, his three books—*The Reality of Psychic Phenomena* (1916), *Experiments in Psychic Science* (1919) and *The Psychic Structures of the Goligher Circle* (1921)—have had a considerable impact on psychical research. They motivated Thomas Glendenning HAMILTON, among others, to investigate physical mediumship, and they inspired L.R.G.

Crandon to try table-tipping, eventually leading to what seems to have been the largely fraudulent mediumship of his wife, "Margery" (see CRANDON, MINA STINSON).

Further reading:
Barham, Allan. "Dr. W.J. Crawford, His Work and His Legacy in Psychokinesis." *Journal of the Society for Psychical Research* 55 (1988):113–38.
Barrett, William. "Report of Physical Phenomena Taking Place at Belfast with Dr. Crawford's Medium." *Proceedings of the Society for Psychical Research* 88 (1920):334–37.
Inglis, Brian. *Science and Parascience: A History of the Paranormal, 1914–1939.* London: Hodder and Stoughton, 1984.

Crewe Circle   See HOPE, WILLIAM.

crisis apparitions   See APPARITIONS; TYRONE, ADMIRAL.

Crookes, Sir William (1832–1919)   One of the 19th century's greatest scientists, an honored chemist and physicist, and an early investigator of mediumship. Crookes sat with D.D. HOME and Florence COOK, among others. For much of his life he was committed to Spiritualism.

Sir William Crookes was born in London on June 17, 1832, one of 16 children of a gifted and prosperous tailor and his second wife (he had five other children by his first). Crookes was largely self-taught; he had had little regular schooling and no university education when, at age 16, he enrolled in the Royal College of Chemistry.

Upon graduation in 1854, Crookes went to Radcliffe Observatory, Oxford, as Superintendent of the Meteorological Department. While there, he invented an automated system for recording instrumental readings on wax paper. In 1855 he accepted a position as professor of chemistry at Chester Training College (a scientific preparatory school), but he resigned after a year when he was not given a laboratory in which to continue his research. Although he tried periodically to get another teaching position, he was never successful in his efforts. Most of his later work was done in the laboratory he established in his home.

In 1856, Crookes married Ellen Humphrey of Lancashire. The marriage was very happy; it produced eight children, of whom four sons and one daughter survived their father.

From his home, Crookes wrote for and edited photography journals, and then in 1859 he founded a weekly, *Chemical News*, which he continued to edit until 1906. He also helped found and edit the *Quarterly Journal of Science*, beginning in 1864.

The year 1861 saw the first of Crookes's major scientific achievements. This was the discovery of the element thallium and the correct measurement of its atomic weight. He was elected a Fellow of the Royal Society in 1863, at age 31.

The death of his youngest brother, Philip, of yellow fever, in 1867, marked a turning point in Crookes's life. He had been close to Philip, and was deeply disturbed by his death. At the urging of Cromwell Varley, a fellow physicist and a convinced Spiritualist, Crookes and his wife attended some seances in order to communicate with Philip. Although the details of these seances have not survived, we know that Crookes believed that they were successful. He became a Spiritualist, although for the most part he kept his beliefs to himself and never associated himself publicly with the religious movement.

Spiritualistic phenomena fascinated Crookes because they lay at the boundary of the known world, something which inspired other areas of his scientific work. His systematic study of mediumship began late in 1869 and continued into 1875.

One of his first seances was with D.D. Home, together with two other famous mediums of the period, Frank Herne and Charles Williams. At this informal seance, held after a dinner party at the home of a friend, Herne and Williams were thrown about and at one point lifted up in the air and set down upon the table. An accordion—Home's trademark instrument—moved around from one sitter to another, playing all the while. Herne and Williams were later unmasked as frauds, but Home's mediumship has survived all criticism.

It was Home, in any event, to whom Crookes chose to devote most of his time. Home always asked that his seances be held in good light, and he welcomed scientific investigations of his abilities. With Home, Crookes observed other levitations and table-tiltings, as well as luminous phenomena and materializations of hands. On one occasion, a hand rose up from between the leaves of a dining table and gave him a flower (he does not tell what kind). He encountered similar phenomena with some other mediums, although none were as powerful as Home.

Crookes was not content simply to observe Home's phenomena; he wanted to see them produced under proper scientific conditions. In his first report of his studies, he described how Home's accordion would play and move around without contact within a metal cage, and how Home could influence a plank with a weight attached to raise or lower at will, while he and two other scientists of repute, William Huggins and Serjeant Cox, watched and took notes. In his discussion, he distanced himself from the belief that spirits were responsible for these effects, and sug-

gested instead that they were due to some "psychic force" emanating from the medium.

Crookes believed the psychic force to be of supreme scientific importance, and he tried in vain to interest other scientists in investigating it with him. He was snubbed by two members of the Royal Society he invited to attend experimental seances with Home, and the same Society (its full name is the "Royal Society of London for Improving Natural Knowledge") rejected the paper he submitted for publication. He published it instead in his *Quarterly Journal of Science*, to great controversy. One of his critics charged that the phenomena he reported could not have occurred because they were impossible, to which Crookes replied, "I never said it was possible, I only said it was true."

Crookes's second major series of investigations was with Florence Cook. These began in 1872 when Cook asked for an investigation in order to clear her name, after a sitter at one of her seances had grabbed Katie King, the alleged full-form materialization of her spirit-guide, and declared it to be none other than Cook herself.

Crookes took control of Cook's seances, and for a period of four months she lived in his home. He was mainly interested in determining whether it was possible for investigators to see both Cook and Katie at the same time, and he claims to have done this, even taking a picture of the two of them together. With a battery of five cameras in his laboratory, he took a series of 44 pictures of Katie. He was also able to hold and measure her, reporting her to be taller, bigger, and somewhat prettier than Cook; Cook, moreover, habitually wore earrings, while Katie did not have her ears pierced.

Cook later was caught in fraud and to this day it remains a question whether her seances with Crookes were genuine, or whether he was fooled by her. The skeptical historian Trevor Hall has suggested that Crookes was having an affair with Cook, but there is no real evidence for this theory, and it is not widely accepted.

Crookes's last series of sittings for research purposes was held in 1875 with another medium of doubtful reputation, Anna Eva Fay. After this, however, he decided that his time was better spent on more tractable scientific problems, and he turned away from his psychic investigations. Although he supported the SOCIETY FOR PSYCHICAL RESEARCH (SPR) after it was formed in 1882, and served as its president in 1886, he did not take an active part in it.

The Royal Society gave Crookes its Royal Medal in 1875. In 1876 he invented the radiometer, a device that demonstrated the effects of radiation on objects in a vacuum, and the special tube called the Crookes' tube to go along with it. This in turn led to his discovery of cathode rays, which were shortly to lead to the discoveries (by others) of x rays and the electron.

Crookes served as president of the Chemical Society from 1887 to 1889 and president of the Society of Electrical Engineers from 1890 to 1894. He was knighted in 1897. In 1898 he was elected president of the British Association for the Advancement of Science, and in his presidential address he made a point of saying he had nothing to retract from his earlier reports on Home and Cook.

Five years later, in 1903, Crookes invented the spinthariscope, an instrument used in the study of subatomic particles. He received the Order of Merit, one of Great Britain's highest civilian honors, in 1910, and from 1913 to 1915 he served as president of the Royal Society, the organization that had so fiercely objected to his psychical investigations.

The death of Lady Crookes in 1916 was a severe blow. Crookes, who had never lost his Spiritualist inclinations, began to try to communicate with her. His first efforts were unsuccessful, but, after a visit to the CREWE CIRCLE, he finally obtained what he considered to be photographic proof of her continued existence; the plate, however, is said to bear signs of having been doubly exposed.

Crookes died on April 4, 1919 in London, at the age of 87. He never wrote the book he was hoping to write on his psychical investigations, but his papers on the subject were collected in an unauthorized booklet, *Researches in the Phenomena of Spiritualism*, first published in 1874. This booklet and related materials are reprinted in *Crookes and the Spirit World* (1972), edited by SPR members R.G. Medhurst and K.M. Goldney.

Further reading:
Barrett, William. "In Memory of Sir William Crookes." *Proceedings of the Society for Psychical Research* 31 (1920): xx.

Fournier D'Albe, E.E. *The Life of Sir William Crookes.* London: T. Fisher Unwin, 1923.

Gauld, Alan. *The Founders of Psychical Research.* London: Routledge & Kegan Paul, 1968.

Hall, Trevor. *The Spiritualists.* London: Duckworth, 1962.

Medhurst, R.G., and K.M. Goldney. "William Crookes and the Physical Phenomena of Mediumship." *Proceedings of the Society for Psychical Research* 54 (1964):25–156.

Medhurst, R.G., and K.M. Goldney. *Crookes and the Spirit World.* New York: Taplinger, 1972.

Oppenheim, Janet. *The Other World: Spiritualism and Psychical Research in England, 1850–1914.* Cambridge: Cambridge University Press, 1985.

cross correspondences Information purportedly from discarnate personalities received by different mediums acting independently. The information is received through trance mediumship or automatic writing.

There are three types of cross correspondences: simple, complex and ideal. In simple cross correspondences, two or more mediums produce the same word, words, or phrases, or similar phrases which are obviously related or interconnected. In complex cross correspondences, messages are indirect and must be deciphered. Ideal cross correspondences involve messages which are incomplete and must be put together like pieces of a puzzle.

There is no natural explanation for cross correspondences. Some psychical researchers believe they provide strong evidence in support of survival after death. Others say the mediums obtain the information from their own unconsciousnesses, or from each other or other living persons through unconscious telepathy or clairvoyance (see SUPER-ESP).

Cross correspondences were studied intently between 1901 and 1932 by the SOCIETY FOR PSYCHICAL RESEARCH (SPR), London. The most important communicators appeared to be three of the founders of the SPR, all of whom had been interested in the question of survival after death: Edmund GURNEY, who died in 1888, Henry SIDGWICK, who died in 1900, and Frederic W.H. MYERS, who died in 1901. Of the three men, Myers was most interested in proving survival after death. In his seminal work, *Human Personality and Its Survival of Bodily Death*, published posthumously in 1903, Myers stated that the influence of science on modern thought might be continued after death, and that the dead would know what constitutes good evidence of survival and would discover how to produce it. He believed that producing this evidence would require a group effort on the part of the dead rather than an individual effort. Myers stated while living that he would attempt to communicate posthumously. Sidgwick had been open to the possibility of survival, while Gurney had been skeptical.

The first cross correspondences were produced by several mediums prior to Myers's death. These were simple, showing similarities among trance utterances and automatic scripts of mediums sitting simultaneously but separate from one another.

After Myers's death in 1901, cross correspondences became more frequent and complicated, especially in the notable cases known as the PALM SUNDAY CASE and the EAR OF DIONYSIUS. The complex and ideal cross correspondences in these and other cases seemed to reveal an intelligent purpose behind masses of fragmentary and symbolic communications. The messages were unintelligible to the individual mediums involved and only became coherent after much analysis and comparison. Clues to links between messages were found in classical literature, poetry, topics that had been of interest to the dead while living, and to events that had taken place in life. Literary clues also seemed to pertain to life events. Sometimes, the discovery of these obscure clues proved difficult; years were spent making sense of the communications. By 1918, the various mediums and investigators working through the SPR concluded that cross correspondences formed large, linked groups.

SPR founding member Frank PODMORE was among those who believed that cross correspondences were the result of telepathic communication among the living. He suggested that one medium telepathically broadcast material, which was picked up by other mediums. However, the fact that the individual messages seemed to have been couched in symbols, were disseminated with apparent deliberation, and were made unintelligible to individual mediums, strengthened the case for survival. The principal SPR investigators of the cross correspondences concluded that the messages were genuine communications from the discarnate personalities involved.

Leonora PIPER and Gladys Osborne LEONARD were among the mediums to participate in cross correspondence research. Interest waned after the 1930s, following the conclusion of the Palm Sunday Case. Cross correspondences have appeared since then in physical research, but have not been the subject of great study.

Further reading:

Balfour, Jean. "The Palm Sunday Case." *Proceedings of the Society for Psychical Research* 52, 189 (Feb. 1960):79–267.

Douglas, Alfred. *Extrasensory Powers: A Century of Psychical Research*. London: Victor Gollancz Ltd., 1976.

Gauld, Alan. *Mediumship and Survival*. London: William Heinemann Ltd., 1982.

Grattan-Guinness, Ivor. *Psychical Research: A Guide to Its History, Principles and Practices*. Wellingborough, Northhamptonshire, England: The Aquarian Press, 1982.

Rhine, J.B., and Robert Brier, eds. *Parapsychology Today*. New York: The Citadel Press, 1968.

Saltmarsh, H.F. *Evidence of Personal Survival from Cross Correspondences*. London: G. Bell & Sons, Ltd., 1938.

crossroads   The meeting and parting of ways are widely associated with magic, the appearances and activities of demons, the Devil, witches, fairies, ghosts and spirits, and various sinister supernatural phenomena. Crossroads superstitions prevail through-out Europe and the British Isles, Greece, India and Japan, and among Native Americans and Mongols.

Crossroads are said to be haunted by various entities who delight in leading confused travelers astray, such as witches, trolls and the Will-o'-the-Wisp. (See IGNIS FATUUS.) Crossroads also are frequented by ghosts. In German lore, a ghostly rider haunts a crossroads in Schleswig; the neck of his mount stretches out across the road and prevents people from passing. In a legend from Pomerania, a traveler is stopped at a crossroads one night after sunset by a shadowy figure wearing a long coat and wooden shoes. To the man's consternation, the figure follows him to his house and haunts it. Finally, the man speaks to the ghost, who asks him to accompany the spirit to a churchyard and say prayers that will allow the restless shade to attain peace.

Spirits of the dead appear at crossroads every ALL HALLOWS EVE, the pagan festival when the veil between worlds is at its thinnest. In Welsh lore, every crossroads is populated by spirits of the dead on this night. In European lore, the dead walk in processions on All Hallows Eve to visit the homes of their relatives, and can be glimpsed by standing in a crossroads with one's chin resting on a forked stick.

At other times, the dead can be conjured to appear at crossroads. A ritual in Danish lore instructs one to go to a crossroads at midnight on New Year's Eve and stand within a rectangle formed by horse-cart tracks. The ghost will appear when his name is called, and will be required to answer three questions. Other folk and magical rituals exist for conjuring the Devil, demons and familiars at crossroads. The Greeks believed that Hecate, the patroness of witchcraft and crossroads, would appear at crossroads on clear nights, accompanied by spirits and howling phantom dogs. Offerings of food were left at crossroads for her. She also was petitioned for help in cases on insanity, which was believed to be caused by spirits of the dead.

One may divine who is going to die by performing rituals at crossroads, especially at certain times of the year, such as All Hallows Eve. In Welsh lore, one goes to a crossroads and listens for the "wind blowing over the feet of the corpses" (the east wind), which bears sighs to the houses of those doomed to die within the coming year. In the Scottish Highlands, one sits on a three-legged stool in a three-way crossroads, and at midnight will hear the names of those who will die. In German lore, one can hear names of the doomed at crossroads between eleven o'clock and midnight on either Christmas or New Year's Eve.

Crossroads also play roles in funeral and burial rites. An old Welsh custom calls for corpses to be laid down at every crossroads and prayed over as they are carried from house to graveyard, perhaps to protect the corpse from the evil spirits lurking about these places, or to prevent the ghost from returning to haunt the living. In Hesse, Germany, the return of a ghost was prevented by smashing the pottery of the deceased at a crossroads. In Finland, earth from crossroads that had been traversed by funeral processions was scattered upon the fields as protection against witchcraft. In many locales, suicide victims traditionally were buried at crossroads, but the reasons are not known. It may have been because the cross shape of an intersection mimicked the consecrated ground of a Christian churchyard, denied to suicides; or, it may have been an attempt to use the supernatural power of crossroads to prevent the ghosts of suicides from returning.

The cross shape of crossroads is in some lore protection against the very spirits alleged to haunt the places. For example, one German superstition holds that spirits and ghosts cannot pass a crossroads. Thus, if one is pursued by a ghost or demonic creature, one should race to a crossroads. The pursuer will vanish, usually with an unearthly shriek. Similarly, Irish lore holds that the powers of fairies can be neutralized at crossroads, and that mortals who are kidnapped by fairies can gain their freedom there.

Further reading:
Guiley, Rosemary Ellen. *The Encyclopedia of Witches and Witchcraft*. New York: Facts On File, 1989.
Puhvel, Martin. "The Mystery of the Cross-Roads." *Folklore* 87 (1976):167–77.

cryptomnesia The repression or forgetting of information learned. Forgotten information that surfaces in mediumship may be attributed to communication by spirits of the dead.

The forgetting of information is an essential process to keep the conscious mind uncluttered. However, during trance or dissociated states of consciousness, repressed information may break free of the subconscious and rise to the surface, where it appears new and "unknown" by the medium. Psychical researchers consider the possibility of cryptomnesia when investigating mediums, as well as cases of alleged past-life recall in reincarnation. If the information said to be obtained paranormally in fact can be found in existing sources, researchers consider the likelihood of the medium or individual seeing those sources in the past.

The earliest known case of cryptomnesia investigated by psychical researchers occurred in 1874, when the English medium William Stainton MOSES purported to contact the spirits of two young brothers who had died in India. The deaths were verified.

However, it was discovered that six days prior to the seance, an obituary of the brothers had appeared in the newspaper. Mose's information contained nothing beyond the obituary; thus researchers concluded he had seen the obituary without making conscious note of it, or had forgotten that he had read it.

Two mediums investigated by psychiatrist Ian STEVENSON claimed not to have read the obituaries of persons they contacted through their Ouija (q.v.). However, one of them regularly worked the crossword puzzles that appeared on the same newspaper page as the obituaries. Stevenson concluded that the obituaries fell within vision range and were absorbed unconsciously.

It is difficult to eliminate cryptomnesia as a natural explanation in many afterlife and reincarnation cases, because it is not known how much information the brain can store and for how long. The difficulty was demonstrated in the 1960s when Finnish psychiatrist Reima Kampman hypnotized secondary school students and directed them to recall "past lives." While the students were still under hypnosis, Kampman asked them for the original sources of their memories. Some cited books they had read as a small child.

Cryptomnesia is ruled out when information goes beyond accessible records to facts that can be verified only by other persons or in personal diaries. However, other theories, such as telepathy and SUPER-ESP, are then proposed and are equally difficult to eliminate.

Further reading:
Gauld, Alan. *Mediumship and Survival*. London: William Heinemann Ltd., 1982.
Stevenson, Ian. "Cryptomnesia and Parapsychology." *Journal of the Society for Psychical Research* 52 (1983):1–30.
Wilson, Ian. *All in the Mind*. Garden City, N.Y.: Doubleday, 1982.

Cult of the Zar (also **Cult of the Sar**) A type of possession among Muslims, which largely affects married women. It seems to provide an opportunity for oppressed women to manipulate men.

The possessing spirits are the *zar*, a malign, man-hating type of *djinn* (genie) which is capricious and much feared. The *zar* attack women and demand beautiful clothes, jewelry, perfume, better treatment and luxurious food and surroundings before they can be persuaded to depart. Such appeasement can get expensive, and many Muslim husbands suspect they are being manipulated, but they acquiesce, fearing punishment by the *zar*.

The possession and exorcism of the *zar* typically proceeds as follows: The victim, suffering from some minor complaint, blames possession by the *zar*, and other female relatives keep her from seeing a medical doctor, preferring the services of a female shaman, called *shechah-ez-Zar*. For a fee, the *shechah* identifies a *zar* as the source of the woman's troubles and interrogates the *zar*, sometimes in a recognizable language and sometimes in *zar* language, understood only by the *shechah*. After repeated conversations, the *zar* offers to leave once the possessed victim receives lavish gifts and attention from her husband.

On the afternoon of the *zar's* scheduled departure, a "beating the *zar*" ceremony is performed. The victim's female friends and relatives join her for the ceremony, much like a tea or party, often accompanied by a flute performance. The *shechah* and her assistants chant the final exorcism rites, with music, and then often sacrifice a lamb. The lamb's blood is rubbed on the victim's forehead and elsewhere. She then dances madly, sways and finally faints. The *zar* leaves.

Zar exorcisms have become part of contemporary urban Islamic culture. In many large cities, such as Cairo, regular exorcisms are held in a public building as often as once a week. Women from all walks of life participate, whirling and dancing until the spirit leaves them and they return home, exhausted but entertained. Relief from the possession may be only temporary, returning upon another infraction committed by a husband. Men are expected to believe in the possession, which, in addition to giving women the freedom to ask for gifts, permits them to scold and upbraid their husbands in a manner that would be forbidden under normal circumstances.

Further reading:

Ebon, Martin. *The Devil's Bride, Exorcism: Past and Present.* New York: Harper & Row, 1974.

Lewis, I.M. *Ecstatic Religion: An Anthropological Study of Spirit Possession and Shamanism.* Middlesex, England: Penguin Books, 1971.

Oesterreich, T.K. *Possession: Demoniacal and Other.* New Hyde Park, N.Y.: University Books, 1966. First published in 1921.

cypress Evergreen tree native to the southern United States, southern Europe and western Asia that is associated with death, burial, regeneration and the immortal soul. In Biblical lore, an angel gave the cypress to Seth to plant under Adam's tongue upon his death. The Egyptians used cypress for mummy cases. The Greeks and Romans associated it with the chthonic (underworld) deities; Athenian heroes were buried in cypress coffins. Cypress is planted along the borders of many cemeteries.

D

daimon   The ancient Greeks believed in the existence of daimons or daemons, intermediary spirits between humanity and the gods. Daimons could be either good or evil. A good daimon protected and gave good advice. Evil daimons led one astray with bad advice.

Socrates claimed he had a lifelong daimon that sounded warnings when things were about to go badly, but never gave orders as to what he should do. Socrates said his daimon was more trustworthy than omens from the flights and entrails of birds, which the Greeks often consulted for matters of great import.

Frederic W.H. MYERS, an English psychical researcher, opined that Socrates' daimon was his own subconscious speaking to him in a form—a spirit—that was acceptable to Greeks at the time. In Jungian psychology, the daimon would be considered the Higher Self, that part of the psyche that looks out for one's well-being, and which communicates with the waking conscious through intuition.

The Christian church considered all such pagan spirits as evil demons, servants of the Devil. (See DEMON.) However, the concept of a protective spirit has survived in the form of a "guardian spirit," believed by some to be attached to all persons from the moment of birth.

See also ANGEL.

Further reading:

Guiley, Rosemary Ellen. *Harper's Encyclopedia of Mystical and Paranormal Experience*. San Francisco: HarperSanFrancisco, 1991.

Myers, Frederic W.H. *Human Personality and Its Survival of Bodily Death Vols. I & II*. New York: Longmans, Green & Co., 1954. First published in 1903.

Davenport Brothers, The   Americans who conducted one of the most successful seance acts of the 19th century. William and Ira Davenport introduced the cabinet—a special room or enclosure—to the medium's repertoire and produced various spirit phenomena, including ghostly hands that played musical instruments. They also developed sophisticated rope tricks and escape illusions unparalleled until the days of Harry HOUDINI.

Ira Erastus Davenport was born September 17, 1839 and his brother William Henry was born February 1, 1841, both in Buffalo, New York. Their father, a local policeman, was intrigued with spirit rappings reported in nearby Rochester. The family tried sitting around a table, and raps appeared almost at once. The senior Davenport told friends that the boys and their younger sister, Elizabeth, could levitate and often floated around the room. At one seance in 1850, the spirits told Ira to fire a pistol in a corner of the room, and the ever-present control John KING appeared for an instant in the gun flash.

Sittings were originally held in the Davenport home, but soon John King ordered the family to rent a hall and begin public performances. The boys, 16 and 14, went on the stage in 1855. Their first performances included such standard fare as table-tipping and rapping, but also featured playful spirit hands which gripped sitters, played musical instruments and twirled umbrellas overhead. John King continued as spirit guide; his alleged daughter Katie, another famous control, also appeared in Davenport seances, but not as the lovely lady manifested by Florence COOK. By the end of the year, the boys appeared in New York City, adding the signature effects that characterized their act: rapidly escaping from complicated rope bindings and knots.

At the suggestion of a member of the audience in New York, suspicious of the Davenports working with confederates in the crowd, a box similar to a closet was erected on stage. Immediately realizing the benefits of working in secret darkness, the Davenports embraced the new arrangement, only asking that an opening be available for the spirit hands to work. The cabinet, as all spiritual enclosures came to be known, was seven feet by six feet wide by two feet deep and sat on three sawhorses. It had three doors in front, exposing the brothers tied to benches on opposite ends and facing a middle bench containing the musical instruments. A diamond-shaped opening in the middle door let in air and showed the phenomena. The entire contraption was quite lightweight and could be disassembled for travel.

Part of the brothers' act involved asking members of the audience to act as binders. Overeager skeptics tied the brothers in elaborate, often torturous ligatures, occasionally drawing blood. Suspicious watchers were invited to sit in the center section of the cabinet, and they too were bound hand and foot to the Davenports. No matter what the bindings, however, as soon as the doors were closed, wondrous spirit music filled the air and spirit hands waved through the aperture. Someone would fling open the doors, and the Davenports would still be found tied up as before.

Their act created quite a sensation. Many Spiritualists hailed the manifestations as proof of spirit intervention, while critics regarded the brothers as conjurers. Neither brother ever admitted being a Spiritualist medium, leaving such a determination to their audience. Their act was billed as a seance, however, and Spiritualists and even several psychical researchers believed the phenomena to be genuine. The brothers were never caught in fraud.

In 1864, the Southern preacher Jesse Babcock Ferguson joined the brothers as their master of ceremonies. A fiery speaker, Ferguson believed in what he called the "supramundane" and was impressed by the Davenports' powers. Additionally, his Union sympathies forced him to take his family out of their home in Nashville and head north. The Davenports and the Fergusons traveled for about four months in Canada and New England, before sailing for England in company with another medium named William Fay.

The Davenports held their first English seance in the home of actor and playwright Dion Boucicault in front of several scientists and journalists. Various phenomena were produced, including the removal of Fay's coat while he was bound (it flew up to the chandelier), the re-dressing of Fay with another jacket while he remained tied, spirit musicianship, the brothers' incredible rope escapes and even spirit hands playing with the hair of Sir Charles Wyke, who sat bound between the brothers in the cabinet. The Davenports also sat for authors Sir Edwin Arnold and Sir Richard Burton.

In February 1865, a hostile crowd in Liverpool rioted, storming the stage and breaking the cabinet, after the Davenports objected to the cruel way they were bound and refused to perform. Similar vio-

lence followed them in performances at Huddersfield and Leeds, causing the Davenports to cancel any more performances in England. Ferguson left the Davenports before they went to France, saying his ignorance of foreign languages made him a liability. He always maintained that after years of intimate travel with the Davenports, he knew of no instance when their phenomena were not genuinely paranormal.

The French authorities delayed giving the Davenports a permit to perform, fearing a repeat of the riots they had suffered in England. But the brothers prevailed, eventually appearing before the Emperor Napoleon III and the Empress Eugenie. From France, the Davenports returned to London, then Ireland, Germany, Belgium and Russia, where they mystified the Imperial Court of Czar Alexander II. After Russia, the Davenports traveled to Poland and Sweden—in all, a four-year tour of Europe.

In 1876 the brothers left for Australia, but William died suddenly in Sydney in July 1877. Ira commissioned a memorial carved with the accoutrements of their performances:—ropes, musical instruments and the cabinet—but cemetery officials refused to erect the Spiritualist monument on hallowed ground. Ira placed it outside the cemetery walls. Lost without his brother, Ira quit performing and retired to New York.

In his book *A Magician Among the Spirits*, Houdini recounts meeting Ira Davenport. He began corresponding with the old showman in 1909 and finally met him at his home in Maysville, New York in 1910, after a long European tour. While in Australia, Houdini visited William's grave and, finding it neglected, had it put in order. He also met Fay, who regaled Houdini with his adventures traveling with the Davenports.

Ira was apparently touched by Houdini's tenderness regarding William's gravesite, and he returned the favor by explaining many of the brothers' escape illusions. The best was the Davenport tie, or the means by which the brothers could so rapidly escape their bonds and just as easily return before the cabinet was opened. The brothers guarded the particulars of this trick so closely that Houdini claimed even the Davenport children did not know how it worked.

When the brothers were seated opposite one another in the cabinet, the rope was wound around their legs, near the knees, then at the ankles. A shorter piece was tied to each pair of wrists with the knots next to the pulse. Once the brothers were enclosed in the cabinet, one brother would extend his feet while the other drew his in, providing enough slack to allow one, then the other, to free himself.

The wrist ropes were knotted in such a way that one hand could twist in the opposite direction and open enough loop to instantly free the left hand. Upon replacing the hand, the hand twisted the rope and appeared to be securely tied. Magician Harry Kellar used the same wrist trick.

Ira died in 1911. Following his death, Houdini maintained that Davenport had confessed the brothers were expert conjurers, not Spiritualists. But many discounted Houdini's claims, noting that the whole affair pitted Houdini—a staunch anti-Spiritualist—against the signed statements of many distinguished believers and scientists.

Further reading:

Brown, Slater. *The Heyday of Spiritualism*. New York: Pocket Books, 1972.

Doyle, Sir Arthur Conan. *The History of Spiritualism Vol. I & II*. New York: Arno Press, 1975.

Fodor, Nandor. *An Encyclopaedia of Psychic Science*. Secaucus, N.J.: The Citadel Press, 1966. First published 1933.

———. *Mind Over Space*. New York: The Citadel Press, 1962.

Houdini, Harry. *Houdini: A Magician Among the Spirits*. New York: Arno Press, 1972.

Mysteries of the Unknown: Spirit Summonings. Alexandria, Va.: Time-Life Books, 1989.

Davis, Andrew Jackson   An early magnetist, Andrew Jackson Davis helped bridge the gap between mesmerism and Spiritualism. He is credited with prophesying the coming of the spirits to the FOX SISTERS and detailing the progressive creation and spiritual evolution of the world through trance revelations.

Davis was born in Blooming Grove, Orange County, New York on August 11, 1826, the sixth child and only son. Only one of his sisters survived girlhood, and young Andrew was sickly and nervous. He often heard voices. His mother was illiterate but deeply religious. His father, a cobbler, drank heavily. The family was quite poor and moved frequently, ending up in Poughkeepsie in 1838. Davis had little formal schooling, and drifted from one small job to another as farm boy, grocery clerk or cobbler. He apprenticed himself to a shoemaker named Ira Armstrong in 1841–1842 but left in 1843.

What enticed Davis away from the trade was animal magnetism. In the fall of 1843, Davis attended the traveling show of magnetist and phrenologist J. Stanley Grimes. Davis volunteered to be magnetized but did not become hypnotized. Nearly all of Poughkeepsie tried mesmerism, however, a local tailor named William Levingston finally succeeded in entrancing Davis in December 1843.

Levingston discovered that Davis was susceptible to trance and while under could see through the

Andrew Jackson Davis. Painting by Thomas Le Clear. Courtesy New-York Historical Society.

body as if it were transparent, making astounding medical diagnoses. For a year, Davis worked as a clairvoyant and healer, becoming known as the Poughkeepsie Seer. Levingston gave up his tailor shop and devoted all his time to Davis's work.

In March 1844, Davis underwent a strange, mystical experience. In a state of semi-trance, he wandered about forty miles from his home into the Catskill Mountains, following an allegorical vision of a flock of sheep. He fell asleep near an altar in the woods, again seeing visions of sheep, mountains and a shepherd he recognized as Christ. Next he met a small old man dressed like a Quaker, who carried a scroll that Davis signed. Hurrying down the mountain, Davis again fell asleep and awoke in a graveyard, where he encountered Galen, the Greek physician.

Galen provided Davis with a long lecture on his healing work, explaining his methods, and then presented Davis with his staff. Following Galen was Emanuel SWEDENBORG, who also lectured Davis and declared the young man would become a vessel for the perception of wisdom, opening the soul's way to harmony. At that, Davis tried to depart over the cemetery wall and lost his temper when he became caught on a post. After his outburst, Galen refused to give him the staff after all, cautioning him to learn control of his emotions. Dazed, Davis walked home.

Repeated visions convinced Davis that he was to serve as an oracle for some divine truth, and for some reason, he did not feel Levingston was capable of drawing this out. While healing in Bridgeport, Connecticut, Davis met a botanic (herb) doctor named S. Silas Lyon, whom he chose as his new mesmerist. Davis and Lyon moved to New York City, where Davis continued his healing business. Within three months Davis selected the Universalist minister Rev. William Fishbough to act as scribe, and in November 1845 he began the great work.

The three men would gather in the parlor of their New York apartment (like Levingston, both Lyon and Fishbough had quit their jobs to be with Davis) and Lyon would hypnotize Davis. After three or four minutes Davis would shudder in convulsive shock, then remain motionless for another five minutes, blindfolded to protect his eyes from the light. Then he would become cataleptic, rigid and cold, hardly breathing. Finally Davis, although still in trance, would appear more normal and begin dictating a phrase or two at a time. Lyon would repeat each phrase to Fishbough, who wrote them down. The sessions lasted anywhere from forty minutes to four hours, producing about five pages.

Usually three witnesses, chosen by Davis, watched the transcription. Edgar Allan Poe, the Fourierist Albert Brisbane and trance poet Thomas Lake Harris were frequently present. The most influential visitor, however, was Dr. George Bush, professor of Hebrew language and literature at New York University. A great biblical scholar and Swedenborgian, Bush enthusiastically endorsed the authenticity of Davis's trance pronouncements as an amazing display of ancient history, Hebrew language, archeology, geology, language and mythology, especially in one so ignorant as Davis.

After 157 sessions, *The Principles of Nature, Her Divine Revelations, and a Voice to Mankind, By and Through Andrew Jackson Davis, the 'Poughkeepsie Seer' and 'Clairvoyant'* was published in January 1847. Lyon and Fishbough claimed they had made no changes except in grammar and spelling. Bush wrote a six-column review in the New York *Tribune* praising the work and Davis, calling him the greatest prodigy since Swedenborg. Four editions appeared before the year was out, and the darkly handsome 21-year-old Davis was an instant celebrity. He was not instantly rich, however, as he had relinquished all rights to copyright and sales of the book to Lyon and Fishbough while in trance. The book eventually went into 34 editions, but there are no records of any beyond the 13th until the 30th.

The 782 pages of complicated and rambling prose challenge the modern reader. But in the mid-19th century, people were fascinated to learn about creation, philosophy and religion in theories that supported America's belief in optimistic and universal progress. Davis gave his readers hope for future regeneration of mankind both in the secular and spiritual worlds.

Briefly outlined, Davis defined God as the Great Positive Mind, the inner divine essence that causes all external effect. This Mind is by its very nature progressive. God created the cosmos out of a great primordial ocean of liquid fire. Life evolved from lower forms to higher, culminating in man, who is composed of the essence of all other existing life. After death man still progresses through the celestial spheres to the seventh, where he becomes one with God's infinite Mind, wisdom and love.

Throughout the book Davis explained the evolution of the solar system, the geological and biological history of the earth, the development of language, the rise of mythology and religion, the probabilities of prophecy, the Old and New Testaments, the life of Jesus, the precepts of Swedenborg, Calvin and Charles Fourier, the spiritual constitution of man, and the real estate of heaven. Finally, he discussed the evils of society, the wickedness of doctors and clergymen, and the benefits of a Fourierist utopia.

Davis claimed only five months of schooling, but educated readers of *The Divine Revelations* recognized the creation theories of Robert Chambers and the spiritual concepts of Swedenborg. Several critics charged Davis with fraud, but it is unlikely that Davis could have recited, blindfolded, all those previous works. Others believed Davis had hypermnesia (unusually exact or vivid memory), or the ability to remember quantities of tiny details while in trance.

Personal scandal gave the book more publicity. As a healer in New York, Davis had counseled a Mrs. Catherine Dodge, née deWolfe, a very wealthy heiress in Bristol, Rhode Island, and 20 years Davis's senior. They struck up a correspondence, and she generously paid all publication expenses for *The Divine Revelations*.

Her generosity extended to buying and furnishing a house for Davis in Waltham, Massachusetts, but Davis declined the gift. Undeterred, Dodge talked editor S.B. Brittan, a friend of Davis's, into renting him an apartment in Brittan's home, which Dodge paid for and furnished. Davis accepted and met her in the apartment, proposing marriage. She accepted, and she browbeat the Brittans into renting her rooms next to Davis. This in itself was shocking, but when the Brittans' maid found that Dodge had spent the night in Davis's room, the couple was forced to move out. They were married in July 1848 after the Rhode Island legislature (Dodge definitely had connections) had passed a law dissolving her marriage. Sadly, their union was short and unhappy, as each came from such different backgrounds. Dodge died in 1853, leaving her estate to Davis.

Also in 1848, Davis predicted the birth of Spiritualism. In his diary of March 31, Davis wrote that he felt warm breath on his face when he awoke and a strong voice telling him that the good work had begun—a living demonstration was born. March 31 is the day Kate and Maggie Fox challenged the Hydesville rapper (see FOX SISTERS).

Davis enjoyed a long career, lecturing on "Harmonial Philosophy" and writing several more books of divine philosophy and healing, including *The Great Harmonia* in 1852, his autobiography *The Magic Staff* in 1857 and various books and treatises on diagnosis and disease. He became a legitimate physician at age 60 with a medical degree and prescribed herbal cures. *The Univercoelum*, a Spiritualist magazine, was founded in 1847 by Brittan, Fishbough and others just to serve as Davis's mouthpiece.

Davis also espoused conjugal love, which critics saw demonstrated in his affair with Dodge. Brittan was so incensed over the scandal that the *Univercoelum* suffered and finally died.

Other projects which interested Davis were the poltergeist haunting of the Phelps home in Stratford, Connecticut in 1850, and the discovery of electrical vibrations in some young girls and children, early evidence of psi (extrasensory perception and psychokeinesis). Davis attributed the Phelps poltergeist phenomena to electrical irregularities from the two older children. He also supported John Murray Spear's "New Motor," allegedly powered by spiritual magnetic forces, some of them sexual.

In his later years Davis ran a bookshop in Boston, all but forgotten by later Spiritualists who had called him their John the Baptist. He died in 1910.

Further reading:

Brown, Slater. *The Heyday of Spiritualism.* New York: Pocket Books, 1972.

Douglas, Alfred. *Extra-Sensory Powers: A Century of Psychical Research.* Woodstock, N.Y.: The Overlook Press, 1977.

Doyle, Sir Arthur Conan. *The History of Spiritualism Vol. I & II.* New York: Arno Press, 1975.

Fodor, Nandor. *An Encyclopaedia of Psychic Science.* Secaucus, N.J.: The Citadel Press, 1966. First published 1933.

Moore, R. Laurence. *In Search of White Crows: Spiritualism, Parapsychology and American Culture.* New York: Oxford University Press, 1977.

Mysteries of the Unknown: Spirit Summonings. Alexandria, Va.: Time-Life Books, 1989.

Somerlott, Robert. *"Here, Mr. Splitfoot": An Informal Exploration into Modern Occultism.* New York: The Viking Press, 1971.

Day of the Dead   A special holiday each year to honor the dead, involving parties, feasts, special foods, songs and parades.

Unlike holidays such as Memorial Day or Veterans Day, in which citizens remember former members of the armed forces with a parade, a gravesite ceremony and a long weekend, the Day of the Dead in most cultures brings the living and the dead together for a great feast and celebration to remember the departed and to placate them for another year. The worship and placation of the spirits of the dead is an ancient and universal practice, and it continues in many parts of the world.

The Chinese, who venerate their ancestors, perform special ceremonies in spring, summer and autumn to ease humankind's two souls: the spiritual and the animal. The spiritual soul is petitioned to give special consideration to the departed's descendants, and the animal soul is discouraged from rousing the corpse and disturbing the living.

Of particular import is the Hungry Ghost Festival, a two-week observance that takes place in the autumn during the Seventh Moon. People prepare offerings of food for those ghosts who have no living descendants to take care of them, and therefore are hungry. The ghosts are symbolized by lotus flower lamps that are carried through streets, and small boats with candles that are floated in streams at dusk.

In Japan, the equivalent of All Souls' Day is Obon, or the "Feast of Lanterns." It is celebrated between July 13 and 16. It is believed that the spirits of the dead come home during this time; they are entertained with food and offerings. Household services are conducted for the dead, and special lights are placed at gates to guide the spirits.

The "shades" of former tribal Africans remain with their families and intercede on their behalf with the divine spirits. To keep them happy, living relatives hold feasts with plenty of food and drink, frequently accompanied by animal sacrifice. The ancestor's kin must attend the meal, since it is a communion among the living and the dead. If any of the family is quarreling, such disagreements are resolved at the feast to ward off witchcraft.

Hindu *sraddha*s, or rituals for the ancestors, last for 10 days. During that time the departed spirit receives food to help it survive the required trips though 10 different hells. Additionally, on the first of the new autumn moon, the head of each Hindu family holds ceremonies venerating the dead of the last three generations.

Perhaps the most elaborate ceremonies for the dead occur in Mexico. The Spanish conquistadores were shocked to find the Aztecs and the Mayans practicing cannibalism and human sacrifice, and they violently discouraged such practices. But to the native Mexicans, personal and collective salvation did not depend on faith in future redemption but on the continuity of life and death: more specifically, the blood and death of humans.

They saw little distinction between life and death, viewing each as merely phases of a cycle. According to Octavio Paz, the well-known Mexican writer and diplomat, for the Aztecs the chief function of life was to die; death was life's natural complement. Conversely, death was not an end but the food of future life. Sacrifice, then, served two purposes: to allow humans a role in the creative process and to pay back their debts to the gods. Celebrating death made continued life possible.

Forced to adopt Catholicism, the native Aztecs and Mayans transferred their death rites into the worship of the martyred saints. Grim religious artworks portray death in graphic detail. Even popular cartoons feature skeletons cavorting in a *danse macabre* representing all walks of life. *Calaveras*, or death's heads, still can be found in any Mexican market or gift shop.

The official day of the dead, *El Dia de los Muertes*, is November 2, All Souls' Day. The natives received this date from the missionaries, but it fit in well with traditional corn festivals. Festivities actually begin on October 31, Halloween, or ALL HALLOWS EVE. The women of each family clean house, make candles and cook great quantites of chicken, tortillas, hot chocolate, sweet corn gruel called *atole* and a special bread baked in the shapes of little animals. The men build small clay altars on which they place offerings of food and toys to the *angelitos*, the little children in the family who have died. Around midnight, as the family prays, the angelitos come and enjoy their presents, then leave.

The next day, All Saints' Day, the children enjoy the food prepared for the *angelitos* while the adults prepare an even bigger feast for the older deceased who will arrive near dawn the next morning. Such a party requires spicier food and plenty of tequila and aguardiente. Older departed spirits deserve a bigger altar as well, complete with gaily decorated skulls and bones made from marzipan or a special bread baked for the occasion. Across the skulls' foreheads appear the names of the departed or even a suitable motto or sentiment, such as "as I am, so shall you be." Up until about the turn of the 20th century, celebrants dug up real skulls and then reburied them under the supervision of the local priest.

Outsiders may find such celebrations morbid, but the Mexicans do not. Walking through the town square, wrapped in banners and streamers, celebrants enjoy amusement park rides, munch on candy bones and tiny coffins, and drink quantities of strong alcohol. Mexicans believe the dead want to have a good time, too, so mixing the sacred and the profane is quite normal.

Later on, the local priest visits his parishioners' home altars, offering prayers and blessings. The shrine is usually hung with photographs of the departed and pictures of the family's patron saints. Yellow marigolds surround the altar (yellow was the color of death before the Spanish conquest). Neighbors go from house to house, sharing food and drink and swapping memories of the deceased, who have now gathered to listen to what the living say about them. No dead soul is neglected for fear it may be sad or revengeful.

These visitations last all night and are followed by a mass at about 8:00 the next morning, All Souls' Day, at which time the departed return to their graves. After a day of rest, everyone proceeds to the cemetery that evening, where each family says prayers, sings songs and shares another meal with the departed in a picnic over the loved ones' graves. These last visitations satisfy the deceased, who are once more able to rest comfortably until they need to rejoin the living again the next year.

See also AFTERLIFE; ANCESTOR WORSHIP; FEASTS AND FESTIVALS OF THE DEAD.

Further reading:

Day, Douglas. "A Day with the Dead." *Natural History* (October 1990):69–72.

Dictionary of Folklore, Mythology and Legend Vol. 1. New York: Funk & Wagnalls Co., 1949.

Sayer, Elizabeth Carmichael Chlöe. *The Skeleton at the Feast: The Day of the Dead in Mexico.* London: British Museum Press, 1991.

dead house In Britain, a small building at railways stations once used as a temporary morgue to house corpses of those who died on railway property, until they could be taken away. Ghosts of the dead who have been placed in the dead houses have been reported at some railway stations.

One such occurrence took place at the Middlebrough station in North Yorkshire, according to Terence Whitaker in his book *Haunted England*. A young telegraphist by the name of Archer always was made uneasy by the strange atmosphere exuded by the dead house, and avoided going near it. One night at about 2 A.M., he steeled himself to walk past the house alone when he suddenly saw a fellow employee, Fred Nicholson, a signalman, standing at the end of the platform. As Archer drew nearer, Nicholson vanished. Archer told the signalman on duty what he had seen, and he was informed that Nicholson had been killed by a train that afternoon—and that his body was lying in the dead house.

Further reading:
Whitaker, Terence. *Haunted England.* Chicago: Contemporary Books, 1987.

Dead Smell Bad Native American legend that explains why the dead are not resurrected back to life. According to the Huchnom of California, the creator deity, Taikomol, intended to resurect the dead, and built a dance house and taught the people the dance of the dead. However, during the dance one man erred and sickened and died. Taikomol buried him, and resurrected him the following morning. When the man returned to the dance house, the people were sickened by his terrible smell. Taikomol was forced to give up his intentions to bring the dead back to life.

Further reading:
Leach, Maria, and Jerome Fried, eds. *Funk & Wagnalls Standard Dictionary of Folklore, Mythology, and Legend.* San Francisco: Harper & Row, 1979.

Dean, James See LITTLE BASTARD, CURSE OF.

deathbed visions Experiences of the dying, most of which are apparitions of the dead or mythical or religious figures, and visions of an afterlife place. Deathbed visions share common characteristics that cut across racial, cultural, religious, educational, age and socioeconomic lines. The importance of deathbed visions is that they are evidence in support of survival after death. Although nearly all cultures assume an afterlife, Western science holds the Aristotelian view that consciousness cannot exist separately from form, the body, and that therefore death is the total destruction of the personality.

Deathbed visions are reported in the biographies and literature of all ages, and have been researched scientifically in the 20th century. Early psychical researchers, including Frederic W.H. MYERS, Edmund GURNEY, Frank PODMORE and James H. HYSLOP, recorded cases of deathbed visions in the late 19th and early 20th centuries. The first systematic study of the phenomena was done in the early 20th century by Sir William BARRETT, a distinguished professor of physics and psychical researcher. Barrett's interest in deathbed visions was aroused in 1924 when his wife, a physician specializing in obstetrical surgery, told him about a woman patient who spoke of seeing

visions of a place of great beauty and her dead father and sister shortly before she died. The visions were very real to the patient, and had transfigured her into a state of great radiance and peace. When shown her baby, she had pondered staying for its sake, and then had said, ". . . I can't stay; if you could see what I do, you would know I can't stay." What struck Barrett was the fact that the woman had not know her sister had died about three weeks earlier, yet she saw an apparition of the sister along with that of the dead father.

Several decades later, Barrett's research interested Karlis Osis, then director of research for Eileen J. GARRETT's Parapsychology Foundation. Under the auspices of the Foundation in 1959–60, and later the AMERICAN SOCIETY FOR PSYCHICAL RESEARCH (SPR) in 1961–64 and 1972–73, Osis collected information from doctors and nurses on tens of thousands of deathbed and near-death experiences in the United States and India. The Indian survey (1972–73) was conducted with Erlendur Haraldsson. Of those cases, more than 1,000 were examined in detail. The findings of these studies confirmed Barrett's findings, as well as the experiences of individuals who work with the terminally ill and dying, such as Elisabeth Kübler-Ross. The findings also are in agreement with many of the findings of research into the near-death experience (NDE) by Raymond Moody and Kenneth Ring and others. (See NEAR-DEATH EXPERIENCE.)

Deathbed visions typically occur to individuals who die gradually, such as from terminal illness or serious injuries, rather than those who die suddenly, such as from heart attacks. The majority of visions are of apparitions of the dead, who typically are glowing and dressed in white, or are beings of light perceived as mythical or religious figures or deities: for example, angels, Jesus, the Virgin Mary, Krishna, Yama (Hindu god of death), Yamhoot (messenger of Yama), or similar figures. Apparitions of the dead invariably are close family members, such as parents, children, siblings or spouses. The purpose of these apparitions—"take-away apparitions," as they are called—is to beckon or command the dying to accompany them; i.e., they appear to assist in the transition to death. The response of most of the dying is one of happiness and willingness to go, especially if the individual believes in an afterlife (deathbed visions occur to those who do not believe as well as those who do). If the patient has been in great pain or depression, a complete turnaround of mood is observed, and pain vanishes. The dying one literally seems to "light up" with radiance.

When take-away apparitions appear, the patient usually is cognizant of the real physical surroundings and other living people present, who in all but rare cases cannot see the apparitions. Approximately one-third of deathbed visions involve total visions, in which the patient sees another world which appears objective and real. The descriptions most frequently given are of endless gardens of great beauty. Some also see gates, bridges, rivers, boats and other symbols of transition, as well as castles and other architectural structures. Regardless of image, the visions are resplendent with intense and vivid colors and bright light. The otherworld places may be populated with apparitions of the dead or spiritual beings. The vision either unfolds before the patient, or the patient feels transported out-of-body to the location. Again, the usual emotional response of the patient is one of happiness and anticipation at going to the beautiful place. Few total vision cases conform to religious expectations about the nature of the afterlife. Osis found only one case of a vision described as hell, from a Catholic woman who seemed to be carrying a great burden of guilt about her ''sins.''

A small number of those studied in the Osis-Haraldsson research reported hearing nonearthly music. The incidence of music appears to have been higher in cases collected around the turn of the century by earlier psychical researchers; perhaps this is a reflection of cultural differences in the role of music in everyday life.

Most deathbed visions are short in duration: approximately 50% last 5 minutes or less; 17% last 6–15 minutes; and 17% last more than one hour. The visions usually appear just minutes before death: approximately 76% of the patients studied died within 10 minutes of their vision, and nearly all of the rest died within one or several hours. In a few cases, one or more visions were seen by a patient over the course of several days, as though they were announcing appointments with death at a certain time. The appearance of the vision seems to have little connection with the physical condition of the patient. Some who seemed to be recovering, then had visions, quickly fell into comas and died.

Similarities are found between deathbed visions and mystical experiences: a sense of the sacred, feelings of great peace, or a heightened sense of elation. However, the ineffable nature of mystical experiences—that they are beyond description—occurs in very few deathbed visions.

Various explanations have been advanced to attribute deathbed visions to natural causes. Drugs, fever, disease-induced hallucinations, oxygen deprivation to the brain, wish-fulfillment and depersonalization have all been advanced as possible causes. While these factors can cause hallucinations, they are

Woodcut of the Duke of Buckingham on his deathbed, attended by the ghost of his father.

found not to concern the afterlife, but to relate mostly to the present. The Osis-Haraldsson research found that deathbed visions are most likely to occur in patients who are fully conscious. Medical factors do not generate true deathbed visions. Nor is wish-fulfillment a likely explanation, as the visions by and large do not conform to expectations of patients, and appear even to those who want to recover and live.

Related to a deathbed vision of the dying is a deathbed vision seen by the living who are in attendance to the dying. As the person dies, clouds of silvery energy are sometimes reported floating over the body. In some cases, the energy is seen to clearly form into the astral body of the dying one, connected by a silvery cord which severs at the moment of death. The living also have reported seeing the "take-away" apparitions both of the dead and of angelic beings. Such visions seen by the living appear in the literature of the early psychical researchers, but not in the later researches by Osis and Haraldsson, who report the living saw no astral bodies and only rarely saw the take-away apparitions. The most likely reason for this apparent decrease is that in earlier times, more people died at home. Familiar surroundings, and constant attendance to the dying, might have been more conducive to such visions than the impersonal surroundings of a hospital.

Deathbed visions are significant to thanatology, the scientific study of death and dying, from physiological, psychological and sociological perspectives, for they demonstrate that the transition of death is not to be feared, but is a wondrous experience. Dying is a rite of passage that ideally should be undertaken with as much dignity and clear-mindedness as possible. There are various arts of dying, as exemplified in the ancient Western mystery traditions and in *The Tibetan Book of the Dead* (see BARDO THÖDOL). Unfortunately, most modern Westerners fear death, and thus have allowed medicine to force the dying to cling to life at all costs until the last possible moment, in great pain or in a benumbed state on drugs and life-support machines. Perhaps the researches into the phenomena of dying, such as deathbed visions, near-death experiences and out-of-body experiences, will help bring about a change in attitude.

See also OUT-OF-BODY EXPERIENCE; SURVIVAL AFTER DEATH.

Further reading:
Barrett, William. *Death-Bed Visions: The Psychical Experiences of the Dying*. Wellingborough, Northamptonshire, England: The Aquarian Press, 1986. First published 1926.

Evans-Wentz, W.Y., comp. and ed. *The Tibetan Book of the Dead*. 3rd ed. London: Oxford University Press, 1957.

Gurney, Edmund, Frederic W.H. Meyers, and Frank Podmore. *Phantasms of the Living*. London: Kegan Paul, Trench, Trubner & Co. Ltd., 1918.

Osis, Karlis. *Deathbed Observations by Physicians and Nurses*. Monograph No. 3. New York: Parapsychology Foundation, 1961.

Osis, Karlis, and Haraldsson Erlendur. *At the Hour of Death*. Rev. ed. New York: Hastings House, 1986.

death cars A folklore motif in which a car carries an ineradicable smell of death because a previous owner died in the car and the body was not discovered until after it began to decompose. The legend is widespread throughout the United States, where it may have originated, perhaps in the 1930s. It appeared in England in the 1950s.

The main story line of the death car legend is that someone knows a person who bought a nice car at an unbelievably cheap price, and then discovered it had a horrible smell of death. The details vary: the type and year of car, the location where the event takes place, and the circumstances of the death. For some unknown reason, Buicks are the most popular make of car in the legend, followed by Chevrolets, Fords and sports cars, not necessarily in descending order. The most common cause of death is suicide, but the cause may also be murder or accident. All efforts to rid the car of the stench fail, and the owner either sells it at a loss, takes it back to the dealer, or turns it into scrap metal.

See also LITTLE BASTARD, CURSE OF.

Further reading:
McNeil, W.K., comp. and ed. *Ghost Stories from the American South*. New York: Dell, 1985.

Winer, Richard, and Nancy Osborn. *Haunted Houses*. New York: Bantam Books, 1979.

death omens In folklore, portents of a person's impending death. Every culture has its own unique death omens.

Death omens can be signs of nature, such as cloud formations or storms; signs that occur naturally, such as the way wax drips from a candle or the appearance of coffin-shaped cinders in a fireplace; or even accidental happenings, such as a chair falling over backward as a person rises from it.

Death is foretold by the appearance of certain animals, insects or birds that are associated with death, the underworld, and spirits of the dead. Black birds and night birds such as rooks, ravens, owls and crows are widely regarded as death omens when they appear in a village or lurk about a particular house. The howling of a dog, which in mythology is guardian of the underworld and guide of souls of the dead, portends the death of someone nearby. In parts of England, if the first lamb born to a farmer is black, it portends a family death within a year.

Death omens also include supernatural phenomena, such as the appearance of an apparition (see BANSHEE). Another common omen is a phantom death coach drawn by phantom black horses and driven by a headless man that stops at the houses where someone will die the next day. Other phantom vehicles,

The raven, a common death omen in folklore.

such as boats, cars and trains, also are death omens; their appearances mean they have come to take away the souls of the dead. Spectral black dogs and other animals are death omens (see BLACK SHUCK; WHISHT HOUNDS; WILD HUNT.)

Luminous phenomena, such as corpse candles and corpse lights—bluish lights seen flickering in the night—are harbingers of death.

Death omens also include various divination charms intended to foretell the future.

Further reading:
Leach, Maria, and Jerome Fried, eds. *Funk & Wagnalls Standard Dictionary of Folklore, Mythology, and Legend.* San Francisco: Harper & Row, 1979.
Opie, Iona, and Moira Tatem. *A Dictionary of Superstitions.* Oxford: Oxford University Press, 1989.

deathwatch beetle Small insect which makes a ticking or tapping sound as it bores into wood. The beetle is especially heard in woodwork, benches and wainscot during the summer months. In folklore beliefs in the United States, Britain and Europe, the sound of the deathwatch beetle is a harbinger of a death in the family. Various specific beliefs exist; for example, in Lancashire, England it is especially ominous if the deathwatch beetle ticks only three times. Records in England dating back to the 17th century attest to the terror the deathwatch beetle held over people.

See also DEATH OMENS.

Further reading:
Opie, Iona, and Moira Tatem. *A Dictionary of Superstitions.* Oxford: Oxford University Press, 1989.

Decatur House The haunted home of one of America's great military heroes, Stephen Decatur, and his wife, Susan. Located at the once-fashionable Lafayette Square in the heart of Washington, D.C., the box-shaped house is said to be haunted by the ghosts of both husband and wife, as the result of Decatur's tragic death by duel.

Stephen Decatur hailed from a family of Maryland seafarers and distinguished himself in the American Navy. In 1803, he was given command of his first ship, and he earned fame for his exploits at sea. He married the beautiful Susan Wheeler, daughter of the mayor of Norfolk, Virginia.

The seeds of his death were sown in 1807, by the actions of Commodore James Barron, the commander of the U.S. frigate *Chesapeake.* At that time, provocative confrontations still occurred between American and British ships, the result of lingering hostility from the War of Independence. In one such incident, the British frigate *Leopold* fired a shot across the bow of

Stephen Decatur. Painting by Gilbert Stuart. Courtesy Independence National Historical Park.

the *Chesapeake.* Barron seized the opportunity to board the *Leopold* and take into custody four sailors whom the British charged were deserters. Barron was court-martialed for not securing permission for such action. Decatur was a member of the naval commission that voted to suspend Barron for five years. The incident was instrumental in the outbreak of the War of 1812. While Barron sat out the war on the sidelines, Decatur, named the new commander of the *Chesapeake,* went on to greater glory.

Following the end of the war, the Decaturs moved to Washington, where they basked in the admiration of the capital's high society. Their Lafayette Square house, designed by the prominent architect Benjamin Latrobe, was the setting of elegant parties.

Barron, meanwhile, nursed an increasing hatred of Decatur. He was reinstated in the Navy at half-pay, and was always passed over for promotion. He was not given another ship to command. He mounted numerous personal attacks on Decatur, until the latter was reluctantly pressed into a duel.

According to legend, the Decaturs hosted a party in their home on March 13, 1820, the eve of the duel.

Decatur was said to be depressed, as though he sensed his imminent death. From his first-floor bedroom window, he stared out gloomily over his estate.

The next morning, he arose before dawn and went with his friend, William Bainbridge, to the appointed dueling place, a field near Bladensburg, Maryland. Pacing off, Decatur and Barron fired almost simultaneously at the count of two. Barron fell first, wounded in the hip; then Decatur fell, mortally wounded in the right side. Decatur was an excellent shot, and it is said that he deliberately avoided killing Barron; perhaps he believed the other would only wound him as well.

Decatur was taken back to his home to die. Susan was so distraught that she could not bring herself to look at him. His burial with full military honors did nothing to assuage her profound grief, and she could not stand to remain in the house where they had been so happy together.

A year after Decatur's death, his apparition was seen late one night, looking out sadly from the bedroom window where he had stood on the eve of his death. The window was walled up, but the ghost continued to return, as though it was loathe to be separated from the elegant house and grounds. The ghost sometimes was reported slipping out the back door early in the morning, black box under one arm, just as Decatur had done on the morning of the fateful duel. In addition, sounds of a woman weeping—said to be the ghost of Susan Decatur—have been heard in the house.

Decatur House is now a museum.

Further reading:
Alexander, John. *Ghosts: Washington's Most Famous Ghost Stories*. Arlington, Va.: Washington Book Trading Co., 1988.

demon detector See MAHER, MICHAELEEN CONSTANCE.

demon queller In Chinese and Japanese folklore, a fierce demigod hero dedicated to saving others from evil demons. He is large and bearded and wields an enormous sword. The origins of the demon queller date to the eighth century during the T'ang dynasty in China, when he is said to have appeared to Emperor Ming-huang in a dream.

In the dream, a demon broke into the royal chambers, stole the emperor's jade flute and his favorite consort's perfume bag, and began dancing around the palace. Just as the emperor was about to summon his guards, a large, bearded man appeared, snatched up the goblin, poked out its eyes and ate it. The stranger said he was Chunk K'uei, a scholar who

had committed suicide approximately 150 years earlier. He had failed his exams and had smashed his head against the palace steps. The Emperor Kao-tsu had graciously granted his corpse an official burial, and out of gratitude, Chung K'uei had sworn to rid the world of demons and suppress all evil.

Emperor Ming-huang might have forgotten his dream, had not it been mysteriously painted by Wu Tao-tzu, the greatest artist of the entire T'ang dynasty. Acting independently and without knowledge of the dream, Wu Tao-tzu recorded the demon queller exactly as the emperor had envisioned it. The emperor was so impressed that he awarded the artist 100 taels of gold.

The demon queller became a popular figure in Chinese folklore. He was adopted by the Japanese, who call him Shoki, as early as the 12th century. Early artists of both nations portrayed him as a fearsome-looking man subduing writhing demons. By the late 18th century, Shoki became associated with the Boy's Festival, which occurs on the fifth day of the fifth month of the lunar year (May 5), and is celebrated by all families with male children under seven years of age. The carp, which represents strength and virility, is the major symbol of the festival. The Boy's Festival also is feared for the presence of evil spirits, bad luck and poisonous insects. Shoki was adopted as a masculine, amuletic symbol for driving these evil influences away. Images of the demon queller were painted on banners to be hung outside the homes of families with young, vulnerable sons. In the 19th century, Shoki images began to appear inside homes as well.

An amusing side to the demon queller also exists. He is sometimes portrayed as a comical figure who does not frighten demons and occasionally is bested by them. In Chinese art, he has been depicted as a drunkard who must be helped along by a retinue of ghosts and goblins. By the 19th century, Japanese artists were fond of showing the demon queller being quelled himself by beautiful courtesans.

Further reading:
Addis, Stephen, ed. *Japanese Ghosts & Demons: Art of the Supernatural*. New York: George Braziller, 1985.

demons Various kinds of spirits, both good and evil, which allegedly have the ability to intervene in the affairs of humankind.

In Christianity, demons are evil and are the minions of Satan. Their sole purpose is to tempt and torment people and lead them into sin. The gods and goddesses of pagan religions became demons in Christianity. In other religions, demons can be either good or evil or have a dual nature.

Demons drowning a monk in the Tiber. After a 13th-century Italian manuscript.

The term "demon" means "replete with wisdom" and is derived from the Greek term DAIMON, which means "divine power," "fate" or "god." Daimons were rather like guardian spirits to the Greeks.

Religions have classified and organized demons into hierarchies. The *Testament of Solomon*, which appeared between 100 and 400 A.D., lists the names and functions of various Hebrew, Greek, Assyrian, Babylonian, Egyptian and perhaps Persian demons. Solomon controlled his demons, called *djinn*, with his magic ring. Ceremonial magic rituals for the summoning and control of demons continue to be practiced worldwide in modern times.

Christian demonologists of the 16th and 17th centuries devised elaborate organizational schemes of demons; for example, Johann Weyer estimated that there were 7,405,926 demons serving under 72 princes of hell. Jewish demonologies also are complex. One class of demons is the night terror, female demons that attack sleeping men, children and women in childbed to suck them of their vitality and blood (see OLD HAG; VAMPIRE).

Demons are often blamed for a host of ills and misfortunes, and in many cultures are routinely exorcised (see CULT OF THE ZAR; SHAMANISM). In Catholic Christianity, demonic possession, in which demons battle for control of a soul, are addressed by formal exorcism rites dating back to 1614.

It is widely believed that sex with demons is possible, albeit unpleasant or horrific. The offspring of a human-demon union usually are monstrous in folklore. Some of the night terror demons also are sexual molesters. In the Middle Ages, Christian authorities put forth the beliefs that sex with demons was a sign of witchcraft. A succubus, or demon masquerading as a voluptuous woman, molested men, while an incubus, a demon masquerading as a man, molested women. Though sterile, the incubi were said to be able to impregnate women with semen collected from the nocturnal emissions of men. Possession cases of the period commonly involved sexual molestation; it is possible that sexual repressions (especially among nuns, who seemed susceptible to possession) were more a factor than actual demonic forces. Some poltergeist cases, even in modern times, feature demonic sexual molestation (see SMURL HAUNTING).

Further reading:

Cavendish, Richard. *The Powers of Evil*. New York: G.P. Putnam's Sons, 1975.

Ebon, Martin. *The Devil's Bride, Exorcism: Past and Present*. New York: Harper & Row, 1974.

Guiley, Rosemary Ellen. *The Encyclopedia of Witches and Witchcraft*. New York: Facts On File, 1989.

depossession   See RELEASEMENT.

Dickie Skull   See SCREAMING SKULLS.

Dieppe Raid Case   Reports of the hearing of ghostly sounds of a bloody World War II air and sea battle fought near Dieppe, France. The case, documented and examined by psychical researchers, attained fame in the 1950s. It is considered to be an example of paranormal collective auditory hallucinations.

The case was reported by two Englishwomen on holiday at Puys, near Dieppe, in late July and early August 1951. The women, identified pseudonymously in reports as Dorothy Norton and her sister-in-law Agnes Norton, stayed in a house that during World War II had been occupied by German soldiers. Dorothy Norton was accompanied by her two children and a nurse.

On the morning of August 4, at about 4:20, the women were awakened by loud noises that started suddenly and at first sounded like a storm arising at sea. The sounds ebbed and flowed, and then they could distinctly hear sounds of gunfire, shellfire, divebombers, and men shouting and crying out. The women got up and went out on their balcony, where they could not actually see the sea, but they detected nothing that could account for the noises. Meanwhile, the noises came in from the direction of the sea, loud and intense, and still seemed like gunfire, divebombing and voices shouting. The roaring abruptly stopped at 4:50 A.M. and resumed at about 5:07 A.M. The noise became so intense that the Norton women were amazed that other occupants of the house were not awakened. As the sky grew light, they heard a rifle shot on the beach below. The noise became more distinct as the sound of divebombing planes that came in waves. It stopped abruptly at 5:40 A.M. The noise resumed at 5:50 A.M., not as loud, but still sounding distinctly like planes. The noise died away at 6 A.M. and resumed at 6:20 A.M., much fainter. The women heard nothing at all after 6:55 A.M.

Both women knew that a battle had taken place in the vicinity during the war, but neither knew the details. They consulted a French guidebook and, during the experience, sat and read the account of the battle. They concluded they might have heard ghostly sounds of the real battle, and agreed to write independent versions of their experience. With a small discrepancy in time (probably due to a difference in watches), their reports matched. Later, they asked several persons if they, too, had been disturbed during the night, but received negative answers.

The sounds bore a remarkable correspondence to the fierce battle that took place in the Dieppe environs on August 19, 1942, at precisely the times experienced by the Nortons. The Royal Regiment of Canada launched a pre-dawn assault on German forces from Puys, about 1.5 miles east of Dieppe, to Berneval, about 5 miles east, to Purville, about 2.5 miles west of Dieppe and to Varengeville about 3 miles further west. Flank landings were scheduled to make surprise arrivals at 4:50 A.M. to destroy coastal batteries. At about 3:47, the Canadians encountered a small German convoy off the coast, and the two forces exchanged fire until after 4 A.M. The Canadians arrived at Dieppe a few minutes late, at 5:07. At 5:12 A.M., destroyers started to bombard Dieppe with shells, and at 5:15 Hurricane planes attacked, at Puys as well as Dieppe. At 5:20 A.M., main landings at Dieppe were made, covered by a bombardment of shells from destroyers and by heavy air attack. A second wave went ashore at about 5:45 A.M. At about 5:50 A.M., new air fighters from England arrived, and German planes were in the sky as well.

The Germans, who were able to man their beach defenses, waited until the landing craft nearly touched shore before opening heavy fire with rifles, machine guns and howitzers. The Canadians were trapped by a high sea wall. Within two or three hours, the Royal Regiment of Canada was nearly destroyed. Thirty-four officers and 727 men were killed. Two officers and 65 men, half of whom were wounded, were rescued and taken away, and another 16 officers and 264 men were captured by the Germans.

A comparison of the Nortons' experience with the phases of the Dieppe raid showed consistencies between times and the changes in the noises they heard, with a few exceptions. The information in the French guidebook was not specific enough for them to have subconsciusly matched their description to the real event after reading about it.

The Nortons, interviewed by psychical researchers G.W. Lambert and Kathleen Gray, came across as well balanced individuals who displayed no tendency to embellish their accounts, and no desire to prove they had had a paranormal experience. Dorothy Norton said she had been awakened by similar, but fainter, noises on the morning of July 30, but had not mentioned the experience to Agnes (who had not heard the noises) because she had not wanted to spoil the holiday with something mysterious.

Skeptics proposed other explanations for the experience, such as surf sounds, noise from commercial airplanes flying a nearby route across the English Channel, or noise from a dredger. Agnes Norton had served in the women's Royal Naval Service during the war, however, and she probably would have been able to distinguish the sounds of the sea and of a single commercial aircraft, had those been the natural sources. The dredger was not in operation at the times corresponding to the Nortons' experience.

Both women were familiar with the VERSAILLES HAUNTING, a similar case in which two Englishwomen on holiday in France felt they had paranormal experiences in encountering the ghostly past. Skeptics also suggested that this familiarity may have subconsciously primed the Nortons to have their own experience. The possibility is remote, since the Norton women were not previously acquainted with the details of the Dieppe case.

See also APPARITION; RETROCOGNITION.

Further reading:
Hastings, Robert J. "An Examination of the Dieppe Raid Case." *Journal of the Society for Psychical Research* 45 (June 1969:55–63.
Lambert, G.W. "Comments on Mr Hastings' Examination of the Dieppe Raid Case." *Journal of the Society for Psychical Research* 45 (June 1969):63–66.
Lambert, G.W., and Kathleen Gray. "The Dieppe Raid Case: A Collective Auditory Hallucination." *Journal of the Society for Psychical Research* 36 (May–June 1952):607–18.

Di Manes See MANES.

direct voice phenomenon The independent speaking of a spirit without using a medium's vocal apparatus. Instead, the voice issues from a point in space near the medium, or, as was common during early Spiritualist seances, from a trumpet (q.v.) that appeared to float about the seance room. The trumpet allegedly acted as a condenser of psychic energy and an amplifier of the spirits' voices. Without a trumpet or megaphone, the spirits were said to construct an artificial larynx that was activated by ectoplasm (q.v.) exuded by the medium.

Most early Spiritualist mediums employed direct voice communication at one time or another; some specialized in it. Direct voice was introduced in the 1850s by the spirit control, John KING, who spoke through a tin horn at the seances of Jonathan Koons, an Ohio farmer. Koons said he had been instructed by a band of spirits to build a Spirit Room and provide fiddles, guitar, drums, a horn, tambourine, triangle and other instruments. During seances put on by him and his wife, a virtual cacophony of noise erupted from the instruments as they sailed about the room. Besides King, other "unearthly" voices sang songs in an undistinguishable language. King also spoke in direct voice through the mediums the DAVENPORT BROTHERS.

Medium William Stainton MOSES described an out-of-body experience in which he saw a "voice box," or artificial larynx, near the ceiling of a seance room. And Mina Stinson CRANDON, known as "Margery," reportedly had an ectoplasmic mass on her shoulder, connected to her ear and nostrils, that enabled her control, Walter, to speak directly.

Psychical researchers often suspected mediums of speaking through trumpets themselves surreptitiously in the dark, or of using ventriloquism. If investigators suspected the medium used a trumpet, they examined the contents of the spirit communication and considered the similarity in voices. As for ventriloquism, it is not possible to throw one's voice to a distant location across a room. Some mediums were tested by being asked to hold water in their mouths while the spirits spoke. Sometimes, the medium and a spirit spoke simultaneously, or several spirits spoke simultaneously from different locations.

Direct voice is rare in modern mediumship. Most mediums purportedly receive mental impressions from spirits, which they relay in their own voices. Or, they allow spirits to use their vocal chords.

See also FLINT, LESLIE.

Further reading:
Brown, Slater. *The Heyday of Spiritualism.* New York: Hawthorn Books, 1970.
Fodor, Nandor. *An Encyclopedia of Psychic Science.* Secaucus, N.J.: Citadel Press, 1966. First published 1933.
Godwin, John. *Occult America.* New York: Doubleday, 1972.

dolphin In classical mythology, a carrier of the souls of the dead to the afterlife world. In Christian myth, the dolphin represents resurrection and sal-

vation, and also represents the Christian Church being guided by Christ.

domovik (also domovoj, domovoy) In Russian folklore, a household spirit that resides in every home. The *domovik* traditionally is the ancestral founder of the family, and moves with it from house to house. He is portrayed as an old man with a gray beard, and is always referred to as "he," "himself" or "grandfather,"—never by a personal name.

The *domovik* lives behind the stove. When a family moves, fire from the old stove is carried to the new, where it is lit to welcome the *domovik* into his new quarters. The *domovik* watches over family members, keeps hostile spirits from entering the house, and, like the brownie, does household chores. But if family members displease him, he makes poltergeist-like noise disturbances. His harshest punishment is to burn down the house.

There are other types of *domoviks*, each of which has its own small domain: the *chlevnik*, who lives in the barn; the *bannik*, who lives in the bathroom; and the *ovinnik*, who lives in the kitchen.

Further reading:
Leach, Maria, and Jerome Fried, eds. *Funk & Wagnalls Standard Dictionary of Folklore, Mythology, and Legend.* San Francisco: Harper & Row, 1979.

doors Various superstitions exist concerning doors and ghosts of the dead. It is widely believed to be unlucky to enter a house through the back door; this perhaps is one reason why corpses traditionally are carried out through the back. However, in certain areas the belief is the reverse: the corpse should be carried out the front door, lest other deaths occur in the household.

There are many charms and spells involving doors that are intended to keep ghosts from entering homes, or to force them out of homes. A circle chalked on doors, or patterns chalked on doorsteps, are believed to prevent ghosts—and the Devil and evil spirits—from entering. The markings must be unbroken and joined together. Slamming a door several times in a row catches a ghost between the door and the frame and forces it to leave the premises. A Norfolk, England charm calls for unhinging the door, turning it around and rehanging it.

Further reading:
Opie, Iona, and Moira Tatem. *A Dictionary of Superstitions.* Oxford: Oxford University Press, 1989.

doppelganger See DOUBLE.

Doris Fischer Case One of the notable cases of alleged spirit possession investigated by James

H. HYSLOP, a psychical researcher and an early president of the AMERICAN SOCIETY FOR PSYCHICAL RESEARCH (ASPR).

The case of Doris Fischer, whose real name was Brittia L. Fritschle, was first reported by Walter Franklin PRINCE, an Episcopal minister and psychologist. Fischer suffered an extreme traumatic incident as a child at the hands of her abusive and alcoholic father, and had exhibited multiple personalities since she was three in 1892. She also displayed striking psychic tendencies and was able to foresee her mother's sudden illness and death. Fischer and her siblings continued to live with their father, but she retreated more and more into the personalities of "sick Doris" and the wicked "Margaret." Fischer was eventually adopted by Prince and his wife. Prince was familiar with the newly recognized syndrome of multiple personality, and he and his wife helped Fischer to regain some normalcy.

Hyslop became involved in the case in 1914. For years, he had postulated that some psychotic states were caused—or at least aggravated—by spirit influence. Although not a Spiritualist per se, Hyslop sympathized with the cult's psychic "cures" and believed that spiritual communication was just as important as physiological therapy. With that in mind, Hyslop took Fischer to sit with medium Minnie Soule, hoping to find and eliminate the possessive spirits who were destroying the girl's peace of mind.

During the seances, Soule communicated lengthy messages to Fischer from her mother. The medium also heard from the spirit of Count Cagliostro. Hyslop did not like Cagliostro's presence and encouraged him to leave the seances and Fischer. Later researchers speculate that "Cagliostro" represented sexual mores that both Hyslop and Fischer suppressed but secretly desired.

Next, Soule heard from the spirit of Richard HODGSON, a former leading member of the ASPR and the SOCIETY FOR PSYCHICAL RESEARCH (SPR), who confirmed Hyslop's suspicions of spirit influence and promised to help all he could. Finally, Soule received messages from a young Indian spirit calling herself "Minnehaha," or "Laughing Water." Hyslop was skeptical of such a spirit, since Minnehaha is the heroine of Henry Wadsworth Longfellow's poem *Hiawatha*. But he went along, impressed with Minnehaha's knowledge of Fischer's case and her claims that she had caused many of Doris's problems. After further communications, Hyslop came to believe that the personality "Margaret" was not an offshoot of Doris's mind but a possessing spirit herself.

Hyslop asked why spirits hurt Fischer, and was told by Soule's communicators that they were evil influences. The controls also told Hyslop that Fischer's case was no different than hundreds of other instances of insanity and multiple personality that could easily be cured through psychic exorcism. By 1915, Hyslop was convinced that Fischer was possessed, and he wrote of his experiences with her in his book, *Life After Death* (1918).

Hyslop believed that Cagliostro was the leader of Fischer's possessing spirits, and he exorcised the count. Whatever other spirits remained were ineffectual, and Hyslop quit the case in the hopes that Fischer had been cured. She returned with the Princes to California and resumed a normal life for a while. But she never recovered, finally dying in a mental hospital after years of dealing with her various personalities and psychic disturbances.

The Fischer case was Hyslop's last major investigation, although he never lost interest in the possibility of spirit possession. He reportedly believed his health had been threatened in 1919 by a spirit he was trying to exorcise through sessions in Boston with Soule, and he was ill for several months. He believed that the existence of discarnate spirits had been proved scientifically, and he dismissed those who did not agree.

Further reading:

Anderson, Roger I., ed. "Autobiographical Fragment of James Hervey Hyslop Part III." *The Journal of Religion and Psychical Research* 9 (July 1986):145–60.

Rogo, D. Scott. *The Infinite Boundary*. New York: Dodd, Mead & Co., 1987.

double   The apparition of a living person that is an exact duplicate, even including details of dress. Doubles fall into two general categories: death omens and a type of possible out-of-body projection or BILOCATION, done either consciously or unconsciously.

The belief that doubles are death omens flourishes in the folklore of Britain and Europe. Doubles are known by a variety of names, including *wraith*, FETCH, *waff*, *fye*, *swarth* and *task*. In Germany doubles are called *Doppelganger*, or "double-goer." As a death omen, doubles typically are seen by others in a distant location just as the individual in question is about to die or has died. The double may appear real, or have a filmy, ghostly look about it (see APPARITIONS). In some rare cases, individuals see their own doubles shortly before they die. Percy Bysshe Shelley saw his double shortly before he drowned. Catherine of Russia saw her double seated upon her own throne, and ordered her guards to fire on it.

Not all cases of doubles are harbingers of death; some seem to be projections of consciousness that somehow assume visible form. Mystics and adepts are said to have the ability to project themselves, or bilocate, at will. Others who project their doubles may not be aware they are doing so. Many cases collected by psychical researchers remain unexplained (see ARRIVAL CASES; RODGERS, LOUIS).

The belief that the spirit or soul exists in a visible double is ancient and widespread, particularly among animistic societies. The Maori believe that the double cannot be distinguished from the real person unless it reveals itself by becoming filmy. The Melanesians, Iroquois and others believe that the soul is a reflection of the body. The Nyassa believe likewise, but also believe that the double can only be seen in dreams.

Further reading:

Gurney, Edmund, Frederic W.H. Myers, and Frank Podmore. *Phantasms of the Living*. London: Kegan Paul, Trench, Trubner & Co. Ltd., 1918.

Leach, Maria, and Jerome Fried, eds. *Funk & Wagnalls Standard Dictionary of Folklore, Mythology, and Legend*. San Francisco: Harper & Row, 1979.

Spence, Lewis. *The Encyclopedia of the Occult*. London: Bracken Books, 1988. Reprint.

Doyle, Sir Arthur Conan (1858–1930) Remembered more for his brilliant detective character Sherlock Holmes, Sir Arthur Conan Doyle was an ardent Spiritualist who tirelessly defended Spiritualism and the legitimacy of mediums. Unlike Holmes, who was shrewd and skeptical, Doyle believed in virtually anyone or anything that claimed to give evidence of survival or life on the Other Side.

Born in 1858, Doyle grew up in the sunshine of the British Empire. He was sublimely self-confident about the rightness of things—white, English, upper class—and his ability to influence events. He was tall; he was opinionated; and he was a successful physician. He loved England, his home and family, and the ordered beauty of life under the reigns of Victoria and Edward. Doyle also was a gifted storyteller.

His first exposure to the paranormal came while he was a physician at Southsea in 1885–88. Doyle participated in table-turning seances at the home of his patient General Drayson, a mathematician, and was intrigued but unconvinced. The subject piqued his interest enough, however, to lead Doyle into further study and membership in the SOCIETY FOR PSYCHICAL RESEARCH.

After 30 years of study, Doyle wholeheartedly embraced the faith of Spiritualism in 1916. His second wife, Jean, lost her brother Malcolm at the World War I battle of Mons that year, and soon thereafter she began automatic writing. The Doyles felt their mission so strongly that they began lecturing on Spiritualism; thousands of bereaved trying to contact fathers, sons and brothers lost in World War I only helped their cause. In 1918 Doyle's eldest son, Kingsley, fell at the battle of the Somme. Doyle was bereaved but sincerely believed Kingsley lived in the beyond. He reported that Kingsley communicated with him and encouraged his spiritual work.

Doyle's lectures, first in Great Britain and then in Australia and New Zealand, followed the publication of his books *The New Revelation* (1918) and *The Vital Message* (1919). For the next 12 years the Doyles traveled ceaselessly, lecturing in America, South Africa, England and northern Europe. He drew large crowds eager to see the famous novelist and find some comfort in his words. And Doyle never failed to entertain as well as instruct. His love for detail sketched a picture of the Other Side as happy, well-ordered and busy, rather like Sussex. Doyle claimed to be uninterested in physical phenomena, but he actively supported manifestations obtained through spirit photography and the search for proof of fairies.

Fairy lore had interested Doyle all his life. In 1920, he was excited to receive a letter from a Spiritualist friend, Felicia Scatcherd, informing him that the existence of fairies had been proven with photographs taken in Yorkshire.

Doyle asked a Theosophist friend, Edward L. Gardner, to investigate. Gardner examined the photographs, which showed diminutive female figures dressed fashionably in Paris gowns, with transparent wings and the traditional double pipe of elves. The photographers were two young girls, Elsie Wright and her cousin Frances Griffiths, who claimed they were able to see the fairies, as well as a gnome who did not want his photograph taken. They said they had taken the photos in July and September of 1917 in the countryside near their Yorkshire village of Cottingley. The bodies of the fairies were white, they said, and the wings were pale green, mauve and pink.

Though the photographs looked suspiciously faked (they were actually cutouts taken from an illustration in *Princess Mary's Gift Book* of 1915), Gardner pronounced them genuine and sent them to Doyle. Doyle asked opinions from the Eastman Co. and from Kodak, but took Gardner's word as the truth. He was further swayed by the testimony of his friend Geoffrey Hodson, a clairvoyant, who said he had seen fairies in the Cottingley area. When Elsie and Frances produced three more photographs (shot by themselves with no witnesses), Doyle was elated.

He published an article about the fairies in the Christmas 1920 issue of *The Strand Magazine*, complete with illustrations. Other fairy-seekers deluged Doyle with "genuine" photographs, but he saw none that had the charm of the Yorkshire sprites. Over and above Doyle's desire to believe, he refused to consider the possibility that girls age 16 and 10, so innocent in their youth, could hatch professional trickery.

In 1922, Doyle published *The Coming of the Fairies*, containing a full account of the girls' encounters and including chapters giving other fairy evidence and the Theosophic case for fairy sightings. He opined that more authentic fairy sightings would be documented. He then left for Australia on a lecture tour. Upon his return, he found himself the laughingstock of the press on both sides of the Atlantic. The photographs had been widely circulated, examined, and deemed false. Doyle finally admitted that perhaps he was the victim of what might be the greatest hoax in history.

It was not until long after Doyle's death that the Wright sisters finally admitted their hoax. In the early 1980s, they stated that they had faked the photographs to get back at adults who had chided them for saying they played with fairies. As girls, they had actually seen fairies, they said. The sisters said that when Doyle became enthusiastically involved, they had been unwilling to embarrass him by admitting that the photos were fake.

Nineteen twenty-two was also the year that Doyle and his friend Harry HOUDINI argued over a seance. Houdini had met the Doyle family after a performance at the Hippodrome in Brighton, England in 1920, and the two families had struck up a friendship. When the Doyles toured America that year, they asked Houdini and his wife Bess to join them in Atlantic City for a short vacation. While there, Doyle told Houdini that his wife Jean, who wrote automatically, felt she could get the magician in touch with his beloved mother, a feat he desperately wanted.

The only sitters in addition to Houdini were Doyle and his wife. Lady Doyle soon was seized with the spirit and began writing furiously. The manuscript was full of messages to "her boy," thanking the Doyles for their intercession and telling Houdini of her love and desire to be with him. Houdini, always the skeptic but wanting to believe, was moved but unconvinced.

He had good reasons for his skepticism. Lady Doyle had started the manuscript with a cross at the top of the page, and Mrs. Weiss (Houdini's real name) was Jewish. The writing was in good English, and Houdini's Hungarian mother spoke broken English. And, most telling to Houdini, the seance was held on his mother's birthday, June 17, and she never

mentioned it. Houdini denied that he had received true communication, and the Doyles never forgave him. The friendship broke under the strain.

By 1924, Doyle and Houdini angrily opposed each other on the question of Mina Stinson CRANDON's mediumship. Crandon, alias Margery, was investigated by a committee of the *Scientific American* to verify the truth of her talents. As a member of the committee, Houdini was outraged that the rest of the group had examined Margery without him and were ready to endorse her. He proposed a series of tests to find her fraudulent but ended up chastised for his ungentlemanly behavior. Doyle called him a bounder and cad and supported Margery without question. Complicating the situation was Doyle's conviction that Houdini, an acknowledged medium-baiter, was himself the world's greatest medium, unable to perform many of his escape stunts without dematerializing his body and then rematerializing. (See MATERIALIZATION.)

Fans of the logical Sherlock Holmes have asked how his creator could be so credulous. Part of the problem was Doyle's supreme self-confidence, and part was his need to believe regardless of the evidence. As time went on, Doyle regarded himself as the messiah of Spiritualism and prophet of the world's future; indeed, he was nicknamed the movement's St. Paul. Consequently, anyone suggesting he might be mistaken was regarded as an ignorant fool.

Not long after Lady Doyle began automatic writing, she heard from an Arabian spirit control named Pheneas, who warned against the evil nature of the world. In 1923, Pheneas told the Doyles the world was sinking fast into a slough of evil and materialism, and that God must intercede to save it. To that end, Pheneas said a team of spiritual scientists were at work connecting vibrating lines of seismic power that would trigger earthquakes and tidal waves, signaling Armageddon. Doyle's task was to prepare people's minds for the revelation.

By 1925, Pheneas was outlining the specifics of the upheaval. Central Europe would be engulfed by earthquakes and storms, followed by a great celestial light. Russia would be destroyed, Africa flooded and Brazil razed by some sort of eruption. America would suffer another civil war. And the Vatican, described as a sink of iniquity, would be swept away. England would be the world's beacon (ideas similar to those of Empire), flashing especially strong from the power station of cosmic energy surrounding the Doyle home. Christ would appear there before making plans for the Second Coming.

Doyle kept a notebook of prophesied events, noting that he would pass over with his entire family after the conflagration. But 1925 passed with no extraordinary upheaval. Shortly before his death, Doyle began to wonder if he and his family had been the butt of a great joke on humans by members of the Other Side, since none of Pheneas' predictions had come about.

Doyle died on July 7, 1930. On the July 13th, his family and friends held a reception at the Albert Hall in London, leaving an empty chair for the old fighter. Medium Estelle Roberts claimed she could see him and passed on a message the family felt was evidential. Others have also claimed communications; the most noteworthy was received by Eileen J. GARRETT that same year.

Further reading:

Brandon, Ruth. *The Spiritualists.* New York: Alfred A. Knopf, 1983.

Doyle, Sir Arthur Conan. *The Coming of the Fairies.* London: Hodder & Stoughton, 1922.

———. *The Edge of the Unknown.* New York: Berkley Medallion Books, 1968. First published by G.P. Putnam's Sons, 1930.

Fodor, Nandor. *An Encyclopaedia of Psychic Science.* Secaucus, N.J.: The Citadel Press, 1966. First published 1933.

Higham, Charles. *The Adventures of Conan Doyle: The Life of the Creator of Sherlock Holmes.* New York: W.W. Norton & Co., Inc., 1976.

Houdini, Harry. *Houdini: A Magician Among the Spirits.* New York: Arno Press, 1972.

Mysteries of the Unknown: Spirit Summonings. Alexandria, Va.: Time-Life Books, 1989.

Drake, Sir Francis (1540–96) English navigator, who, in legend, is reputed to have been a wizard. He supposedly remains in eternal slumber, ready to spring once again to life whenever Britain is in danger. Few historical figures in Britain have accumulated so many legends as has Sir Francis Drake.

Drake, a native of Devon, was the first Englishman to circumnavigate the globe, between 1570 and 1580, in his ship the *Golden Hind.* He fought Spanish vessels and settlements, and navigated the Strait of Magellan. He pillaged North and South America and returned to Queen Elizabeth I in 1580 with great treasures. For his deeds, he was knighted.

In 1588, King Philip II of Spain launched the Spanish Armada to invade England. The 130 ships, bearing some 30,000 men, were delayed by storms. When they met the English fleet, of which Drake was an admiral, they were severely battered and scattered. The Armada fled north, sailing around Scotland and Ireland, where it was buffeted by more storms; it finally returned to Spain, with only half of its original force. It was said among the Spaniards that Drake possessed a magic mirror that enabled him to see ships in all parts of the world.

Sir Francis Drake.

According to legend, Drake sold his soul to the Devil in exchange for prowess at sea. In concert with Devon witches, he cast spells that raised the storms against the Spanish Armada. The ghosts of those witches are said to still haunt Devil's Point, the headland overlooking the entrance to Devonport. The Devil was so pleased with Drake that he built him a house at Buckland Abbey in only three days.

Drake also reputedly used his magical skill to give Plymouth a new water supply: he said a spell over a Dartmoor spring and commanded the water to follow him to Plymouth. Still another legend tells of how Drake sat whittling one day on the cliff of Plymouth Hoe. Each wood chip that fell into the water sprang into a fully armed ship.

Drake fell in love with Elizabeth Sydenham, a noblewoman. Her family refused to allow her to marry a commoner. Drake retreated to sea. Elizabeth waited, then grew weary and became betrothed to another man. At their wedding, according to legend, a huge cannonball fell at the feet of Elizabeth—fired from Drake's cannon from across the world. She cancelled the wedding. In 1585, she and Drake were married. The "cannonball" is identified as a football-sized meteorite now kept at Coombe Sydenham House.

Despite his legendary magical powers, Drake eventually was defeated by the Spanish in the West Indies in 1595. In 1596, he died aboard his ship off Puerto Bello, Panama. As he lay dying, he ordered his drum, which he had taken around the world with him, to be sent back to his home, Buckland Abbey in Devon. He said that if anyone beat on the drum when his beloved England was in danger, he would return and lead his country to victory. In this, Drake joins other legendary national heroes such as King Arthur and WILD EDRIC, who will return from the dead to defend their country.

The story about Drake's drum has varied, and the drum has since been said to beat of its own accord whenever the country is threatened. It reportedly was heard in the West Country in 1914 at the start of World War I, and it was said to have beaten again when the German fleet officially surrendered in 1919. In the latter instance, a single drum beat was heard aboard British ships as they closed around the Germans ships. A search was made, but no unauthorized drummer was found. Sailors were convinced it was the sound of Drake's drum, celebrating the victory. The drum also was reported to have been heard at the start of the World War II.

Drake also appears in folklore as the leader of the WILD HUNT, a spectral night train in pursuit of lost souls.

It is believed by some that Drake reincarnated in other British admirals, including Viscount Horatio Nelson (1758–1805).

Further reading:
Folklore, Myths and Legends of Britain. London: Reader's Digest Assoc., 1977.
Guiley, Rosemary Ellen. *The Encyclopedia of Witches and Witchcraft*. New York: Facts On File, 1989.
Maple, Eric. *The Realm of Ghosts*. New York: A.S. Barnes & Co., 1964.
Russell, Jeffrey B. *A History of Witchcraft*. London: Thames and Hudson, 1980.

drop-in communicator An unknown entity who appears unexpectedly and uninvited at a seance. Drop-in communicators have provided fascinating data to psychical researchers to support the contention that mediums do communicate with spirits of the dead and are not merely manifesting secondary personalities. The potential importance of drop-ins was recognized as early as 1874 by William Stainton MOSES, an English medium, and a few years later by early English psychical researchers such as Frederic W.H. MYERS, a founder of the SOCIETY FOR PSYCHICAL RESEARCH (SPR).

True drop-ins are unknown to both medium and sitters. Thus, they are evidence that contradicts the theory of "SUPER-ESP," which holds that mediums obtain their information from clairvoyance of published sources and telepathy of facts from the minds of sitters, not from discarnate entities. In the best cases, drop-ins provide information which has never been in print in a public source, which is known to, and can be verified by, a small circle of family or friends.

Some drop-ins, through automatic speech, speak in foreign languages unknown to the medium. There is no known way for knowledge of a foreign language to be transmitted by telepathy. In rare cases, the appearance of a drop-in is accompanied by physical phenomena such as table-tilting, rappings, mysterious lights, apports, scents, and strange whistles, whisperings and breathing.

Some drop-ins drop out as quickly as they appear, showing up once or twice without making their motive clear. Most cases are inconclusive.

Many drop-ins appear with a motive. Like lonely people who finally find a receptive audience, they love to talk about themselves in their most recent life, and reveal personal information that may be verified upon research. One of these was "Harry Stockbridge" (a pseudonym used by investigators to protect the family of the deceased), a spirit who dropped in on the Ouija seances of a group in Cambridge, England between 1950 and 1952. Stockbridge said he had been a second lieutenant in the Northumberland Fusiliers and had died on July 14, 1916. He offered a physical description of himself, personality traits and other facts. His information was verified through old military records and interviews with surviving family members.

Some drop-ins do not want to talk about themselves, but are intent on accomplishing a mission. One such case was that of Runolfur RUNOLFSSON, a hard-drinking, rough-talking Icelander who dropped in on medium Hafsteinn Bjornsson in 1937, looking for his missing leg bone.

Another drop-in with a mission was Patience WORTH, who dropped in on Pearl Curran and a friend in 1913 as they used a Ouija board. The entity demurred to talk much about herself, but dictated through Curran a prodigious literary outpouring of novels and poetry.

The biggest hazard with drop-in communicators is unwitting self-deception on the part of the medium. One such case is that of English medium Margo Williams, whose first drop-in, "Jane," appeared in 1976; Williams eventually claimed to be visited by more than 100 drop-ins, including Mary Todd Lincoln. The Lincoln drop-in stated some minor errors about Abraham Lincoln; the same errors were later discovered in material at the local library, which Williams frequented.

Further reading:

Gauld, Alan. "A Series of Drop-in Communicators." *Proceedings of the Society for Psychical Research* 55 (July 1971):1966–72.

———. *Mediumship and Survival.* London: William Heinemann Ltd., 1982.

Stevenson, Ian. "A Communicator Unknown to Medium and Sitters." *Journal of the American Society for Psychical Research* 64 (January 1970):53–65.

Stevenson, Ian, and John Beloff. "An Analysis of Some Suspect Drop-in Communicators." *Journal of the Society for Psychical Research* 50 (September 1980):427–47.

Drummer of Cortachy   A poltergeist haunting of the Scottish Earls of Airlie, the Ogilvys, of Cortachy Castle. The ghostly drumming was said to presage the death of an Ogilvy.

The origin of the legend dates to medieval times. It was said that a messenger of a despised chieftain appeared at Cortachy Castle one day with an unpleasant message, and the Ogilvys had him stuffed into his drum and tossed over the castle battlements. Just before he perished, the drummer vowed to haunt the family ever afterward.

For hundreds of years, the family was haunted by ghostly drumming, always followed by a death in the family. Whenever the sound was heard, the family was stricken with terror wondering who would be the next to die, and when.

One of the most famous drumming incidents occurred at Christmas 1844, when a Miss Dalrymple was staying as a guest in the castle. The evening of her arrival, she was dressing for dinner when she heard the sound of music below her room. The music presently changed to the sound of drumming, but she could not see who was doing it. She asked the maid, who knew nothing. At dinner, Dalrymple inquired of her hosts, Lord and Lady Airlie, who was the drummer. To her astonishment, Lord Airlie turned pale and Lady Airlie looked upset. Lady Airlie explained the legend, adding that the last time the drumming had been heard, the Lord's first wife had subsequently died.

The next day, Dalrymple again heard the drumming, which spooked her so badly that she cut short her visit and left the castle.

Six months later, Lady Airlie died at Brighton, leaving behind a note that said she knew the drumming had been for her. It was speculated that she had brought about her own death to fulfill the curse.

On August 19, 1849 the ghostly drumming was again heard by an Englishman who was a guest of Lord Ogilvy, the heir to the Earldom of Airlie. The

A ghostly drummer, from Barham's Ingoldsby Legends.

guest was traveling across the moors en route to his hosts's shooting-box when he heard the faraway sound of band music, highlighted by drumming. He asked his Highlander guide about it, but the man said he heard nothing. Upon entering the shooting-box, the guest was informed that Lord Ogilvy had departed unexpectedly, upon news that his father, the ninth Earl of Airlie, was seriously ill in London. The next day, the earl died.

However, when the succeeding earl died in the Boer War in 1900, his death apparently was not presaged by drumming—or at least no one admitted to hearing it. The drummer has not been heard since.

Further reading:

Harper, Charles G. *Haunted Houses: Tales of the Supernatural With Some Accounts of Hereditary Curses and Family Legends.* Rev. and enlarged ed. London: Cecil Palmer, 1924.

Drummer of Tedworth   English poltergeist case for which a living agent, an irate man, took credit, and insinuated that his ability to cause the disturbances was due to witchcraft.

The case took place in 1661 in Tedworth, Wiltshire. In March of that year, an anonymous drummer began annoying the nearby town of Ludgarshall with his incessant drum beating. He demanded money from the bailiff with what appeared to be a counterfeit pass signed by a Colonel Ayliff and a Sir William Cawly. John Mompesson, who lived in Tedworth, complained of the noise and also declared the pass to be counterfeit. Mompesson had the man arrested and his drum, a demobilized roundhead, confiscated. The drummer confessed his fraud and begged for his drum back. Mompesson refused, saying that he would get his drum back if Colonel Ayliff vouched for him. The bailiff took the drum.

The drummer soon persuaded the constable to release him, and he left the area. In April, the bailiff sent the confiscated drum to Mompesson, who was about to leave on a trip to London. During his absence, violent poltergeist activity erupted in his house, terrifying his wife, children and servants. The first disturbances were drumming noises heard outside the house and on top of it, which then moved indoors to the room where the confiscated drum was kept.

The noises, joined with other disturbances, escalated and seemed to focus upon the children. Objects were moved about, rude animal snortings, pawings and noises were heard, disembodied human voices spoke, and the children were pestered in their beds. Objects also were thrown at people in the house, and terrible smells, including sulfur, wafted about. Drumming noises continued for days on end; after a short break, they would resume for days on end. The children and servants saw apparitions, and the younger children were levitated in their beds. Mompesson's manservant woke up one night to see a dark body with red, glaring eyes staring at him from the foot of the bed; the apparition soon vanished. The family scattered ash on the floor to attempt to identity the culprit; the next morning claw-like marks were found in the ashes, along with unintelligible letters and numerous circles.

The disturbances went on for more than two years. They created widespread interest and drew curious visitors. They also caused the family much distress: servants were difficult to retain, skeptics derided the family, and the pious proclaimed that they were being punished by God for wickedness. Some of the lesser phenomena—scratchings and animal purrings and pantings heard near the childrens' beds—were heard by Joseph Glanvil, who chronicled the case in *Sadiucismus Triumphatus* (1661). During Glanvil's visit, one morning his horse appeared to be exhausted, as though it had been ridden all night (see OLD HAG). It collapsed and died within days.

Other phenomena included glimmering lights that appeared in the children's bedroom; a disembodied voice that repeatedly cried, "a witch, a witch"; the chasing of a servant by a stick of wood, while another was held by an invisible force; the sounds of coins jingling; doors opening and shutting violently by

The Drummer of Tedworth, from Joseph Glanvil's Sadiucismus Triumphatus *(1661).*

themselves; footsteps and the rustling of invisible, silk-like clothing; lighted candles floating up the chimney; singing heard in the chimney; a horse found with its hind leg stuffed into its mouth so firmly that it took several men to pry it out with a lever; chamberpots emptied onto beds; a knife found in one bed; and pocket money mysteriously turned black. Through all this, the drum continued to beat.

Meanwhile, the drummer turned up in custody again and was tried and convicted for stealing. He was incarcerated at the Gloucester Gaol. He asked a visitor about news in Wiltshire. When the visitor said he had none, the drummer reportedly said, "Do you not hear of the drumming at a gentleman's house in Tedworth? That I do enough, I have plagued him (or to that purpose) and he shall never be quiet, til he hath made me satisfaction for taking away my drum." This remark earned the fellow a trial at Sarum on charges of witchcraft. He was "condemned to transportation," or made to leave the area. It was rumored that he raised storms and frightened seamen.

Despite his sentence, the drummer periodically returned to the area. As long as he was gone, the Mompesson house was quiet, but whenever he returned, the disturbances began again. It is not known if the Mompessons were plagued indefinitely.

Further reading:

Glanvil, Rev. Joseph. *Sadiucismus Triumphatus: Full and Plain Evidence Concerning Witches and Apparitions.* London, 1689. First published 1661.

Sitwell, Sacheverell. *Poltergeists: Fact or Fancy.* New York: Dorset Press, 1988. First published 1959.

dybbuk In Jewish folklore, an evil spirit or doomed soul that possesses a person body and soul, speaking through the person's mouth and causing such torment and anguish that another personality appears to manifest itself. Such evil spirits have existed in Judaism since the earliest times, but they were called evil *ibbur* (spirits) until the 17th century. At that time, the term "dybbuk" (also spelled dibbuk) was coined from the language of German and Polish Jews. It is an abbreviation of two phrases: *dibbuk me-ru'ah* ("a cleavage of an evil spirit"), and *dibbuk min ha-hizonim* ("dibbuk from the demonic side" of man).

In early folklore, dybbukim were thought only to inhabit the bodies of sick persons. Possessive evil spirits appear in the Old Testament, in Samuel I, which describes the possession of Saul and how David exorcised the spirit by playing the harp. In the Book of Tobit, the angel Raphael instructs Tobit in the ways of exorcisms. In the rabbinical literature of the first century, exorcisms called for the ashes of a red heifer, or the roots of certain herbs, burned under the victim, who was then surrounded with water. Other methods included incantations in the name of Solomon, repetition of the Divine Name, reading from Psalms, and the wearing of herbal amulets.

By the 16th century, the concept of possessive evil spirits changed. Many Jews believed the spirits were transmigrated souls that could not enter a new body because of their past sins, and so were forced to possess the body of a living sinner. The spirits were motivated to possess a body because they were tormented by other evil spirits if they did not. Some thought the dybbukim were the souls of people who were not properly buried, and thus became demons.

The Kabbalah, a body of medieval esoteric and mystical writings of Judaism, contains many procedures and instructions for exorcising a dybbuk, which were still employed as of the 20th century. The exorcism must be performed by a *ba'al shem*, a miracle-working rabbi. Depending on how the exorcism is done, the dybbuk either is redeemed or is cast into hell. It usually exits the body of its victim through the small toe, which shows a small, bloody hole as the point of departure.

Further reading:

Scholem, Gershom. *Kabbalah.* New York: New American Library, 1974.

Dzibai (Ghost Midewiwin).

The Mide Society (formerly the Midewiwin Society), the medicine society of the Ojibwa (Native Americans), a fraternity of initiates into the mysteries and healing arts, performs a ceremony called the Dzibai to speed the journey of souls of the newly dead to the Land of the Ghosts. The Dzibai is one of the society's most important functions.

It is believed that at death, the soul leaves the body and wanders about the earth, longing to be with loved ones. It may cause trouble in its wanderings.

In the Dzibai, a proxy takes the place of the dead person, and a shaman enacts a ritual in which the soul is encouraged to journey on to the Land of the Ghosts, which is believed to lie in the western land of Nanabozho, the Great Hare, the culture hero. In addressing the dead, the shaman says:

> You are ready to leave me now; be sure not to look back for the glance that draws us with you. Look straight ahead as you were told by the Chief Mide. We live here as long as we are supposed to. Never wish for us to hasten and join you. For you will find your brothers there, and your mother, father and grandparents there also. Do not trouble us; we will do all you requested before you died.

The ritual is simple and fees are paid by the family of the deceased are minimal, in order to speed the soul on its way as quickly as possible.

See also SHAMANISM.

Further reading:

Grim, John A. *The Shaman: Patterns of Religious Healing Among the Ojibway Indians.* Norman, Okla.: University of Oklahoma Press, 1983.

Ear of Dionysius Famous mediumistic case involving cross correspondences. This type of case is something like a jigsaw puzzle, in that a series of references in a variety of communications must be brought together in a certain way before the whole can be understood. For another example, see PALM SUNDAY CASE.

The "Ear of Dionysius" refers to a Sicilian cave to which Dionysius the Elder, Tyrant of Syracuse from 405 to 367 B.C., was in the habit of going to eavesdrop on the Athenian prisoners of war he held in adjoining stone quarries. The first reference to this situation was given in trance communication from a medium who went by the name of Mrs. Willet, in August 1910. At one point Mrs. Willet said, "Dionysius Ear the lobe." The allusion meant nothing to the sitter, Mrs. Verrall, and she asked her husband, the classical scholar A.W. Verrall, to explain it to her.

No further reference to the Ear of Dionysius was made in any of Mrs. Willet's scripts for another three years, and in the meanwhile Dr. Verrall died. Then in January 1914, Mrs. Willet, doing automatic writing in the presence of Sir Oliver LODGE, produced a script that included a passage that was expressly sent by the deceased Dr. Verrall to Mrs. Verrall. This passage contained references to acoustics, hearing, ears, a Tyrant and Syracuse. An attempt was evidently made to get out "Dionysius" as well: Mrs. Willet wrote, "Dy Dy and then you think of Diana Dimorphism."

Both Verralls were closely connected with the SO-CIETY FOR PSYCHICAL RESEARCH (SPR), which emphasized the importance of private and evidential communications as evidence for survival after death, so it made sense that Dr. Verrall would try to signal his continued existence to his wife in this way. This message, however, turned out to be only the beginning of a series of communications relating to the same theme, coming through Mrs. Willet from both Dr. Verrall and another communicator, also a deceased classical scholar, over the next year and a half.

As the series progressed, allusions to Ulysses and Polyphemus (the Cyclops), Acis (a shepherd boy murdered by Polyphemus), his lover Galatea, jealousy, music, a zither, Aristotle's poetics and satire began to appear as well.

Finally, in August 1915, the second communicator, S.H. Butcher, in a script communication through Mrs. Willet with Mrs. Verrall as sitter, sent a message which tied all the various allusions together. It referred to a certain Philoxenus, who had been imprisoned in the quarry by the Tyrant of Syracuse because he had managed to seduce the Tyrant's mistress, Galatea. Philoxenus wrote a satirical poem based on his experience, in which he portrayed himself as Ulysses and the Tyrant as Polyphemus. This was the type of poem usually recited to the accompaniment of a zither, and it was mentioned by Aristotle in his *Poetics*, a work that Dr. Butcher had translated while he was alive.

The Ear of Dionysius case seems to provide clear evidence of cooperation between two deceased communicators. Drs. Verrall and Butcher had been close friends while alive, and that friendship would seem to have continued after death. Cooperation of this sort is evident in other similar cases. On the other hand, this case is unusual in that only a single medium was involved—more often the pieces to be fitted together come through a variety of mediums. And this difference is a major weakness of the case, because it means that one could argue that Mrs. Willet either overheard a discussion of the key points, or managed to learn of them through extrasensory perception (ESP), and then wove this knowledge into her trance communications (unconsciously—no deliberate deception is required by such a scenario). In fact, one critic raised just this objection to the case soon after it was published, pointing out that the details of the story are given in a book that was then being used as a textbook at the University of Cambridge.

As is so often true of research on survival, one's evaluation of this case comes down to which explanation one finds more plausible—the idea that the deceased Drs. Verrall and Butcher cooperated to send a complex series of messages through Mrs. Willet to Mrs. Verrall, or that Mrs. Willet exercised extensive powers of ESP (see SUPER-ESP) to gain the necessary information, which she then unconsciously produced in a series of automatic writings while in trance.

Further reading:

Balfour, Gerald William. *The Ear of Dionysius.* New York: Henry Holt, 1920.

Gauld Alan. *Mediumship and Survival: A Century of Investigations.* London: William Heinemann Ltd., 1982.

earth lights   See GHOST LIGHTS.

ectoplasm   A lifelike substance, solid or vaporous in nature, which allegedly extrudes from the body of a medium and can be transformed into materialized limbs, faces or even entire bodies of spirits. Ectoplasm often appears milky white in color and smells like ozone.

Coined by French physiologist Charles Richet in 1894 to explain the strange third arm, or pseudopod, emanating from Eusapia PALLADINO, ectoplasm comes from the Greek words *ektos* and *plasma*, meaning "exteriorized substance." But ectoplasm-like vapors had been observed surrounding D.D. HOME by Sir William CROOKES. And medium Madame d'Esperance described being covered with luminous spider webs which eventually developed into a living organism. Earlier, a 17th-century philosopher named Vaughn described a substance he called "first matter" or "mercury" which seemed to be like ectoplasm.

These extrusions often seemed warm to the touch, had weight, produced carbonic acid and seemed to wax and wane from the medium's body. They could also be cold and rubbery or dough-like. Emanation usually came from a body orifice, such as the mouth, ears and nose, but could also pour from the eyes, navel, nipples or vagina. Their structure varied from amorphous clouds to thin rods to a wide membrane resembling a net. Ectoplasm disappeared altogether in the light, preferring red incandescent light and darkness. If suddenly exposed to light, the ectoplasm snapped back violently, perhaps causing injury to the medium or nearby sitters. The substance could be light and airy, like smoke, or sticky and viscous. And like all other physical manifestations, ectoplasm appeared best in an atmosphere of faith, not skepticism.

Ectoplasm allegedly must be released from the medium's body before materialization may occur. Gustave GELEY, head of the Institute Metapsychique in Paris, described ectoplasm as an externalization of decentralized energy in solid, liquid or vapor states. This decentralization expended great vital energy, which could manifest through rapping, phosphorescence, telekinesis or the production of ectoplasm. Complete materialization was the final product of the ectoplasmic process.

William J. CRAWFORD, of Queen's University in Belfast, opined that ectoplasm was the basis of all psychic phenomena. It gave consistency to all physical structures during the seance and gave these structures the ability to come into contact with ordinary forms of matter, thereby forming hands and faces. He also found ectoplasm responsible for direct voice phenomena.

Rev. Robert Chaney, himself a medium, described ectoplasm as the spiritual counterpart of protoplasm. He said that the medium's ectoplasmic body exists in the inter-cellular spaces of her physical body in vibration halfway between the physical and spiritual forms. In order to materialize spirits, the medium projects ectoplasm from her own body and draws it magnetically from the bodies of the sitters. The spirit is then clothed in this astral substance and appears. If the transformation is incomplete, the medium takes the spirit drapery and assumes the part of the spirit, a process called transfiguration.

Although Palladino's knobby pseudopods were fascinating, the real experts at ectoplasmic manifestations were Marthe BERAUD, alias Eva C., and Mina Stinson CRANDON, known as Margery. Another successful ectoplasmic medium was Kathleen Goligher (see GOLIGHER CIRCLE).

In experiments in the early 1900s with her colleague, Juliette Bisson, and later with German physician Baron Albert von SCHRENCK-NOTZING, Beraud would produce masses of amorphous white or gray material. She was thoroughly examined before each sitting, often wearing tights or a veil. Schrenck-Notzing even had Bisson examine Beraud's genitalia to verify that she was concealing nothing.

Schrenck-Notzing described Beraud's ectoplasm as similar to sticky, gelatinous icicles dripping from her mouth, ears, nose and eyes and down her chin onto the front of her body. When touched by hand or light, the ectoplasm writhed back into Beraud's body like the tentacles of an octopus. He found the stuff could go through fabric and not leave a trace. After forming, the ectoplasm often assumed faces or shapes, some resembling President Wilson and other popular government or historical figures.

In seances held with Beraud and Bisson alone, Bisson testified that Beraud produced copious extrusions from her breasts and vagina—even an ectoplasmic pseudobirth. She also materialized a tiny

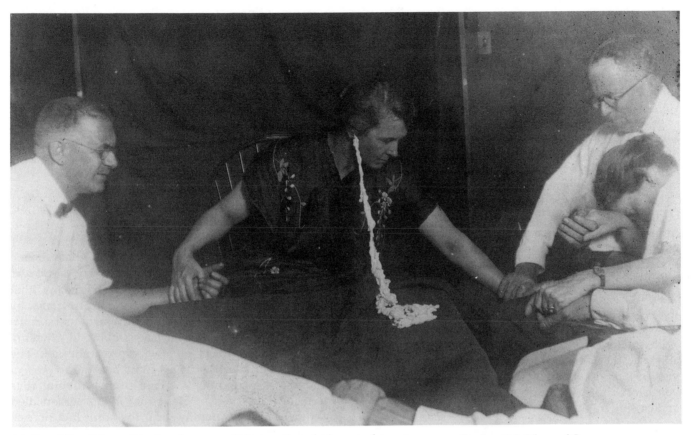

Medium Mina Stinson Crandon, known as "Margery," producing ectoplasm at a seance. Courtesy U.S. Library of Congress.

naked woman, eight inches high, with long flowing hair. Few researchers gave much credence to these testimonials, however, surmising that they were not so much paranormal manifestations as sexual.

From 1917 to 1920, Crawford studied the Goligher family, especially their daughter Kathleen. Crawford was convinced that Kathleen Goligher could lift tables using a pseudopod, or what he called a psychic structure or rod. Crawford's work intrigued Dr. LeRoi Crandon, a Boston surgeon, who began experiments with his wife, Mina.

Mina Crandon's mediumistic talents soon developed, complete with the production of ectoplasm. Famous photographs show long strings of ectoplasm, like umbilical cords, pouring from her mouth, ears and nose. They seemed to hang by tiny threads. Other extrusions came from between her legs; psychical researcher Eric J. Dingwall suspected Crandon concealed the ectoplasm in her vagina and extruded it by muscular contractions. She even produced a third hand, grossly formed, from her naval.

Analysis of small pieces of ectoplasm yielded few clues. Several critics claimed the stuff was either chewed paper, gauze or other fabric, probably regurgitated, or even animal tissue. Beraud's ectoplasm was most likely paper, and Harvard biologists found Crandon's pseudopod to be animal lung cleverly carved to resemble a hand.

Magician Harry HOUDINI, who attempted to expose fraudulent mediumship, once commented that he couldn't believe the Almighty would allow the production of such disgusting substances from a human body.

Ectoplasm was investigated by psychical researchers well into the 20th century. Fraudulent mediums were known to produce ectoplasm composed of nothing more than strips of muslin, or mixtures of soap, gelatin and egg white. Scientific interest in ectoplasm has declined along with the practice of physical mediumship. Some modern mediums reputedly produce ectoplasm.

Further reading:

Brandon, Ruth. *The Spiritualists.* New York: Alfred A. Knopf, 1983.

Chaney, Rev. Robert G. *Mediums and the Development of Mediumship.* Freeport, N.Y.: Books for Libraries Press, 1972.

Douglas, Alfred. *Extra-Sensory Powers: A Century of Psychical Research.* Woodstock, N.Y.: The Overlook Press, 1977.

Doyle, Sir Arthur Conan. *The History of Spiritualism Vol. I & II.* New York: Arno Press, 1975.

Fodor, Nandor. *An Encyclopaedia of Psychic Science.* Secaucus, N.J.: The Citadel Press, 1966. First published 1933.

Houdini, Harry. *Houdini: A Magician Among the Spirits.* New York: Arno Press, 1972.

Mysteries of the Unknown: Spirit Summonings. Alexandria, Va.: Time-Life Books, 1989.

Edgar Allan Poe House   The tiny Baltimore house once occupied by Edgar Allan Poe reportedly is haunted, but not by the famous author of mystery and horror himself.

The house, located in what is now a poor neighborhood of Baltimore, was new when Poe lived there from 1832–1835. Other occupants were his grandmother, Elizabeth Poe, his aunt, Maria Clemm, and his cousin, Virginia Clemm, who later became his wife. Elizabeth Poe died in the house in 1835. Subsequently, various other persons lived in the house. It was vacant from 1922 to 1949, when it became a historical site open to the public.

Phenomena have been reported since the 1960s, and include lights being on when no one is inside; visitors feeling tapped on their shoulders; mysterious voices and noises, and doors and windows opening and closing by themselves. Most of the activity seems to center in Poe's attic room and Virginia's bedroom. None of the phenomena seems threatening or hostile.

Different psychics have claimed to clairvoyantly see the ghost of an old, heavy woman dressed in period clothes, with gray hair. Her identity is unknown.

Further reading:

Myers, Arthur. *The Ghostly Register: Haunted Dwellings: Active Spirits, A Journey to America's Strangest Landmarks.* Chicago: Contemporary Books, 1986.

Edison, Thomas Alva   See ELECTRONIC VOICE PHENOMENON; PHONE CALLS FROM THE DEAD.

ekimmu   In ancient Assyria, the evil ghost of one who was denied entrance to the underworld and was doomed to wander the earth. "Ekimmu" means "that which is snatched away." One became an *ekimmu* by dying a violent or unsavory death, such as by murder, in battle, drowning, or succumbing to exposure in the desert, which left the corpse unburied. The spirits of buried corpses also could become an *ekimmu* under other conditions: if the proper funeral rites were not observed at graveside; if the person died without surviving family; or if the spirit had no one to care for it.

The *ekimmu* was greatly feared, for it would attach itself quite easily to virtually any living person regardless of whether that person had been acquainted with the dead one. So much as looking at an impure corpse could result in being haunted by the *ekimmu*. At the least, the *ekimmu* was a nuisance, and at the worst, it could cause the deaths of an entire household. Once attached to the living, it was extremely difficult to exorcise.

The *ekimmu* also appeared as a death omen outside of houses, wailing in the same manner as the Irish BANSHEE.

Further reading:

Hurwood, Bernhardt J. *Passport to the Supernatural: An Occult Compendium from All Ages and Many Lands.* New York: Taplinger, 1972.

electronic voice phenomenon   A form of modern spirit communication in which the voices of spirits of the dead are recorded directly onto magnetic audio tape. The electronic voice phenomenon (EVP) is controversial; EVP researchers believe they do capture the voices of the dead, as well as of extraterrestrials, but skeptics contend the voices come from radio, television and citizen band (CB) radio transmissions, or are imagined from static and white sound.

EVP is the most modern of attempts to communicate with the dead and other discarnate beings.

Edgar Allan Poe. Courtesy National Archives, Brady Collection.

Thomas Alva Edison believed that an electronic device could be built for such communication. Edison announced in the October 1920 issue of *Scientific American* that he was working on such a device, but it was not completed prior to his death in 1931. Little serious work in this field was done until the 1950s, when George Hunt Williamson attempted to tape paranormal voices, particularly of extraterrestrials. In 1956, a medium named Attila von Sealay began experiments with researchers (including Raymond Bayless and D. Scott ROGO) to capture voices on electromagnetic tape. Von Sealay said that he had begun to hear a "tiny voice" in the air near him in 1938. He believed the voice belonged to his dead son, Edson. The experiments yielded what sounded like male and female voices, whistles and rappings.

Despite this precedence, the credit for discovery of the EVP goes to Friedrich Jurgenson, a Swedish opera singer, painter and film producer, perhaps because Jurgenson's work became widely known and inspired others. In 1959, Jurgenson tape recorded bird songs in the Swedish countryside near his villa. On playback, he heard a male voice discuss "nocturnal bird songs" in Norwegian. At first he thought it was interference from a radio broadcast, but he nonetheless made other recordings to see if the same thing happened. Though he heard no voices during taping, many voices were heard on playback. The voices gave personal information about him, plus instructions on how to record more voices.

Jurgenson wrote about his experiments in *Voices from the Universe*, published in 1964 with a recording of EVP sounds. In 1965, he met Konstantin Raudive, a psychologist and philosopher, who was so intrigued by EVP that he devoted himself to researching it. Over the years Raudive recorded more than 100,000 voices. He published his research in German in "The Inaudible Made Audible," translated into English in 1971 under the title *Breakthrough*. EVP voices also are called "Raudive voices" after him.

EVP research is conducted worldwide by a number of organizations. The greatest interest is in Germany and the United States. In Germany, the VTF (Association for Voice Taping Research) was founded in the 1970s, followed by a second organization a few years later, the FGT (Research Association for Voice Taping). In 1982, Sarah Estep founded the American Association-Electronic Voice Phenomena in the United States. Conferences and seminars are conducted all over the world by enthusiasts. Many are engineers and electronics experts who devise sophisticated experimental equipment for capturing the voices. Generally, headphones must be used to hear EVP voices.

Estep rates voices according to three categories: Class C are faint, whispery voices that can barely be heard and are sometimes indecipherable; Class B voices are louder and clearer and can sometimes be heard without headphones; and Class A voices are clear, can be heard without headphones and can be duplicated onto other tapes.

EVP voices typically speak in short, cryptic and sometimes grammatically poor phrases. They speak in a variety of languages, regardless of the languages known to the listeners, and sometimes sing in indistinguishable lyrics. Sometimes one or two voices are heard, at other times a multitude of them. The voices are identifiable as men, women and children. Animal sounds have been recorded as well. Some voices have said they are able to communicate on tape through ectoplasm (q.v.). Voices also report that they communicate through one of many "central transmitting agencies" on the Other Side.

There are various ways to attempt to record EVP voices. The simplest is to turn a recorder on and leave it running. Enthusiasts record at any time of day and night, but they say night is best because of a lower risk of broadcast interference. Serious researchers employ sensitive microphones, amplifiers and high-quality tape. Some researchers ask questions and leave a tape running to capture answers that are inaudible during taping, but audible on playback.

Many investigators doubt EVP voices are paranormal. Between 1970 and 1972, the SOCIETY FOR PSYCHICAL RESEARCH, London, commissioned D.J. Ellis to investigate EVP voices. He concluded that the interpretation of the sounds was highly subjective and was susceptible to imagination, and that the voices most likely were a natural phenomenon. Such conclusions are supported by the Rorschach sound test, which demonstrates that a person can listen to a medley of sounds and hear whatever one wishes. Other skeptics propose that the voices are due to psychokinesis in which sounds are imprinted on the tape due to the intense desire of the experimenter to capture "paranormal voices."

Raudive, who died on September 2, 1974, expressed no particular theory about EVP.

In 1982, the EVP field received an international publicity boost with the announcement by George Meek, a retired engineer, that he and a medium, William O'Neill, an electronics expert, had built a device called Spiricom that could communicate with the Other Side. Meek, who had long been interested in survival after death, had been given the idea for building a device by a discarnate scientist who communicated during a seance. The dead scientist told Meek he would cooperate in giving instructions.

Meek then met O'Neill in 1977. O'Neill's spirit communicator identified himself as "Doc Nick," a former radio ham operator, and delivered the technical information used by Meek and O'Neill to build Spiricom. According to Doc Nick, Spiricom would make available thousands of sensitive frequencies to the Other Side. Meek founded the MetaScience Foundation of North Carolina and invested more than a half million dollars of his own money in the research.

Spiricom allegedly enabled sustained, two-way conversations between the living and the dead, a vast improvement over the cryptic phrases characteristic of most EVP voices. Meek made available the plans for Spiricom devices to anyone at no cost. Unfortunately, no one who constructed the device reported success. EVP researchers theorized that Spiricom's success rested largely on the unique mediumship abilities of O'Neill. Meek went on to pursue increasingly sophisticated systems intended to reach astral levels where "higher minds" resided.

Despite such spotty experimental records, EVP researchers strive to capture something on tape that will prove survival after death. Seances, at which attempts are made to capture voices live for audiences, are conducted for individuals, groups and even the media. Research also is pursued with capturing evidence on video and film cameras, and on computers.

See also PHONE CALLS FROM THE DEAD.

Further reading:

Bander, Peter. *Carry On Talking: How Dead Are the Voices?* Gerrards Cross, England: Colin Smythe Ltd., 1972.

———. *Voices From the Tapes: Recording from the Other World.* New York: Drake Publishers, 1973.

Ellis, D.J. *The Mediumship of the Tape Recorder.* Pulborough, England: Self-published, 1978.

Estep, Sarah. *Voices of Eternity.* New York: Fawcett Gold Medal, 1988.

Fuller, John G. *The Ghost of 29 Megacycles.* New York: Signet/New American Library, 1981.

Ostrander, Sheila, and Lynn Schroeder. *Handbook of Psi Discoveries.* New York: Berkley, 1974.

Raudive, Konstantin. *Breakthrough: An Amazing Experiment in Electronic Communication with the Dead.* New York: Taplinger, 1971.

Enfield Poltergeist

Poltergeist case in a London suburb that involved trickery along with some evidently genuine phenomena.

The house in Enfield, North London, was an ordinary suburban townhouse. It was occupied by Peggy Harper and her four children: Rose, age 13; Janet, 11; Pete, 10; and Jimmy, 7. The disturbances began the night of August 30, 1977, shortly after Janet and Pete had retired to the bedroom they shared (the other children slept with their mother in another room). Their beds began jolting up and down—"going all funny," as Janet expressed it to Peggy. By the time Peggy got to the room, the strange movements had stopped, and she was not at all sure the children were not making it up. All remained quiet for the rest of that night, but then the next night, things got going in earnest.

At around 9:30 in the evening, Peggy was called to Janet and Pete's room by their excited chatter. This time they claimed to hear shuffling sounds coming out of the floor. Janet suggested that it sounded like one of the chairs moving, so Peggy carried it downstairs to the living room, then went back up and turned out the light, thinking this would help to settle the children down. But then she also heard something odd. It did indeed sound like shuffling, like someone moving across the floor in slippers. Peggy switched the light back on, but all the furniture seemed to be in place, and Janet and Pete were lying in their beds with their hands under the covers. She turned the light off again, and immediately the sound started as before.

Then there were four loud, distinct knocks that seemed to come from the wall adjoining the neighboring house. What happened next was even more bizarre. With the light on, and all three watching, a heavy chest of drawers moved away from the wall. After moving out about a foot and a half, it stopped. Peggy shoved it back again, but the chest returned to its former position, and this time when she tried to push it, it refused to budge. Shaking with fear, she ordered the children downstairs to the living room, and tried to decide on a course of action. Janet noticed the next door neighbor's light was still on, and that decided things. The entire Harper family trooped over in their night clothes.

When the neighbors walked through the Harper house, they could find nothing to explain the knocks, which continued at intervals, and which they also heard plainly. The next to be called were the police, who responded to the scene expecting to find a domestic quarrel of some sort. Instead, they too heard knocks, now on different walls, and one of the officers was in the living room when a chair suddenly slid several feet across the floor. The officer examined the chair at once, but found nothing to explain how it had moved. It did not seem that anyone was breaking the law, so the police left, promising that they would keep an eye on the house for the next few days.

The following day brought a new phenomenon—flying marbles and plastic Lego bricks. With the police unable to help, the Harpers and their neighbors turned to the press. The *Daily Mirror* sent out a reporter and photographer, who stayed in the house for several hours without anything happening and were about to leave, when the barrage started up. A piece of Lego flew across the room and hit the photographer on the forehead hard enough to leave a bruise that lasted over a week, just as he was taking a picture. When he developed the negative, he noticed some strange things about it: the negative had an inexplicable hole in it, the flying Lego brick was not pictured, and the two people who were pictured were standing in such a way that it was clear that they had not thrown the brick.

The *Daily Mirror* called the SOCIETY FOR PSYCHICAL RESEARCH (SPR), which in turn contacted Maurice Grosse, a resident of North London, who had been hoping to find a case to investigate. Grosse arrived at the Harper house for the first time on September 5, exactly a week after the disturbances had begun. His presence had an immediate calming effect on the family, and for a few days nothing out of the ordinary occurred. Then on the night of September 8, when Grosse and three men from the *Daily Mirror* were keeping watch, they heard a crash in Janet's bedroom. Investigation showed that her bedside chair had been thrown about four feet across the room, where it was now lying on its side. Janet was asleep at the time, and no one saw the chair move—but when it happened again an hour later, a photographer was ready, and captured the event on film.

Shortly thereafter, Grosse was joined in the investigation by writer Guy Lyon Playfair. The two men were to spend the next two years studying the case, which took various twists and turns before the strange occurrences at the Harpers' finally ceased.

Many poltergeist cases center around children who are about to reach or have recently reached puberty. Peggy Harper had one of each—Rose, at 13, was already well developed, and Janet, 11 was soon to come of age. The case also had another feature typical of such cases: interpersonal tension. Peggy had never altogether resolved her feelings surrounding her divorce from the children's father. After she realized that this might have something to do with the phenomena, and came to terms with her emotions, the disturbances ceased. Or rather, they took a hiatus, and when they started up again, they had a somewhat different character. Now more than ever they seemed to focus on the two girls, Janet and Rose, and on Janet's bedroom.

When SPR researchers Anita Gregory and John Beloff visited the Harpers some months later, all they saw was trickery. Over and over again, Anita Gregory wrote in her review of Playfair's book on the case, *This House is Haunted* (1980), they would hear

"a thump and a squeal," and Janet would be found sitting on the floor of her room (from which everyone was now barred), where she said she had been thrown by an "entity." Janet and Rose would also produce muffled voices (many of which used strong profanity), their mouths covered by sheets. A video camera set up in the room next door caught Janet bending spoons and attempting to bend an iron bar in an entirely normal manner, then bouncing up and down on the bed while she made little flapping movements with her hands.

The case appears to be one which began with some genuine phenomena, but which devolved into trickery by the two girls, probably prompted by the attention the case received from the media and from the investigators.

Further reading:

Gregory, Anita. "Review of *This House Is Haunted.*" *Journal of the Society for Psychical Research* 50 (1980):538–41.

Playfair, Guy Lyon. *This House Is Haunted*. London: Souvenir Press, 1980.

Epworth Rectory   Poltergeist haunting of a lonely rectory in Lincolnshire, Isle of Axholme, England, in the early 18th century. For about two months, the household of Rev. Samuel Wesley was plagued by characteristic poltergeist disturbances such as rappings and the movement of furniture. The poltergeist, however, had some unusual habits.

Epworth Rectory had been presented to Rev. Wesley by Queen Mary, to whom he dedicated a poem on the life of Christ. Members of his family, however, had a low opinion of the locale: one daughter, Hetty, described the nearest village, Wroot, as "a place devoid of wisdom, wit or grace." In 1709, the rectory was burned down, and Wesley's cattle were maimed, by villagers who disapproved of Rev. Wesley's Hanoverian principles. The rectory was rebuilt.

For 20 years of their marriage, Mrs. Wesley was either in a state of pregnancy or post-delivery. She bore 19 children, 14 of whom died in infancy. Her only year of respite occurred in 1701–02 when Rev. Wesley deserted her on account of her Jacobite sympathies. As their son, John, recorded:

> The year before King William died my father observed that my mother did not say Amen to the prayer for the King. She said she could not, for she did not believe the Prince of Orange was king. My father vowed he would never cohabit with her till she did. He, then, took his horse, and rode away; nor did she hear anything of him for a twelvemonth. He, then, came back and lived with her as before. But I fear his vow was not forgotten before God.

This conflict between the two apparently was never resolved; Rev. Wesley gave in and returned home of his own accord. It is possible that deep and repressed hostility, especially on the part of Mrs. Wesley, played a role in the poltergeist disturbances which broke out without warning on December 1, 1719 (some accounts give the date as 1716).

The servants were the first to hear the unusual noises. On December 1 or December 2, one of the maids and Rev. Wesley's manservant, Robin (also given as Robert) Brown, heard groans, like those of a dying person, at the dining room door at about 10 P.M. Thinking it was a neighbor, Mr. Turpine, who was very ill and who visited on occasion, Brown opened the door, but no one was there. The knocks sounded again two or three times, and each time Brown opened the door to find nothing. The servants then went to bed. When Brown went to his room in the garret, he saw at the top of the stairs a hand-mill whirling swiftly. The hand-mill was empty. As he lay in bed, Brown then heard sounds of someone walking about in jack boots and stumbling over Brown's shoes and boots. He also heard a turkey-cock gobble. Again, no one was present.

The children began to hear noises at night: knockings, rumblings by the stairs and in the garret, sounds of dancing, footsteps running up and down the stairs, chains clanking and door latches being rattled.

Rev. Wesley seemed to be the only member of the household oblivious to the noises, and at first, no one wanted to advise him of them, out of fear that they heralded his death or the death of someone else in the family. Finally, however, the knocks sounded in Rev. and Mrs. Wesley's bedchamber.

A pattern began to develop. The noises would begin every night about 9:45, always preceded by 15 minutes of sounds variously described as a jack winding up, a saw creaking, or the planing of a windmill as it changed direction. It was as though the poltergeist was winding up its energy for the evening. Raps and knockings would then sound all over the house, and sometimes the house itself shook. Once, sounds like bottles being dashed to pieces were heard below the stairs; an inspection revealed nothing out of place. Similarly, it once sounded like the pewter was being thrown about the kitchen, yet nothing was out of place when family members went to check. Brown was so frightened by the nightly visitations that he took the family mastiff to his room. The first night the dog was there, it barked violently just before the noises began. After that, it whined and ran and afforded the poor man no comfort at all.

Mrs. Wesley was for a time convinced that the disturbances were caused by rats, and she called for a horn to be blasted throughout the house to scare

The stairway at Epworth Rectory favored by "Old Jeffrey."

them away. After that, the noises sounded during the day as well as at night, as though the spirit were getting even for the horn.

The children, who were quite frightened at night by the noises, nicknamed the unknown spirit "Old Jeffrey." It was also speculated that the spirit might be "Old Ferries," the name of someone who had died in the house. Daughter Emilia blamed witchcraft, as there had recently been a disturbance nearby that "undoubtedly" had been caused by witches.

Attempts to communicate with the poltergeist had limited success. If a member of the family rapped, the spirit would rap back in the same fashion. It never, however, responded to questions, and never spoke with a voice of its own. One night, hearing knockings in the nursery, Rev. Wesley followed them and became angry at the spirit. According to son John's account:

He . . . said sternly, "Thou deaf and dumb devil, why dost thou frighten these children that cannot answer for themselves? Come to me to my study that am a man!" Instantly it knocked his knock (the particular knock which he always used at the gate) as if it would shiver the board in pieces, and we heard nothing more that night. Till this time my father had never heard the least disturbance in his study. But the next evening, as he attempted to go out into this study (of which none had the key but himself), when he opened the door it was thrust back with such violence as had like to have him thrown down.

The poltergeist was particularly active when the family said their prayers, knocking furiously when Rev. Wesley said prayers for King George and the prince, and at the utterance of "Amen." If prayers for the king were omitted, the poltergeist did nothing.

Other manifestations included a bed levitation with one of the daughters, Nancy, on it, and two spectres. One, seen by Brown in the kitchen, appeared to look like a rabbit. Another, seen by Emilia in the nursery, looked like a badger.

Others urged Rev. Wesley and his family to leave the house, but Wesley was determined not to be run off by "the devil." He did decide to summon his oldest son from London, but he canceled the visit when the disturbances stopped, as mysteriously as they had started, at the end of January 1720.

There is reason to think that the poltergeist was not supernatural, but was psychokinetic energy unleashed by one or more of the Wesley family members. Certainly Mrs. Wesley must be suspected, especially since the poltergeist was its noisiest at the mention of the names of King George and the prince, the sovereignty of whom was of sufficient issue to split the Wesley marriage for a year. Mrs. Wesley also may have harbored long-term frustrations, resentment and weariness at producing a child every year, only to see most of them die.

Of all the children present in the house during the disturbances, daughter Hetty was most troubled. When the noises occurred, she did not wake up, but slept fitfully and with skin flushed. It is not known how old she was at the time—estimates are from ages 14 to 19—but she may have been a prime agent. She harbored bad feelings about her surroundings, and perhaps may have been deeply affected by the rift between her father and mother.

Further reading:
Sitwell, Sacheverell. *Poltergeists: Fact or Fancy.* New York: Dorset Press, 1988. First published 1959.

Estep, Sarah See ELECTRONIC VOICE PHENOMENON.

Eva C. See BERAUD, MARTHE.

exorcism The expulsion of ghosts, spirits, demons or other entities believed to be possessing or disturbing a human being or a place that humans frequent. Depending on the severity of the possession and how evil the spirit seems, exorcisms can range from friendly, persuasive conversations to elaborate rituals commanding the entity to leave in the name of God or a god.

The word "exorcism" comes from the Greek *exousia*, meaning "oath," and translates as *adjuro*, or "adjure," in Latin and English. To "exorcise" does not mean to cast out so much as it means "putting the spirit or demon on oath," or invoking a higher authority to compel the entity to act in a way contrary to its wishes. Such compulsion also implies binding. The Anglican pamphlet "Exorcism" (1972) states that exorcism binds evil powers by the triumph of Christ and through the application of His power in and by His Church. Christian exorcism rituals, especially in the Roman Catholic Church, begin with the following words, in Latin: *"Adjure te, spiritus nequissime, per Deum omnipotentem,"* which translate as "I adjure thee, most evil spirit, by almighty God." The gospels tell that Jesus Christ cast out many devils, but he did not exorcise, because he had no need to call on any higher authority than Himself.

Rites of exorcism have existed universally since ancient times. In many cultures, where spirits are believed to interfere frequently in the affairs of man, exorcism plays a role in daily life; one consults an exorcist for spirit-caused maladies as one would consult a medical doctor for physical ailments. Exorcisms of spirits, demons, ghosts, poltergeists, and unwanted or negative spirits, energies or "thoughtforms" (an artificial spirit created through magical ritual) are commonplace around the world. Who the exorcist is depends upon context and culture, but includes such persons as priests, rabbis, lamas, shamans, witch doctors, medicine men, witches and psychics. It may be said that forms of exorcism occur in the psychiatric or psychological treatment of personality disorders in which patients feel taken over by alien personalities.

In Christianity exorcism is associated with demonic possession, which is regarded as evil and the work of Satan. As evidence of demonic possession, the victims may levitate, exhibit superhuman strength, forswear all religious words or articles, and speak in tongues. This last trait offers the strongest proof to the Catholic Church, allowing the attending bishop to permit an exorcism.

Priests and ministers perform most demonic exorcisms, assisted by a junior cleric, a physician and perhaps a family member. Both physical and spiritual violence dominate a demonic exorcism. The victim may suffer pain, unbelievable physical contortions and spasms, disgusting body noises, diarrhea, spitting, vomiting and swearing. Waves of cold and heat may roll over the room. Objects that can be moved, such as furniture, clothing, rugs, lamps and toys, are taken out to keep them from flying about the room and breaking.

Spiritually, the Christian exorcism is a duel between the Devil and the exorcist for the victim's soul, and no holds are barred. The exorcist and his assistants must be relatively guiltless at the time of the exorcism, for the Devil may hurl their sins in their faces and criticize them cruelly. For every invective snarled by the Devil, the exorcist must be prepared to counter with firm demands to depart in the name of Christ, promising everlasting pain and damnation if the Devil does not go. Above all else, the exorcist must stand firm in his conviction that the power of Jesus Christ supercedes everything.

Among Christians, only the Roman Catholics offer a formal rite of exorcism: the *Rituale Romanum*, dating back to 1614. Less formal exorcisms are performed by Protestant ministers.

Without established procedures, exorcists rely on prayer, stern language, electric shock, beating and starvation, fumigations with strong odors, and foul-tasting substances given to victims. Hellebore, attar of roses and rue are said to perform quite well. Salt, a precious commodity in medieval Europe and believed to represent spiritual purity, has always figured prominently in exorcism rituals and still does today. Wine works well also, as it represents the blood of Christ.

Catholics have received the most publicity for exorcisms—some priests have even performed mass exorcisms in public squares, calling for the demons Lucifer, Nambroth, Bechet, Ashtaroth and Nabam to depart. In the 20th century, the Church has downplayed possession and exorcism. However, in 1991, officials allowed the American Broadcasting Company television network to broadcast a real exorcism of a young girl. The girl had received psychiatric treatment, but was still afflicted by what family and Church officials believed to be a demon. The exorcism, which aired on the show "20/20," was a first in the history of the Church. Although the victim vomited, exhibited fits and used foul language in an altered voice, the exorcism was far less dramatic than television audiences were conditioned to expect due to sensational treatments in films such as *The Exorcist* (see ZUGUN, ELEANORE). Skeptics remained unconvinced. The exorcism failed to effect permanent relief, and the girl soon returned to psychiatric treatment. Nonetheless, Church officials expressed their belief in the Devil's continuing torment of human beings.

The idea that demons can invade innocent human beings is an important tenet of the approximately eight million Pentacostal Christians in the United States. The Pentacostals, and other so-called "Charismatics," practice what is known as "deliverance ministry," where those who claim to possess the gift cast out devils and heal through the laying on of hands. The minister or healer and his assistants, often the entire congregation, confront the devil with

An exorcism rite being performed in an English home in the early 19th century.

prayer and exhort the demons to depart. If the victim is truly possessed, the demons eventually are forced to reveal themselves, usually calling themselves by the vice they exhibit, such as Lust, Envy or Greed. Prayers of thanksgiving and cries of joy envelop the congregation as the victim returns to Christ.

Exorcism has played a smaller and different role in Judaism. The Old Testament mentions possession and exorcism by evil spirits; in Samuel I, a spirit possesses Saul and is exorcised when David plays his harp. In Tobit, Tobit learns about exorcisms from the angel Raphael. As early as the first century, rabbinical literature mentions exorcism rituals. Perhaps the best-known exorcisms concern the dybbuk.

In Hinduism, Buddhism, Islam and animism, a wide variety of spirits and ghosts may be deemed responsible for various maladies or situations, and may be ritually exorcised (see CULT OF THE ZAR). In some shamanic traditions, the shaman enters an ecstatic trance to search for and recover the soul of the patient, which has been possessed by a demon, and then drives the demon out (see SHAMANISM).

More moderate views on possession and exorcism have been exposed by secular and nonsecular experts. Carl WICKLAND, an American physician and psychologist, and his wife, Anna, believed that spirits were rarely evil, but were confused and trapped in the aura of a living person. They caused apparent multiple and dissociated personalities, and insanity ranging from "simple mental aberration to . . . all types of dementia, hysteria, epilepsy, melancholia, shell shock, kleptomania, idiocy, religious and suicidal mania . . . amnesia, psychic invalidism, dipsomania, immorality, functional bestiality, atrocities, and other forms of criminalities," as Wickland described in his book, *Thirty Years Among the Dead*

(1924). The Wicklands used coaxing and mild electric shock to send the spirits on their way.

Canon John D. Pearce-Higgins, an Anglican clergyman, also has used coaxing. Dr. Martin Israel, a clergyman and senior lecturer in pathology at the University of London, has agreed, adding that most discarnates are family members or friends of the victim trying to finish their worldly business.

Another Anglican priest, the Rev. J.C. Neil-Smith of Hampstead, England, has claimed to have performed more than 800 successful exorcisms of both people and places. He believes in both confused spirits and evil demons, finding that restless entities fill a room with cold, devils with searing heat. Although he recites a liturgy to expel the entities, Rev. Neil-Smith places more faith in the conviction of the exorcist that the spirits will depart and that he is capable of causing this event to happen.

Donald Page, a medium and exorcist, has depended on spirit guides to help him remove the unwanted spirits and send them on their way. He senses the spirit's vibrations to determine its level of wickedness, sometimes detecting an unpleasant smell. Page claims to be able to see a patient's aura, and if a spirit has penetrated the aura, Page removes it and takes it into himself before sending it on. The patient then watches the spirit transform Page into itself, exhibiting whatever characteristics defined the spirit: hostility, timidity, imbecility, aggressiveness or even evil. Depending on the degree of possession, more than one exorcism session may be necessary. Page believes that by watching his transformation, the patient will be more reluctant to encounter spirits in the future.

In California, psychiatrist Dr. Ralph Allison writes in his book *Minds in Many Pieces* (1980) that various of his patients over the years, especially sufferers of multiple personality, exhibited signs of demonic possession and required exorcism as well as conventional treatment. One multiple personality patient, named Carrie, suffered from drug addiction and from fears of choking to death and of dying on the next New Year's Eve. A psychic described Carrie as being possessed by the spirit of a young woman named Bonnie who had died in 1968 of a drug overdose. Allison at first dismissed the story, but as Carrie's condition worsened, he decided to try an exorcism. First Allison hypnotized Carrie and then talked to her, trying to determine if Bonnie was just another of her personalities. Carrie claimed she was not, and under deeper hypnosis she begged to be rid of Bonnie. Then Allison suspended a crystal ball over Carrie and exhorted Bonnie to leave the victim in peace, saying that when the ball stopped swinging, he would

know Bonnie had gone. Bonnie left, and Carrie never feared New Year's Eve or choking to death again.

In Christianity, there are no formal exorcism rituals for exorcising ghosts from places. Such a rite might consist of a priest sprinkling holy water and burning incense and exhorting the ghost to depart.

Various magical rites allegedly can vanquish troublesome ghosts from cemeteries, especially those of a murderer or suicide. One must ritually cast a magic circle over the grave, which protects the person against the ghost. At midnight, the exorcist stands in the circle and summons the ghost, who materializes with a great crash. The exorcist then demands an explanation for the ghosts's hauntings. According to lore, the ghost will answer all questions in hollow tones. Usually the reason has to do with unfinished business, and if the exorcist promises to carry out the ghost's final wishes, then the ghost vanishes, never to haunt again.

If the troublesome ghost haunts a house, then the ritual is somewhat different. The exorcist enters the house at midnight carrying a candle, compass, crucifix and Bible. He draws a magic circle, and inside the circle draws a cross. Upon the cross he places a chair and table. He sits in the chair and places the Bible, lighted candle and crucifix on the table. The ghost enters noisily, and submits to all questions before meekly departing. If the exorcist is a priest, he will sprinkle holy water on the ghost or wave the crucifix at it. In reality, exorcism rituals seldom are performed that way, or follow such a neat plan. Ghosts do not respond to questions, and sometimes exorcisms performed by the most holy of clergy fail.

In China, the traditional means of exorcising ghosts from houses is done by a Taoist priest. First, an altar is erected at the spot frequented by the ghost, and lit tapers and sticks of incense are placed upon it. The priest enters the house dressed in a red robe, blue stockings and a black cap. He carries a sword, which in Chinese lore is held to be an effective weapon against the supernatural, and is hung over beds and elsewhere in rooms to repel unwanted influences. The exorcism sword must be made of peach or date tree wood, and the hilt must be covered by a red cloth. An exorcism charm is written on the blade. The priest places the sword on the altar.

He then prepares a mystic scroll, burns it and collects the ashes into a cup of spring water. He holds the cup in his left hand and the sword in his right, takes seven steps to the left and eight to the right, and intones: "God of heaven and earth, invest me with the heavy seal, in order that I may eject from this dwelling-house all kinds of evil spirits.

Should any disobey me, give me the power to deliver them for safe custody to the rulers of such demons.'' Addressing the ghost, the priest adds, "As quick as lightning depart from this house." He lays down the sword, picks up a bunch of willow, dips the willow in the cup and sprinkles the ash-water in the corners of the house according to the cardinal points. He picks up the sword again, and, with the cup, goes to the eastern corner and says, "I have the authority, Tai-Shaong-Loo-Kivan." He drinks from the cup and spits on the wall, saying, "Kill the green evil spirits which come from unlucky stars, or let them be driven away." This ritual is repeated at the other three corners, with the colors red, white and yellow substituted in place of green.

The priest's attendants beat gongs and drums. The priest says, "Evil spirits from the east [west, south, north], I send back to the east [west, etc.]." The priest goes to the entrance of the house, makes mystical signs in the air with his hands and sword, and proclaims the house free of ghosts.

Further reading:

Baroja, Julio Caro. *The World of the Witches*. Chicago: The University of Chicago Press, 1964.

Crabtree, Adam. *Multiple Man: Explorations in Possession and Multiple Personality*. New York: Praeger, 1985.

Ebon, Martin. *The Devil's Bride, Exorcism: Past and Present*. New York: Harper & Row, 1974.

Eliade, Mircea. *Shamanism*. Princeton, N.J.: Princeton University Press, 1964.

Guiley, Rosemary Ellen. *The Encyclopedia of Witches and Witchcraft*. New York: Facts On File, 1989.

Hill, Douglas, and Pat Williams. *The Supernatural*. London: Aldus Books, 1965.

Kapferer, Bruce. *A Celebration of Demons*. Bloomington: Indiana University Press, 1983.

Martin, Malachi. *Hostage to the Devil*. New York: Harper & Row, 1976.

extrasensory perception (ESP)   Paranormal sensing of sight, sound, taste, smell and touch. Extrasensory perception (ESP) is divided into two categories, telepathy and clairvoyance, which deliver information relevant to the present, past or future that cannot be obtained through normal senses. ESP occurs in mediumship, possession, cases of apparitions, some cases of poletergeists, hauntings, near-death experiences and out-of-body experiences.

Though called an extra sense, ESP does not function like normal senses. Research into its nature shows that it cannot be explained or quantified by physical laws; it seems to operate in an alternate reality (see GARRETT, EILEEN J.) Theories have proposed that an individual experiences ESP when information in the subconscious, the collective unconscious or the superconscious (the soul) is somehow accessed.

The term "ESP" was used in the late 19th century by researchers of mesmerism to describe a subject's ability to externally sense without using the known senses. Other researchers called it by other names, including "hidden sense" and "telesthesia." The latter was coined by Frederic W.H. MYERS, a founder of the SOCIETY FOR PSYCHICAL RESEARCH (SPR), and eventually gave way to "clairvoyance." Early psychical researchers believed that ESP required a receiver and a sender; this assumption was disproved later.

In the 1930s, American parapsychologist J.B. RHINE used the term "ESP" to refer to paranormal phenomena analogous to sensory functions. Rhine also coined the term "general extrasensory perception" (GESP) to include both telepathy and clairvoyance, but GESP never caught on in popular usage. Modern Parapsychologists refer to ESP as "psi," a term that also includes psychokinesis (PK).

According to research by Louisa E. Rhine, wife of J.B. Rhine, ESP occurs most often in realistic dreams, followed by intuition, unrealistic or surreal dreams and hallucinations. Hallucinations include the seeing of apparitions and visions of distant places in geography or time. Most episodes of ESP are spontaneous and involve trauma or crisis, such as premonitions of death, or crisis apparitions in which a person appears to another at the approximate moment of death. (See APPARITIONS.)

Information that comes through ESP is not always accurate, perhaps because it is affected by the thoughts and biases of the waking consciousness.

Everyone probably experiences ESP, but certain individuals, such as mediums, seem to possess unusual ESP ability. Persons who are sensitive to ESP may be more likely to experience paranormal phenomena at a haunted site than those who are not so sensitive. This may explain why some individuals are bothered at haunted sites and others claim those same sites are not haunted at all.

Further reading:

Edge, Hoyt L., Robert L. Morris, John Palmer, and Joseph H. Rush. *Foundations of Parapsychology*. Boston: Routledge & Kegan Paul, 1986.

LeShan, Lawrence. *Alternate Realities*. New York: M. Evans & Co., 1967.

Murphy, Gardner. "Direct Contacts with Past and Future: Retrocognition and Precognition." *Journal of the American Society for Psychical Research* 61 (1967):3–23.

Rhine, J.B. *New Frontiers of the Mind*. New York: Farrar & Rinehart, 1937.

Rhine, Louisa. *ESP in Life and Lab: Tracing Hidden Channels*. New York: Collier Books, 1967.

Swann, Ingo. *Natural ESP*. New York: Bantam Books, 1987.

Faceless Gray Man of Pawleys Island Legend of an apparition of a gray man with no face who appears just before hurricanes strike at Pawleys Island off the coast of South Carolina. In times past, before modern technology enabled advance warning of hurricanes, the Gray Man was credited with saving thousands of lives.

The identity of the Gray Man is unknown. It is believed by some that he is the ghost of Percival Pawley, the first to settle the island and name it. Popular theory, however, contends that the ghost is that of an 18th-century Charleston belle's cousin and lover.

According to legend, the Charleston belle was beautiful, gracious and accomplished, and could have had her pick of fine husbands. She disappointed her family by falling in love with a cousin, a young man who was a bit of a scoundrel. The parents of both agreed to break up the romance by sending the young man off to France. Although he swore he would return and marry the belle, she was informed several months later that he had been killed in a dual. Grief-stricken, she withdrew from the world.

She was drawn out of her grief by a male friend who had recently been widowed. The two married and took up residency on a plantation near Charleston. From May to October, they lived on Pawleys Island, where sea breezes kept away the mosquitoes that spread malaria on the coastal mainland.

The husband joined the army during the American Revolution, and in 1778 was away fighting with Francis Marion, the "Swamp Fox." Meanwhile, his wife left for Pawleys Island when the "fever months" arrived.

While she was there, a hurricane arose and sank a brigantine off the island's shore. It was thought that everyone aboard was drowned. That night, however, a man made it to shore and arrived at the young woman's house, seeking shelter. When she opened the door, she was horrified to see that it was her cousin, who had not died in a duel after all. The cousin fled. He later reached the mainland, where he died of fever.

The young woman resumed her life with her husband, which appeared normal in every respect. Whenever they went to Pawleys Island, however, she was troubled by a gray figure who lurked about in the dunes, watching her. Once she drew close enough to see that the figure was that of a man who had no face.

The apparition soon became visible to others, and established the pattern of appearing before hurricanes. Residents say the Gray Man appeared before the hurricanes of 1822, 1893, 1916, 1954, and 1955.

Further reading:

Anderson, Jean. *The Haunting of America.* Boston: Houghton Mifflin, 1973.

fairies A type of supernatural being, neither ghost, god nor demi-god, which exists on earth and either helps or harms humankind. Fairy beliefs are universal and are strikingly similar. They probably arose to explain illnesses, deformities and untimely deaths among children; epidemics among livestock; and various disasters of weather. Fairies have a close connection with the dead.

Fairy beliefs are particularly strong in Celtic Europe and Britain, and especially so in Ireland. Celtic fairy lore was transplanted to the American Colonies, where it settled in the Appalachians, Ozarks and other rural mountainous areas. Fairy lore abounds in Asia, but not in Africa. Native Americans have their own fairy lore; the Crow, for example, refer to the "Little People" who live in the Pryor Mountains of south-central Montana. The Little People possess powerful medicine for healing, war and horse theft, and are incredibly strong with canine teeth.

The term "fairy" comes from the Latin *fata*, or fate, which refers to the Fates of mythology, three women who spin, twist and cut the threads of life. Fairies

Revenge of the fairies, drawn by George Cruikshank.

were known as *fays* in archaic English, a term which means "enchanted" or "bewitched." Fairies are said to possess magical powers and the ability to cast spells; in Celtic lore, they are frequently identified with witches or said to be their familiars, or their tutors in the magical arts.

Fairies are given various names and descriptions, but in almost all cases are diminutive, even tiny. They may be beautiful or ugly, may resemble humans, or have wings and carry wands and pipes. They usually are invisible save to those with clairvoyant sight; they can make themselves visible to humans if they so desire. Some are morally ambivalent, while others are always benevolent, and still others are always malevolent.

The origins of fairies are given in several main theories: (1) they are the souls of the pagan dead, caught between heaven and earth because they were not baptized; (2) they are the guardians of the dead; (3) they are the ghosts of venerated ancestors; (4) they are fallen angels, cast out of heaven with Lucifer but condemned by God to remain in the elements of the Earth; (5) they are nature spirits who are attached to particular places or elements; and (6) they are small-statured human beings. In various cultures, fairies fall into more than one of these categories.

In Irish mythology, the fairies are the Tuatha de Danaan, the divine race who are children of the goddess Danu. The Tuatha De, or "people of the goddess," as they are called, came over the sea from the east in clouds and mist in the 15th century B.C. They were strong and beautiful people, skilled in the magical arts. After taking control of Ireland, they retired into the hills and mounds (side or sidhe) and became underground dwellers who evolved into fairies. In some myths, Tuatha De also remained above ground, where they were renowned for their warrior skills, beauty, wizardry and magic. They were part mortal, part spirit and part god, and they intermarried with humans.

Medieval romances portrayed human characters as fairies; up to the 13th century, having fairy blood was considered desirable. It is possible that these medieval fairies were descendants of small races, such as the Lapps, Picts and Romano-British-Iberian peoples, who populated Britain, Europe and Scandinavia in the Neolithic and Bronze Ages and were pushed out by larger races such as the Celts. As they retreated more and more into the woodlands, successor races increasingly associated them with superstition. Some of the little people were pressed into servitude, while others married into larger races.

Where fairy lore exists, it is believed that at least some of them live as a fairy race or nation; the Land of Fairy, also called Elfland, has characteristics of the land of the dead: it exists underground and is accessed through barrows and mounds; time ceases there. The fairies customarily come out at night, when they dance, sing, travel about, make merry and make mischief. They are believed to steal human women away for wives, and to steal unprotected human children and leave their own in place (changelings). In order to stay in the good graces of "the little people," "the good people" and "the good neighbors," as they are called, humans are to keep clean houses and leave out food and drink. In return, fairies bestow gifts and money and help humans with their chores.

Fairies also are traditionally propitiated with offerings and rites at sacred wells, fountains, lakes and tree groves so that humans may ward off illness and misfortune. Samhain, the Celtic pagan festival of the dead, November 1, includes recognition of fairies (see ALL HALLOWS EVE). Such rites and observances were absorbed into Christianity: saints assumed the roles of gods, spirits and fairies, and All Saints' Day, the festival of saints and martyrs known and unknown, replaced the festival of the dead.

In Celtic lore, ancient burial sites such as tumuli, dolmens, menhirs and megaliths are haunted by fairies and other beings. It is the fairies' custom, according to lore, to come out and dance circular dances at these sites on moonlit nights. Stories of sightings of such revelries continue into modern times.

See also DOYLE, SIR ARTHUR CONAN.

Further reading:

Briggs, Katherine. *The Vanishing People.* New York: Pantheon Books, 1978.

———. *An Encyclopedia of Fairies: Hobogoblins, Brownies, Bogies, and Other Supernatural Creatures.* New York: Pantheon Books, 1976.

Evans-Wentz, W.Y. *The Fairy Faith in Celtic Countries.* New York: Carroll Publishing Group, 1990. First published 1911.
Guiley, Rosemary Ellen. *The Encyclopedia of Witches and Witchcraft.* New York: Facts On File, 1989.
Murray, Earl. *Ghosts of the Old West: Desert Spirits, Haunted Cabins, Lost Trails, and Other Strange Encounters.* Chicago: Contemporary Books, 1988.

feasts and festivals of the dead Celebrations that are part of the cycle of funerary activities in tribal societies around the world (see FUNERAL RITES AND CUSTOMS).

In the system of beliefs about souls and spirits called animism, the spirit after death has a treacherous road to travel to the Land of the Dead (see AFTERLIFE). The journey typically begins a few days after death and may take several months, up to about a year, to complete. The feasts that are held at this time are intended partly to celebrate this journey, but also partly to help it along. Once the spirit reaches the Land of the Dead, it will find the means of sustaining itself, but while on the way, it requires nourishment from surviving members of the community.

Food may be left out for the spirit, in which case it is believed to eat its material as well as its spiritual essence, or else the food may be consumed or burned, in which case the spirit is thought to partake of its spiritual essence only. Sometimes there are a series of feasts, at intervals, over a course of months, with the last, rather than the first, being the biggest one.

The last feast is the biggest because it celebrates the arrival of the spirit in the Land of the Dead, and its final transformation from a deceased person into an ancestor. Significantly, in many societies it is not until this time that a widow ends her mourning, whatever goods the deceased possessed are transferred to his heirs, and if he held an office, a successor is named. Until the spirit has reached its final destination, the entire society remains in limbo.

See also DAY OF THE DEAD.

Further reading:
Bendann, Effie. *Death Customs: An Analytical Study of Burial Rites.* London: Kegan Paul, Trench, and Trubner, 1930.
Radin, Paul. *Primitive Culture: Its Nature and Origins.* New York: Dover Publications, 1957.
Tylor, Edward Burnett. *Religion in Primitive Culture.* New York: Harper and Row, 1956.

fetch In Irish and English folklore, the term for one's double, an apparition of a living person. The fetch is also called a "co-walker" in England. In general, seeing a fetch is a sign of ill-boding, although in Irish lore, to see a fetch in the morning means one

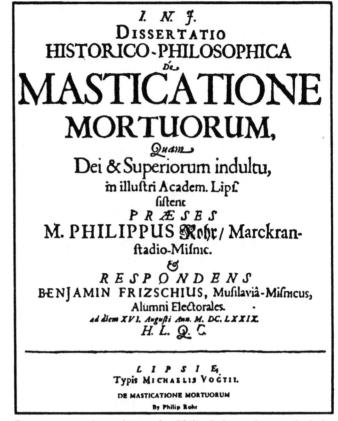

Poster announcing a lecture by Philip Rohr on how to feed the dead, given at the University of Leipzig in 1679.

will have a long life. When seen at night, however, the fetch is believed to foretell a person's death.

Fetches are seen by persons with clairvoyant ability, or by friends or family of the living person just prior to, or at the moment of, that person's death. As such, the fetch is the equivalent of certain crisis apparitions, a term applied in psychical research and parapsychology. Sometimes the fetch is witnessed by the person who is to die several days or weeks prior to his or her death. A case (undated) cited in *Haunted England* (1940) by folklorist Christina Hole is that of Sir William Napier, who stopped at an inn while traveling from Bedfordshire to Berkshire. When he was shown his room, he saw a corpse lying on the bed. Upon closer inspection, he was astonished to see that the corpse was himself. Shortly after arriving in Berkshire, he died.

See APPARITIONS; DEATH OMENS.

Further reading:
Briggs, Katherine. *An Encyclopedia of Fairies: Hobgoblins, Brownies, Bogies, and Other Supernatural Creatures.* New York: Pantheon Books, 1976.
Hole, Christina. *Haunted England.* London: B.T. Batsford Ltd., 1940.

Leach, Maria, and Jerome Fried, eds. *Funk & Wagnalls Standard Dictionary of Folklore, Mythology, and Legend.* San Francisco: Harper & Row, 1979.

fetch candles   See CORPSE CANDLES.

fetch lights   See CORPSE CANDLES.

fetish   An object believed to embody spirits or be inhabited by, or attached to, them. A fetish represents the spirits to its owner and creates a bond between the human and supernatural realms. Usually a doll or carved image, a fetish may also be an animal tooth, snake vertebrae, beautiful stones or even the hut where a witch doctor communes with his spirit guides. Fetishes are widely used in animistic religions. They are often worn as ornamental talismans or amulets, but they are not the same as traditional talismans or amulets, which do not carry inhabiting spirits.

"Fetish" derives either from the Latin *factitius*, "made by art," or the Portuguese *feitico*, for "charm" or "sorcery." The term usually is associated with the West African *juju*, meaning "sacred object." *Juju* may be a European translation of the native expression *grou-grou*, or it may refer to the French word *joujou*, meaning a doll or plaything. Early European traders on the West African coast may have mistaken fetishes, which are sacred, for mere playthings. A slight variation of *grou-grou* is *gris-gris*, a modern term for a charm or talisman kept for good luck or to ward off evil.

ANCIENT EGYPTIAN FETISHES

The ancient Egyptians, who practiced an animistic religion in pre-dynastic times, had numerous gods and goddesses of fetish origin, especially those associated with magic, luck, increase, health and life, fecundity and virility, childbirth and war. Egyptian animism was succeeded by magic cults and then cults of animals, birds and trees, the totemism and fetishism of which enabled the higher spirits to evolve into deities.

AFRICAN-AMERICAN FETISHES

Africans captured for the slave trade brought their fetishes with them to the New World. Possession of a fetish, however, was punishable by torture and death. Not only were the fetishes graven images of a god other than the Christian one, they also represented tribal ways feared by white masters. Eventually, the slaves began carrying stones or small bags filled with herbs or oils for good luck, for such items were not seen as threatening. Most gris-gris today are made the same way.

In New Orleans, the traditional headquarters for American Vodoun, many persons, even some police officers, carry gris-gris bags for protection. Legends about the famous New Orleans "voodoo" queen, Marie LAVEAU, tell that her gris-gris contained bits of bone, colored stones, graveyard dust (also called "goofer dust"), salt and red pepper. More elaborate gris-gris might have been made of tiny birds' nests or horsehair weavings. A red-flannel bag containing a lodestone, or magnet, was a favorite gris-gris for gamblers, sure to bring them good luck.

In Santería, the gris-gris bags are called *resguardos*, or "protectors." A typical *resguardo* under the protection of the thunder god, Chango, might be made of red velvet and filled with herbs, spices, brown sugar, aloes and other ingredients and then stitched with red thread. Finally, the preparer attaches a tiny gold sword, the symbol of Saint Barbara (Chango's image as a Catholic saint), and if the sword breaks, Chango has interceded on the owner's behalf.

Gris-gris also can be used to cause someone else ill luck. Throwing a gris-gris bag filled with gunpowder and red pepper in someone's path or on his doorstep supposedly makes that person get into a fight. Leaving a gris-gris at the front door tells a person he is out of favor with "the voodoos" and had better watch his step. Another term for gris-gris is "charm bag."

NATIVE AMERICAN FETISHES

Fetishes are part of the traditions of various North American tribes. In some traditions, fetishes are owned individually, while in others they are primarily collective. The Crow and the Dakota, for example, have fetishes of societies of visionaries, while the Sauk and the Fox of Wisconsin have clan fetishes and the Pawnee of Nebraska have village fetishes. The Midewiwin, or Grand Medicine Society of the Great Lakes region, had a collective fetish of the sacred white shell, which empowered initiates.

The strongest fetish tradition has existed for centuries among the Pueblo, and particularly the Zuñi, the most ceremonial of the Pueblo. Zuñi fetishes are animals, birds and reptiles carved from stone or horn or made from shell; they are regarded as extremely powerful and are used only for religious purposes. The most traditional forms are the mountain lion, bear, coyote, wolf and eagle, which are valued for their prowess in game hunting. Carried in leather pouches around a hunter's neck, they are believed to aid the success of the hunt. Small ornaments of turquoise, shell, beads or arrowpoints are tied to the backs of the fetishes to increase their power. Besides hunting, fetishes aid luck, gambling and war, protect households and play a role in various initiations and curing rituals.

Some fetishes represent deities, such as the Earth Mother and Creator God. The Corn Mother aspect of the Earth Mother is represented by a sacred corn ear or similar fetish and is kept by each individual throughout life. The fetish contains a seed or seeds, so that the cycle of life may continue. The Acoma, a Pueblo tribe, destroy the corn fetish upon a person's death; the Zuñi break up their similar fetish and plant the seeds in the deceased's fields.

If not kept in a pouch, fetishes are housed in jars. They must be properly cared for or they will visit ill fortune upon their owners.

The most powerful Zuñi fetishes are collective ones which belong to ceremonial societies. The Rain Priests own the most holy, called *ettowe*, which provide the priests' source of power. The *ettowe* represent the nourishing forces of the Earth Mother and the soul power or life-giving breath of Awonawilona, the bisexual creator god. Fetishes of frogs, which are associated with water, are used in rain-making ceremonies and are buried near water sources to ensure a continuing supply of potable water.

Zuñi medicine societies have large, animal-like fetishes which represent the Beast Gods (gods of the most sacred animals), which are housed in jars and fed daily. The Ant Society uses its fetish, an effigy of a red ant tied to a horn medicine pouch, to cure skin diseases. The fetish is placed on the pillow near the patient's face, where it draws out the illness through the patient's mouth. The healing also involves 12 mornings of chanting.

Among the Acoma, the Corn Mother fetish is used in curing illness.

In general, ceremonial fetishes carved from deer antler are highly valued, since the antler once was a part of a living creature. Horn fetishes are associated with sea-serpents, whose power is believed to be greater than that of the Beast Gods.

The Zuñi fetishes are regarded as petrified supernatural beings and have their origin in myth. When the first ancestors emerged from the four caves of the Lower Regions—the underworld—they were greeted by a new world covered with water, shaken by earthquakes and filled with monstrous beasts of prey. The Children of the Sun took pity on them and dried and hardened the earth with lightning arrows. Then the Children of the Sun traveled over the land and touched every animal they met, shrinking them and turning them to stone. A few animals escaped, and became the ancestors of the present-day animals. Natural stones that resemble animal shapes are believed to be the original petrified beings, and thus possess the greatest potency.

The Zuñi traded fetishes to the Navajo. Following the publication of a book, *Zuñi Fetiches* (sic), by Frank Cushing in 1883, a tourist and collector's market for them developed among whites. Around 1945, the Zuñi began producing replica fetishes for sale to the public.

See also ANIMISM.

Further reading:
Budge, E.A. Wallis. *From Fetish to God in Ancient Egypt.* New York: Dover Publications, 1988. First published 1934.
Tallant, Robert. *Voodoo in New Orleans.* Gretna, La.: Pelican Publishing Co., 1983. First published 1946.
Gonzales-Wippler, Migene. *Santeria: African Magic in Latin America.* New York: Original Products, 1981.
Hultkrantz, Ake. *Native Religions of North America.* San Francisco: Harper & Row, 1987.
Tyler, Hamilton A. *Pueblo Gods and Myths.* Norman, Olka.: University of Oklahoma Press, 1964.

Fifty Berkeley Square Home in London's fashionable Berkeley Square known in Victorian days as "the most haunted house in London." The house acquired a reputation for being haunted merely because the owner allowed the property to deteriorate. Once the reputation was established, reports emerged of terrifying phenomena at the house, and even several deaths were attributed to its ghosts and evil nature.

Fifty Berkeley Square was once the residence of George Canning, Prime Minister of England, who owned it until his death in 1827. The house was then leased to a Miss Curzon, who occupied it until her death in 1859 at the age of 90. The tenancy then passed to a Mr. Myers, the man allegedly responsible for its haunting.

The story goes that Mr. Myers was jilted at the last moment by his fiancée, and he turned into a bitter recluse. He took to living in a small room in the garret, and would open the door only to receive food from his manservant. But at night, he would wander forlornly about the dark house with a single lighted candle.

As the years went by, Myers became more eccentric, and the house began to fall into disrepair and ruin. The windows became caked with black dust and dirt. Myers failed to pay his taxes, and he received a summons in 1873 from the local council. He even failed to respond to that. He was not prosecuted further, as the local officials declared that his house was known to be haunted, as if that explained Myers's bizarre behavior.

By 1879, 50 Berkeley Square had such a bad reputation that stories about it were played up in the press, including the magazine *Mayfair* (it is not known whether Myers was still living at the house). The magazine emphasized the house's "ghostly feeling" and the fact that it "always seems oppressed into dullness by a sense of its own secret grandeur."

Mayfair also reported anecdotes about evil happenings at the house in the past. Once upon a time a new maid was given an upper room. Not long after the family had retired for the night, it was awakened by terrible screams coming from upstairs. The maid was found standing in the middle of her room, "rigid as a corpse, with hideously glaring eyes," unable to speak. "However, this, of itself, did not mean much, even when taken in connection with the house and with the room—women may go mad now and then without any ghostly dealings," *Mayfair* intoned drily.

The maid was given a new room (in another version she died insane the next day in the hospital), and the family refused to use the haunted room. Then a visitor arrived, and they had no other place to put him. The man scoffed at the story about the maid, but said he would ring his bell once to indicate that he was all right, and twice to summon someone if he needed help. After he retired, he rang the bell once. Shortly thereafter, the family heard the bell ring madly. They dashed upstairs to find the man dead in the middle of the room. *Mayfair* appealed to the owner of the house to come forward and confirm or deny the tales, but no response was made.

Another version of the second story identifies the victim as Sir Robert Warboys, who accepted the challenge of his club to prove that the tales about the house were "poppycock." After the bell began to jangle wildly, rescuers heard a shot. They dashed upstairs and found Warboys dead across the bed—but not from being shot. He appeared to have been frightened to death.

Other stories added to the house's reputation. Lord LYTTLETON reportedly spent a night in the haunted upper room, protecting himself with two shotguns loaded with buckshot and silver sixpence coins. During the night he fired at a shape that lunged out of the darkness at him, and that something dropped to the floor "like a rocket." No evidence but buckshot holes in the floor was visible the next morning.

According to another story, the house is haunted by the ghost of a woman who lived there with her lecherous uncle. To escape him, she threw herself out of the garret window, and her ghost still clings to the ledge and screams.

The most chilling story of all concerns two sailors from the frigate HMS *Penelope* who came to town on December 24, 1887. They found a "to let" sign on the house, but it was empty, so they let themselves in. They went to sleep in a second-story bedroom. In the middle of the night, footsteps were heard in the corridor outside the room, and a dark and shapeless "thing" (later described as a white-faced man with a gaping mouth) entered and attacked them. One sailor escaped. The second was found impaled on the railings of the basement steps as though he had fallen through the bedroom window.

During the 1870s and 1880s, neighbors of the house complained it was the source of loud noises, cries, moans and poltergeist phenomena such as ringing bells, furniture being moved about, objects, stones and books being thrown out of the house, and windows being thrown open. One natural explanation put forward by Charles Harper in *Haunted Houses* (1924) is that the house was owned by a Mr. Du Pre of Wilton Park who kept his lunatic brother imprisoned in the garret. The man was violent and threw objects about, and cried and moaned a great deal.

Other possible explanations are that natural noises and movements came from the proximity of the house, but were associated with the haunting because of the house's reputation; or, that the phenomena were imagined or exaggerated for the same reason.

In 1939, the house was leased by the Maggs Brothers, antiquarian booksellers. No phenomena have been reported in recent years.

Further reading:

Brooks, J.A. *Ghosts of London: The West End, South and West.* Norwich, England: Jarrold Colour Publications, 1982.

Harper, Charles G. *Haunted Houses: Tales of the Supernatural With Some Accounts of Hereditary Curses and Family Legends.* Rev. and enlarged ed. London: Cecil Palmer, 1924.

Whitaker, Terence. *Haunted England.* Chicago: Contemporary Books, 1987.

Findlay, J. Arthur See SPIRITUALISTS' NATIONAL UNION.

Fischer, Doris See DORIS FISCHER CASE.

Flight 401 The ghosts of the captain and flight engineer of an ill-fated Eastern Airlines Flight 401 L-1011 jumbo jet have been reported to visit the crews and passengers of other Eastern L-1011 jets containing parts salvaged from Flight 401's 1972 wreckage. Eastern crew members and passengers reportedly saw the ghosts and heard them speak on the planes' public address systems or received verbal messages and warnings from them. Witnesses also reported experiencing abnormally cold sensations and invisible presences. Further strange happenings attributed to the ghosts were one plane's power suddenly coming on, and a tool inexplicably appearing in a mechanic's hand when no one was in the immediate area.

Bob Loft was captain, and second officer Dan Repo was flight engineer, when Flight 401 crashed in the Florida Everglades on Friday night, December 19, 1972. They and 100 passengers and crew members lost their lives. Initially, Loft and Repo were among the survivors, but Loft succumbed in the cockpit about an hour after the crash, before rescuers could remove him to a hospital. Repo, critically injured and seemingly angry when pulled from the wreckage, lingered about 30 hours before dying.

An investigation concluded that the cause was a combination of equipment failure and pilot error. A printout of the flight recorder indicated that the plane had a problem with either its landing gear or the gear's warning light as it approached the Miami airport. As the crew became preoccupied with finding the source of the problem, they did not notice that the plane was steadily losing altitude. When they finally realized the extent of their descent, it was too late to correct and the plane crashed.

To save costs, Eastern ordered the plane's salvageable parts to be incorporated into other Eastern planes. Soon after, reports of the ghosts of Repo, Loft and even some unidentified flight attendants were sighted on various Eastern flights. For the next year or so, they were most often seen on Eastern's plane number 318, or on other L-1011s that Eastern leased to other airlines, all of which contained many of those salvageable parts.

Substantiation of the sightings was difficult, however. Eyewitness reports made to Eastern's management were met with skepticism mixed with fear of tarnishing the airline's reputation and losing business. Management's suggestions to a few employee witnesses to see the company's psychiatrist were viewed as precursors to getting fired. Thus, eyewitnesses were reluctant to talk to anyone investigating the hauntings. The story was made public in *The Ghost of Flight 401* (1976) by John G. Fuller.

Adding to the mystery was the discovery that the log sheets containing the sighting reports, as well as the names of witnesses, were missing from logbooks on those planes where the ghosts had been seen. Normally, a logbook would contain entries for several months. Nevertheless, the eyewitness reports continued and were so widely circulated throughout the aviation community that Eastern finally removed the parts associated with Flight 401.

The reports apparently were numerous because the ghosts allegedly visited different parts of the plane at various times of the day or night, thereby exposing themselves to a wide range of potential witnesses. Moreover, Repo and Loft were often rec-

ognized by crew members who had once worked with them.

Repo was reportedly seen more often than Loft. Repo was said to have visited the galley where flight attendants saw his face reflected in the oven door. These attendants often reported that the galley felt unusually cold and clammy, or that there was a powerful feeling of someone present in the room. During one haunting, Repo fixed an oven that had an overloaded circuit. It wasn't until another engineer came to fix the oven, and told the attendant that he was the only engineer on the plane, that she realized something was strange. She looked up Repo's picture and identified him as the man who had first appeared and made the repairs.

But Repo's ghost seemed to be especially concerned about the safety and operation of the plane. When his ghost appeared, it often made suggestions or gave warnings to crew members who only realized he was an apparition after he had vanished. Repo's ghost was seen in the cockpit, either sitting at the engineer's instrument panel or with just his face reflected on it. During one visit, a flight engineer was making a pre-flight inspection when he recognized Repo's apparition. Before vanishing, Repo told the engineer that he had already made the inspection.

Repo's ghost once warned a flight engineer that there would be an electrical failure, and a check discovered a faulty circuit. Another time, his ghost warned an attendant about a fire on the plane. On still another occasion, his ghost pointed out a problem area in the plane's hydraulic system. Repo's ghost even told a captain that there would be another crash on an L-1011, but that "we will not let it happen."

On several occasions, Captain Loft's uniformed ghost was seen sitting in a plane's first-class section. During one sighting, a flight attendant asked Loft why his name was not on her passenger list. When there was no response, she sought the aid of her supervisor and a flight captain. It was the captain who recognized Loft, whose ghost then immediately disappeared. Loft's ghost also appeared in the crew compartment, and it was suspected of being the voice that spoke over the public address system to warn passengers about seat belts and smoking rules, when no one claimed to have made such an announcement.

The alleged hauntings remain a mystery.

Further reading:
Fuller, John G. *The Ghost of Flight 401*. New York: Berkley, 1976.

Flint, Leslie (1911?–   ) British medium noted for his 35 years of "independent direct voice mediumship," a rare mediumistic gift in which voices of the dead allegedly spoke from a point above and slightly to the left of Flint's head.

The various voices manifested around Flint were sometimes quite clear and other times gravelly or hoarse. Flint rarely went into trance, but he remained aware of what the voices were saying throughout the sitting. He only used trance, he said, when the power was weak and spirits urgently wanted to communicate. He claimed the spirits did not use his own vocal cords.

In addition to bringing messages from the dead, Flint also brought messages from living individuals who were in a state of deep sleep or coma. Psychical researchers tested him and never found any evidence of fraud.

Flint was born in a Salvation Army home in Hackney, England. His mother, a factory worker, was unemployed. His father served in the army in World War I. He was raised primarily by his mother and maternal grandmother at their home in St. Albans.

Flint had his first psychic experience during the summer of 1918. He was in the kitchen of his home with his grandmother when his Aunt Nell came in crying. She had just learned her husband had been killed in France in World War I. Flint saw her followed by a soldier carrying a kit bag containing his uncle's belongings, and by another soldier who appeared to be lost. This second soldier kept trying to get his aunt's attention, but to no avail. Finally he vanished. Later, Flint was shown a photograph of his dead uncle and recognized him as the woebegone soldier in the kitchen.

After this experience, Flint began hearing the voices of the dead. When he attempted to describe these experiences to his family, he was reprimanded, and so decided to keep quiet about them.

In his later teens, he became interested in Spiritualism. He attended a Spiritualist service and witnessed the mediumship of Annie Johnson, who described a spirit guide around him, a being who seemed to be an Arab but was not really an Arab. This guide, said Johnson, wanted Flint to develop his ability as a medium. Flint initially ignored this message, though it was repeated to him by other mediums. He was propelled to act on it when he received a letter from a Munich woman who told him a spirit claiming to be Rudolph Valentino was trying to contact Flint, and had given her his name and address. This apparently explained to Flint the mysterious "Arab" guide who was not really an Arab.

Flint then attended a home circle where Valentino allegedly manifested with rappings, spirit writing, movements of the table and other physical phenomena.

Flint pursued his mediumship by participating in seances. After a time, his clairvoyance developed and he could see the spirits in attendance at a circle. Then independent direct voices manifested. Their first appearances occurred in movie theaters. As Flint watched films, he became aware of strange whisperings around him. Others could hear them as well and thought they were Flint. He was sometimes hounded out of theaters for not keeping quiet. This phenomenon began to happen so often that he quit going to movies. The theater whisperings led to the manifestation of independent spirit voices at Flint's seances. The first spirit to speak claimed to be Valentino.

Through Flint's involvement in home circles, he met an older woman, Edith Mundin, a widow with a son named Owen. Edith became one of his champions, and they eventually married.

With the manifestation of the voices, Flint felt ready to take his mediumship to the public. He held seances at which the voices of dead friends and relatives would speak to those present. In order for the voices to manifest, the seances had to be conducted in absolute darkness and with a limited number of sitters. Flint had control spirits, one of whom professed to be a Cockney boy named "Mickey." In addition to Valentino, other spirits alleging to be famous persons came through, such as Thomas Alva Edison, Sir Arthur Conan DOYLE and Professor Charles Richet, a noted psychical researcher.

With Edith and other Spiritualists, Flint formed an association called the Temple of Light and moved to Hendon, a suburb of London. He gave numerous public appearances in London, attracting thousands at a time. In order to fulfill his need for darkness before a large crowd, Flint sat on a chair enclosed in a small cabinet (q.v.). While most of his seances were successful, some were not; on some occasions, no spirits manifested at all.

When World War II broke out, Flint attempted to get conscientious objector status but was denied and was drafted into the army. He was not sent to the front, but performed clerical work and bomb defusion duties.

Flint's popularity attracted the attention of psychical researchers, who sought to test him. Some members of the SOCIETY FOR PSYCHICAL RESEARCH (SPR) thought perhaps Flint received messages clairaudiently and then surreptitiously used his own voice. Flint agreed to be tested on numerous occasions; he even referred to himself as "the most tested medium in this country."

Tests were devised by the Reverend Charles Drayton Thomas, a member of the Confraternity, a group of clergymen interested in Spiritualism, and a member of the Temple of Light governing committee. The first tests were conducted in 1948, but not before members of the SPR. Flint's lips were sealed with adhesive tape and his mouth was tied with a scarf. His hands were tied to a chair and he was unable to bend his neck. He sat behind a curtain. The test was done again for the benefit of the SPR. Voices manifested, but one of the researchers concluded that Flint could speak through his stomach.

Another researcher theorized that the voices were not real, but were auditory hallucinations produced by hypnotism on the part of Flint and subconscious longing on the part of sitters. However, that theory was disproved when the voices were subsequently recorded on gramophone records.

In 1949, Flint gave a successful tour in the United States.

In 1970, Flint underwent perhaps his most significant tests, administered both in London and New York by William R. Bennett, a professor of electrical engineering at Columbia University. Flint's lips were sealed with plaster, a throat microphone was attached to his throat and wired to amplifiers, his hands were held by sitters, and an infrared telescope was used to detect any movements. The throat microphone registered nothing despite the manifestation of the voices, which were weaker than customary. Bennett verified that Flint's vocal cords were not used in the manifestation of the voices, and also concluded that infrared somehow weakened mediumship.

In 1976, Flint retired from public seances. In 1977, he was named "Spiritualist of the Year" in a poll of readers of *Psychic News*, a British periodical.

One of Flint's most famous clients was the actress Mae West, who had private sittings with him in London in the 1940s. Shaw Desmond, the Irish novelist and poet, also sat frequently with him during his home circle days.

See also DIRECT VOICE MEDIUMSHIP.

Further reading:

Flint, Leslie. *Voices in the Dark: My Life as Medium*. Indianapolis: Bobbs-Merrill, 1971.

Shepard, Leslie A., ed. *Encyclopedia of Occultism and Parapsychology*, 2nd ed. Detroit: Gale Research Co., 1984.

Flying Dutchman   Phantom ship legend involving a rash oath or punishment for sins or evil. It is the best-known of PHANTOM SHIPS legends.

The Flying Dutchman legend has various versions. In the Dutch version, the captain, named van Straaten, was a stubborn man who vowed to sail around the Cape of Storms, now known as the Cape of Good Hope, in bad weather. The ship was lost, and as a result the ship, its crew of dead men and the dead captain are condemned to sail the spot forever. Their phantom vessel reportedly can be seen at the Cape in stormy weather, and is an omen of disaster.

In the German version of the legend, the captain is known as von Falkenberg, and he sails in the North Sea. In this tale, the Devil visited periodically and engaged the captain in a game of dice on deck, playing for the captain's soul. The captain lost the game and his soul and became one of the phantom condemned.

In a version published in a British magazine in 1821, the ship was sailing around the Cape of Good Hope when a storm arose and the crew begged the captain to head for safe harbor. He refused and taunted them for their fear. As the storm grew worse, he shook his fist and challenged God to sink the ship. Instantly an apparition appeared on the deck, but the belligerent captain ordered it away lest he shoot it. When the apparition did not leave, he drew out his pistol and fired at it, but the gun exploded in his hand. The apparition then cursed him to sail forever, always tormenting his crew. Anyone who sighted the doomed ship would have misfortune.

There are still other variations of the legend. In one, the ship was condemned to eternal wanderings because of cruelty on the part of the captain. In another, a goddess appeared on deck one day and was treated sacrilegiously by the captain. In revenge, she condemned the ship to sail forever until doomsday.

Heinrich Heine, the great German writer, romanticized the Flying Dutchman story. Heine injected the element of redemption by allowing his captain to go ashore once every seven years in order to try to regain his freedom by winning the hand of an unsullied maiden. Composer Richard Wagner took this version for his opera, *Die Fliegende Hollander*. Wagner called the captain van Derdeeken, and the maiden to whom he makes advances, Senta.

An apparition of a phantom derelict ship believed to be the Flying Dutchman was seen at the Cape in 1923. It was witnessed by four seamen, one of whom reported the incident years later to Sir Ernest Bennett, a member of the SOCIETY FOR PSYCHICAL RESEARCH. Bennett included the account in his book, *Apparitions and Haunted Houses: A Survey of the Evidence* (1934).

According to Fourth Officer N.K. Stone, the apparition was sighted at about 15 minutes past midnight on January 26, 1923. Earlier in the day, the ship, en route from Australia to London, had left Cape Town. Wrote Stone:

> About 0.15 A.M. we noticed a strange "light" on the port bow; . . . it was a very dark night, overcast, with no moon. We looked at this through binoculars and the ship's telescope, and made out what appeared to be the hull of a sailing ship, luminous,

Sailors terrified by a vision of the Flying Dutchman's phantom ship.

with two distinct masts carrying bare yards, also luminous; no sails were visible, but there was a luminous haze between the masts. There were no navigation lights, and she appeared to be coming close to us and at the same speed as ourselves. When first sighted she was about two-three miles away, and when she was about a half-mile of us she suddenly disappeared.

There were four witnesses of this spectacle, the 2nd Officer, a cadet, the helmsman and myself. I shall never forget the 2nd Officer's startled expression—"My God, Stone, it's a ghost ship."

Stone drew a picture of the ship, which he kept for many years. His account was corroborated for Bennett by the second officer; the other two seamen could not be located.

In theorizing what causes such apparitions as this, Bennett agreed with Frederic W.H. MYERS that some form of consciousness survives death and is capable of telepathically projecting images, including those of material objects, to the living, which are perceived as phantoms. If such were the case, then the Flying Dutchman apparition was an image projected telepathically by her dead crew. The telepathic projection theory has since been discounted as a plausible explanation of apparitions.

Further reading:

Bennett, Sir Ernest. *Apparitions and Haunted Houses: A Survey of the Evidence.* London: Faber and Faber Ltd., 1934.

Leach, Maria, and Jerome Fried, eds. *Funk & Wagnalls Standard Dictionary of Folklore, Mythology, and Legend.* San Francisco: Harper & Row, 1979.

Fodor, Nandor (1895–1964) Journalist, lawyer, psychoanalyst and psychical researcher best known for his pioneering theories on the psychological and sexual aspects of mediumship and poltergeist phenomena. Some of his theories were far ahead of his day, causing controversy and bringing him much criticism, especially from Spiritualists. His views were supported by subsequent research by others in later years.

Nandor Fodor was born on May 13, 1895 in Berengszasz, Hungary. He earned a law degree from the Royal Hungarian University of Science in Budapest in 1917. He also earned a doctorate. From 1917 to 1921 he worked as a law assistant. In 1922 he married Amarai Iren; the couple had a daughter.

From 1921 to 1928, Fodor worked as a journalist. One of his posts was staff reporter for the *Amerikai Magyar Neszava (American Hungarian People's Voice)* based in New York. In the year of his arrival in New York, he discovered Hereward CARRINGTON's book *Modern Psychic Phenomena* (1919), which so intrigued him that he made psychical research his primary activity for the rest of his life. Fodor used his position as a journalist to meet Carrington, who in turn introduced him to others prominent in psychical research, including Sir Arthur Conan DOYLE. Fodor and Carrington became close friends, and Carrington served as an influential model for Fodor's later psychical investigations.

A second major influence upon Fodor was his meeting of Sandor Ferenczi, a psychoanalyst and an associate of Sigmund Freud, whom Fodor interviewed in 1926. The meeting stimulated his interest in psychoanalysis. In his later research, Fodor would approach psychical phenomena from the viewpoint of a psychoanalyst.

In 1927, Fodor was introduced to the world of Spiritualism when he attended a seance of William Cartheuser, a direct voice medium in New York. Fodor was overwhelmed to receive a message purportedly from his dead father. Cartheuser's mediumship was questioned by some psychical researchers—in 1926, one of his allegedly dead communicators had been discovered to be alive after all—but the seance reinforced Fodor's interest in psychical phenomena. (He later became disillusioned with Cartheuser.)

In 1928, Lord Rothermere, the owner of a number of British newspapers, hired Fodor as a secretary to work with him on Hungarian projects. Fodor moved to London, where he worked for Rothermere until 1937.

In London, he became more involved in Spiritualism and psychical research, giving lectures and writing articles. In 1934 he became assistant editor of *Light*, the oldest British Spiritualist journal, a post he held through 1935. He worked with the London Spiritual Alliance in conducting experiments with mediums.

In 1934, the International Institute for Psychical Research was formed, including both Spiritualists and non-Spiritualists, and Fodor was appointed research officer in 1935. The following year, Fodor became London correspondent to the AMERICAN SOCIETY FOR PSYCHICAL RESEARCH.

The position afforded him the opportunity to conduct numerous investigations of mediums, mediumistic phenomena, poltergeists and hauntings. At about the same time, he renewed his interest in psychoanalysis, and began applying it to his research.

Prior to this, scant consideration had been given to emotional states and unconscious drives as causes or contributors to some psychical phenomena. Fodor's theories ignited controversies. Psychoanalysis itself, with its focus on sex, was not well regarded in Britain; also, many Spiritualists resented the implication that the phenomena might have (at least in some cases) a natural, non-otherworldly explanation. What was more, Fodor found that research and analysis did not necessarily mix, due to their unique relationships with the subject/patient.

Nonetheless, Fodor's work was profoundly influential, especially in his two most famous cases, the ASH MANOR GHOST and the THORNTON HEATH POLTERGEIST. In the Ash Manor Ghost case, investigated beginning in 1936, Fodor determined that suppressed sexual energies apparently contributed to a haunting. In the Thornton Heath case, investigated beginning in 1938, a woman's personal and emotional problems seemed to be at the root of poltergeist phenomena and alleged vampire attacks.

Fodor came under severe attack from the Spiritualists, especially for his Thornton Heath work, until he finally sued one Spiritualist newspaper, *Psychic News*, for libel in 1938. J. Arthur Findlay, a Spiritualist

and a founder and chairman of the International Institute for Psychical Research, resigned his post in protest of Fodor's theories. Shortly after, Fodor was dismissed from his post as research officer.

Fodor responded to these attacks by stepping up his own criticism of mediumistic fraud. He was comforted by an encouraging letter from Freud, who read Fodor's manuscript on the Thornton Heath case and stated, "I hold it very probable that your conclusions regarding this particular case are correct . . ."

In 1939, Fodor won two of his four charges of libel, but he was awarded only minor monetary damages. He quit his role as London correspondent to the ASPR and returned to New York, where he became a successful psychoanalyst. He eventually became an editor of *The Psychoanalytic Review*, the oldest psychoanalytic journal in the United States, and served on the teaching staff of the Training Institute of the National Psychological Association for Psychoanalysis.

In the United States, Fodor found a more favorable attitude to his psychoanalytic approach to psychical research. He resumed his association with Carrington, and worked with Eileen J. GARRETT, whom he had met previously in England. He wrote numerous articles for Garrett's journal, *Tomorrow*.

In his later years, Fodor came to believe that psychical research "has tried to be too scientific for years and has gone bankrupt as a result." Mediums do not function well if treated like guinea pigs, he said. He defended posthumous criticism of ghost-hunter Harry PRICE and psychical researcher Sir William CROOKES.

Fodor died on May 17, 1964. He left a legacy of nine major books and numerous articles and essays. His most important work, *An Encyclopedia of Psychic Science* (1934), is a classic and is still regarded as one of the most important reference books in the field, providing an in-depth picture of psychical research from about the late 19th century to its year of publication. He compiled the encyclopedia after moving to London, spurred by his own need for a concise reference to assist him in his reading and research. The encyclopedia was reissued with corrections in 1966, and later was combined with Lewis Spence's *Encyclopedia of the Occult* (1929) to become *The Encyclopedia of Occultism and Parapsychology*. An updated second edition of that work was issued in 1984, and a third edition was issued in 1990.

Other significant books were *These Mysterious People* (1936); *Haunted People* (1951; published in 1953 in the U.K. as *The Story of the Poltergeist Down the Centuries*); *On the Trail of the Poltergeist* (1958; the story of the Thornton Heath case); *The Haunted Mind* (1959; includes the Ash Manor case); *Mind Over Space* (1962);

Between Two Words (1964); *Freud, Jung and the Occult;* and *The Voice Within* (published posthumously).

Fodor was a past member of the Free and Accepted Masons.

See also BALTIMORE POLTERGEIST.

Further reading:
Fodor, Nandor. *On the Trail of the Poltergeist.* New York: The Citadel Press, 1958.
———. *The Haunted Mind.* New York: Helix Press, 1959.
———. *Between Two Worlds.* West Nyack, N.Y.: Parker Publishing, 1964.
Shepard, Leslie A., ed. *Encyclopedia of Occultism and Parapsychology,* 2nd ed. Detroit: Gale Research Co., 1984.

Ford, Arthur Augustus (1897–1971)   American medium who gained international fame for his ability to communicate with the dead through a control named Fletcher. Once hailed by some as the greatest leader of the American Spiritualist movement, Ford worked to convince mainstream churches to integrate Spiritualist beliefs into their doctrines. Although he was invited to speak in many mainstream churches, he had little effect on changing doctrine.

Ford's personality was like the moon. The bright side, always turned toward the public, was charming, witty and urbane—the life of the intellectual party. The dark side, glimpsed only by close friends and associates, was tormented, lonely and mysterious.

Like most talented psychics, Ford was drawn involuntarily to his calling. He was born into a Southern Baptist family on January 8, 1897 in Titusville, Florida, the second oldest of four children. As a child, he had no profound psychic experiences, although later in life he recalled anticipating what people were about to say, and sensing when they were lying. But his psychic visions and voices did not begin until he was a young adult.

As a boy, Ford was drawn to religion, and he liked to pray for the dead because he believed he helped them that way. But he questioned orthodox church doctrines concerning life after death, angering his Baptist church so much that he was excommunicated at the age of 16. Throughout his life, Ford opposed traditional church concepts of "heaven" and "hell." That anyone would suffer eternal punishment for wrongdoings on earth was "blasphemous and heart-rending," he said.

He entered Transylvania College in Lexington, Kentucky on a scholarship in 1917, determined to become a minister, but his studies were interrupted by World War I. He joined the army in 1918 and became a second lieutenant, but he never saw action overseas.

It was during his army stint that Ford's psychic gifts emerged. Frightening voices and visions bombarded him. As a deadly influenza epidemic swept through Camp Grant in Sheridan, Illinois, he dreamed the next day's death list. Then voices began to whisper the names of soldiers overseas who soon were killed in action. Ford's first clairvoyant experience was a waking vision of his distant brother, George, accompanied by an ominous feeling. He learned later that George had become ill with the flu on that same day, and had died shortly thereafter.

At first Ford thought he was going crazy. Back at Transylvania College, a psychology professor, Dr. Elmer Snoddy, convinced him he was psychic, not insane, and Ford slowly began to develop his extrasensory ability.

He graduated with a mediocre academic record, but an outstanding track record in leadership and preaching. In 1922, he was ordained a minister of the Disciples of Christ Church in Barbourville, Kentucky. He also married a Kentucky belle, Sallie Stewart, but the union would last only five years.

Ford's popularity at the pulpit gained him a great deal of attention. He left the church to join the Swarthmore Chatauqua Association of Pennsylvania, doing the lecture circuit on Spiritualism topics. He moved to New York, where he lectured often to full houses at Carnegie Hall. He taught himself to enter a "half-hypnotized" state in which he could hear voices, sometimes audibly, sometimes as an "inner awareness." The voices claimed to be people who were dead, and Ford delivered messages from them to people in the audience.

Ford's psychic talent remained spotty until he met the Hindu Swami Yogananda, who became his guru and taught him how to achieve a Yogic trance state that enabled him to stay in control and not be helplessly bombarded by voices. Ford did his yoga exercises nearly every day, even into his 70s.

In 1924, a spirit named "Fletcher" announced he would become Ford's control. Fletcher had been a boyhood friend of Ford's and had been killed in action during World War I. Fletcher opted to be known by his middle name only in order not to embarrass his Roman Catholic family.

To communicate with Fletcher, Ford wrapped a black silk handkerchief around his eyes to shut out the light, and then did deep, rhythmic breathing to induce a trance and let Fletcher come through. He was never aware of Fletcher's speaking with his vocal cords and could never remember anything that was said in trance.

With Fletcher's help, Ford's psychic ability grew more impressive. Though skeptics accused him of trickery—fraud was rampant among mediums—Ford often astounded even some of his harshest critics. He rode the crest of the Spiritualism movement all over the world, hobnobbing with royalty, nobility and the elite.

In the late 1920s, Ford founded the First Spiritualist Church of New York, the first of several organizations that he would conceive or lead. He traveled to England, where he took Spiritualists by storm. Sir Arthur Conan DOYLE, a staunch Spiritualist, was impressed with Ford, and urged him to devote himself to mediumship, advice which Ford took to heart.

In other countries, reaction to Ford was much the same. In Europe, Australia and New Zealand, he drew huge audiences to his lectures and sessions with Fletcher. The press called him the "international ambassador of Spiritualism." Skeptics challenged him in public; he invariably won by delivering compelling evidence that he could, indeed, communicate with the dead.

In 1929, Ford conducted a sitting for Harry HOUDINI's widow, Beatrice. Houdini had died in 1926. Prior to his death, he and Beatrice had agreed on a coded phrase, "Rosabelle, believe," that Houdini would try to send his wife from beyond the grave, to prove that there was life after death. Until she had a reading with Ford, no medium had produced the secret message. Ford did, and Beatrice was so convinced she had communicated with Houdini that she signed a sworn statement to the fact. Later, she wavered, but she never officially denied her sworn statement.

In 1930, Ford suffered a traumatic auto accident. He was driving through North Carolina, with his sister and another woman as passengers, when a truck went out of control and struck the car broadside. The two women were killed. Ford suffered serious internal injuries, a broken jaw and crushed ribs. He was hospitalized.

His doctor, who was interested in psychic phenomena, discovered that Ford had out-of-body experiences (q.v.) while on morphine. To experiment, the doctor gave him more and more morphine, until he was addicted. Ford's struggle to overcome the addiction made him an insomniac. He drank to sleep, and over the course of a decade he became alcoholic.

Ford was at the height of his career in the late 1930s. He hid his personal problems from the public and most of his friends. Professionally, he kept himself aloof from other mediums, and denounced fraud. No psychic can perform one hundred percent of the time, he declared. He was accused of trickery himself, but it was not until after his death that evidence surfaced among his private papers to indicate that he might have cheated from time to time by researching the backgrounds of famous people who came to his sittings. He was said to have a photographic memory, and he kept voluminous files of newspaper clippings and notes, which could have provided "evidential" material for his readings.

Ford remarried in 1938, to Valerie McKeown, an English widow he met while on tour. They settled in Hollywood, and for a time, Ford felt the happiest in his life. Then the alcohol began taking a serious toll. Ford missed lectures, suffered blackouts and appeared drunk in public. Fletcher rebuked him and threatened to go away, but Ford would not quit drinking. Soon, his psychic powers diminished and Fletcher disappeared. His wife divorced him. His health deteriorated, and he was plagued by recurring illnesses and bouts with depression. By 1949, he was hospitalized with a complete physical breakdown.

Alcoholics Anonymous helped Ford get back on his feet. Except for occasional wild benders, he managed to control his drinking but never gave it up. He kept a huge stash in a closet wherever he lived. His health was further aggravated by his tendency to plunge into fad diets. Despite his regular yoga and daily intake of dozens of vitamin pills, Ford suffered angina and heart attacks, and comas from mild diabetes. Each time he was in a crisis, he seemed to subconsciously send out psychic distress signals to friends, who got sudden urges to check up on him and rescue him.

In the 1950s, Fletcher returned and Ford resumed his mediumistic work. To his satisfaction, he began having an impact on mainstream churches, who invited him to speak to their congregations. But while the churches were willing to hear him, they still were not willing to change their doctrines to incorporate Spiritualism.

In 1956, Ford helped found SPIRITUAL FRONTIERS FELLOWSHIP, an organization dedicated to awakening man to his spiritual nature.

Beginning in 1964, the Reverend Sun Myung Moon had several sittings with Ford. Moon's followers were anxious for Ford to declare the charismatic Korean as the reincarnated Christ and World Savior, but Ford refused to do so. He allowed only that Moon was psychic himself and a prophet, and that God was working through Moon, as He was through many persons.

Ford was 71 when he conducted the most famous seance of his life, on television for Bishop James PIKE. Pike's 20-year-old son had committed suicide in 1966, and the distraught bishop was anxious to make contact with him. At first, Ford was opposed to the idea of a televised seance, and he said afterward that if he had had any idea of the publicity it would generate, he would have turned it down flat. But friends convinced him to proceed, and the show was taped in Toronto in September 1967. Ford delivered information that Pike considered evidential. The seance was widely debated in the press.

Ford spent the last three years of his life in Miami. He died of cardiac arrest on January 4, 1971. His last words were, "God help me." He was cremated and his ashes were scattered over the Atlantic Ocean.

Following his death, mediums around the world claimed to receive communication from him. Author Ruth Montgomery, one of Ford's close friends, claimed to receive communication from him through automatic writing.

Further reading:

Ford, Arthur, with Margueritte Harmon Bro. *Nothing So Strange: The Autobiography of Arthur Ford.* New York: Harper & Brothers, 1958.

Montgomery, Ruth. *A World Beyond.* New York: Fawcett Crest, 1971.

Spraggett, Allen. *Arthur Ford: The Man Who Talked with the Dead.* New York: New American Library, 1973.

Fox Sisters   The birth of Spiritualism historically is credited to the three Fox sisters of New York, Margaretta (Maggie), Catherine (Katie) and Leah. Their discovery that they could communicate with spirits by rappings helped fuel an explosion of mediumship and belief in survival after death on both sides of the Atlantic. They rose to the heights of fame, but their careers ended in disgrace and confessions of fraud.

In 1848, Leah Fox, 34, was living in Rochester, New York with her daughter, in poverty. Her husband had deserted her. Maggie, 15, and Katie, 12, lived in Hydesville with their parents, John and Margaret Fox. In March of that year, the Fox family in Hydesville was disturbed by strange thumping noises at night. Mrs. Fox believed the noises were made by a ghost.

On the night of March 31, Maggie and Katie discovered that if they clapped their hands, the raps answered back. Neighbors were summoned to witness this astonishing phenomenon. By rapping for "yes," "no," and letters of the alphabet, the spirit claimed to be a murdered peddler named Charles Rosa, whose throat had been slashed by John Bell, a former occupant of the house, who had buried the remains beneath the cellar floorboards. Digging in the cellar yielded some human teeth, hair and a few bones.

The press sensationalized the story. At the time, mesmerism and Swedenborgianism were popular, and provided fertile ground for a new "religion" to take hold. The opportunity was seized by Leah, who took charge of her younger sisters and their spirit demonstrations.

The rappings seemed to follow Maggie and Katie wherever they went. In Rochester, the girls held seances in parlors, contacting other spirits of the dead with their raps. Then, allegedly at the instruction of the spirits, Leah rented a public hall for a stage show, where the girls were mobbed by the curious.

Publicity was intense. Some newspapers denounced them as frauds who played parlor tricks, others hailed them as sensations. People flocked to see them and willingly paid for the privilege.

With Leah as manager, Maggie and Katie toured other cities. They were a sensation everywhere. The seances grew more elaborate, with objects moving, tables rising, and the spirit of Ben Franklin joining in. Suddenly others began discovering their own mediumistic powers, and seances became the popular rage.

The Fox sisters were routinely "exposed" by persons who advanced various theories, including toe, ankle and knee cracking, ventriloquism and assorted electrical gadgets. No trickery was found despite numerous tests.

P.T. Barnum brought the girls to New York City to perform. Despite denunciations from skeptics, they impressed William Cullen Bryant, James Fenimore Cooper, George Ripley and other literati. Horace Greeley, editor of the *Tribune,* took them under his wing and provided quarters at his mansion.

But the fame took its toll. By 1855, Maggie and Katie were on their way to alcoholism. Maggie, disillusioned with Spiritualism, converted to Catholicism and wanted out of the act, but family pressure kept her in. She fell into a deep depression when her fiancé, Elisha Kane, a naval surgeon, died before the two could be married. Disapproval by both families had postponed their wedding plans. Nevertheless, she considered herself a widow, and began using the Kane name.

In an effort to control the alcoholism, the family separated the two sisters. Maggie responded once to treatment, but returned to drinking. Leah abandoned them in 1857, when she married a wealthy businessman and retired from the stage acts.

Katie managed to continue performing, achieving new heights with mirror-writing, or backward automatic script which had to be held up to a mirror to be read (see SLATE-WRITING). In 1861, she purportedly manifested the spirits of the dead in materializations. Her performances were irregular due to drinking. In 1871, she went to England, where she recovered sobriety long enough to impress British Spiritualists.

The Fox sisters. From left to right: Kate, Margaret, Leah.

Sir William CROOKES declared that no one approached her in talent.

In 1872, Katie married an Englishman, Henry Jencken, and she bore two sons. The first, Ferdinand, born in 1873, was hailed as a medium by the time he was three. Spirits reportedly took over his body and caused unearthly light to stream from his eyes. By age five, he did automatic writing, penning in Greek, "He who trusts me shall live." Jencken died of a stroke in 1885, and Katie returned to New York with her sons.

In the United States, interest in Spiritualism began to wane, and investigations of fraud increased. In 1884, an ill Maggie was called before a commission and failed the tests. Her enduring reputation enabled her to continue a modest career as a medium in New York.

Leah succeeded in having the Society for the Prevention of Cruelty to Children take Katie's sons away from her because of Katie's drinking. The blow was devastating.

In 1888, Maggie and Katie made a public appearance in New York, at which Maggie denounced Spiritualism as a fraud and an evil characterized by sexual licentiousness. She confessed that she and Katie had created the rappings in Hydesville to play a trick on their mother, and they were able to do so by surreptitious toe cracking. They had learned to use muscles below the knee which are supple in children but stiffen with age; their practice had kept the muscles flexible. Maggie demonstrated on stage how she rapped with her toes. She also stated that Leah had led them around like lambs because she wanted to create a new religion, and that they had rapped at seances in response to body cues from Leah.

Devoted Spiritualists hissed and discounted the confession as the ravings of a sick woman. Katie, who did not speak at the public appearance, later said she did not agree with Maggie. Leah maintained a low public profile. Maggie and Katie went on tour exposing Spiritualism; Katie also continued to work as a medium. In 1891, Maggie recanted her confession for unclear reasons.

Leah died on November 1, 1891. Katie drank herself to death on July 2, 1892, at age 56. Her body was found by one of her sons. Maggie died on March 8, 1893, at age 59, at a friend's home in Brooklyn; she was ill and destitute.

On November 21, 1904, the Hydesville house finally gave up its mysterious remains, when school children discovered a skeleton buried behind a crumbling cellar wall. To Spiritualists, it was proof of the truth of the Fox Sisters' beginning, even though the skeleton was not beneath the floor. Critics said the skeleton probably had been planted. The house burned to the ground in an accidental fire in 1955, and it was rebuilt 13 years later as a tourist attraction.

Further reading:

Brandon, Ruth. *The Spiritualists.* New York: Alfred A. Knopf, 1983.

Brown, Slater. *The Heyday of Spiritualism.* New York: Hawthorn Books, 1970.

Douglas, Alfred. *Extrasensory Powers: A Century of Psychical Research.* London: Victor Gollancz Ltd., 1976.

Jackson, Herbert G., Jr. *The Spirit Rappers.* Garden City, N.Y.: Doubleday, 1972.

Moore, R. Laurence. *In Search of White Crows*. New York: Oxford University Press, 1977.

funeral rites and customs Societies have a wide variety of ways of disposing of their dead, ranging from exposure of the body on the ground or in the branches of a tree, to burial in boxes, tombs, or graves, and cremation. In many tribal societies, a buried body is dug up after a certain time, cleaned, and reburied in a collective grave.

The various funerary practices are often accompanied by rites, which anthropologists have shown to have the important function of reuniting a society following the rift caused by the death of one of its members. The overt purpose of these rites, however, is different. They are intended to assist the safe passage of the deceased's spirit to the land of the dead and to ensure that it will not turn into a malevolent ghost. In many societies, the rites also are intended to effect the reincarnation in the society of one of the deceased's souls or some part of his or her spirit.

A good deal of attention has been given to the problem of when in history the first burials occurred. The interest in this question derives from the assumption that burial implies an awareness of death and of mourning, and that the beginning of burial practices therefore implies the dawn of a religious sense. However, given the variety of ways of disposing of bodies, this assumption would seem to be unfounded. Anthropologists have studied societies in which burial was proscribed, because it was thought to make the soul's departure from the body and ascension to the heavens more difficult. There is no reason to think that human beings had no religious sense—or did not care about the future of their dead—before burial practices became commonplace. The attention that has been given to burial is probably a consequence of the fact that burial is the norm in modern European and American society.

To some extent, the form of mortuary treatment favored by a society depends on factors such as environment and general life-style. Hunting-and-gathering peoples, particularly nomadic ones, are more inclined to practice exposure, whereas more settled people often prefer burial. No strict correlation of this sort has been discovered, however, and little can be concluded except that the preferred method of disposal is usually rationalized in terms of the society's religious beliefs.

Fear of the dead is widespread. According to Sir James Frazer, author of *The Golden Bough*, it was this fear, rather than reverence for the dead, that inspired the entire range of practices associated with death in tribal societies. Many things are done to make it difficult for the ghost to find its way back home. If death occurs inside a house, a hole may be made in a wall for the carrying out of the corpse and then blocked back up again, even if doors or windows are large enough to transport the corpse. In the Solomon Islands, the funeral procession returns home by a route different from the one by which they carried the corpse to the grave, lest it follow them back home (see CHARMS AGAINST GHOSTS). In many societies, the corpse is tightly bound, perhaps even mutilated, with the idea that this will keep the ghost from "walking." In southeast Australia, the Aboriginal tribes of the Herbert River used to break both legs and bore holes in the lungs, stomach, and other organs, in order to render the ghost harmless (compare to VAMPIRE). Ghosts are particularly to be feared in the first days after death, for they have not yet begun their journey to their new home, and are at their most potent (see GHOST SICKNESS).

At the same time as things are done to prevent the return of the ghost, certain other things are done to start the spirit on its journey. The Herbert River tribes buried a man with all his personal belongings, and put food and water at the burial place. His personal belongings he would take with him, and the food and water would nourish him on his way. In other places, slaves or animals may be sacrificed and buried with the corpse, especially if the person had been of some stature in the community. The body may also be positioned with its face away from the village and toward the land of the dead. The motive behind all such practices is similar: to assist the spirit to reach the land of the dead safely and with dispatch. Muslims bury their dead facing toward Mecca; Christians generally toward the west; many tribal societies toward the land of their ancestors.

Gravestones praise the dead and express hope for their immortality. In some cases, magical objects or pieces of iron may be placed on a grave to prevent the soul from wandering (see IRON).

All cemeteries are sacred grounds. The term "cemetery" is derived from the Greek for "sleeping chamber." Originally it was applied to the catacombs of the dead in Rome, then to the consecrated grounds of a church, and now to any place where the dead are buried. Certain trees are planted in cemeteries. For example, cypress and pine in China are believed to give the departed strength for their journey (see CYPRESS).

Animistic soul concepts are more complex than Western religious ones, and it is not uncommon to find beliefs in more than one soul or spiritual entity, each of which has a different destiny after death, or passage of the spirit to the land of the dead, and facilitate the reincarnation of the soul in the community. The nature of the rites and rituals varies, but everywhere a successful outcome is thought to be dependent on carrying them out properly; if anything goes wrong, it is typically blamed on not having done everything as prescribed. In many societies there are a series of rites, which may include feasts and other festivals (see FEASTS AND FESTIVALS OF THE DEAD).

Sometimes there is a lengthy period—of a year or more—between the funeral and the final ceremony. In such cases, the final ceremony is often held in conjunction with a secondary burial, during which the body of the deceased is dug up and the bones are cleaned and then reburied, often with others in the same family line, or lineage. The wait is because a part of the deceased's soul resides in the flesh, and it is only released as the flesh rots away. The French sociologist Robert Hertz, who first drew attention to these practices, considered that cremation originated as a way of speeding up this process. In any event, it is only after the final service that the spirit of the deceased is believed to have passed on to the land of the dead, and only then may his successor be appointed, his belongings be passed to his heirs, and his former wife remarry.

Modern American beliefs about the fate of the soul and funerary practices make an interesting contrast to tribal ones. Although there are many varying and sometimes conflicting beliefs about the afterlife among the heterogeneous American population, funerary practices are similar throughout the country; some are mandated by health laws. The general features include a rapid removal of the corpse to a funeral parlor, embalming, institutionalized "viewing," and disposal by burial. The difference is perhaps because there is no longer a direct connection made between how a person is buried and what will happen to him or her in the afterlife.

Further reading:

Bendann, Effie. *Death Customs: An Analytical Study of Burial Rites.* London: Kegan Paul, Trench, Trubner, 1930.

Dickson, D. Bruce. *The Dawn of Belief: Religion in the Upper Paleolithic of Southwestern Europe.* Tucson: University of Arizona Press, 1989.

Hertz, Robert. *Death and the Right Hand.* Glencoe, Ill.: Free Press, 1960.

Huntington, Robert, and Peter Metcalf. *Celebrations of Death: The Anthropology of Mortuary Ritual.* London: Cambridge University Press, 1979.

Leach, Maria, and Jerome Fried, eds. *Funk & Wagnalls Standard Dictionary of Folklore, Mythology, and Legend.* San Francisco: Harper & Row, 1979.

Offerings to the dead painted on the wall of an ancient Egyptian tomb.

a spirit which divides after death (see ANIMISM). Thus, in addition to traveling to the land of the dead, a different soul or spiritual part of a person may be thought to reincarnate, and certain funerary practices are intended to facilitate this process. This is especially true with regard to the place of burial or abandonment. Although fear of ghosts sometimes leads to the destruction of the deceased person's house, burials may also occur within houses, which then continue to be occupied. This is especially true in the case of infants or of young children, whose spirits are thought to be too undeveloped to cause harm. By burying children inside the house (or just outside it), it is believed that their spirits would have an easier time finding their way back to the same mother (see REINCARNATION).

Not only the method of disposal of the body, but rites and rituals which accompany the disposal, are designed to serve this triple function—prevent the ghost from returning to harm the living, assist the

G

galleytrot See BLACK SHUCK.

Garrett, Eileen J. (1893–1970) Irish medium and founder of the PARAPSYCHOLOGY FOUNDATION (PF) in New York City. Eileen J. Garrett was a leader in encouraging the scientific study of paranormal phenomena, and she volunteered for numerous research projects as a subject.

She was born Eileen Jeanette Vancho Lyttle on March 17, 1893 at Beau Park, County Meath, Ireland. She exhibited paranormal ability at an early age, including clairvoyance of the dead.

Garrett married three times. Her first marriage, to Clive Barry, produced three sons, all of whom died young, and a daughter, now Eileen Coly, who is president of the PF. Following divorce, Garrett ran a hostel for wounded soldiers during World War I. Many of them returned to the front, and Garrett had precognitive visions of those who were destined to die there. One of her patients proposed marriage to her, probably as a last act—he had his own premonition of his own death. She agreed. One month after the wedding he was reported missing in action. Garrett sensed that he and several others had been killed in an explosion. Just before the end of the war in 1918, she married J.W. Garrett, a wounded soldier. After divorcing Garrett, she remained unmarried for the rest of her life.

Garrett's mediumship began after the war, when she joined a group of women who wanted to contact the dead through seances. Garrett went into an involuntary trance and began relaying information about the spirits of the dead, whom she saw around the seance table.

Garrett was disturbed by this and underwent hypnosis. Her control, Uvani, appeared and announced Garrett's new role as a medium. At first Garrett resisted. However, psychical researchers whom she met at the BRITISH COLLEGE OF PSYCHIC SCIENCE, especially James Hewat McKenzie, helped her not only to come to terms with her ability, but to develop it as well. Garrett worked with McKenzie, Sir Oliver LODGE, Hereward CARRINGTON, Nandor FODOR and others from 1924 to 1929, the year McKenzie died.

In 1931, she was invited to the United States by the AMERICAN SOCIETY FOR PSYCHICAL RESEARCH. At Duke University, she worked with J.B. RHINE and William McDougall. Rhine considered her to be one of the finest mediums of the day. McDougall, she said later, persuaded her to continue in the new field of parapsychology at a time she thought of ending her participation in experiments.

Garrett became a U.S. citizen in 1947. She established a publishing venture for books and a periodical on parapsychology; neither is presently in operation.

In 1951, she founded the PF to encourage organized scientific research through grants and international conferences. Garrett championed this research in the hopes of bringing together science and religion in order to restore a spiritual power to religion. The PF continues to sponsor university research around the world, and to conduct international congresses on parapsychology, the first of which was held in 1953 at the University of Utrecht, The Netherlands.

In the 1960s, Garrett worked with psychologist Lawrence LeShan in his studies of alternate realities. She helped him describe the "clairvoyant reality," a state of consciousness comparable to mystical states in which paranormal abilities function. In this state, there is a central unity of all things in a larger pattern; time exists in an eternal now; there is no "good" or "evil," for the pattern of the universe is beyond that; and paranormal senses are better than ordinary senses at obtaining information. For Garrett, the clairvoyant reality could be accessed through controlled breathing. Her experience in the state of clairvoyant reality, in which she could perceive past, present and future simultaneously, was exhiliarating, and she had to learn to control her powers to avoid exhaustion.

While many other mediums believed in the literal existence of spirits of the dead and of their spirit controls, Garrett retained an objectivity and even skepticism about them. More than most of her medium contemporaries, she possessed and understanding of a mystical side to her abilities. As early as World War I, she had begun to contemplate such matters, especially after meeting Edward Carpenter, whose social and political writings interested her. Carpenter told her she had been born to a state of cosmic consciousness which others spent their entire lives searching for in vain. She began to see her perceptions not as fantasies or pathological hallucinations, but as capacities for inner comprehension. This resulted in a dramatic spiritual experience in which she saw that her living in two selves (the "normal" woman and the medium) was the result of "positive powers beyond the range of contemporary understanding." She felt her powers were not supernatural in origin, but came from within her own deep unconscious.

Garrett had other controls besides Uvani, but remained detached from them. She regarded them as "principles of the subconscious" formed by her own inner needs.

Garrett died on September 15, 1970 in Nice, France following years of declining health. In addition to her legacy of the PF, she left seven nonfiction books on the paranormal, plus novels under the pseudonym Jean Lyttle.

Further reading:

Angoff, Allan. *Eileen Garrett and the World Beyond the Senses.* New York: William Morrow, 1974.

Garrett, Eileen. *Adventures in the Supernormal: A Personal Memoir.* New York: Garrett Publications, 1949.

———. *Many Voices: The Autobiography of a Medium.* New York: G.P. Putnam's Sons, 1968.

———. *My Life as a Search for the Meaning of Mediumship.* London: Rider & Co., 1939.

LeShan, Lawrence. *The Medium, the Mystic, and the Physicist.* New York: Viking Press, 1974.

Geley, Gustave (1868–1924)

French physician and psychical researcher, first director of the INSTITUT METAPSYCHIQUE INTERNATIONAL (IMI).

Gustave Geley was born in Montceau-les-Mines, France in 1868. He became a physician, though he was interested in the unconscious and in psychical research. His first book was concerned with the origin of species. With his second book (*L'etre subconscient*, 1899, untranslated), he took a stand against strict materialism, arguing for an interaction between the mind (or soul) and the physical body. In Geley's "dynamo-psychism," a dynamic power of the mental and spiritual realms is capable of directly affecting atoms of matter.

With the approach of World War I, the French materialization medium Marthe BERAUD ("Eva C.") was cut off from her German investigator, Baron Albert von SCHRENCK-NOTZING, and Geley took up the study of her mediumship. Between 1916 and 1918, he had twice-weekly sittings with Beraud at her home in Paris. When she arrived for a sitting, Beraud was undressed in his presence (as a doctor, he was allowed to see her unclothed), and then was literally sewn into a tight-fitting garment something like a body stocking. After she had entered a trance, she was led to a curtained cubicle that shielded her from the light in the room, and in which she sat during the seance. Geley observed formations of ectoplasm very similar to those reported by Schrenck-Notzing and others. He never saw full form materializations, but he did watch hands or heads form out of the ectoplasmic substance. Investigators would sometimes touch these formations, which would dissolve at their touch.

In his third book, *From the Unconscious to the Conscious* (1919; English translation, 1920), Geley reviewed a variety of data from psychical research and sought to develop further his idea of mind-body interaction. Unlike most of his colleagues in psychical research, Geley was a Spiritualist at heart, and he accepted the reality of reincarnation as well as the possibility of communication with the dead through mediums (see SURVIVAL AFTER DEATH).

In 1918, when the French industrialist Jean Meyer gave money to establish the Institut Metapsychique International in Paris, Geley gave up his medical practice to become its director. Geley held additional sittings with Beraud at the IMI. Sittings with the Pole, "Franek Kluski," began in 1920. Wax casts of limbs materialized by Kluski were successfully produced and placed on exhibit at the IMI. Geley studied another Polish materialization medium, Jan GUZIK, in Warsaw in 1921, and at the IMI in 1922 and 1923. He recorded his later work with Beraud and his work with Kluski and Guzik in *Clairvoyance and Materialisation* (1924; English translation, 1927).

Geley died in an airplane crash on his way back to Paris from Warsaw, where he had attended a sitting with Kluski, on July 15, 1924. He was 56.

Twenty-five years after his death, an article by R. Lambert suggesting that Geley had covered up evidence of fraud by Beraud appeared in the *Journal of the Society for Psychical Research*. In psychical research, the mere levying of a charge is often enough to condemn mediums and investigators, and Lambert's communication has hung like a dark cloud over Geley's reputation ever since. However, it constitutes the type of hearsay evidence that would be heavily discounted if it ran in favor of a medium's ability, and a similar discounting would seem to be appropriate in this case.

Further reading:

Inglis, Brian. *Science and Parascience: A History of the Paranormal, 1914–1939.* London: Hodder and Stoughton, 1984.

Lambert, Rudolph. "Dr. Geley's Reports on the Medium 'Eva C.' " *Journal of the Society for Psychical Research* 37 (1954):380–86.

Lodge, Oliver. "In memorium: Gustave Geley." *Proceedings of the Society for Psychical Research* 34 (1924):201–11.

Pleasants, Helene, ed. *Biographical Dictionary of Parapsychology.* New York: Helix Press, 1964.

ghost   An alleged spirit of the dead. The term "ghost" enjoys popular use, especially in connection with hauntings. Parapsychologists generally use the term "apparition." Ghosts may be visible, though only a small percentage of cases involve visual images. Generally, a ghost makes its presence known through mysterious noises, smells, cold breezes and movements of objects.

In its archaic meaning, the term "ghost" refers to the animus or disembodied soul. After death, souls go to live in an underworld or afterlife, often at the bottom of a lake, across the ocean, in the sky or on the moon, or to the west where the sun sets. Beliefs vary as to what happens to the soul. For example, Melanesians believe the soul separates into a dual nature at death: *adaro,* the ghost which is the bad part of the soul, and *aunga,* the good part. Ghosts make their home in nearby islands or underground. Ghosts travel to their home by land or on a ship of the dead. Upon their arrival, they are segregated according to their good or bad nature by a ghost ruler. Beliefs vary by island. On some, the *adaro* eventually die, while the *aunga* live happily forever. Throughout Melanesia, souls of the dead are worshipped, as they are in other animistic societies. On San Cristoval in particular, the *adaro* are worshipped. The ghosts are distinguished from the *figaro,* which are spirits who have never had human form.

Similarly, the Chinese believe in at least two, and possibly three, aspects of the soul, which accounts for the fact that the dead can make their presence felt in more than one place. There are superior and inferior parts of the soul, as well as a third that dwells in an ancestral altar, where it can receive the blessings of its family. (See also the Egyptian concepts of BA and KA).

Virtually all cultures have believed at one time or another in the ability of the ghosts of the dead to return to the world of the living, either in solid form

Marley's ghost visiting Scrooge in Charles Dickens's A Christmas Carol.

(the "walking dead") or in sensory form (see REVENANT). When they return, they may have either benevolent or malevolent intent. In cultures where ancestor worship exists, the returning dead are taken as matter of fact; they are often assumed to dwell in the same house as the living.

In the West, the soul is supposed to depart for an eternal resting place with God in heaven or with Satan in hell (or perhaps in between in purgatory). Consequently, the returning dead are regarded as unnatural and frightening, and possibly demonic. Catholicism acknowledges that souls in purgatory might return as phantasmal, but not solid, ghosts to ask for prayers from the living. In earlier centuries, Protestants generally believed that the dead could not return, and ghosts were diabolical entities masquerading as the dead. This belief still continues in modern times, especially among Fundamentalist Christians. In Eastern European lore, the returning dead who assault the living may be vampires.

Followers of Spiritualism believe that ghosts are souls of the dead trapped on earth, either because they are confused, or because they don't yet realize they are dead. Mediums believe they can communicate with ghosts and help them move on.

Many stories of the return of the dead follow motifs: the ghost returns to avenge its wrongful death (see GREENBRIER GHOST); to take care of unfinished business; to deliver vital information not given during life (see CHAFFIN WILL CASE); to punish living enemies; to protect loved ones or give advice; to reward the living (see GRATFFUL DEAD); or simply to reenact its death. In folklore, ghosts are believed to take part in normal activities, such as eating and drinking, and seem so lifelike that they fool others until they vanish, or until others find out they are dead.

Every culture has superstitions concerning ghosts. In European folklore, for example, it is widely believed that one should never touch a ghost; that ghosts cannot cross running water (nor can witches, vampires, demons and anything with evil attributes); that ghosts only appear at night; and that ghosts have noticeable smells. Smells are the second most common characteristic of hauntings.

It is not true that ghosts appear only at night; many appear during the day. It is possible that filmy visual apparitions may be more readily seen at night, or that a person is more receptive to clairvoyance when relaxed or asleep at night (many ghosts appear in dreams, or awaken people from sleep). Conversely, the very same conditions may foster mere hallucinations of ghosts. Ghosts reported to have been seen at twilight in many cases are what American ghost investigator Dale KACZMAREK calls "bedroom episodes": people claim to be wide awake, when in fact they are drifting off to sleep or are already asleep. Many ghosts are reported under foggy conditions, and are probably tricks of light. Many also are reported in conjunction with thunderstorms, and may be caused by excessive electrical charges in the atmosphere.

And, contrary to popular belief, most ghosts are not seen in graveyards, but in structures—houses and buildings. In Hong Kong, the greatest number of ghosts are associated with buildings that were occupied by the Japanese during World War II. Many buildings were used as interrogation centers, and hundreds of Chinese were said to have been executed in them. After Japanese-occupied buildings, the second most common ghost sites in Hong Kong are hospitals.

Psychical researchers have found that the overwhelming majority of ghost reports that have been investigated in fact have natural explanations (see GHOST HUNTING). Still, the small percentage—perhaps as few as 2%—of unexplained cases continue to perplex researchers. In more than a century of scientific inquiry in the West, no one has definitive answers about ghosts and their natures. There is no consensus among psychical researchers as to whether ghosts have objective reality or are fantasies, or if they have intelligence and personality, or are psychic remnants of past events. Possibly, different types of ghosts exist that would fall into all theories.

Frederic W.H. MYERS, a founder of the SOCIETY FOR PSYCHICAL RESEARCH (SPR), London, defined a ghost as "a manifestation of persistent personal energy, or as an indication that some kind of force is being exercised after death which is in some way connected with a person previously known on earth." Myers did not believe that ghosts were conscious or intelligent entities, but rather believed they were automatic projections of consciousness which had their centers elsewhere. More recent researchers have disagreed, arguing that at least some ghosts may possess an awareness, perhaps within themselves.

Every society has procedures and rituals for dealing with troublesome ghosts. Exorcisms cast out ghosts who are causing bad luck, illness and misfortune (see also DYBBUK). In Christianity, there are formal religious rites for the exorcism of demonic entities, blamed for possession, but not for mere ghosts. Nonetheless, clerics of various denominations conduct rites to "rescue," "lay" or "release" the ghost. See EXORCISM; RELEASEMENT.

Further reading:

Emmons, Charles F. *Chinese Ghosts and ESP.* Metuchen, N.J.: The Scarecrow Press, 1982.

Haynes, Renee. "What Do You Mean By A Ghost?" *Parapsychology Review* 17 (1986):9–12.

Lang, Andrew. *The Book of Dreams and Ghosts.* Hollywood, Calif.: Newcastle Publishing, 1972. First published 1897.

Leach, Maria, and Jerome Fried, eds. *Funk & Wagnalls Standard Dictionary of Folklore, Mythology, and Legend.* San Francisco: Harper & Row, 1979.

Myers, Frederic W.H. *Human Personality and Its Survival of Bodily Death Vols. I & II.* New ed. New York: Longmans, Green & Co., 1954. First published 1903.

Thurston, Herbert. *Ghosts and Poltergeists.* Chicago: Henry Regnery, 1954.

Ghost Club   Private organization based in London devoted to psychical research and investigations of paranormal phenomena, including—but not limited to—ghosts, apparitions, mediumship, hauntings and poltergeists.

The Ghost Club is the oldest existing organization associated with psychic matters, and has had several incarnations since its origins circa 1862. It apparently was predated by another club known as the Cambridge Ghost Club, which is no longer in existence.

The Ghost Club was formed by a select group of London gentlemen with the idea of unmasking fraudulent mediums and investigating psychic phenomena. They investigated the DAVENPORT BROTHERS, conjurers who came to London in the fall of 1862 and claimed to contact the spirits of the dead. Little is known about the club's earliest activities. Members included Charles Dickens, who had numerous psychic experiences during his life, including visions of ghosts, yet was an opponent of Spiritualism.

The Ghost Club eventually became inactive. It was revived on All Souls' Day in 1882; the activity lasted until 1936. During that time, the club was a private circle of 82 men (no women were allowed to join), whose members included many eminent psychical researchers, including Sir William BARRETT, Sir Arthur Conan DOYLE, Sir William CROOKES, Sir Oliver LODGE, Frederic Bligh BOND, Harry PRICE, Nandor FODOR and William Butler Yeats.

In 1936, the Club disbanded and made arrangements to deposit its records and papers in the British Museum, where they were to remain sealed for 25 years. The papers were not deposited until July 1938.

Four months earlier, Price revived the Club in a third incarnation with himself as chairman. Price limited membership to 500 persons, and women were admitted for the first time. Price emphasized that the club was not and never had been a Spiritualist organization; in fact, he aptly described it as "a body of extremely skeptical men and women who get together every few weeks to hear the latest news of the psychic world and to discuss every facet of the paranormal . . ." Members included people such as Professor C.E.M. Joad, Sir Julian Huxley, Algernon Blackwood, Sir Ernest Jelf (Master of the Supreme Court), Sir Osbert Sitwell and Lord Amwell. The club continued until World War II curtailed its activities.

In 1947 Price invited Peter UNDERWOOD to join (number 496). The following year, meetings ceased soon after Price's sudden death.

The present club, in which membership is strictly by invitation only, was revived in 1954. Underwood has been president since 1960. In November 1963, the sealed papers at the British Museum were opened, and the full history of the club became public.

The Ghost Club does not subscribe to any particular creed or belief about the paranormal or survival after death, nor does it follow any single approach to a given subject. The club does not undertake any investigations on an official basis; members pursue their own inquiries. Members include scientists, lay investigators, authors, Spiritualists, philosophers, skeptics and others; most live in Britain, and especially in the greater London area. Other members are in the United States and elsewhere around the world.

Among members are Tom PERROTT (chairman), Air Chief Marshall Lord Dowding, Donald Campbell, Beverly Nichols, Henry Williamson, Colin Wilson, Dennis Wheatley, Sheila Scott, Arthur Koestler and Colonel John Blashford-Snell.

Meetings feature discussions and talks by leading experts on a wide variety of subjects in all branches of psychic investigation. *The New York Times* has described the club as "the place where skeptics and spiritualists, mediums and materialistists, meet on neutral ground."

Further reading:
Underwood, Peter. *No Uncommon Task: The Autobiography of a Ghost-hunter.* London: Harrup Ltd., 1983.

Ghost Dance Native American religious movement that arose in the mid-19th century in the plains and western portion of America in opposition to the oppression of whites. The Ghost Dance envisioned the end of white civilization, a paradisal new world order for Native Americans in which they would have eternal life free of suffering, and the return of Native dead to enjoy the new world along with the living.

The Ghost Dance religion took its name from the Ghost Dance, a circle dance during which dancers experienced mystical visions of the dead and the new world to come. The dance was intended to facilitate the return of the dead.

Although aimed at the white enemies, the Ghost Dance movement was an expression of an old Native myth about the end of the world, its renewal, and the return of the dead to coexist with the living. As animosity against the whites increased, however, various Native prophets specifically addressed the end of white civilization. The movement began to spread in the 1850s. Such prophecies figured prominently in the Nez Percé War of 1877, which the whites won.

One of the primary prophets of the Ghost Dance was Wowoka, the son of a Paiute mystic, who began preaching in 1886. He advocated pure and harmonious living, nonviolence against whites, and a cessation of mourning for the dead, since they were due for imminent return.

The Ghost Dance movement was quick to find followers. The dance was celebrated in elaborate rites that would span four or five days. Entranced dancers spoke of glorious visions of their dead ancestors coming back to the world, and of heaven-like fields and enormous herds of buffalo.

Perhaps the most enthusiastic of Ghost Dance followers were the fierce Sioux, who defeated General Custer at Little Big Horn and rejected the tenet of nonviolence. The Sioux began Ghost Dancing in earnest in the summer of 1890. Dancers wore magical shirts that supposedly would stop bullets. Whites took this as a sign of building hostilities, and banned the dance on all Sioux reservations in November 1890. The Sioux continued to dance.

The whites responded with a military presence on the Rosebud and Pine Ridge reservations in South Dakota. In fighting, some Native leaders were killed (Chief Sitting Bull among them) and others were arrested. Those who surrendered were ordered to camp at Wounded Knee Creek. On December 29, 1890 fighting broke out when a gun went off (it is uncertain which side fired the shot), and the result was a tragic massacre of Native Americans. The Wounded Knee massacre effectively ended the Ghost Dance movement, and also brought to a close the frontier wars.

Further reading:

Hultkrantz, Ake. *Native Religions of North America.* San Francisco: Harper & Row, 1987.

Underhill, Ruth M. *Red Man's Religion.* Chicago: University of Chicago Press, 1965.

Waldman, Carl. *Atlas of the North American Indian.* New York: Facts On File, 1985.

ghost hunting   Various methods of investigating reports of ghosts, apparitions and poltergeists to determine if the phenomena are paranormal or have natural explanations. Scientific investigations became well established in the late 19th century, as a result of interest in Spiritualist phenomena.

Ghost investigators estimate that 70% to 98% of all reports of haunting phenomena have natural explanations, such as tricks of light and shadow, hallucinations, peculiar atmospheric conditions, geological or electromagnetic influences, and animal noises. Some cases are exposed as tricks. Other cases seem to have human agents, especially poltergeist cases, in which phenomena are caused by unconscious psychokinesis (PK).

The SOCIETY FOR PSYCHICAL RESEARCH (SPR), London, has established guidelines for investigations of hauntings, apparitions and poltergeists. Effects are divided into five classifications: (1) unaccountable movement of objects; (2) unaccountable noises (including voices and music) and smells; (3) apparitions, mysterious lights and shadows; (4) unaccountable touches, pushes and feelings of heat and cold; and (5) feelings of fear, horror, disgust, and of unseen "presences."

The investigator must be an open-minded skeptic, and must look first for all possible natural causes. These fall into two classes, mechanical and personal.

Mechanical causes include machinery vibrations and lights, road noises, and the like. Personal are those effects caused by people, whether unconscious or deliberate, such as floorboards creaking when stepped upon, or tricks. Determining and eliminating these potential causes requires a thorough investigation of a site during daytime and nighttime to determine natural lights, shadows and noises. Maps are consulted to show fault lines; power lines; underground streams, mines or tunnels; or other features that might be responsible. Investigators evaluate their evidence for significant patterns, and to determine which effects are primary (the first to occur) and which are secondary. Effects that are "veridical," that is, possibly paranormal, occur when a percipient receives information unknown to him or her and not obtained by ordinary means, and which can be verified through research. Veridical experiences are the most valuable to the scientific community.

Investigators also must do historical research concerning a site, especially geological conditions and construction activity. Earlier press accounts of hauntings at a site are taken into consideration by some ghost hunters and not by others. Those who reject such reports feel that they are likely to contain distortions and errors.

Three basic investigative techniques are used: description, experimentation and detection.

The description technique involves taking eyewitness accounts. Witnesses should be interviewed separately to avoid influence upon one another's accounts. In addition to details of the experience, witnesses are asked to provide information about their circumstances, health and states of mind; previous knowledge, if any, of similar experiences; and any previous paranormal experiences. Investigators must keep in mind that in the reconstruction of an experience, the "Rashomon" effect may occur; that is, every witness may see the same experience quite differently.

The experimental technique involves bringing in a psychic or medium to see if his or her impressions tally with those of the eyewitnesses. The medium will also mark a floor plan of the house or building to show spots where hauntings occurred, based upon their sensations of "cold spots" (unusually cold areas) and clairvoyant impressions.

Opinions vary concerning the use of mediums. Some investigators feel that mediums will most likely reiterate what they pick up through telepathy and clairvoyance with those individuals involved; also, that mediums will not be objective, but will be predisposed to consider hauntings as always caused by a spirit or spirits of the dead. Some investigators have mediums conduct "circles" (see SEANCE) at haunted sites in an effort to communicate with a haunting entity.

The detection technique involves such procedures as securing rooms and objects to test their disturbance; setting up electronic surveillance equipment (such as cameras, tape recorders, temperature sensors or Geiger counters); and spreading flour, sugar or sand on floors to detect footprints.

Harry H. PRICE was among the first to use modern technology in his ghost investigations, the most celebrated of which was BORLEY RECTORY in England. Price leased the rectory and created a laboratory. Conducting tests with 48 volunteers, and with the use of modern technology which included felt overshoes, steel tape measures, a still camera, a remote-control movie camera, fingerprinting equipment, telescope and portable telephone, Price still was not able to prove the existence of ghosts. Price wrote about his investigation in a book, *The Most Haunted House in England,* published in 1940. Several years after his death, critics contended that he had manipulated certain facts in an attempt to prove that the rectory was haunted.

Critics contend that ghost investigation is imprecise and not a true science because it is heavily reliant upon the anecdotal testimony of witnesses. Also, despite the greatest precautions taken on the part of the investigator, it is virtually impossible to rule out telepathy and SUPER-ESP as factors in experiencing a haunting.

Despite the impressive research of hauntings, scientists remain in the dark about the nature of hauntings and the laws, if any, which govern them.

Further reading:

Auerbach, Loyd. *ESP, Hauntings and Poltergeists: A Parapsychologist's Handbook.* New York: Warner Books, 1986.

Underwood, Peter. *The Ghost Hunter's Guide.* Poole, Dorset, England: Blandford House, 1986.

ghost lights Luminous phenomena, usually in the shape of balls or irregular patches of light, reported around the world, that defy natural explanation. Most ghost lights are yellow or white, while others are red, orange or blue. The lights may change color as they are observed. They appear randomly or regularly at particular sites, varying in size and configuration, and may be active for years. Some appear and become "inactive" after short periods of time. Ghost lights are widely reported in remote areas throughout the United States, Britain, Japan and other countries.

The GHOST RESEARCH SOCIETY, based in Oak Lawn, Illinois, collects data on ghost lights and investigates some sites where they are active. Research has identified common characteristics: (1) they appear in remote areas; (2) they are elusive and can only be seen from certain angles and distances; (3) they react to noise and light by receding or disappearing; (4) they are accompanied by hummings, buzzings or outbreaks of gaseous material; and (5) they are associated with local folklore surrounding a haunting due to a terrible accident or tragedy which took place at the site, involving loss of life. For example, a person loses his head in an accident, and his headless ghost returns to the site to look for it. The ghost light supposedly is the ghost's lantern.

Perhaps the most famous ghost lights are the Marfa lights, named after Marfa, Texas and first reported in 1883 by a settler, Robert Ellison. The lights are seen often to the southwest of the Chinati Mountains, bouncing up and down or racing across the ground like a grassfire. Witnesses say the lights sometimes seem playful, as though directed by an intelligence.

The Brown Mountain lights have been reported at Brown Mountain near Morganton, North Carolina since 1913. They are multicolored lights with limited lateral and horizontal movements. The lights were investigated by the U.S. Geological Survey, which attributed them to automotive and locomotive headlights and brush fires. The findings have been disputed by numerous witnesses. In the 1970s, research by the Oak Ridge Isochronous Observation Network (ORION) did show that some, but not all, sightings could be explained by light refractions from points beyond Brown Mountain. Many sightings of the lights remain unexplained.

Near Joplin, Missouri, another active site, yellow and orange ghost lights are reported every night from dusk until dawn. The lights have defied attempts to explain them and appear to be true anomalies. Dale KACZMAREK, president of the Ghost Research Society, has viewed the Joplin lights through high-powered binoculars from a distance of 300–400 feet and describes them as diamond-shaped with hollow and transparent centers. As they move, they leave behind luminous pinpoints of light dancing in the air.

Many reports of ghost lights can be explained naturally, such as car headlights or phosphorescences known as *ignis fatuus* (q.v.) Ghost lights have the power to fascinate, and some individuals who see them do not want the mystique spoiled by an explanation.

Megalith sites, ancient stone circles and monuments once used as burial grounds or for astronomical observations or unknown sacred ritual, have manifestations of mysterious lights, called "earth lights" by some researchers. Various theories propose that these lights are caused by natural earth energies, such as ionized gas escaping from faults (luminous phenomena are associated with earthquakes), or some as-yet unidentified electromagnetic energy. The fault theory may explain some of the Brown Mountain lights; the Grandfather Mountain fault, old and not very active, runs close to Brown Mountain. Other theories propose that the lights are associated with extraterrestrial vehicles that home in on megalith sites.

Further reading:

Devereaux, Paul. *Earth Lights Revealed.* London: Blandford Press, 1990.

Frizzell, Michael A. "The Brown Mountain Lights." In Sharon Jarvis, ed., *True Tales of the Uninvited.* New York: Bantam Books, 1989.

Guiley, Rosemary Ellen. *Harper's Encyclopedia of Mystical and Paranormal Experience.* San Francisco: HarperSanFrancisco, 1991.

Ghost Research Society   Lay psychical research organization founded in the late 1970s in the Chicago area by Martin V. Riccardo, a hypnotherapist who also founded the Vampire Studies information clearinghouse. Membership is international.

The organization originally was called the Ghost Tracker's Club. The name and format were changed in 1981. In 1982, Dale KACZMAREK, research director, became president, and also editor of *The Ghost Tracker's Newsletter,* the society's journal. In 1991, Howard E. Heim of Chicago was named research director, becoming the second person to fill that post. Headquarters of the society are in Oak Lawn, Illinois.

The Ghost Research Society (GRS) researches, investigates and collects data on ghosts, hauntings, poltergeists, survival after death and related phenomena. Society investigations center in the Chicago and northern Indiana area; some members who live elsewhere undertake their own field investigations. Major field investigations of haunted sites are conducted twice a year for sustaining members.

In investigating a site, society members utilize tape recorders, still cameras and video cameras. Psychics occasionally are involved in attempts to communicate with spirits that might be present; seances and mediumistic techniques, however, generally are eschewed. According to Kaczmarek, seances can provide unreliable results due to unpredictable influences from those present and unknown factors concerning the environment. If contact is made with haunting entities, they are urged to move on, but no formal exorcism rites are used. Investigators have found that most spirits of the dead haunting a site do not realize they have died.

Most GRS investigations are of private residences. More than 80% involve individuals of Roman Catholic background. The GRS has undertaken a study to determine the influence of Catholic beliefs on the incidence of paranormal experience.

Of particular interest to the GRS is spirit photography (q.v.). The society maintains one of the world's largest collections of spirit photographs, and analyzes them by digitizing them with a computer. According to Kaczmarek, approximately 90 percent of them have natural explanations.

The GRS also researches ghost lights (q.v.), which are mysterious luminous phenomena, and collects information on the electronic voice phenomena (q.v.) and personal anecdotal accounts of reported ghost and poltergeist experiences.

The GRS receives approximately 100 reports of ghosts and poltergeists annually. Like other paranormal research organizations, the GRS finds that the overwhelming majority of cases—70 to 85% or more—have natural explanations. However, most GRS members, including Kaczmarek, have seen enough unexplained phenomena to conclude that ghosts do exist, and that there is survival after death.

ghost seers   In folklore throughout the world, it is thought that persons born at a certain time of day, or on a particular day, possess the clairvoyant power to see ghosts and things that other persons cannot see. In Lancashire, England, children born during twilight are believed to have the ability to know which of their acquaintances will die next. In other parts of England, the magical birthing hour is twelve o'clock at night or the hour after midnight.

In parts of Europe, it is the day of birth that predicts the power to see clairvoyantly. In Denmark, children born on a Sunday will be able to see certain things, such as an impending death. In Scotland, people born on Christmas Day or Good Friday are said not only to be able to see spirits but to order them about.

Among other peoples, it is believed that only certain persons can see the ghosts, or can see them only at certain times. According to Finnish lore, the ghosts of the dead can be seen only by shamans, and that other men can see them only in their dreams. In the Antilles, some tribes believe that the dead can be seen on the road only when a person travels alone.

In some parts of the world, seers take consciousness-altering substances to enhance their powers and provide information that could be useful to themselves or the community. In the Amazon and North Brazil, seers traditionally are given narcotics to induce visions that might provide information about such matters as who committed a crime.

Similarly, Native Americans in California once gave children intoxicants so that they could envision their enemies.

Further reading:
Leach, Maria, and Jerome Fried, eds. *Funk & Wagnalls Standard Dictionary of Folklore, Mythology, and Legend.* San Francisco: Harper & Row, 1979.

ghost sickness   The belief that the ghosts of the dead can cause illness and death.

In the animistic system of beliefs characteristic of tribal societies around the world, the spirit of a deceased person is thought to remain close to the corpse for a few days before beginning its journey to the land of the dead, and during this in-between or "liminal" period it is particularly dangerous to the living. The ghost is portrayed as lonely in its new existence, and so inclined to seek company from among the living. Children in particular are susceptible to ghost sickness, because their souls are less strong or less firmly attached to their bodies. Among the Kwakiutl Indians of British Columbia, children are sometimes disguised or referred to as adults, in order to confuse the ghosts into thinking that they are older than they are (see ANIMISM; SOUL LOSS).

Fear of ghost sickness accounts for the widespread fear of the dead as expressed in such practices as carrying the corpse out of the house through a hole in the wall rather than through a window or door (see FUNERAL RITES AND CUSTOMS), which is intended to make it difficult for the ghost to find its way back home. Although ghosts are most feared immediately after a death, in many societies any sighting of an apparition or sounds suggestive of a poltergeist are harbingers of disease or death (see DEATH OMENS).

Further reading:
Hultkrantz, Ake. *Conceptions of the Soul Among North American Indians.* Stockholm: Ethnographic Museum of Sweden, 1953.
Tylor, Edward Burnett. *Religion in Primitive Culture.* New York: Harper, 1956.

ghoul   A demon in Islamic lore who feeds on the flesh of human beings, especially travelers, children or corpses stolen out of graves. The name comes from the Arabic terms *ghul* (masculine) and *ghula* (feminine). Ghouls are nocturnal creatures who inhabit graveyards, ruins and other lonely places. Sometimes they are described as dead humans who sleep for long periods in secret graves, then awake, rise and feast on both the living and the dead. Ghouls

also personify the unknown terrors held by the desert, and may be compared to the lamia and Lilith night terror demons. In classical mythology, lamia are monsters who feed on the flesh and blood of the young. Lilith, traditionally the first wife of Adam, is the wife of the Devil, whose children are the *djinn* demons.

In Islamic lore, there are several varieties of ghouls, but the most feared is a female type that has the ability to appear as a normal, flesh-and-blood woman. Such a creature marries an unsuspecting man, who becomes her prey.

See also VETALA.

Further reading:
Leach, Maria, and Jerome Fried, eds. *Funk & Wagnalls Standard Dictionary of Folklore, Mythology, and Legend.* San Francisco: Harper & Row, 1979.

Glamis Castle   The oldest inhabited castle in Scotland, built in the 14th century, has more supernatural lore than perhaps any other castle in the United Kingdom. It is reputed to be the home to a legendary monster, a vampire and a fearsome menagerie of ghosts, some of whom are unknown for their connection to the castle while living. The castle curiously is said to have more windows when seen from the outside than when seen from the inside.

Glamis Castle (the birthplace of Princess Margaret) originally was the home of the lords of Glamis, who, according to legend, were drinking, gambling spendthrifts who lost their family fortune. By the mid-17th century, the castle was in ruins. It was then inherited by Patrick Lyons, who rebuilt the family fortune and the castle, for which he was made the earl of Strathmore. But in the 18th century, the family's bad habits resumed.

In the early 1800s, according to legend, the Strathmores were confronted with an unpleasant situation. The first son of the 11th earl of Strathmore was born a hideously deformed, egg-shaped monster with no neck, tiny arms and legs, and a large, hairy torso. The Monster of Glamis, as he became known, was the true heir to the family estate. However, the child was not expected to live, and so the family hid him away in a secret chamber. His existence was known only to the earl, his second son, the family lawyer and the factor of the estate. To everyone's horror, the monster did not die, but remained strong and hearty. The estate was unlawfully passed on to the second son. In successive generations, as the monster lived on, each earl of Strathmore was informed on his 21st birthday of the true heir's existence and was shown the creature. The earls were permanently changed by this revelation, and became silent, moody and withdrawn. It is said that the monster lived a remarkably long life and died around 1921 or 1941.

While the monster's existence has not been proved, there are records of a secret and yet unknown chamber constructed somewhere in the depths of the castle. In 1880, a newspaper in Scotland told of a workman who accidentally knocked through a wall in the castle and found a secret passage to a locked room. After he informed the steward, the man disappeared, and it was said that he had been given a large sum of money and was sent off to Australia.

A ghost frequently reported seen at Glamis is that of Alexander, the fourth earl of Strathmore who lived in the late 17th century and early 18th century, and was better known as "Earl Beardie." According to one legend, Earl Beardie, a Lord Glamis and two chieftains gambled one night in the tower (now uninhabited). They quarreled and cursed God. The Devil appeared and doomed them to play dice there until Judgment Day. According to another version, Earl Beardie, drunk one Sunday, could find no one to play cards with him, and became so enraged that he said he would play cards with the Devil himself. The Devil obligingly appeared in the form of a tall, dark man wearing a black coat and hat. The two retired to a small room, from which issued sounds of loud shouting and swearing. The earl at last protested that he had lost all his money, and he apparently sold his soul. The Devil vanished and took the soul with him. Earl Beardie died about five years later.

Sounds of stamping, swearing and the rattling of dice still are said to drift from the tower. Earl Beardie's ghost also has been seen flitting around other parts of the castle.

The ghost menagerie includes a woman, thought to be Janet Douglas, wife of James Douglas, the sixth lord of Glamis. James died one morning after eating his breakfast, and Janet was suspected of poisoning him, though no evidence linked her to the deed. Six years later, in 1537, she was accused of attempting to poison King James V. She was condemned and burned at the stake at Castle Hill, Edinburgh. Her ghost appears above the clock tower, wrapped in flames or a reddish glow. Another ghost, of a madman, walks the roof along a spot called "The Mad Earl's Walk" on stormy nights.

Other ghosts include the unidentified GRAY LADIES who haunts the chapel; a tongueless woman who races across the grounds, tearing at her mouth; "Jack the Runner," a thin man who races up the drive to the castle; a black boy—perhaps once a badly treated page—who sits by the door of the Queen Mother's sitting room; a woman with mournful eyes who clutches at an upper window as though imprisoned; and a tall figure dressed in a long, dark cloak.

Modern poltergeist phenomena at the castle include a door which allegedly opens by itself every night, no matter how well secured or barricaded; strange hammerings and knockings; and bedclothes that are pulled off of overnight guests.

Glamis's vampire is said to be a woman servant who was caught sucking the blood of a victim. Legend has it that she was walled up alive in the secret chamber, where she continues to sleep the sleep of the undead, until someone finds her and she is loosed once again.

Two legendary murders are said to have been perpetrated at Glamis Castle, though it is unlikely to be true. Macbeth's murder of King Duncan is believed to have been committed there because Shakespeare mentions Glamis Castle in *Macbeth*; Macbeth's tortured ghost thus is said to haunt the place. Oddly, the murder of King Malcolm II, who reigned during the 11th century, also is placed at Glamis, despite the fact that the castle was not built until three centuries later. Nonetheless, lore has it that a mysterious bloodstain from Malcolm's murder could not be scrubbed off the floor, and the entire floor in the room had to be boarded over. This latter tale is an example of how some ghost legends persist even when historical fact demonstrates otherwise.

Compare to HAM HOUSE.

Further reading:

Folklore, Myths and Legends of Britain. London: Reader's Digest Assoc., 1977.

Harper, Charles G. *Haunted Houses: Tales of the Supernatural With Some Accounts of Hereditary Curses and Family Legends*. Rev. and enlarged ed. London: Cecil Palmer, 1924.

goblin Generally, any type of small, hideous, mischievous or evil spirit. In some cultures, putting the prefix "hob" in front of the word differentiates them from mean-spirited to helpful and kind spirits, although still full of mischief. The Puritans, however, did not subscribe to this notion, and used the term to describe any nasty little creatures.

In French folklore, goblins are wandering spirits who attach themselves to households, where they alternately help and plague the residents, depending on their whims. Goblins are believed to live in grottoes, but are attracted to homes that have beautiful children and lots of wine. When they move in, they help by doing household chores at night and by disciplining children—giving them presents when they are good and punishing them when they are

A 16th-century illustration of minor devils, demons, satyrs and hobgoblins.

naughty. Goblins have an unpredictable, mischievous nature. On some nights, instead of doing chores, they will keep everyone awake by banging pots and pans, moving furniture, knocking on walls and doors, and snatching bedclothes off sleeping persons. Goblins who become tiresome can be persuaded to leave by scattering flaxseed on the floor. The sprites get tired of cleaning it up every night and decide to depart for more hospitable surroundings.

Goblins are similar to brownies, household spirits in England and Scotland, DOMOVIKS in Russia, and other sprites in other countries. In Germany, they are called KOBOLDS, and they work industriously in the mines; they are sometimes thought of as earth elementals. (See KNOCKER.)

Goblins in general have become associated with ALL HALLOWS EVE and are said to roam that night when the veil is thinnest between the world of the living and the world of the dead.

See also BOGEY; BOGGART; POLTERGEIST.

Further reading:

Briggs, Katherine. *An Encyclopedia of Fairies: Hobgoblins, Brownies, Bogies, and Other Supernatural Creatures.* New York: Pantheon Books, 1976.

Leach, Maria, and Jerome Fried, eds. *Funk & Wagnalls Standard Dictionary of Folklore, Mythology, and Legend.* San Francisco: Harper & Row, 1979.

Goligher Circle   Members of an Irish Spiritualist family who formed the mediumistic circle studied by William Jackson CRAWFORD, a lecturer in mechanical engineering at Queens University, Belfast. The Goligher Circle consisted of a father and his four daughters, a son and a son-in-law. All the daughters were mediumistic, although one, Kathleen, was the most powerful. Only Kathleen would go into trance and speak for the spirits the family believed to be pro-

ducing the rappings, table levitations and other phenomena that occurred when they sat together. Their seances were held as part of a religious observance and were ordinarily private, but in 1914 Crawford learned about them and persuaded the family to let him study the manifestations.

Crawford wrote three well-known books about the Golighers: *The Reality of Psychic Phenomena* (1916), *Experiments in Psychic Science* (1919) and *Psychic Structures of the Goligher Circle* (1921). He accepted the seance phenomena as paranormal and was principally interested in studying their physical characteristics. Through experimentation, he discovered evidence of what he called "psychic rods" which appeared to emanate from Kathleen's vagina, and by which the table levitations and other physical effects were accomplished. These "rods" seem to have been composed of ectoplasm (q.v.) and would sometimes solidify into visible forms that could be seen, felt and photographed.

Crawford killed himself in 1920, inevitably raising the suspicion that he had learned that the Golighers had been engaged in trickery. Another investigator, E.E. Fournier d'Albe, who had 20 sittings with the Golighers after Crawford's death, reported few phenomena and concluded that what he did see was fraudulently produced.

W.W. Carington, who observed the Golighers in 1916 and in 1920, believed that genuine phenomena had occurred at the earlier sittings, though not at the later ones. If either Kathleen alone or the Goligher family as a whole had turned to fraud around 1920, this may have been because Kathleen's abilities were suffering the decline that typically accompanies aging with physical mediums, both male and female. She was about 16 in 1914, and thus about 22 in 1920. It is interesting that by 1920 the Golighers had begun to accept donations from observers, something they had not done earlier.

After Fournier d'Albe, the Golighers ceased to give public seances and permitted no further outside studies of their mediumship. However, Kathleen continued to give seances privately, some of which have been reported in print. She married S.G. Donaldson in 1926, and in 1933 he conducted a series of five sittings with her that he reported in the *Psychic Science* the following year. In these experiments, he employed infrared photography, which had then only just become commercially available. No physical phenomena except raps are reported, but photographs of what appears to be ectoplasm (q.v.) were obtained at all five sittings (which would seem to have been held in darkness). Although no further reports of Kathleen's mediumship are available, the sittings with infrared photography were continued. The photographs, however, unfortunately were destroyed during the bombing in World War II.

Kathleen Goligher was last heard from in 1962. It is not known whether she is still alive.

Further reading:

Barham, Allan. "Dr. W.J. Crawford, His Work and His Legacy in Psychokinesis." *Journal of the Society for Psychical Research* 55 (1988):113–38.

Donaldson, S.G. "Five Sittings with Miss Kate Goligher." *Psychic Science* 12 (1934):89–94.

Inglis, Brian. *Science and Parascience: A History of the Paranormal 1914–1939.* London: Hodder and Stoughton, 1984.

Goodwin Sands   See PHANTOM SHIPS.

Grateful Dead   Motif in folklore in which ghosts of the dead return to the world of the living to bestow rewards upon deserving people. For example, a hero comes upon a group of people who refuse to bury a corpse because there is no money to pay the costs. The hero pays for the burial and continues on. He is then joined by a mysterious traveler who gives him astonishing aid, such as saving his life in great peril, finding a princess for him to marry, slaying monsters, or finding great treasure. Sometimes the companion demands half the spoils, which he relinquishes at the very end, just before he reveals himself to be the ghost of the corpse.

In Chinese folklore, the grateful dead often act as agents of social control. The purpose of their appearance is to copiously reward those who gave their corpses proper burial and their spirits continuing respect (thus ensuring the continuation of ANCESTOR WORSHIP). They also honor brave persons, and grace deserving relatives with drop-in visits.

Further reading:

Emmons, Charles F. *Chinese Ghosts and ESP.* Metuchen, N.J.: The Scarecrow Press, 1982.

Leach, Maria, and Jerome Fried, eds. *Funk & Wagnalls Standard Dictionary of Folklore, Mythology, and Legend.* San Francisco: Harper & Row, 1979.

graves and graveyards   See FUNERAL RITES AND CUSTOMS.

gray ladies   The ghosts of women who reportedly died violently for the sake of love or pined away from loss of love. Gray ladies take their name from their frequent appearance as women dressed in gray. Some, however, appear clothed in white, black and brown.

According to lore, gray ladies haunt a house because of their intense desire to be reunited with a loved one. Their hauntings often are associated with

A man startled by the white apparition of a woman.

poltergeist activity. Gray ladies appear around the world, but have been most extensively documented in England.

Speke Hall near Liverpool Airport, for centuries the home of the Norris family, has a ghost believed to be that of Mary Norris, the daughter of the last male Norris, who died after the Restoration. Mary reportedly was so unhappily married to Lord Sidney Beauclerk that she held her son Topham in her arms and jumped into the moat to end both their lives. Mary's ghost is said to still rock the child's cradle in the tapestry room.

A woman who died in a shipwreck has haunted Chambercombe Manor, at Ilfracombe, North Devon, since the 17th century. According to the legend, Alexander and William Oatway were a father and son team who used a lantern on stormy nights to lure ships to the coast. Instead of finding safety, the ships crashed on the rocks and the men would plunder them.

Years later, when William was grown and the father of a married daughter, Kate Wallace, who lived in Dublin, he again lured a ship but was surprised by a survivor. Lying on the rocks was a woman who had been so badly battered during the storm, that her face was unrecognizable. William and his wife took the woman back to the house, but she died during the night. The couple could not resist taking the dead woman's jewelry and money belt.

Two days later, the Admiralty inquired about a missing passenger who turned out to be none other than the Oatways' own daughter, Kate. The devastated Oatways walled up her body in a secret room and moved away. More than a century later, the secret room was discovered with the skeleton lying on a bed. The bones were buried in a pauper's grave, but Kate's ghost continues to visit the house where she grew up.

A few miles from Speke Hall and about seven miles from Ormskirk is Rufford Old Hall, a 15th-century manor house whose resident and anonymous gray lady allegedly died from despair. Shortly after their wedding, her husband left for war. A soldier told her that her husband was due to return in the near future, but when he did not, the hapless girl deteriorated with each passing day. Her dying wish was for her spirit to remain in the house to wait for her husband.

A marriage that never took place was the cause of death for the gray lady of Samlesbury Hall. The house, located between Preston and Blackburn in Lancashire, belonged to the Southworth family for centuries. Sir John, the last male heir of this Catholic family, had a daughter, Dorothy, who fell in love with the heir of a nearby Protestant family.

Despite Sir John's attempts to keep them apart, the young couple met secretly and made arrangements to elope. Unbeknownst to them, one of Dorothy's brothers was hiding in the bushes and overheard the designated time and place. Determined to save his sister from disgrace, the brother hid on the fateful night and killed the young man and two of his friends who were helping him. Their bodies were secretly buried near Samlesbury Hall's chapel; three skeletons were found there in the 19th century.

Dorothy was sent abroad to a convent, where she is said to have gone insane, and shortly after, to have died. The ghosts of Dorothy and her lover have been seen walking on the grounds and on the road, and embracing on the spot where the young lover is believed to have been buried. Crying and wailing have also been heard.

A violent death reportedly produced the gray lady of Heskin Hall, near Blackburn. Heskin Hall often served as a hiding place for Catholic priests during the English Civil War. During a visit by Cromwell's Roundheads, a priest was discovered. In order to save his own life and prove his faith to Puritanism, the priest offered to hang the Catholic daughter of the house. It is believed that his offer was accepted and the girl was hanged in front of her parents. Her ghost, often accompanied by strange tappings and bangings, is said to haunt the Scarlet Room.

Other gray ladies are of special interest because of unique characteristics. The white lady of Bolling Hall at Bradford is credited with saving the lives of all the men, women and children of Bradford. The Earl of Newcastle had ordered their deaths in retaliation for the killing of the Earl of Newport during the English Civil War. The white lady disturbed the sleep of the visiting Earl of Newcastle by pulling at the bedclothes three times during the night and pleading with him to take pity on the town. He rescinded the order the next morning.

The gray lady at the famous Levens House in Cumbria was only a passing visitor, never an occupant. The ghost is said to belong to a Gypsy who laid a curse that there be no male inheritor of the house until the River Kent stopped flowing and a white fawn was born. The house's 17th-century owners reportedly had refused to give the beggar food, and she later died of starvation. The curse was lifted and a male heir was born only when the Gypsy's prophecy came true.

Liberty Hall in Frankfort, Kentucky, reportedly is haunted by a benevolent gray lady who does household chores and is seen gazing out a window.

See RAYNHAM HALL; WILLINGTON MILL.

Further reading:

Folklore, Myths and Legends of Britain. London: Reader's Digest Assoc., 1977.

Green, Andrew. *Our Haunted Kingdom.* London: Wolfe Publishing Ltd., 1973.

Underwood, Peter. *A Gazeteer of British Ghosts.* Rev. ed. London: Pan Books, Ltd., 1973.

Whitaker, Terence. *Haunted England.* Chicago: Contemporary Books, 1987.

Green, Andrew Malcolm (1927–   )

English investigator of ghosts, poltergeists, hauntings and possessions; author, lecturer and media personality.

Andrew M. Green was born on July 28, 1927 in Ealing, London. He earned a bachelor of science degree in 1971 from the London School of Economics, and in 1975 he received a master of philosophy degree from Goldsmiths College, London University. In 1951, he married Hazel Hunter; they were divorced in 1971. Green lives in Robertsbridge, Sussex, with his second wife, Norah Bridget Cawthorne, nee Styles, whom he married in 1979. His stepson and Nora's son, Paul Michael Cawthorne, BSc. (b. 1960) is a linguist and English teacher.

From 1945 to 1990, Green had a varied career, holding jobs as a chemist, office administrator, advertising and publicity manager, publications editor and tutor. From 1968 to 1972, he operated his own publishing house, Malcolm Publications, which produced house journals and tourist material. In 1990, he took retirement and resumed work full time in psychical investigations, which had been a part-time pursuit for more than four decades.

Green's interest in the paranormal was sparked in 1944. His father, who then worked as a rehousing officer, was called upon to assess a house at 16 Montpelier Road in Ealing that had been vacant for 10 years. The elder Green found the structure acceptable for the storage of goods, but noticed a peculiar, sulphurous smell in a small room on a mezzanine. He reported the smell, and was informed that the floor and plaster in the room had been

Andrew M. Green's photo of the house at 16 Montpelier Road, taken in 1944. Notice the filmy shape in the upper lefthand window. Courtesy Andrew M. Green.

replaced, but the smell persisted. Workmen who later brought in goods to be stored in the house claimed it was haunted. They had heard footsteps and sensed an "atmosphere."

His curiosity aroused, Mr. Green senior visited a friend at the metropolitan police and inquired about the history of the house. He was told that since it had been constructed in 1883, and until 1934 when it became vacant, there had been 20 suicides and one murder there. All had occurred by jumping or being thrown from the integral 70-foot-high top tower. The murder involved an infant that had been tossed from the top of the tower.

Green and his father then visited the house. During the tour of the building, young Green thought he felt invisible hands at one point helping him up the staircase to the tower top. Looking out from the roof, he thought he heard a voice whispering to him urging him to go into the garden by going over the parapet. He nearly went over the edge when his father grabbed him from behind and showed him that the drop was certainly fatal.

Green photographed the exterior of the house from the back garden. Although he noticed nothing strange at the time, one photograph revealed a shape in an upstairs window. The image appears to be that of a female in Victorian style dress. The figure might be that of a 12-year-old girl who either fell, jumped or was pushed from the tower in 1886. The photograph remains unexplained.

The Montpelier case launched Green on his second career as investigator of hauntings. His work has

Andrew M. Green. Courtesy Andrew M. Green.

included assisting authorities in alleviating "possession" phenomena, and lecturing and writing.

In 1949, he founded the Ealing Society for the Investigation of Psychic Phenomena, and served as its first chairman until 1953, when he resigned. He was co-founder of the National Federation of Psychic Research Societies in 1951.

In the late 1960s, Green conducted a trial survey of psychic sensitivity and established that children of seven years of age seem to be at the peak of this faculty, which then diminishes with age, learning and increased reliance on intellect rather than intuition. Thus, seven-year-old children might be helpful in assessing an allegedly haunted side. Green's research concerning peak sensitivity was subsequently confirmed by research conducted by another parapsychologist at Surrey University, England.

Green defines a ghost as a form of electromagnetism. He does not believe that ghosts have personalities or intelligence, but that they are merely impressions created by the living at times of shock and stress. When a person receives a severe shock, such as learning of the unexpected death of another person, he or she immediately and uncontrollably creates a mental image of the deceased in circumstances under which they were last seen, according to Green. Under certain circumstances, the dying may create their own ghosts through mental impressions. Apparitions of the living, he says, are created under similar conditions that create an intense desire in a person to be in another, distant spot.

He believes that the most disturbing hauntings are not genuine impressions left at a site, but are created by imagination and PSYCHOKINESIS (PK) on the part of the living. A successful exorcism alleviates the mental conditions that create the haunting.

Smells associated with hauntings usually have natural explanations, Green says. For example, smells can be absorbed into various materials and remain for considerable periods of time, becoming noticeable periodically under the right conditions of moisture and temperature. Sounds likewise usually have natural explanations; or, he says, they can remain imbedded in a building for long periods of time.

Green does no believe in survival after death due to insufficient evidence.

Green lectures on ghosts and hauntings and makes frequent appearances on radio and television shows throughout the U.K. He is the author of 10 nonfiction books and numerous articles on ghosts and hauntings. Books include: *Mysteries of Surrey* (1972), *Mysteries of Sussex* (1973), *Mysteries of London* (1973), *Ghost Hunting, A Practical Guide* (1973), *Our Haunted Kingdom* (1973), *Haunted Houses* (1975), *Ghosts of the South*

East (1976), *Phantom Ladies* (1977), *The Ghostly Army* (1980) and *Ghosts of Today* (1980).

Greenbrier Ghost   West Virginia murder case that, according to legend, was exposed and solved by the ghost of the victim. The case went to trial, during which testimony concerning the ghost's appearances was entered into the record. The case is the only known case (at least in the United States) in which a ghost helped to convict a murderer.

The victim, later known as the "Greenbrier Ghost," was Elva Zona Heaster Shue, who lived near Greenbrier, West Virginia with her new husband, Trout Shue. Zona (the name she used) was born probably in 1873—records give different dates—and bore an illegitimate child in 1895.

In 1896, she met Erasmus (also given as Edward) Stribbling Trout Shue, an out-of-towner who moved to Greenbrier to work as a blacksmith and start a new life for himself. The two were quickly attracted to each other, and they married shortly after meeting, on October 26, 1896. The marriage was opposed by Zona's mother, Mary Jane Robinson Heaster, who did not like Shue or the idea of her daughter marrying a stranger.

On January 23, 1897, Zona's body was discovered inside her house by a black boy, Andy Jones, who had been sent to the house by Shue with instructions to ask Zona if she required anything from the store. Jones found Zona lying on the floor, stretched out straight with feet together, one hand by her side and the other lying across her body, and her head inclined slightly to one side. Jones ran home to tell his mother.

The local physician and coroner, Dr. George W. Knapp, was summoned and arrived at the Shue household in about an hour. By then, Shue had already carried his wife's body upstairs and dressed it up in her Sunday best: a dress with a high neck and stiff collar secured by a big bow, and a veil covering her face. While Knapp attempted to determine the cause of death, Shue remained planted by his wife's head, cradling her head and upper body and sobbing in great distress.

Because of Shue's tremendous display of grief, Knapp made only a cursory examination. He observed slight discolorations on the right side of Zona's neck and right cheek. When he tried to examine the back of her neck, Shue erupted into such protests that Knapp ended the examination and left. Initially, Knapp announced that Zona had died of "an everlasting faint," then officially recorded the cause as "childbirth." It is not known for certain whether Zona was pregnant. For two weeks prior to the tragedy, Knapp had been treating her for an undisclosed "trouble." In those times, one of the most common causes of death among young women was complications from childbirth, and Knapp may have fallen back on that for lack of anything more specific.

Zona's body was laid out for her wake. Neighbors who came to pay their respects observed odd behavior in Shue. He changed from overwhelming grief to manic energy to agitation. He did not want anyone near Zona. He had placed a pillow at one side of her head and a wadding of cloth on the other side, explaining that the ministrations were to enable Zona "to rest easier." He said the big scarf around her neck was her favorite, and that she had wanted to be buried in it. Nonetheless, people noticed that when time came for the corpse to be moved to the cemetery, there was a strange looseness of the head. Tongues wagged.

Heaster, Zona's mother, took the sheet from inside the coffin, and later attempted to return it to Shue. He refused it. Heaster noticed it had a peculiar smell, so she washed it. The water turned red, but when she scooped the water out of the basin, it was clear. The sheet was stained pink. Heaster tried boiling the sheet and hanging it outdoors in freezing weather for several days, but the stain remained. To her, it was a sign that her daughter had met with foul play.

Hester prayed that her daughter would come back from the dead and reveal the truth about how she died. Specifically, Heaster said later, she wanted Zona to "tell" on Shue, as she suspected the blacksmith of murder.

Heaster's prayers were answered within weeks. On four nights, Zona's ghost reportedly appeared and awakened her from sleep, and described in detail her murder. Her husband had been abusive and cruel, she said. He had attacked her in a fit of rage because he thought she had no meat cooked for supper, and had broken her neck. To illustrate, the ghost's head turned completely around on the neck.

Heaster went to the prosecutor, John Alfred Preston, and demanded an investigation. It is unlikely that he agreed simply on the basis of a ghost's story. However, the local rumor mill continued to grind about Zona's mysterious and untimely death, the odd appearance of her corpse and her husband's strange behavior.

Preston ordered Zona's body exhumed. Shue vigorously opposed the inquest. He publicly said that he knew he would be arrested, "but they will not be able to prove I did it," thus indicating at least knowledge that his wife had been murdered.

Zona's body was exhumed on February 22, 1897. An autopsy revealed a broken neck and a crushed windpipe from strangulation. There was no evidence of violence to other parts of her body. Shue said, "They cannot prove I did it." He was arrested and charged with murder. He pleaded not guilty.

While he awaited trial in jail, information came out about his unsavory background. He had served time in jail for stealing a horse. He had been married twice before. He had abused his first wife, and had forced her to divorce him by throwing her things out of the house. His second wife had died under mysterious circumstances from a head injury, due, according to different accounts, to a fall or a rock falling upon her.

In jail, Shue remained in good spirits, his grieving long since over. He said that he wanted to have seven wives, and since Zona had been his third and he was only 35, he stood a good chance of realizing his ambition. He said repeatedly that his guilt could not be proved. He wondered why no one suspected the 11-year-old black boy, Jones. (If Shue did indeed commit the murder, he may have set the boy up for possible blame.)

Despite the fact that all the evidence against Shue was circumstantial (it is doubtful the case would have ever been tried in modern times), the trial commenced in late June. Numerous people testified against Shue. Heaster's ghost story was inadmissible as evidence because it was heresay. However, the defense raised the matter when she was on the stand, perhaps in an effort to make her appear to the jury to be unbalanced and insane. Heaster recounted the ghost's assertion that Zona's neck had been "squeezed off at the first vertebrae" by Shue.

Shue took the stand in his own defense, passionately denying everything said about his alleged guilt. It was to no avail. The jury quickly found him guilty, but voted for life imprisonment instead of death by hanging due to the circumstantial nature of the evidence.

The verdict did not satisfy many in Greenbrier. A lynching party was formed on July 11, but was thwarted due to a tip. Shue was moved to the state penitentiary in Moundsville, West Virginia. He died on March 13, 1900, possibly from an epidemic of infectious diseases that swept the community at that time. There is no record of what happened to his remains.

A highway historical marker near Greenbrier commemorates the case. It reads:

> Interred in nearby cemetery is Zona Heaster Shue. Her death in 1897 was presumed natural until her spirit appeared to her mother to describe how she was killed by her husband Edward. Autopsy on the exhumed body verified the apparition's account. Edward, found guilty of murder, was sentenced to the

state prison. Only known case in which testimony from ghost helped convict a murderer.

Despite the resolution, many questions remain about the case. In all likelihood, Shue did murder his wife in a fit of rage, and then attempted to cover up the crime. Afterward, there was speculation among the Greenbrier townsfolk that Zona had died a natural death, and her mother had broken her neck in the coffin in an attempt to frame the hated Shue of a crime. There also was talk that Zona had been pregnant with another illegitimate child (accounting for her quick marriage to Shue), and that Knapp had been trying to abort the baby and had killed Zona. Her neck was broken to cover it up. Or, that Shue killed Zona when he discovered her pregnant with a child that couldn't possibly be his. Though stories circulated of a dead baby being wrapped in the coffin wadding next to Zona's head, the autopsy mentioned nothing about pregnancy.

Doubts have been raised that Zona's mother ever saw the ghost. Instead, it is theorized that Heaster concocted the ghost story to validate her own suspicions and give credence to a request for a post-mortem inquest. It does seem odd that the ghost of a young country woman would specifically announce that her neck had been "squeezed off at the first vertebrae" rather than simply broken. Perhaps at trial time Heaster conformed her ghost story to the findings of the autopsy.

In investigating the case, historian Katie Letcher Lyle found an overlooked clue that would indicate that Heaster had made up the ghost story. Zona's death was announced in the *Greenbrier Independent* on January 28, 1897. In the same issue, on a nearby page, was a story about how a murder case in Australia had been solved because numerous people had seen the ghost of the murdered man sitting on a rail of a horse pond into which his body had been thrown. Years later, a dying man confessed that he had made up the story of the ghost, which others had then believed to the point that they had claimed to see the apparition. The man said he had witnessed the murder, but had been threatened with death if he divulged details. He concocted the ghost in an effort to get the body discovered.

Lyle proposes the plausible theory that Heaster read the story and took a similar course of action to avenge her daughter's death. It is impossible to say whether she undertook the action deliberately, or was subconsciously influenced by the story and actually believed in Zona's ghost.

The case of the Greenbrier Ghost features three motifs prominent in folklore concerning ghosts: the inability of a murder victim to rest until the truth is known; the return of the dead for revenge; and the disturbance of a sleeping person by a ghost.

Further reading:

Lyle, Katie Letcher. *The Man Who Wanted Seven Wives.* Chapel Hill, N.C.: Algonquin Books of Chapel Hill, 1986.

gremlin   A small, pesky spirit that first appeared in British military aircraft during World War I. Royal Air Force pilots sent out on dangerous missions reported seeing misty, goblin-like spirits in their aircraft. The pilots named them "gremlins." Nothing public was said about them until 1922, perhaps out of superstitious belief that it might be bad luck to acknowledge the spirits. The term "gremlin," after Grimm's *Fairy Tales*, was not used until 1939 during World War II, when a British bomber squadron in India suffered numerous incidents of seeming sabotage to their craft. Gremlins have since expanded their presence to military and civilian aircraft elsewhere around the world.

Gremlins seem to be generally friendly in nature, though they are wont to play poltergeist-like pranks upon crew. They are ascribed great knowledge of technology, meteorology, engineering and aerodynamics. They have been said to drink fuel, bore holes in the aircraft, bite through cables, sever fuel lines, slash wings with invisible scissors, and punch and pinch gunners and bombardiers as they line targets up in their sights. They have been blamed for poor landings by pilots. On the other hand, they also have been credited with helping pilots to fly badly damaged aircraft to safety.

Gremlins also have been reported to appear in factories. They perhaps may be modern, high-tech versions of brownies, kobolds, domoviks, blue-caps and other such spirits who, according to lore, like to live among humans and keep them alert.

Various descriptions have been given of gremlins. During World War II, some were said to be six inches tall with horns and black leather suction boots, while others looked like a cross between a jack rabbit and a bull terrier. Still others were humanoid and about one foot tall, wearing ruffled red jackets and green breeches. Some had webbed feet with fins on the heels.

When Charles Lindbergh made his historic solo flight across the Atlantic Ocean in 1927, he reportedly saw spirits in his cabin that may have been gremlins or gremlin-like. By the ninth hour of his journey, which took thirty-three and one-half hours, Lindbergh became fatigued and began to feel detached from his surroundings. He became aware that the fuselage was filled with vaporous forms that moved freely about. They spoke in friendly voices and discussed navigation. They reassured him of his safety and also imparted, he said, information of a mystical nature. Lindberg did not reveal his strange experiences until the publication of his book, *The Spirit of St. Louis*, in 1953.

More recently, cases have been recorded of gremlin-like voices speaking audibly to civilian pilots, delivering instructions to turn, land, change course, and so on, in order to avert unforeseen disasters.

Compare to KNOCKER.

Further reading:

Caidin, Martin. *Ghosts of the Air: True Stories of Aerial Hauntings*. New York: Bantam Books, 1991.

Guiley, Rosemary Ellen. *Harper's Encyclopedia of Mystical and Paranormal Experience*. San Francisco: HarperSanFrancisco, 1991.

Haining, Peter. *A Dictionary of Ghost Lore*. Englewood Cliffs, N.J.: Prentice-Hall, 1984.

Leach, Maria, and Jerome Fried, eds. *Funk & Wagnalls Standard Dictionary of Folklore, Mythology, and Legend*. San Francisco: Harper & Row, 1979.

Griffin See PHANTOM SHIPS.

Grottendieck Stone-Thrower The island of Sumatra, formerly a part of the Dutch East Indies and now a part of Indonesia, is a place where poltergeist activities seem to be commonplace, and are often reported in the newspapers. A famous incidence, and one that is still unexplained, occurred in September 1903 when a Dutch engineer working for a Dutch oil company witnessed a strange phenomenon of falling stones. The story was published in the British *Journal of the Society for Psychical Research* in 1906.

The engineer, W.D. Grottendieck of Dordrecht, Holland, had returned from a tiring trip in the steamy Sumatran jungle with some 50 coolies when he found that his regular quarters had been temporarily taken by another member of his company. He decided to stay in a new house that had just been erected on bamboo poles. The roof was thatched with large, dried leaves, known as *kadjang* leaves, in an overlapping shingle style.

Exhausted, Grottendieck laid out his sleeping bag and mosquito netting on the wooden floor and immediately fell asleep. At about one o'clock in the morning, he was partially awakened by something falling near his head outside the netting. A few minutes later, he was awakened by the realization that something was falling on the floor beside him. In the darkness, he was able to see that the falling objects were small black stones, all less than one inch in diameter. Grottendieck turned up his kerosene lamp and was amazed to see that the black stones looked as though they were falling *through* the roof, though there were no apparent holes in the thatching.

Grottendieck went into the next room to wake up his Malay servant boy. Thinking that someone was playing a joke on him, he told the boy to go outside to see if he could see anyone. While holding a flashlight to light the way for the boy, Grottendieck could see the stones continue to fall right through the roof onto the floor of his room.

The boy returned without finding anything. Grottendieck then ordered him to investigate the kitchen. Grottendieck returned to his sleeping room and tried to catch a few of the falling stones. Unbelievably, he was unable to catch even one of them. Just as he thought one would be caught in his grasp, it mysteriously changed direction in midair and floated away. Meanwhile, more stones were falling and hitting the floor beside him. He noticed that the stones seemed to fall slowly, and that the movements of the boy seemed unusually slow as well.

Grottendieck climbed up the partition between his room and the servant boy's room in order to examine the spot from which the stones seemed to be falling. He could not see any holes or cracks in the roof. Once again, he tried to catch the stones, but they elude him.

The servant boy then entered the room to say there was no one in the kitchen. Grottendieck, frustrated that somebody was so successfully tricking him, grabbed his Mauser rifle and fired five rounds into the air above the jungle to scare off the invisible prankster. The stones, however, continued to fall.

The servant boy, frightened, announced that the situation was the work of Satan, and fled into the jungle. Grottendieck never saw him again. At the departure of the boy, the stones stopped falling. Grottendieck touched a few of them and found them warm. Although mystified, he returned to his sleeping bag and dozed off.

The next morning, only about 18 to 24 of the little stones remained on the floor, although the five cartridge shells from his rifle were still there. Grottendieck observed that the stones had fallen within a radius of not more than three feet, and that they all had come through a single *kadjang* leaf. He thought perhaps he had been visited by a shower of meteors, but he abandoned the idea after he once again examined the roof and found no torn holes.

The cessation of stones upon the departure of the boy suggested that the boy was unconsciously a poltergeist focal point. However, Grottendieck discounted that theory in his subsequent correspondence with the SOCIETY FOR PSYCHICAL RESEARCH (SPR), explaining that while he was bending over the sleeping boy, he could still hear the stones falling through the half-open door to his room.

Prior to this incident, Grottendieck had been a skeptic in occult matters, but now he began to wonder about poltergeists and spiritism. His sister had died three months before, and Grottendieck thought there could be a connection between her death and the falling stones—perhaps it was her way of communicating with him. Consequently, he obtained a book about spiritism in an attempt to ascertain if this might be the case. If he arrived at a conclusion, he did not share it with the SPR.

Grottendieck told the SPR that similar phenomena were commonplace in the Dutch East Indies. Frank PODMORE opined that the boy servant had thrown the stones, or that Grottendieck was hallucinating because of his impressions that the stones and boy were moving slowly. Podmore's views were refuted by other members, including Andrew LANG. A member living in Singapore suggested that the "stones" were really fruit seeds dropped by bats which fly into houses at night and eat the fruit while they hang from rafters.

The case remains inconclusive.

Further reading:
"A Poltergeist Case." *Journal of the Society for Psychical Research* 12 (1906):260–66.
"Correspondence." *Journal of the Society for Psychical Research* 12 (1906):278–331.

guardian spirit   A personal protective spirit, also called a "tutelary spirit," or "genius," believed by some persons and some societies to be present with one from birth, and by others to be acquired through a dream or visionary experience. Guardian spirits play an important role in animism as well as in spiritualism. They also figure in the Christian concept of guardian angels.

The major function of the guardian spirit is, as its name implies, to look out for its possessor, which means keeping him or her out of trouble, and making sure life runs smoothly. Misfortune may be attributed to failure on the part of the guardian spirit, and good fortune to its successful guidance. Messages from the guardian spirit may sometimes be precognitive or clairvoyant.

In tribal societies, guardian spirits have varying relationships with the rest of the spirit-soul complex associated with the human being (see ANIMISM; SOUL). In some societies they are conceived of as independent spirits, whereas in others they are thought to be surviving ancestors or are connected to an ances-

tor in some intimate way. For some of the Australian Aborigines, a person's soul and his or her guardian are united before birth and reunited after death, but during life they have different existences and serve different functions.

Guardian spirits may be acquired in various ways. If one is not born with a guardian, one may have to deliberately seek one. This is the case with many Native American peoples, for whom a part of the traditional "vision quest" for boys and girls at puberty is the finding of their own guardian. Alternatively, one's guardian is revealed to one in a dream. Because in animism dreams are believed to represent the experiences of the soul at night, this is the same as saying that one meets one's guardian while out of one's body, in other words while in spirit form. Whether the encounter occurs in a vision or dream, however, it is not always at this time that one has acquired one's guardian. It may be that the guardian has been with one from birth, but one has only now become aware of it.

In the animistic tradition, guardian spirits are related to shamanism, totemism and reincarnation. In many cases shamans, whose business it is to make contact with the spirit world, have more than one guardian or assistant, often in the form of a "power animal." Totemism is a subclass of animistic beliefs which concerns aspects of the human relationship to animals. People are often associated with particular animals, which may also be their guardians. The connection between guardian spirits and reincarnation is especially complex, as the Aborigine example suggests. Many of the Aborigines believe in reincarnation, and thus, by continually reuniting with the soul between lifetimes, the guardian is assured of always being associated with the same soul while it is incarnate.

In Spiritualism and in some Christian denominations, a person is believed to have a guardian from birth, although one may not always be aware of its existence. In general, however, the guardian performs the same function of looking out for one as it does in tribal societies.

Further reading:
Hultkrantz, Ake. *Conceptions of the Soul Among North American Indians*. Stockholm: Ethnographic Museum of Sweden, 1953.
Radin, Paul. *Primitive Religion: Its Nature and Origins*. New York: Dover Publications, 1957.
Tylor, Edward Burnett. *Religion in Primitive Culture*. New York: Harper & Row, 1956.

Guppy, Agnes (also known as **Mrs. Samuel Guppy**) (**1838–1917**)   The first medium to perform full-form materializations in Great Britain, Agnes Guppy was the queen of Spiritualist circles from the mid-1860s to the early 1870s.

She was born Agnes or Ann Nichol (also spelled Nicholl) in 1838 in London. She was orphaned before her first birthday and raised by her grandfather, Mr. Nichol, a sculptor. She began having visions of spirits at age nine and could not shake them, no matter how her grandfather laughed, cajoled, or prescribed cold baths and rigorous exercise.

By the time she came of age, Agnes, now called Elizabeth or Lizzie, had become a photographer and painter, aligning herself with Mr. and Mrs. Sims. Mrs. Sims, referred to both as sister and sister-in-law of the naturalist Alfred Russel Wallace, encouraged Lizzie's mediumistic talents and introduced Wallace to her. On December 14, 1866, Lizzie first aported fresh flowers at a seance attended by Wallace. He enthusiastically supported her gifts, which included levitation as well as teleportation. Lizzie also trained as a mesmeric healer.

In December 1867, Lizzie married the wealthy but elderly Spiritualist Samuel Guppy. For the next two years, the Guppys lived abroad, continuing to hold seances and dazzle Continental sitters with Mrs. Guppy's spectacular apports. They returned in the summer of 1870 to England with a son and resumed their Spiritualist endeavors. Mrs. Guppy sponsored Frank Herne and Charles Williams, even participating in a so-called "apport post" among Herne and Williams, herself, James Burn, Catherine Berry and Mrs. MacDougall Gregory. Items "mailed" from house to house included a white cat and a Maltese dog.

Mrs. Guppy's most amazing apport was herself. In June 1871, she allegedly was teleported to a seance at the Herne-Williams home in High Holborn, London, dressed in only her robe and holding her pen and household account book. One of the sitters, W.H. Harrison, had jokingly asked the spirit controls John and Katie King if they could bring Mrs. Guppy, by now a very large woman, and they obliged.

Mrs. Guppy materialized the first full-form human in 1872 via a completely light-tight cabinet which supposedly allowed the medium to gather psychic power and display the materialization. One observer also found Mrs. Guppy's voluminous skirts to be the source for materialized forms. Not long thereafter, Herne and Williams materialized the ever-popular John King, with Mrs. Guppy's approval.

But full-form materializations of Katie King by Florence COOK did not have the jealous Mrs. Guppy's endorsement. Florence's youthful, petite beauty, contrasted with Mrs. Guppy's enormous figure, attracted many of Mrs. Guppy's former sitters. In January 1873, Mrs. Guppy conspired to have vitriol acid thrown in Florence's "doll face" to permanently disfigure her, but as her hoped-for accomplices, mediums Mr. and Mrs. Nelson Holmes, refused to cooperate, she instead exposed them as frauds the next month. Her spiteful actions effectively ended her career as London's reigning medium.

Mrs. Guppy got her revenge on Florence Cook, however. In December 1873, William Volckman grabbed the materialized Katie King during a seance, believing the spirit to be Florence in costume. He was condemned by Spiritualists for risking Florence's life while her "essence" was merged into Katie's, but the public's faith in Florence Cook was shaken. Perhaps in gratitude, Mrs. Guppy married Volckman after Mr. Guppy died, and she called herself Mrs. Guppy-Volckman until her death in 1917.

Further reading:

Brandon, Ruth. *The Spiritualists.* New York: Alfred A. Knopf Inc., 1983.

Fodor, Nandor. *An Encyclopaedia of Psychic Science.* Secaucus, N.J.: The Citadel Press, 1966. First published 1933.

———. *Mind Over Space.* New York: The Citadel Press, 1962.

Mysteries of the Unknown: Spirit Summonings. Alexandria, Va.: Time-Life Books, 1989.

Gurney, Edmund (1847–1888)   Classical scholar, musician, psychologist and psychical researcher, a founding member of the SOCIETY FOR PSYCHICAL RESEARCH (SPR), best known as principal author of the classic work *Phantasms of the Living* (1886). He was also one of the foremost authorities of his day on hypnotism and contributed several important papers on the subject to the SPR *Proceedings* and to the journal *Mind*.

Edmund Gurney was born March 23, 1847 in Hersham, Surrey, England. He attended Trinity College, Cambridge, where he studied classics. His original choice of vocation was music, to which he devoted the five years 1872 to 1877, and about which he wrote his first book, *The Power of Sound* (1880). When he failed to reach concert standard, he switched to medicine; but he found the hospital too stressful, and briefly took up law instead. He married Kate Sibley in 1877 and by her had a daughter, Helen May.

Gurney's active interest in psychical research began in 1874 when he and Frederic W.H. MYERS attended a seance with William Stainton MOSES. Gurney and Myers, along with Henry SIDGWICK, Arthur Balfour (see BALFOUR FAMILY) and others, subsequently sat with several mediums over a period of years, but they encountered little in the way of genuine paranormal ability, let alone phenomena suggestive of survival after death. This group nevertheless is important because it included many of those who came to be centrally involved in the SPR when it was established in 1882. Gurney himself served on the SPR's governing council from its inception and was its secretary and the editor of its *Proceedings* from 1883. In psychical research he found the career for which he had been searching.

Gurney's early work with the SPR concerned experiments using hypnosis in tests for ESP. In one of the first series, he and Myers tested two men, G.A. Smith and Douglas Blackburn, in London and in the town of Brighton. Good results were gotten, especially with drawings and diagrams, and Gurney hired Smith as a private secretary; Smith's hypnotic susceptibility made him valuable in the experimental work as well. Gurney continued working with hypnosis until 1888, varying and improving the conditions under which the tests were made.

Gurney was responsible for writing most of *Phantasms of the Living* (1886), a massive two-volume study of the evidence for telepathy, particularly from crisis apparitions. Crisis apparitions are those that appear coincidentally with a death or life-threatening crisis. Gurney built a careful case to explain them as hallucinations of the percipient, resulting from an impression of the agent's crisis gained via telepathy. Besides breaking new ground theoretically, *Phantasms of the Living* also for the first time set forth standards of evidence and methods of investigation appropriate to the study of psychic phenomena.

Many of Gurney's papers on various subjects, from diverse fields, were collected in *Tertium Quid* (1887). He died suddenly and prematurely (he was forty-one) on the night of June 23, 1888, at a hotel in Brighton.

Gurney had suffered for some time from insomnia and neuralgia, and took chloroform to relive the pain. He was found lying in bed, with a sponge-bag pressed over his nose and mouth and a small empty bottle on the table. The death was ruled accidental, but the suspicion that it was a suicide remains to this day. There are hints that Gurney admitted taking his own life in some private (and otherwise evidential) communications through Leonora PIPER to Sir Oliver LODGE, when Piper visited England in 1889–90.

Gurney is said to have gone to bed in good spirits, but he had alternating periods of exhilaration and despair throughout his life (he seems to have been manic-depressive), and he could conceivably have passed into one of the latter phases that night. The skeptical historian Trevor Hall has suggested that Gurney killed himself when he learned that it was true (as Blackburn had claimed) that Smith and Blackburn had cheated in their series of tests. Hall, however, offers no real evidence for his conjecture, and in the absence of convincing evidence one way or the other, the exact circumstances of Gurney's death are likely to remain a mystery.

Further reading:

Gauld, Alan. *The Founders of Psychical Research*. London: Routledge & Kegan Paul, 1968.

Hall, Trevor H. *The Strange Case of Edmund Gurney*. London: Duckworth, 1964.

Oppenheim, Janet. *The Other World: Spiritualism and Psychical Research in England, 1850–1914*. Cambridge: Cambridge University Press, 1985.

Guzik, Jan (1875–1928)   Polish materialization medium. Jan Guzik was the son of a weaver, a native of Warsaw. He was apprenticed to the tanning trade, but began to manifest poltergeist disturbances, and at the age of 15 he became a professional medium. He was in the habit of taking brandy before seances, of which he would sometimes hold five in one day.

The first systematic study of Guzik's mediumship was a series of 50 sittings conducted by Gustave GELEY of the INSTITUT METAPSYCHIQUE INTERNATIONAL (IMI) in 1921. Geley witnessed the movement of objects without contact (see PSYCHOKINESIS) and various materializations, including that of a head and face, seemingly alive and speaking. Impressed, he arranged for Guzik to visit Paris in 1922 and 1923.

The IMI seances were attended not only by Geley but by several other psychical researchers, including Eugene OSTY, Charles Richet, Camille Flammarion, and Sir Oliver LODGE. Footsteps were sometimes heard passing around the circle. At times, small lights would appear in the air not far from the sitters. These would draw together to form pairs, which developed pupils. A mass of cloudy matter would them form around the eyes, and gradually a human shape would appear in the darkness. The experimental conditions were such that the investigators believed that trickery was ruled out, and all signed a statement to that effect.

Characteristic of Guzik's mediumship were touches that seemed to be those of animals, and the "full-form" materialization of an "ape man," whom Geley nicknamed "Pithecanthropus."

Like the Italian Eusapia PALLADINO, Guzik was not above helping out the phenomena, if given the chance. This was well known by November 1923, when a committee of four professors at the Sorbonne in Paris held a series of 10 seances with him. Unaccustomed to psychical research, the professors were lax in their controls of Guzik's arms and legs, and as a result found that he would sometimes use his hand or knee to produce "spirit touches" or move objects. Although the professors were unable to explain all the seance phenomena in this way, they declared that he was a complete fraud.

Some psychical researchers—notably Harry PRICE, who saw Guzik in action in 1923, and Walter Franklin PRINCE, who sat with him in 1927—were no kinder in their evaluations. The continental European investigators who worked most closely with him were, nonetheless, convinced that, like Palladino, Guzik was capable of producing genuine phenomena, if properly controlled.

Guzik died in 1928.

Further reading:

Inglis, Brian. *Science and Parascience: A History of the Paranormal, 1914–1939*. London: Hodder and Stoughton, 1984.

Geley, Gustave. *Clairvoyance and Materialization*. London: T. Fisher Unwin, 1927.

Prince, Walter Franklin. "Experiments for Physical Phenomena with Noted Mediums in Europe." *Bulletin 7* (1928). Boston Society for Psychical Research.

H

hag See OLD HAG.

Halcyon House Historic home of Benjamin Stoddert, the first Secretary of the U.S. Navy, said to be haunted, perhaps as a result of its strange history. The house is located in the Georgetown district of Washington, D.C.

After the Revolutionary War and the establishment of Washington as the capital of the United States, Stoddert built Halcyon House on a bluff overlooking the Potomac River. He named it after a mythical bird that calms the sea. The original structure was small and elegant. Stoddert commissioned the renowned planner Pierre Charles L'Enfant to design his terrace.

Stoddert ran his own shipping business, which fell on hard times. By the time his tenure as Secretary of the Navy in 1801 ended, the last year of the John Adams administration, Stoddert was nearly destitute. He died virtually penniless in 1813.

The house then passed to a series of owners. During the Civil War, its basement was connected to a tunnel from the Potomac that was part of the Underground Railroad for runaway slaves. According to legend, some slaves died in the basement, and began haunting it with ghostly moans and cries. The entrance to the tunnel was walled up around the turn of the 20th century, but the moans and cries continue to be heard. In addition, mysterious shapes and a ghostly woman reportedly were seen floating about the house at night.

In the 1930s, Halcyon House was acquired by a peculiar man named Albert Adsit Clemons, who believed that as long as he added on to the house, he would not die. He added apartments and facades, and made haphazard alterations, including a staircase that went nowhere, doors that opened to walls and rooms without walls. He also refused to wire the house for electricity, which discouraged prospective tenants.

Clemons's fervor failed to stave off death, and he died in 1938. Oddly, he left a will, and it instructed that upon his death his attending doctor should pierce or puncture his heart—just to make sure he was dead.

After Clemons's death, haunting phenomena in the house increased. Residents and guests reported finding that closed windows had been opened, an engraving hung on a wall was repeatedly found on the floor, and odd sounds were heard, especially coming from the attic when no one was there. On two separate occasions a male tenant and a female guest awoke at night to find themselves floating above their beds. A phantom of an old, balding, fat and short man was repeatedly seen; the description matched a portrait of Stoddert. A phantom woman also continued to be seen until the mid-1970s. In 1972, a couple who were housesitting were reportedly reversed in their bed the first night they slept in the master bedroom.

Hubert Humphrey, Vice President during the Lyndon B. Johnson administration in the 1960s, considered living in Halcyon House, but restoration work was deemed to be too extensive. The house is privately owned and is a historical landmark.

Further reading:

Alexander, John. *Ghosts: Washington's Most Famous Ghost Stories.* Arlington, Va.: Washington Book Trading Co., 1988.

Halloween See ALL HALLOWS EVE.

Ham House Elegant house in Dubuque, Iowa, now a museum, reported to be haunted and to have various paranormal and poltergeist phenomena. The house has an interesting history, but the legends credited with some of the phenomena have not been verified by historical fact.

The original owner of the house, Mathias Ham, was a prosperous 19th-century businessman with lumbering, agriculture and shipping interests. In 1837 he married Zerelda Marklin, who bore him five children before she died in 1856. In 1857, Ham purchased a quantity of limestone at a bargain price; the stones had been rejected by a federal inspector for a government project because of inferior quality. With these stones, Ham constructed a luxurious 23-room Victorian gothic mansion on a bluff overlooking the Mississippi River.

In 1860, Ham married his second wife, Margaret McLean, who bore him two children. The Hams lived peacefully in the house, and hosted lavish parties that were the talk of Dubuque society. In his spare time, Ham liked to retire to a cuppola above the third floor, where he could watch activities on the river. Once he spied pirates in action, and his report led to their capture and arrest. The pirates vowed revenge.

Margaret Ham died in the house in 1874; Ham died in 1889. Two daughters remained in the house, the other siblings having departed for their own households. In the 1890s, May Ham died in the house, leaving Sarah Ham alone.

According to legend, the haunting activity was caused by a murder committed by Sarah. One night Sarah thought she heard a prowler and feared the pirates had returned for their revenge. She told a neighbor that if she heard noises again, she would turn on a light in a window as a signal for help. Several nights later, she heard noises again. She lit a lamp in her window, locked her door, picked up a gun and waited. She heard footsteps ascend the stairs and approach her bedroom door. She fired two bullets through the door. The intruder staggered down the stairs and fled. Later, the body of a pirate, shot twice, was found dead near the riverbank.

Sarah died in 1911. The house was bought by the Dubuque Park District to be used as a home and office for the parks superintendent. He, his wife and seven children made no reports of being haunted.

The house was turned into a museum in 1964 by the Dubuque Historical Society. Since then, numerous employees have reported strange phenomena. A window in the upstairs hall, securely locked every night, is often found open in the morning. A light fixture in the same hall works erratically and comes on by itself, despite the fact that nothing is wrong with it. Icy breezes, cold spots and noises have been reported in various parts of the house, especially near the stairway leading to Ham's hideaway cuppola. According to another unsubstantiated legend, a man hanged himself in the tower sometime before the turn of the century.

The front lights in Ham House are turned off by unscrewing a fuse. A former employee once unscrewed the fuse and heard organ music coming out of the box. The sound ceased when she rescrewed the fuse, then started again when she unscrewed it once more. Ham House does have a pump organ, but it is in disrepair.

In 1978, an employee spent the night in the house to investigate the phenomena, and claimed to hear women's voices in the yard at around 3 A.M., as well as footsteps and shuffling noises in the house.

There are no reports of visual apparitions. It is possible, as some staff suggest, that the phenomena are misinterpreted or produced by expectation and imagination. The murder legend is undermined by the fact that none of the doors in the house—all original—show any evidence of patched holes. Nonetheless, Ham House is believed by many to be the home of unknown presences.

Further reading:

Riccio, Dolores, and Joan Bingham. *Haunted Houses USA.* New York: Pocket Books, 1989.

Scott, Beth, and Michael Norman. *Haunted Heartland.* New York: Warner Books, 1985.

Hamilton, Thomas Glendenning (1873–1935)

Physician of Winnipeg, Manitoba. Founder and president of the Winnipeg Society for Psychical Research, Hamilton conducted systematic research on physical mediumship in a laboratory in his home over a period of 15 years.

T. Glen Hamilton, or "TGH," as he came to be known, was born on November 26, 1873 into a farmer's family in Agincourt, Ontario, now a part of Toronto. The Hamiltons moved in 1891 to Winnipeg, where Thomas attended college and taught school for a period before studying medicine. After graduating from Manitoba Medical College in 1903, he did a year's internship as house surgeon at Winnipeg General Hospital, and established a private medical practice. In 1906, he married Lillian Mary Forrester, a nurse. The Hamiltons were to have four children, including a son, James, and a daughter, Margaret.

TGH was active in community and medical affairs, serving on the Winnipeg School Board for nine years, from 1906 until his selection as Liberal Member for Elmwood to the Manitoba Legislative Assembly in 1915, a position he held until 1920. In 1916, he became the first chairman of the Winnipeg Committee on Mothers' Pensions. He was elected president of the Manitoba Medical Association for 1921–1922, and from 1923 to 1934 he was the Manitoba representative on the Executive of the Canadian Medical Society. He also taught medical jurisprudence and acted as an examiner in clinical surgery.

TGH was first attracted to psychical phenomena as an undergraduate, when he read an article by the

Spiritualist W.T. STEAD in the *Review of Reviews*. In 1918, he came across the Patience WORTH publications, which greatly impressed him. The following year he devised and carried out a telepathy experiment, and began reading widely in psychical research. His first practical experience with the psychic came in 1920, at a table-tipping session arranged by his wife in their home, at which the deceased Stead and Frederic W.H. MYERS purported to communicate.

The Hamiltons became interested in the work of W.J. CRAWFORD, whose books on the GOLIGHER CIRCLE were then being published. Mrs. Hamilton was struck by an apparent similarity between Kathleen Goligher and Elizabeth Poole, the medium at the Hamilton's table-tipping session, and wondered whether Poole might have greater untapped abilities. Poole was willing to find out, and the women began to hold weekly seances in the Hamilton home. Nothing unusual happened for several months, and they were about to give up the sittings, when suddenly their table reared up on two legs. It remained so for several minutes, despite efforts to push it down. TGH was called in, and the phenomenon was repeated.

His curiosity aroused, TGH formed a small group of sitters, with Poole as the medium. By March 1922, after some 40 seances, he had satisfied himself about three things: (1) a 10-pound wooden table would make powerful movements under Poole's touch; (2) it would continue to make strong movements after she had removed her hands; and (3) the rappings he and the other sitters heard showed signs of intelligence in their responses to questions. He accepted the table movements as evidence of paranormal activity, but he was skeptical of the idea that the raps really were communications from Stead and Myers.

TGH decided to give up the psychic work. He had satisfied his curiosity, and he was much aware how this research would be regarded by his medical colleagues. But it was a decision he found impossible to carry through. Nine months later, at an impromptu seance held for a visiting friend, Stead advised him to go on with his work, predicting that there was more to come. Impressed, TGH told his wife that if she could get together a suitable group of people, he would find the time to continue.

The sitter group which Mrs. Hamilton then formed consisted of four medical doctors, a lawyer, a civil engineer, and an electrical engineer, in addition to the Hamiltons. Poole and two other nonprofessional mediums were engaged. And, perhaps most significantly, a special seance room was outfitted in the Hamiltons' house. This room was furnished with an open medium's cabinet, a 12-pound wooden table, and chairs arranged in a half-circle facing the cabinet. There was a ruby-colored light in the ceiling, equipped with a dimmer (most seances were held in the dark). There was also a large battery of cameras of various types, some of them stereoscopic, positioned at the end of the room and in the ceiling. These could be operated by remote control with the aid of a push-button device TGH invented. TGH loaded all film and did all the developing, printing and enlarging. A secretary took verbatim notes during seances. These arrangements, together with TGH's standing in his community, greatly impressed many who heard him speak about his work in later years.

The new sittings began in April 1923. Many movements and partial levitations of the table occurred, some without physical contact. Thirty of these were photographed, from various angles. Soon Poole (in reports, she is called "Elizabeth M.") began to enter a spontaneous trance. At first, her deep trances would last only a few minutes, but gradually they became longer. During these deep trances, Poole would be "invaded" by trance personalities, two of which—those purporting to be the writer Robert Louis Stevenson and the missionary-explorer David Livingstone—became regular communicators. It was as a consequence of messages from them that TGH became convinced of survival after death and the correctness of the Spiritualist view of mediumistic communication. However, in 1928, when Stead predicted that a materialization medium would soon appear, TGH rejected the idea and continued with plans to disband the sitter group.

His mind was to be changed and Stead's prophecy borne out once again. A woman who had demonstrated some mediumistic ability in her occasional appearances with the group started to attend regularly in January 1928. In February, a control calling himself "Walter" and identifying himself as Mina Stinson CRANDON's control of the same name attached himself to this woman, Mary Marshall (also known as Mary M. or "Dawn"). At Walter's insistence, TGH built a bell-box of the sort used in Crandon's seances. This was a box with a hinged lid which, when pressed down, would bring two strips of metal into contact, and cause a bell to ring. Walter instructed TGH to place this bell-box on a shelf in the seance room, where it could be heard to ring periodically at sittings. In July, Walter suggested that TGH photograph Marshall while the bell was ringing. The developed plate showed very fine, thin cords connecting Marshall's head to the bell-box, some three feet above. Walter explained that he had constructed the cords from ectoplasm, allegedly a substance exuded by physical mediums that enables materializations to take place.

In October 1928, Walter announced that he would try something new. A photograph taken at this session revealed a lump of ectoplasm on Marshall's neck, in the center of which Stead's face appeared. Other faces appeared in later sessions, and not long thereafter the circle underwent another major development, with some of the regular sitters falling into trances along with the designated mediums. Marshall, however, was the only one to produce ectoplasm. Photographs showed some of these to be attached to her head, others separated from it. They ranged in size from a silver dollar to substantial growths three or four feet in height and several inches thick. Several showed faces, and a few represented more fully formed figures, replete with hair and clothing.

As his research continued, TGH began to speak about it openly. He gave a presentation, which included displays of photographs, to the British Medical Association at its convention in Winnipeg in 1930. He was convinced that European psychical researchers were wrong in interpreting materialization as a psychokinetic action of the medium, and believed that the production of ectoplasm was under the control of the trance personality, as Walter claimed. TGH published a series of articles on his work in Spiritualist publications such as *Light* and *Psychic Research* in the early 1930s, but his only book, a compilation of his notes edited by his son, James, appeared posthumously in 1942 as *Intention and Survival*. The title expressed TGH's conviction that seance communications were purposeful, providing evidence of intention, and therefore of a surviving intelligence.

TGH died of a heart attack on April 7, 1935, at the age of 61. After a hiatus of some months, the sittings were continued by Mrs. Hamilton, partly for the purpose of giving him the opportunity to communicate himself. As the Hamiltons' daughter Margaret tells in her book *Is Survival A Fact?* (1969), the most significant of these new sittings occurred in February 1939, once more at Walter's suggestion. TGH's likeness was produced in ectoplasm, and through Marshall a TGH communicator referred to events that were known only to Mrs. Hamilton, and that had been forgotten consciously even by her. She and the other sitters were confident that TGH had indeed communicated his continued existence from the beyond.

Further reading:

Dean, K.F., comp. *Register of the Thomas Glendenning Hamilton Collection*. Winnipeg: Elizabeth Dafoe Library, University of Manitoba, 1980.

Hamilton, Margaret. *Is Survival A Fact?* London: Psychic Press, 1969.

Hamilton, T. Glen. *Intention and Survival*. Edited by James Hamilton. Toronto: Macmillan of Canada, 1942.

Hampton Court Palace given to King Henry VIII by Cardinal Thomas Wolsey, his disgraced chancellor, that is said to be haunted by the ghosts of royalty and commoners.

Two of the ghosts are associated with the construction of the palace. Wolsey built the palace, and his ghost was seen under one of the archways by a member of the audience viewing a sound and light show in 1966. Also, mysterious, unexplained footsteps and other strange happenings occur on the anniversary of the death of the architect Sir Christopher Wren at the Old Court House. Wren lived there while supervising the palace's renovation, and he died there on February 26, 1723.

The palace, however, is most frequently haunted by people who were associated with King Henry VIII. The sovereign lived there with five of his six wives, and two of them make visits as ghosts.

Jane Seymour, the king's third wife, died there one week after she had given birth to the boy who later became King Edward VI. Her ghost, carrying a lighted taper, has often been seen on the anniversary of his birth.

The motherless Edward was cared for by a nurse, Mistress Sibell Penn, and her ghost has also appeared at the palace. Penn lived there, and in 1568 she caught smallpox and died. She was buried at nearby St. Mary's Church, which was destroyed by lightning in 1829 and had to be rebuilt. Her tomb was moved to the new church, but her grave was tampered with and her remains were scattered.

Shortly after, strange whirring sounds and mutterings could be heard coming from behind a wall in the palace. A sealed chamber was discovered after the wall was knocked down. A spinning wheel and other feminine items were found, and they were thought to be Penn's because two sentries had seen an old woman in a gray robe pass through that area. Penn's ghost was given the name the Lady in Gray after Princess Frederica of Hanover, who knew nothing about the nurse, saw her ghost in a long gray robe with a hood over her head.

The ghost of Catherine Howard, the allegedly adulterous fifth wife of King Henry VIII who was beheaded in 1542, has been sighted so frequently that she is mentioned in the castle guidebooks. Her spirit likes to roam what is known as the Haunted Gallery, that passage through which she ran in terror from her captors and screamed for mercy from her

Catherine Howard.

Henry VIII.

husband on the night of her arrest. Howard's ghost often appears on that night's anniversary. Years ago when the gallery was open to the public, an artist sketching a picture repeatedly saw a ringed hand in front of the picture. The artist drew what he saw and the jewel in the ring was later identified as belonging to Howard.

Other ghosts are not royal. Two ghostly officers who fought for King Charles I haunted the palace's Fountain Court with loud noises in the middle of the night until they were given a Christian burial. Another ghost, known as the White Lady of Hampton Court, and the headless Archbishop Laud have been seen on the grounds. During World War II a constable was startled to see an entourage of ghosts, including two men and seven women, walking about the grounds.

Further reading:

Hole, Christina. *Haunted England.* London: B.T. Batsford Ltd., 1940.

Underwood, Peter. *A Gazeteer of British Ghosts.* Rev. ed. London: Pan Books, Ltd., 1973.

Hart, Hornell Norris (1888–1967) Sociologist and psychical researcher, especially interested in apparitions, out-of-body experiences (OBEs), and the question of survival after death.

Hornell Hart was born on August 2, 1888 in St. Paul, Minnesota, of Quaker parents. His father, Hastings Hornell Hart, was secretary of the Minnesota State Board of Correction and Charities at the time. Later he served as superintendent of the Illinois Children's Home and Aid Society and was secretary of the state committee which devised one of the first juvenile court laws in the United States.

Hart graduated from Oberlin College in 1910; he received his M.A. from the University of Wisconsin in 1914 and his Ph.D. from the State University of Iowa in 1921. He shared his father's concern for child welfare, serving as research associate and as associate professor at the University of Iowa's Child Welfare Research Station from 1919 to 1923, and then, in 1924, as executive secretary of the Iowa Child Welfare Commission. His academic career began in 1924, when he joined the faculty of Bryn Mawr College, where he was professor of social economy from 1930 to 1933. From 1933 to 1938 he was professor of ethics at Hartford Theological Seminary in Hartford, Connecticut.

In 1915, Hart married Ella Brockhousen. The couple had three daughters, all of whom became professional women, and a son, Robert. Robert was born and died before the first of his sisters was born, and his early death may have helped to stimulate Hart's interest in psychical research, particularly in the question of survival. He retained his interest in psychical research along with his personal religious convictions throughout his life, and all of his writings reflect these concerns. He first dealt with psychical research in his textbook *The Science of Social Relations* (1927).

Hart's first major contribution to psychical research came in 1933 with the publication of a paper, coauthored with his wife, in the *Proceedings* of the SOCIETY FOR PSYCHICAL RESEARCH. Entitled "Visions and Apparitions Collectively and Reciprocally Perceived," this paper included quantitative comparisons of various types of apparitions, especially collective apparitions and reciprocal apparitions. In the latter type of case, one person (the agent) has an OBE during which he or she seems to travel to a distant place and see someone else, while this person (the percipient) simultaneously sees the agent as an apparition (see WILMOT APPARITION). The Harts concluded that "the collectively observed apparitions of the dead seem to be closely similar in character to the conscious apparitions of the living."

In 1938 Hart was appointed professor of sociology at Duke University, where J.B. RHINE had his Parapsychology Laboratory. Hart, as one of the first sociologists to employ statistics in his research, was well equipped to understand Rhine's experimental approach. He joined the editorial staff of the *Journal of Parapsychology* and stayed in close touch with the Parapsychology Laboratory throughout his career at Duke, although in the later years relations between them became strained as a result of the laboratory's conservative position on the survival question and on the problem of everyday psychic experiences (so-called spontaneous cases).

Hart continued to write on OBEs and apparitions and published several important papers in the *Proceedings* of the Society for Psychical Research and the *Journal* of the AMERICAN SOCIETY FOR PSYCHICAL RESEARCH. In 1953, he proposed a "psychic fifth dimension" and showed how such an idea could make sense of the data of psychical research. His 1956 paper, "Six Theories about Apparitions," written in cooperation with colleagues, has become a classic.

At the same time, Hart was making important contributions to sociology and political science. He was actively involved in the movement for world government following World War II. He won the Edward J. Bernays Award for Best Action-Related Study of the Social Effects of Atomic Energy in 1948, and his pamphlet "McCarthy Versus the State Department" (1952) was widely distributed and is credited

with going far to establish the inaccuracy of many of McCarthy's charges.

Upon his retirement from Duke in 1957, Hart became the John Hay Whitney Foundation Professor of Sociology at Centre College of Kentucky in Danville, Kentucky. From 1960 until his death in 1965 he was chairman of the Sociology Department at Florida Southern College in Lakeland, Florida. In these last years of his life he turned his attention more and more to psychical research.

To this period belongs his only book devoted entirely to psychical research, *The Enigma of Survival: The Case For and Against an After Life* (1959). Here Hart contrasted the two points of view on the evidence of apparitions and mediumship, and sought to reconcile them through his own "persona theory." According to this idea, what is seen as an apparition and what attempts to communicate through a medium is not the deceased person himself, but rather a projected "persona" that interacts with the perceptual faculties of the percipient and the unconscious of the medium to produce the reported effects.

In the same book, Hart introduced the label "SUPER-ESP" to refer to a hypothetical ESP capacity that extends beyond the bounds that have been established in laboratory experimentation or field work with spontaneous cases. Super-ESP has often been employed by critics to account for evidence suggesting survival after death.

Hart died on February 27, 1967 of a heart attack, on a visit to Washington, D.C. Shortly before his death he had completed the manuscript of a book, "Survival After Death," that he described to a colleague as his most important contribution to psychical research, superseding *The Enigma of Survival*. This manuscript, however, has not been published.

Hart's more important writings in psychical research have already been mentioned. His last major contribution to the field was a monograph, *Toward a New Philosophical Basis for Parapsychological Phenomena* (1965). His books in other areas include *The Science of Social Relations* (1927), *The Technique of Social Progress* (1931), *Personality and the Family* (1941), *Living Religion* (1937), *Autoconditioning* (1956) and *Your Share of God* (1958).

Further reading:

Pleasants, Helene, ed. *Biographical Dictionary of Parapsychology*. New York: Helix Press, 1964.

Pratt, J.G. "In Memory of Hornell Hart: A Personal Appreciation." *Journal of the American Society for Psychical Research* 1 (1968):80–83.

Harvard Exit Theater   Cinema in Seattle, Washington said to be haunted during the early 1970s through the mid-1980s. Some of the phenomena remain unexplained, but some are confessed practical jokes.

The cinema, established in 1968 and named after a freeway exit, occupies part of a three-story, turn-of-the-century building on Capitol Hill, one of Seattle's older neighborhoods. The rest of the building is occupied by the Womans Century Club, once active in the suffragist movement and now a civic organization.

Under its original owners, the Harvard Exit Theater gained popularity for its foreign and independent films, and for its homey atmosphere, with waiting parlors furnished in old pieces. The main auditorium is on the second floor; a second auditorium was later added to the third floor. The third floor is where most of the alleged phenomena occurred.

Tales of a ghostly woman dressed in turn-of-the-century clothing haunting the place began to circulate in the early 1970s. The manager at the time, Janet Wainwright, reportedly saw the female apparition, which on one occasion was sitting in a chair by the fireplace and vanished as Wainwright drew near. Wainwright also reported finding lights on and a fire going in the fireplace when she was the first to arrive some mornings to open up. Once she found chairs arranged in a semicircle around the fire. On the third floor, she reported seeing several apparitions of women. Other employees reported hearing sounds of a woman sobbing, and the projectionist allegedly arrived one day to find the projector already running.

In 1982, Wainwright left and was replaced by Alan Blangy, who managed the theater until 1988. One night, shortly after Blangy began his job at the theater, he and his assistant manager were closing up when Blangy thought he heard a noise in the third-floor auditorium. Entering it, he saw the door to the fire escape close, and he thought an intruder had been in the building. But as he attempted to pull the door shut, something on the other side pulled back in strong jerks. A tug-of-war ensued. Blangy called to his assistant, who arrived just as he managed to pull the door shut. Together, they then pushed the door open, expecting to see an intruder fleeing down the fire escape or out into the street. They found nothing. Nor had they heard any sounds of feet running down the stairs. The incident spooked Blangy, who from then on never wanted to be in the theater alone.

Around 1985, a group of ghosthunters set up equipment in an effort to record evidence of haunting, but results were inconclusive. They claimed to record ghostly voices on tape and to see a ball of light float across the third-floor auditorium. Blangy never heard the tapes, and the ghosthunters eventually left. The phenomena ceased in the mid-1980s. In 1987, an independent filmmaker, Karl Krogstad, moved his goods into rental quarters in the theater and experienced his stacks of boxes falling over repeatedly for several days. No explanation was found.

Blangy theorized that the theater may have been haunted by the ghost of Seattle's first and only woman mayor, Bertha K. Landes, an early feminist and reformer. A leader of the Womans Century Club and other women's organizations, she served as mayor from 1926 to 1928 and made significant inroads against government corruption. She died in 1943.

Blangy was told by early staffers that some of the phenomena were outright jokes on Wainwright. After Wainwright reported seeing an apparition, other staff members played pranks of lighting the fire prior to her morning arrival and setting up the chairs in the semicircle. According to Blangy, some of the other phenomena may have been exaggerations, or may have had natural explanations. For example, since movies were screened by the staff during the day, it is possible that someone left the projector running prior to the arrival of the projectionist for the public showings.

At about the time the phenomena ceased at the Harvard Exit, a museum opened in downtown Seattle with objects and photographs pertaining to Landes. An account in one of the local newspapers mentioned that workmen at the museum site reported strange incidents such as tools and materials being misplaced. Blangy theorized that the ghost of Landes relocated to the museum to look after her things. However, museum officials have claimed no knowledge of any unusual happening during or after construction. In 1988, some of the Landes objects were sent to another museum in Seattle, whose officials claimed likewise.

Hateful Thing, The   See BLACK SHUCK.

haunting   The repeated manifestation of strange and inexplicable sensory phenomena—smells, sounds, tactile sensations and hallucinations—said to be caused by ghosts or spirits attached to a certain locale.

The term "haunt" comes from the same root as "home." Typically, a haunted location is the former home of the deceased, or the spot where the deceased died. Haunted sites also include places that apparently were frequented or favored by the deceased, and sites of violent death. Other hauntings are "aimless," occurring without explanation.

There is no general pattern to a haunting. Some phenomena manifest periodically or continually over durations that may be short—a matter of days—or long, going on for centuries. Some hauntings occur only on certain "anniversary" dates: the ghost of Sir Christopher Wren is said to be heard hurrying up and down the stairs of HAMPTON COURT every February 26, the date of his death in 1723.

Not everyone who visits or lives in a reputedly haunted location will experience phenomena. Hauntings sometimes can be brought to an end through exorcisms conducted either by clergy or by mediumistic individuals who reportedly can communicate with the ghost or spirit believed to be responsible for the haunting. Some hauntings end of their own accord for reasons not known. Those that seem to be "psychic recordings," or impressions that certain people can receive, do not respond to exorcisms. Such hauntings seem to be endless reenactments of events (see DIEPPE RAID CASE; RETROCOGNITION; VERSAILLES GHOSTS).

It is popularly assumed that most hauntings involve apparitions, or ghosts, of the dead. In fact, apparitions are associated with a minority of reported cases. Most hauntings involve noises, such as mysterious footsteps, rustlings, whisperings, animal sounds and howlings, thumps, tappings and rappings; smells, especially of flowers, perfume, burned wood or rotting flesh or matter; tactile sensations such as a cold prickling of the skin, cold breezes and feelings of being touched by an invisible hand. Some hauntings feature poltergeist activities such as rearranged furniture, stopped clocks, smashed glassware and mirrors, and the paranormal movement of objects.

Percipients often experience negative emotions at a haunted site, including anger, fear or hatred. They also may sense a presence of evil. Other hauntings seem to involve friendly or benign ghosts. Some mediums say they can contact trapped spirits of the dead who are haunting sites, and are able to send them on their way to the Other Side (see RELEASEMENT).

Some hauntings also feature phantom animals, such as pet dogs, cats and horses, which are seen, felt or heard in their familiar spots.

Objects as well as sites may be haunted. In Britain, for example, numerous tales exist of haunted skulls that seem to cause unearthly screaming whenever they are removed from their places in a home (see SCREAMING SKULLS).

Poltergeist (q.v.) hauntings are characterized by violent physical disturbances such as flying and levitating objects, banging doors, assaults on humans, and rapping and thumping noises. These disturbances often seem to be caused by living persons;

A haunting ghost awakening sleeping people.

there is evidence that some poltergeists may be discarnate spirits.

Little is known about why or how hauntings occur. Thousands of hauntings have been systematically investigated by psychical researchers and parapsychologists since the late 19th century. Many explanations have been proposed, but there is no conclusive evidence to support one more strongly than another. Frederic W.H. MYERS, one of the founders of the SOCIETY FOR PSYCHICAL RESEARCH (SPR), London, who did extensive research of apparitions in the late 19th century, believed that most hauntings are fragmentary and meaningless, the bits and pieces of an energy residue left by the living after their death. Others who have built on Myers' theory propose that hauntings do not involve ghostly personalities, but are those recordings of energy that take on personalities to percipients who are psychically sensitive. Psychic sensitivity may account for diverse experiences in a haunted site: why one person experiences phenomena and another does not.

Eleanor SIDGWICK, former secretary of the SPR, theorized that hauntings are a form of psychometry. Just as an object appears to absorb and retain the "vibrations" of its owner, which manifest as impressions when the object is handled by a MEDIUM or psychic, then houses might also retain memories or psychic impressions. A house could incorporate the thoughts, actions and feelings of its former occupants, which then manifest as a haunting to psychically sensitive individuals.

Oxford philosopher Harry H. Price and American parapsychologist William G. ROLL are among those who have elaborated upon Sidgwick's theory. Price's theory, called "deferred telepathy," posits that there exists a "psychic ether" that is a bridge between mind and matter and impregnates all matter and space. Certain thoughts and events are impressed upon this ether and remain on it for long periods, even years. When tragedies occur, the appropriate psychic conditions are created and lasting impressions result. Sensitive persons coming into contact with a haunted house might telepathically contact these thoughts and emotions which are then "replayed" as hauntings. "Deferred telepathy" has been criticized by others for not explaining movements of objects that are sometimes reported in hauntings.

Roll has proposed that all objects have a psi field that pervades and exudes from them. A sensitive individual contacts and reads the impressions of a house from its psi field during a haunting. This theory has suffered some of the same criticism as Price's theory, particularly since persons who have little or no demonstrable psychic ability have witnessed hauntings.

Italian parapsychologist Ernesto Bozzano studied several hundred cases of hauntings and analyzed their characteristics, relating them to the different theories of hauntings and to his Spiritistic theory. Bozzano came to five conclusions in support of his belief that hauntings were spirits of the dead: phantoms of the dead can haunt sites where they did not die and had not lived; hauntings consist of telekinetic movement of objects that suggests some type of physical presence; hauntings are associated with deaths to a greater extent than other types of tragedies or emotions; hauntings are intermittent; and when such actions as exorcism and prayers for the dead are performed, the hauntings end.

Numerous remedies to end hauntings exist around the world. Some are simple, such as sweeping out the offending spirits with a broom. Others are more elaborate, such as formal rites of exorcism (q.v.). Such measures do not always succeed.

See also GHOST HUNTING.

Further reading:
Auerbach, Loyd. *ESP, Hauntings and Poltergeists: A Parapsychologist's Handbook.* New York: Warner Books, 1986.

Cochran, Tracy. "The Real Ghost Busters." *Omni* 10 (August 1988):35–36+.

Gauld, Alan, and A.D. Cornell. *Poltergeists.* London: Routledge & Kegan Paul, 1979.

Greeley, Andrew. "Mysticism Goes Mainstream." *American Health* (January/February 1987):47–55.

MacKenzie, Andrew. *Hauntings and Apparitions.* London: William Heinemann Ltd., 1982.

Myers, Frederic W.H. *Human Personality and Its Survival of Bodily Death Vols. I & II.* New ed. New York: Longmans, Green & Co., 1954. First published 1903.

Owen, George, and Victor Sims. *Science and the Spook: Eight Strange Cases of Haunting.* New York: Garrett Publications, 1971.

Underwood, Peter. *The Ghost Hunter's Guide.* Poole, Dorset: Blandford Press, 1986.

Hermitage Castle   Redcap Sly, the familiar spirit of the evil Lord Soulis, is said to haunt the ruins of this 13th-century castle near Newcastleton, Roxburgshire, Scotland. Here Mary, Queen of Scots nearly died of fever.

Redcap (red is the color of witches) is described as a horrible old man with long fangs. He allegedly told his master, Lord Soulis, owner of the castle, that he could be bound only by a three-stranded rope of sand.

Soulis is alleged to have practiced black magic. He kidnapped young farm children, imprisoned them in the castle's dungeon, and sacrificed them in his dark rites. There are different versions of the lord's demise. According to one story, the enraged parents of the murdered children stormed the castle and attacked Soulis. He was bound in iron chains and a blanket of lead, and boiled to death. According to another story, he abducted the Laird of Branxholm, a crime for which he was bound in a sheet of lead and boiled to death.

Ghostly sounds of the young murder victims reportedly are heard coming from within the castle.

Further reading:
Folklore, Myths and Legends of Britain. London: Reader's Digest Assoc., 1977.

Green, Andrew. *Our Haunted Kingdom.* London: Wolfe Publishing Limited, 1973.

Herne the Hunter   Spectral huntsman who haunts the ancient forest of Windsor Great Park near Windsor Castle in England, according to legend. Herne wears chains and has stag's antlers growing from his head. He appears riding on a spectral black horse, accompanied by baying phantom hounds.

According to legend, Herne was a royal huntsman of a king, said to be either Richard II, Henry VII or Henry VIII. On a hunt, Herne saved the king from being killed by a wounded stag by throwing himself in front of the animal. He was mortally wounded. As he lay dying, a wizard appeared and advised the king that Herne could be saved by cutting off the stag's antlers and tying them to his head. This the king did, and Herne recovered. The grateful king bestowed favors upon the huntsman for several years, until the other huntsmen became so jealous that they convinced the king to dismiss Herne. Devastated, Herne went out to an oak tree in the park and hanged himself. He has haunted the grounds ever since.

English ghost investigator Peter Underwood has suggested that the real Herne the Hunter was the huntsman of Richard II (r. 1377–99). This huntsman did hang himself on an oak tree near the castle. The oak tree blew down in 1863 and was replanted by Queen Victoria.

Herne may have much older, pagan roots, however. His stag antlers give him the appearance of Cernunnos ("the horned"), the Celtic horned god of fertility, the hunt and the underworld.

Herne the Hunter is supposed to always appear in times of great national crisis, which he did in 1931 prior to the Depression and again before the start of World War II.

In 1962, he made a dramatic appearance with horse and hounds one night to a group of youths in the forest. They found a hunting horn and blew on it at the edge of a clearing. The call was answered by another horn and the baying of hounds. Suddenly Herne and his company appeared charging through the forests. The youths dropped the horn and ran in panic. Some sightings of Herne are reported in connection with alleged witchcraft activity in the forest; some modern Witches worship Cernunnos.

Herne also is a leader of the Wild Hunt, a nocturnal procession of the dead. His name is associated with another leader of the dead, Herlechin, or Harlequin, who is associated with the Devil.

Similar spectral horned huntsmen exist in German and French lore.

See also WILD HUNT; WINDSOR CASTLE.

Further reading:

Folklore, Myths and Legends of Britain. London: Reader's Digest Assoc., 1977.

Guiley, Rosemary Ellen. The Encyclopedia of Witches and Witchcraft. New York: Facts On File, 1989.

Underwood, Peter. A Gazeteer of British Ghosts. Rev. ed. London: Pan Books, Ltd., 1973.

Higginson, Gordon   See SPIRITUALISTS' NATIONAL UNION.

Hodgson, Richard (1855–1905)   Psychical researcher, best known for his investigation of the controversial Theosophist Helena P. Blavatsky and for managing the AMERICAN SOCIETY FOR PSYCHICAL RESEARCH (ASPR) from shortly after its formation in 1885 until his death in 1905.

Richard Hodgson was born in Melbourne, Australia on September 24, 1885. He was interested in psychic phenomena as a youth, but there was not yet an organized effort to study them, and other interests took precedence for some years. He attended the University of Melbourne and received an LL.D. (doctor of law) degree from that institution in 1878. Finding the legal field less congenial than he had supposed, he moved to England and enrolled in St. John's College, Cambridge, in 1881, in order to study poetry. His major professor was Henry SIDGWICK, who was about to become the first president of the SOCIETY FOR PSYCHICAL RESEARCH (SPR). When the SPR came into being in 1882, Hodgson joined at once.

Hodgson was 29 in 1884 when the SPR sent him to India to look into the claims of Blavatsky, the colorful leader of the Theosophical movement, that she was in supernatural contact with a group of Tibetan adepts. These adepts, called Mahatmas, were said to be able to astrally project themselves to the Theosophists, to whom they appeared as apparitions (see APPARITIONS). They were also said to deliver letters or to cause letters to be written on previously blank sheets of paper (see SLATE-WRITING). But shortly before Hodgson left England, another set of letters was published in India, purportedly written by Blavatsky to a trusted couple (the Coulombs) with whom she had had a falling out. The Coulomb letters, if genuine, made it clear that the Mahatma incidents were fraudulent, but Blavatsky claimed that the letters were forgeries.

Hodgson spent three months in India interviewing various people involved in the case, inspecting the Coulomb letters, and searching the room in which the Mahatma incidents were said to occur. In the room he discovered sliding and hinged panels that reinforced the conclusion he was reaching from his interviews, namely, that the Coulomb letters were genuine. This conclusion was later supported by British handwriting experts, and the SPR committee charged with looking into the Mahatma phenomena concluded that they were staged by Blavatsky.

The Theosophical Society objected; they accused Hodgson of bias, and broke off relations with the SPR. The controversy continues to this day, although in 1986 the SPR made an effort to patch things up by publishing the report of another handwriting expert, who concluded that the Coulomb letters were forgeries after all.

The Blavatsky investigation had interested Hodgson in conjuring, and he soon made a name for himself as one of the SPR's most knowledgeable members in that area. His work with S.J. Davey to duplicate the slate-writing of the medium William Eglinton continues to be cited as a study of misperception. Davey had worked with Eglinton for a while, then had branched out on his own, finding that he had no trouble fooling his audience into thinking his tricks were paranormal events. He and

Hodgson made a systematic study, comparing what Davey did to what sitters at his seances reported having seen. They were able to show how unreliable such testimony can be. William JAMES considered their report "the most damaging document concerning eye-witness evidence that has ever been produced."

James, himself keenly interested in psychic phenomena, was at the center of the SPR's sister society, the ASPR, which had been launched in Boston in 1885. The ASPR, however, in contrast to the SPR, wanted for members and money, and James was forced to appeal to the SPR for help. In 1887 Hodgson was sent to see what he could do, and he soon made himself invaluable as secretary.

Hodgson took over from James responsibility for managing research with the extraordinary mental medium Leonora PIPER. He began the regular recording of seances, and hired private detectives to have her shadowed (she was never caught in any suspicious behavior).

Hodgson's two reports on Piper for the SPR *Proceedings* are classics. In the second report, published in 1897, he stated his conviction that survival after death was the most reasonable interpretation of the results obtained from her seances. The conclusion astonished many of his friends, who had expected him to unmask Piper, as he had earlier unmasked Blavatsky and Eglinton. However, Hodgson was only one of a long list of psychical researchers to become convinced of survival on the basis of Piper's mediumship.

In 1897 Hodgson returned to England to become an SPR Council member and editor of the SPR *Journal* and *Proceedings,* but he did not stay long. A year later, he was back in Boston at the ASPR, again working with Piper.

Hodgson died December 20, 1905, at the age of 50, of a heart attack while playing handball at the Union Boat Club in Boston. There is some evidence that in the last years of his life he began to experiment with automatic writing.

Soon after his death, Piper began to be controlled by a communicator calling itself Richard Hodgson. Reception to these communications was mixed; James thought the deceased Hodgson might be behind them, but Hodgson's British friends were less convinced.

Although Hodgson contributed several important papers to the SPR *Proceedings,* he wrote no books. He did, however, co-edit Frederic W.H. MYERS' great work, *Human Personality and Its Survival of Bodily Death* (1903). Myers had died in 1900, asking that Hodgson together with the SPR's Gertrude Johnson complete the book if he should not live to finish it himself.

Further reading:

Berger, Arthur S. *Lives and Letters in American Parapsychology: A Biographical History, 1850–1987.* Jefferson, N.C.: McFarland, 1988.

Gauld, Alan. *The Founders of Psychical Research.* London: Routledge & Kegan Paul, 1968.

Harrison, Vernon. "J'accuse: An examination of the Hodgson Report of 1885." *Journal of the Society for Psychical Research* 53 (1986):286–310.

Hodgson, Richard. "Mr. Davey's Imitations by Conjuring of Phenomena Sometimes Attributed to Spirit Agency." *Proceedings of the Society for Psychical Research* 8 (1892): 253–310.

"Report of the Committee Appointed to Investigate Phenomena Connected with the Theosophical Society." *Proceedings of the Society for Psychical Research* 3 (1885):201–380.

home circle   Also known as a home sitting, a home circle is a seance held in a home, with or without the services of a professional medium, for the purpose of achieving spirit communication.

Following the revelations of the FOX SISTERS in 1848, people on both sides of the Atlantic began organizing sittings with their friends to see if any of those seated in the circle could reach the Other Side. *The Spiritualist,* a weekly magazine published in the 1870s in England, carried instructions for home circles each week, advising readers how to form spirit circles in their own homes, with no Spiritualist or professional medium present. At least one person possessing mediumistic talent could be found in any household. Powerful mediums were described as persons of impulsive, genial, affectionate nature. Any individuals not getting along should not be seated in the same circle.

Usually the participants gathered around a table, either holding hands or placing all hands flat on the tabletop, but sitters could merely arrange their chairs in a circle. Trumpet medium James M. Laughton recommended holding the circle in the same room each time, so that the spirits became comfortable with the surroundings and routine. (A trumpet medium enabled spirits to speak through trumpets.)

Clifford L. Bias, a voice and trumpet medium, felt that the circle should be composed of equal numbers of both sexes, arranged alternately in the circle. He started his circles at the same time each night, using the twilight for the first half and the darkened room for the latter. Further instructions in *The Spiritualist* recommended keeping the room comfortably cool.

Like religious ceremonies, meetings most likely began with hymn-singing and the recitation of prayers. Another trumpet medium, Mable A. Riffle, always commenced the sitting with the Lord's Prayer and a hymn, believing such actions kept her desires on a spiritual plane.

Although anyone could organize a circle, few did unless they had heard of Spiritualist phenomena. Home circles were at their most popular in the late 19th and early 20th centuries.

See also BROWNING CIRCLE.

Further reading:

Brandon, Ruth. *The Spiritualists*. New York: Alfred A. Knopf, 1983.

Chaney, Rev. Robert G. *Mediums and the Development of Mediumship*. Freeport, N.Y.: Books for Libraries Press, 1972.

Home, Daniel Dunglas (1833–1886)

Scottish medium renowned for his remarkable physical feats. Daniel Dunglas Home repeatedly moved objects, stuck his head into fires without burning himself, levitated, elongated and shrank his body, and materialized spirits. He was often accused of fraud, though no one was ever able to prove it in a single instance. Home was a vain man who used his paranormal ability to circulate among the aristocracy and upper classes. He never accepted money for his performances, but lived off the largess of his wealthy patrons.

Home was born in Edinburgh, Scotland on March 20, 1833. His father was a carpenter. His mother was clairvoyant and claimed her family was related to the 17th-century Brahan Seer, Kenneth MacKenzie. Home's own budding mediumistic talent allegedly manifested in infancy: his aunt reported that his cradle rocked on its own, as if moved by a spirit hand. At age four, Home predicted the death of a cousin.

When he was nine, his family moved to Connecticut. Home was sickly, with a tendency toward tuberculosis. He read the Bible a great deal and spent much time alone in the woods. At age 13, he had a vision of a boyhood friend at the moment the friend died far away.

Home was 15 when the FOX SISTERS created a stir with table-rapping spirits, and Spiritualism began to catch fire. His own paranormal experiences began to increase, especially following the death of his mother in 1850. Home was living with an aunt, Mary Cook, in Norwich, Connecticut. Rappings began in her home, and Cook blamed Home for bringing the Devil into her house. She called in ministers to free him from the evil spirits, but the ministers were convinced the young man had a God-given gift. For Home, that marked the turning point in his life. His

Daniel Dunglas Home.

dead mother appeared to him in a vision, as she would do throughout his life, and told him not to be afraid and to do good things with his gift. Cook threw Home out.

For most of the rest of his life, Home had no home of his own, but lived as a guest in various households. He attended seances, but felt most mediums were frauds. In the burgeoning Spiritualism movement, fraud became rampant, and many of Home's critics tried unsuccessfully to expose him. Home avoided contact with other mediums, saying he had nothing to learn from them.

He held his own seances in rooms which were lit, which was opposite of the prevailing custom of darkened rooms. He produced spectral lights, rappings, and ghostly hands which ended at the wrist and shook hands with those persons present. He moved tables, chairs and objects, and tipped tables without spilling the objects on the tops. He produced visions of ghostly guitars which played eerie music. He spelled out messages from the dead by pointing at letters of the alphabet written on cards. He sometimes appeared to be possessed, and played the piano or accordion himself in great frenzy. He also was seen to stretch or shrink his body, increasing his height by 11 inches to 6.5 feet while his feet were on the floor, or shrinking to 5 feet, with his shoes disappearing into his trousers. He often asked his guests to hold his hands and feet, to prove that he was not secretly manipulating any hidden devices or machinery.

Home said his feats were made possible by friendly spirits whom he could not control, but who came and went as they pleased. The most reliable was one named "Bryan." When in trance, Home referred to himself in third person as "Dan."

Home was 19 when he experienced involuntarily his first levitation in the Connecticut home of a silk manufacturer. He reportedly rose about a foot off the ground, then bobbed up and down several times, going all the way to the ceiling. Later, he learned to contol his levitation; witnesses reported that he seemed to literally fly.

He entered the Theological Institute in Newburgh, New York to study religion. In 1853, too sick to study and preoccupied with death, he experienced an out-of-body trip which lasted for 11 hours and was intended, he said, to show him what was on the Other Side.

In 1855, he traveled to England and Europe, where he began to realize his dreams of associating with the royal, rich and famous. His seances generated much controversy in the press. His supporters included Sir Arthur Conan DOYLE and Elizabeth Barrett Browning. Edward Bulwer-Lytton remained unimpressed. Foes included David Brewster, noted scientist, and Robert Browning, who so disliked Home that he wrote a 2,000-line poem about him called *Mr. Sludge the Medium.* (See BROWNING CIRCLE.)

In February 1856, Home announced that his spirits had informed him they intended to withdraw from him for a year. He went to Naples and Rome, where he had an audience with Pope Pius IX. Impulsively, he converted to Catholicism and said he would enter a monastery.

A year later, as promised, his spirit friends returned and restored his health. In France, he had an audience with Napoleon III and Empress Eugenie. The emperor had expected to find Home a fraud, but was convinced of his authenticity when Home produced the spirit of Napoleon I, who shook hands with Napoleon III and his wife.

In Rome, Home met Alexandrina, the wealthy sister-in-law of a Russian nobleman, Count Gregoire de Koucheleff. They fell in love and were married in St. Petersburg on August 1, 1858. Their son, Gregoire, was born in 1859. Alexandrina died of illness in 1862, and her estate remained tied up in Russia for years, forcing Home to depend once again on patrons.

In 1866, the Spiritual Athenaeum was founded in England with Home as secretary, and he hoped that fashionable society would support it. However, support was small and slow in coming, perhaps because founders insisted on a quasi-religious nature that required a professed belief in orthodox Christianity.

Home's financial needs soon embroiled him in a lawsuit with a wealthy widow, Mrs. Lyon, who was 75 years old. Her husband had died seven years earlier, and had informed her prior to his death that she would only survive him by seven years. Mrs. Lyon sought out Home at the Spiritual Athenaeum to contact her husband to find out if she was soon to die. The dead man allegedly communicated through Home with raps, and relieved the widow of the prospect of imminent death. She enthusiastically sought more visits with Home. Her husband began telling her that Home was to be their new son, and was to be given independent means with an allowance of 700 pounds. By January 1867, all on the alleged instructions of the dead Mr. Lyon, Home had taken the Lyon family name, had received 60,000 pounds in cash and securities, and had been made beneficiary in Mrs. Lyon's will.

On June 10, 1867, Mrs. Lyon made affectionate advances to Home, who "repulsed her," she claimed later. The next day, she asked for her money back from him and would not relent. Home attempted to appease her by offering to give back all but 30,000 pounds. Mrs. Lyon had him arrested and filed suit against him.

The trial was a tawdry affair, with Mrs. Lyon appearing deranged during her testimony. There were intimations that she and Home had been more than "affectionate." Home's supporters, embarrassed, deserted him, and critics had a field day. Despite the poor performance of Mrs. Lyon, the court found in her favor, and Home was forced to return the 60,000 pounds. The court denounced Spiritualism as "mischievous nonsense, well calculated on the one hand to delude the vain, the weak, the foolish and the superstitious. . . ." Home did not appeal.

Home's low point of scandal was followed by some of his most remarkable alleged feats, including a levitation in 1868 in the London home of Lord Adare, where he had never before visited. Home went into a trance and reportedly floated out a window on the third floor, then floated back in another window. However, skeptics contend the feat may have been hallucination on the part of the witnesses, and point to inconsistencies in descriptions of the event written by Lord Adare.

In 1868 Home also performed remarkable feats with fire and hot coals. He could carry red-hot coals without being burned, and had the ability to enable others to do the same. He stuck the top of his head directly into flames in a fireplace, yet his hair was not even singed.

To earn money, Home toured England and Scotland reading poetry. He worked briefly as a war correspondent in the Franco-Prussian war of 1870. Later, back in Russia, he met Julie de Gloumeline, a wealthy woman who married him in 1871.

That same year, Home began a series of tests in London with Sir William CROOKES, a scientist intensely interested in Spiritualism. To determine if Home somehow manipulated electromagnetic energy, Crookes wrapped an accordion with copper wire and placed it inside a wire cage. He ran an electric current through the wire, which he believed would block any electromagnetic force from Home. Home still was able to make the accordion play without touching it. Crookes concluded that Home possessed an independent psychic force; his findings brought severe criticism from fellow scientists.

When he was finished with Crookes in 1873, Home announced his retirement as a medium. Restless and suffering from bad health, he traveled about with his wife and his son from his first marriage. Julie bore a baby girl, who died in infancy. Home died of tuberculosis on June 21, 1886 in Auteuil, France and was buried at St. Germain-en-Laye. Julie returned to Russia with Home's son. She wrote two books about her husband, *D.D. Home: His Life and Mission* (1888) and *The Gift of D.D. Home* (1890).

Home's published works include two autobiographies, *Incidents in My Life* (1862) and *Incidents in My Life, 2nd Series* (1872), and an exposé of fraudulent mediumistic techniques, *Light and Shadows of Spiritualism* (1877).

Explanations abounded of how Home allegedly accomplished his paranormal feats through trickery, though none was ever proved. The most prominent stage magicians of America and England, Harry HOUDINI, John Nevil Mackelyne, and John Mulholland, all claimed they could duplicate Home's feats on the stage. They never did. Houdini promised that he could levitate out a window, as Home did at Lord Adare's home. Shortly before it was to be done, the feat was canceled by Houdini, who said his assistant was ill. Houdini said he would reschedule it the next time he was in London, but he never did.

Further reading:

Brown, Slater. *The Heyday of Spiritualism*. New York: Hawthorn Books, 1970.

Earl of Dunraven. *Experiences in Spiritualism with D.D. Home*. Glasgow: University Press, 1924.

Edmonds, I.G. *D.D. Home The Man Who Talked With Ghosts*. Nashville: Thomas Nelson, 1978.

Fodor, Nandor. *An Encyclopaedia of Psychic Science*. Secaucus, N.J.: Citadel Press, 1966. First published 1933.

Hall, Trevor H. *The Enigma of Daniel Home*. Buffalo, N.Y.: Prometheus Books, 1984.

Pearsall, Ronald. *The Table-Rappers*. New York: St. Martin's Press, 1973.

home sitting   See HOME CIRCLE.

Hope, William (1863–1933)   Famous spirit photographer, considered a genuine master by some, but a consummate trickster by others. Although often accused of fraud, he was never actually caught in trickery.

William Hope was born in 1863 in Crewe, England. He became a carpenter. His talent for spirit photography first emerged about 1905, when he and a friend took turns photographing each other. In the picture which Hope took there was an "extra"—the image of a figure who was not physically present when the picture was taken—who turned out to be none other than his friend's deceased sister.

After this episode, a group of six persons organized in the Spiritualist Hall at Crewe for the purpose of spirit photography. This group became renowned as the "Crewe Circle," and Hope was at its center. This early group destroyed all its original negatives, out of fear of being suspected of being in league with the Devil, until the Archdeacon Thomas Colley joined them. Colley had been a lifelong enthusiast of the psychic and of Spiritualism, and his support gave credence to the enterprise.

Ironically, Hope's first brush with exposure came in Colley's first sitting. When Hope doctored the spirit photograph, he mistakenly used the wrong extra, substituting another elderly woman for Colley's mother. When Hope sought to confess to Colley, however, the clergyman dismissed it as nonsense, insisting that he could recognize his mother when he saw her. To prove his case, Colley put a notice in the newspaper asking for all who remembered his mother to meet him at the rectory. No fewer than 18 persons selected Hope's photograph from among several others, as definitely representing the late Mrs. Colley.

A few years later, in 1921, there was another exposure—one which almost backfired on the accuser, and about which there are questions to this day. Hope had by this time moved to London and established himself at the BRITISH COLLEGE OF PSYCHIC SCIENCE. The SOCIETY FOR PSYCHICAL RESEARCH (SPR) saw the opportunity for an investigation of Hope's claims and sent a new member, Harry PRICE, who had good knowledge of conjuring. Price reported what he claimed was evidence of trickery by Hope, but questions immediately arose about whether it was Price, and not Hope, who had tampered with the photographic plates. Author Brian Inglis observes that if Hope was a fraud, he almost certainly used a more sophisticated technique than the one Price charged him with.

Like all self-proclaimed mediums, Hope had his supporters as well as his detractors. Sir Arthur Conan DOYLE produced *The Case for Spirit Photography* (1923) in response to Price's "exposure." One of those who allied himself with Doyle at that time, Fred Barlow, of the Society for the Study of Supernormal Pictures, later reversed himself. In the SPR *Proceedings* for March 1933, Barlow said that further experience enabled him to say quite definitely that Hope's abilities were not psychic. No less than Sir William CROOKES and Sir William BARRETT endorsed Hope, although Sir Oliver LODGE wrote that he had "not the slightest doubt" that the sealed packet of plates he sent to Hope had been opened before being returned to him. There is also reason to suspect trickery in Crookes' case. The physicist was in his 80s in 1916 when he had his sitting, having just lost his wife. His assistant at the time, J.H. Gardiner, told Crookes' biographer, E.E. Fournier d'Albe, that the negative from which Hope's photograph of Lady Crookes was reproduced showed clear signs of double exposure, but that Crookes preferred to ignore these signs.

The Japanese researcher of "thoughtography," Tomokichi Fukarai, used Hope as a subject when he visited London in 1928. (Thoughtography, a term coined by Fukarai, is a type of paranormal photography in which a living person psychically projects images onto photographic film, with or without the aid of a camera.)

Hope died on March 7, 1933 at the age of 70.

Further reading:

Barlow, Fred, and W. Rampling-Rose. "Report of an Investigation into Spirit Photography." *Proceedings of the Society for Psychical Research* 41 (1933):121–38.

Inglis, Brian. *Science and Parascience: A History of the Paranormal, 1914–1939.* London: Hodder and Stoughton, 1984.

Oppenheim, Janet. *The Other World: Spiritualism and Psychical Research in England, 1850–1914.* London: Cambridge University Press, 1985.

Houdini, Harry (1874–1926) A master illusionist and escape artist, Harry Houdini was perhaps the greatest magician of all time. He also spent most of his adult life trying to expose fraudulent Spiritualist mediums as nothing more than conjurers like himself. At the same time, he desperately sought someone who could convince him of the truth of Spiritualism and enable him to contact his dead mother.

Houdini was born Ehrich Weiss in Appleton, Wisconsin on April 6, 1874, to Dr. Mayer Samuel Weiss, a rabbi, and his wife Cecilia. The Weisses were from Hungary. Even as a baby, his mother worried about Ehrich because he slept so little, often lying in his crib staring keen-eyed at the walls and ceiling. He learned to pick locks early on to steal jam tarts. By age six he was conjuring, making a dried pea appear in any of three cups. He was quite agile and athletic.

When a circus came to town, young Ehrich astonished the manager with his rope tricks. He performed during the circus's stay, but his father refused to let him travel with the circus. He worked with a local locksmith at age 11 and could pick any lock submitted to him. Ehrich also worked odd jobs as a newspaper seller, bootblack and necktie cutter.

His goal was to be a magician, however. A book by the famous French magician Jean Robert-Houdin provided Ehrich with some conjuring tricks and secret codes for sleight-of-hand, and he worked up his first professional act with a friend named Hayman. They called themselves the Houdini Brothers, adding an "i" to the French magician's name. When they parted later, Ehrich's real brother Theodore joined the act. The boys appeared in dime museums and sideshows, escaping from packing cases and handcuffs.

In 1893, Houdini performed at a girls' school and accidently spilled acid on a young girl's dress. Mrs. Weiss made the girl, Beatrice (Bess) Rahner, a new dress, and Houdini delivered it to her home. Not long after, she and Houdini were married. Bess, who had been strictly brought up, at first thought Houdini was the devil disguised as a handsome man, but she soon came to be his greatest supporter, even becoming his assistant in mind-reading performances. They remained deeply in love all their lives but had no children.

During the early lean days, Houdini offered to sell his conjuring tricks to newspapers, but no one was interested. He and Bess resorted to holding "psychic" demonstrations, in which local tipsters provided them with enough information to impress the audience. The crowd's eager acceptance of their me-

Harry Houdini.

diumship, which both knew to be a trick, scared the Houdinis.

By 1900, Houdini had escaped from handcuffs in a Chicago prison and even had broken free of handcuffs at Scotland Yard. His notoriety gained him more lucrative engagements, and his career soared. For the next 26 years, Houdini performed some of the most spectacular feats ever witnessed: escaping from fetters in icy cold water; emerging in minutes from boxes, coffins, kegs, mailbags, safes and gigantic paper bags; hanging from ropes off the ledges of tall buildings, then freeing himself; even coming back to life after being buried alive. There was no rope knots or contraptions that could hold him.

Throughout his life, Houdini was a devoted son to his mother, sending her part of his earnings and remaining in constant touch. After her death, he searched desperately for a way to reach her. He contacted medium after medium with no success. After each failure he would stand over his mother's

grave and say that he'd heard nothing yet. He wanted passionately to believe in Spiritualism, yet was convinced that the movement was nothing more than conjuring tricks.

In 1920, during a tour of England, Houdini and Bess met Sir Arthur Conan DOYLE and his family. The two struck up a friendship and an active correspondence. Both had an interest in Spiritualism, but from opposite sides, as Doyle was as ardent a believer as Houdini was a skeptic.

During the Doyles' first American lecture tour on Spiritualism, the Houdinis joined them for a vacation in Atlantic City in June 1922. On the afternoon of June 17, Doyle reported that his wife, an "inspired" (automatic) writer, felt she could get Houdini through to his mother. Bess was asked not to attend to prevent diluting the spiritual force. Bess had told Lady Doyle all about Houdini's mother the night before, and she cued her husband in their mind-reading code language that Lady Doyle was so informed.

Nevertheless, Houdini determined to be as open-minded and religious about the experience as possible. He wrote that he wanted to believe and emptied his mind of all skepticism. For Houdini, June 17 was a holy day, as it had been his mother's birthday.

Presently, Lady Doyle was seized by the spirit and began shaking convulsively. She asked the spirit if it believed in God, and receiving affirmative raps, made a cross at the top of the paper and began writing furiously. The message was an emotional outpouring of love for Mrs. Weiss's "darling boy," describing her happiness on the Other Side and joy that the Doyles had enabled her to finally get through to him. When Houdini asked if his mother's spirit could read his mind, she claimed that she could, and thanked the Doyles for helping her pierce the spiritual veil. She asked God's blessing, and then departed.

When Lady Doyle came out of trance, Houdini asked Sir Arthur if he, or anyone, could try automatic writing. Urged to try, Houdini picked up a pencil and wrote "Powell." Sir Arthur was dumbfounded, asserting that Houdini had been contacted by the spirit of his recently deceased friend Dr. Ellis Powell. Doyle claimed that Houdini was profoundly moved by the whole seance.

Within six months, however, Houdini publicly renounced the communication, finding it a noble try but again a failure. In the first place, his mother was Jewish and would not have started her message with a cross. Doyle countered that Lady Doyle always placed such a holy symbol on her manuscripts to guard against evil influence. Secondly, Mrs. Weiss spoke only broken English and could not write the language at all. Again Doyle had a ready answer, saying that a good medium in trance can receive message in a language and try to translate them into her own; it was the inspiration, not the tongue, that was important. Lastly, the message did not mention his mother's birthday at all, and Houdini believed that if the communication were truly from his mother she would have commented on that fact.

As for the Powell reference, Houdini refused to believe he had heard from Doyle's friend, noting that he and Bess had recently been talking about their magician friend Frederick Powell, whose wife and assistant was ill. That the two should have the same last name was mere coincidence. Doyle disagreed, saying another medium had revealed in a seance later on June 17 that Powell had tried to reach him and apologized for his abruptness.

The Doyles were angry and hurt by Houdini's refusal to believe. Although Doyle and Houdini tried to remain friends after that, speaking of anything but Spiritualism, the rift could not be repaired. By 1924, they were antagonists.

In January 1923, *Scientific American* magazine offered $2,500 to the first person who could produce a spirit photograph under test conditions and another $2,500 to anyone who could produce physical paranormal phenomena and have it recorded by scientific instruments. The magazine's test committee was composed of William McDougall, Harvard professor of psychology; Daniel F. Comstock, formerly of the Massachusetts Institute of Technology; Walter Franklin PRINCE, head of the AMERICAN SOCIETY FOR PSYCHICAL RESEARCH; Hereward CARRINGTON, a psychic investigator; Malcolm Bird, assistant editor of *Scientific American*; and Houdini.

The committee's first assignment was the medium Mina Stinson CRANDON of Boston, alias Margery. Her enthusiastic husband had written Doyle about his wife's talents, and he recommended her to the committee without ever meeting her. They began their investigation in November 1923, and Bird prepared a glowing endorsement of her for the July 1924 issue. Unfortunately, the committee had acted without Houdini, who learned of their activities from press clippings while he was on tour. Furious, he arrived in Boston in July to see Margery for himself.

The Crandons suspected Houdini from the beginning and were uncooperative. He, in turn, resorted to trickery to discredit her. For the first seance, Houdini wore a tight bandage around his upper calf for hours before the sitting, making his leg extraordinarily sensitive. Margery's spirit control, her brother Walter, was accustomed to ringing bells during the seance, and Houdini asked that the bell box be placed

between his feet. Sitting on Margery's left, Houdini claimed his tender leg detected Margery's almost imperceptible movements to work the box with her left foot.

Houdini caught Margery in several other tricks: throwing a megaphone with her head as if it had flown by spirit intervention, lifting a table with her head, and again sliding her foot. He waited to expose her, however, until more tests could be conducted. The press claimed Margery had stumped Houdini, further antagonizing him against the Crandons.

Houdini vowed to outwit Margery. In August, he arrived in Boston with a special box for Margery to sit in during the seances. The box enclosed her body completely, except for her head, neck and arms, allowing little movement of her legs and feet. Margery objected to the cage, stating that such pressure showed little regard for the psychic process. But it did not hamper her performance, as the lid was ripped off, ostensibly by Walter.

The next night Houdini replaced the lid and added locks. The Crandons examined the box and found it satisfactory. Bird burst into the seance demanding to know why he had been excluded, and Houdini accused him of betraying the committee's investigation. After he left, Houdini repeatedly reminded Prince to hold Margery's right hand. Irritated, Margery asked why he kept saying that, and Houdini replied that if her hands were held she could not manipulate anything she might have hidden in the box during the earlier examination.

Soon thereafter, Walter accused Houdini of leaving some articles in the box. Houdini denied this, but Walter explained that Houdini's assistant had placed a folding ruler in the box which, when found, would be seen as a reaching tool for Margery's use. Walter screamed out that Houdini was a son of a bitch, should go to hell, and that if he didn't leave the Crandons, he, Walter, would return. Many years later Houdini's assistant admitted his own complicity, saying that Houdini was bent on discrediting Margery.

Doyle and other Spiritualists attacked Houdini for his ungentlemanly actions; Doyle even called his former friend a bounder and a cad. Complicating the whole affair was Doyle's insistence that Houdini himself was probably the greatest medium of modern times. Doyle refused to believe that Houdini could perform his amazing escapes without first dematerializing and then reappearing, and others shared Doyle's opinion. All of this put Houdini the medium-baiter in the embarrassing position of demurring without really revealing the secrets of his act.

Actually, Houdini believed that if anyone could escape from the Other Side to the physical realm, it was he. Before his death, he and Bess worked out a code using their mind-reading secrets that would tell her that he had succeeded in coming back.

On October 22, 1926, a student visiting Houdini backstage in Montreal took him unawares and punched him in the stomach to test Houdini's claim of extraordinarily firm muscles. The blow was too hard, however, and Houdini died of peritonitis from a ruptured appendix nine days later, on Halloween.

Mediums claiming communications from Houdini besieged Bess Houdini immediately. Lonely and in poor health, Bess fell down a set of stairs on New Year's Day 1929, calling out to Harry for help. A week later, Arthur FORD, pastor of the First Spiritualist Church of New York, delivered a message purportedly from Mrs. Weiss containing the word "forgive," a word Houdini had vainly sought. Bess contacted Ford for a seance.

On January 8, 1929, Bess and several friends sat with Ford, who entered a trance immediately. First his control, Fletcher, spoke, then Houdini allegedly took over, saying, "Rosabelle, answer, tell, pray, answer, look, tell, answer, answer, tell." The communication sounded incoherent, until Bess removed her wedding band, in which were inscribed some of the words of a song she had sung on stage with Houdini in the early days: "Rosabelle, sweet Rosabelle, I love you more than I can tell. Over me you cast a spell, I love you my sweet Rosabelle." After singing the song, Bess fainted.

When she revived, Fletcher the control explained the message as a coded communication dating back to the couple's mind-reading days; decoded it meant "Rosabelle, believe." Bess promptly confirmed that the message was indeed the secret password. She signed a statement affirming its legitimacy and even wrote columnist Walter Winchell about the affair. Spiritualists rejoiced that Houdini, who had never believed, confirmed the truth of the movement after death.

Within a few years, however, Bess retracted her statements after hearing from radio mentalist Joseph Dunninger that he had read Houdini's code word in a 1927 biography. She condemned the Ford seance, attacked all mediums as charlatans and planned to make a movie exposing their trickery, but never did. Bess continued to hold seances on Halloween for a few years, trying to reach Houdini, but he was silent. In resignation, Bess told her friends that when she died, she would not try to come back.

As Houdini himself once said, anyone can talk to the dead, but the dead do not answer.

Further Reading:

Brandon, Ruth. *The Spiritualists*. New York: Alfred A. Knopf, 1983.

Cannell, J.C. *The Secrets of Houdini*. New York: Bell Publishing Co., 1989.

Doyle, Sir Arthur Conan. *The Edge of the Unknown*. New York: Berkley Medallion Books, 1968. First published by G.P. Putnam's Sons, 1930.

Houdini, Harry. *Houdini: A Magician Among the Spirits*. New York: Arno Press, 1972.

Mysteries of the Unknown: Spirit Summonings. Alexandria, Va.: Time-Life Books, 1989.

Somerlott, Robert. *"Here, Mr. Splitfoot": An Informal Exploration into Modern Occultism*. New York: The Viking Press, 1971.

Hull House   A Chicago landmark, now a museum, which in 1913 was widely believed to house a living "Devil Baby." The Hull House is still included in some "haunted tours" of Chicago and is said by some to exude an uncomfortable atmosphere.

Hull House was built in 1856 as the residence of Charles J. Hull. In the late 1880s, it became the United States' first welfare center, founded by Jane Addams and Ellen Starr. The center provided numerous services to the large numbers of immigrants who settled in the area. The Hull House welfare organization moved to new quarters in 1963, and the original house was preserved as a museum.

The Devil Baby rumor that arose in 1913 seemed to come from nowhere and gather great speed as it spread throughout the communities of immigrants. The rumor split into various ethnic versions, all of which wove the story around the moral of the need to adhere to one's religion.

According to the Italian version, a young Italian woman defied her family and married an atheist. She became pregnant right away. A few months later, she hung a picture of the Virgin Mary on the wall. This angered her husband, who tore it down, ripped it up and swore he would rather have the Devil in the house. The couple was punished with the birth of a baby that looked like a miniature Satan, with horns, cloven feet, pointed ears, a tail and a scaly body. It could walk and talk, and would run about the house threatening the father. Finally the father took it to the Hull House and beseeched Addams to take it in.

Other ethnic versions varied only in the sins that brought on the monstrous birth:

- An Irish girl failed to confess to her priest that prior to her marriage, she had conducted an affair with another man.

- A Jewish girl married a gentile without her parents' permission. Her enraged father said he would rather have the Devil as a grandchild than have a gentile for a son-in-law.
- Two young Jewish women, one of them pregnant, attended a performance of the play *Faust*. The pregnant one looked too intensely at the stage devil.
- An orthodox Jewish woman hid the truth about an illegitimate child, claiming that her second child, born in wedlock, was her first. Her next child was the Devil.

The rumor evidently appealed primarily to elderly women with Old World mores and superstitions. Once it took hold, the Hull House was beseiged for six weeks by hundreds of callers and visitors asking to see the Devil Baby. Addams and the exasperated staff repeatedly denied the existence of such a monster, but many refused to believe them. Rumors even circulated that discounts were being given to view the child. One man from Milwaukee called to say he wanted to organize a tour. Another woman, from the poorhouse, borrowed a dime to ride the trolley to Hull House in hopes of seeing the monster, only to be crushed to hear the truth.

The rumor finally diminished. Addams wrote about the event in her book *The Second Twenty Years at Hull House*, in which she theorized that the story had fired the imaginations of women who largely felt left out of life in America; the Devil Baby was something they could grasp and understand.

The story has refused to die, however. Reports continue in present times that the Devil Baby still can be glimpsed in an attic window of Hull House. Individuals also have claimed to photograph unusual lights and ectoplasm present inside the house, but such photographs are inconclusive as evidence.

Further Reading:

Riccio, Dolores, and Joan Bingham. *Haunted Houses USA*. New York: Pocket Books, 1989.
Scott, Beth, and Michael Norman. *Haunted Heartland*. New York: Warner Books, 1985.

Hungry Ghost Festival   See FEASTS AND FESTIVALS OF THE DEAD.

Hyslop, James Hervey (1854–1920)   Philosopher and psychical researcher, author of many books, monographs and articles on psychic phenomena. He was particularly interested in the process of mediumship. Although respected as a careful worker by some, he was considered by others to be too ready to believe in survival after death. From 1906 until his own death in 1920, he was secretary-treasurer of the AMERICAN SOCIETY FOR PSYCHICAL RESEARCH (ASPR).

Hyslop was born August 18, 1854 to devout Presbyterians who lived on a farm near Xenia, Ohio. A twin sister died soon after birth and an older sister a few years later. When Hyslop was 10, a younger brother and sister died of scarlet fever, and for the next two years, he wrote in his autobiography, he became preoccupied with death. He was so affected by this experience, in fact, that it remained with him for the rest of his life.

As a youth Hyslop intended to enter the ministry as his parents expected, but while at the College of Wooster, from which he graduated with a bachelor of arts degree in 1877, he suffered a crisis of faith that over the next five years led him to reject the divinity of Christ and embrace a materialist philosophy instead. The climax came during a trip to Europe, and he went to study philosophy at the University of Leipzig under Wilhelm Wundt, founder of the first formal psychology laboratory in 1879. He received a Ph.D. in psychology from Johns Hopkins University in 1887, taught briefly at Bucknell University, then joined the faculty at Columbia, teaching logic and ethics. In 1891 he married Mary Fry Hall, an American woman he had met while in Germany.

He knew nothing about the psychic until 1886, when his attention was caught by an article on telepathy in *Nation*. The article concerned a young boy who reportedly saw an apparition of his father and a team of horses going over a bank into a stream some 25 miles away. Hyslop suspected the story was "some illusion of memory or error in judgment as to the facts." He wrote to the author of the article and received answers to his questions that convinced him the phenomenon might be genuine.

Hyslop became involved in psychical research after hearing Richard HODGSON lecture in 1889. He immediately joined the British SOCIETY FOR PSYCHICAL RESEARCH (SPR) and the Boston-based ASPR. He helped to organize a New York chapter of the latter and soon was assisting Hodgson in the investigation of cases. Hyslop was very aware of the implications of psychical phenomena for philosophy, although his materialism left no room for life after death. The study of Leonora PIPER and other mediums, however, converted him to a belief in survival. His sitting with her began in 1888. Initially skeptical, he was astonished when Piper began relaying personal messages from his dead father and various relatives. By his 12th sitting, he was convinced he had communicated with the spirits of his family.

Hyslop's wife died suddenly in 1900, leaving him a widower with three small children. The following year he suffered a nervous breakdown, and in 1902, on the advice of a physician, he resigned his position at Columbia. Friends thought he would never regain his former strength, but he proved them wrong. Within a year, he was back in full swing, now able to devote all his time to psychical research.

Hyslop's first book on psychical research, *Science and a Future Life*, was published in 1905. It was to be followed by several others; but he is best remembered today for his leadership of the ASPR and his contributions to its publications.

The ASPR had been founded in 1885 as an independent society, but in 1887 had been forced for financial reasons to affiliate with the SPR as the latter's American branch. Hyslop dreamed of returning the ASPR to American control, and when Hodgson died unexpectedly in 1905, he had a plan well underway. This called for the establishment of an American Institute for Scientific Research, modeled after the Carnegie Institute, with a board of directors. The ASPR was to be one section, with another section devoted to abnormal psychology.

Hyslop succeeded in getting the funding to set up his Institute and the ASPR; the section devoted to abnormal psychology, however, was never established. The ASPR was back in operation in 1906, and in 1907 began the publication of a *Journal* that has continued without interruption to this day. An annual series of *Proceedings* was also begun. Hyslop served as president of the ASPR from 1906 until his death in 1920.

Hyslop's output between 1907 and 1920 was prodigious. In addition to fund-raising and administrative duties, he investigated many cases and wrote lengthy reports for ASPR publications. For most of this time he was unassisted except by a secretary; from 1917 he was joined by Walter Franklin PRINCE. He suffered a stroke at the end of 1919, and died June 17, 1920.

At least part of the difficulty Hyslop experienced in getting a hearing for psychical research in the scientific community, and in getting help at the ASPR, was due to his irascible personality. He irritated and angered many people, including William James, who had been a central figure in the ASPR's early years, and he is said to have run the ASPR like a dictator. However, no one disputes that his loss was a blow to psychical research in America.

His other books include *Borderland of Psychical Research* (1906), *Enigmas of Psychical Research* (1906), *Psychical Research and the Resurrection* (1908), *Life After Death: Problems of a Future Life and Its Nature* (1918) and *Contact with the Other World* (1919).

HYSLOP'S CASEWORK

Beginning in 1907, he worked with a number of mediums—principally Minnie Soule—to investigate spirit possession and obsession. His most famous cases are the THOMPSON-GIFFORD CASE and the DORIS FISCHER CASE. He also investigated the story of S. Henry, a coachman in New Jersey who was tormented by the death of his wife and by his increasingly frightening psychical experiences. Henry described feelings of a strange fluid in his stomach which forced him to breathe in a certain way, then rose to his brain and drove him crazy. He also felt he could leave his body through an opening in the back of his head. Hyslop did not recognize Henry's symptoms as those of *kundalini* (in Yoga, an intense spiritual energy) or out-of-body experience. By 1908, almost two years after Hyslop had first met him, Henry was suffering from delusions and had gone insane. Hyslop took Henry to New York to the ASPR, where he hypnotized him and tried to encourage him to forget his troubles. The simple treatment worked. Never having confronted out-of-body experiences before, Hyslop attributed Henry's problems to spirit possession.

In 1909, Hyslop met Etta De Camp, a medium then living in New York City who had been psychic since her childhood in Ohio. She was an editor and proofreader for *Broadway* magazine, but had never written anything other than letters until 1908. After reading about spirit communications received by W.T. STEAD through automatic writing, De Camp decided to try. She reported a tingling in her arm, like electric shock, and after two or three days began writing copiously.

De Camp experienced terrible headaches and earaches at this time, usually if she tried to resist the writing. She found some relief while in trance, but she refused to lose conscious control. The scripts made little sense to her, and she complained to the spirits that if they could not write well, they should bring someone to her that could. From that point on, the scripts became more coherent. Her first comcmunicator was an Indian brave, who reported that she would hear from a man, a writer who wanted someone to finish the stories he had left when he died.

Very soon her pencil wrote that the spirit of Frank R. Stockton had arrived and wished to communicate. She felt intense pain, but once Stockton took control of her the pain subsided. De Camp began writing short stories in Stockton's style, and she showed them to her employer, George Duysters, who introduced her to Hyslop.

Stockton had been popular in the late 19th century, writing whimsical stories for children. His most famous, "The Lady or the Tiger," is still popular. He had a distinctive style, full of humor, cynicism and bizarre situations. Duysters showed some of the De Camp transcriptions to the late author's editor at *Harper's*, who found them quite real. De Camp also began hearing from her dead father.

De Camp continued to write in Stockton's style, although Hyslop lost contact with her from 1910 to 1912 while he investigated other matters. In 1912, De Camp was close to a complete breakdown, and Hyslop agreed to participate in sittings which would finally reveal Stockton's presence. Through a series of seances with Soule, both Stockton and the recently deceased Duysters revealed themselves, proving again to Hyslop the reality of spirit possession and survival. De Camp wrote of her experiences in *The Return of Frank R. Stockton* in 1913, including all of the transcribed Stockton stories. After initial publicity, De Camp later married and settled down to a private life, hearing no more from Stockton.

A third case involved a woman identified as Ida Ritchie, really Ida Marie Rogers. Rogers claimed to be receiving communications from the great opera singer Emma Abbot, who had died in 1891. Rogers was a budding singer herself, and had made remarkable progress for a person with little formal training. When she contacted Hyslop, Rogers said that Emma Abbott, Rogers' mother, and the late William James, a Harvard philosopher and psychologist and friend of Hyslop's, were all talking to her through automatic writing. Again through sittings with Soule, Hyslop contacted Abbott and Rogers's mother. Their communications indicated great efforts on the part of the spirits to help Rogers's singing career, but she never became a great star.

Further reading:

Anderson, Roger I. "The Life and Work of James H. Hyslop." *The Journal of the American Society for Psychical Research* 79 (April 1985):167–204.

Anderson, Roger I., "Autobiographical Fragment of James Hervey Hyslop." *The Journal of Religion and Psychical Research* 9 (April 1986):81–92.

———. "Autobiographical Fragment of James Hervey Hyslop Part III." *The Journal of Religion and Psychical Research* 9 (July 1986):145–160.

Berger, A.S. *Lives and Letters in American Parapsychology: A Biographical History, 1850–1987.* Jefferson, N.C.: Scarecrow Press, 1988.

Rogo, D. Scott. *The Infinite Boundary.* New York: Dodd, Mead & Co., 1987.

I

ignis fatuus A wide variety of spectral lights, whose alleged purpose is either to herald death or to play tricks on travelers out alone at night. "Ignis fatuus" literally means "the foolish fire" and is so named because anyone who follows such a light is foolish.

Ignis fatuus lights appear as bluish flames, blue or yellow globes, and candle lights that float and bob mysteriously through the countryside at night. They appear around the world and are universal throughout folklore.

As death omens, they include the corpse candle, dead candle, will-o'-the-wisp, and such. Numerous names exist for pesky travelers' lights, including jack-o'-lantern, jenny-burnt-tail, Kit-in-the-candlestick and a host of other appellations. The lights that plague travelers are said to be fond of luring people off a trail or path until they become lost.

Various legends exist to explain such lights. One of the most popular holds that the light is a ghost of a sinner whose soul cannot rest, and is doomed to wander the earth forever. In some parts of Britain, such as the Lincolnshire fen country, the ignis fatuus lights, called Will-o'-the-Wykes, are evil. In German lore, the light is named the *Irrlicht*, and is either a forest spirit or a wandering soul that accompanies an invisible funeral procession.

In Swedish lore, the light is that of a soul of an unbaptized child who tries to lead travelers to water in hopes of receiving baptism. Ignis fatuus appears in the lore of Native Americans; the Penobscot call it "fire creature" or "fire demon," a death-omen spirit who spins his lighted fingertips in a wheel to skim the milk at dairies during the night. In parts of Africa, such lights are called "witch-fire" and are believed to be witches flying through the air, or lights sent by witches to scare wrongdoers.

Natural explanations given for such lights include marsh gas, electrical and magnetic phenomena and some form of unknown "earth energy." See GHOST LIGHTS.

Further reading:
Briggs, Katherine. *An Encyclopedia of Fairies: Hobgoblins, Brownies, Bogies, and Other Supernatural Creatures.* New York: Pantheon Books, 1976.
Guiley, Rosemary Ellen. *The Encyclopedia of Witches and Witchcraft.* New York: Facts On File, 1989.

incubus See DEMONS.

Indridason, Indridi (?–1912) Remarkable Icelandic medium who exhibited numerous paranormal feats and was never exposed of fraud.

Indridi Indridason was a young printer in Reykjavik when he was discovered by psychical researchers who had started a seance circle for investigating mediumistic phenomena. Indridason had been raised in the countryside in Iceland, and professed to know nothing about Spiritualism or psychical research. His abilities were so great that the researchers, among them Haraldur Nielsson, professor of theology at the University of Reykjavik, began sitting with him once or twice a week between September and the end of June each year from 1904 to 1909.

Initially, Indridason communicated with spirits of the dead through trance speaking and automatic writing. Soon, he began to produce psychokinesis (PK) of objects; levitations; materializations; luminous phenomena and direct voice mediumship. These feats began to take place at every sitting. Sometimes as many as 26 spirit voices would speak directly at sittings; those who were known to sitters while living sounded the same as they had in life. Occasionally, the spirits would use Indridason's voice to sing. He had a good voice of his own, but had never had singing lessons. In trance, Indridason would state that his singing was controlled from the Other Side.

Indridason's numerous control spirits said he also had exceptional healing ability. His primary control claimed to be a brother of Indridason's grandfather, who had been a professor at the University of Copenhagen. Other controls included three physicians

175

(one English, one Dutch and one Norwegian), four Icelandic clergymen, an Icelandic farmer, a Danish manufacturer, a German officer, a Norwegian singer, a French singer (female) and an Icelandic girl. In addition, other spirits also manifested, including a troublesome one named "John" who claimed to have committed suicide and was seeking to possess the medium. John—whose real identity was verified by researchers—eventually mellowed and began to assist Indridason.

Various phenomena seemed to have their own cycles of power. During the winter of 1906–07, Indridason produced mostly materializations and luminous phenomena, while during the winter of 1908–09, he produced mostly levitations and direct voices.

The researchers established the Psychic Experimental Society for the express study of Indridason and supported him with housing and a salary. The Society invited people to attend seances, but mediumship had not caught on in Iceland as it had in Britain and the United States, due to the popularity of Spiritualism, and only a few literary individuals accepted. Nonetheless, sometimes 60 to 70 persons would come, and even before such crowds Indridason produced his phenomena. Skeptics became convinced that unknown powers truly were at work. The Society became popularly known as "The Ghost Society," a reference to the spirits of the dead in Spiritualism.

Indridason's powers were at a peak in June 1909. His career was cut short that summer when he contracted typhoid fever, and soon thereafter contracted consumption. He died of tuberculosis in August 1912.

Shortly after his death, the Society broke up. An outgrowth of the research, however, was the formation in 1918 of the Icelandic Society for Psychical Research.

Further reading:

"Remarkable Phenomena in Iceland." *Journal of the American Society for Psychical Research* 18 (1924):233–59.

Institut Metapsychique International

French psychical research organization, located in Paris.

The Institut Metapsychique International (IMI) was founded in 1918 with backing from the French industrialist Jean Meyer, a dedicated Spiritualist. Charles Richet was the first president of its governing committee, which included several other important men of science and politics. The first director was Gustave GELEY. The IMI began publication of a bimonthly journal, the *Revue Metapsychique*, in 1919.

Under Geley, the IMI studied physical mediums such as Marthe BERAUD ("Eva C."), Jan GUZIK and

Franek Kluski. When Geley died in an airplane crash in 1924, Eugene OSTY was named to replace him.

As Geley had before him, Osty gave up a private medical practice to take the job. Osty continued Geley's research program, but placed his own stamp on it. With Meyer's assistance, he built a laboratory, outfitting it with some of the most advanced instruments available. Osty's experiments with Rudi Schneider (see SCHNEIDER BROTHERS) at the IMI in 1930 are regarded as some of the most important in the history of psychical research.

The first period of the IMI's history, from its inception until Osty's death in 1934, was its heyday. World War II forced the closing of the IMI in 1940, and although it reopened after the war, it has never since had the luster of the early years. This is reflected in the publishing history of the *Revue Metapsychique*, which has ceased publication more than once only to be revived after a few years. The last issue of the most recent series appeared in 1983.

Although the IMI is technically still in business today, one must call and make an appointment to visit there. It does not have the public support that attend its British and American counterparts, the SOCIETY FOR PSYCHICAL RESEARCH (SPR) and the AMERICAN SOCIETY FOR PSYCHICAL RESEARCH (ASPR).

Further reading:

Inglis, Brian. *Science and Parascience: A History of the Paranormal, 1914–1939.* London: Hodder and Stoughton, 1984.

Lodge, Oliver. "In memoriam—Gustave Geley." *Proceedings of the Society for Psychical Research* 34 (1924):201–11.

iron   Cold iron protects against witches, fairies and evil spirits, who are unable to cross it, according to widespread superstition. In India, iron is believed to repel the djinn, the demonic children of Lilith and the Devil. In classical times, iron was used to ward off illness and bad luck, which were believed to be caused by evil spirits; it was especially important in the protection of women in childbirth and of small children, who were more vulnerable to evil than others. Pliny, in his *Natural History*, writes that a circle traced three times with iron or a pointed weapon would protect a woman and her infant from all noxious influences.

Iron lore is found in the United Kingdom, and was exported from there to the American colonies. Large pieces of cast iron or iron ore traditionally are laid at the threshold of dwellings or set in the main door frame in order to prevent undesirable beings from entering. Other iron amulets include knives buried under doorsteps or gates, horseshoes hung over doorways, and fire irons crossed over or beneath a cradle. Similarly, iron scissors placed in a cradle prevent fairies from stealing an infant and replacing it with a changeling. Iron coal rakes, scythes, hoops, hooks and shears also serve as a deterrent to evil, and if kept in the bedroom will ward off the nightmare (see OLD HAG). Nails carried in the pocket serve protection while traveling.

Iron seems to have little or no effect against ghosts or vampires. The Saxons, however, did not put iron rune wands in cemeteries because they feared the iron would scare away the spirits of the dead. Many a house with an iron threshold or charm reputedly has been haunted. A few classic ghosts haunt with their rattling of iron chains. (See ATHENODORUS, HAUNTING OF.) Vampires must be warded off with silver, garlic, wolfbane and other charms.

See also AMULETS.

Further reading:
Garrad, Larch S. "Additional Examples of Possible House Charms in the Isle of Man." *Folklore* 100 (1989):110–12.
Guiley, Rosemary Ellen. *The Encyclopedia of Witches and Witchcraft*. New York: Facts On File, 1989.
Tebbett, C.F. "Iron Thresholds as a Protection." *Folklore* 91 (1980):240.

J

Jack-in-Irons A specter said to haunt the lonely roads of Yorkshire, England. A tall, demoniac figure draped in chains, the Jack-in-Irons reportedly jumps out at travelers and gives them a fright. The chains make Jack-in-Irons an unusual specter, for few ghosts have them in folklore and legend, despite a popular portrayal of ghosts in chains in art and literature (see ATHENODORUS, HAUNTING OF).

Jack-o'-lantern (also jacky lantern) A type of IGNIS FATUUS, or "foolish fire." In British folklore, the jack-o'-lantern is a spectral light that drifts about at night, scaring travelers and beckoning them to follow it until they become lost.

According to lore, the jack-o'-lantern is a soul who has been denied entry into both heaven and hell. It is doomed to wander about the earth clothed in a luminous garment or carrying a lighted wisp of straw.

Numerous stories explain the origin of the jack-o'-lantern; perhaps best-known is the Irish tale of the ne'er-do-well man named Jack, who was notorious for his drunkenness and meanness. On one ALL HALLOWS EVE (Halloween) night, Jack got so drunk at the local pub that his soul began to slip out of his body. Immediately the Devil appeared to claim his victim. Jack, desperate to avoid his fate, begged the Devil to have one last drink before they departed. The Devil agreed, but told Jack he would have to pay for the drinks, as the Devil carried no money. Jack said he had only sixpence left. He suggested that the Devil, who could assume any shape he wanted, take on the shape of sixpence so that Jack could pay for the drinks. Then the Devil could change back.

The Devil thought this was a reasonable suggestion, and so changed himself into a sixpence piece. Jack snatched up the coin and stuffed it in his wallet, which had a cross-shaped catch. The Devil could not get out, and began cursing.

Jack told the Devil he would release him if the Devil promised to leave him alone for a year. The Devil agreed.

Jack intended to reform his ways for the next year, being nice to his wife and children, paying his bills instead of squandering his money at the pub, going to church and giving to the poor. But soon he had slipped back into his mean ways.

The next All Hallows Eve, Jack was hurrying home from the pub when the Devil appeared by his side and demanded to collect his soul. Once again Jack tried to trick the Devil. He pointed to apples hanging from a tree and suggested the Devil wanted one. He offered to let the Devil stand on his shoulders so that the Devil could pick them.

As soon as the Devil had climbed up into the tree, Jack took out his pocket knife and carved the sign of the cross on the tree trunk. The Devil could not come down. He ranted and raved to no avail. In despair, he offered Jack 10 years' peace in exchange for his freedom. Jack insisted that the Devil never bother him again. The Devil, desperate, agreed.

Jack returned to his mean ways. But before the next All Hallows Eve, his body gave out, and he died. He tried to enter the gates of heaven, but was turned away because of his meanness in life. He then went to the gates of hell. The Devil refused him, saying he had promised never to bother him. He told Jack to return whence he had come. To help Jack find his way in the dark, the Devil threw out a piece of coal from hell. Jack put it inside a turnip. It became a jack-o'-lantern and has been Jack's light on his eternal wanderings around the earth ever since.

Different versions of this story were created in America. In the south in the 1800s, one popular version in black culture told of Grandpappy, who lost his way in the woods, saw a light and started to follow it. The light led him astray. When Grandpappy realized he had been tricked by a "jack-ma-lantern," he was mad as a hornet. But he knew what to do. He turned his pockets inside out, drew a ring in his path, made a cross on the ground, and said, "In the name of the Father and the Son and the Holy Speret, drive these witches away with their evil jack-ma-lanterns."

An American version of the Irish Jack story says that Jack sold his soul outright to the Devil at midnight one night at a crossroads. He bargained a seven-year grace period, during which he could do whatever he pleased. At the end of the period, the Devil came to collect Jack's soul. Jack put the sole of an old shoe above his door and asked the Devil to retrieve it for him. When the Devil reached up, Jack nailed his hand to the wall and left him hanging. He released the Devil only upon extracting a promise never to bother him again. When Jack died, he could enter neither heaven nor hell. The Devil threw a piece of fire at him, saying Jack was too smart for him. Jack was forced to wander eternally, and his only entertainment was leading people into swamps and mudholes at night. One can protect oneself from a jack-o'-lantern by carrying an object made of iron, which is believed to repell evil spirits. In Scottish lore, sticking an iron knife into the ground does the trick. Irish lore warns children who are caught outdoors after dark to wear their jackets inside out in order not to be lured astray by a jack-o'-lantern. By doing so, the wearer is disguised, and shows the evil spirits that he or she has nothing for them. These remedies were transplanted to America, along with the procedure of flinging oneself to the ground, shutting the eyes, holding the breath and plugging the ears until the jack-o'-lantern passes.

Jack-o'-lantern lights that are part of Halloween festivities descend from an old Irish custom of using carved-out turnips or beets with candles as lanterns. On Halloween, such lights represented the souls of the dead or goblins freed from the dead. The Irish who immigrated to America found pumpkins a suitable substitute for turnips and beets. In America, pumpkin jack-o'-lantern have been an essential part of Halloween celebrations since Victorian days.

Further reading:

Bannatyne, Lesley Pratt. *Halloween: An American Holiday, An American History.* New York: Facts On File, 1990.

Guiley, Rosemary Ellen. *The Encyclopedia of Witches and Witchcraft.* New York: Facts On File, 1989.

Linton, Ralph, and Adelin Linton. *Halloween Through the Centuries.* New York: Henry Schuman, 1950.

James, William (1842–1910)

American philosopher and psychologist who made significant contributions to psychical research, in particular the study of mediums.

William James was born in New York City to a wealthy family. His father, Henry James, was a renowned philosopher who became a follower of the teachings of Emanuel SWEDENBORG. James earned a medical degree from Harvard University at age 27, and two years later he began teaching there on physiology, psychology and philosophy. He was particularly interested in trance and mystical states, and had his own profound experiences in middle age.

As early as 1869, he showed interest in paranormal phenomena, and throughout his lifelong involvement in the subject, he maintained an open mind and was thorough about fact-gathering. In London in 1882, he met the key founders of the newly-formed SOCIETY FOR PSYCHICAL RESEARCH (SPR)—Henry SIDGWICK and Eleanor SIDGWICK, Frederic W.H. MYERS, Edmund GURNEY, Frank PODMORE and Richard HODGSON—and participated in their research. In particular he admired Myers, and Myers's theory of the subliminal self, a secondary consciousness or psychic region in which higher mental processes occur; the theory echoed his own theory of a "hidden self," developed prior to meeting Myers.

In 1885, James helped found the AMERICAN SOCIETY FOR PSYCHICAL RESEARCH with William BARRETT and others. He also founded the Lawrence Scientific School at Harvard where psychical research was conducted. He was vice president of the SPR from 1890 to 1910 and president from 1894 to 1895.

James's most significant contribution to psychical research was his discovery of the Boston medium Leonora PIPER in 1885. Her ability so impressed him that he researched mental mediums for the rest of his life (he had little interest in physical mediumship). He was never quite convinced that her spirit controls were truly spirits of the dead, but he leaned toward that belief. In 1890, he delivered his famous "white crow" lecture, stating that "to upset the conclusion that all crows are black, there is no need to seek demonstration that no crows are black; it is sufficient to produce one white crow; a single one is sufficient." Thus Piper, he said, was a white crow.

While James remained committed to empiricism, he also believed that researchers should be strict with mediums. By being yielding, better results were obtained. He desired to see scientific research include paranormal phenomena.

Although James never explicitly stated he believed in SURVIVAL AFTER DEATH, he did hope that Myers and Hodgson would provide proof after their deaths in 1900 and 1905, respectively. Hodgson, who allegedly became one of Piper's controls, seemed most promising, but James became disappointed in the lack of proof.

William James.

James died on August 26, 1910 in his summer home in Chocurua, New Hampshire. He is frequently cited as communicating through mediumship, and if all such claims are to be believed, he is one of the busiest spirits on the Other Side.

Further reading:
Burkhardt, Frederic, and Fredson Bowers, eds. *The Works of William James: Essays in Psychical Research.* Cambridge, Mass.: Harvard University Press, 1986.

Feinstein, Howard M. *Becoming William James.* Ithaca, N.Y.: Cornell University Press, 1984.

Murphy, Gardner, and Robert O. Ballou, eds. *William James on Psychical Research.* New York: Viking Press, 1960.

Myers, Gerald E. *William James: His Life and Thought.* New Haven, Conn.: Yale University Press, 1986.

Jesus Christ, exorcisms of   The gospels of Matthew, Mark and Luke refer to many instances where Jesus "cast out demons" or "unclean spirits." Such acts are differentiated from healing diseases or defects, implying that Jesus' contemporaries believed in Satan and his capacity to send devils into man separately from illness.

To "exorcise," however, actually comes from the Greek word *exousia*, meaning to put under oath and command, invoking a higher authority to force compliance. To exorcise, then, is to adjure (in Latin, *adjuro*) the spirits to depart in the name of God. As such, Jesus was not an exorcist, for He needed no higher authority than Himself.

The first instance of Jesus casting out demons occurred not long after His baptism by John the Baptist. Immediately following the baptism, Jesus spent 40 days in the wilderness, tempted by Satan. Upon returning, Jesus began selecting his disciples and went into Capernaum to teach. Both Mark (1:23–27) and Luke (4:33–36) tell the story; the text appears in the King James translation in Mark:

> And there was in their synagogue a man with an unclean spirit; and he cried out, Saying, Let us alone; what have we to do with thee, thou Jesus of Nazareth? art thou come to destroy us? I know thee who thou art, the Holy One of God. And Jesus rebuked him, saying, Hold thy peace, and come out of him. And when the unclean spirit had torn him, and cried with a loud voice, he came out of him. And they were all amazed, insomuch that they questioned among themselves saying, What thing is this? what new doctrine is this? for with authority commandeth he even the unclean spirits, and they do obey him.

The man's possession and exorcism follow the traditional pattern. First, the demon recognizes Christ. Second, the spirit's departure causes great pain to the possessed, coupled with loud voices and cries. Third, the demon must ultimately yield to Jesus' higher power.

Jesus's method of simple command over the demons differed greatly from that practiced by other holy men of his time. Most exorcists of the period relied on ritual, chants, signs and artifacts to expel evil spirits. Professor Merrill F. Unger of the Dallas Theological Seminary wrote in his book *Biblical Demonology* that Christ's method differed from other approaches because it "consisted neither in magical means nor in ritualistic rigmaroles, but in His own living word of infinite power. He spoke and the demons obeyed Him as Lord of the spirit world."

Not long after the episode in Capernaum, Mark and Luke describe Jesus healing the sick and casting out more demons (Mark 1:32–34; Luke 4:38–41), with the significant comment that Jesus would not let the demons speak, because they knew Him.

After finally naming all 12 disciples—to whom He gave the power to cast out demons also—Jesus returned home, welcomed by great crowds of the faithful and curious. Some of His friends believed He was temporarily insane, and some of the Jewish scribes considered Him possessed by the devil Beelzebul, or

Beelzebub. Matthew (12:24–29), Mark (3:22–27) and Luke (11:14–22) recount the incident:

> And the scribes which came down from Jerusalem said, he hath Beelzebub, and by the prince of devils casteth he out devils. And he called them unto him, and said unto them in parables, How can Satan cast out Satan? And if a kingdom be divided against itself, that house cannot stand. And if Satan rise up against himself, and be divided, he cannot stand but hath an end. No man can enter into a strong man's house, and spoil his goods, except he will first bind the strong man; and then he will spoil his house.
>
> (Mark 3:22–27)

Beelzebub, also known as Baal-zebub, literally means "lord of the flies." The name is a distortion of Baal-zebul, the chief Canaanite or Phoenician god, meaning "lord of the divine abode" or "lord of the heavens." In the prophet Elijah's day, the god Baal was the main rival to the Israelite god Yahweh (Jehovah), and his name came to represent Satan to the Jews (1 Kings 18; 2 Kings 1:3). This incident also presents the idea of binding Satan to the will of God before he can be thrown out of the "house," or the body of the possessed victim.

The episode most often told about Jesus casting out the devils concerns the Gerasene or Gadarene demoniac, according to Mark, Luke, and the two demoniacs in Matthew. Although identified differently, the story is the same. After delivering the Sermon on the Mount, Jesus and His disciples trav-

Unclean spirits falling down before Jesus as described in Mark 3:11.

eled by boat to the country of the Gerasenes, or Gadarenes. There they were met by a man possessed of an unclean spirit, as told in Mark:

> And they came over unto the other side of the sea, into the country of the Gadarenes. And when he was come out of the ship, immediately there met him out of the tombs a man with an unclean spirit, Who had his dwelling among the tombs; and no man could bind him, no, not with chains: Because that he had been often bound with fetters and chains, and the chains had been plucked asunder by him, and the fetters broken in pieces; neither could any man tame him. And always, night and day, he was in the mountains, and in the tombs, crying, and cutting himself with stones.
>
> But when he saw Jesus afar off, he ran and worshipped him, And cried with a loud voice, and said, What have I to do with thee, Jesus, thou Son of the most high God? I adjure thee by God, that thou torment me not. For he said unto him, Come out of the man, thou unclean spirit. And he asked him, What is thy name? And he answered, saying, My name is Legion: for we are many. And he besought him much that he would not send them away out of the country.
>
> Now there was there nigh unto the mountains a great herd of swine feeding. And all the devils besought him, saying, Send us into the swine, that we may enter into them. And forthwith Jesus gave them leave. And the unclean spirits went out, and entered into the swine: and the herd ran violently down a steep place into the sea (they were about two thousand); and were choked in the sea.

Like other possessed souls, the Gadarene demoniac suffered great physical pain and spiritual anguish. He ran to Jesus for help, but the demon within denied Jesus's power and *adjured* Jesus (to adjure— to exorcise) not to cast him out. Another important part of this story is the naming of the demon, a vital point in the exorcism ritual. A legion is a major unit in the Roman army (also considered devils by many) consisting of four to six thousand men. The estimate of two thousand may be low. Finally, however, the demons could not stand up to Jesus any longer and begged to enter the herd of swine. The pig was already deemed an unclean animal in Jewish law, so the choice of pigs was appropriate. People in Jesus's day believed that devils hated water, so when the pigs drowned, the devils were destroyed.

Jesus continued to cast out devils during His ministry, even cleansing the unclean spirit from the daughter of a Gentile woman who accepted Him as the messiah (Mark 7:25–30; Matthew 15:21–28). Obviously, such acts were crowd-pleasers, and the disciples tell Jesus of an exorcist who claims to cast out devils in His name (Mark 10:38–41; Luke 9:49–50). Jesus tells them not to worry, for anyone who performs such a mighty act in His name cannot speak ill of Him. And later, 70 other followers, sent out as disciples but not specifically given the power to exorcise, found they were also able to cast out demons. Jesus reminded them that the joy was not in being able to exorcise, but in the fact that God had found them worthy (Luke 10:17–20).

After Jesus's death, the power of His name grew, so that a band of "vagabond Jews, exorcists" (Acts 19:13–16) decided to invoke the name of Jesus Christ in their exorcism rituals, saying, "We adjure you by Jesus whom Paul preacheth." Not to be fooled, the evil spirit answered, "Jesus I know, and Paul I know, but who are ye?" At that moment the demon left the possessed man and overcame the exorcists, sending them running out of the man's house "naked and wounded"—an early example of the dangers of exorcism to the exorcist.

These stories in the gospels provided proof to medieval thinkers that not only was Satan real, but he took possession of innocent souls at will. And if not only Jesus Christ but also his disciples—even those not specifically chosen but only devoutly faithful—were able to cast out demons, then holy men of the Church everywhere had the same power to exorcise in the name of the Lord. Whether Jesus actually expelled evil spirits, or merely ministered to the people in terms they were familiar with, continues to be debated in theological circles.

Further reading:

Ebon, Martin. *The Devil's Bride, Exorcism: Past and Present.* New York, Harper & Row, 1974.

Jimmy Squarefoot   In English folklore, a phantom of a man with a pig's head and two huge tusks like those of a wild boar. Jimmy Squarefoot, the name of the man who became the odd phantom, haunts the Grenaby district of the Isle of Man. According to lore, at one time it was a giant pig which was carried around by a stone-throwing giant, a Foawr. As a mortal, Jimmy, too, was a stone-thrower; his favorite target was his wife. She ultimately left him, after which it seems he assumed his semi-human form and roamed the land.

Stone-throwing is a common phenomenon of poltergeist cases.

K

ka To the ancient Egyptians, the double of the soul. Upon death, the *ka* retained its own consciousness and prepared the way to the underworld for the soul. It then resided in the tomb with the corpse, while the soul stayed in the underworld. Animals and objects, as well as human beings, had *ka*s. Some kings were believed to have many *ka*s.

To accommodate the *ka*, a special "house of *ka*" was constructed in the tomb. A priest was appointed to minister to the needs of the *ka* and to see that offerings of food, drink and objects were left to it. The *ka* would eat the *ka*s of the offerings. If insufficient offerings were made, the *ka* would be forced to leave the tomb and wander about as a ghost, eating and drinking whatever it could find. The Egyptians believed that periodically the soul would return to the tomb to visit its *ka*.

See also BA.

Kan Hotidan In Native American lore, a powerful and feared elf-like tree spirit who lives in tree stumps and casts spells over unwary travelers. The name means "Tree-Dweller." The Kan Hotidan also could bestow magic to ensure success in hunting. Effigies of the elf were kept in a box which symbolized its tree-stump dwelling.

See also TREE GHOSTS.

kachinas Among the Pueblo Native Americans of the southwestern United States and parts of Mexico, supernatural beings or the spirits of the ancestral dead who are intermediaries to the gods. "Kachina" (a Hopi term) means "spirit father," "life," or "spirit." Spirit fathers are associated with the dead. Kachinas bring rain and perform other mostly beneficial functions.

According to myth, the kachinas live in the sacred San Francisco Mountains. In a distant time, they periodically descended to visit the villages, where they danced and performed their ministrations to the living. The people asked them to take the souls of the newly dead back with them to the mountains. This became so onerous that the kachinas ceased their visitations. Instead, they declared that they should be impersonated. The cult of kachinas came into being, comprised of men who, at the appointed times, dress in elaborate costumes and masks and perform the kachinas' dances.

Most kachinas are perceived as benevolent beings who, in addition to bringing rain, will entertain and discipline children. There are evil kachinas who attack and kill.

The Hopi dead go to the sacred mountains, where they become kachinas and are transformed into clouds. The living ask them to bring rain.

The Zuñi call their kachinas *koko*, the spirits of men who come in the form of ducks to bring rain and supervise hunts. Like Hopi kachinas, some *koko* live in mountains. Most, however, live in a great village at the bottom of the mythical Lake of the Dead, which exists in Listening Spring Lake at the junction of the Zuni and Little Colorado rivers. Offerings of food are thrown into the rivers to be carried to the Lake of the Dead. There the *koko* have happy lives and dress beautifully. They visit the living as clouds.

In Zuñi myth, the original *koko* were children who died by drowning after the emergence of people from the underworld (the Zuñi creation myth), and people who died and returned to the underworld. *Koko* also include persons who have recently died, and who may or may not make rain, and ancestors who have been long dead and who can bestow health, rain and good corn crops. As for the newly dead, only those men who were initiated into the cult of *koko* during life can become *koko* after death. Women apparently may join their husbands, but spirits of children are turned into *uwanammi*, or water monsters (also empowered to bring rain).

Kachina dolls are not idols, but are made for the education of children, or as fertility charms for women.

SIO HUMIS   SIO HUMIS TAAMÛ

SIO AVATC HOYA   WÜWÜYOMO

Hopi kachinas.

Further reading:

Fewkes, Jesse Walter. *Hopi Kachinas.* New York: Dover Publications, 1985. First published 1903.

Hultkrantz, Ake. *Native Religions of North America.* San Francisco: Harper & Row, 1987.

Tyler, Hamilton A. *Pueblo Gods and Myths.* Norman, Okla.: University of Oklahoma Press, 1964.

Kaczmarek, Dale (1952–   ) American lay psychical researcher, especially of phenomena associated with ghosts and poltergeists; president of the GHOST RESEARCH SOCIETY in Oak Lawn, Illinois.

Dale Kaczmarek was born in Chicago on December 19, 1952. He graduated from high school and later served in the U.S. Army from 1972 to 1974. While stationed at Fort Polk, Louisiana, he attended the University of Louisiana-Nagadoches. Following his discharge, he returned to the Chicago area. Kaczmarek has worked as a manager for the McDonald's fast food chain and K-Mart retail merchandise chain, and as a frozen food selector loader for Certified Grocers Midwest. He lives in Oak Lawn, Illinois, a suburb of Chicago, with his wife, nee Ruth Bosley, whom he married in 1992.

Kaczmarek's early childhood interest in the paranormal was stimulated by his Army post as a chaplain's assistant, which brought him into contact with diverse spiritual beliefs and views. After returning to Chicago, he attended numerous lectures and programs on the paranormal, and through them met Martin V. Riccardo, founder of the Ghost Tracker's Club, which later became the Ghost Research Society. Kaczmarek became the organization's first research director. Since 1982, he has served as president of the GRS, as well as editor of its journal, *The Ghost Tracker's Newsletter.*

Kaczmarek investigates Chicago-area reports of hauntings by ghosts and poltergeists. He also has devoted particular attention to researching ghost lights around the United States and in other countries.

He believes in survival after death and in the existence of ghosts. He has a two-fold definition of ghosts, dividing them into categories of ghosts and apparitions. Ghosts include the disembodied spirits of once-living persons, as well as phantom replays of events. Ghosts manifest as sounds, smells, tactile sensations and images that have no recognizable forms, such as streaks of light, cloudy patches and balls of light. The phantom replays are lingering

Dale Kaczmarek. Courtesy Dale Kaczmarek.

vibrations of events in certain locations that can be sensed by certain persons under as yet unknown conditions. Neither ghosts nor phantom replays have any intellligent center and cannot engage in interactive communication. Apparitions, however, are recognizable and often lifelike forms of humans, animals and objects. Human and animal apparitions are earthbound spirits, and mediumistic communication with them is possible; human apparitions can engage in interactive communication. Kaczmarek acknowledges that it is difficult to eliminate the possibility of thought-forms—thoughts and emotions among the living—that a psychic or medium might receive and attribute to a ghost.

Kaczmarek believes that poltergeists are not nonphysical entities, but are the "psychic explosions" of human agents, most likely females from adolescence to late teens (see POLTERGEIST). Poltergeist phenomena, such as rappings, movement of objects and apports (q.v.) also occur in some ghost hauntings, and are attached to a site.

He has observed a trend toward greater public openness to the possibility of ghosts and poltergeists. Reasons, he says, include greater media coverage and more credible reporting; movies and other entertainment pertaining to the paranormal; and interest in so-called New Age topics.

Kaczmarek is a contributor to *True Tales of the Unknown: The Uninvited*, edited by Sharon Jarvis (1989). He conducts ghost bus tours, called "Excursions Into The Unknown," in the Chicagoland area. He is a member of the Society for the Investigation of the Unexplained, the International Fortean Organization and the American Association-Electronic Voice Phenomena.

Kardec, Allan (1804–1869)

The pseudonym of French physician Hippolyte Leon Denizard Rivail, who founded SPIRITISM (also known as Kardecism) and promoted psychic healing.

Born in Lyons, France in 1804, Rivail was the son of a barrister. By 1850, he had become a practiced doctor and writer but was intrigued by the Spiritualist fervor sweeping across Europe. He participated in seances with two daughters of a friend, but he eventually sat with Celina Japhet, formerly Celina Bequet, a professional somnambulist.

During these sessions, spirits speaking through Japhet supposedly revealed to Rivail his past lives in which he was known as Allan and Kardec. Automatic writing scripts produced while in trance explained the necessity of compulsory reincarnation. The spirits also exhorted Rivail, now Kardec, to publish these truths in *Le Livre des Esprits (The Spirits' Book)*, in 1856.

The 1857 revised version became the guidebook of spiritist philosophy, appearing in more than 20 editions. Drawing on the communications of spirits, Kardec expanded Spiritualism beyond mere survival after death to claim that reincarnation through many lives was necessary to achieve spiritual progress and to better understand and heal current suffering—especially epilepsy, schizophrenia and multiple personality disorder—most of which was caused by the interference from past incarnations.

As a consequence, Kardec—described as rather unimaginative and cold and a logical reasoner—accepted spirit communication on faith and denied the need for physical manifestation or investigative proof. Through the monthly magazine *La Revue Spirite*, which he founded, and the Society of Psychologic Studies, of which he was president, he actively discouraged the kind of psychical research prevalent in Britain or America.

Following on the success of *Le Livre des Esprits*, Kardec published *Le Livre des Mediums (The Mediums' Book)* in 1864; *The Gospel as Explained by Spirits*, also in 1864; *Heaven and Hell*, in 1865; *Genesis*, in 1867; and *Experimental Spiritism and Spiritualist Philosophy* not long after. In 1881 his English translator and supporter, Ann Blackwell, published *The Four Gospels*, a three-volume work described as further explanations of Kardec's religious philosophy.

Shortly before his death in 1869, Kardec organized "The Joint Stock Company for the Continuation of the Works of Allan Kardec" with the power to buy and sell stock, receive donations and bequests and continue the publication of *La Revue Spirite*.

European Spiritism faded with the passing of Allan Kardec, replaced by Spiritualism and the appeal of physical phenomena. Kardecism remains a potent force in Brazil, however, with Kardecist healing centers operating alongside conventional hospitals. Many Brazilians, professing Catholicism, still claim to be *espiritas*.

Further reading:

Doyle, Sir Arthur Conan. *The History of Spiritualism, Vol. I and II*. New York: Arno Press, 1975.

Fodor, Nandor. *An Encyclopaedia of Psychic Science*. Secaucus, N.J.: The Citadel Press, 1966. First published 1933.

Guiley, Rosemary Ellen. *Harper's Encyclopedia of Mystical and Paranormal Experience*. San Francisco: HarperSanFrancisco, 1991.

Playfair, Guy Lyon. *The Unknown Power*. New York: Pocket Books, 1975.

Kardecism See SPIRITISM.

kelpie

In Scottish folklore, a malevolent water spirit believed to inhabit every lake and stream, and a death omen if seen. According to lore, kelpies usually appear in the shape of a horse, but may also assume the form of a shaggy-looking man. They are invariably terrifying to humans.

As horses, they appear on lake and river banks, grazing peacefully, and lure travelers to mount them, only to plunge into the waters and drown the hapless victims. Or, the kelpies plunge the victims into the water, where they eat them, save for the livers, which float to the surface. Kelpies also jump on solitary riders and try to crush them in their grip. They have even been said to tear people into pieces and eat them. They make sounds like thunder to frighten travelers.

When in the form of a horse, a kelpie sometimes has a magic bridle. Anyone who forces a kelpie to do something against its will, however, risks being cursed by it and meeting with nothing but misfortune in the future.

To see a kelpie is a harbinger of death by drowning, and nothing will prevent the tragedy from coming to pass. In one Scottish legend called "The Hour is come but not the Man," a kelpie took the form of a female nymph by a false ford in the River Conan in Ross-shire. A group of reapers in a nearby field saw the water spirit as it called out, "The hour is come but not the man," and then plunged into the waters. Just then, a rider on a horse dashed up to the false ford as though to dive in after the kelpie, but the reapers interceded, stopped the horse and dragged the man, kicking and screaming, into a nearby church. They told him they would keep him locked there for an hour—the "Ill Hour," they called it, as the kelpie was trying to work evil for that period of time. When the hour was up, the reapers returned to the church, only to find their man dead—he had fallen into a stone trough of water and drowned himself. Other versions of this legend are found in Britain, Norway and Denmark.

Further reading:
Briggs, Katherine. *An Encyclopedia of Fairies: Hobgoblins, Brownies, Bogies, and Other Supernatural Creatures.* New York: Pantheon Books, 1976.
Leach, Maria, and Jerome Fried, eds. *Funk & Wagnalls Standard Dictionary of Folklore, Mythology, and Legend.* San Francisco: Harper & Row, 1979.

keres   The spirits of the dead in ancient Greece. It was believed that they escaped from the pithos, the jars used to contain the bodies of the dead, and devoted themselves to pestering the living. They were exorcised by ritual and incantation. Sticky tar was painted on doorframes to catch them and prevent them from entering a dwelling. Plato observed,

"There are many fair things in the life of mortals, but in most of them there are as it were adherent *keres* which pollute and disfigure them."

In mythology, *keres* are akin to goddesses of death who originally escaped from Pandora's box. They served the will of the gods, and their chief functions were to carry off the corpses of the dead and to afflict the living with disease and illness.

Kidd, James (1879–1949?)   American prospector who disappeared in 1949, and left a will stating that his estate of nearly $200,000 should be given to scientific research to prove the survival of the human soul after death. The will was contested and the money sought by numerous parties in a controversial trial nearly 20 years later.

That a poorly educated, reclusive miner would bequeath his estate to researching the soul created a mystery that was never solved. Little is known about Kidd. He arrived in Arizona in 1920, and lived alone in a rented room. He worked at a copper mine and prospected. He never married. He told others that he was from Ogdensburg, New York, though no records exist of his birth there. He never gave any indication of metaphysical interests.

On November 9, 1949, he went out to prospect at his claim and never returned. His body was never found; it was speculated that he perished in a fall into a canyon in the Superstition mountains.

Seven years later, when Kidd was declared legally dead, authorities gathered together what was an astonishing amount of assets in cash and stocks: slightly more than $174,000 dollars. A safety deposit box held his unwitnessed will, written in his own hand on lined notebook paper. It read:

> this is my first and only will and is dated the second of January 1946. I have no heirs and have not married in my life and after all my funeral expenses have been paid and #100. one hundred dollars to some preacher of the gospel to say fare well at my grave sell all my property which is all in cash and stocks with E.F. Hutton Co Phoenix some in safety deposit box, and have this balance money go in a research or some scientific proof of a soul of the human body which leaves at death I think in time their can be a Photograph of soul leaving the human at death, James Kidd

The will was declared legal. Relatives of Kidd contested and attempted to have the will declared invalid and the estate divided up among themselves. In 1964, the University of Life Church, an Arizona nonprofit organization, filed suit against the heirs apparent in support of the will. These suits were the beginnings of a lengthy court battle over the money by numerous interested parties.

Kidd's will was probated in Superior Court in Phoenix in 1967. Judge Robert L. Myers heard 133 petitions from various individuals, universities and research organizations, all claiming to be best suited to carry out Kidd's intent. The media called it "the Ghost Trial of the Century." Myers awarded the estate to the Barrow Neurological Institute of Phoenix, stating that they were best equipped to carry out the research "in the combined fields of medical science, psychiatry, and psychology."

The ruling was appealed. A higher court awarded a large portion of the estate to the AMERICAN SOCIETY FOR PSYCHICAL RESEARCH, which used some of it to finance research in deathbed visions (q.v.)

Science nonetheless has been unable to prove that the soul exists and survives death.

Further reading:
Fuller, John G. *The Great Soul Trial.* New York: Macmillan, 1969.

King, John   Probably the busiest spirit of the dead in the history of Spiritualism, John King served as the spirit control for many major 19th-century mediums, including the DAVENPORT BROTHERS, Eusapia PALLADINO, Mary Marshall, Agnes GUPPY, Frank Herne and Charles Williams, Mr. and Mrs. Nelson Holmes, W.T. STEAD and even Madame Helena P. Blavatsky. His erstwhile daughter, Katie, performed similar duties principally for Florence COOK but also worked for Herne and Williams and the Holmeses in Philadelphia.

According to his own account given from the Other Side, John King had been Henry Owen Morgan, the English pirate who plundered Jamaica in the 17th century and then became the island's governor after being knighted by King Charles II. He first appeared as John King, the spirit, in 1850, in the gunflash of young Ira Davenport's pistol. The Davenport Brothers called him John, or Johnnie, King, and he acted as their main control and master of ceremonies throughout their career. King allegedly pushed the brothers to give performances in large halls and reputedly gave them the construction specifications for their famous CABINET.

But King was an adept moonlighter and an eager participant in the common practice of spirit-lifting: borrowing another medium's spirit control. In 1852, while still guiding the Davenports, he appeared to Jonathan Koons in backwoods Ohio to lead the raucous gatherings in the Koonses' Spirit Room. To Koons, King introduced himself as King Number One, chief of a band of 165 spirits described as part of an ancient and primal order of man that antedated Adam by many thousand years. King Numbers Two and Three were Number One's adjutants. King Number Three also called himself the Servant and Scholar of God.

King relinquished his royal ancestors after his experiences in Ohio to appear at the London seances of Mrs. Guppy and her protégés, Frank Herne and Charles Williams. He also regularly appeared to Mr. and Mrs. Nelson Holmes, both in London and in Philadelphia. Guppy first heard from King through direct voice at a seance conducted by Mary Marshall. King had been communicating by direct voice mediumship and trumpet—a conduit he is credited with inventing—to both the Koonses and the Davenports since the mid-1850s. By 1872, King appeared regularly to Guppy and to Herne-Williams fully materialized. Sitters at a Herne-Williams seance could shake the former blackguard's hand, and once King materialized so completely that a sketch was made. Working with Katie King, the two performed the greatest apport feat of all time, allegedly transporting Guppy herself to a seance at the Herne-Williams home.

While staying at the Nelson Holmeses, Madame Blavatsky became acquainted with John King. His swashbuckling past appealed to her, and he frequently appeared in her early letters and Spiritualist meetings. V.S. Solovyoff, a Russian journalist and longtime friend of Blavatsky, speculated that the Mahatma Koot Hoomi was nothing more than John King dressed in Eastern clothing. (The mahatmas were, according to Blavatsky, spiritual masters who transmitted the teachings that formed the basis of the Theosophical Society she co-founded.)

In the early 1870s, King added Naples to his itinerary. The Italian medium Signor Damiani found the psychic gifts of Eusapia Palladino remarkable, and his wife heard from John King at a seance that she should seek out a powerful medium named Eusapia; he even gave Palladino's street address to Signora Damiani. From that time on, King was Palladino's principal control. The scientists that investigated Palladino throughout her career described King as most anxious to help her produce convincing phenomena. Speaking in Italian through the medium, King claimed that Palladino was his daughter reincarnated. One sitter, a Chevalier Francesco Graus, testified that King psychically drew out Graus's cerebral fluid during a seance and administered it to Palladino to relieve her agitation and anxiety.

In most Spiritualist circles, however, John's daughter was Katie King, the former Annie Owen Morgan. Quite a colorful character herself, Katie died at about age 23 after murdering her two children and committing various other crimes. She said she had returned to try and expiate her sins, and attached herself mainly to Florence Cook for that purpose.

Like her father, Katie first appeared to the Davenport Brothers. A sitter at one of the Davenports' seances, Robert Cooper, described Katie as a person of low social station who talked too much and had little wit. She next surfaced in London at the Herne-Williams gatherings but was believed to be a Negro after a black hand materialized during a seance. As such, Katie's true parentage is cloudy. Some called Katie John's sister. Florence Cook, Katie's most famous medium, met her at a Herne-Williams sitting and appropriated Katie as her own thereafter. Cook's Katie possessed much more charm and beauty than the woman at the Davenports' sittings.

Katie also guided the Nelson Holmeses in Philadelphia, but after a scandal in which a local woman, Eliza White, claimed to have impersonated Katie, she no longer served as their control.

John King's true identity was no less obscure than Katie's. Sir Arthur Conan DOYLE described King as tall and swarthy with a full black beard. He had a deep voice and a distinctive rap, and was a master of many languages, even Georgian. Doyle had a picture of the historical Sir Henry Morgan from a book on pirates and found the likeness to be completely different from the materialized King. In King's defense, however, Doyle said that King had revealed knowledge of Morgan's will during a seance with a lady from Jamaica, calling the document his. Doyle also commented that men who pursued rude, open-air occupations in life seemed to be drawn to spirit activity after death. Both John and Katie appeared for the last time in February 1930 at a seance conducted by Thomas Glendenning HAMILTON in Winnipeg.

Why would a 17th-century pirate and his daughter be the ones to promote spirit communication? In his book *Mind Over Space*, Nandor FODOR speculated that the Kings were not reincarnations of anybody, but were archetypes of psychic manifestation, able to appear at any seance and produce phenomena under the leadership of a master medium. Author Ruth Brandon postulated a simpler explanation: once the Kings had re-established contact with the human world, they acquired a taste for it.

Further reading:
Brandon, Ruth. *The Spiritualists.* New York: Alfred A. Knopf, 1983.
Brown, Slater. *The Heyday of Spiritualism.* New York: Hawthorn Books, 1970.
Doyle, Sir Arthur Conan. *The History of Spiritualism, Vol. I and II.* New York: Arno Press, 1975 (originally published by George H. Doran Co., 1926).
Fodor, Nandor. *An Encyclopaedia of Psychic Science.* Secaucus, N.J.: The Citadel Press, 1966. First published 1933.
———. *Mind Over Space.* New York: The Citadel Press, 1962.
Mysteries of the Unknown: Spirit Summonings. Alexandria, Va.: Time-Life Books, 1989.
Somerlott, Robert. *"Here, Mr. Splitfoot": An Informal Exploration into Modern Occultism.* New York: The Viking Press, 1971.

King, Katie   See FLORENCE COOK.

knocker   In the folklore of Cornwall, England, a spirit that lives and works in mines, especially tin mines. Knockers are friendly and helpful, but can be mischievous; they are not evil and malicious like the German KOBOLD mine spirit. Knockers also are called BUCCAS (the Cornish term for sea-going GOBLINS), as well as Gathorns, Knackers, Nickers, Nuggies and Spriggans. In mines north of Cornwall, the spirits are called BLUE-CAPS and Cutty Soams. In American folklore, mine spirits are known as tommyknockers.

Knockers are so named because of the knocking sounds they make in mine shafts as they work, perhaps in imitation of human miners. They are believed to be the ghosts of Jews who worked the mines, or of the Jews who crucified Christ and were punished by being sent to work below the earth. Historically, Jews did not work in Cornish mines until the 11th and 12th centuries. Perhaps because of their alleged associations with punishment for Christ, knockers cannot tolerate the sign of the cross, and so miners avoid marking anything with a cross or an X. The aversion may also stem from the Christian displacement of pagan religions and spirit beliefs.

According to lore, knockers are industrious beings, toiling away through the night. They are associated with rich lodes of ore; thus, miners pay attention to the locations where they heard the supernatural knockings. Knocker laughter and footsteps are said to be heard, and sometimes the spirits are said to manifest in doll-sized form. They have been said to help miners in trouble. Whistling, however, offends them; consequently, it is unlucky to whistle in mines. Food and tallow must be left for them in payment, otherwise they will cause trouble.

In American mines, tommyknockers mirror the behavior of their Cornish counterparts, though some have been attributed vicious streaks akin to the kobolds. In the late 19th century, the Mamie R. Mine on Raven Hill in Cripple Creek, Colorado was said to be haunted by malicious tommyknockers that beckoned to miners and then jumped up and down on beams until they collapsed upon the men. The tommyknockers also were blamed for snapping cables and for premature blasts, and they were said to snicker at the miners as they wrought their evil deeds.

Friendlier tommyknockers in other Colorado mines were said to be protective and helpful, although they yielded to practical jokes upon occasion. Miners generally regarded their supernatural companions with fondness, and liked to talk about them and make space for them at the bar at the end of a shift. Tommyknocker stories frequently were written up in the press.

Mine spirits of all names are said to continue to haunt abandoned mines.

Further reading:

Briggs, Katherine. *An Encyclopedia of Fairies: Hobgoblins, Brownies, Bogies, and Other Supernatural Creatures.* New York: Pantheon Books, 1976.

Folklore, Myths and Legends of Britain. London: Reader's Digest Assn. Ltd., 1973.

Martin, Maryjoy. *Twilight Dwellers: Ghosts, Ghouls & Goblins of Colorado.* Boulder: Pruett Publishing Co., 1985.

kobold In German folklore, a mischievous spirit, occasionally malicious. There are two types of kobolds: a household kobold that is comparable to the BROWNIE and BOGGART of British folklore, and a mine kobold that is comparable to the Cornish KNOCKER and the American tommyknocker.

The household kobold, when in a good mood, helps with chores, looks after horses, finds lost objects and sings to children to keep them occupied. Food must be left for him, otherwise he becomes angry and turns to pranks, such as pushing someone over just as they stoop to pick something up, or hiding household objects. Kobolds are given names, such as Heinze, Chimmeken and Walther.

In Saxon lore, a *biersal* is a type of household kobold who lives in the cellar. In exchange for a daily jug of beer, he will clean bottles and jugs.

The mine kobolds are almost always evil and malicious, and try to hinder the miners by causing accidents and rockfalls.

Further reading:

Haining, Peter. *A Dictionary of Ghost Lore.* Englewood Cliffs, N.J.: Prentice-Hall, 1984.

Leach, Maria, and Jerome Fried, eds. *Funk & Wagnalls Standard Dictionary of Folklore, Mythology, and Legend.* San Francisco: Harper & Row, 1979.

L

La Llorona (also called **The Weeping Woman)** In Mexican folklore, a spectral weeping woman who drifts about at night looking for her murdered child or children. *Llorona* is Spanish for "weeper."

There are numerous versions of the Llorona legend, which also exists in the American Southwest and as far away as the Philippines. According to one version, the ghost is searching for her lost boy and is lost herself. In another version, she murdered the boy and now wanders about demented. Or, she murdered the child and therefore is condemned to eternal wanderings as a ghost. In still another version, she once had several children but fell in love with a man who wanted none. To please him, she drowned them all, then drowned her self.

Most folklorists believe that the legend derives from Aztec mythology. The goddess Civacoatl (also known as Chihuacohuatl or Tonantzin) dressed in white and carried a cradle on her shoulders. She walked among Aztec women and left the cradle, which was discovered to contain an arrowhead in the shape of a sacrificial knife. Civacoatl also walked the cities, screaming and crying, eventually disappearing into lakes. Another theory points to a historical basis for the legend. According to that story, which took place in Mexico City around 1550, Doña Luis de Olveros, an Indian princess, fell in love with a nobleman, Don Nuno de Montesclaros. She bore him two children (some versions say twins). Montesclaros promised to marry her, but instead married someone else. The Doña visited him on the night of his wedding party and was spurned by him. Insane with rage and humiliation, she went home and stabbed her children to death with a dagger that Montesclaros had given her previously as a gift. She then wandered the streets, in torn and bloody clothing, crying for her children. She was found guilty of sorcery and was hanged. Her ghost is said to be cursed to wander the earth forever looking for her children.

La Llorona has numerous shapes and appearances. Usually she has a seductive figure and dresses either in white or black and has long black hair. She has long fingernails, sometimes described as claws. She is faceless, or has the face of a bat or a horse. She also is described as a vampire. In the El Paso, Texas area, she has appeared as a faceless woman in white with shiny claws.

La Llorona's mournful, shrouded ghost usually is seen by riverbanks, the woods and along deserted streets, especially at midnight, the traditional "witching hour." Sometimes she is seen in daylight. She may not bother the living, or may ask someone if her missing child has been seen. She often entices men when they are drunk and out and about lonely areas. As a phantom hitchhiker, she sometimes waits along lonely roads and tells motorists who pick her up her woeful tale of her lost or murdered child. She is feared, however, for, like the demon Lilith of Hebrew lore, she preys upon young men and kills them.

La Llorona also may be compared to the banshee of Irish lore, in that to see her presages one's death within a year, or, at the very least, bad luck within the year.

A version of La Llorona has been reported as far north in the United States as Gary, Indiana; it may be two ghost legends, La Llorona and the phantom hitchhiker, blended into one. A woman in white, often said to be La Llorona, has been reported drifting about Cudahey, a suburban community once largely populated by Mexican-Americans who worked in the steel mills. The ghost is said to have killed her illegitimate children in Gary by drowning them in the Calumet River. She usually hitches rides to the Calumet Harbor, disappearing from the car en route. Sometimes, she is said simply to appear in a car and vanish a few minutes later.

Further reading:

Leach, Maria, and Jerome Fried, eds. *Funk & Wagnalls Standard Dictionary of Folklore, Mythology, and Legend.* San Francisco: Harper & Row, 1979.

McNeil, W.K., comp. and ed. *Ghost Stories from the American South.* New York: Dell, 1985.

Scott, Beth, and Michael Norman. *Haunted Heartland.* New York: Warner Books, 1985.

labyrinth   See MAZES.

Lady Lovibond   See PHANTOM SHIPS.

Lafitte, Jean   See PHANTOM SHIPS.

Lang, Andrew (1844–1912)   Author of more than 70 books and hundreds of magazine articles on classical subjects, mythology, folklore, anthropology, psychical research and religion. A scholar by training, an artist by inclination, and a writer by profession, Lang believed passionately in both psychical research and anthropology, and never lost an opportunity to point out the relevance of each to the other.

Andrew Lang was born in the town of Selkirk, near the Scottish border with England, on March 31, 1844. Intellectually precocious, he learned to read when he was only four years old. Fairy tales were among his favorites, and he later wrote that as a youngster he "knew all the fairies in *A Midsummer Night's Dream*, and every ghost in Sir Walter Scott." No special incident seems to have triggered his interest in the paranormal. It was simply something he grew up with—perhaps not surprising, given the place and time.

When he was 10, Lang was sent to Edinburgh Academy, a preparatory school, and at 17 he went to St. Andrews University. Two years later, in 1864, he was admitted to Balliol College, Oxford. Upon graduation in 1868, he accepted a teaching fellowship at Merton College. There he stayed until 1875, when he married Leonora Blanche Alleyne, moved to London, and embarked on his journalistic career.

Lang contributed an important article on "Apparitions" to the ninth edition of the *Encyclopaedia Britannica* (1875). In this, he argued that veridical apparitions were not satisfactorily explained as coincidental but suggested that crisis apparitions, which are seen about the time of the agent's death, were telepathically induced hallucinations, an argument very close to that which was to be made 11 years later by Edmund GURNEY in *Phantasms of the Living* (1885). Although he did not discuss his own experience, Lang's views may have been influenced by an apparition he had observed a few years earlier, in 1869. He had seen an Oxford professor standing by a street light in front of the college where he had taught at the same time this man lay dying elsewhere.

In *Cock Lane and Common Sense* (1894), Lang championed the work of both anthropologists and members of the SOCIETY FOR PSYCHICAL RESEARCH (which had been founded in 1882), even while he chided them for ignoring each other's data. His title was taken from an 18th-century London poltergeist case (see COCK LANE GHOST), which Lang showed to be strikingly similar in form to cases reported from tribal societies around the world. The book met a chilly but predictable response from both sides. Anthropologists continued to reject the idea that there was any substance to claimed paranormal experiences, while psychical researchers replied that strictly anecdotal accounts such as those commonly reported by anthropologists could not hope to reach a satisfactory standard of evidence. Evidence of belief or experience alone was not the same as establishing paranormality.

The Book of Dreams and Ghosts (1897) was aimed at a more general audience. Lang brought together a variety of real-life ghost stories from throughout history and around the world, arranged in chapters that progress from dreams and visions to hallucinations, apparitions and hauntings. He included a chapter on "wraiths," as he called the apparitions of living persons. Again he did not comment on his personal experience, but it is perhaps noteworthy that Lang had seen such an entity himself. This was a girl, a relative of his, whom he saw dressed in blue, crossing a brilliantly lit hall. Although he called out to her, she said nothing, and he went on in to the dining room, where he found her dressed in white, seated at the table.

In *The Making of Religion* (1898), based on his series of Gifford lectures at the University of Edinburgh, Lang renewed his attempt to bring psychical research and anthropology together. He also discussed his own crystal gazing experiments. After some number of trials with different people, he discovered one woman, whom he called "Miss Angus," who was able to see in the crystal the image of a person or scene related to a person who was present with her at the time. The images Miss Angus saw were not necessarily in the mind of the sitter, and might contain veridical information not known to the sitter at the time. Thus, they suggested the operation of some extensive network of telepathy, what today would be called SUPER ESP. This led Lang to doubt the evidence for survival after death from the trance communications of Leonora PIPER, which some SPR researchers found convincing.

Lang was one of the most widely read writers of his day, and he reached both the public and scholars. It is of some significance for the SPR, therefore, that he never lost the chance to publicize its work. Although Lang never succeeded in bringing anthropology and psychical research together in the way he would have liked, he did much to raise awareness of the issues. He was the principal contributor of articles on psychical research topics to the great 11th edition of the *Encyclopaedia Britannica* (1910), and W.H.R. Rivers, an anthropologist of stature, wrote that thanks to Lang's efforts, psychical research was no longer a disreputable field of study.

Lang showed in his handling of his case material that he was aware of appropriate standards of evidence, and thus earned the respect of the SPR as well. Although he was late in joining the Society (he did not join until 1904), he contributed many articles to its publications, including one on the "voices" of Joan of Arc (later incorporated into his book, *The Maid of France*, 1908). He was elected president of the SPR in 1911.

In 1901 Lang saw a third wraith, which he described in the *Monthly Review* for March 1903. But he regretted that he had had so few such experiences. In one of his magazine articles, he wrote, "I have passed nights in a haunted castle, with the whole of the haunted wing to myself, and that when I was young, ill, and over-worked: I have occupied the ghostly chamber where the original of Dickens's Miss Haversham lived and died in her mouldy bridal raiment; but in spite of expecting with fear and trembling all sorts of horrors, I never saw or heard anything to establish the existence of a bogey."

A few months before his death, Lang saw his final apparition: his family's death omen, a monstrous cat. He died on July 20, 1912 of a heart attack, while on a visit to his native Scotland, and was buried in St. Andrews.

Further reading:

Cocq, Antonius Petrus Leonardus de. *Andrew Lang, A Nineteenth Century Anthropologist.* Tilburg, Netherlands: Zwijsen, 1968.

Gauld, Alan. "Andrew Lang as a Psychical Researcher." *Journal of the Society for Psychical Research* 52 (1983):161–76.

Green, Roger Lancelyn. *Andrew Lang: A Critical Biography.* Leicester, Eng.: Edmund Ward, 1946.

Haynes, Renee. *The Society of Psychical Research, 1882–1892: A History.* London: William Heinemann Ltd., 1982.

lares   In the beliefs of ancient Romans, good spirits of the dead. Lares were believed to take up occu-

pancy in households, cities, or regions, and to act as protectors. There also were lares for the public in general. The household lares were members of a family, and the most important spirit was that of the founder of the family. Lares were worshipped privately along with penates (household guardian deities) and manes, a category which included both ancestral spirits and underworld deities. Food offerings were made to them at every meal. As household and ancestral spirits, the lares are similar to the ancestral spirits of the dead in Shinto. As spirits of the dead, they are similar to the djinn, the demonic children of Lilith and the Devil.

See also MANES.

larvae   In ancient Rome, evil spirits which sought to harm and frighten the living. Larvae usually were associated with lemures, the evil spirits of the dead.

See LEMURES.

Laveau, Marie (1794?–1881); Laveau Glapion, Marie (1827–1897)   The most famous voodoo queens, mother and daughter by the same name, reigned over New Orleans in the late 19th century, and in death are believed to haunt the city still. Their lives have become legend.

Marie Laveau I reputedly was born in New Orleans in 1794, the illegitimate daughter of Charles Laveau and Margeurite Carcantel. A mulatto of mixed black, white and Indian blood, she was from birth a free woman of color. As a young woman, she was tall and statuesque, with curling black hair, flashing black eyes, reddish skin and "good" features, meaning more white than Negroid. On August 4, 1819 she married Jacques Paris, a quadroon (three-fourths white, one-fourth black) free man of color from Saint Domingue (now Haiti). They lived in a house in the 1900 block of North Rampart Street that had been given to them by Charles Laveau as part of his daughter's dowry.

Not long after the marriage, Paris disappeared, perhaps returning to his homeland. Marie began calling herself the Widow Paris, and supported herself by working as a hairdresser to the wealthy white and Creole women of New Orleans. Her clients confided their most intimate secrets to Marie, about their husbands, their lovers, their estates, their husbands' mistresses, their business affairs, their fears of insanity and of anyone discovering a strain of Negro blood in their ancestry. At this time, Marie also was likely involved in voodoo activities, for she took careful note of these confessions, and later used them to strengthen her powers as voodoo queen. About five years after Paris's disappearance, his death was reported, but there is no certification of burial.

Around 1826, Marie became the lover of Louis Christophe Duminy de Glapion, another quadroon from Saint Domingue, who lived with her on North Rampart until his death in June 1855. They never married, but they produced 15 illegitimate children. After establishing her relationship with Duminy de Glapion, Marie gave up hairdressing and began to devote all her energies to becoming the supreme voodoo queen of New Orleans.

The voodoo practiced by black African slaves was a mixture of African and Caribbean rites. The rites were held in secret deep in the bayous. Stories circulated that they involved worship of a snake called Zombi, orgiastic dancing, drinking and lovemaking. Nearly a third of the worshippers were whites who sought magical power for their own ends.

By the early 1830s, there were many voodoo queens in New Orleans, fighting over control of the Sunday Congo dances and the secret ceremonies out at Lake Pontchartrain. Marie handily bested them all—some said by powerful magic. A devout Catholic, she added elements of Catholic worship, such as holy water, incense, statues of the saints and Christian prayers, to the already sensational voodoo ceremonies.

She turned the rites at Lake Ponchartrain into large spectacles. The police, the press, young New Orleans roues and any other thrill-seekers interested in forbidden fun were invited to attend, provided they paid an admission fee. Marie added to the carnival atmosphere with such acts as praying over a black coffin and sacrificing roosters. Meanwhile, other, more secret orgies were organized for wealthy white men looking for beautiful black, mulatto and quadroon mistresses. Marie then gained control of the dances at Congo Square, entering the gated area before any of the other dancers and performing with her 20-foot snake for the fascinated onlookers.

Eventually, the information learned from her former hairdressing clients, her considerable knowledge of spells and her own style and flair made Marie the most powerful woman in the city, sought by both whites and blacks for magical concoctions and advice. She charged whites high fees, but few blacks paid for services.

Stories about Marie abound. Most of the tales are no doubt exaggerations, but some of the best are these, as told in Robert Tallant's *Voodoo in New Orleans* and *Mysterious Marie Laveau, Voodoo Queen* by Raymond J. Martinez:

Around 1830, the son of a very prominent and aristocratic New Orleans family apparently raped a young girl of lower but respectable class. Evidence against the young man was strong; out of desperation, either the father or the son (both are credited) went to Marie Laveau to enlist her help in an acquit-

tal. The father promised Marie a new house if she could succeed.

At dawn of the morning of the trial, Marie went to pray at St. Louis Cathedral, remaining at the altar rail for several hours with three Guinea peppers in her mouth. Then she sneaked into the Cabildo, the old seat of French-Spanish justice, and placed the peppers under the judge's chair. On his doorstep Marie placed a gris-gris (a charm bag) of powdered brick, and she pinned a note on the front door declaring the young man's innocence. She even brazenly signed the note, believing in her own power and prestige.

The jury reportedly was made up of other young, aristocratic Creole playboys, many of whom had committed similar crimes but had not been punished. The prosecuting attorney pleaded passionately for conviction, appealing to the jury's Biblical sense of right and wrong. Marie watched silently from the gallery, finally flipping a piece of paper containing one of her hairs onto the prosecutor's shoulder. The verdict: not guilty.

In gratitude, the father kept his promise and gave Marie a new house on St. Ann Street, in the French Quarter near Congo Square. Marie and her family, including Glapion, lived there until she died in 1881, and it pleased Marie to claim that the cottage was one of the oldest in New Orleans, part of the Laveau family for seven generations. The house became voodoo's headquarters, and the small outbuildings probably housed assignations between other white men and their black lovers.

But this is not the end of the story. The freed young man began attending church to give thanks for his good fortune, and finally repudiated his wild friends in remorse for his sins. He determined to marry the woman he had wronged, but she refused. Again the young man appealed to Marie Laveau, who promised him that the girl would marry him within one month. Marie made the man a gris-gris bag containing ''love powder'' (talcum), feathers, pulverized lizard eggs and donkey hair, which he had to wear around his waist. Then she took hair from various parts of the young man's body and spread them on the lady's doorstep.

The lady continued to spurn the young man, but unfortunately she met him coming into church as she was leaving. She turned to run, fell and sprained her ankle. He tenderly picked her up, begging her to let him get a doctor and take her home. Impressed with his solicitude, she yielded, and he kissed her. The next day she married him, albeit limping down the aisle.

Another affair of the heart concerned a wealthy old bachelor who was madly in love with the daughter of another Creole gentleman. The girl was young enough to be the man's granddaughter, and rejected his advances. But her father, suffering from financial reversal, tried to convince his daughter of the benefits of the match, and when she refused, he locked her up in a cabin near the lake. Every night the old man, attended by the girl's father, came to the cabin and tried to woo her, but still she refused. Her father cajoled, threatened and even beat her, but she held fast, swearing to die first. She had already given her heart to a dashing young adventurer, who was expected to return from the West Indies any day with his new-found fortune.

Having no other alternatives, the father and the old suitor turned to Marie Laveau, who promised that the wedding would take place. She gave love powders to the father to put in the girl's food, and made the old man a gris-gris containing the dried testicles of a black cat. He was to wear the bag near his own genitals to cure his impotency and bring back virility. Finally, Marie advised patience, telling the men to refrain from begging for the girl's hand for two weeks.

At the end of a fortnight, the girl, very pale and weak, agreed to marry the old man. Both men were overjoyed, and plans commenced for the wedding to take place at once. Two weeks later, all of New Orleans society crowded St. Louis Cathedral for the ceremony, gossiping about the lovely young bride taking the hand of an old man with bent knees and a toupee. Everyone was invited to a huge reception that night at the groom's mansion, replete with champagne and rare delicacies.

As the party became livelier, the celebrants demanded that the bride and groom lead the first dance. Flushed with his conquest, he led his wife out into the ballroom and began to waltz. For a moment he was young again. Then he stopped, face turning purple, and crumpled to the floor. The bride shrieked, a doctor rushed to help, but it was too late.

The new bride inherited all the old man's fortune, enabling her to call her lover home from the West Indies. After a year of conventional mourning, they married and reportedly lived happy ever after. Questioned about her role in the affair, Marie Laveau would reply that she had promised only that "the wedding would take place."

Although love provided more business for Marie Laveau than anything else, she was also known for her work with convicted prisoners. Marie had always performed acts of Christian charity, helping Pere (Father) Antoine, New Orleans' much-beloved priest who had married her and Jacques Paris, with yellow fever victims. By the 1850s, her influence with local authorities allowed her to enter and exit the prison with impunity, taking food and solace to the men in their cells. She donated an altar to the prison chapel and decorated it with her own hands. None of these visits exhibited any outward signs of voodoo, only devout Catholicism.

In 1852, Jean Adam and Anthony Deslisle were convicted to hang for the murder of a young mulatto servant girl named Mary in the employ of a Madame Chevillon while stealing a large sum of money from Madame's home. Marie Laveau visited the condemned men every day while they awaited execution, taking them food, talking and praying. The morning of the hanging she took them a pot of gumbo and stayed until the very last minute. Then she joined the enormous crowd outside waiting to watch the execution (all executions in New Orleans were then public).

When the men were brought out, they were highly intoxicated, although Marie had not given them any obvious drinks. Deslisle shouted at the spectators—hundreds of people, with their children, enjoying the clear, sunny day and the upcoming show—that he was innocent, and begged that the people attend his funeral and see that he had a decent burial and a long funeral procession. Then he claimed he was a Frenchman, willing to die only for France and not at the hands of "barbarous" American justice. Deslisle raised his arms, stared at the gathering clouds above the gallows, screamed and fainted.

By now the clear, sunny sky had filled with heavy, black clouds. Wind roared through the trees, children cried, and one woman reportedly shouted, "It's just like the Crucifixion!" But the execution proceeded as planned. Arms bound, the men were placed in chairs on the platform, their heads covered with black hoods, and the ropes placed around their necks. Just as the executioner released the trap doors at the sheriff's signal, rain began falling in torrents and lightning filled the sky.

The crowd gasped in horror as people realized the men lay on the ground, bleeding but not dead, the ropes frayed and broken. Deslisle crawled on his hands and knees, sobbing, and Adam was unconscious. The mob surged forward, and the police had to use their clubs to force them back. Prison officials carried Deslisle and Adam back into the jail, then hauled them out 10 minutes later and tried again, this time successfully. The sky cleared as a tall woman, recognized in whispers as Marie Laveau, left the throng.

Newspaper accounts described the execution as a "painful spectacle . . . the seldomer such exhibitions are public the better." Everyone who was there, and anyone who heard the story, believed Marie Laveau had caused the storm and almost saved the lives of the murderers. The whole affair caused such an uproar that the Louisiana State Legislature outlawed public executions in the state forever.

In 1869, Marie was past 70 years of age, and her followers decided she should retire. She did not completely retreat from active service until 1875, when she entered her St. Ann Street home for the last time; she did not leave until her death in 1881. Her role as voodoo queen was assumed by one of her daughters, also named Marie Laveau, who bore a striking resemblance to her mother, save for a lighter skin.

Marie Laveau Glapion was born on February 2, 1827. It is not known whether Marie I appointed her daughter to follow her or Marie II chose the role herself. Marie II apparently lacked the warm compassion of her mother and inspired more fear and subservience. Like her mother, she started out as a hairdresser, but then graduated to running a bar and brothel on Bourbon Street between Toulouse and St. Peter streets.

Marie II continued assignations at "Maison Blanche" (White House), the house her mother had built for secret voodoo meetings and liaisons between white men and black women. The police looked the other way because they were afraid of crossing her and ending up "hoodooed" (bewitched).

One of the most important events in the New Orleans voodoo calendar was June 23, St. John's Eve, the observance of the summer solstice. The event was celebrated by voodoo rites at Bayou St. John on Lake Ponchartrain. Originally, the rites were religious, but Marie I had turned them into a circus. By the time of Marie II, most St. John's Eve rites were led by underling voodoo queens, but Marie II presided more than once.

According to one newspaper account of St. John's Eve, 1872, the crowd sang to Marie II, then built a large fire to heat a cauldron. The cauldron was filled with water from a beer barrel, salt, black pepper, a black snake cut in three pieces (representing the Trinity), a cat, a black rooster and various powders. Marie ordered everyone to undress, which they did while singing a repetitive chorus. At midnight they jumped into the lake for about half an hour to cool off, then came out and sang and danced for another hour. Marie then preached a sermon, then gave the celebrants permission for a half-hour's "recreation," or sexual intercourse.

Afterward, everyone ate and sang some more, until the signal was given to extinguish the fire under the cauldron. Four nude women threw water on the fire, then the contents of the kettle were poured back into the barrel. Marie told everyone to dress again, then she preached another sermon. By now it was daybreak, and everyone went home.

Marie I died in her St. Ann Street home on June 16, 1881. Her obituaries described her as a saintly woman who had nursed the sick and prayed incessantly with the diseased and the condemned, and said her alleged beauty had attracted the attention of Governor Claiborne, French General Humbert, Aaron Burr and even the Marquis de Lafayette. The obituaries further claimed she had lived her life in piety, surrounded by her Catholic religion, and made no mention of her voodoo activities. Even one of her surviving children, Madame Legendre, claimed her saintly mother had never practiced voodoo and in fact had despised the cult. The faithful, however, knew better.

With her mother's passing, Marie II faded into obscurity. She had been so closely identified with her mother that she apparently had little persona of her own. She continued to reign over the voodoo ceremonies among the blacks and ran the Maison Blanche, but she never regained media attention. According to legend, she drowned in a big storm in Lake Pontchartrain during the 1890s. Some people, however, claimed to see her as late as 1918.

Marie I is reportedly buried in the family crypt at St. Louis Cemetery No. 1. The cemetery is quite small, but the tomb seems to appear out of nowhere when walking among the crypts. The vault does not bear her name; according to the inscription, it belongs to "Marie Philome Glapion, deceased June 11, 1897." Nonetheless, the tomb still attracts the faithful and the curious. Petitioners leave offerings of food, money and flowers, then ask for Marie's help after turning around three times and marking a cross with red brick on the stone.

One popular legend holds that Marie I never died, but changed herself into a huge black crow which still flies over the cemetery. The crow's head feathers supposedly stick up in tufts, after the fashion in which Marie wore a *tignon*, or kerchief, over her hair, tied in seven knots with the points sticking up.

Marie II is believed to be buried in St. Louis Cemetery No. 2, where another crypt marked "Marie Laveau" bears red-brick crosses and serves as the "Wishing Vault" for young women seeking husbands. Other stories place Marie in cemeteries on Girod Street, Louisa Street and Holt Street as well.

Both Maries are said to haunt New Orleans in various human and animal forms. In addition to being seen as a crow, one or the other has been seen as an old woman in a long white dress and blue *tignon*, as a snake, and as a Newfoundland dog. The apparitions have been sighted floating up and down St. Ann Street. And on St. John's Eve, when Marie I slipped off to St. John's Bayou on Lake Ponchartrain for secret voodoo rites, residents of the bayou hear an ethereal singing and see a shadowy figure who looks like a woman clinging to a floating log.

Further reading:

Guiley, Rosemary Ellen. *The Encyclopedia of Witches and Witchcraft.* New York: Facts On File, 1989.

Tallant, Robert. *The Voodoo Queen.* Gretna, La.: Pelican Publishing Co., 1983. First published 1956.

lemures In ancient Rome, ghosts of people who died without a surviving family, or a ghost evil in nature. The lemures were one of two classes of ghosts in Roman belief (see LARES), and were associated with larvae, or evil spirits.

The Romans considered it a curse to die without surviving issue. Thus, those who did so were doomed to become lemures. Other lemures included the spirits of those who had died prematurely and were trapped on the earth until their allotted lifespan was up; victims of murder and violent death; executed criminals; and drowning victims. To prevent a lemure from returning from the grave, the Romans burned black beans around the tomb as the body was interred. If a lemure succeeded in haunting the living, it was exorcised by banging on drums.

Lemures were propitiated each year at a festival called LEMURIA.

See also BEANS.

Further reading:

Haining, Peter. *A Dictionary of Ghost Lore.* Englewood Cliffs, N.J.: Prentice-Hall, 1984.

Leach, Maria, and Jerome Fried, eds. *Funk & Wagnalls Standard Dictionary of Folklore, Mythology, and Legend.* San Francisco: Harper & Row, 1979.

Lemuria (also Lemuralia) Ancient Rome's annual three-day festival for appeasing the LEMURES, the spirits of the dead, especially those of an evil nature. According to legend, the festival was inaugurated by Romulus after his murder of his brother, Remus, and was called Remuria. The festival took place on the 9th, 11th and 15th of May, which made the entire month unlucky for all sorts of activities, especially marriages.

During Lemuria, businesses and temples were closed, and people observed rituals for the dead. On the third and final day, the merchants held a festival intended to resume normal activities and help business prosper. Images made of rushes were cast into the Tiber River.

The most important ritual of Lemuria was performed during the last night by heads of households to protect their homes against ghosts. In the middle of the night, each participant washed his hands three times, placed black beans in his mouth, and walked barefoot through the house tossing other black beans over his shoulder while calling out, "With these beans I do redeem me and mine." The incantation was repeated nine times without looking backward. It was thought that any ghosts present would follow along, pick up the beans and then leave until Lemuria the following year. While walking, the man also kept one hand in the sign of the horns—the thumb crossed over the two middle fingers and the index and little fingers extended—an amuletic gesture which protected him against any ghosts he might unexpectedly encounter (see AMULET; CHARMS AGAINST GHOSTS). To close the ritual, he washed his hands again, and then banged brass cymbals while urging all uninvited spirits to depart the premises.

The ancient Greeks had a similar festival for propitiating ghosts, and the Romans absorbed some of the customs into Lemuria. The Greek observances were held over three days earlier in the year in February or March. Temples and businesses were closed. Residents were careful to avoid contact with ghosts by smearing their doors with pitch and chewing whitehorn, a type of hawthorn used in folk remedies to lower blood pressure and the heart rate (and also considered an effective amulet against vampires). On the final day, sacrifices were made to Hermes, the wing-footed messenger god who escorted the souls of the dead to Hades, and ghosts were invited to leave.

See also BEANS.

Further reading:

Finucane, R.C. *Appearances of the Dead: A Cultural History of Ghosts.* Buffalo, N.Y.: Prometheus Books, 1984.

Leach, Maria, and Jerome Fried, eds. *Funk & Wagnalls Standard Dictionary of Folklore, Mythology, and Legend.* San Francisco: Harper & Row, 1979.

Leonard, Gladys Osborne (1882–1968) One of the world's truly great mediums, she worked closely with the SOCIETY FOR PSYCHICAL RESEARCH (SPR) throughout her career, and produced a substantial body of evidence for survival after death.

Gladys Osborne Leonard was born on May 28, 1882 at Lytham, Lancashire, England. Her parents kept the fact of death from her as a young child, and she afterward attributed the impulse of her mediumship to the realization of mortality at age eight. Her father was in the habit of taking her with him on Sunday afternoon visits to one of his friends. When they arrived at this man's house one week, they found the shades drawn, and the parlor maid told them he had gone. Gladys asked where he had gone, but was told not to ask questions. Later the maid told her he had been buried, which she learned meant he had turned "from ashes to ashes, from dust to dust."

The awareness of death affected her deeply, but it was tempered by her blissful visions of a "Happy Valley." Her surroundings would suddenly be transformed into scenes of gentle slopes and banks covered with flowers, with radiantly happy people walking around. Although she did not consider these visions unusual, by some instinct she refrained from mentioning them to her parents, until one morning when her father was about to set off on a trip. She commented on the scene she was seeing on the wall. What scene? he wanted to know. She described it, and he forbade her to look upon her Happy Valley ever again. After this, the visions became less frequent, until the young Gladys stopped seeing them altogether.

When in her teens, Leonard saw an advertisement for a Spiritualist meeting, and went. She returned home delighted. She thought her parents would be equally happy to hear that the dead still lived, but they were horrified.

Leonard trained to be a professional singer, and had hopes of entering the opera. Unfortunately she contracted diphtheria, which affected her voice. She turned to performing with a touring theatrical company instead.

One morning while on the road, Leonard awoke at 2:00 A.M. to see her mother standing in her room, smiling at her. Mrs. Osborne was surrounded by a bright light, looking years younger than she actually was. The next day, Leonard received a telegram which stated that her mother had died at 2:00 A.M. (see APPARITIONS). Leonard had no doubts that her mother's spirit had visited her in her room that night. She decided to try to develop her mediumship, and began table tipping exercises with friends backstage between acts. After some 26 futile attempts, a long name which they could not pronounce was spelled out. They asked whether they might contract this name to "Feda," and the communicator assented. From this point on, Feda was to be Leonard's principal control. Feda sounded and behaved like a child, and claimed to be the spirit of one of Leonard's great-great-grandmothers, a woman of India who had died in childbirth at age 14, around 1800. Feda made her first appearance in 1913, and the following year she began to urge Leonard to hold sittings for the public. "Something big and awful is going to happen to the world," Feda insisted, and Leonard must be ready to provide comfort. By this time, Gladys Osborne

had married Frederick Leonard, a fellow actor. He too was interested in psychical phenomena, and he gave up his career to assist her in her professional mediumship. Mrs. Leonard, as she was to be known, made every effort to provide a clear "channel" for discarnate communicators. She gave up smoking and drinking and became a vegetarian. Her first seances were given to small groups of sitters, but after the outbreak of World War I, she was besieged by such large crowds that she began to hold private sittings.

A major turning point in Leonard's life came when she gave a sitting to a widow who had lost two sons in the fighting. This woman was so impressed with Leonard's exact descriptions of the young men that she mentioned them to a friend of hers, Lady Lodge, wife of physicist Sir Oliver LODGE. When the Lodges lost their son, Raymond, in 1915, Lady Lodge made an appointment with Leonard. What she heard so impressed her that she persuaded her husband to attend a sitting, which he did under an assumed name. He in turn was so impressed that he continued the sittings. During this series, "Raymond" described a photograph which had been taken shortly before his death. The Lodges were not then aware of such a photograph, but when one finally came to their attention, Raymond's pose was found to be exactly as described.

Lodge gave an account of his sittings with Leonard in his book, *Raymond: A Life* (1916). This caused a great sensation, and brought Leonard even more publicity and sitters. At Lodge's suggestion, she raised her fee to a pound per sitting, providing an increased income that allowed the Leonards to rise above the poverty in which they had been living up until this time.

In 1916, Lodge arranged for Radclyffe Hall (author of *The Well of Loneliness*) and her friend, Una Troubridge, to sit with Leonard, in hopes of contacting Hall's deceased friend, Mabel Batten. When the first sittings showed promise, he trained them in seance procedure. Troubridge and Hall continued to have weekly sittings with Leonard over a period of eight years. They published a report on the first year of their work in the *Proceedings of the Society for Psychical Research*. Not only did the Batten communicator (called "A. V. B." in the report) refer to many private moments with Hall, she showed a good knowledge of events in Hall's life since Batten's death, and commented on some things (later shown to be correct) unknown to either Hall or Troubridge at the time. A striking feature of the sittings was the way Batten's personality came through. This would be manifested in the choice of subjects and words, characteristic gestures, and an overall attitude toward life.

Perhaps because of her experience with her parents, Leonard understood the importance of strict seance procedures, aimed at obtaining the best possible evidence of survival. In 1918, she agreed to give sittings arranged by the SOCIETY FOR PSYCHICAL RESEARCH (SPR) exclusively for three months. As a condition of employment, she promised never to read an SPR publication, a promise she kept to the end of her life. Although Leonard returned to professional mediumship after this engagement, she continued to make herself available to the SPR.

The researcher who worked most closely with Leonard was Charles Drayton Thomas, who had more than 500 sittings with her. It was with Thomas that Feda first suggested an experiment which came to be called the book test (see SURVIVAL TESTS). A communicator would instruct a sitter to go to a certain room, and take a book from a certain shelf on a bookcase there; on such-and-such a page would be a passage of interest to the sitter. Later on, newspaper tests were introduced. In these, a communicator would predict in advance of printing what would appear in a newspaper.

Many of the sittings with Leonard scheduled through the SPR over the years were not attended by the persons interested in contacting deceased loved ones, but by proxies who knew nothing about the people or subjects involved in the communications. Such "proxy sittings" came to be standard methodology in psychical research, because they minimized the possibility of the medium getting information directly from the sitter, via either "fishing" or ESP. Many Leonard proxy sittings were highly successful.

Feda would sometimes have trouble understanding what a communicator was trying to say to her. On these occasions, sitters would sometimes hear a voice, different from Feda's, from a point elsewhere in the room, a phenomenon known as direct voice mediumship. Sometimes Feda and the direct voice would talk to each other. This might happen when Feda stumbled on a word, as in the following instance. Feda said, "He says you must have a good working . . . What? Hippopotamus?" "Hypothesis," said the direct voice. "Hippopotamus?" Feda said, somewhat louder. "Hypothesis," the direct voice said again. "And don't shout." "I'm not shouting," replied Feda. "I'm only speaking plainly."

Leonard's mediumship was of such a superior quality that it led to a number of attempts to explore the nature of mediumistic trance and trance communication. The philosopher C.D. Broad made a major contribution to this subject in his *Lectures on Psychical Research* (1962). He and others judged Feda to be a facet of Leonard's personality, rather like what occurs in cases of multiple personality, rather than the independent entity she claimed to be.

In the mid-1950s, Feda instructed Leonard to take no new sitters, and to reduce the number of those she had. Leonard died on March 10, 1968 of cerebral thrombosis, at her home in Tankerton, Kent. She was 85.

Further reading:

Gauld, Alan. *Mediumship and Survival*. London: William Heinemann Ltd., 1982.

Heywood, Rosalind. "Mrs. Gladys Osborne Leonard: A Biographical Tribute." *Journal of the Society for Psychical Research* 45 (1969):95–104.

Leonard, Gladys Osborne. *My Life in Two Worlds*. London: Two Worlds Publishing Co., 1931.

Pleasants, Helene, ed. *Biographical Dictionary of Parapsychology*. New York: Helix Press, 1964.

Radclyffe Hall, [Marguerite], and Lady Troubridge, Una. "On a Series of Sittings with Mrs. Osborne Leonard." *Proceedings of the Society for Psychical Research* 30 (1919):339–554.

Smith, Susy. *The Mediumship of Mrs. Leonard*. Hyde Park, N.Y.: University Books, 1964.

levitation The lifting up into the air of objects, persons and animals without apparent natural means and in defiance of gravity. Levitations occur in mediumship, shamanistic trance, mystical rapture and trance, magic, bewitchment, hauntings and possession. In parapsychology, levitation is considered a phenomenon of psychokinesis (PK), or "mind over matter." Most levitations last only a few seconds or perhaps a few minutes.

Levitations of a spiritual nature are numerous in religions. Saints and mystics reportedly levitate as proof of the powers of God, or in rapture, or because of their saintly nature. The 17th-century Christian saint, Joseph of Cupertino, allegedly could levitate and fly about in the air for long periods of time. In Eastern mysticism, levitation is a feat made possible by mastery of concentration and breathing techniques that control the universal life energy.

The Western view of levitation is dichotomous: saints can levitate by the grace of God, but ordinary persons who levitate are often believed to be under the evil influence of witches, fairies or demons. Levitation is one of the certain signs of the diabolical, according to the Catholic Church's criteria for demonic possession. In 1906, a 16-year-old possessed schoolgirl from South Africa, Clara Germana Cele, levitated up to five feet high, sometimes vertically and sometimes horizontally. She fell if sprinkled with holy water.

Poltergeist cases and hauntings are sometimes characterized by levitating and flying objects, blamed

Levitations of the victims of bewitchment (lower left and middle left) depicted in an illustration from Sadiucismus Triumphatus *by Joseph Glanvil (1661).*

on ghosts or discarnate beings. In some poltergeist cases, investigators theorize that a human focal point, typically an adolescent or an adult with intense, repressed emotions, unwittingly creates psychokinetic energy that causes the activity.

Levitation was a phenomenon of the physical mediumship popular in the early days of Spiritualism. Spirits allegedly caused mediums to rise up out of their chairs at seances, and similarly caused tables and objects to rise and float about the room. Floating trumpets, through which the spirits were said to amplify their voices, came into vogue in the 1850s. The most spectacular levitations were credited to D.D. HOME, who reportedly caused furniture and objects to rise on many occasions during his career as a physical medium. Home levitated himself on

more than 100 occasions before witnesses, and in 1868, he reportedly floated out and in windows. Unlike most other mediums, Home was not always in trance during levitations and so was aware of what was happening and how he felt. He said an unseen power lifted him, and he had "an electrical fulness (sic)" in his feet. The Catholic Church expelled him as a sorcerer; perhaps if he had been a saint instead of a medium, the church would have championed him. Home was never exposed as a fraud, but many other mediums were caught "levitating" objects with hidden wires and contraptions.

Levitation in controlled experiments is rare. Parapsychologists achieved table-tipping, most likely due to PK, in the PHILIP experiments to create an artificial poltergeist in the 1970s.

Skeptics argue that levitations may be explained by hallucination, hypnosis or fraud; Home was accused of using hypnosis to trick his witnesses into thinking he levitated, when in fact he sat in a chair. According to stage magicians, a medium skilled in ventriloquism could easily have faked the type of levitation in the dark that characterized most early Spiritualist seances. The medium removed his (or her) shoes or boots and placed them on top of his hands. He would say, "I am rising," and sitters would be convinced they saw the dim shapes of the boots rising in the air.

Not all levitations have a plausible natural explanation.

See also PALLADINO, Eusapia.

Further reading:

Brandon, Ruth. *The Spiritualists.* New York: Alfred A. Knopf, 1983.

Edge, Hoyt L., Robert L. Morris, John Palmer, and Joseph H. Rush. *Foundations of Parapsychology.* Boston: Routledge & Kegan Paul, 1986.

Fodor, Nandor. *An Encyclopaedia of Psychic Science.* Secaucus, N.J.: Citadel Press, 1966. First published 1933.

Guiley, Rosemary Ellen. *Harper's Encyclopedia of Mystical and Paranormal Experience.* San Francisco: HarperSanFrancisco, 1991.

liekko (omlatt)   In Finnish folklore, an ignis fatuus light, comparable to the British jack-o'-lantern. The *liekko,* which means "the flaming one," is believed to be the soul of a child who was buried in the forest. It presides over plants, roots and trees.

See IGNIS FATUUS.

Lincoln, Abraham (1809–1865) The 16th president of the United States may have had his politics influenced by his experiences at Spiritualist seances. He dreamed of his own death, and his ghost and phantom funeral train reportedly still haunt several locations.

Abraham Lincoln showed personal interest in Spiritualism early in his political career (he was elected to the Illinois state legislature in 1834). After the death of his favorite son, Willie, he attended seances in an effort to contact Willie's spirit. Most historians attribute Lincoln's interest and involvement to the Spiritualist influence of his wife, Mary Todd. Yet there is evidence that Lincoln's interest was independent of Mary and was deeply rooted in his own sense of purpose and destiny. In a letter to his friend Joshua F. Speed in 1842, Lincoln observed that he had "always had a strong tendency to mysticism" and had often felt controlled "by some other power than my own will," which he felt came "from above."

Lincoln's experiences with several mediums may have been an influence on his issuance in 1863 of the emancipation proclamation that freed slaves in America. His antislavery position was in fact well established before then; he regarded slavery as an evil and had opposed its extension. His election to the presidency in 1860 incited the secession of the Southern states and the ensuing Civil War (1861–65).

During his presidency, Lincoln sat with various mediums, including J.B. Conklin, Nettie Colburn, Mrs. Miller, Mrs. Cranston Laurie and Cora Maynard. Maynard, a favorite of Mary Todd Lincoln, took credit for the emancipation proclamation, saying in her autobiography that Lincoln issued it at the direction of her spirits. Nettie Colburn also claimed credit, citing an hour-and-a-half trance during which she lectured Lincoln that the war would not end until he freed the slaves. While it is unlikely that Lincoln made his decision because of such spirit utterings, they may have reinforced his own inner conviction to take such action.

Similarly, medium Cora Richmond claimed that Lincoln and the Joint Congressional Committee on Reconstruction sought her advice, a claim refuted by historians.

Lincoln's position on slavery led to his assassination by John Wilkes Booth on April 14, 1865. Booth shot Lincoln in the back of the head as he and his wife sat in his box at Ford's Theater in Washington, DC. He died within a few hours.

Lincoln had two startling premonitions of his own death. Shortly before his election in 1860, he saw a vision of himself in mirrors on several occasions that upset him. He would see two separate and distinct images of his face, one of which was very pale, and which vanished as he gazed at it. Mary Todd Lincoln interpreted it as a sign that he would be re-elected to a second term but would not survive it.

Ten days before the assassination, Lincoln had a dramatic and prophetic dream of his own death. He wrote in his journal:

> I retired late. I soon began to dream. There seemed to be a deathlike stillness about me. Then I heard subdued sobs, as if a number of people were weeping. I thought I left my bed and wandered downstairs. There the silence was broken by the same pitiful sobbing, but the mourners were invisible. I went from room to room; no living person was in sight, but the same mournful sounds of distress met me as I passed along.
>
> It was light in all the rooms; every object was familiar to me; but where were all the people who were grieving as if their hearts would break? I was puzzled and alarmed. What could be the meaning of all this? Determined to find the cause of a state of things so mysterious and so shocking, I kept on until I arrived at the East Room, which I entered. Before me was a catafalque, on which rested a corpse wrapped in funeral vestments. Around it were stationed soldiers who were acting as guards; and there was a throng of people, some gazing mournfully upon the corpse, whose face was covered, others weeping pitifully. "Who is dead in the White House?" I demanded of one of the soldiers. "The President," was his answer. "He was killed by an assassin." Then came a loud burst of grief from the crowd, which awoke me from my dream. I slept no more that night; and although it was only a dream, I have been strangely annoyed by it ever since.

The night before he was killed, Lincoln told a member of his cabinet that he had dreamed he would be assassinated. The day of his assassination, Lincoln confided to his bodyguard, W.H. Crook, that he had dreamed for three nights straight that he would be assassinated. Crook beseeched him not to go that night to Ford's Theater, but Lincoln demurred, saying he had promised his wife they would go. Perhaps he knew he would be shot that night, for when they departed for Ford's, Lincoln said "good-bye" to Crook instead of "good-night."

A funeral train bore Lincoln's body home to Springfield, Illinois for burial. Since then, every April at the anniversary of the assassination, a phantom funeral train is reported traveling the tracks along the route taken by the official funeral train, from Washington through New York state and west to Illinois. The train never reaches its destination.

(According to some stories, there are two phantom trains. The first steam engine pulls several cars draped in black and belching black smoke. One is a military car, from which issues the sounds of a dirge. The second steam engine pulls only a flatcar bearing the president's coffin.)

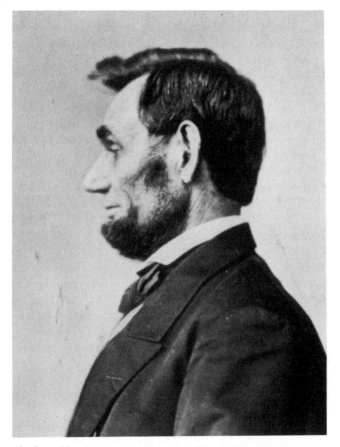

Abraham Lincoln. Courtesy New-York Historical Society.

Mary Todd Lincoln. Courtesy New-York Historical Society.

The Albany (New York) *Evening Times* once gave the following account of the phantom train passing through town:

> Regularly in the month of April, about midnight the air on the tracks becomes very keen and cutting. On either side of the tracks it is warm and still. Every watchman, when he feels the air, slips off the track and sits down to watch. Soon the pilot engine of Lincoln's funeral train passes with long, black streamers and with a band of black instruments playing dirges, grinning skeletons sitting all about.
>
> It passes noiselessly. If it is moonlight, clouds come over the moon as the phantom train goes by. After the pilot engine passes, the funeral train itself with flags and streamers rushes past. The track seems covered with black carpet, and the coffin is seen in the center of the car, while all about it in the air and on the train behind are vast numbers of blue-coated men, some with coffins on their backs, others leaning upon them.
>
> If a real train were passing its noise would be hushed as if the phantom train rode over it. Clocks and watches always stop as the phantom train goes by and when looked at are five to eight minutes behind.

> Everywhere on the road about April 27 watches and clocks are suddenly found to be behind.

After Lincoln's death, spirit photography was in vogue, and Mary Todd Lincoln sat for William Mumler under an assumed name. The resulting photograph shows a misty likeness of the dead president as well as the portrait of his wife.

Lincoln's ghost reportedly continues to haunt the White House. Ghostly footsteps attributed to him were reported first in the second floor corridors by staff. The first person to see his alleged ghost was Grace Coolidge (wife of Calvin Coolidge, the 30th president of the United States, from 1923 to 29), who observed his silhouette standing at a window in the Oval Office, looking out over the Potomac. Since then, his ghost has been seen or sensed in this pose; the poet Carl Sandburg once said he felt (but did not see) Lincoln stand by him at the window. The haunting recreates a real scene observed one night during Lincoln's presidency by Army Chaplain E.C. Bolles. Bolles had arrived in the Oval Office to meet with Lincoln; the president was gazing mourning out the window. "I think I never saw so sad a face in my life, and I have looked into many a mourner's face," wrote Bolles of the episode.

Lincoln's bedroom, called the Lincoln Room, also is a site of hauntings. It is the quarters of visiting heads of state, many of whom report strange phenomena, from footsteps to visual hallucinations. When Queen Wilhelmina of The Netherlands once visited President Franklin D. Roosevelt (1933–45), she told of hearing footsteps in the corridor outside and a knock at the door. When she opened the door, she was astonished to see Lincoln standing before her, dressed out in frock and top hat. The queen fainted. At least one other guest saw Lincoln sitting on the bed, putting on his boots.

Eleanor Roosevelt often sensed Lincoln's presence, usually late at night when she was writing. Sometimes the Roosevelt's dog, Fala, would bark excitedly for no apparent reason.

President Harry Truman (1945–52) also believed he heard Lincoln walking about. After Truman's presidency, the ghost seemed to disappear from the White House. During the Ronald Reagan administration (1981–88), the president's daughter Maureen reported seeing Lincoln's ghost in the Lincoln Room.

In addition to being heard at the White House, Lincoln's ghostly footsteps are reported near his gravesite in Springfield, Illinois. Popular legend has it that the grave is empty.

Further reading:

Alexander, John. *Ghosts: Washington's Most Famous Ghost Stories.* Arlington, Va.: Washington Book Trading Co., 1988.

Cohen, Daniel. *The Encyclopedia of Ghosts.* New York: Dodd, Mead & Co., 1984.

Fodor, Nandor. *An Encyclopaedia of Psychic Science.* Secaucus, N.J.: Citadel Press, 1966. First published 1933.

Moore, R. Laurence. *In Search of White Crows.* New York: Oxford University Press, 1977.

Scott, Beth, and Michael Norman. *Haunted Heartland.* New York: Warner Books, 1985.

Lindbergh, Charles. See GREMLIN.

Little Bastard, Curse of The life and promising film career of the American actor James Dean were cut short by a fatal car accident in September 1955. Dean once said he believed he was predestined to die in a speeding car, and the legend which grew up around the circumstances of his death attributes a curse on the car in which he met his violent fate. Following Dean's death, the curse affected others who came into contact with the wreck.

James Bryan Dean, born February 8, 1931 in Marion, Indiana, rose to fame in the film industry as the prototypical disaffected, rebellious young man. His

leading roles in *East of Eden* and *Rebel Without a Cause* turned him into a superstar. He never finished his last film, *Giant,* costarring Elizabeth Taylor and Rock Hudson; it was completed without him following his death.

Like his celluloid image, Dean liked to live on the dangerous, thrill-seeking edge. He loved fast sports cars and motorcycles; his favorite hobby was racing. He was an adroit driver and performed well behind the wheel, taking top honors in his first several races.

For most of the summer of 1955, Dean was on location near Marfa, Texas for *Giant.* His employer, Warner Brothers, fearful of a mishap, forbade him from racing during production. He did not, however, stop driving pell-mell on his own.

After the location filming, Dean returned to Los Angeles, where his eye was caught by a new sports car, a silver-gray 1955 Porsche Spyder. Thinking it would make a fine entry in upcoming races at Salinas on October 1, he bought it, but on the condition that one of Porsche's top mechanics, Rolf Wuetherich, accompany him as mechanic to all races. The deal was struck.

Although Dean was thrilled with the car—he puckishly named it the "Little Bastard"—several of his friends allegedly were not. Ursula Andress, Alec Guiness, Nick Adams (star of the TV series *The Rebel*) and George Barris, a car designer who had worked on Dean's other sports cars, all apparently expressed feelings of unease about the car. As authors Richard Winer and Nancy Oborn report in *Haunted Houses* (1979), Guiness told Dean to get rid of the car, to no avail. Barris said the car seemed to give off "a weird feeling of impending doom." When Adams mentioned his own unease about the car to Dean, Dean shrugged it off, saying he was destined to die in a speeding car. The final warnings of caution came from Dean's uncle, Charlie Nolan, just before Dean set out to drive to Salinas.

On the trip out of Los Angeles, Wuetherich rode with Dean. They were followed much farther behind by Bill Hickman, an actor friend of Dean, and Stan Roth, a photographer from *Collier's,* which planned a photo story on Dean at the races. Hickman and Roth drove a Ford station wagon which towed a trailer.

Out on the open and nearly empty highway, Dean happily raced along. The car was topless and the windshield had been replaced by a much smaller racing shield. At about 3:30, a highway trooper near Bakersfield pulled the speeding Porsche over and gave Dean a ticket.

At Blackwell's Corner, a small roadstop at the intersection of Route 466 (now State Highway 46) and Route 33, Dean spotted a Mercedes-Benz 300 SL gull-wing sports car, and stopped. The car belonged to Lance Reventlow, son of Barbara Hutton, heiress to the Woolworth fortune. Reventlow also was en route to the Salinas races.

After a short visit with Reventlow, Dean and Wuetherich climbed back in the Little Bastard and resumed their journey. They began the ascent of the Diablo Range mountains. Meanwhile, traveling in the opposite direction in a Ford sedan was Donald Gene Turnupseed, a student at California Polytechnic Institute, who was driving home for the weekend. At 5:59 P.M., Dean's car bore down upon Turnupseed as he attempted to make a left-hand turn across the highway. Faced with a split second to decide whether to accelerate or swerve to avoid a collision, Turnupseed did neither, but slammed on the brakes. Dean saw the impending crash but was powerless to stop it. The two cars crashed head-on into each other.

Dean was killed instantly with a broken neck and other injuries. Wuetherich was thrown free and suffered a fractured jaw, broken leg and internal injuries. The Porsche was badly mangled and nearly torn in two. Turnupseed suffered minor cuts and was not hospitalized.

Dean's death stunned Hollywood. Then a subsequent series of macabre events gave rise to the legend that Dean's death car was somehow cursed.

The incidents began after Barris bought the wreck for its parts. Upon its arrival at Barris's garage, the wreck slipped during its unloading and fell on a mechanic, breaking one of his legs. Then two physicians, Troy McHenry and William F. Eschrid, bought the engine and drive train, respectively, to place in their own race cars. On October 2, 1956 both doctors then raced their cars at Pomona, California, using the Little Bastard parts for the first time. McHenry was killed when his car went out of control and struck a tree, and Eschrid was seriously injured when his car mysteriously rolled over going into a curve.

Two of the Little Bastard's tires were not damaged in the crash, and Barris sold both to a young sports car enthusiast. A few days later, the young man told Barris that both tires had blown simultaneously, causing him to run off the road and nearly wreck his car.

Souvenir-seeking fans sought out the wreck at Barrie's garage. One young man, attempting to steal the steering wheel, ripped his arm open on a jagged piece of metal; at least one other person was injured while trying to steal a piece of bloodstained upholstery.

Spooked by these incidents, Barris decided to store the wreck. He was persuaded by the California Highway Patrol, however, to allow the wreck to be used as part of a traveling highway safety exhibit. Two exhibits took place without incident, but prior to the third, in Fresno, the garage used to house the Little Bastard went up in flames during the night. All vehicles inside were destroyed—except the Little Bastard, which barely suffered scorched paint.

Wherever the Little Bastard went, injury, death and mishap occurred. On display at a Sacramento high school, the car fell off its pedestal, breaking a student's hip. Later, the wreck was sent by flatbed truck to Salinas. En route, the driver, Geroge Barkuis, lost control of the truck and was thrown free; the Little Bastard fell off the truck on top of him, crushing him to death. Two years later, on another flatbed truck, the wreck fell off and crashed onto the freeway, causing an accident. In 1958, yet another strange mishap took place. A truck carrying the car was parked on a hillside in Oregon. The brakes slipped, and the truck crashed into a car shattering its window. Luckily, no one was hurt. In 1959, the Little Bastard was sent to New Orleans for exhibit. While on display, it suddenly broke and fell into 11 pieces. Barris was unable to determine the cause of the breakage.

The last mishap took place in 1960. The Little Bastard was lent to the Florida Highway Patrol for a safety exhibit in Miami. Afterward, it was crated and placed onto a truck for return to Barris in Los Angeles. It never arrived. Somewhere, out on the open road, the car vanished.

Those who believe in the Curse of the Little Bastard also point to the workings of misfortune in the lives of those whom Dean knew. Nick Adams, who dubbed his voice for Dean's in several scenes of *Giant*, died in 1968 of an overdose of paraldehyde. The same year, Wuetherich was convicted of murdering his wife and sentenced to life in prison; he pled insanity at his trial. Lance Reventlow was killed in a plane crash. Sal Mineo, Dean's costar in *Rebel Without a Cause*, was stabbed to death in 1976.

Was the Little Bastard cursed when Dean bought it—even though it was brand-new—or did it become cursed as a result of his violent death? According to superstition, objects—as well as places—can become cursed when they are associated with violence and tragedy. If Dean truly was destined to lose his life in a car crash, then perhaps any car that became the death vehicle might have become cursed. According to psychometry, objects absorb the emotions of their owners and those around them, and remain a repository of those emotions indefinitely. Is it possible that in the final, blinding, terrible seconds of James Dean's life, he experienced emotions of such intensity that they were literally seared into his car, along with the violence of his death? The answer will remain forever a mystery.

Further reading:
Winer, Richard, and Nancy Osborn. *Haunted Houses*. New York: Bantam Books, 1979.

Little-Washer-By-The-Ford　See BANSHEE.

Lodge, Sir Oliver Joseph (1851–1940) Physicist, educator, and psychical researcher, a prominent member of the SOCIETY FOR PSYCHICAL RESEARCH (SPR). Although he made important contributions to both physics and psychical research, Lodge is perhaps best known today for his book *Raymond: A Life* (1916), which dealt with mediumistic communications received from his son, who was killed in World War I.

Oliver Lodge was born on June 12, 1851 in Penkhull, Staffordshire, England (near Stoke-on-Trent). Oliver's father was the 23rd of 25 children, and Oliver was the eldest of seven sons and a daughter. His father was a successful businessman, who supplied clay to the local potteries. Oliver was sent away to a boarding school when he was eight, but he was unhappy there, and his father brought him home at 14 to help in his business. For the next seven years, Oliver traveled as an agent for his father.

When he was 16, his maiden Aunt Anne had him visit her in London, where he attended university classes in physics, and these stimulated his interest in that subject. He entered his first full course at the Royal College of Sciences in 1872. In 1874 he enrolled in University College, London; he received his B.S. from that institution in 1875 and his D.Sc. in 1877. Upon earning his doctorate, he was appointed assistant professor of physics at University College. That same year he married Mary Marshall, by whom he was to have his own large family of six sons and six daughters.

Lodge was present at the meeting of the British Association for the Advancement of Science at which Sir William BARRETT read his paper on his telepathy experiments, but he had no interest in it, and did not hear it. His involvement in psychical research was soon to begin, however. Edmund GURNEY attended one of his lectures, and invited Lodge to his home, where he was busy classifying accounts of apparitions for a book that would be published a few years later as *Phantasms of the Living*. The cases struck Lodge as ''a meaningless collection of ghost stories,'' but he was impressed by Gurney, and through him met Frederic W.H. MYERS.

In 1881, Lodge was appointed the first professor of physics at the new University College in Liverpool. As it happened, Liverpool was the home of Malcolm Guthrie, the proprietor of a drapery establishment, who had discovered that two of his employees were successful ESP test subjects. He contacted University College, and Lodge responded to the opportunity to conduct his own experiments. Rather to his surprise, he obtained good results. He joined the SPR and began traveling to Cambridge to attend its meetings, deepening his acquaintance with Gurney and Myers (both of whom were closely involved in the Society).

The next milestone in Lodge's contact with the paranormal was the American trance medium, Leonora PIPER, whom the SPR invited to England for sittings in 1889. Lodge had his first sittings with Piper in Cambridge. He was much impressed to receive messages from his beloved Aunt Anne, who had recently died, and he invited the medium to Liverpool so that he could study her further. During these later seances, Piper told Lodge of long-departed relatives of whom he knew nothing, and of incidents which were later verified. He concluded that telepathy—which he was already satisfied operated between the living—would need to be extended to include the possibility of communication between the living and the dead.

Five years later, in 1894, Lodge had his first experience with a physical medium: Eusapia PALLADINO. He and Myers journeyed to the summer home of Charles Richet on the Isle de Ribaud. The meeting was a polyglot one, because the researchers and medium had no common language between them, but he and Myers were impressed enough by what they witnessed to invite Palladino to Cambridge for another series of sittings.

In 1900 Lodge accepted the post of principal of another new university, this one in Birmingham, on the condition that he be allowed to continue his work in psychical research. He was elected president of the SPR to succeed Myers in 1901, and again in 1902 and 1903. Later, in 1932, on the 50th anniversary of the founding of the society, he served as president of honor jointly with Eleanor SIDGWICK.

Lodge was well aware of the possibility that mediums read the minds not of their supposed deceased communicators, but of their sitters or other living persons. Messages given through mediums had to be verified if they were to stand as evidence of the beyond, and this required them to be recorded somewhere or known to someone—which at the same time meant that in theory the medium could have gained the knowledge through her (or his) ESP.

This was a key problem in the interpretation of seance material. So it was a major development in psychical research when several different mediums, on different continents, began to make fragmentary statements, attributed to the same communicators, that made sense only when brought together. These communications (which became known as CROSS CORRESPONDENCES) could be understood as the products of a single guiding intelligence. Gurney (who died in 1888) and Myers (who died in 1901) were among those apparently involved. Lodge saw the potential value of such communications at once, and became a major figure in their explication.

Lodge was by now convinced of survival after death (q.v.), but it was only after an extraordinary series of events that his belief turned to faith, and he became a dedicated follower of Spiritualism. In August 1915, Piper, in Boston, delivered a message to Lodge, ostensibly from Myers, to the effect that he would ease the blow; this became meaningful a few days later when it was learned that Lodge's son, Raymond, had been killed in battle in France.

Lodge and his wife began to attend seances with other mediums in England, and at one of these Lady Lodge was told that Raymond appeared in a group photograph, with his walking stick. Through another medium (GLADYS OSBORNE LEONARD) came a more detailed description of this photograph, including the fact that someone was leaning on Raymond's shoulder. The Lodges had no such photograph at the time, and were inclined to mark these communications down as meaningless, when a friend (who knew nothing of these events) offered to send them one. When the photograph arrived, it proved to match Raymond's communications exactly.

Lodge describes these events and the subsequent sittings he had with his son in *Raymond: A Life*. Much of the book is less evidential, Lodge using it to advance his ideas about the afterlife. The book created a sensation and brought Lodge both ridicule from the scientific establishment and praise from the Spiritualist community.

Alongside his contributions to psychical research and his involvement in Spiritualism, Lodge was responsible for important advances in physics, and was highly honored. He did early research in electricity, worked on the radio before Marconi, and developed a spark plug, known as the Lodge plug. Some of his work was useful to Einstein in his development of the theory of relativity. He was knighted in 1902, while he was serving as president of the SPR. In 1913 he was elected president of the British Association for the Advancement of Science.

Lodge died on August 22, 1940 at home at Normanton House, Amesbury, Wiltshire, England. He left a sealed envelope, the contents of which he was to try to communicate after death, with the SPR, but no satisfactory message seems to have been received from him (see SURVIVAL TESTS). However, there is supposed to have been a communication of another

sort. The journalist Paul Tabori, in a short biography, reports that "in September 1940 hundreds besieged a big Spiritualist church in New York where Lodge's 'whispy form' was alleged to have floated over the altar, announcing itself as Sir Oliver."

Lodge wrote numerous books on psychical research and Spiritualism, and in the later ones, especially, he tried to relate these areas to physics. Drawing on the widely-accepted 19th-century concept of "ether," which was said to pervade the entire universe, he held this to be the common basis of both physical and psychical worlds.

Lodge's other books include: *Man and the Universe* (1908), *Survival of Man* (1909), *Modern Problems* (1912), *Science and Religion* (1914), *Ether and Reality* (1925), *Evolution and Creation* (1926), *Why I Believe in Personal Immortality* (1928), *Phantom Walls* (1929) and *My Philosophy* (1933). His autobiography, *Past Years*, appeared in 1931. A comprehensive *Bibliography of Sir Oliver Lodge*, compiled by SPR librarian Theodore Besterman, was published in 1935.

Further reading:
Haynes, Renee. *The Society for Psychical Research, 1882–1892: A History*. London: Heinemann, 1982.
Jolly, W.P. *Sir Oliver Lodge*. London: Constable, 1974.
Lodge, Oliver. *Past Years: An Autobiography*. London: Hodder and Stoughton, 1931.
Oppenheim, Janet. *The Other World: Spiritualism and Psychical Research in England, 1850–1914*. Cambridge: Cambridge University Press, 1985.
Pleasants, Helene, ed. *Biographical Dictionary of Parapsychology*. New York: Garrett Press, 1964.
Tabori, Paul. *Pioneers of the Unseen*. New York: Taplinger, 1973.

Lord Castlereagh   See RADIANT BOYS.

lucks   Objects, such as ornate dishes, cups or goblets, which are kept by families for generations as tokens of good luck and protection against evil. Lucks were once common throughout the British Isles among the gentry and nobility; as long as they remained intact, so tradition goes, the family line would prosper.

Most lucks are fragile objects that have required careful preservation throughout the generations. They invariably have romantic legends attached to them to explain how they came to be in the possession of the family. Lucks cannot be purchased, but must be given to a family. The customary bestowers are royalty, supernatural beings such as fairies, or magical individuals such as witches. It is possible that some lucks originally were tokens of tenure. In days when few people could read or write, tenancy and land ownership was acknowledged by the bestowal of an identifying possession of the landlord or owner.

One of the most famous lucks is the Luck of Edenhall, a cup made of thick yellow-brown glass decorated in blue, red and gold enamel, and kept in its own leather case. Edenhall, located in Cumberland, northern England, was the property of the Musgrave family since the middle of the 15th century. There are various versions of how the luck came into the possession of the family. The most popular version is that one day the butler went down to draw water from a fairy well named after St. Cuthbert. There, he found a group of fairies dancing and drinking around the well. His intrusion caused the fairies to scatter, and they left behind their intriguing drinking cup, which the butler picked up. As they departed, the faires called after them:

> If this Cup should ever break or fall,
> Farewell the Luck of Edenhall.

The exact date of the appearance of the luck is not known. There is a written reference to an unusual cup at Edenhall in 1689. The fairy legend, however, did not emerge until 1791. The luck was made famous in the 18th century by the Duke of Wharton, who visited Edenhall in 1721 and nearly broke the luck by letting it fall during a drinking bout. The butler prevented disaster by catching the cup in a napkin. Wharton later immortalized the luck in a ballad, *The Drinking Match.*

Different theories have been put forth on the origins of the Edenhall cup. It has been described as Moorish in design. The leather case, inscribed with the letters IHS, has led to speculation that the cup was once a Spanish Communion vessel. According to another theory, it may have been drafted in or near Damascus in the 13th or 14th century, as its style and composition is consistent with glasswork done there at that time. The IHS may have been added to the case much later, perhaps as a superstitious charm to keep the fairies from returning to reclaim their possession. Still other theories hold that the cup is of French or English origin from the 13th or 14th century.

Another famous luck in the Cumberland region is the Luck of Muncaster, kept by the Pennington family in Muncaster Castle. The luck is a small bowl made of green glass and decorated in gold and white enamel. According to legend, it was bestowed upon Sir John Pennington by King Henry VI, one of the most luckless of monarchs. During the Wars of the Roses (1455–85), Henry was forced to leave his throne in 1461 and flee into the countryside with only one companion. Either in that year or in 1464, he was in Cumberland, and one night sought shelter at Ireton Hall but was turned away. As he and his companion stumbled about in the middle of the night, they came upon shepherds who guided them to Muncaster Castle, where Pennington took them in. In gratitude, Henry gave the cup to his host and declared that as long as the family preserved it unbroken, they would prosper and never lack a male heir. Henry allegedly claimed that the cup was his own holy water stoup.

The king's own luck had nearly run out, however. He had already gone insane in 1453. When he was restored to the throne in 1470, his reign lasted only a year before his son, Edward V, retook the throne. Henry was sent to the Tower of London, where he was murdered.

Nonetheless, the Luck of Muncaster lasted until the 18th century, when the family died off without male heirs. Although Henry did stay at the castle during his flight, the luck legend may not have been born until much later, in the 18th century, at the doing of Sir John Pennington, the first Lord Muncaster. He is most likely responsible for a painting of Henry holding the cup, and for the inscription of the legend on the tomb of his ancestor, Sir John Pennington.

Another luck, the Luck of Burrell Green, a shallow brass dish, is said to have been given to the Lamb family by a witch, who intoned,

> If this dish be sold or gi'en
> Farewell the Luck of Burrell Green.

With the decline of the great families of aristocracy, lucks have been sold at auction.

See also AMULETS.

Further reading:
Lockhart, J.G. *Curses, Lucks and Talismans.* Detroit: Singing Trees Press, 1971.

Lyttleton, Lord Thomas (1744–1779) The case of Lord Thomas Lyttleton, called the "Wicked Lord" and the "Bad Lord Lyttleton" because of his ill reputation, involves both a death omen apparition and a crisis apparition.

In 1779, Lyttleton returned from Ireland to his house in Hill Street, Berkeley Square, in London. He was visited by several guests, among them Lord Fortescue, Lady Flood, two unmarried sisters by the name of Amphlett, and a friend who recorded the account of Lyttleton's mysterious death.

Lyttleton was not in good health, and had suffered suffocating fits during the preceding month. According to the friend's account:

It happened that he dreamt, three days before his death, that he saw a fluttering bird, and that afterwards a Woman appeared to him in white apparel, and said to him, "Prepare to die; you will not exist three days."

His lordship was much alarmed, and called to a servant from a closet adjoining, who found him much agitated and in a profuse perspiration. The circumstance had a considerable effect all the next day on his lordship's spirits. On the third day, which was a Saturday, his lordship was at breakfast with the above personages [the guests], and was observed to have grown very thoughtful, but attempted to carry it off by the transparent ruse of accusing the others at the table of unusual gravity. "Why do you look so grave" he asked. "Are you thinking of the ghost? I am as well as ever I was in my life."

Later on he remarked, "If I live over tonight, I shall have jockeyed the ghost, for this is the third day."

The whole party presently set off for Pit Place [Lyttleton's gloomy mansion in Epsom, now a suburb of London], where they had not long arrived before his lordship was visited by one of his accustomed fits. After a short interval, he recovered, dined at five o'clock, and went to bed at eleven. When his servant was about to give him a dose of rhubarb and mint-water, his lordship, perceiving him stirring it with a toothpick, called him a slovenly dog, and bid him go fetch a teaspoon.

On the man's return, he found his master in a fit, and, the pillow being placed high, his chin bore hard upon his neck; when the servant, instead of relieving his lordship on the instant from his perilous situation, ran, in his fright, and called out for help; but on his return he found his lordship dead.

Thus, the apparitional dream warning proved to be true.

Yet another apparition was connected to Lyttleton's death. On the day of his demise, Lyttleton and others planned to visit a nearby good friend of Lyttleton, Miles Peter Andrews, Esq., who lived at Dartmoor. At the last moment, Lyttleton excused himself, perhaps because he was anxious about the death warning. He sent along no excuse to Andrews.

That night, Andrews went to bed early because he was not feeling well himself. Shortly after he retired, he was startled when the curtains of his four-poster bed were drawn aside by Lyttleton, who was dressed in one of his distinctive nightgowns. Andrews assumed that Lyttleton had decided to visit after all, and was playing a joke on him. He said to the figure, "You are up to some of your tricks. Go to bed, or I'll throw something at you." Lyttleton, however, merely gazed at him mournfully and responded, "It's all over for me, Andrews." Andrews, still thinking his friend was playing a joke, picked up one of his slippers and threw it at Lyttleton, who then seemed to glide into the adjoining dressing room.

Angry, Andrews jumped up and searched both bedroom and dressing room, but he found both empty and the doors bolted from the inside. He rang his bell for his servants and asked them about Lyttleton, but the servants, puzzled, said he had not been in the house all evening. Andrews still did not suspect anything strange, and ordered the servants to deny Lyttleton a bed, saying he could instead go to one of the inns at Dartford.

The news of Lyttleton's death during the night reached Andrews the next day. He fainted when he heard it, and reportedly "was not his own man" for three years following.

Premonitory death dreams are not uncommon, though the symbolism usually is more couched and not as direct as the Woman in White telling Lyttleton directly that he would be dead in three days. The initial appearance of the bird is significant, for birds are symbols of spirit and the soul, and are associated with heaven. The Woman in White also is a heavenly messenger. However, as was typical of the day, the dream apparition and death were blamed on the revenge of an allegedly evil woman, the late Mrs. Amphlett, who was rumored to have died of a broken heart because Lyttleton had callously seduced both daughters.

Premonitory death dreams often are met by great resistance by the living, and by a determination not to die. Such efforts invariably are in vain. (See DEATH-BED VISIONS).

The accounts of Lyttleton's death and apparitional appearance before Andrews do not mention timing, but it is most likely that Lyttleton appeared to his friend at his moment of death, as is the case in other crisis apparitions. He was dressed in his nightgown; typically, the dying who appear are clothed as they are at the moment of death.

Further reading:

Harper, Charles G. *Haunted Houses: Tales of the Supernatural with Some Accounts of Hereditary Curses and Family Legends.* Rev. and enlarged ed. London: Cecil Palmer, 1924.

M

McLoughlin House Haunted home of pioneer Dr. John D. McLoughlin (1784–1857), located in Oregon City, Oregon, a community in the Willamette Valley near Portland, Oregon. Phenomena include a shadowy figure thought to be McLoughlin's ghost, mysterious footprints and voices, and various poltergeist activities. A possible link exists between the phenomena and the historic home's curator, Nancy Wilson.

Dr. John D. McLoughlin is one of the most colorful figures in the pioneer history of Oregon State. He founded Oregon City and is popularly known as "the Father of Oregon." A towering man with streaming white hair, he was renowned for his generosity yet was spurned by many of his contemporaries.

McLoughlin was born to a Quebec farming family in 1874. He became a physician for the Hudson's Bay Company. In 1821, he was sent to the Oregon Country to preside over the company's new headquarters at Fort Vancouver, across the Columbia River from Oregon (now Vancouver, Washington). The company never had clear title to the land it claimed, however, and when the fur trade dwindled and the wagon trains of American pioneer settlers moved in, McLoughlin saw the writing on the wall: British claims to the land were doomed. He began to aid the settlers, sending them south to the Willamette Valley and extending them generous credit for food and supplies. He rescued settlers who became stranded on treacherous portions of the Oregon Trail.

In 1829, McLoughlin founded Oregon City. He laid out the town himself and gave away more than 300 lots to settlers, churches, schools and organizations. In 1845, he placed the land in his name in exchange for $20,000 paid to the Hudson's Bay Company. He was forced to resign from the company in a power struggle, and so retired to his new home in Oregon City in 1846. He devoted himself to serving the growing community as coroner, physician, mayor and councilman.

McLoughlin's saltbox home was luxurious by local standards—most of the pioneers lived in one-room log cabins at best—and locals dubbed it "the house of many beds" because of McLoughlin's famous hospitality. The doctor also was renowned for his many loans to business enterprises and to individuals.

Even so, many in the community resented him because he was British, wealthy, a Catholic (in a Protestant town) and was married to a Chippewa woman. So when the American government disputed his claim to the land, few were on his side.

In an effort to retain his title, McLoughlin became an American citizen. Nonetheless, Congress stripped him of ownership, and as insult to injury affirmed the rights of others to land given them by McLoughlin. He was still bitter and disillusioned at the time of his death in 1857. His home was then used to board Chinese laborers and later became a bordello for a time before it was abandoned. In 1909 it was moved to another site, its present location on a hill overlooking the city. It was restored in the 1930s and opened to the public. In 1970, the graves of McLoughlin and his wife were moved to the new grounds.

Although McLoughlin might be said to have had plenty of reasons to haunt his home, no phenomena manifested for nearly 120 years, until Nancy Wilson became curator in the mid-1970s. Wilson, who had no beliefs in ghosts, was surprised when inexplicable things began happening on the average of once a week, typically during hours when the house was closed to the public.

One of Wilson's earliest and eeriest experiences was receiving a firm tap on her shoulder while she cleaned the upstairs one day. She turned around, but no one was in sight. The only other person in the house was another employee, who was downstairs. It gave Wilson a fright.

The phenomena increased. Wilson and others on the staff began seeing a hulking shadow—Mc-

Dr. John McLoughlin. Painting by William Cogswell. Courtesy McLoughlin House National Historic Site.

Loughlin was six-foot-five—walk in the upstairs hall and duck into McLoughlin's bedroom. Footsteps of heeled boots have sounded on the upstairs hall when no one is up there. When carpet was installed in the mid-1980s, the footsteps became muffled. The smell of pipe tobacco and brewed coffee have wafted about the dining room occasionally. Every year on September 3, the anniversary of McLoughlin's death, his portrait that hangs over the downstairs drawing room fireplace emits a strange glow as sunlight strikes it. Hanging prisms on candle lampshades have swayed unaccountably, without aid of wind or vibration. One night in the 1980s as one of the tour guides was closing the home, she went into the drawing room where a pair of prismed candle lamps was located and found the prisms of one shade swinging wildly while the prisms on the second shade remained still.

Other phenomena include a child's bed that mysteriously appears slept in when staff arrive to open

up in the morning; a ladder-back rocker in one of the bedrooms that rocks by itself; tracks that resemble chicken feet trailed across a carpet vacuumed the night before; and the movement of objects, such as a button lost by a visitor which suddenly appeared rolling in the middle of another room. Once the cash register turned up 10 dollars short; Wilson later found the money in a drawer that had been locked. Wilson also has heard mysterious voices, including a woman weakly calling for help, and noises of phantom objects crashing to the floor.

The phenomena reached a peak of activity around 1981, when Wilson organized an exhibit of pioneer women's clothing inside the McLoughlin House. One of the dresses was a wedding dress belonging to Mrs. Forbes Barclay, wife of an associate of McLoughlin. The activity remained high during the entire length of the exhibit, with something happening daily.

Around the late 1980s, the house became fairly quiet, though McLoughlin's presence continued to be felt. None of the staff ever felt menaced by the ghost or sensed any negative energy in connection with the hauntings.

Wilson believes her family history played a role in activating the phenomena. After the hauntings began, she researched her past and found a link to McLoughlin. Among her ancestors is a family named Wells, pioneers who arrived in Oregon City in 1842. Less than one year after their arrival, Mr. Wells died, leaving behind his wife and children. McLoughlin gave them financial help. Mrs. Wells later married another man named Wells, but she never paid back all of the money. At the time of McLoughlin's death, she still owed him $43. Wilson thinks that perhaps McLoughlin's ghost saw an opportunity to collect on one of his many outstanding debts. Or, perhaps he wished to express his satisfaction with Wilson, who has a great interest in preserving the home and promoting the good name of McLoughlin.

Next to the McLoughlin House is the historic Barclay House, once owned by Dr. Forbes Barclay. It, too, is said to be haunted, though it is less active than the McLoughlin House. A small red-haired boy has been seen on separate occasions, appearing so real that visitors ask who he is. One guide even called the police, thinking the boy to be lost or an intruder. A phantom black-and-white dog that leaves its paw prints on the carpet may be associated with the boy, Wilson speculates.

The Barclay House also has been haunted by "Uncle Sandy," the seaman brother of Forbes. In times past when the house was still used to shelter guests overnight, Uncle Sandy sometimes appeared beside his former bed, apparently to see who was sleeping there. Around the turn of the century, a woman who slept in Uncle Sandy's bed said she felt that a boy had died in the house, though there are no supporting records.

None of the phenomena at either house has been scientifically investigated.

Further reading:

Melvin, Robert. ''Does McLoughlin's Ghost Haunt Oregon City Mansion?'' *The Oregonian* (January 4, 1983).

Riccio, Dolores, and Joan Bingham. *Haunted Houses USA.* New York: Pocket Books, 1989.

Mad Anthony   Major General Anthony Wayne, an American, was known as ''Mad Anthony'' for his daring military exploits during the Revolutionary War, perhaps because he was unable to let go of his passion for fighting. His ghost reportedly lingers on, appearing in many different places and in many different roles. Major hauntings include a military post, a lake, a mountain pass in northern New York State and a country house in Virginia.

Wayne's ghost is said to appear at Fort Ticonderoga, where he was commandant in 1771. Wayne was known as a ladies' man, and he was particularly attracted to two ladies present at one of his dinner parties. One lady was a guest, Penelope Haynes, the daughter of Prescott Haynes, a rich Vermont landowner. The other lady was Nancy Coates, a local woman who served at the party.

Shortly after, Wayne and Nancy became lovers. In time, Nancy set her heart on marrying him, but he successfully fended off her entreaties. Meanwhile, the British were making military advances, and some prominent citizens asked for protection for their womenfolk, among them Prescott Haynes. General George Washington commanded Wayne to bring the women to Ford Ticonderoga.

While Wayne was away on this mission, some people at the fort maliciously told Nancy that he had gone to fetch his bride. When the cavalry returned, Wayne rode at its head, followed by Penelope Haynes sitting on the pillion of a wagon train. Nancy gently touched Wayne's boot as he rode past, but since he was glancing back at Penelope, he did not feel her touch. Nancy was devastated, and she fled to the lake, where she sat until dawn and then ended her misery by walking into its waters.

Nancy's ghost has been seen in and around various parts of the fort, running along the lake paths, and even floating face up in the lake. The sounds of a sobbing woman often accompany the apparition. Wayne's ghost is said to appear in the dining room of the commandant's quarters, or is seen sitting in a

Mad Anthony Wayne, after a painting by Chappel.

wing chair before the fireplace. The ghost smokes a churchwarden pipe and drinks from a pewter mug, copying the pose in Wayne's portrait hanging on the room's wall.

Wayne's ghost also is said to visit Lake Memphremagog. In 1776, Wayne and two guides from Laurentian Canada went there to search for a bald eagles' nest. If caught early and trained, eagles were thought to make good hunting companions.

They found a nest with two bald eaglets. Wayne tried to remove them when one of them raked him across the cheek and the bridge of his nose. He had the scar for the rest of his life, and kept the eagles for the rest of their lives. He taught them to hunt, and they were his constant traveling companions wherever he went.

After Wayne died, his ghost was reportedly seen at the log fort at the lake, which had become a fur traders' post. Dressed as an Indian scout, Wayne's apparition would walk along the lake's shore with one eagle sitting on each outstretched wrist. Trappers claimed that Wayne's ghost crossed the lake with his feet barely touching the water.

Wayne's ghost has also been seen making a midnight ride on his beloved horse, Nab, in an assumed replay of what has been called one of the most daring ventures of the Revolutionary War. In 1779, General George Washington commanded Wayne to warn the American troops at Storm King Pass of an impending attack on a nearby British garrison. Wayne and Nab often enjoyed riding through the dangerous, lonely mountain hills. On this night during a violent storm, Wayne rode Nab to warn the troops, and then returned to successfully lead his men in the bayonet attack on Stony Point.

On similarly stormy nights, Wayne's cloaked ghost is reportedly seen hunched over Nab while darting in and out of the mountain tunnels. The apparition is accompanied by blue and orange sparks made by Nab's shoes hitting the flint, and from his hide hitting branches. The ghostly pair is said to appear to local residents before an impending storm.

Another Wayne ghost has been associated with a house of which he grew fond. In 1777, Wayne surrendered Fort Ticonderoga to General Burgoyne. While riding to join General Lafayette in Virginia, Wayne anticipated seeing once again a half-built, Georgian brick house belonging to an acquaintance, Philip Noland.

Noland's house was never finished for unknown reasons. It reportedly is haunted by the ghosts of two Hessian prisoners who, during the Revolutionary War, escaped from their nearby camp and hid in the empty house, only to be discovered and shot to death. It is said that their ghosts prowl through the cellar, and hit and scratch on the walls. Followers of Mad Anthony folklore believe that his own ghost visits the house, perhaps to wonder why it was never completed.

Further reading:
Reynolds, James. *Ghosts in American Houses*. New York: Paperback Library, 1967. First published 1955.

Madame Pele
Pele, Hawaii's goddess of the volcano, reportedly has been seen in ghostly form off and on for centuries. Most of the sightings are on the island of Hawaii, where she is said to reside in Kilauea Crater on the eastern side of Mauna Loa, one of the island's highest peaks.

Various Polynesian myths explain the origins of Pele. In one, she came from a family of distinguished Hawaiian deities. Her original home was the island of Kauai, which she left for Mauna Loa. Once there, she dug until she found the molten center of the mountain, thus creating Kilauea Crater. When the volcano is quiet, she lives in the crater and presides over a family of fire gods, but prior to eruption, she descends to warn islanders of the coming danger.

According to another myth, Pele originated in Tahiti, which she left to escape the wrath of her sister,

whose husband she had seduced. Still another myth says she escaped a flood, while another claims she simply loves to wander. Her jealousy of her sister is the cause of the lava she sends streaming down Mauna Loa.

As a ghostly form, Madame Pele, as she is called, always appears as a young, beautiful woman dressed in a brilliant red muumuu, accompanied by a small white dog. She is often spotted in the wee hours of the night, standing or walking along a lonely road. It is advisable to stop and offer her a lift, for to ignore her is to invite her wrath in the form of excessive death and destruction in the coming eruption.

According to tradition, Pele is propitiated by islanders who lay roasted chickens on the crater's rim.

Further reading:
Beckwith, Martha. *Hawaiian Mythology*. Honolulu: University of Hawaii Press, 1970. First published 1940.

Maher, Michaeleen Constance
New York parapsychologist who specializes in the investigation of haunted houses, using quantitative techniques rather than the traditional qualitative method of case investigation (see APPARITIONS; HAUNTINGS).

Michaeleen (Mikki) Maher was born in the town of Maywood, near Los Angeles, in southern California. Her father was a career officer in the U.S. Navy, and her family moved repeatedly during her early years. Thanks to several visits to New York, she got to know that city, and finally settled there. In 1967 she married photographer Don Snyder, and by him had two children.

While attending City College of the City University of New York (CUNY), Maher took a course in parapsychology with Gertrude Schmeidler, who introduced her to experimental parapsychology. Maher received her B.A. from City College in psychology in 1974, and, encouraged by Schmeidler, went on to earn her Ph.D. in basic and applied neurocognition from the CUNY Graduate School in 1983. In 1986, she began to teach a course in parapsychology at the New School for Social Research.

Maher heard about her first haunting case from a family friend, a woman whom she knew to have a history of psychical experiences. This woman, her sister, and their mother had all seen what seemed to be dark figures moving along the hall of their apartment near Washington Square Park, in New York's Greenwich Village. The figures invariably turned into the bathroom or the master bedroom before disappearing.

Maher modeled her investigation on a pioneering study by Schmeidler, published in the *Journal of the American Society for Psychical Research* in 1966. Making

Michaeleen C. Maher. Photo by Liza Stelle. Courtesy Michaeleen C. Maher.

a floorplan of the apartment, she designated the areas where the family reported seeing the apparitions moving and heading as the target, and asked psychics who knew nothing about the haunting to go through the apartment and mark on the floorplans any place they sensed something unusual. She asked skeptics to go through the same apartment, but this time to mark floorplans according to where they thought people would imagine they saw ghosts.

The psychics and skeptics also circled items on a checklist that they thought were descriptive of what the family had reported and crossed out items that they believed were inapplicable. When she evaluated the results of her tests statistically, Maher found that the psychics had given responses that came closer to the family's reports than chance would allow, whereas the skeptics' responses fell within chance expectation.

Maher also used infrared photography and a Geiger counter in order to see whether physical signs of something paranormal could be detected in the apartment. One infrared photograph showed an unusual

light effect in the hall, but in her 1975 report (written with Schmeidler) Maher downplayed this, saying she could not rule out imperfections in the manufacturing or handling of the film. Although the Geiger counter went haywire in a room where one of the psychics had felt something peculiar, the overall results averaged to chance.

Maher routinely employs infrared photography and videotape, and in several investigations she has introduced a device she and its inventor, colleague George P. Hansen, affectionately call the "Demon Detector." The Demon Detector is actually a computer that generates a series of random numbers. When the sequence departs too far from chance, a red light flashes on. The assumption is that DEMONS prefer red light, and that they will therefore be motivated to affect the generator in such a way as to keep the light on. But when Maher and Hansen have

Unexplained diffusion effect documented with infrared photography in hallway of apartment in New York City. Photo by Marilyn Krauss. Courtesy Michaeleen C. Maher.

used the Demon Detector, the red light has tended to stay off significantly more often than chance would predict. In explaining this unexpected result, Maher observes that ghosts, after all, are not the same as demons. Ghosts, unlike demons, are traditionally thought to prefer darkness.

Several of Maher's investigations have been covered by the media. The Washington Square case was described in an article featuring Maher and fellow parapsychologists Karlis Osis and William G. ROLL in *Omni* magazine in August 1988, and she has since reinvestigated the case for *Frontiers of the Unknown*, a series on "alternate realities" for the cable television Discovery channel. Another investigation, that of Philadelphia's General Wayne Inn—whose ghost dates from the American Revolution (see MAD ANTHONY)—provided a segment for the popular NBC show, *Unsolved Mysteries*.

Maher keeps the book open on all of her investigations, she said in an interview, because haunting phenomena often continue indefinitely. Although her studies routinely produce statistically significant results, she prefers not to generalize about these, beyond saying that she believes they point to something paranormal and may even indicate that some deceased entity is physically present in the houses she investigates. She believes research is not yet sufficient to permit definite conclusions.

Further reading:

Maher, Michaeleen, and Gertrude Schmeidler. "Quantitative Investigation of a Recurrent Apparition." *Journal of the American Society for Psychical Research* 69 (1975):341–52.

Maher, M.C., and G.P. Hansen. "Quantitative Investigation of a Reported Haunting Using Several Detection Techniques." In G. Schmeidler (Chair), *Proceedings of Presented Papers, Parapsychological Association 33rd Annual Convention*, pp. 151–167. Durham, N.C.: Parapsychological Association, 1990.

manes In ancient Rome, spirits of the dead. Generally, the manes were "good spirits"; the Di Manes were divine spirits. The term "manes" also referred to an individual spirit of the dead, to underworld deities and to the underworld. The Romans placated manes with offerings called *religiousae*.

Manning, Matthew British psychic with extraordinary powers. Matthew Manning writes and draws automatically, communicates with spirits, bends metal, starts and stops mechanical devices, apports objects, communicates telepathically and predicts future events.

In his first book, *The Link* (1974), Manning describes how he learned of his abilities at age 11 in 1967 with the onset of poltergeist activity in his home at Shelford, in Cambridge, England. Rooms tidy one minute would be found in complete disarray; objects appeared and disappeared, sometimes on command; furniture moved unaided; and knocks and raps were heard throughout the house. These phenomena went on for several weeks, stopped, then resumed with more force in late 1970 and early 1971, even following young Manning to his boarding school and frightening his housemates. Pebbles, knives and glass flew around the dormitory bedroom, often nearly missing a student; heavy beds moved across the floor; and strange lights and cold air plagued the building. At home, childish scribbling with pencil covered the walls, and pools of liquid would appear on the floor. Manning began having out-of-body experiences, even projecting himself astrally into the past, he said, to see the Mannings' "new" old house in Linton, also near Cambridge, as it looked in the 16th through 18th centuries.

While viewing his house in the past, Manning also began communicating with spirits, first by apparitions and voices and then through automatic writing. Surprisingly, the onset of spirit communication caused the poltergeist activity to decline and then cease altogether. Many of the messages were incoherent or trivial, but some were accurately predictive. Manning received messages in many languages, including French, German, Italian, Greek, Latin, Russian and Arabic, and sometimes in early or medieval forms.

He heard from all types and ages of people; some famous, like Bertrand Russell, and others long forgotten. One Robert Webbe (c. 1733), connected with the past of the Mannings' house, communicated often and prompted 503 of his relatives and peers to sign the Mannings' walls, ostensibly to fill in the gaps in Manning's study of the Webbe family history. Manning also received communications from Greek Orthodox bishop Kephalas Nektarios, who used him and a few others to convince His Eminence Archbishop Athenagoras of Great Britain to build a monastery at Aegina, the bishop's burial place.

In 1971, Manning's mother suggested he try drawing automatically. Because Manning claims to have no artistic ability, any pictures he produced supposedly would have had another inspiration. Since that time, Manning has drawn pictures in the styles of Thomas Bewick, Paul Klee, Aubrey Beardsley, Albrecht Dürer, Thomas Rowlandson, W. Keble Martin, Henri Matisse, Arthur Rackham, Francisco Goya, Isaac Oliver, Pablo Picasso, Leonardo da Vinci and Beatrix Potter, as well as anonymous artists. Most are done in pen and ink, and some are copies of the artist's work while in life. They are drawn rapidly with few changes (see AUTOMATISMS).

As early as 1974, Manning began undergoing extensive tests and investigations of his psychic powers. By then, he discovered that, like Uri Geller, he could bend spoons, handcuffs and other metal objects. He also could cause clocks, engines, faucets and electronic appliances to start and stop; set off alarms; cause objects to appear and disappear; and predict future events. He foresaw a 1975 plane crash at New York's Kennedy Airport and a London subway disaster the same year. He predicts his own early death. By 1977, he had experienced enough startling phenomena to fill another book, *In the Mind of Millions*.

Perhaps most interesting, studies of Manning's abilities by doctors and scientists at a 1974 conference in Toronto have raised theories about the location of psychic ability in the brain. Using an electro-encephalograph (EEG), doctors traced the source of Manning's brain waves during psychic demonstrations to a part of the brain believed to be defunct and dysfunctional—part of the "old animal brain" of early man. If their hypothesis is correct, it is possible that every person possessed psychic abilities centuries ago but lost them over time. Since many persons with extraordinary psychic or mediumistic gifts have experienced an electrical shock before age 10, some experts speculate that perhaps this part of the brain can be activated with electric shock treatment.

Like many other psychics, Manning has endured criticism of his abilities and has been accused of outright fraud. Consequently, he gives few interviews and tries to remain out of the public eye. In 1977 he relinquished the term "psychic," preferring to be known as a "mentalist."

Further reading:

Manning, Matthew. *The Link.* New York: Ballantine Books, 1974.

Shepard, Leslie A., ed., *Encyclopedia of Occultism and Parapsychology, Second Edition.* Detroit: Gale Research Co., 1984.

Marfa lights See GHOST LIGHTS.

Margery See CRANDON, MINA STINSON.

Marian apparitions Visions or supernatural manifestations of the Blessed Virgin Mary. The experiences are accompanied by other paranormal phenomena, such as heavenly music and singing, miraculous healing, luminosities, extrasensory perception and mediumship.

Untold numbers of Marian apparitions have been reported over the centuries, but only a handful have been deemed authentic by the Catholic Church. In most sightings, a luminous lady appears and identifies herself as Mary. Typically, she bears messages urging people to pray more and lead a more devout life; she also asks for churches and shrines to be built to her. Miraculous healings often are reported in the wake of sightings. In a number of cases, children are the percipients.

According to the Catholic Church, religious apparitions are not ghosts but are mystical phenomena permitted by God. Both corporeal and incorporeal apparitions are recognized, and are mentioned in both the Old and New Testaments of the Bible. Marian apparitions are not accepted as articles of faith, but those which are deemed authentic are celebrated.

AUTHENTICATED APPARITIONS

Authentic sightings occurred in Guadalupe, Mexico in 1531; in Paris in 1830; in La Salette, France on September 19, 1846; in Lourdes, France from February 11 to July 16, 1858; in Knock, Ireland on August 21, 1879; in Fatima, Portugal from May 13 to October 13, 1917; in Beauraing, Belgium from November 29, 1932 to January 3, 1933; and in Banneaux, Belgium in 1933. Of those, the most famous and celebrated are:

Guadalupe, Mexico

In 1531, Mary appeared five times to Juan Diego, a middle-aged Aztec convert to Catholicism. The apparitions were recorded in various documents, including the Codex of Seville. The first episode occurred before dawn one morning as Juan was on his way to attend Mass:

". . . he suddenly heard a great choir, as of thousands of birds singing . . . He was enchanted and looked up to the hilltop where the music seemed to come from and saw there a shining cloud of brightness in that dusk before dawn, and started to climb up the barren rocks towards it. Suddenly the heavenly music stopped and then through the silence he heard a lady's voice call him by name: 'Juan, Juan Diegito'. . . ."

(Coley Taylor in *Our Lady of Guadalupe: Marian Library Studies No. 85*, 1961)

Diego then saw a woman "standing in the luminous cloud of mist, iridescent with rainbow hues." She immediately identified herself as Mary, saying, "You must know, and be very certain in your heart, my son, that I am truly the eternal Virgin, holy Mother of the True God, through Whose favor we live, the Creator, Lord of Heaven, and the Lord of Earth."

One another occasion, the apparition told Juan to pick flowers. Although it was a cold time of the year, he found a garden of roses at a site where no flowers had grown before. The flowers were Roses of Castile, a species not grown in Mexico at that time. Mary told him to wrap the flowers in his *tilma*, or cape, and take them to the bishop, which he did.

When Diego revealed the flowers and cape to the bishop and others who were present, a beautiful image of the Immaculate Conception was found to be imprinted on the cape: a woman with the sun and stars, standing on a new moon, with an angel at her feet. The style of the "painting" is not in the Maya-Toltec-Aztec tradition of the time, which resembled primitive hieroglyphics. The cape was made of *ayate*, a coarse fabric made of cactus fiber, and had a maximum life span of about 30 years. Both the cape and the "painting" have lasted to the present day, and are on display in the church-shrine that was built at Mary's request.

Specialists have examined the figure's eyes in the "painting" and confirm what appear to be images of a man, perhaps Juan Diego, in each eye.

Pope Pius XII (1939–58) said that "on the *tilma* of humble Juan Diego—as tradition relates—brushes not of this earth left painted an Image more tender which the corrosive work of the centuries was marvellously to respect."

Lourdes, France

On 18 occasions, from February 11 to July 16, 1858, 14-year-old Bernadette Soubirous reportedly saw Mary in a grotto along the Gave du Pau river near Lourdes. Bernadette said she saw "a girl in white, no taller than I, who greeted me with a little bow of her head." On one occasion, the Lady spoke, in the Lourdes dialect, and said, "Will you please come here every day for a fortnight. I do not promise to make you happy in this world but in the next." In the last apparition, the woman identified herself, "I am the Immaculate Conception."

As a result of the apparitions, Bernadette reportedly experienced trances or ecstasies, some lasting an hour. After her series of visions ceased, a spring near the site became credited with miraculous healing powers. The spring has no known natural therapeutic properties; believers attribute its curative powers to the patronage of Mary. Numerous other claims of visions and miracles proved to be spurious. The

Catholic Church authenticated Bernadette's apparitions four years later, and canonized Bernadette as a saint on December 8, 1933.

The identification of the apparition as the Immaculate Conception is important to Catholicism, and has been taken by many Catholics to be heavenly confirmation of the doctrine of the Immaculate Conception, which had been defined as a Catholic dogma in 1854. The "immaculateness" of Mary is a theme of the apparitions at Guadalupe and Fatima.

At Mary's request, a chapel was built in 1871 at the Lourdes site; it has grown to be one of the great churches of southern France.

Up to six million pilgrims visit Lourdes each year. Supervision and examination of people who claim to be healed is done by the Bureau des Constatations Medicales, established in 1882 as an independent group of doctors, which also is open to qualified visiting physicians. There are documented cases of cures associated with both the waters and the site.

Fatima, Portugal

In 1917, after three appearances of a being who identified itself as the Angel of Portugal, Mary appeared to three children: Lucia dos Santos, 10, and her two cousins, Jacinta and Francisco Marto, 7 and 9 respectively. The two girls saw a "young lady" and heard her speak; the boy saw her but did not hear her speak. The children said the lady was dressed in white and stood above a small tree. She asked them to return to the same place at the same hour of the same day for six consecutive months. Tens of thousands of spectators showed up at the appointed time and place to witness the six apparitions. All but the August appearances took place at Cova da Iria, a grazing ground near Aljustrel, a village in the parish of Fatima, north of Lisbon.

At the final sighting on October 13, a crowd of 50,000 or more gathered in the rain. Mary appeared to the children and told them to build a chapel in her honor. She said she was the "Lady of the Rosary," and that people must say the Rosary daily. Lucia saw in succession Mary as Our Lady of Sorrows and as Our Lady of Mount Carmel; St. Joseph with the Child; and Jesus as a man. Then the rain stopped, and a phenomenon now known as the "miracle of the sun" occurred. The sun appeared suddenly through a rift in the clouds and seemed to rotate, throwing off multicolored light. It appeared to plunge to the earth, giving off heat. Some in the crowd feared it was a signal of the end of the world, and panicked. Fear then gave way to awe as the sun returned to normal in the sky. The "miracle of the sun" was witnessed miles away, and lasted an estimated 10 minutes. The significance of it is not known. Photographers at the event documented the unusually fast change from wet to dry environment, but not the phenomenon of the rotating sun.

According to Mary, the purpose of her apparitions was to deliver messages to the people of the need for daily recitation of the Rosary; prayer and mortification for the conversion of sinners; prayers for priests; and offering of the Holy Communion of reparation on the first Saturday of every month. In addition, all people of the world needed to be devoted to the Immaculate Heart of the Blessed Mother. In return for these acts, many souls would be saved; Russia would be converted; another and more terrible world war would be averted; and there would be world peace.

In 1927, the Catholic Church authorized pilgrimages to the site. In accordance with the apparition's instructions, construction of a basilica was begun in 1928. Hospitals, hospices and other religious institutions also have been erected.

The story of the Fatima apparitions was a vehicle for a 1952 movie, *The Miracle of Our Lady of Fatima*. The film did not present the spiritual aspects effectively, but used the story as a vehicle for an anti-Communist statement.

UNAUTHENTICATED APPARITIONS

Alleged sightings of Marian apparitions have a powerful effect on witnesses, even if the apparitions are not authenticated by the Church. Investigations can take years before a decision on authenticity is made; meanwhile, sites of apparitions continue to draw new pilgrims who hope to have miraculous experiences. Among unauthenticated sightings are:

Zeitoun, Egypt

Beginning April 2, 1968, and lasting approximately 14 months, more than 70 Marian apparitions and other unusual phenomena were reported in the vicinity of the St. Mary's Coptic Church in Zeitoun, a suburb of Cairo. The first eyewitnesses were three Muslim mechanics, who reported seeing a woman dressed in dazzling white, standing on top of the central dome of the church in the late night hours. The light was so brilliant that they could not make out facial features. Others saw it, and a crowd gathered within minutes; someone recognized the apparition as Mary. The crowd shouted and the figure acknowledged by bowing. After a few minutes, it ascended rapidly into the night sky and disappeared.

The first sighting was followed by hundreds of alleged spontaneous cures of all manner of diseases and illnesses. One of the mechanics, who suffered a gangrenous finger and was due for surgery the next day, completely recovered.

From April 2 until August 1969, Marian apparitions occurred two to three times a week, then were sporadic for the remainder of 1969. They were most frequent on early Sunday mornings and on the 32 Marian feast days of the Coptic Church. The total number of eyewitnesses was estimated at 250,000 to 500,000.

The apparitions included full and partial figures in at least 10 different shapes, which bowed and waved to the witnesses; reddish clouds of sweet incense which appeared and disappeared with great rapidity; unusual lights shooting across the sky; and luminous doves or dove-like objects of silver and other brilliant colors, some of which appeared in the shape of a Christian cross. None of the apparitions was accompanied by sound. The shortest lasted about one minute, while the longest, on June 8, 1968, lasted for more than seven hours. The General Information and Complaints Department of the Egytian Government investigated and declared it "an undeniable fact" that Mary had appeared to both Christians and Muslims.

Medjugorje, Yugoslavia

A remote village tucked into the mountains of Yugoslavia, Medjugorje has been the site of pilgrimages and tourist visits since Mary first appeared on a hill to six adolescent villagers on June 24, 1981. Four were girls and two were boys; they ranged in age from 10 to 17. For the next 18 months, there were daily apparitions to one or more of the adolescents, who came to be called the "seers" or "visionaries." Nearly 2,000 Marian apparitions were recorded by 1985. Most have occurred in the "chapel of apparitions," the rectory behind the St. James Roman Catholic Church in Medjugorje, and have lasted three to four minutes (the first apparitions lasted 20 to 30 minutes).

In addition to the apparitions, miraculous healings have been reported of a range of physical and psychological conditions, from eye diseases and vascular problems to substance addictions. Other miracles occurred nearly daily. In August 1981, the Croatian word for peace, Mir, was seen written in the sky at night above the cross on the hill where Mary first appeared, now known as the Hill of Apparitions. Her silhouette has also been seen on the hill. Like the "miracle of the sun" at Fatima, the sun has been reported to either pulsate, spin hypnotically, change into a white disc, or shine in a rainbow of brilliant colors. The cross behind the church has been seen to spin or disappear. On October 28, 1981, a bush spontaneously ignited on the hill. People rushed to extinguish it, but by the time they reached it, it had burned itself out, leaving no charring or burned evidence.

According to the adolescent seers, the purpose of the apparitions is to bring a message from Christ, which the seers would then communicate to the world. Essentially, the message is that atheists must convert and return to the ways of God, to change their lives to peace with God and with their fellow man. Returning to God can be achieved through peace, conversion, fasting, penance and prayer. Peace is the most important, for it makes everything else possible. Prayer is vital because faith cannot be maintained without it. Prayer must be directed to Jesus, and Mary will intercede with Him. The purpose of the supernatural events, according to Mary, is to give credence to the apparitions and underscore the importance of the message.

Mary further communicated that Medjugorje was selected because the village of about 400 families included many good believers who were capable of restoring their faith and serving as an example to other people in the world regarding the need to convert.

After their first vision, the adolescent seers spent at least six hours in prayer, and fasted up to three times a week. They said they conversed with Mary in normal conversational tones, and in their native Croatian. They learned that each of them would be given 10 secrets, after which time Mary would cease to appear to them, except on special occasions. The children did not receive their secrets at the same time; four messages were to concern mankind as a whole, while the rest would be directed to individuals or the village of Medjugorje.

As a result of the apparitions, the villagers, with few exceptions, converted and began attending daily church services.

Pilgrims who visit the church and rectory say Mary appears to them during prayer. Others report unusual experiences, such as the changing of silver Rosary chains to gold. Photographs appear to show images of the figure of Jesus on the cross on the hill, Mary in prayer against the cross, Mary and child in the sky, and unnatural rays of light striking the cross. In some cases, the images are evident only after the film is developed.

By the fall of 1987, Mary was appearing on the 25th day of each month, giving messages to vision-aries to spread throughout the world about the need for prayer and the need to dedicate time to Jesus.

Lubbock, Texas
In February 1988, three parishioners of the St. John Neumann Roman Catholic Church reported that during their weekly Rosaries, Mary had appeared to them. In a situation similar to Medjugorje, the three were to be messengers of the need for prayer, faith, love and peace.

Mary said that she would reveal herself at an August Feast of the Assumption celebration, the day when Catholics celebrate the ascension of Mary into heaven, and told her messengers that healings and other miracles would be seen. An estimated 20,000 people attended the outdoor Feast at the church. Many claimed to have seen Mary's apparition, as well as the head of Jesus, as the sun moved behind a mass of clouds. The community of Lubbock responded as had Medjugorje. More parishioners began attending church services. Miraculous healings for conditions as disparate as heart disorders and bad knees were reported.

Further reading:
Arintero, Juan. *Mystical Evolution in the Development and Vitality of the Church Vol. I.* St. Louis: B. Herder, 1949.
Attwater, Donald. *A Dictionary of Mary.* New York: P.J. Kennedy, 1960.
DeVincenzo, Victor. "The Apparitions at Zeitoun, Egypt: An Historical Overview." *Journal of Religion and Psychical Research* 11 (1988):3–13.
Hancock, Ann Marie. "Signs and Wonders of Her Love." *Venture Inward* (September/October 1988):12–15.

Marylebone Spiritualist Association, Ltd. See SPIRITUALIST ASSOCIATION OF GREAT BRITAIN.

materialization The process of forming seemingly solid spirit faces, body parts or complete spirit figures by a medium during a seance. Full-body materializations once were considered the ultimate feat of physical mediumship, requiring great concentration, harnessing of psychic energy and even loss of weight on the part of the medium.

In her book *The Spiritualists,* author Ruth Brandon speculates that early manifestations such as rapping, ghostly hands playing instruments and spirit lights were merely the lead-in acts to the real business of seances: bringing the whole bodies of spirits to the people. A popular handbook for mediums in the mid-19th century advised practitioners to follow the lead of their spirit guides, as not all spirits were capable of materializing. All mediums have the potential, the handbook claimed, but few can gather the necessary energy or have the patience to wait for the phenomenon to appear.

Materialization manifestations usually followed a similar routine. The medium would enter a cabinet (q.v.) in order to collect the psychic energy necessary to produce ectoplasm (q.v.). Soon a spot of white light, or flakes of whiteness, would appear, spreading into a cloud of vaporous whiteness. Next a face would appear, usually on or in front of the dark cabinet curtains; in fortunate circumstances, an entire person would appear. After the spirit had circulated throughout the circle, it returned to the cabinet, or with spectacular effect, melted away. The medium, always found in the cabinet, could lose substantial weight during the process and was quite weak afterward.

Author Rev. Robert Chaney postulated that the medium must project ectoplasm from her own body, plus that gathered from the sitters through magnetization, to facilitate materialization. The spirit is then clothed in this astral substance and appears. If the transformation is incomplete, the medium takes the spirit drapery and assumes the part of the spirit, a process called transfiguration.

Although making only a brief appearance, the famous spirit control John King materialized in the light from Ira Davenport's gunflash in 1850. The first full-form materialization appeared to Robert Dale Owen in 1860 through Leah Underhill, Kate and Maggie Fox's older sister (see FOX SISTERS). Owen reported that a veiled and luminous figure materialized and walked about the room, then disappeared. Not to be outdone, Kate Fox produced the figure of a Mrs. Livermore, deceased wife of one of her clients, and frequently brought the spirit of Benjamin Franklin into her circle.

Agnes GUPPY claimed to be the first English medium to materialize spirits, bringing John King's ghost to her astonished sitters in 1872. John King also appeared in the seances of Mr. and Mrs. Nelson Holmes and those of Mrs. Guppy's protégés Frank Herne and Charles Williams. Sitters at a Herne-Williams seance could even shake John King's hand. But all of their efforts were soon surpassed in the materializations of Katie King by medium Florence COOK.

Cook specialized in materialization from the beginning, starting with faces in 1872. By mid-1873, she introduced Katie King, allegedly John's daughter, as a white-veiled, barefoot figure who walked about the seance room, touching and caressing the sitters and allowing herself to be touched in return. She felt warm to the touch, seemed possessed of flesh and blood, and was an instant sensation.

Katie strongly resembled Cook. In December 1873, during a seance for the Earl and Countess of Caithness, sitter William Volckman grabbed Katie and struggled with the apparition, claiming that Katie was no ghost but Cook in costume. Katie put up a good fight, scratching Volckman's nose and pulling out some of his whiskers. The other sitters separated the two and returned Katie into the cabinet to rejoin Cook, who was found five minutes later disheveled but still bound and sealed. Spiritualists strongly condemned Volckman for his behavior, saying he could have caused Cook severe injury or death. It was believed that mediums were quite vulnerable during materializations.

One of Cook's strongest supporters was the eminent scientist Sir William CROOKES, who investigated her after the Volckman affair. Crookes pronounced the materialization of Katie King completely genuine. He described Katie in rapturous terms, citing her loveliness and good nature, coupled with Cook's innocence, as proof of the spirit's existence. Katie even sang lullabies to Crookes's children, telling them stories of her glory days in 17th-century Jamaica. Crookes photographed Katie and Cook together, but unfortunately destroyed the plates. Several pictures remain of Katie alone, however, one on the arm of Crookes.

In her early days under her real name, Marthe BERAUD, medium Eva C. materialized the Indian Brahmin Bien Boa. Photographs show Bien Boa as a tall man wearing a white garment like a monk's habit, with the hood pulled over a metal helmet. He was bearded and in no way resembled Beraud. Although strange in appearance, Bien Boa was real. He would return from behind the cabinet curtains to acknowledge applause for his performance. Unfortunately, Bien Boa was a little too life-like; his real name was Areski, and he was a former coachman, and very much alive.

Later, Beraud (going by the name Eva C.) materialized the faces and forms of several government and historical figures, most notably U.S. President Woodrow Wilson, King Ferdinand of Bulgaria and the actress Mona Delza. Critics found the materializations flat and two-dimensional, charging they were most likely cutouts from magazines and newspapers draped with muslin. One face even had part of the words *Le Miroir*, a French magazine, on the forehead. Baron Albert von SCHRENCK-NOTZING, one of Beraud's investigators, attributed such coincidences to *hypermnesia*, very acute memory, and *cryptomnesia*, the ability to recall mental images buried in the subconscious. Such reproductions, dug up from Beraud's past, were called "ideoplasts."

Recipes circulated among mediums for preparing the best ghostly effects. One required 21 yards of fine white silk veiling, very gauzy, washed carefully seven times. While still damp, the fabric was dipped in one jar of Balmain's Luminous Paint, a half-pint of Demar varnish, one pint of odorless benzine and 50 drops of lavender oil. Then the fabric dried for three days, at which time it was washed with naphtha soap to remove all odor. Only silk would hold the paint through so many washings and look so soft and luminous in the seance.

Rosina Showers, another young materialization medium and a friend of Florence Cook, described in a confession of fraud how to materialize the spirits: The medium should wear a dress she can easily take off in two or three minutes, wearing two or three shifts underneath. She conceals a filmy muslin veil in her underwear; this veil is her only clothing over the shifts. A pocket handkerchief conceals her hair. After emerging from the cabinet, the "ghost" circulates among the sitters, easily charming them. She then returns to the cabinet and re-dresses. Showers was surprised that none of the investigators thought of checking in the medium's drawers.

In his work for the Seybert Commission, Dr. H.H. Furness attended more than 20 materialization seances. He found some mediums more practiced than others, but applauded the charming work of most as they gracefully appeared as spirits, lightly appearing and disappearing through the cabinet curtains. Throughout it all, he never ceased to be amazed at the faith of the sitters, who recognized their husbands, fathers, mothers, wives and children in the costumed persona of the medium.

Further reading:

Brandon, Ruth. *The Spiritualists.* New York: Alfred A. Knopf, 1983.

Chaney, Rev. Robert G. *Mediums and the Development of Mediumship.* Freeport, N.Y.: Books for Libraries Press, 1972.

Douglas, Alfred. *Extra-Sensory Powers: A Century of Psychical Research.* Woodstock, N.Y.: The Overlook Press, 1977.

Doyle, Sir Arthur Conan. *The History of Spiritualism Vol. I & II.* New York: Arno Press, 1975.

Fodor, Nandor. *An Encyclopaedia of Psychic Science.* Secaucus, N.J.: The Citadel Press, 1966. First published 1933.

Oppenheim, Janet. *The Other World: Spiritualism and Psychical Research in England 1850–1914.* New York: Cambridge University Press, 1985.

Mysteries of the Unknown: Spirit Summonings. Alexandria, Va.: Time-Life Books, 1989.

mazes Mazes have ancient associations with the underworld and with souls of the dead. They represent a path to the underworld that can be negotiated only by the initiated.

Mazes exist universally around the world. The oldest, in ancient Egypt, is believed to have been built about 5,000 years ago. According to the Greek historian Herodotus, the labyrinth was built by 12 kings as a memorial to themselves, and as the tomb of sacred crocodiles. The Egyptian earth god, Geb, assumed the shape of a crocodile and was worshipped by the souls of the dead, according to the *Egyptian Book of the Dead.* Herodotus said the labyrinth far surpassed the pyramids in magnificence.

In myth and legend, mazes are difficult and fraught with dangers. They are presided over by various deities and supernatural beings and creatures, some of whom help travelers and some of whom hinder. To negotiate a maze successfully is to gain access to the secret mysteries of life and death. The river Lethe ("oblivion") that separates Hades from the world of the living in Greek myth was said to be a watery labyrinth. The Labyrinth of Crete had no way out; at its center was the mythical beast, the Minotaur, half man and half bull, who devoured people who were sent into the maze as sacrificial victims. The hero, Theseus, navigated the maze, slew the monster, and found his way out.

Mazes have many different shapes and patterns; they are symmetrical and balanced. One of the most common shapes is the spiral, a symbol of Goddess, which was the shape of the mythical Labyrinth of Crete, presided over by a Goddess-figure, the Mistress of the Labyrinth.

The Tor, the hill at the ruins of Glastonbury Abbey in Wiltshire, England, is associated with Arthurian and Grail legends. It is believed to have a hollow space inside, which can be approached only by threading one's way through a real maze which exists on the outer face of the hill. The maze is said to lead to a point of entry to Annwn, the Celtic Underworld or Otherworld ruled by the demi-god Gwyn ap Nudd. According to legend, St. Collen successfully negotiated the maze and entered Annwn, where he met the demi-god. In Celtic myth, Annwn holds a magic cauldron kept by nine maidens. Magic cauldrons, the source of unlimited physical and spiritual nourishment, inspiration and regeneration, figure prominently in mythologies. For example, there are the magic cauldrons of the Celtic goddess Cerridwen and the Greek goddess Medea.

According to Christian Grail legends, Annwn holds the Grail, the chalice said to have been used by Christ at the Last Supper, and which was used by Joseph of Arimathea to catch Christ's blood at or after the crucifixion. The Grail is a variant of the magic cauldron.

During the Middle Ages, mazes were built in the great Gothic churches and cathedrals. In modern times they are created primarily as turf and topiary designs in gardens.

Further reading:
Matthews, W.H. *Mazes and Labyrinths: Their History and Development.* New York: Dover Publications, 1970. First published as *Mazes and Labyrinths: A General Account of Their History and Developments.* London: Longmans, Green & Co., 1922.

mediums and mediumship   Throughout history and in all cultures, humankind has attempted to communicate with spirits, spirits of the dead and the gods through mediums, or persons ascribed supernormal powers who receive information not available through the normal senses. Mediums heal and cause physical phenomena, such as the movement of objects and the control of weather (see PSYCHOKINESIS). Mediums have been known by various names, among them oracle, soothsayer, wizard, cunning woman, wise woman, witch, medicine man, sorcerer, shaman, fortune teller, witch doctor, mystic, priest, prophet and channeler.

The term "mediumship" usually is applied to mesmeric and Spiritualist communication with spirits of the dead. The origins of mediumship began in research of mesmerism during the 19th century. Some subjects who were "magnetized," or hypnotized, into trances fell under the control of spirits and delivered messages from the Other Side. Like shamans who communicate with the spirit world by becoming possessed by godlings, spirit animals and deities, the mesmeric subjects became temporarily "possessed" by discarnate spirits. As Spiritualism grew, first in America and then in Britain, mesmeric mediums were absorbed into it. Mediums demonstrated their abilities either at private seances held in a home, or in public in a lecture hall.

Mediumship is divided into two categories: mental and physical. In mental mediumship, the medium communicates through inner vision, clairaudience and mental impressions. Physical mediumship was popular toward the end of the 19th century, and is characterized by feats attributed to the spirits, such as rappings, table-tipping, levitation of objects or the medium, movement of objects, materializations, apports, ghostly music, "spirit lights," and strange scents. The medium's communications with spirits are governed by one or more entities called controls. Some psychical researchers contend that controls are

not external spirits, but secondary personalities of the medium.

WHO BECOMES A MEDIUM?

Mediumship often begins early in life, when a child sees and hears things others do not. Often this ability is repressed in response to disapproving adults. Mediumship also can begin at any age later in life as the result of a trauma, such as a blow to the head, a near-death experience, extreme emotional shock or profound grief. Many mediums come from ordinary, working-class or middle-class backgrounds.

Most Western mediums were, and still are, female. In other cultures, the reverse is true. Most shamans, for example, are male. Cultural expectations play a major role in the predominance of a sex in the psychic realm.

During the height of Spiritualism, from the mid- to late-19th century, it was no accident that most mediums were housebound women, who undoubtedly were bored with the creative and educational limitations placed upon them by society. Mediumship provided attention and freedom, and permitted outrageous, masculine behavior, which could be blamed on the "spirits." The press criticized female mediums for being corrupted of their femininity, and lambasted male mediums for being too feminine.

The popularity of Spiritualism prompted hundreds of housewives to begin holding tea parlor seances for their friends. Mediumship seemed to run along bloodlines, with all the women in a family claiming to share the gift. Many avoided publicity and would not accept money; the diversion was all they sought. Others became professional, advertised and charged money.

Of the mediums who took to the lecture circuit, most of them by far were women. They delighted in shocking their audiences with deep trance voices and theatrics. Cora Richmond, famous on both sides of the Atlantic, gave "trance lectures." The audience selected a jury—usually all male—which selected a topic of discourse, usually science or some "masculine" subject. Richmond entered a trance and gave an instant "spirit" lecture on it. Her audiences invariably were impressed, though skeptics noted that the talks were bland, monotonous and predictable.

Other mediums were more dramatic. Some reveled in their possession by male spirits, who "forced" them, for example, to swear and drink whiskey from a bottle. Some told stories of being strangled by pirate spirits. In America, two female mediums engaged in a fist fight on stage because their spirit controls hated each other.

Aspects of sexual liberation were part of Spiritual mediumship as well. Both mediums and their clients frankly enjoyed the physical contact of holding hands, knees, legs and feet during seances, and caressing and kissing "spirit" materializations. Some mediums engaged in affairs under the direction of their spirits. It was not unusual for mediums to leave their husbands—also under the direction of their spirits—and to counsel other women to divorce their mates as well. Mediums claimed to consort with their spirits; the illegitimate offspring that resulted were called "spirit babies."

Despite the fame and freedom, mediumship seldom led to riches. The lucky mediums attracted wealthy benefactors; D.D. HOME enjoyed the rarified company of royalty and nobility. In America, the average medium earned five dollars for a night's performance away from home, and one dollar per hour at home. Female mediums complained bitterly about their low incomes.

Another hazard was ostracization. Despite the adulation of clients, many women-turned-mediums found themselves cast out by family and friends who disapproved of their behavior.

FRAUD

Physical mediumship was fraught with fraud during the competitive height of Spiritualism, with mediums resorting to stage magic tricks for the special effects necessary to attract an audience. Numerous mediums who claimed to materialize spirits were caught impersonating the spirits themselves. Sir William CROOKES, an eminent British physicist and chemist who investigated mediums, said he believed that nearly all mediums resorted to tricks at times. Strangely, he vouched for Florence COOK, who was exposed of fraud more than once. Mediums who were caught, such as Eusapia PALLADINO, complained that public expectations for a performance pressured her into cheating. Fraud, however, does not explain all phenomena associated with physical mediumship.

Fraud also has existed in mental mediumship, particularly toward the mid-20th century, when Spiritualist camps were at their peak of popularity. Arthur FORD, who was often accused of fraud but was never exposed, said no medium could perform 100% of the time; rather than admit an off day, most would cheat.

IS MEDIUMSHIP A MENTAL DISORDER?

Some of the phenomena associated with mediumship also occur in schizophrenia: altered states of consciousness, visions, disembodied voices, and the temporary possession of a medium by a spirit entity or personality. Many prominent mediums have been extensively interviewed and observed by psychiatrists and psychologists, some of whom conclude that mediumship is a form of schizophrenia, and that the "spirits" manifested are merely subpersonalities of the medium which emerge from deep layers of consciousness to seek their own independent expression.

Mediumship cannot be dismissed, however, as a mental disorder. Schizophrenics have no control over the voices, visions and personalities; they occur spontaneously, often without warning, and in many cases will not cease despite the desperate attempts of the victim to turn them off. Mediumship is a psychic gift that the medium learns to control. Schizophrenics become disoriented by their experiences, which are nonproductive; mediums use mediumship for spiritual growth and to help others. Schizophrenics lose their ability to function in normal reality; mediums, for the most part, carry on normal lives.

SURVIVAL AFTER DEATH

Mental mediumship may offer the best evidence for survival after death (q.v.). Some information obtained from spirits of the dead may be verified through research. Some researchers argue, however, that information might be obtained paranormally from the medium from existing sources (see SUPER-ESP) or from the subconscious (see CRYPTOMNESIA).

The parapsychology establishment has had little interest in mediumship since about the mid-20th century.

See also CHANNELING; EXORCISM; SHAMANISM.

Further reading:
Douglas, Alfred. *Extrasensory Powers: A Century of Psychical Research*. London: Victor Gollacz Ltd., 1976.
Gauld, Alan. *Mediumship and Survival*. London: William Heinemann Ltd., 1982.
Moore, R. Laurence. *In Search of White Crows*. New York: Oxford University Press, 1977.
Oppenheim, Janet. *The Other World: Spiritualism and Psychical Research in England, 1850–1914*. Cambridge: Cambridge University Press, 1985.

Meek, George See ELECTRONIC VOICE PHENOMENON.

megaliths See GHOST LIGHTS.

meteors Shooting stars that blaze across the nighttime sky are associated in many cultures with the spirits of the dead. The ancient Romans believed that every person had a star, and when he died, it fell to earth. From this evolved the folklore belief in Europe and America that a meteor is the soul of one who has just died. Similar beliefs are held by tribal societies, such as the Inuit of North America and the Aborigines of Australia; in some places, shooting stars are said to be the souls of murdered men. The Lolos of western China also believe that each person has a star that remains in the sky as long as he is alive. When a person dies, a hole is dug for the star so that it does not fall on someone else. Some NativeAmerican tribes believe stars are the souls of the dead and when they fall, it is the soul coming to be reborn (see REINCARNATION).

Miami Poltergeist   First poltergeist cases in which scientifically controlled experiments were conducted to determine the nature of the activity. A human focal point was identified.

The Miami Poltergeist case began in late 1966 or early 1967, when an unusual number of objects in the warehouse of Tropican Arts, a wholesaler of novelty items, spilled and broke under mysterious circumstances. At first, carelessness on the part of shipping clerks was blamed. On January 14, 1967, the Miami police were called by the warehouse manager, Alvin Laubheim, who complained that a "ghost" was in his warehouse breaking things. The investigating officer arrived and witnessed objects falling off shelves of their own accord.

After the case came to public awareness, parapsychologists, including William G. ROLL and J. Gaither Pratt, investigated. Almost immediately Roll suspected that a human focal point was responsible, and that the person was a 19-year-old shipping clerk named Julio. The breakages and movements of objects always took place when Julio was in the vicinity, and the activity was most intense when Julio seemed to be irritated or upset. Julio's proximity to the activity had led coworkers to accuse him of being the culprit, which he vehemently denied. He did confess, however, that the breakages made him happy. The researchers found no evidence that he was responsible for the incidents, or that any trickery was used to stage effects.

No objects moved when attempts were made to film activity. Also, activity in general decreased whenever Roll was on the scene, although he did manage to witness 13 of the 224 incidents that were documented.

Julio's father-in-law to be, Jose Diaz, a medium, was brought to the warehouse by management, and

he claimed to see an "alligator spirit" that allegedly was responsible for the mischief. Diaz placed items about the warehouse to serve as diversionary "playthings" for the spirit, but the breakages continued.

Roll and Pratt examined all shelves to make sure that boxes and items were pushed as far back as possible, to eliminate the possibility of vibrations or jarring causing them to fall naturally. To see if objects rose up in the air before falling, Roll placed notebooks as a barrier in front of rows of glasses on shelves. When broken glass was discovered and the notebooks stood undisturbed, it indicated that the glasses had risen up into the air before falling to the ground.

The case also enabled Roll to test his "psi field" theory (see POLTERGEIST), which holds that phenomena reduce with distance from the agent due to a weakening psi field, comparable to a magnetic field. Activity was reduced with distance from Julio; however, objects farthest away from him traveled the longest distances, while objects nearest him traveled the shortest distance. To explain this, Roll proposed that the psi field rotates in a circular motion around an agent similar to a vortex. This explanation has been widely contested by other parapsychologists.

Julio agreed to take a battery of personality and psychological tests. Results that might indicate unconscious PSYCHOKINESIS (PK) at work included anger, rebellion, a sense of unworthiness, guilt, rejection, detachment, passivity and inaction, a feeling of being apart from the social environment, and a feeling that he did not get what he felt he deserved, and dissociation, especially in terms of expressing aggression. Julio also acknowledged disliking his boss. It also was discovered that 10 days prior to the start of the phenomena at the warehouse, Julio had had some upsetting experiences at home, with his stepmother trying to get him to move out of the house. He suffered nightmares and had suicidal feelings.

On January 30, a break-in occurred at the warehouse and some items and petty cash were taken. Julio was suspected, and he later confessed. The owner and manager did not press charges. The police sergeant also said that Julio claimed he had caused the poltergeist activity with trickery using threads; the sergeant, however, never examined the warehouse, and Roll and Pratt doubted the claim. Several days later, Julio stole a ring from a jeweler for his fiancee. He was convicted and sent to jail for six months. After his departure from the warehouse, phenomena ceased.

Upon Julio's release, Roll and others attempted to arrange financial support for him so that he could undergo laboratory research for extrasensory perception (ESP) and PK. Julio declined, and pursued marriage and a tumultous job history. He eventually did undergo tests, and showed significant results for PK but not for ESP. He indicated an ability to control his PK. Later, his father-in-law attempted to help him improve his control of PK in mediumistic sittings.

The Miami case is evidence in support of the theory that at least some cases of poltergeist outbreaks are caused unwittingly by human agents, perhaps due to repressed emotions and hostilities.

See also BALTIMORE POLTERGEIST; FODOR, NANDOR.

Further reading:
Roll, William G. *The Poltergeist.* Garden City, N.Y.: Nelson Doubleday, 1972.

Milky Way   See BRIDGE OF SOULS.

mine spirits   See BLUE-CAP; KNOCKER; KOBOLD.

mirror writing   See SLATE-WRITING.

mirrors   Many superstitions exist concerning mirrors, ghosts, souls and death. In primitive societies, beliefs still are held that mirrors reflect the soul, and must be guarded against lest the soul be lost. In Russian folklore, mirrors are the invention of the Devil because they have the power to draw souls out of bodies. Similarly, superstition holds that mirrors, and in some places of the world all shiny surfaces, must be covered in a house after a death to prevent the soul of the living from being carried off by the ghost of the newly departed. The mirrors are covered for a variety of reasons, depending on the local lore: one will see the corpse looking over one's shoulder and be frightened; if the corpse is seen in the mirror the soul of the dead one will have no rest; one will see a ghost; the soul of the dead will be carried off by a ghost. Covering is also done out of respect for the dead.

Mirrors should be removed from a sick room, it is widely believed, because the soul is more vulnerable in times of illness. It is considered very unlucky for the sick to see their reflections, which puts them at risk of dying.

It is also considered very unlucky to look into a mirror at night or by candlelight—one will see ghosts, the Devil or something uncanny, which will portend death. An old Persian spell claims that ghosts may be seen in a mirror by standing in front of it and combing the hair without thinking, speaking or otherwise moving.

Many cultures have beliefs that a person who sees his reflection in anything will soon die. In Greek myth, Narcissus saw his reflection in water and then pined and died. The ancient Greeks also believed that even dreaming of seeing one's reflection was a death omen. A widely held superstition is that looking into a mirror following a death means one will die. In Ozark lore, the appearance of a distant friend in a mirror means he or she will soon die.

Breaking a mirror means seven years of bad luck, and also means death in the family or household. For example, if a child breaks a mirror, one of the children in the house will die within the year.

Further reading:
Guiley, Rosemary Ellen. *Harper's Encyclopedia of Mystical and Paranormal Experience.* San Francisco: HarperSanFrancisco, 1991.
Leach, Maria, and Jerome Fried, eds. *Fund & Wagnalls Standard Dictionary of Folklore, Mythology, and Legend.* San Francisco: Harper & Row, 1979.
Opie, Iona, and Moira Tatem. *A Dictionary of Superstitions.* Oxford: Oxford University Press, 1989.

moon   In mythology, the moon is often the destination point or repository of souls after death. The gods and goddesses of the underworld, the realm of the dead, often are lunar deities. The association of the moon with death and rebirth is due to its waxing and waning: every 28 days, the moon "dies" and then is reborn.

The ancient Greeks believed the moon to be a midway point for souls making the transition either from earth to heaven or from heaven to earth. The souls of the newly dead went first to the moon, where their astral bodies were purified before continuing on to the heavens. The souls of heroes and geniuses, in preparing to reincarnate on earth, went to the moon's face, which is always turned toward earth, where they became clothed in appropriate bodies.

According to Plutarch, the first-century Greek philosopher, human beings had two deaths. The first occurred on earth in the domain of Demeter, goddess of fecundity. The body was severed from soul and mind and returned to dust. Soul and mind went to the underworld, the domain of Persephone, where a second death separated the two. The soul returned to the moon, where it retained the memories of life, while the mind went to the sun, where it was absorbed and then was reborn. The mind then went back to the moon and joined with the soul, and together they went to earth to reincarnate in a new body.

According to the *Upanishads,* sacred Hindu texts, the souls of unenlightened people go to the moon after death, where they await reincarnation. Enlightened souls who have been liberated from reincarnation go to the sun.

Further reading:

Eliade, Mircea. *Patterns in Comparative Religions.* New York: New American Library, 1974. First published 1958.

Guiley, Rosemary Ellen. *Moonscapes: A Celebration of Lunar Astronomy, Magic, Legend and Lore.* New York: Prentice-Hall, 1991.

Schure, Edouard. *The Great Initiates: A Study of the Secret Religions of History.* San Francisco: Harper & Row, 1961.

Morton Case   See CHELTENHAM HAUNTING.

Moses, Rev. William Stainton (1839–1892)

University-educated medium, among the most prominent of British Spiritualists.

William Stainton Moses was born November 5, 1839 in Donnington, Lincolnshire, England. His father was headmaster of the Donnington Grammar School.

Only one unusual incident has been recorded from Moses' early years. He would occasionally walk in his sleep; once when in this state he went down to the living room, wrote out a homework assignment, and returned to bed without waking. His essay was judged the best of those turned in the next day.

Moses began attending Bedford College in 1852 and then won a scholarship to Exeter College, Oxford. There he proved to be an ambitious and diligent student until his health broke down from overwork; he left his studies, traveled for some time, and spent six months in a monastery on Mount Athos in Greece. When he had recovered his health, he returned to Oxford and took his B.A. degree. He was ordained as a minister of the Church of England at the age of 24 in 1863 and was sent to Kirk Maughold, near Ramsey, on the Isle of Man.

In 1869, Moses fell seriously ill and was administered to by a Dr. Stanhope Templeman Speer, who was visiting from London. The association proved to be the beginning of a lifelong friendship with Dr. Speer and his family. During his convalescence, Moses spent some time in the Speer home, and for seven years he tutored the Speer's son, Charlton.

In 1871, Moses accepted a mastership at University College School in London. Until this time he had had little interest in Spiritualism, but in 1872 he was persuaded by Mrs. Speer to attend a seance. It was to be the first of several, including some with the remarkable medium D.D. HOME. Within about six months, Moses found himself convinced of the truth of Spiritualism, and he soon began to show signs of possessing mediumistic powers himself.

In the home circle (q.v.) Moses established with the Speers, he revealed powerful paranormal physical abilities, including levitations (of himself), apports and table tiltings. Objects left in his bedroom were often found arranged in the shape of a cross. Lights, sounds and scents of varying description were produced at his seances. There were also materializations of luminous hands and columns of light that vaguely suggested human forms. Phenomena of this type continued with gradually lessening frequency until 1881.

Also in 1872, Moses began automatic writing, and this continued until 1883. He recorded his scripts in a series of notebooks and serialized many in a widely read newspaper, *The Spiritualist*, under the pseudonym "M.A. Oxon." They later formed the basis of the books *Spirit Identity* (1879), *Higher Aspects of Spiritualism* (1880) and *Spirit Teachings* (1883).

Many of these scripts take the form of dialogues between Moses and a group of spirit controls calling themselves the "Imperator" group. They present a coherent Spiritualist cosmology, and in content and influence they may be compared to the work of the American Andrew Jackson DAVIS. *Spirit Teachings* quickly became the "Bible of British Spiritualism."

Now and then Moses' scripts included evidential communications, and these, along with his physical demonstrations, were sufficient to attract the notice of psychical researchers, as well as Spiritualists. Sir William CROOKES was an occasional sitter at Moses' seances, and it was after attending one in 1874 that Frederic W.H. MYERS persuaded Henry SIDGWICK to join in organizing a group to investigate mediumship; this proved to be a forerunner of the SOCIETY FOR PSYCHICAL RESEARCH (SPR) established in 1882.

The SPR was originally intended as an alliance between Spiritualists and researchers for the serious investigation of psychic phenomena. Moses sat on the first council as a vice president. He and many other Spiritualists were impatient with the critical attitude displayed by the researchers, however. Following Eleanor SIDGWICK's comments on the fraudulent slate-writing medium William Eglinton in 1886, Moses withdrew from the SPR's council and resigned from the society. Several others left with him or shortly thereafter.

Already in 1884 Moses had founded his own organization, the London Spiritualist Alliance (LSA). This was intended to replace the British National Association of Spiritualists (BNAS), which had been in existence from 1872 to 1882. Moses had been associated with the BNAS for most of that time; but he had become disenchanted with it and had left in 1880. The new LSA began to issue a Spiritualist journal, *Light,* under Moses's editorship. This journal continues to be published today by the COLLEGE FOR PSYCHIC STUDIES, successor to the LSA.

Moses remained in his teaching position at the University College School until failing health forced his resignation in 1889. He died three years later, on September 5, 1892, of complications brought on by Bright's disease.

He willed the notebooks of automatic writings and seance records to two fellow Spiritualists, Charles Massey and Alaric A. Watts, who lent them for study to Frederic Myers. Myers in turn reported on them in the SPR *Proceedings.* He was impressed by the similarity of Moses' phenomena to those associated with D.D. Home and he stressed (as did many others throughout Moses's life) his moral uprightness and probity.

Other writers have pointed out that unfortunately most of his seances were private and were not ordinarily attended by outsiders, and the records, although detailed, were kept either by Moses himself or by the Speers. These last factors unavoidably reduce the significance that may be attached to the mediumship, although Moses remains, along with Home, the only major physical medium never caught as a fraud, nor even seriously suspected.

Moses's other books, also published under the pseudonym "M. A. Oxon," include *Psychography* (1878) and *Ghostly Visitors* (1882).

Further reading:

Gauld, Alan. *The Founders of Psychical Research.* London: Routledge & Kegan Paul, 1968.

Myers, F. W. H. "The Experiences of W. Stainton Moses—I." *Proceedings of the Society for Psychical Research* 9 (1894):245–352.

Oppenheim, Janet. *The Other World: Spiritualism and Psychical Research in England, 1850–1914.* Cambridge: Cambridge University Press, 1985.

Mount, The   Author Edith Wharton's one-time country retreat in Lenox, Massachusetts, called The Mount, is said to be haunted by various ghostly figures, including Wharton, her husband Edward, and author Henry James.

Wharton (1862–1937), born to New York's high society, built the neo-Georgian mansion between 1900 and 1902. There she did much writing and hosted numerous guests who were the cream of society and the literati. One frequent visitor was Henry James. Wharton left The Mount in 1908 and sold it in 1912. The house passed through a succession of owners. For a while, it was occupied by Foxhollow School, a boarding school for girls. In 1978, the house was taken over by Shakespeare & Company, a troupe of

Edith Wharton. Courtesy American Academy of Arts and Letters.

actors that lives and performs plays there and opens the house to tourists in the summer. Shakespeare & Company purchased the house in 1980.

Rumors of hauntings have circulated for many years. Strange noises, rustlings, thuds and footsteps have been heard. Sounds of young girls laughing are thought to be connected with the residents of Foxhollow. Must unusual have been the number of visual apparitions reported there, particularly by members of the acting troupe. The phantoms have been seen both during the day and at night. An unidentified apparition of a man with a ponytail was reported in the Henry James Room. The figure of a woman, recognized as Wharton, has been seen in a second-floor hallway, alone and with another ghostly figure who resembles James. A ghost believed to be Wharton also has been spotted walking back and forth on the terrace. Encounters have been reported with a seemingly hostile figure, dressed in a hooded cloak, who manifests at bedside and presses down on the individuals.

One of the most unusual and interesting encounters took place in 1979 and is recorded in Arthur Myers's *Ghostly Register* (1986). Andrea Haring, an actress and voice teacher, lay down to rest late one night on a mattress in Edith Wharton's otherwise bare writing room. She awakened at 4:00 A.M. and sensed presences in the room, which had become extremely cold. She saw three figures and furniture that included a small divan and a desk with a chair. Both figures and furniture seemed real. A woman, whom Haring recognized as Wharton, was on the divan, talking. A man with muttonchop whiskers was at the desk, writing and gesturing to the woman. Standing with arms folded was another man, whom Haring recognized as Edward (Teddy) Wharton. The three seemed engaged in activity, as though they could hear each other, but Haring could not hear them. Wharton seemed to be dictating to the man at the desk. Haring thought about leaving the room, and at this thought, the ghosts turned to her and acknowledged her presence, then resumed their activity. Haring got up and left. She returned minutes later and found the room empty of apparitions, and warm once again. Later, after examining photographs in a book, Haring concluded the figure at the desk was Wharton's secretary of sorts, who may also have been her lover.

Further reading:

Myers, Arthur. *The Ghostly Register: Haunted Dwellings—Active Spirits, A Journey to America's Strangest Landmarks.* Chicago: Contemporary Books, 1986.

Riccio, Dolores, and Joan Bingham. *Haunted Houses USA.* New York: Pocket Books, 1989.

Mount Rainier Poltergeist Poltergeist cum possession case that inspired William Peter Blatty's bestselling novel, *The Exorcist.*

Blatty made numerous changes in dramatizing the story, among them making the afflicted child a girl rather than a boy. The subject of the actual case, "Roland," was thirteen and a half in January 1949, when his family began to be disturbed by scratching sounds coming from the ceilings and walls of their house in the Maryland suburb of Washington, D.C. called Mount Rainier. Thinking they had mice, his parents called an exterminator. This man could find no signs of rodents, and his efforts failed to end the scratching, which only became louder. Noises that sounded like someone walking about in squeaky shoes began to be heard in the hall. At times, dishes and furniture moved for no evident reason.

The noises and movements were frightening enough, but then Roland himself began to be attacked. His bed shook so hard that he could not sleep. His bedclothes were repeatedly pulled off the bed, and once, when he tried to hold onto them, he was pulled off onto the floor after them.

After a few weeks, Roland's parents were convinced that an evil spirit, possibly that of a recently deceased relative, was behind the disturbances and they appealed to their Lutheran minister, Luther Schulze, for help. Schulze tried praying with Roland and his parents in their home, and then with Roland alone in his own home. He led prayers for Roland in church. Reverend Schulze ordered whatever was possessing the boy to leave him in the name of the Father, the Son and the Holy Ghost, but the affliction continued.

The boy was tormented by the weird noises and movements of objects day and night, with the result that he was unable to sleep. In February, Schulze offered to let Roland spend a night at his house, to which his parents agreed.

That night, Mrs. Schulze went to a guest room, while Roland and the Reverend retired to twin four-poster beds in the master bedroom. Some time after they had said goodnight, Schulze heard Roland's bed creaking. He grasped the bed and felt it vibrating rapidly. Roland himself was wide awake, but was lying absolutely still.

Schulze suggested that Roland try to sleep in an armchair, while he kept an eye on him from his bed. Before long, the heavy chair began to move. First it scooted backward several inches. Schulze suggested Roland raise his legs, to add his full weight to the chair, but that was not enough to stop it from continuing until it had slammed into the wall. The chair then began to turn, as if in slow motion, until it had deposited the boy, unhurt, on the floor. Schulze noticed that Roland appeared to be in a trance, and made no effort to move out of the chair, even though it had been moving slowly enough for him to do so.

After this night, Schulze was able to persuade Roland's parents to have him tested in a mental health clinic, but he began to act wildly, and the message "Go to St. Louis!" appeared scratched on his skin in blood-red letters. Roland's favorite aunt lived in St. Louis, and since it was thought that he might benefit from being closer to her, he was sent to St. Louis Hospital. But more and more he began to act like someone possessed. He began to cough up phlegm and drool in a steady stream, and more scratches mysteriously appeared on his arms.

An exorcism eventually seemed to offer the only hope. Over the next 35 days, a Lutheran minister, an Episcopal priest and some Jesuit priests took turns performing the appropriate ritual. Roland was exorcised no fewer than 20 times. During the exorcisms, Roland's body would jerk in violent spasms. He seemed to be super-strong, and he repeatedly spat into the exorcist's eye. Gradually, however, his attacks subsided, and some time after his return to Washington in April they disappeared altogether.

Meanwhile, Schulze had contacted J.B. RHINE, who was then famous as the director of the Parapsychology Laboratory at Duke University. Rhine and his wife Louisa drove up to Washington, where they discussed the case with Schulze. Unfortunately the phenomena had ceased by this time and Rhine was not able to observe them for himself.

Roland's parents, Reverend Schulze, and the exorcists were all convinced that this was a genuine case of spirit possession, but Rhine's position as he represented it in his laboratory's *Parapsychology Bulletin* was very different. He believed that the phenomena were expressions of the boy's own unconscious ability to influence the objects in his environment and his own body through the power of his mind (see PSYCHOKINESIS).

In fact, although the case is not particularly dramatic as such cases go, the noises heard in Roland's home are typical poltergeist behavior. Bedclothes have been pulled off the bed in other cases. Another typical feature is Roland's age—many poltergeist cases involve children in late childhood or early adolescence. Psychical researchers theorize that most such cases are due to psychokinesis on the part of the "focal personality." Very often there is some conflict in the family, and the outbreak seems to form an outlet for the child's tension. The scratches and marks Roland suffered also appear in other poltergeist cases (see ZUGUN, ELEANORE). Roland's apparent trances and his coughing up phlegm, on the other hand, are more characteristic of cases of possession.

William Peter Blatty was a student at Georgetown University in Washington in August 1949, when he read an Associated Press account of the case in the *Washington Post*. He began to look into the story and soon had made himself thoroughly familiar with it. When he turned to writing his bestselling novel 20 years later, however, he changed so many details and added so much new material that the original story is almost entirely obscured.

Further reading:

Blatty, William Peter. *William Peter Blatty on The Exorcist.* New York: Bantam, 1974.

Brian, Dennis. *The Enchanted Voyager: The Life of J.B. Rhine.* Englewood Cliffs, N.J.: Prentice-Hall, 1982.

Gauld, Alan, and A.T. Cornell. *Poltergeists.* London: Routledge and Kegan Paul, 1979.

"Report of a Poltergeist." *Parapsychology Bulletin* 15 (1949): 2–3.

moving coffins Mysterious disturbances of coffins inside sealed crypts have been recorded in cases around the world. For reasons unknown, heavy, lead coffins in a vault are found in disarray, as though tossed about by some tremendous force. They are restored to their proper positions, only to be found tossed about again the next time the vault is opened for burial.

No satisfactory natural explanations have ever been found. It has been theorized that the coffins were moved when crypts flooded with water: they floated to new positions and were left at ungainly angles as the water receded. While these circumstances have been demonstrated in a church in London, flooding crypts have been unlikely in other cases of moving coffins, especially in locales above sea level. Paranormal theories attribute the disturbances to poltergeists or to the restless dead, especially if persons buried within a disturbed vault had committed suicide.

THE CHASE CRYPT OF BARBADOS

The most famous of moving coffin cases concerns the family crypt of Colonel Thomas Chase, of Christchurch, Barbados. For several years in the early 19th century, lead coffins were found hurled about inside the vault. The mystery was never solved.

Chase was a well-to-do Englishman who had a reputation among the natives as a cruel and short-tempered man who treated both family and slaves poorly. In the early years of the 19th century, Chase purchased an ornate coral and stone crypt with a huge slab door, located on a headland, to serve as his family tomb.

The first family member to be interred there was a Mrs. Goddard, a relative of Chase, who died on July 31, 1807. She was placed inside the crypt in a lead coffin so heavy that it took four strong men to lift it. Mrs. Goddard was followed a few months later by Chase's infant daughter, Mary Anna, who died of disease. On July 6, 1812, Dorcas Chase, another of the colonel's daughters, was buried. When the crypt was opened this third time, nothing unusual was noted; the heavy coffins of the other two family members remained as they had been placed originally.

In August 1812, Chase himself died. As the vault was opened for his burial, family members and spectators were shocked to see the other three coffins in disarray, as though they had been tossed about like toys. Little Mary Anna's coffin looked as though it had been thrown diagonally to the opposite corner of the crypt. It was assumed that vandals had broken into the crypt and somehow managed to move the coffins.

Workmen restored the coffins to their original positions, laid side by side, and placed Chase's coffin on top and across them. To detect further vandalism, someone spread a layer of sand on the floor.

The crypt was not opened again until 1816, when another family baby died. Again the family was shocked to find all four coffins scattered wildly throughout the crypt. Even more astonishing, the sand was undisturbed. The scene was repeated a few weeks later when the body of Samuel Brewster, a family member, was removed from its grave at the parish of St. Phillip and reburied in the Chase crypt. Once again, the coffins were found in disarray with the sand undisturbed.

The natives began to speak of "duppies," as they called evil spirits. It also was rumored that the spirits of the previous family dead were reacting vehemently to the unwanted presence of Colonel Chase. Stories circulated that he had been so cruel toward Dorcas that she had starved herself to death, and that in turn he had committed suicide.

The rumors caused a great deal of anxiety among the superstitious natives, causing the English governor of Barbados, Lord Combermere, to attempt to put the matter to rest. In July 1819, Chase family member Thomasina Clarke was buried in the crypt. Combermere and his wife were present when the tomb was opened, and once again the coffins were found strewn madly about. No marks appeared in the sand. Once again, all coffins were restored to their original positions. Mrs. Combermere wrote in her diary:

> In my husband's presence, every part of the floor was sounded to ascertain that no subterranean passage or entrance was concealed. It was found to be perfectly firm and solid; no crack was even apparent. The walls, when examined, proved to be perfectly secure. No fracture was visible, and the sides, together with the roof and flooring, presented a structure so solid as if formed of entire slabs of stone. The displaced coffins were rearranged, the new tenant of that dreary abode was deposited, and when the mourners retired with the funeral procession, the floor was sanded with fine white sand in the presence of Lord Combermere and the assembled crowd. The door was slid into its wonted position and, with the utmost care, the new mortar was laid on so as to secure it. When the masons had completed their task, the Governor made several impressions in the mixture with his own seal, and many of those attending added various private marks in the wet mortar . . .

After nine months, Combermere ordered the vault unsealed on April 18, 1820. Hundreds of persons turned out to witness it.

Combermere found his seal and all other marks in the mortar undisturbed. He ordered the stone slab to be opened, but workmen could not budge it. After a great deal of effort, the slab finally was moved just enough to allow entry.

To Combermere's surprise, but not to the natives', the coffins were tossed about. One had been on end resting against the slab door, accounting for the great difficulty in opening it. One of the baby coffins apparently had been thrown against the stone wall with such force as to leave a deep gash. Another coffin appeared to have been thrown down the steps to the bottom of the tomb.

Horrified, the Chase family removed all the coffins and buried them elsewhere. The vault was closed, never to be used again.

OTHER CASES OF MOVING COFFINS

In the mid-18th century in Staunton, England (now Stanton All Saints, near Bury St. Edmunds), coffins were found disturbed on three occasions in a vault belonging to a family named French. One of the displaced coffins was so heavy that eight men were required to move it back to its proper position. Flooding was advanced as a cause, though the vault showed no signs of having held water at the times it was opened.

Similarly, coffins were found in disarray twice in the Gretford family vault near Stamford, England, in the early 19th century. Water again was supposed as the cause, though no signs of it were found.

A disturbance similar to the Chase case of Barbados occurred in 1844 in the Buxhowden crypt on the Island of Oesel, now called Saare Maa, located in the Baltic Sea, the home of a largely Lutheran population. In 1844, horses tethered near the vault became frantic when a loud crash was heard to emanate from within the crypt. Subsequently, other loud crashes were heard. When the vault was opened for a burial, several coffins were found scattered about and even lying one atop another. Three were not disturbed: they contained the body of an old woman said to have been very devout, and the bodies of two young children. Villagers inferred that demonic forces were responsible, since the coffins of the devout and the pure were untouched.

So much popular excitement ensued that a commission was appointed to investigate. The coffins were restored to order. The pavement was torn up to make certain there was no secret access to the vault. The vault's floor and steps were covered with fine ash to reveal footprints of intruders, and guards were posted around the clock.

After three days, the Buxhowden vault was reopened. According to an anecdotal account, all coffins but the three were scattered about in even greater confusion. The ash was undisturbed. Many coffins had been set on end, so that the heads of their corpses faced downward. The lid of one coffin had been forced open, and a shriveled right arm poked out. The deceased had committed suicide by cutting his throat with a razor; the blood-stained tool allegedly was found clutched in his right hand. According to religious observances, suicides are not to be buried on hallowed ground. The family apparently had conducted a normal burial, hoping to hush up the tragedy.

The family then buried each coffin separately. There were no further disturbances. An official report by the commission was alleged to have been written, but could not be located by later investigators.

Further reading:

Knight, David C. *The Moving Coffins: Ghosts and Hauntings Around the World.* Englewood Cliffs, N.J.: Prentice-Hall, 1983.

Thurston, Herbert. *Ghosts and Poltergeists.* Chicago: Henry Regnery Co., 1954.

Mrs. Guppy   See GUPPY, AGNES.

Murphy, Gardner (1895–1980)

Eminent psychologist and psychical researcher, often compared to William JAMES in his academic stature and range of interests. As with James before him, his support of psychical research brought the field a visibility and status it probably would not have enjoyed otherwise.

Gardner Murphy was born on July 8, 1895 in Chilicothe, Ohio, but grew up in Concord, Massachusetts. His mother's father was the medium Leonora PIPER's attorney, and his parents, although evangelical Christians, were much interested in the work of James and Richard HODGSON at the AMERICAN SOCIETY FOR PSYCHICAL RESEARCH (ASPR), then based in Boston. When he was 16, Murphy found William BARRETT's *Psychical Research* (1911) in his grandfather's library, and this stimulated in him a life-long passion for the subject.

Murphy attended Yale, where, determined on a career in psychical research, he majored in psychology. He received his B.A. from Yale in 1916 and his M.A. from Harvard in 1917. His education had caused him to question the religious faith of his upbringing, but he decided to continue to pursue psychical research, which he had theretofore conceived of as a support for his religion, for its intrinsic interest.

World War I was then getting under way, and in 1917 Murphy joined the army and went to France.

He also joined the SOCIETY FOR PSYCHICAL RESEARCH (SPR), and, upon being discharged in 1919, stopped by its office in London. The secretary kindly wrote out a list of books and articles which guided his reading after he returned to the United States and a doctoral program at Columbia.

So impressed was Murphy by his visit to the SPR that in 1922 he asked William McDougall, who was then at Harvard, what he thought were Murphy's chances of obtaining a position at the university. McDougall responded by offering him the support of Harvard's Hodgson Memorial Fund, set up by Hodgson's friends to support psychical research following his unexpected death in 1905. Murphy applied for and was granted the money, and for the next three years he made numerous trips from New York to Cambridge to conduct research. During this period he had several sittings with Piper, some of the last of her career.

Murphy received his Ph.D. from Columbia in 1923 and, with the offer of a full-time teaching position there in 1925, gave up the Hodgson Fund support. He had already met his future wife, Lois Barclay, whom he married in 1926. She shared his strong interest in psychical research and admired him for going against the academic trend, but she persuaded him that he could help psychical research more by establishing himself in psychology than by committing himself entirely to the former field.

Murphy's decision to redirect his energies toward mainstream psychology was also influenced by the unprecedented turmoil in American psychical research at the time. In 1925 control of the ASPR (in New York since 1907) passed into the hands of a liberal faction, and the society's more conservative members left to found a rival BOSTON SOCIETY FOR PSYCHIC RESEARCH. In sympathy with the defectors, Murphy accepted a seat on the council of the Boston Society, but he was little active in research for several years.

He did not move out of close contact with the field, however. When J.B. RHINE approached him about supervising J.G. Pratt, a Duke graduate student who had been working at the Parapsychology Laboratory, Murphy agreed, and Pratt spent the years 1935–1937 in New York. Murphy also gave Rhine strong support at a meeting of the American Psychological Association in Columbus, Ohio in 1938, at which he and experimental psychical research (parapsychology) came in for a severe attack.

In 1940 Murphy accepted a position as chairman of the Department of Psychology at City College, a branch of the City University of New York. This new position brought a lighter teaching load, and he was able to devote more time to psychical research. In 1940 and 1941 he and Bernard Reiss of Hunter College edited the *Journal of Parapsychology*, which Rhine had established at Duke in 1937.

The situation at the ASPR changed in 1941; the liberal group who had run the society since 1925 were ousted in a "palace revolution." Murphy became a vice president of the new board of trustees, and he began to spend mornings at the ASPR five or six days a week. He was a man with a vision, and his presence brought the ASPR a sense of purpose and direction it badly needed. The society began both to conduct experimental research and to collect and analyze reports of psychic experiences as they occurred in life.

Meanwhile, his stature in psychology also was increasing. He was elected president of the American Psychological Association in 1944, and in 1950 the United Nations sent him to India to look into the growing unrest there. Upon his return, Murphy was offered a position as director of research at the Menninger Foundation in Topeka, Kansas. He remained in this job until his retirement in 1968, when he and his wife moved to Washington, D.C., and he became a visiting professor at George Washington University.

Murphy was elected president of the SPR in 1949, and from 1962 to 1971 he served as president of the ASPR. In 1967 and 1968, while he was at the Menninger Foundation, he was instrumental in getting the estate of James KIDD for the ASPR and the PSYCHICAL RESEARCH FOUNDATION.

Gardner Murphy died on March 18, 1980, in Washington, D.C. In his last years he had developed Parkinson's disease, a nervous disorder that made him unable to write or participate in many of the outdoor activities which he enjoyed.

He had contributed more than 100 articles to psychical research journals and many more to journals in mainstream psychology. He was the author or coauthor of numerous books, in many of which he sought to show the relevance of psychical research to psychology, particularly to social psychology and personality. He had a breadth and depth of knowledge in all these areas equaled by few if any of his peers.

Murphy's experiences as an experimental investigator were disappointing, and he came to doubt the value of experimental psychical research. He believed that everyday psychic experiences were much more important, and although he never became satisfied that research on survival after death had demonstrated this to occur, he nevertheless considered it a vital area of study.

Murphy's last book on psychical research, *The Paranormal and the Normal* (1980), coauthored with Morton Leeds, was published shortly after his death. His other books include *William James on Psychical Research*, edited with Robert Ballou (1960), and *Challenge of Psychical Research*, written with Laura Dale (1961). A collection of his papers on psychology and parapsychology, edited by Lois Murphy, was published by McFarland in 1990.

Further reading:

Berger, Arthur S. *Lives and Letters in American Parapsychology: A Biographical History, 1850–1987.* Jefferson, N.C.: McFarland, 1988.

Murphy, Gardner. "Notes for a Parapsychological Autobiography." *Journal of Parapsychology* 21 (1957):165–78.

Murphy, Lois B. "The Evolution of Gardner Murphy's Thinking in Psychology and Psychical Research." *Journal of the American Society for Psychical Research*, 82 (1988): 101–14.

Osis, Karlis. "The American Society for Psychical Research 1941–1985: A Personal View." *Journal of the American Society for Psychical Research* 79 (1985):501–30.

"Tributes Honoring the Memory of Gardner Murphy." *Journal of the American Society for Psychical Research* 74:1 (1980).

Myers, Frederic William Henry (1843–1901)

Poet, classical scholar, psychologist, and psychical researcher, a founding and leading member of the SOCIETY FOR PSYCHICAL RESEARCH (SPR), best remembered for his great two-volume work, *Human Personality and Its Survival of Bodily Death* (1903).

Frederic W.H. Myers was born February 6, 1843 in Keswick, Cumberland, England, into the family of a clergyman. He was an impressionable, sensitive child. When he was little more than four years old, he saw a mole that a cart had run over. He was brightened by the thought that the mole's soul had gone to heaven, but his mother, a woman with her own strong religious convictions, crushed him by telling him that the mole had no soul. The horror of this thought haunted him for the rest of his life.

Myers began to write poetry in his youth, and in 1859, when he was 16, he placed second in a national competition. The following year he entered Trinity College, Cambridge, to study classical literature. He passed through an intense religious phase, but then began to experience doubts which eventually led to a loss of faith.

Following his graduation from Trinity in 1864, Myers became a lecturer in classics at Cambridge; he was made a fellow of Trinity College in 1865. In 1869 he resigned his lectureship to work for the education of women. In 1872 he took a position as a school inspector.

In 1873 Myers fell passionately in love with his cousin's wife, Annie Hill Marshall. Her marriage was a difficult one, marred by chronic ill health. Although she seems to have returned Myers's affection, and the two spent many hours together walking in the valley at her estate at Hallsteads, the affair was never consummated. Annie Marshall's suicide in August 1876, following her husband's commitment for insanity, was a blow from which Myers never recovered.

Myers's love for Annie overshadowed his marriage to the beautiful Eveleen Tennant in 1880. She was devoted to him, but she lacked his intellectual inclinations and could not support him in the research and writing that came to occupy a central place in his life. The marriage, nonetheless, was happy, and produced three children.

The first outward sign of the direction Myers's life's work was going to take came in the summer of 1871 on a starlight walk with Henry SIDGWICK. Myers asked Sidgwick "almost with trembling, whether he thought that when Tradition, Intuition, Metaphysic had failed to solve the riddle of the Universe, there was still a chance that from any actual observable phenomena—ghosts, spirits, whatever they might be—some valid knowledge might be drawn as to the World Unseen." Sidgwick replied that he thought there might be, and thus was born in spirit the organization that was to become known as the Society for Psychical Research.

Myers began to sit with mediums in 1872, sometimes in the company of Sidgwick, but the most decisive event of this period was sitting with William Stainton MOSES that he attended with Edmund GURNEY in 1874. After this sitting, Myers, Sidgwick and Gurney formed a group for the study of mediumship. The SPR itself came into being in 1882.

Sidgwick served as the SPR's first president, and Myers had a seat on its governing council. He was also named to four of five investigatory committees, including the most important one, the Literary Committee, whose responsibility it was to collect cases for publication in the Society's *Journal* and *Proceedings*. Myers proved to be an especially sensitive analyst of the case material. He also participated in important investigations of Leonora PIPER and Eusapia PALLADINO, among others.

Myers was listed as second author of *Phantasms of the Living*, a landmark book published under the SPR's auspices in 1886 (Gurney was first author, Frank PODMORE third). Myers wrote an introductory chapter and a lengthy dissent from the theoretical position on apparitions taken by Gurney.

One of Myers's most significant accomplishments was his concept of the "subliminal consciousness." This anticipated Sigmund Freud's "unconscious" by some years, and differed from the latter in being conceived not as a reservoir of repressed thoughts, but as the ground from which conscious thought sprang. The subliminal consciousness, according to Myers, was receptive to extrasensory input and, in a dualistic conception of mind and body, survived physical death. William JAMES ranked Myers as among the greatest psychologists of his day on the basis of his ideas about the subliminal consciousness.

Myers served as the SPR's secretary from 1888 to 1899 and as its president in 1900, at the same time as he was undergoing his eventually fatal illnesses. In March 1898 he suffered a sharp attack of the flu which turned into pneumonia; he had another attack of the flu in February 1899, and that November he was diagnosed as having Bright's disease. Doctors ordered him to the Riviera to recuperate, but he was not to do so. He died on January 17, 1901, at age 58, at a clinic in Rome to which he had gone on the advice of William James.

Myers's contributions to psychical research, however, were not yet over.

In the last years before his death he had been working on a book that would summarize and systematize the findings of psychical research. *Human Personality and Its Survival of Bodily Death* was completed (at Myers's request, by Richard HODGSON and the SPR's Alice Johnson) and published posthumously in 1903.

But it had one major omission. Myers had intended to give a prominent place to the mediumistic communications he had received from his beloved Annie through Mrs. Thompson and Mrs. Piper; they had been decisive in convincing him that there was survival after death. But his wife found out about them and, immensely jealous, succeeded in having them suppressed. She evidently destroyed them as well; no sign of them has been found since.

Eveleen Myers also excised all mention of Annie from *Fragments of an Inner Life*, which she published in an edited form as *Fragments of Prose and Poetry* in 1904. Myers had had *Fragments of an Inner Life* privately printed and had given copies to several of his friends, but in sealed envelopes which he had asked them not to open until after his death. The pamphlet was not published in its unabridged form until 1961, by which time it was clear that the passages Mrs. Myers had cut out were key to understanding the meaning of communications allegedly received from Myers shortly after his death.

Before he died, Myers wrote on a sheet of paper, "If I can revisit any earthly scene, I should choose the 'Valley' in the grounds of Hallsteads, Cumberland," and sealed it in an envelope which he gave to Sir Oliver LODGE for safekeeping (see SURVIVAL TESTS). A few days after his death the medium Mrs. Verrall renewed her automatic writing so that Myers could give the contents of this envelope through her if he wished, and in time she produced the following: "I have long told you of the contents of the envelope. Myers' sealed envelope left with Lodge. You have not understood. It has in it the words from the Symposium—about Love bridging the chasm." The envelope was then opened and the test was judged a failure.

Closer study, however, revealed that although the test was literally a failure, there was nevertheless an association of ideas between what Myers wrote in life and what he communicated after death. The valley at Hallsteads clearly refers to his walks with Annie, and the passage from Plato's *Symposium* is concerned with soul mates—which is how Myers felt about himself and Annie. When the full text of *Fragments of an Inner Life* came to light (one copy had been put away and could not be found when Mrs. Myers went looking for it), it was discovered that Myers himself had made the association in a poem printed there.

Related ideas and images from that and other poems were, moreover, found to correspond to images that had been cropping up in Mrs. Verrall's automatic writing from the time she had taken it up following Myers's death, consistent with the statement from the Myers communicator that he had "long told" of the contents of the envelope.

Other mediums, notably Leonora Piper, were also involved in these communications, which provide an example of what are known as cross correspondences (q.v.). The deceased Myers was seemingly one of the originators of this type of communication, which is considered among the most evidential for survival after death in the mediumistic literature.

Myers's other books include a long poem called *St. Paul* (1867), *Essays, Classical and Modern* (1885) and *Science and a Future Life* (1893).

Further reading:

Gauld, Alan. *The Founders of Psychical Research*. London: Routledge & Kegan Paul, 1968.

Haynes, Renee. *The Society for Psychical Research, 1882–1892: A History*. London: Heinemann, 1982.

Oppenheim, Janet. *The Other World: Spiritualism and Psychical Research in England, 1850–1914*. Cambridge: Cambridge University Press, 1985.

Salter, W.H. "F.W.H. Myers' Posthumous Message." *Proceedings of the Society for Psychical Research* 52 (1958):1–32.

name soul   See REINCARNATION.

near-death experience (NDE)   A range of phenomena, some paranormal, that reportedly occur in many cases where individuals have clinically died and then been revived, or have come close to death. The term "near-death experience" (NDE) was coined in the 1970s by the American physician Dr. Raymond Moody, who heard his patients talk about the phenomena.

NDEs have been recorded throughout history. With the advent of increasingly sophisticated technology that saves lives in crisis, they have become more common. A Gallup poll in 1982 showed that in the United States alone, approximately eight million adults reported having NDEs. All evidence for NDEs is anecdotal, however, meaning that the phenomenon itself eludes scientific proof.

Many NDEs have common phenomena, though each experience is unique, such as deathbed visions (q.v.). Common phenomena include having a sense of being dead, or having an out-of-body experience in which the person experiences floating above his body looking down; cessation of pain and a feeling of bliss; traveling down a tunnel toward a light at the end; meeting apparitions of nonphysical beings dressed in glowing white, many of whom are spirits of dead friends and relatives; coming in contact with a guide or Supreme Being, such as an angel, who shows the person a review of his or her life; and returning reluctantly to life.

Natural explanations for the NDE are similar to those put forward to explain deathbed visions: hallucinations brought about by a lack of oxygen, or the release of endorphins (natural painkillers), or increased levels of carbon dioxide in the blood. NDE-like phenomena can be induced in laboratory experiments with hallucinogenic drugs such as LSD; yet, those who experience the real thing say there is an ineffable mystical quality to it that subsequently changes their lives.

Studies show that religious beliefs seem to have no bearing on whether a person has an NDE, or what phenomena are experienced. All but about 3% of reported NDEs are positive experiences, influencing individuals to become more spiritual or develop a belief in God. Most lose their fear of death and begin believing in survival after death. In some cases, the persons acquire psychic or mediumistic abilities. Most individuals experience varying degrees of difficulty readjusting to daily life.

An NDE may enable an individual to access higher realms of consciousness. There are similarities to the experiences of shamans (see SHAMANISM).

Further reading:

Atwater, P.M.H. *Coming Back to Life.* New York: Dodd, Mead, 1988.

Moody, Raymond A. Jr. *Life After Life.* New York: Bantam Books, 1975.

———. *Reflections on Life After Life.* Harrisburg, Pa.: Stackpole Books, 1977.

———. *The Light Beyond.* New York: Bantam Books, 1988.

Ring, Kenneth. *Life at Death.* New York: Coward, McCann & Geoghegan, 1980.

———. *Heading Toward Omega.* New York: William Morrow, 1984.

Zaleski, Carol. *Otherworld Journeys: Accounts of Near-Death Experience in Medieval and Modern Times.* New York: Oxford University Press, 1987.

necromancy   The conjuring of the dead or the spirits of the dead for magical purposes, especially prognostication. Though considered to be a dangerous and repulsive practice, necromancy is universal and ancient, and is based on widespread belief that the spirits of the dead know everything about the past, present and future. Thus, if they can be conjured and commanded, a wizard or magician can learn the future, cast spells to bind others, and find hidden riches. Some necromantic rites are intended to command the dead to attack the living.

Francis Barrett, author of *The Magus* (1801), said necromancy "has its name because it works on the bodies of the dead, and gives answers by the ghosts and apparitions of the dead, and subterraneous spirits, alluring them into the carcasses of the dead by certain hellish charms, and infernal invocations, and by deadly sacrifices and wicked oblations.''

Necromantic rites purport to either raise a corpse itself to life, or, more commonly, to summon the spirit of a corpse. Necromantic rites usually involve corpses or pieces of corpses, and take place in cemeteries and graveyards. Elaborate preparations—which can go on for days—call for meditating upon death, dressing in clothing stolen from corpses, and eating food associated with death, such as dog flesh (dogs are associated in mythology with the underworld and the dead), unleavened black bread and unfermented grape juice. In the Middle Ages, it was believed that necromancers ate the flesh of the corpses themselves.

If a corpse has been recently deceased, the necromancer may try to force its soul back into the body

The Witch of Endor (right) summoning the ghost of Samuel for Saul.

Alleged communication from the philosopher and theologian Pierre Abelard, produced in a necromantic rite.

to reanimate it and speak. If a corpse has been dead a long time, the necromancer will try to summon an apparition of the soul. When the ritual is over, the corpse should be burned or buried in quicklime to prevent trouble from the disturbed spirit.

Perhaps the most famous story of necromancy is the Witch of Endor, told in the Bible. The witch was hired by King Saul to conjure the dead prophet Samuel; the spirit foretold Saul's doom. The Catholic Church condemns necromancy as ''the agency of evil spirits,'' and in Elizabethan England it was expressly outlawed by the Witchcraft Act of 1604.

In Vodoun, corpses are allegedly ''raised'' from graves in rituals in which appeals are made to Baron Samedi, the scarecrow-like god of graveyards and zombies. The rites are performed by a magician who is the incarnation of the god of death.

Further reading:

Cavendish, Richard. *The Black Arts.* New York: Putnam, 1967.

Marwick, Max, ed. *Witchcraft and Sorcery.* New York: Viking Penguin, 1982.

Nechanesmere, Battle of   See RETROCOGNITION.

New London Ledge Lighthouse   Turn-of-the-20th-century lighthouse near New London, Connecticut, said to be haunted by the anguished spirit of one of its early keepers, according to local legend. The light, which was established in 1910, rises three stories above a square pier. The lighthouse was the lonely home of Ernie, a civilian keeper known only by his first name, and his wife.

According to legend, one day Ernie found his wife gone. A note left behind said she had run off with the captain of the Block Island Ferry. Shattered, Ernie walked up the stairs to the roof of the building and threw himself to his death in the waters below.

The log books at New London Ledge do not record such a suicide, but the story is believed so strongly that for decades, the personnel assigned to the light-house reported Ernie's ghostly presence. Phantom footsteps were heard echoing up and down the stairs, and warm rooms suddenly became chilly. There were poltergeist phenomena of chairs that moved of their own accord and doors that opened and closed by themselves.

Ernie's presence was reported right up to the day the New London Ledge became automated: May 1, 1987. The last entry in the log book reads, "Rock of slow torture. Ernie's domain. Hell on Earth—may New London Ledge's light shine forever because I'm through. I will watch it from afar while drinking a brew."

If there was no suicide, the haunting may be explained in terms of sufficient popular belief in the story that caused hallucinations. These may have been due in part to mental strain caused by isolation for prolonged periods. In the light's later years, Coast Guard personnel were assigned 18-month tours of duty. Daily duties called for 12-hour shifts. Six days of shore leave were permitted every one to two weeks. Thus, the personnel themselves may have unwittingly acted as poltergeist agents, or interpreted natural phenomena as being of ghostly origin.

The haunting cannot be discounted completely, however. Lighthouses are renowned for their ghostly inhabitants. It is possible that over the years, events and emotions accumulate to take on the form of phantoms.

newspaper test   See SURVIVAL TESTS.

O

O'Donnell, Elliott (1872–1965) British ghost hunter who gained fame through his more than 50 books on ghosts and related occult lore. Most of his books were nonfiction, though he did write some occult fiction. Critics have speculated that his fiction crept into his nonfiction, and that his "true" ghost tales were embellished by fancy.

Elliott O'Donnell was born in England to a family that claimed to be descendants of famous Irish chieftains, including Niall of the Nine Hostages and Red Hugh, the latter of whom fought fiercely against the English in the 16th century. O'Donnell was educated at Clifton College in Bristol, England and at the Queen's Service Academy in Dublin. After school, he went to America for a time; he worked on a ranch in Oregon and then as a policeman in Chicago during the Railway Strike of 1894. He returned to England and worked as a schoolmaster while training for the theater. His first book, an occult novel, *For Satan's Sake*, was published in 1905. When World War I erupted, he joined the British Army. After the war, he acted on stage and in film.

O'Donnell wrote other occult novels and eventually became an amateur ghost hunter, investigating hauntings and collecting occult stories, which he chronicled in his nonfiction books. He also wrote numerous articles. His writings gained him great popularity on both sides of the Atlantic. He lectured often and made radio and television appearances in Britain and the United States.

O'Donnell said he believed in ghosts but was not a Spiritualist. He claimed to have had his first psychic experience at age five, when he saw an elemental (a type of nature spirit) covered with spots in a house. He also claimed that as a young man, he had nearly been strangled by a phantom once while in Dublin. His family was reputed to have a banshee, but it is not known if the banshee wailed to presage his own death. He died on May 6, 1965 at the age of 93. His nonfiction books continue to be repackaged and reissued.

Further reading:
Ludlam, Harry, *Elliott O'Donnell's Great Ghost Stories*. New York: Arco Publishing, 1984.
Shepard, Leslie A., ed. *Encyclopedia of Occultism and Parapsychology*. 2nd ed. Detroit: Gale Research Co., 1984.

Obon See FEASTS AND FESTIVALS OF THE DEAD.

Ocean-Born Mary A six-foot tall ghost of a woman who has red hair and green eyes, and dresses in white, said to appear in a house near Henniker, New Hampshire. The legendary ghost belongs to a woman who lived there at the invitation of a man who played a most unusual role from the very first day of her life.

Ocean-Born Mary's life began in 1720 with a shipload of emigrants who left Londonderry, Ireland for its namesake town in New Hampshire. As their little ship, *The Wolf*, was approaching Boston Harbor, it was overtaken by pirates. The pirate ship's Captain Pedro soon boarded *The Wolf* and informed the terified crew and passengers that their lives would shortly end.

At the next moment, when the captain and his men had their pistols aimed at the group, the cry of a baby came from the companionway, stopping Captain Pedro. He walked away from the group, and upon his return his smile told everyone that their fortunes had turned.

The young wife of the captain of *The Wolf*, Mrs. James Wilson, had given birth to a girl that very day. When Captain Pedro learned that the baby was still unnamed, he promised to spare everyone's life if Mrs. Wilson named her Mary, after his own mother. After a grateful consent from Mrs. Wilson, the captain went back to his ship for a moment and soon returned to *The Wolf* with a christening gift, a bolt of greenish-blue brocaded silk. He said that he hoped it would one day be made into Mary's wedding gown. When Mary married Thomas Wallace in Londonderry, New Hampshire 22 years later, she indeed had her gown made of the silk. Within 10 years she was the mother of four sons, and then she became a young widow as had her mother before her.

Mary, however, had not seen the last of Captain Pedro on that fateful day of her birth. He had given up his life of piracy, and in 1760 he was building a Georgian mansion near Henniker. Now old and alone, he located Mary and began making periodic visits, often taking her and the boys to watch the house being built. He invited Mary to become his housekeeper and in turn he would support her and the boys.

Captain Pedro was true to his word and generously lavished gifts upon his five guests, including a coach-and-four in which they took almost daily drives. For the next 10 years, all lived happily together.

One night, Captain Pedro had returned from a trip to the seacoast and Mary heard the sounds of digging while he buried a heavy chest outside the house. About one year later, she found Captain Pedro lying in the garden, murdered with a sailor's cutlass stuck between his shoulders. Mary and her sons buried him beneath the hearthstone fronting the kitchen fireplace as he had requested. Mary lived alone in the house until her death in 1814 at the age of 94, having outlived all her sons.

The house remained in the Wallace family's hands for more than 100 years, during which it became a target of curiosity seekers, treasure hunters and vandals. In 1916, the house was purchased by the Roy family, which soon heard tales about the house—how someone or something seemed to be guarding it, and how a number of owners had tried but could never live in it.

But it was evident to the Roys that the house could be lived in if the occupants loved and cared for it. Although they heard strange noises in different parts of the house, and their dog refused to venture near the cellar, they noticed that when the house was in some kind of danger, something would always happen to avert it. For example, a passerby once stopped a group of boys from burning the house down. And Louis Roy, the son of the first Roy family occupants, suffered 17 near-fatal accidents while living in the house and survived.

Mary's ghost once was seen helping Louis Roy fix the garage during a storm. It is still reported that she opens the door when guests knock, fills the house with light and walks down the carved stairway. Every October, usually around Halloween, Mary's ghost is said to leave the house and take off in her waiting couch-and-four at midnight.

Various psychics have said that treasure is buried beneath the slab in the kitchen, but the treasure has never been discovered. Perhaps it is because legend says that anyone disturbing the hearthstone will meet death. Indeed, a man set to dig up the stone died in a strange manner just the week before the event was to take place.

Louis Roy was still in possession of a small remaining piece of Mary's brocaded silk. But he considered an even greater personal treasure to be the feeling that Mary's ghost not only visited the house she could not forget, but also protected him from harm because she knew that he cared about the house as much as she did. Some subsequent owners also reported that an inexplicable power seemed to protect the house by putting a sudden end to potentially dangerous events such as a fire.

Further reading:
Anderson, Jean. *The Haunting of America*. Boston: Houghton Mifflin, 1973.
Roy, Louis M.A., as told to Pauline Saltzman. "The House That Haunts a Ghost." *Tomorrow* 6 (Winter 1958):51–57.
Smith, Susy. *Prominent American Ghosts*. New York: World Publishing Co., 1970.

Octagon, The   Elegant and odd-shaped house in Washington, D.C. reportedly haunted by numerous ghosts, including that of Dolley Madison, wife of James Madison, the third president of the United States. The Octagon is said to be the site of the most hauntings in Washington, save for the Capitol Building and the White House.

The three-story house was built in the early 1800s for Colonel John Tayloe, a Virginia plantation owner and friend of George Washington, on an odd-shaped piece of property near the White House. It was designed by Dr. William Thornton, the architect of the Capitol Building, who gave the house six sides in order to fit its unusual property (even though only six-sided, the Tayloes dubbed the house "The Octagon"). Its features included a stunning, oval central staircase, odd-shaped rooms and closets, and rear tunnels said at one time to have led to the White House.

The Tayloes and their fifteen children (eight daughters and seven sons) lived in the house until 1855, with the exception of a period during the War of 1812. The first spirit said to haunt the house was that of one of the daughters. According to legend, the Tayloe daughters indulged in some stormy love affairs, and the house was often the scene of arguments and broken hearts. One daughter fell in love with a British officer in the early 1800s, but John Tayloe would not allow the man to even enter the house. One stormy night, so the legend goes, Tayloe and his daughter had an argument over the matter, which ended when she took her candle and flounced upstairs. Suddenly there was a piercing shriek, and the daughter tumbled over the railing and down the stairwell to her death. It is not known whether she tripped and fell, or whether she flung herself over the railing in suicide.

Regardless, her restless spirit soon haunted the house. On some nights, the shadow of a flickering candle moved slowly up the wall along the staircase, followed by a shriek and the sound of something heavy hitting the bottom of the stairwell.

During the War of 1812, Tayloe moved his family to his plantation and rented the house to the French ambassador to the United States. The Octagon was one of the few buildings spared by the British during the fighting.

The White House was burned down during the war, and Tayloe then lent The Octagon to the Madisons during the reconstruction of the presidential home. The Madisons moved in during 1814 and remained through the end of Madison's second term. Dolley, a gracious woman who loved the scent of lilacs, hosted huge and frequent parties.

After the Madisons left, the Tayloes moved back in. Much to Tayloe's horror, the staircase claimed the life of a second daughter. She had eloped against his will and had returned to ask his forgiveness. They met on the staircase, and the angry Tayloe tried to move the girl aside to pass by her. She lost her footing and, like her ill-fated sister, fell to her death. Her ghost, too, is said to haunt the scene of the tragedy.

After Mrs. Tayloe died in 1855, John Tayloe sold the house. It had various owners, who let it deteriorate. Shortly before the Civil War, a gambler was killed on the upper floors during a dispute over his alleged cheating. He grabbed the bellpull as he was shot to death. His ghost reportedly has been seen reenacting his final moments over and over again.

During the latter part of the 19th century, numerous witnesses reported glimpsing Dolley Madison's ghost, clad in elegant fashions of the day, and smelling of lilacs, standing or dancing in the house. Witnesses also reported seeing the apparitions of footmen attending to ghostly carriages. Other haunting phenomena have been reported over the years, some well into the late part of the 20th century: thumpings within the walls, moans, screams, sighs, and clanking of swords, smells of phantom food cooking in the kitchen, the scent of lilacs, and the appearance of human footprints in otherwise undisturbed dust. Other reports include unearthly presences sensed in the bedroom used by Dolley Madison, and ghostly shapes flitting through the rear doors to the gardens and walking up and down the staircase.

The thumping within the walls, which plagued residents of The Octagon for more than 100 years, is attributed to a legend that during the French occupancy of the house, a British soldier killed his slave girl lover and interred her body within an unknown wall. Another legend holds that during the Civil War, the tunnels of the house were used as part of the Underground Railroad for runaway slaves, and also housed wounded and dying Union Army soldiers.

The Octagon House is now a museum.

Further reading:

Alexander, John. *Ghosts: Washington's Most Famous Ghost Stories.* Arlington, Va.: Washington Book Trading Co., 1988.

Old Hag   A nocturnal phenomenon involving suffocation, paralysis, and supernatural smells, sounds and apparitions, blamed on night terror, demons or witches. The Old Hag syndrome has similarities to characteristics of poltergeists and also has associations with reported cases of vampire attacks. The Old Hag also is related to the *mara* (from which the term "nightmare" is derived), a demon that attacks humans at night and sexually assaults them.

The Old Hag has been documented since ancient times. In the second century, the Greek physician Galen attributed it to indigestion. Modern research has found that approximately 15% of the adult population worldwide experiences at least one Old Hag attack. Some individuals suffer repeated attacks over a limited period of time; others have repeated attacks for years. Science has proposed no adequate explanation for what causes the attacks and why certain persons experience them.

The syndrome takes its name from a term for witches. In the Middle Ages, it was believed that witches, or "hags" or "old hags," would sit on a person's chest at night and "ride," causing exhaustion and feelings of suffocation—thus the term "hag-ridden" to describe a rundown feeling.

Characteristics of Old Hag attacks vary, but some are common to most incidents. The victim awakens abruptly, feeling an invisible weight pressing on the chest. He or she tries to move, struggle or scream, to no avail. The attack ends just when the victim is on the verge of losing consciousness. The victim feels drained for a prolonged period of time.

Some Old Hag attacks begin with sounds of phantom footsteps approaching the victim. Monstrous shapes, some with glowing red eyes, may be perceived. Repulsive smells may fill the air, and rasping breath may come from the demonic shape.

Old Hag attacks can occur during the day or night.

Galen's theory of indigestion is still proposed as an explanation for these attacks, as are sleep disorders such as narcolepsy, and repressed sexual tensions. These may explain some cases, but cannot explain all.

Some victims of Old Hag attacks say they know they were magically attacked by an enemy, who cast a spell to send a demon. Various amulets such as religious objects are believed by many to ward off Old Hag attacks.

Further reading:

Guiley, Rosemary Ellen. *Vampires Among Us.* New York: Pocket Books, 1991.

Hufford, David J. *The Terror that Comes in the Night: An Experience-Centered Study of Supernatural Assault Traditions.* Philadelphia: University of Pennsylvania Press, 1982.

Old Shuck See BLACK SHUCK.

Osty, Eugene (1874–1938) French physician and psychical researcher, for many years director of the INSTITUT MÉTAPSYCHIQUE INTERNATIONAL (IMI) in Paris.

Eugene Osty was born on May 16, 1874. His father was a restaurateur, and later a farmer. He studied medicine, and, after obtaining his degree in 1901, established a practice in a small town in central France.

Osty first became interested in the psychic in 1909, when a palmist impressed him with her apparently accurate knowledge of subjects known to him but not to her. After an intensive study of palm reading, he became convinced that clairvoyance was the operative function, and that the palm merely served to focus the mind. He began to divide his time between his medical practice and the study of professional sensitives, resulting in his book, *Lucidité et Intuition* (translated as *Lucidity and Intuition* in 1913). He began close collaboration with other European researchers, including Henri Bergson and Charles Richet.

After serving with the French Army Medical Corps in World War I, Osty published *The Meaning of Human Life* (1919), in which he linked the mental evolution of human beings with their psychic potentials. In 1921, he settled permanently in Paris, began to lecture on his work with psychics, and became a member of the governing committee of the IMI, which had been founded in 1918. An important book, *Supernormal Faculties in Man*, in which he summed up his thinking on clairvoyance and human nature, appeared in 1923. Following the death of Gustave GELEY

in an airplane crash in 1924, Osty took over as director of IMI. He was by this time well respected for his work on clairvoyance, and his appointment was hailed, even in the public press, as a brilliant move.

During his period at the IMI, which lasted until his own death in 1938, Osty took up the study of physical mediumship. Innovative in his research methodology, he developed a technique of photography using ultraviolet light for use in the seance room, and he devised a system of control involving an infrared beam, which if crossed would cause a battery of automatic cameras to take pictures. The idea was to catch any trickery in the act, but every time the beam was crossed and the cameras went off, the medium, Rudi Schneider (see SCHNEIDER BROTHERS), was hunched in his chair, in deep trance. At the same time, however, objects on the table or elsewhere in the room were displaced.

In this way, Osty was able to establish that some invisible emanation from the medium was responsible for the movement of objects at a distance (see PSYCHOKINESIS). His 1930 experiments with Schneider are widely regarded as among the most important in psychical research history. They are reported in his book, *The Unknown Powers of Mind over Matter* (1932), coauthored with his son, Marcel.

Eugene Osty died on August 20, 1938, at the age of 64.

Further reading:

Inglis, Brian. *Science and Parascience: A History of the Paranormal, 1914–1939.* London: Hodder and Stoughton, 1984.

Osty, Marcel. "Eugene Osty: Pioneer Researcher." *Tomorrow Magazine* (Winter 1959):96–102.

Pleasants, Helene. *Biographical Dictionary of Parapsychology.* New York: Helix Press, 1964.

ouija A device marketed as a game in which answers to questions are divined. The Ouija was invented as an oracle game in 1892 by an American, Elija J. Bond. The name is derived from the French and German words for "yes," *oui* and *ja.*

The Ouija is similar to the planchette (q.v.) The board features letters of the alphabet and numerals zero through nine, and the words "yes" and "no." The pointer is a platform that rests on three felt-tipped legs. The user asks a question, places fingertips on the pointer and then allows the pointer to spell out the answer. Most likely, the user moves the platform subconsciously without realizing it, but many people feel the movements are directed by discarnate beings and spirits of the dead.

Shortly after its invention, the Ouija enjoyed great popularity due to the interest in Spiritualism and to the thousands of bereaved people after World War I who tried to find ways to communicate with their loved ones who had been killed in the war. Since then, its popularity often has coincided with popular interest in the occult. Since 1966 the Ouija has been marketed by the Parker Brothers game company of Beverly, Massachusetts, which states that it is a game for entertainment purposes.

In experimenting with the Ouija, some users find that they can do automatic writing with it. Skeptics contend that such writings really come from the user's own subconscious. Others, however, theorize that such users might have natural mediumistic abilities, and the Ouija has enabled them to contact discarnate beings or spirits of the dead.

Some critics contend that such contact is inherently dangerous, and that any beings who communicate through such a device are likely to be demonic and attempt to possess the user. However, many cases of Ouija use in automatic writing and alleged communication with spirits of the dead have been benign, even productive, in nature. The entity Seth, popularized by the writings of Jane Roberts in the 1960s and 1970s, initiated his communication with Roberts through a Ouija board. The communication then rapidly progressed to direct automatic writing with a pen and then into trance mediumship in which Seth allegedly used Roberts' vocal cords to speak.

The Ouija also served as the initial means of communication with alleged spirits of the dead in 1913 for Pearl Curran (see WORTH, PATIENCE), and in 1919 for Stewart Edward White and his wife, Betty. The Whites spent 17 years studying Betty's mediumship with a group of discarnate beings who called themselves "the Invisibles." After initial contact was made through the Ouija, Betty began using automatic writing and then trance mediumship, in which the spirits allegedly used her own vocal cords. The product of this mediumship is the now classic book, *The Betty Book* (1937), in which the Invisibles talk about the importance of spiritual development among humanity.

Further reading:

Guiley, Rosemary Ellen. *Harper's Encyclopedia of Mystical and Paranormal Experience.* San Francisco: HarperSanFrancisco, 1991.

Roberts, Jane. *The Seth Material.* Englewood Cliffs, N.J.: Prentice-Hall, 1970. First published in 1966 as *How to Develop Your ESP Power.*

White, Stewart Edward. *The Betty Book: Excursions into the World of Other-Consciousness.* New York: Berkeley Medallion Books, 1969.

out-of-body experience (OBE) Phenomenon in which a person feels projected from the body to distant locations, even to nonphysical worlds. Out-of-body experiences (OBEs) are not considered paranormal. Although descriptions of them date to ancient times, the phenomenon has never been proved scientifically, and no satisfactory explanation for it exists. OBEs also are known as "astral projection," "astral travel" and "exteriorization." Approximately one-quarter of Western adults claim to have had at least one OBE.

Bilocation, the appearance of a double, crisis apparitions, reciprocal apparitions and near-death experiences may involve OBEs. Mystics such as Emanuel SWEDENBORG, who had visions of heaven and hell, may experience OBEs to other planes of existence.

In some OBEs, a physical or ghostly form of the projector is visible to others (see WILMOT APPARITION), while in other cases, the projecting individual sees others but is not visible. If a double is seen by witnesses, it appears as an exact duplicate of the real person, including clothing details.

Some projectors say they feel like points of light or energy; some say they perceive a silvery cord, called the astral cord, that connects their projection to their physical body. Projectors say they travel with the speed of thought and penetrate physical matter like apparitions.

Researchers who have studied OBEs cannot define precisely what an OBE is. Various theories propose that: it is an actual projection of some kind of form, like an astral body; it is the projection of consciousness which others may perceive as having a physical form; it is a hallucinatory experience; it is a mental projection characterized by extrasensory perception, either clairvoyance or telepathy or both. If some form exists that is capable of separating from the body and then reentering it, it has never been scientifically detected or measured. Psychiatrist Carl G. Jung opined that in at least some cases of OBEs, the projections were of archetypes, hypothetical contents of the primordial collective unconscious Jung said is shared by all humanity.

Despite the lack of proof, the belief that consciousness can separate from the body is universal. The ancient Egyptians believed in a traveling *ka*, a vehicle of the mind and soul (*ba*). Plato also held that the soul could leave the body and travel. Other ancient Greek and Roman philosophers, such as Socrates, Pliny, Plotinus and Plutarch, wrote of experiences that resemble OBEs. In shamanism, the shaman's work is performed out-of-body in an alternate reality.

OBEs most often occur spontaneously, and often during times of great trauma or stress, as seen in cases of crisis apparitions, in which the dying appear to be projected to distant living persons. Some persons apparently have the ability to project at will (see BILOCATION).

Studies of OBEs have been done since the late 19th century. One of the most famous experimenters, Sylvan Muldoon, began experiencing OBEs spontaneously at age 12. Muldoon, an American, researched OBEs from 1915 to 1950. He said he traveled about in a ghostly double. Muldoon was a sickly child, and as his health improved with the years, his OBEs decreased in frequency. He wrote a book about his experience and research, *The Projection of the Astral Body?* (1929), coauthored with psychical researcher Hereward CARRINGTON.

Modern laboratory experiments with persons who claim to be able to project out-of-body at will have produced conflicting and disappointing results. Subjects who project to distant locations often give erroneous descriptions of what they allegedly saw. ESP tests during OBEs have had sporadic results. Tests with animals, involving a person's influence of an animal's behavior while allegedly out-of-body, have been more promising, but still are inconclusive. Tests done during sleep have shown that the OBE does not correspond to the dream state, which occurs during the REM (rapid eye movement) stage of sleep.

Further reading:

Black, David. *Ekstasy: Out-of-the-Body Experiences.* Indianapolis: Bobbs-Merrill, 1975.

Blackmore, Susan. *Beyond the Body: An Investigation of Out-of-the-Body Experiences.* London: William Heinemann Ltd., 1982.

————. *Parapsychology and Out-of-the-Body Experiences.* Monograph. London: Transpersonal Books, 1978.

Green, Celia. *Out-of-the-Body Experiences.* London: Hamish Hamilton, 1968.

Mitchell, Janet Lee. *Out-of-the-Body Experiences: A Handbook.* Jefferson, N.C.: McFarland, 1981.

Monroe, Robert A. *Journeys Out of the Body.* Garden City: N.Y.: Doubleday, 1971.

P

Palatine light, The In the folklore of New England, a phantom ship, seen off Block Island in the North Atlantic waters. The story of *The Palatine*, like many folk tales, is based on fact but probably is greatly embellished with fancy. There are different versions of the tragedy.

According to one version, the Dutch ship, *The Palatine*, left Holland in 1752 with a load of immigrants bound for Philadelphia. Off the coast of New England, the ship suffered damage by storms. Then the crew mutinied, killed the captain, robbed the passengers, and abandoned them, taking off in the lifeboats. The ship ran aground on Block Island, off Rhode Island, a place so notorious for shipwrecks that it supported a band of land pirates called the Block Island Wreckers, who made their living salvaging wrecks. This time, however, the Wreckers humanely saved the survivors before plundering the wreck. One survivor, a woman who had gone insane from the trouble at sea, refused to leave the ship, even though the Wreckers planned to set it afire once they had finished scavenging. She remained aboard, and as the tide carried the flaming wreck out to sea, her screams could be heard by those ashore.

According to another version, the ship bore German immigrants and was deliberately run ashore by the captain and crew for the sake of plunder. Still another version holds that the ship was lured aground one stormy night by the decoy lights of the land pirates. In both of these versions, the pirates did not save the survivors, but plundered the ship and set it afire with the living still on board.

The blazing *Palatine* light, as the phantom is called, was seen periodically by the inhabitants of Block Island in the late 18th through 19th centuries, and came to be a harbinger of stormy weather. Family recollections recorded by one Thomas R. Hazard in *Recollections of Olden Times* in 1879 tell of one unnamed resident "who was generally well and in his right mind except at the season of the year when the *Palatine* ship was wrecked." At that time, the old man

> became madly insane, and would rave about seeing a ship all ablaze, with men falling from her burning rigging and shrouds, and ever and anon shrink in horror from the spectres of two women, whose hands he cut off or disabled by blows from a cutlass, as they sought to cling to the gunwale of the last boat that left the burning ship and all on board to their fate that not one might remain alive to bear witness of the terrible catastrophe and crime.

During the 19th century, it was commonly believed among Block Islanders that the *Palatine* light had been sent by God to punish the wicked men who murdered her passengers and crew, and that when the last of the pirates was dead the ship would be seen no more. Reports of the *Palatine* light continue, however, into the 20th century.

Further reading:
Botkin, B.A., ed. *A Treasury of New England Folklore.* Rev. ed. New York: American Legacy Press, 1989.

Palladino, Eusapia (1854–1918) One of history's most outstanding yet controversial physical mediums, investigated by a record number of scientific communities, largely in her native Europe, but also in England and the United States. She would indulge in trickery when given the chance, but if properly controlled she was capable of producing phenomena such as rapping, levitation and materialization.

Eusapia Palladino was born on January 21, 1854 in the mountain village of Minerverno Murgo in southern Italy, a child of peasants. She gave investigators contradictory stories of her early life; according to one version, her mother died giving birth to her, and her father was killed by outlaws when she was eight. According to another and more widely accepted version, her mother died soon after her birth and her father died when she was 12.

In any event, after she was orphaned, Palladino was taken into the family of friends in Naples. This family dabbled in Spiritualism, and there came a time when the young Palladino was invited to participate in a seance. The table tilted and then rose completely into the air. She began to sit as a medium, it seems, to avoid being put into a convent, although she was afraid of her powers and avoided using them.

Palladino's control was identified as the spirit of the deceased pirate, John KING, as the result of a curious incident. One day an unknown woman came to the house where Palladino was staying. At a recent sitting in another place she had received a message from King to the effect that there was a powerful medium, residing at this address, through whom he intended to produce many marvelous phenomena. After this, King began to announce himself as soon as Palladino sat at the seance table; he remained her control throughout her career.

Palladino married a merchant named Raphael Delgaiz and worked in his shop. Evidently she had begun to sit professionally by the time she came to the attention of Neapolitan professor Ercole Chiaia. Chiaia encouraged the development of her powers and, in 1888, published an open letter to the renowned psychiatrist Cesare Lombroso, who had expressed an open-minded skepticism about seance phenomena. Lombroso waited until 1891 to respond to Chiaia's invitation to sit with Palladino, but the experience he then had marked a turning point in her life.

With Lombroso and another professor holding Palladino's hands, a bell that had been placed on a small table a yard away from her sounded above the heads of the sitters. They struck a match and saw the bell suspended in the air. The bell then fell to the table and traveled from there two yards to a bed. This seance was enough to convince Lombroso of the reality of physical phenomena, and he arranged for Palladino to undergo a longer series of tests in Milan the following year.

At the 17 sittings in Milan, some conducted in light rather than darkness, levitations of the table and alterations of the medium's weight were observed. The sittings were attended by several eminent scientists, including Lombroso and physiologist Charles Richet. A detailed report was published in the bulletin of the Psychological Section of the Medico-Legal Society of New York, and other investigations followed with other scientists in Naples and Rome.

A series held in 1894 is particularly noteworthy because it involved, for the first time, investigators from the London-based SOCIETY FOR PSYCHICAL RESEARCH (SPR). Richet hosted these sittings at his summer home on the Ile de Roubaud off the coast of France. The SPR's Frederic W.H. MYERS and Sir Oliver LODGE were present from the start, with Henry SIDGWICK and Eleanor SIDGWICK also there later on. The SPR group were impressed by what they saw and prepared a report for the Society's *Proceedings.*

When this report was published, however, Richard HODGSON, then in Boston as secretary of the SPR's American Branch (see AMERICAN SOCIETY FOR PSYCHICAL RESEARCH), criticized some of the research as leaving room for trickery. As a result of Hodgson's comments, a series of sittings was arranged in Cambridge, England in 1895. This Cambridge series was to prove disastrous.

It was the first time Palladino had sat outside Europe, and little happened at the first few seances. Hodgson then deliberately let go of Palladino's hand, and found her to be adept at cheating. The Sidgwicks and Myers declared that the trickery, which clearly had been practiced and perfected over many years, invalidated all the earlier findings from work with Palladino, including those from the Ile de Roubaud.

Palladino's European investigators were not happy with the SPR's pronouncement. They asserted that Palladino's propensity to cheat had been known all along, but that if properly controlled, she could nonetheless produce striking effects. Another lengthy series of studies followed, with reportedly good results, and eventually the SPR decided to take another look. In 1908 it commissioned three experienced investigators, all of whom had knowledge of conjuring methods and had reputations for exposing mediumistic fraud, to sit with Palladino in Naples.

The three investigators were Everard Feilding, W.W. Baggally, and Hereward CARRINGTON (Hodgson had died in 1905), and they were as surprised as were SPR officials when their study vindicated Palladino. Their detailed report, published in the SPR *Proceedings* in November 1909 (later reprinted in the book *Sittings with Eusapia Palladino and Other Studies* in 1963), is widely considered to be among the most important documents in the literature of psychical research.

But there was more to come. Carrington was so impressed with what he witnessed in Naples that he arranged for Palladino to visit the United States. She arrived in November 1909 and left in June 1910, having given 31 seances. The first 27 of these were under Carrington's supervision, and he restrained her when she tried to cheat. But the last four seances were held at Columbia University in Carrington's absence, and they were a disaster. Palladino was not restrained, and two detectives, hired for the purpose, were easily able to spot her tricks.

The Columbia exposure was well publicized, and it brought the end of American public interest in Palladino, although it had little effect upon the European investigators who had worked with her for years. The American sittings also produced one unlikely convert: the well-known American stage magician Howard Thurston. Thurston stated that he had witnessed one of Palladino's levitations, and he offered to give one thousand dollars to charity if it could be proven that she could not levitate except by trickery.

Palladino died on May 16, 1918. She had never learned to read or write, was unkempt in personal appearance and could be rather boorish in manner. Yet she had been one of the best-studied mediums in history. One book about her, by the psychiatrist Enrico Morselli, contained a 29-page bibliography of reports and discussions of her mediumship, published through 1909. If her cheating places her in a second class to D.D. HOME, against whom no serious charge was ever levied, history may nevertheless choose to regard her as having helped to establish the reality of what today is called "Macro-PK" (see PSYCHOKINESIS).

Further reading:

Carrington, Hereward. *Eusapia Palladino and Her Phenomena.* New York: B.W. Dodge, 1909.

Dingwall, E.J. *Very Peculiar People.* London: Rider, 1950.

Feilding, Everard. *Sittings with Eusapia Palladino and Other Studies.* Hyde Park, N.Y.: University Books, 1963.

Tabori, Paul. *Pioneers of the Unseen.* New York: Taplinger, 1973.

Palm Sunday Case Unique English case famous in the annals of psychical research for its evidence of survival after death (q.v.). The Palm Sunday Case spanned more than 30 years and involved complex and ideal cross correspondences, mental mediumship and automatic writing. Principal participants included several automatists, several investigators for the SOCIETY OF PSYCHICAL RESEARCH (SPR), London, and several deceased "communicators." There were two apparent motives to the communications. One seemed to be a group effort on the part of the communicators to provide evidence for survival. The second seemed to be the effort of one communicator to communicate with her beloved, one of England's renowned statesmen. The case is considered by some psychical researchers to be compelling evidence in support of survival after death. However, it remains beyond proof scientifically.

The Palm Sunday Case takes its name from the death date of one of the communicators, Mary Catherine Lyttleton, known as May, who was born in 1850. A vivacious and beautiful young woman, she attracted Arthur James Balfour upon their meeting in 1870. Both were from prestigious families. Lyttleton was daughter of the fourth Baron Lyttleton (Viscount Cobham). Balfour was the first Earl of Balfour, a statesman and philosopher, and was named after his godfather, Arthur Wellesley, the first Duke of Wellington, who had distinguished himself in the defeat of Napoleon at Waterloo.

For Balfour, it was love at first sight, but his relationship with Lyttleton progressed slowly. Eventually she apparently returned his ardor, which was known to her sister, Lavinia, but not to the rest of the family. Early in 1875, Balfour told Lyttleton he intended to propose. After this meeting, he never saw her again. Lyttleton fell ill with typhus fever, and after several weeks collapsed and died on the morning of March 21, 1875. It was Palm Sunday.

Balfour was so grief-stricken that it took him years to recover any sense of joy in living. He never married. He became involved in philosophy and politics. Though he was cordial and sociable, he remained aloof from others. For 55 years, until his death in 1930, he visited the home of Lavinia and her husband, Edmund Talbot, every Palm Sunday and spent the day in quiet commemoration of May's death. He earnestly believed in survival.

The first apparent communications in the Palm Sunday Case began in 1901, shortly after the death of Frederic W.H. MYERS, one of the founders of the SPR. Myers had believed ardently in survival and had stated while living that he would make an effort to communicate after death. As a psychical researcher, he knew that evidence would consist of information that was not known and could not have possibly been obtained by the living recipient.

Shortly after his death, Margaret Verrall, a friend of Myers and a classical lecturer at Newnham College, began receiving communications through automatic writing that seemed to come from Myers. They were veiled in symbolic references and laced with Latin and Greek terms and classical material.

In 1903, automatic writing scripts began to come through to Alice Kipling Fleming, sister of Rudyard Kipling (and who went by the pseudonym "Mrs. Holland") and to Helen Verrall, Margaret Verrall's daughter, who married psychical researcher W.H. Salter. In 1908, Winifred Coombe-Tennant (later Willett) began to receive scripts, purportedly from Myers. She was related by marriage to Myer's wife. These were the principal automatists; scripts were also received by other individuals.

All the scripts, like those of Margaret Verrall, were fragmentary and full of obscure and classical references. All of the automatists had mediumistic abilities of varying degrees. None knew of the story of the Balfour-Lyttleton romance cut short by death. Willett's scripts later were determined to have provided introductory material to what would emerge later in her trance mediumship.

The scripts were analyzed by the SPR. It became apparent over the years that a group of discarnate beings seemed to be producing the scripts. Some sense could be made out of them by piecing them all together, yet the overall meaning and purpose of the communications remained elusive. The investigators eventually included Gerald William Balfour, Second Earl of Balfour and Arthur Balfour's younger brother; John George Piddington; Alice Johnson; Sir Oliver LODGE; and Eleanor SIDGWICK.

The apparent purpose of the early fragmentary messages was to reveal the continuing, post-death personal identities of Lyttleton and Francis M. Balfour, one of Arthur's brothers, who had been killed in the Alps in 1882. In addition to Myers, Balfour and Lyttleton, other communicators allegedly included Henry SIDGWICK (1838–1900), a founder of the SPR; and Edmund GURNEY (1847–1888), an SPR founder and close friend of Myers.

All of the messages seemed to be directed at Arthur Balfour, though that was not immediately known. Many of the symbolic references had personal meaning only to him concerning Lyttleton and the circumstances surrounding her death.

In the messages, Lyttleton was referred to as "the Palm Maiden," and Arthur was referred to as "the Faithful Knight." Lyttleton also was identified by mentions of cockleshells or scallop shells, apparently in reference to the nursery rhyme, "Mary, Mary, quite contrary."

The use of symbols apparently was the preference of the communicators, who did not explain why they used them rather than speak more directly. Apparently, they were in no hurry to say much of anything until Arthur Balfour himself became involved.

Around 1910, the case began to change. Alice Kipling Fleming ceased to receive scripts. By 1911, Willett's mediumship had developed dramatically. Initially, Gurney seemed to be her control, and then he was succeeded by Francis Balfour, known as the "Dark Young Man." In time, Willet seemed to be able to communicate directly with discarnate personalities without need of a control. She was able to remain aware of what she said during a trance, and to recall details afterward. In 1911, Willett met Arthur Balfour for the first time. Upon shaking his hand, she suddenly felt "very queer."

In 1912, the case took a dramatic turn. Lyttleton began to communicate through Willett in trance. It then became clear that the purpose behind the communications was her effort to reach Balfour and impress upon him that she survived death and loved him deeply.

When approached with this stunning information, Balfour at first refused to believe it, despite his desire to believe in survival. He was 64 years old. Thirty-seven years had passed since Lyttleton had died, and 30 since his brother, Francis, had been killed in the Alps.

Balfour consented to have sittings with Willett, during which she would "try" for messages. Like the automatic scripts, they were cryptic and indirect, and full of symbols. With the trance sessions, the automatic scripts then began to make more sense; the symbols in them could be interpreted in terms of the Palm Sunday story. The trance sessions became the focus of the case, though Margaret Verrall and Helen Verrall Salter continued to receive automatic scripts. Margaret Verrall died in 1916.

Over the years, Balfour seemed to accept that Lyttleton was communicating with him. However, he never sought a sitting of his own volition and never volunteered comment on anything that came out of the sessions. It was not until late in his life, when his health deteriorated, that the messages visibly excited him.

In 1926, Balfour contracted pneumonia, and his health began an irreversible decline. During one sitting in 1926, Willett said she saw a phantasm of a young lady with thick, beautiful hair dressed in an old-fashioned dress. The phantasm communicated that Balfour was never alone, implying her spirit was always with him, and that she wanted him to know that she was "absolutely alive, and herself, and unchanged." She said she was with Francis Balfour on the Other Side.

In October 1929, six months before Balfour died, Lyttleton communicated that she was finished with trying to provide evidence of survival, and now was interested only in companionship with Balfour, or "deep calling unto deep." Lyttleton said, "Tell him he gives me Joy," which made Balfour visibly happy. Spiritually, he seemed renewed though his body continued to deteriorate. On March 19, 1930, he died. He was 81. His death brought the case to a close.

Despite the dramatic nature of the case and the fact that the automatists received material of which they had no personal knowledge, in the final analysis there was nothing revealed that was not known to someone living somewhere. Therefore, the possibility of telepathy and clairvoyance among the living cannot be ruled out. However, the participants in the case believed that they were truly communicating with discarnate spirits.

Some of the material in the scripts did seem to arise from the minds of the automatists, or perhaps from telepathy among them, yet the source of the symbolisms is unlikely to have come from their individual unconsciousness. The scripts do seem to build in support of a discarnate group working to gain the attention and scrutiny of the living. Nothing like this had happened before in the history of psychical research. There did seem to be a purpose, and the symbols seem to have been accurately applied to the Palm Sunday case.

On the surface, it appears that Lyttleton ultimately loved Balfour more than he loved her, for she seemed to have devoted many years to the effort of communicating with him. Lyttleton's family speculated that she never knew until after death how much she loved him. By modern standards, it seems odd that this passion would be expressed in indirect and cryptic messages. Perhaps this was due, at least in part, to the prevailing social formalities of the time. The Balfour-Lyttleton relationship had, in life, been hampered by the fact that they were never married and never even formally engaged; thus the public expression of intimate emotions was either alluded to or repressed.

If not for the Palm Sunday case, very little would be known about Balfour. He was an enigmatic man and left behind no private papers. The case was not made public until 1960, long after the deaths of all the participants.

See also EAR OF DIONYSIUS.

Further reading:
Balfour, Jean. "The Palm Sunday Case." *Proceedings of the Society for Psychical Research* 52 (February 1960):79–267.

Parapsychology Foundation Organization founded in New York City in 1951 by medium Eileen J. GARRETT. A non-profit, educational organization, the Parapsychology Foundation supports scientific research into the mind and consciousness through grants and international conferences. The foundation maintains the Eileen J. Garrett library at its New York City headquarters. The library is open to parapsychology researchers.

parsley Plant associated with death, the dead and ghosts. The ancient Greeks and Romans considered parsley to be sacred to the dead, and placed it on graves. In the Celtic world, parsley acquired a reputation for bad luck due to its association with the dead: in the lore of Devon, England, for example, it is considered unlucky to transplant it, for that would cause a death in the family and the Devil would take control of the garden. It is also most unlucky to be given parsley.

Conversely, parsley is a folklore remedy for those who are unfortunate enough to witness the spectral WILD HUNT, which results in blinding, swelling of the head and even death. All one need do is ask one of the ghosts for a bit of parsley.

Pele See MADAME PELE.

periwinkle Trailing evergreen plant, also called myrtle or creeping myrtle, often used as a ground cover in gardens. In superstition, periwinkle has powers pertaining to ghosts, witches and bewitchment. Periwinkle, which blooms in five-petaled blue-purple or white flowers, is called *violette des sorciers* (violet of the sorcerers) in France, where it wards off evil spirits. Hung over doorways, periwinkle is said to keep out both witches and spirits. It is effective in the exorcism of demons. In Welsh superstition, if one plucks periwinkle off a grave, one will be haunted by the dead in dreams for a year. In order for the plant to be magically effective, one must harvest it only on the first, ninth, eleventh and thirteenth nights of the moon. The harvester must not be unclean.

Perrott, Tom (1921–   ) English lay investigator of hauntings, apparitions and related phenomena; chairman of the GHOST CLUB, London.

Tom Perrott was born on December 28, 1921 in Bridport, Dorset. In 1925, his family moved to London. He attended Highgate School, not far from Highgate Cemetery, where reports of a vampire scared the public in the 1970s (most likely, the "vampire" was created by imagination and hysteria). Perrott married Doris Norton in 1949; the couple have four daughters. During World War II, he served in the Reconnaissance Corps and the Office for Prisoner of War Intelligence, the latter of which involved the interrogation of prisoners of war. Following his discharge in 1946, he pursued a career in business. In 1984, he took an early retirement from his post as personnel manager at a bakery factory, and devoted himself full time to his studies of folklore and the paranormal, subjects of life-long interest.

Perrott specializes in collecting information on cases of apparitions and hauntings. He has collected rec-

Tom Perrott. *Courtesy Tom Perrott.*

ords of nearly 3,000 reports at sites around Britain and has investigated cases for the SOCIETY FOR PSYCHICAL RESEARCH (SPR), which he joined in 1964. He has devoted special effort to collecting British ghost stories and legends so that they are recorded for history, and to researching Gypsy folklore.

Although numerous cases have been authenticated, Perrott finds most are subjective and can be explained by ordinary causes, such as atmospheric changes, effects of medication or drugs, imagination, emotional stress, biases or expectations. A small number of cases may involve telepathic transfer of impressions from a percipient to others. On rare occasion, atmospheric and other environmental conditions may give perceptible form to strong emotions, such as love, hate or grief, that linger at a site.

Perrott prefers not to use electronic equipment when making an inquiry, and does not rely on electronic or photographic evidence because of the ease with which trickery can be used.

Perrott also remains skeptical of survival after death, because of insufficient evidence. A theory that some hauntings may be due to psychic vibrations left at a

site is feasible, he believes. Collective apparitions may be caused by telepathy or mass hysteria.

Perrott lectures widely around the United Kingdom and has taught his own courses in parapsychology at various universities. He makes numerous media appearances for radio and television programs in the United Kingdom, France and Canada. In addition, he leads tours of haunted U.K. sites.

Perrott has written books, columns and articles and is a co-author of *Ghosts of Dorset, Devon and Somerset* (1974) and *Strange Dorset Stories* (1991).

He joined the Ghost Club in 1967 and became chairman in 1971. He also is a member of the Folklore Society and the GHOST RESEARCH SOCIETY, based in Oak Lawn, Illinois.

Further reading:

Neesom, Dawn. " 'Ghosts Terrorized My Family for Two Years.' " *Woman's Own* (May 27, 1991):16–17.

Strange Dorset Stories. St. Teath, Cornwall, England: Bossiney Books, 1991.

Underwood, Peter. *The Ghost Hunters.* London: Robert Hale, 1985.

phantasmagoria   A ghost-making machine used for popular entertainment from the late 18th century through the 19th century. The device, developed by Belgian optician E.G. Robertson in the 1790s, projected convincing figures before an audience.

phantasm   See APPARITION; GHOST.

Phantom Hitchhiker (also Vanishing Hitchhiker)   One of the most popular and widespread of modern ghost legends, appearing around the world and especially throughout the United States. There are countless variations, and the story continues to be reported in contemporary times.

In most versions, the phantom hitchhiker is a girl or woman, sometimes in distress. She is spotted late at night, standing by the side of a lonely stretch of road. Sometimes she stands in the middle of the road, looming up suddenly in the headlights. She is often dressed in white, and if the night is stormy she is bedraggled from the rain. The driver, who usually is a man alone, stops and asks if he can help, or where she is going. She tells him, and she always is going to the same town as he is. He offers to take her straight to her home. She accepts and gets in the back seat. He may give her his coat to keep warm. As they drive on, the man cannot help but notice how stunningly beautiful she is. But she is painfully shy and withdrawn, perhaps even exhausted, for she rarely says another word. She may give her name.

When the driver reaches the address she has given him, he stops the car and turns around in his seat, and is astonished to see that she has vanished. Typically, she leaves behind a piece of clothing or an object, such as a book, pin, purse or scarf. The seat may still be wet where she sat. The driver goes up to the door of the house, which is answered usually by a woman and sometimes by a man and woman. The driver explains the mysterious event. He is told that it has happened before—the girl or woman is their daughter who was killed some time ago, and the night is the anniversary of her death. She was either murdered or killed in a tragic accident at about the spot where the driver picked her up. Every anniversary of her death, her ghost attempts to come home. The driver is shown a photograph of the dead girl—she is the same one he picked up, wearing the very same clothes. Later, the driver visits her grave. If he had given her his coat in the car, he then finds it draped across her tombstone.

The phantom hitchhiker may appear and pick up traveling companions at locations other than lonely roads. Sometimes she is met at a club or dance hall and is driven home. In one version from the American South, the phantom hitchhiker is a young woman in a cemetery who meets a man walking home alone late one night. He offers to walk her to her home and she accepts. They talk along the way. Later, he decides to call on her, and he is shocked to hear from the man who answers the door that the young woman, his daughter, has been dead for 12 years.

Despite its widespread popularity in the United States, the phantom hitchhiker legend probably originated in Europe with legends of PHANTOM TRAVELERS. It also appears in Asian folklore as a young woman who walks behind a man to the home of her parents, but vanishes when the destination is reached and he turns around. In America, the phantom hitchhiker legend appeared as early as the late 19th century. It may have gained a prominent role in American lore because of the emphasis on automobiles in American culture, and the romance of the open road, especially beginning in the mid-20th century. There also are sexual undertones in the vulnerable-female-in-distress motif.

In some versions, the phantom hitchhiker story takes on characteristics of the legends of eternally wandering ghosts, such as the FLYING DUTCHMAN and LA LLORONA.

See also MADAME PELE; RESURRECTION MARY.

Further reading:

Goss, Michael. *The Evidence for Phantom Hitch-Hikers*. Wellingborough, Northamptonshire, England: The Aquarian Press, 1984.
Leach, Maria, and Jerome Fried, eds. *Funk & Wagnalls Standard Dictionary of Folklore, Mythology, and Legend*. San Francisco: Harper & Row, 1979.
McNeil, W.K., comp. and ed. *Ghost Stories from the American South*. New York: Dell, 1985.
Scott, Beth, and Michael Norman. *Haunted Heartland*. New York: Warner Books, 1985.

phantom monks   Ghosts of monks and other ecclesiastical persons said to inhabit abbey ruins, churches and vicarages built on the sites of former monasteries, present cathedrals and churches, and houses where they were born. Some spirits belong to monks who suffered violent deaths for their faith during times of religious prosecution, or to monks and priests who simply wish to remain at beloved sites in spirit. Some phantoms are clergymen, while others are monks seen walking alone or in processions. Phantom monks are heard chanting and singing, and have even been said to speak to visitors. Numerous phantom monk hauntings are reported throughout the U.K.

At the ruins of Whalley Abbey, near Clitheroe in Lancashire, England, witnesses have heard the singing of a *Te Deum* and have seen a procession of monks with heads bowed and hands clasped together as if in prayer. The monks first came to Whalley in the 13th century, but the property was forfeited to the state after the abbot, John Paslew, was tried and executed for treason in 1537. Paslew's ghost is often accompanied by poltergeist activities.

Two phantom monks have appeared at Chingle Hall, at Goosnargh, Lancashire, a 13th-century house located six miles north of Preston. During the 16th-century Reformation, the Catholic owners, the Singletons, allowed secret masses to be celebrated and priests to be hidden in its myriad rooms and passages.

In the next century, the house passed to relatives, the Wall family, and it was the birthplace of St. John Wall, who was hanged for his religion in 1679. It is believed that his head was taken back to the house and buried in its cellars. His ghost has been seen in the house and on the grounds, often accompanied by footsteps, stamping feet, scratchings, rappings and tappings.

Visitors report seeing objects and wall pictures move as though manipulated by invisible hands, as well as being touched and shoved by the ghost.

The ghost known as the Black Canon haunts Bolton Priory, eight miles east of Skipton, North Yorkshire, so-called because it is dressed in a black cassock, cloak and hat. According to eyewitnesses, the ghost visits the ruins, sometimes in daylight, and belongs to a man in his late 60s.

Some phantom monks allegedly have spoken to visitors, giving them advice or instructions. At Bury St. Edmunds in Suffolk, the site that once housed the shrine of St. Edmund, King of the East Angles, who was murdered by the Danes in 870, a local rector was given information for a book he was writing about the saint. The monk reportedly said that the saint's body had been removed from its tomb and safely buried elsewhere in the church in order to protect it against defilement.

In 1928, a visitor to Beaulieu Abbey, in Hampshire, was of service to a phantom monk who told her to dig in a certain spot where she found a coffer with two round stones and some bones. She gave them a Christian burial, and since that time, phantom monks have been heard chanting.

In addition to a speaking phantom monk, there is a ringing phantom bell at the vicarage of Elm in Cambridgeshire, which stands on the site of a 12th-century monastery. The ghost reportedly told the vicar's wife that he was Ignatius the bell-ringer. Villagers had reported that the sound of the bell foretold a death in the parish within the next 24 hours.

The ghost explained that his job had been to sound the bell when the floodwaters were rising. One night he had fallen asleep and failed to warn the brothers when the water became too high. The water rushed into the monastery and some monks were drowned. This same vicar's wife claimed that she was the victim of an attempted strangulation by a ghost while she slept. She related the story to the phantom monk, who told her that the room where she slept had once been the scene of a murder and the victim's spirit had attacked her. It further explained that it had stopped the attack, a move that it hoped would count toward completing its penance for the loss of brother monks.

Further reading:

Folklore, Myths and Legends of Britain. London: Reader's Digest Assoc., 1977.

Underwood, Peter. A Gazeteer of British Ghosts, Rev. ed. London: Pan Books, Ltd., 1973.

Whitaker, Terence. Haunted England. Chicago: Contemporary Books, 1987.

phantom nuns Ghosts allegedly belonging to women of the church some of whom met violent ends, either as victims of religious persecution or because they were punished for transgressions. Phantom nuns haunt religious buildings or buildings built on the former site of religious institutions. Many cases have been documented in England.

Holy Trinity church in Micklegate, York is said to be haunted by the ghosts of an abbess, a woman and child. The abbess was associated with a Benedictine priory that once stood on the site. She met her death when she defied soldiers who came to destroy the priory during the Reformation by saying they would enter only over her dead body. They killed her, and as she lay dying she promised to haunt the site until another sacred building was built. She kept her promise until the abbey ruins were destroyed, whereupon she moved into the church.

The other adult female ghost is believed to belong to the woman who is buried near the organ window; the child's ghost belongs to her. The woman's husband died and was buried near the organ window. Shortly after, their only child died of the plague and was buried outside the city walls. The plague soon claimed the woman, who was buried alongside her husband. It is thought that the spirit of the abbess brings the child from its grave to visit the parents' graves, because the mother's spirit could not rest without her child.

During the Middle Ages, it was common practice for nuns to have their cell doors bricked up, leaving just a small window for receiving food. The ghost that haunts the Theatre Royal in York belongs to a nun from the time that a hospital run by nuns stood on the theater site from the 12th to 18th century. Supposedly, the nun broke her vows and her punishment was to be walled up alive. Visitors and actors alike have seen the gray and white apparition, most often in a small room near the dress circle.

See BORLEY RECTORY.

Further reading:

Underwood, Peter. A Gazeteer of British Ghosts. Rev. ed. London: Pan Books, Ltd., 1973.

Whitaker, Terence. Haunted England. Chicago: Contemporary Books, 1987.

phantom ships Legends and reports of ghostly ships are universal. Most commonly, they are linked to disasters and shipwrecks. Phantom ships usually appear at the scene of the disaster and may reenact their wrecks, especially on stormy nights.

Numerous phantom ship stories come from the British Isles; ghost ships continue to be reported in modern times, especially off the Atlantic Coast. The most haunted area, however, lies on the opposite coast facing the English Channel: the Goodwin Sands, about five miles off Deal in Kent. According to legend, this dangerous sandback was once the island of Lomea, which was flooded and drowned in the 11 century when the Earl of Goodwin neglected to maintain the sea walls. There is no evidence that such an island ever existed, yet the phantom bells of its drowned churches are reported to toll beneath the sea. Legend also has it that some 50,000 people have lost their lives in shipwrecks on the sandbank. Their phantom ships still ply the waters.

The most famous of the Goodwin Sands ghosts is the three-masted schooner *Lady Lovibond*, which was bound for Oporto when it was wrecked on February 13, 1748. All aboard were drowned. The voyage was considered to be most unlucky from the start, for the captain's bride, Annetta, was on board; in the superstitions of sailing, it is bad luck to take a woman to sea. The mate was said to have been a rival for the lady's affections, and one story holds that he murdered the helmsman and deliberately wrecked the ship for revenge.

Every 50 years, on February 13, the *Lady Lovibond* is seen running aground on the sands. On its first appearance in 1798, the crew on at least two ships reported seeing it. The phantom was so real that the master of the coaster *Edenbridge* thought his ship nearly collided with it. In 1848, the phantom again appeared so real that Deal seamen thought a wreck had actually occurred, and set out in lifeboats to rescue survivors. None was found, nor were any traces of a wrecked ship. The *Lady Lovibond* appeared in 1898 and 1948, and is due in 1998 and 2048.

Another Goodwin Sands victim is the *SS Violet*, a paddle steamer which ran aground crossing the channel in a snowstorm more than 100 years ago. Everyone on board was killed. Curiously, the wreck was reenacted at the start of the World War II, and was witnessed by the lookout at the East Goodwin lighthouse. A lifeboat was sent out to investigate, but nothing was found.

On the Atlantic coast, mysterious tall-masted sailing ships are seen floating offshore before they vanish into the mist. Many are unknown. According to one Cornwall legend, a ship was once seen one moonlit night sailing straight for shore between Land's End and Penzance. Just as it seemed the ship would wreck itself, it lifted out of the water, sailed through the air over land and vanished.

The Cape of Good Hope, the treacherous southernmost tip of South America, is another oft-haunted site. (See FLYING DUTCHMAN.)

Pirates, who plied the seas in the 17th and 18th centuries, are associated with phantom ship lore. In American lore, the ghost ship of Captain Kidd is said to sail up and down the New England coast as Kidd searches for his buried treasure. Pirate Jean Lafitte's ship is said to prowl the waters off Galveston, Texas, which is thought to be the area where his ship went down in the 1820s.

The most haunted waterways of America are the Great Lakes, which have claimed numerous ships during violent winter storms. The Great Lakes are more dangerous than any ocean to navigate because of fast-rising, powerful storms that can sink a ship in minutes.

One of the most famous lost ships of the Great Lakes is the *Griffon*, built at Niagara, New York and owned by the French explorer Rene Robert Cavalier, Sieur de La Salle. The *Griffon*, at 60 feet in length and 45 tons in weight, was the largest ship built to sail the lakes in her time. During construction, the workers were taunted by local Iroquois, who considered the ship an affront to the Great Spirit. The Iroquois prophet, Metiomek, cursed the ship and said it would sink. The *Griffon* commenced her maiden voyage on August 7, 1679. At Detroit Harbor at Washington Island, Wisconsin, La Salle loaded fur and then left the ship to continue his own explorations for the source of the Mississippi River by canoe. The *Griffon* set out to return to Niagara on September 18, 1679. It never arrived. No one knows what happened to it; according to legend, it "sailed through a crack in the ice" and vanished. In 1900, a wreck believed to be that of the *Griffon* was discovered off Bruce Peninsula in Lake Huron. The identity of the wreck was announced in 1955 after historical evidence had been examined; however, others have disputed the claim, and the true identify of the wreck remains unconfirmed. Meanwhile, the ghost of the *Griffon* reportedly is still seen drifting about Lake Huron on some foggy nights.

An unusual phantom ship appeared at New Haven, Connecticut in 1648, wrecking itself before a crowd of astonished witnesses. It was interpreted as a sign from God revealing the fate of a ship that had disappeared.

The event was recorded in Cotton Mather's ecclesiastical history of New England, *Magnalia Christi Americana*, as reported to him in a letter by the pastor of New Haven at the time, James Pierpont. According to the story, the merchants of New Haven, former Londoners, found themselves on hard times. They pooled the last of their resources to build a ship to send to England with goods. The ship was built in 1647 in Rhode Island. The master, a Mr. Lamberton, perhaps with a bit of prescience, commented that the ship would prove to be their grave. The ship set sail in January, bearing about five or six of New Haven's most prominent citizens among the passengers. It never reached England and presumably was lost at sea. For months, the citizens of New Haven anguished over the fate of the ship, and prayed for the souls aboard.

In June of the following year, a violent thunderstorm came out of the northwest one afternoon. The sky then grew calm. About one hour before sunset, Pierpont told Mather:

> . . . a ship of like dimensions with the aforesaid, with her canvas and colours abroad (though the wind northerly) appeared in the air coming from our harbor's mouth, which lyes southward from the town, seemingly with her sails filled under a fresh gale, holding her course north, and continuing under observation, sailing against the wind for the space of half an hour.
>
> Many were drawn to behold this great work of God; yea, the very children cryed out, 'There's a brave ship!' At length, crowding up as far as there is usually water sufficient for such a vessel, and so near some if the spectators, as that they imagined a man might hurl a stone on board her, her *main-top* [Pierpont's emphasis] seemed to be blown off, but left hanging in the shrouds; then her *mizzen-top;* then all her *masting* seemed blown away by the board: quickly after the *hulk* brought unto a careen, she overset, and so vanished into a smoaky cloud, which in some time dissipated, leaving, as everywhere else, a clear air. The admiring spectators could distinguish the several colors of each part, the principal rigging, and such proportions, as caused not only the generality of persons to say, 'This was the mould of their ship, and this was her tragick end,' but Mr. Davenport [an official or preacher] also in publick declared to this effect, 'That God had condescended, for the quieting of their afflicted spirits, this extraordinary account of his sovereign disposal of those for whom so many fervent prayers were made continually.'

See also PALATINE LIGHT, THE.

Further reading:
Botkin, B.A., ed. *A Treasury of New England Folklore.* Rev. ed. New York: American Legacy Press, 1989.

Cohen, Daniel. *The Encyclopedia of Ghosts.* New York: Dodd, Mead & Co., 1984.

Folklore, Myths and Legends of Britain. London: Reader's Digest Assoc., 1977.

Hole, Christina. *Haunted England.* London: B.T. Batsford Ltd., 1940.

Scott, Beth, and Michael Norman. *Haunted Heartland.* New York: Warner Books, 1985.

phantom travelers   Ghosts of humans and animals which haunt travel routes, stations and vehicles. Phantom travelers are universal in folklore and legend. Typically, they seem to be associated with tragedies which have occurred in the course of travel. They also seem to be associated with the lure and romance of travel, and with the strong emotions of meetings and partings. The tradition of traveling phantom tales is quite old, and was documented as early as the 1600s in Europe and Russia. Legends often grow up around phantom travelers.

The most interesting type of phantom traveler is the specter who appears real to the casual observer. Some hauntings include no visual apparitions, but only sounds, lights, sensations and smells. Lord Halifax, who collected ghost tales of Britain, recorded one tale of a phantom traveler who rode the rails as a passenger. The account was given him by the nephew of a man, Colonel Ewart, who claimed to have encountered the spectral woman. Once on the train from Carlisle to London, Ewart secured a compartment by himself and dozed off. He awoke feeling stiff and strange, and suddenly noticed that a woman in black was seated opposite him. Her face was obscured by a black veil, and she seemed to be looking at something on her lap, though nothing was visible. Ewart spoke to her but she did not respond. She began to rock back and forth and sing a soft lullaby. However, there was no child with her.

Before Ewart could probe further, the train screeched and crashed into something. Ewart was knocked unconscious by a flying suitcase. When he came to, he left the train and ascertained that the accident was not serious. He then remembered the woman in black and returned to the compartment, but she was gone and was nowhere to be found. No one he questioned had seen her; in fact, Ewart was told that his compartment had been locked after he had entered it, as was customary, and no one had gone in after him.

Months later, Ewart was told by a railway official that the woman in black was a ghost who haunted the line. According to legend, she and her bridegroom had been traveling on the train when he stuck his head too far out the window and was decapitated by a wire. The headless body fell into the young woman's lap. When the train arrived in London, she was found sitting in the compartment, holding the corpse and singing a lullaby to it. She never regained her sanity, and died several months later.

Other hauntings and phantom traveler legends center around railway and underground stations and airports. At the Darlington rail station in Durham, England, the ghosts of a man and a black retriever have been seen in the porter's cellar. The ghost is said to be a man who committed suicide by throwing himself in front of a train. He had owned a black retriever. The phantom dog reportedly bit an old porter, but the bite left no marks. At the Dearham Bridge station at Maryport in Cumbria, a baby's screams still are heard on certain nights just before a train passes by. The story goes that one evening a couple were out walking with their baby, and the father inexplicably snatched the child and threw it over the bridge in front of a train. He was hanged for the crime. At the Mayfield station in Manchester, the scene of at least two suicides and other fatal accidents, phantom footsteps are heard on the platform. In London's underground, the Aldgate station on the Circle line is one of several haunted stations, with so many sightings that they are entered into the station log.

Perhaps one of the most intriguing phantom travelers is a gentleman in a dark suit and bowler hat who has haunted Heathrow International Airport since 1948, when a DC3 Dakota of the Sabena Belgian Airways crashed on landing in heavy fog, killing all 22 persons on board. While rescue workers dug through the wreckage, they were interrupted by the man, who appeared suddenly out of the fog and said, "Excuse me. Have you found my briefcase?" Since then, the ghost has been seen numerous times at the airport, walking along Runway 2-8-right where the crash occurred. It is believed the ghost was a victim of the tragedy.

Other Heathrow ghosts include an invisible presence that pants like an animal down the backs of people's necks, and "the ghost in the light gray suit," a man who haunts the VIP lounges. One witness saw only the bottom half of the ghost.

Manchester International Airport also seems to be home to ghosts, including one of an old man seen daily in 1971 on the premises of C. Claridge & Co., Ltd., a freight forwarding company at the airport. The ghost was seen sitting in a store room and walking along barefoot. The haunting also included strange noises, an unexplained scream, and the movement of office equipment. The ghost has been seen sporadically since 1971.

Phantom travelers move about in the travel mode of their day: they walk, ride phantom horses, ride phantom bicycles or motorcycles, or drive phantom carriages, cars, buses and trucks. If on foot, they may suddenly appear standing in the middle of the road. Drivers of vehicles may swerve to avoid hitting them, sometimes causing an accident with their own vehicle, or may think they have struck the person. However, when they stop and inspect the area, there is no sign of anyone or any damage to the vehicle caused by impact. (See also PHANTOM VEHICLES.)

In the United States, the vicinity of Elmore, Ohio is said to be haunted by a headless motorcyclist who appears yearly on the night of March 21, the anniversary of his death. According to legend, the cyclist was a young soldier who, after being discharged from the army after the end of World War I, bought a motorcycle to impress the girlfriend he had left behind. When he arrived at her farm, he was shocked to find out that she had become engaged to another man in his absence. He sped off on his cycle and lost

control on a curve just before a bridge. He and his motorcycle hurtled into the ravine. He was decapitated and his headlight was shorn off. His phantom appears only as a speeding headlight which races down the road and vanishes halfway over the bridge. Legend has it that the phantom can be summoned on the death anniversary by blinking car lights and honking the horn three times each.

In 1968, two men tried to record the phantom on film and audiotape. They summoned the phantom twice. The third time, one of them stood in the middle of the bridge, and was found by his friend beaten up and lying in a ditch. He said he had no recall of what happened. Nothing showed up on the movie film. A strange light registered on the still film, and their audiotape recorded some odd, high-pitched noises, all inconclusive as evidence of paranormal phenomena.

Some phantom travelers seem doomed to eternal wandering as punishment for some folly or sin. The FLYING DUTCHMAN is perhaps the most famous example. Another such legend is that of Peter Rugg, which dates to the early 19th century in the Boston area. One eyewitness, a man named William Austin, claimed to have encountered the spectral Rugg in 1826 while riding in a coach out of Boston. Austin, who was sitting with the driver, noticed the horses becoming nervous. The driver remarked that the "storm breeder" was approaching, and they would encounter a storm, despite the fact that no clouds were in the sky. The "storm breeder" turned out to be a man and child in an open carriage accompanied by rain clouds. The driver related that he had seen the two often on the road, and that the man had asked directions to Boston but had paid no attention when told he was headed in the opposite direction.

Three years later, Austin, while staying in a hotel in Hartford, Connecticut, again saw the mysterious carriage, which was heading toward the hotel. Another man told him the occupants were Peter Rugg and his child; Rugg always asked directions to Boston but paid no heed to them.

Austin flagged the carriage down and, he claimed, carried on a conversation with the ghost. Rugg identified himself by name and said he lived on Middle Street in Boston. He and his child had left the city "some time ago" and had gotten wet in a rain shower. He asked Austin for directions to Boston, and refused to believe that he was in Connecticut. He drove off in a hurry.

Austin located individuals in Boston who told him the story of Rugg, a stubborn man who lived in Boston around 1730. Rugg had set out one day with his daughter to drive to Concord. On the return trip, he was warned by a friend that a storm was coming, but he vowed he would get home that night in spite of it, or never see home at all. He and his daughter never reached home, and never were found. Their ghosts, apparently, strive continually to reach home.

The PHANTOM HITCHHIKER is another common phantom traveler.

See also FLIGHT 401.

Further reading:
Cohen, Daniel. *The Encyclopedia of Ghosts.* New York: Dodd, Mead & Co., 1984.
Halifax, Lord. *Lord Halifax's Ghost Book.* London: Geoffrey Bles, Ltd., 1936.
McNeil, W.K., comp. and ed. *Ghost Stories from the American South.* New York: Dell, 1985.
Scott, Beth, and Michael Norman. *Haunted Heartland.* New York: Warner Books, 1985.
Whitaker, Terence. *Haunted England.* Chicago: Contemporary Books, 1987.

phantom vehicles Ghostly vehicles which suddenly appear on the road, usually traveling at high speed, are a widespread type of haunting. The vehicles appear to be real; some are driverless. Drivers of other vehicles in their approaching path swerve violently to avoid a collision, sometimes colliding with something else, resulting in injury and death. Some phantom vehicles are associated with sites where murders or tragic accidents occurred, or sites reputed to be otherwise haunted. Some have unknown origins but are seen by many over the course of time, always hurtling down the same piece of road or highway.

On the night of June 15, 1934, a young man driving his car in the North Kensington area of London suddenly found himself on a collision course with a bus. Headlights blazing, the bus was speeding to the intersection of St. Mark's Road and Cambridge Gardens. The young man swerved but collided with another car. He was killed. The bus allegedly was a phantom vehicle which continues to be reported over the years, and has caused other accidents. Other drivers have had minor accidents trying to avoid the bus, said by at least one witness to be driverless.

At Christmas time along the Lamberhurst-Frant Road in Kent, a phantom truck appears, sometimes during the day, to cause other drivers to swerve out of the way. In 1960, one truck almost overturned in the driver's attempt to avoid the ghost truck; the driver investigated but could find no sign of the vehicle. The phantom truck also has been reported, to suddenly back out into oncoming traffic.

At BACHELOR'S GROVE CEMETERY near the Rubio Woods Forest Preserve near Chicago, an area where numerous haunting phenomena have been reported, phantom cars have mystified and terrified various

witnesses at dusk and at night. Phantom cars and trucks which suddenly disappear have been reported along or near the Midlothian Turnpike, which runs past the cemetery. Drivers have reported having their own cars struck by speeding phantom cars which appeared out of nowhere; some even hear the sounds of splintering glass and crumpling metal. When they get out to inspect the damage, however, there is no sign of an impact and no sign of the other car. There are no legends of accidents or tragedies that attempt to explain the phantom cars at this site.

See also PHANTOM TRAVELERS.

Further reading:
Jarvis, Sharon, ed. *True Tales of the Unknown Vol. II.* New York: Bantam Books, 1989.
Scott, Beth, and Michael Norman. *Haunted Heartland.* New York: Warner Books, 1985.
Underwood, Peter. *A Gazeteer of British Ghosts.* Rev. ed. London: Pan Books, Ltd., 1973.
Whitaker, Terence. *Haunted England.* Chicago: Contemporary Books, 1987.

"Philip" An artificial poltergeist created by experiment by eight members of the Toronto Society for Psychical Research, under the direction of parapsychologists A.R.G. Owen and Iris M. Owen.

The group, none of whose members had any demonstrable psychic ability, set out in 1972 to determine if they could mentally create a collective thought-form, or artificial ghost, by intense and prolonged concentration. They fabricated a man named "Philip" and gave him a fictitious history. He was born "Philip Aylesford" in 1624, joined the military at age 15 and was knighted at age 16, was befriended by Prince Charles (Charles I), fought for the crown in the English Civil War, worked as a secret agent for Charles II, and knew Cromwell. He had an affair with a Gypsy. His wife discovered his infidelity and accused the girl of witchcraft. The Gypsy was burned at the stake and "Philip" committed suicide at age 30 in 1654.

With "Philip's" life story set, the group in September 1972 began convening at the Owens' house in Toronto, where they meditated and tried to establish communication with him. They visualized him and discussed the details of his life, hoping that eventually an apparition would materialize. No visual apparition appeared, but sometimes various members of the group reported feeling a presence in the room, or receiving an unusually vivid mental picture of "Philip."

After months with no success, the group tried Spiritualist techniques for table-tilting, in which psychokinetic (PK) effects sometimes manifest when a group sits around a table with their hands placed lightly on it. The idea for this came from the work of British psychologist Kenneth J. Batcheldor, who had achieved PK effects in seance-like settings. It was Batcheldor's theory that the atmosphere of belief and expectation that permeates a seance in effect creates the phenomena that Spiritualists attribute to spirits.

On the third or fourth table-tilting session, the group felt a vibration within the tabletop. The vibrations became raps and knocks, and the table moved beneath their hands. When one member of the group wondered out loud if "Philip" was responsible, a knock sounded in answer. Using a simple code of one rap for yes and two for no, the group communicated with the spirit, who claimed to be the very man they had created. Although the spirit was able to give historically correct answers concerning events and persons—perhaps due to cryptomnesia or extrasensory perception (ESP) among members of the group—it was unable to provide any information about itself which had not previously been manufactured as part of his life's history.

"Philip" sometimes greeted latecomers to the sessions by moving the table toward them, and on occasion he even managed to maneuver the table so as to trap some members in the corner of the room. With raps, he would play and beat times to tunes.

Sessions with "Philip" continued for several years. In 1974, a film was made in which the table levitated about one inch off the carpet and glided about four feet in distance. In 1975, the group was invited to participate in PK experiments at Kent State University. Interest in the electronic voice phenomenon (q.v.), in which attempts are made to record spirit voices on magnetic tape, led the group to try to evoke a vocal response from "Philip" in answer to questions. The group thought they obtained whispered responses, some clear, especially to questions posed by Iris Owen.

The group's results encouraged other groups to try similar experiments to create artificial personalities. Another Toronto group created "Lilith," a French-Canadian spy during World War II, and a group of French students from Quebec created "Sebastian," a medieval alchemist, and "Axel," a man from the future. The personalities communicated by rapping. One evening, the French students and the Owens group conducted a joint session, which produced an amusing evening of rapping. Each personality had its own identifiable character of raps.

The Owens experimenters believed that they succeeded in demonstrating that a group's subconscious could produce physical effects characterizing a poltergeist—"PK by committee," as they called it. The

messages rapped out came from the group's collective subconscious. The experimenters further believed they were only a step away from producing a physical manifestation of a spirit. That, however, was not achieved. After about 1977, interest waned and activities eventually were discontinued. The experiments were time-consuming, and after several years, the group felt they had made little headway in understanding the basic physical phenomena that were occurring.

Since then, the Owens have from time to time assembled small groups to pursue more experiments, with small successes. Raps are easy to produce, but progressing beyond that point is difficult.

Further reading:

Owen, Iris M., with Margaret Sparrow. *Conjuring Up Philip.* New York: Harper & Row, 1976.

Owen, Iris M. " 'Phillip's' Story Continued." *New Horizons: Journal of the New Horizons Research Fund* 2 (April 1975):14–20.

phone calls from the dead   Alleged contact with the dead has occurred universally throughout history, taking various forms of dreams, waking visions and auditory hallucinations, either spontaneous or induced through trance. In many cultures, the spirits of the dead have been sought for their wisdom, advice and knowledge of the future. The dead also seem to initiate their own communication, using whatever means seem to be most effective. With the advent of electromagnetic technology, mysterious messages have been communicated by telegraph, wireless, phonographs and radio. A curious phenomenon of modern times is the communication via the telephone.

Phone calls from the dead seem to be random and occasional occurrences that happen without explanation. The great majority are exchanges between persons who shared a close emotional tie while both were living: spouses, parents and children, siblings, and occasionally friends and other relatives. Most communications are "intention" calls, initiated by the deceased to impart a message, such as farewell upon death, a warning of impending danger, or information the living needs to carry out a task. For example, actress Ida Lupino's father, Stanley, who died intestate in London during World War II, called Lupino six months after his death to relate information concerning his estate: the location of some unknown but important papers. Some calls appear to have no other purpose than to make contact with the living; many of these occur on emotionally-charged "anniversary" days, such as Mother's Day or Father's Day, a birthday or holiday. In a typical "anniversary" call, the dead may do nothing more than repeat a phrase over and over, such as "Hello, Mom, is that you?"

Persons who have received phone calls from the dead report that the voices sound exactly the same as when the deceased was living; furthermore, the voice often uses pet names and words. The telephone usually rings normally, although some recipients say that the ring sounded flat and abnormal. In many cases, the connection is bad, with a great deal of static and line noise, and occasionally the faint voices of other persons are heard, as though lines have been crossed. In many cases, the voice of the dead one is difficult to hear and grows fainter as the call goes on. Sometimes, the voice just fades away but the line remains open, and the recipient hangs up after giving up on further communication. Sometimes the call is terminated by the dead, and the recipient hears the click of disengagement; other times, the line simply goes dead.

The phantom phone calls typically occur when the recipient is in a passive state of mind. If the recipient knows the caller is dead, the shock is great and the phone call very brief; invariably, the caller terminates the call after a few seconds or minutes, or the line goes dead. If the recipient does not know the caller is dead, a lengthy conversation of up to 30 minutes or so may take place, during which the recipient is not aware of anything amiss. In a minority of cases, the call is placed person-to-person, long-distance with the assistance of a mysterious operator. Checks with the telephone company later turn up no evidence of a call being placed.

Phone calls allegedly may be placed to the dead as well. The caller does not find out until sometime after the call that the person on the other end has been dead. In one such case, a woman dreamed of a female friend she had not seen for several years. In the disturbing dream, she witnessed the friend sliding down into a pool of blood. Upon awakening, she worried that the dream was a portent of trouble, and called the friend. She was relieved when the friend answered. The friend explained that she had been in the hospital, had been released and was due to be readmitted in a few days. She demurred when the woman offered to visit, saying she would call later. The return call never came. The woman telephoned her friend again, to be told by a relative that the friend had been dead for six months at the time the conversation took place.

In several cases studied by researchers, the deceased callers make reference to an anonymous "they" who have allowed the communication to take place, and caution that there is little time to talk. The remarks imply that communication between the liv-

ing and the dead is not only difficult, but not necessarily desirable.

Most phone calls from the dead occur within 24 hours of the death of the caller. Most short calls come from those who have been dead seven days or less; most lengthy calls come from those who have been dead several months. One of the longest death-intervals on record is two years.

In a small number of cases, the callers are strangers who say they are calling on behalf of a third party, whom the recipients later discover is dead.

Several theories exist as to the origin of phantom phone calls: they are indeed placed by the dead, who somehow manipulate the telephone mechanisms and circuitry; they are deceptions of elemental-type spirits who enjoy playing tricks on the living; they are psychokinetic acts caused subconsciously by the recipient, whose intense desire to communicate with the dead creates a type of hallucinatory experience; they are entirely fantasy created by the recipient.

For the most part, phantom phone calls are not seriously regarded by parapsychologists. In the early 20th century, numerous devices were built by investigators in hopes of capturing ghostly voices; many of them were modifications of the telegraph and wireless. Thomas Alva Edison, whose parents were Spiritualists, believed that a telephone could be invented that would connect the living to the dead. He verified that he was working on such a device, but apparently it never was completed before his death. "Psychic telephone" experiments were conducted in the 1940s in England and America. Interest in the phenomenon waned until the 1960s, following the findings of Konstantin Raudive that ghostly voices could be captured on electromagnetic tape. (See ELECTRONIC VOICE PHENOMENON.)

Similar to phone calls from the dead are "intention" phone calls occurring between two living persons. Such calls are much rarer than calls from the dead. In a typical "intention" call, the caller thinks about making the call but never does; the recipient nevertheless receives a call. In some cases, emergencies precipitate phantom calls: a surgeon is summoned by a "nurse" to the hospital to perform an emergency operation; a priest is called by a "relative" to give last rites to a dying man.

Some persons who have had UFO encounters report receiving harassing phantom phone calls. The calls are received soon after the witness returns home, or within a day or two of the encounter. In many cases, the calls come before the witness has shared the experience with anyone; they also are placed to unlisted phone numbers. The unidentified caller warns the witness not to talk and to "forget" what he saw.

Further reading:
McAdams, Elizabeth, and Raymond Bayless. *The Case for Life After Death*. Chicago: Nelson Hall, 1981.
Rogo, D. Scott, and Raymond Bayless. *Phone Calls from the Dead*. Englewood Cliffs, N.J.: Prentice-Hall, 1979.
Smith, Susy. *The Power of the Mind*. Radnor, Pa.: Chilton Book Co., 1975.

Pike, Bishop James A. (1913–1969) A former official of the Episcopal Church in America, James Albert Pike became a Spiritualist after the death of—and subsequent communication from—his oldest son. The bishop's own untimely death in the Israeli desert, and messages purportedly sent by him through mediums, further strengthened Spiritualists' case for survival after death (q.v.).

James Pike was born in Oklahoma City on February 14, 1913, the only child of James Albert and Pearl Agatha Pike. He was raised a devout Roman Catholic, attended mass daily and planned to be a priest. But he disagreed with the pope's encyclical on birth control and left the Church. Pike earned a doctorate in jurisprudence from Yale in 1938 and practiced law in Washington, D.C., before joining the Episcopal Church in 1944 and again pursuing the priesthood. He was ordained in 1946.

Several of his relatives on both his mother's and father's sides of the family possessed psychic ability. While Pike was in college in 1933, on a visit his Aunt Almah Chandler showed extraordinary extrasensory perception (ESP) when tested with Zener cards (now called ESP cards), getting 21 out of 25 right (5 out of 25 is average according to probabilities). And his mother had a clear vision of him in trouble during World War II, slogging around in a muddy field. Fortunately, her vision did not describe a battle scene but only a misguided Pike lost in a new housing development in Arlington, Virginia. Another relative, physician Alfred Pike, received a premonition of his aged mother's death and a visit from an apparition who was able to lead him to information concerning Isaiah Pike, the missing piece in Alfred Pike's genealogy of the family.

Pike experienced poltergeist phenomena in at least two of his homes. As the new rector of Christ Church in Poughkeepsie, New York in 1947, Pike occupied the rectory that had recently been vacated by the former pastor of 46 years. Pike heard books being moved and found candles mysteriously extinguished. Medium Ethel Meyers investigated the rectory and verified its occupation by the former pastor. She also said Pike possessed psychic talents.

In 1953, Pike became dean of the Cathedral of St. John the Divine in New York City. Pike often worked and studied in the library, one floor above his residence. While there, he heard shuffling feet and footsteps on the floor and stairs. The senior canon, Canon West, told Pike that the sounds belonged to Bishop Greer, a former resident of the Cathedral, who was still looking for a misplaced jeweled pectoral cross lost during his tenancy. In 1968, again via Ethel Meyers, psychic evidence came through that not only Bishop Greer but also a young priest was searching for the cross; the cleric had committed suicide over its loss.

But although Bishop Pike found such events fascinating, he did not pursue any psychical research until February 1966. Pike, who by then was separated, lived in an apartment in Cambridge, England, with his secretary, Maren Bergrud, and chaplain Rev. David Barr. Pike had long been estranged from his eldest son, James Jr., but the two had reconciled at the end of the year previous, and Jim Jr. had lived with his father for four and a half months. The 21-year-old Pike was involved in the hippie scene in San Francisco's Haight Ashbury district and often used hallucinogenic drugs.

On February 4, prior to returning to Cambridge, Jim Jr. took an overdose of pills and died in New York City. Bishop Pike was devastated. He had his son cremated and spread his ashes over the Pacific Ocean just beyond the Golden Gate Bridge.

Beginning February 20, something began to haunt the Cambridge flat. Postcards, which Jim Jr. had liked to save, appeared on the floor near the bishop's bed, carefully arranged in a 140-degree angle. Books were found placed in the same manner. From February 22 to 24, Maren Bergrud's bangs were gradually singed off in a straight line, higher and higher until they were gone; Jim Jr. had hated her hair cut that way. The bishop was found sitting up in bed the night of February 23, entranced, spouting his son's ideas on the drug culture. Safety pins were sprung open in the same 140-degree angle. Fresh milk turned sour. The heat would turn up without explanation. Butts from Jim's cigarettes appeared. And a broken clock, stopped for months at 12:15, read 8:19—the probable time in Cambridge corresponding to Jim's suicide in the States. The clock hands made a 140-degree angle.

Bishop Pike remembered a conversation on psychic research he had had some months before with Canon John Pearce-Higgins, vice-provost of Southwark Cathedral and an expert on Spiritualism. He called the canon, who suggested communication through a planchette. When that failed, Bishop Pike called the canon again, and he arranged a seance with medium Ena TWIGG.

On March 2, 1966, Bishop Pike, Maren Bergrud and Canon Pearce-Higgins called on Twigg; the canon took notes during the session. After examining a passport belonging to Jim Jr., Twigg became very distressed and reported that he was there and trying desperately to get through to his father. He asked forgiveness for the suicide, saying it was an accident, and expressed his love. He liked having the ashes spread at the Golden Gate Bridge. He also urged his father to continue fighting the church officials opposed to the bishop's controversial beliefs.

Twigg said that Jim Jr. was accompanied by a German intellectual, to whom the bishop had dedicated his most recent book, *What Is This Treasure?*, which was not yet off the presses. Bishop Pike was shocked, identifying the spirit as liberal theologian Paul Tillich, a great friend and his son's godfather. Tillich also urged Pike to fight church officials charging the bishop with heresy, and promised to watch over Jim Jr.

On March 14, just four hours before leaving England for the United States, Bishop Pike again sat with Twigg. This time she went into a trance, allowing Jim Jr. to speak directly through her. At this session, Jim prophesied his father would soon leave his post and would be going to Virginia. Pike denied the likelihood of either event, but both happened.

In response to the bishop's question of how to reach Jim in the States, Jim Jr. recommended finding Father William V. Rauscher, an Episcopal priest in Woodbury, New Jersey and president of the SPIRITUAL FRONTIERS FELLOWSHIP (SFF). Twigg knew nothing of this organization.

By the summer, Pike resigned his post as Episcopal bishop of California and joined the Center for the Study of Democratic Institutions in Santa Barbara, where he had more freedom to write. In August and September, Pike sat with medium George Daisley, who again spoke for young Jim and revealed many evidential details. Jim urged his father to stand fast against the charges of doctrinal heresy leveled against him by the bishop of South Florida, charges which Pike countered with his book *If This Be Heresy*. He founded the New Focus Foundation, led by his secretary Maren Bergrud, as a nonprofit channel for his unorthodox views and calls for church reform. But by fall, Pike's faith was shaken again as Bergrud killed herself with an overdose of sleeping pills. Pike tried repeatedly to reach her, but with no success.

On September 3, 1967, Pike agreed to sit for a televised seance on Canadian television with medium Arthur FORD. Ford had met the bishop at Easter the year before in New York and had revealed his connections with the SFF. First, Pike was interviewed by Allen Spraggett, the religion editor of the Toronto *Star*, at which time he revealed that he had had communications with his son. Up to that time, Pike was known for his unorthodoxy; now his involvement in Spiritualism was broadcast to millions. Unexpectedly, Ford lapsed into trance during the program, and again Jim Jr. came through with evidential detail.

Pike and Diane Kennedy, Bergrud's replacement as director of the New Focus Foundation, along with her brother Scott, had sat with Ena Twigg earlier that year. During the seance, Jim had told his father that he was making spiritual progress and finding inner peace. The bishop published these communications with Jim Jr. in his book *The Other Side*. In December, Pike and Kennedy sat with Arthur Ford. Accompanying them was Rev. Rauscher of the SFF and a friend of Kennedy. Jim came through easily and explained many of the unanswered questions about the suicide, and claimed that soon his father would no longer need mediums like Ford to communicate. Bergrud also came through, acknowledging the passing of her position to Diane Kennedy.

Bishop Pike married Kennedy on December 20, 1968. Three days later, Pike's successor as bishop of California, the Right Rev. C. Kilmer Myers, requested of all bishops and lower clergy that Pike be kept from performing any priestly function—preaching, speaking, public service or administration of the sacraments—in any church in his diocese or elsewhere.

As a result, Pike left the Church and formed the Foundation for Religious Transition in April 1969. That summer, the couple took a long-awaited trip to the Holy Land. On September 1 the Pikes became lost in the desert, and Diane Pike had to leave her husband behind to get help. When she returned, he was missing.

As soon as she heard of Pike's disappearance, Twigg began trying to reach Jim Jr. for help. On September 4, in a sitting with Canon Pearce-Higgins and her husband Harry, Twigg received a long, painful message from Pike. The men taped her trance utterances, during which Pike struggled with his death and transition to the Other Side. Twigg reached Diane Pike in Jerusalem with her sad news, and searchers finally found his body on September 7. Other mediums, including Ford, had tried to reach Pike.

Before they found his body on a cliff in the Judaean desert near the Dead Sea, Diane Pike had a vision of her husband's death, in which his spirit, described as white and cloud-like, ascended from his body to join hundreds of people in a joyful celebration. She published the story of the hunt for Pike—and his spiritual journey—in the book *Search*. She believes in the survival of his spirit.

Further reading:

Pike, Diane Kennedy. *Search: The Personal Story of a Wilderness Journey*. Garden City, N.Y.: Doubleday & Co., 1970.

Pike, James A., and Diane Kennedy. *The Other Side*. New York: Doubleday & Co., 1968.

Twigg, Ena, with Ruth Hagy Brod. *Ena Twigg: Medium*. London: W.H. Allen, 1973.

Unger, Merrill F. *The Mystery of Bishop Pike: A Christian View of the Other Side*. Wheaton, Ill.: Tyndale House Publishers, 1971.

Piper, Leonora Evelina Simonds (1859–1950)

Celebrated medium, known throughout her career simply as "Piper." Discovered by the family of William JAMES and investigated by psychical researchers on both sides of the Atlantic, she provided some of the first good evidence for survival after death (q.v.).

Leonora Simonds was born in Nashua, New Hampshire on June 27, 1859. The first sign of her future career came when she was 8 years old and was playing in the garden. She suddenly felt a sharp blow to her right ear, accompanied by a hissing sound and then the words: "Aunt Sara, not dead, but with you still." Terrified, she ran into the house in search of her mother who, besides comforting her, made a note of the day and time. Several days later they learned that Aunt Sara had died at that moment.

In 1881, when she was 22, Leonora Simonds married William Piper of Boston, by whom she was to have two daughters, Alta and Minerva. Alta was to write what is still the standard biography of her mother, *The Life and Work of Mrs. Piper* (1929). It is thanks to this book that much about her personal life is known.

According to Alta, the mediumship began in earnest in 1884, after Piper's father-in-law took her for a medical consultation to J.R. Cook, a blind clairvoyant who was becoming famous for his psychic diagnoses and cures. She lost consciousness, and seems to have fallen into a trance herself. When she later attended Cook's circle, she again fell into a trance, and wrote out a message for one of the other persons present. This was regarded by its recipient to be the finest he had received in 30 years' experience in Spiritualism.

Piper thereafter began to give private sittings in her home, to one of which she admitted William James' mother-in-law, Alice Gibbons. Gibbons was so impressed that she convinced her daughter, James's wife's sister, to go. Finally, James himself went, with

the intention, as he later admitted, of learning how the trick was done so that he could explain it to his in-laws. But the detailed knowledge Piper showed of his family stumped James. He made appointments for 25 of his friends, and thus began the research that was to continue for the remainder of Piper's career.

James was in the perfect position to begin this research, because he was then (1885) involved in establishing the AMERICAN SOCIETY FOR PSYCHICAL RESEARCH (ASPR) and was on the lookout for promising subjects. James secured from Piper the right to manage all of her sittings. He continued sending sitters to her for the next two years, then turned over responsibility for the investigation to Richard HODGSON, who had arrived from England to take charge of the ASPR.

Like James, Hodgson began his work with Piper assuming her to be a fraud. He had accused the Theosophist Helena P. Blavatsky of fraud and had become the scourge of English physical mediums; in the process he had learned a good deal about conjuring. He made appointments for 50 more sitters, keeping their identities secret from Piper; he began to keep detailed records of all her sittings; and he hired private detectives to have her followed. Although Piper behaved in no suspicious way, she continued to make remarkably accurate statements about people she had never met and about whom she had never even heard.

During this early period, Piper's trance control was an entity named "Phinuit," who claimed to be a French doctor. Phinuit, however, knew little medicine and less French, and was unable to give a verifiable account of his supposed life on earth; his name (pronounced "Finney") suggested he was modeled (unconsciously) after J.R. Cook's control, who also was called "Finney." Eleanor SIDGWICK suggested that Phinuit was best considered a secondary personality, but a secondary personality endowed with considerable psychic talent. Phinuit was not who he said he was; but Piper, through Phinuit, was able to tell things about other people she had no normal way of knowing.

Piper's talent was considered so extraordinary that a trip to England was arranged for her in 1889. Between November 1889 and February 1890 she held 83 sittings under the supervision of SPR investigators Frederic W.H. MYERS, Sir Oliver LODGE and Walter Leaf. Although she was in a place she had never been before, was closely watched, and consented to have her mail opened, Mrs. Piper continued to perform with astonishing success.

Hodgson published a cautious report on his work with Mrs. Piper in the SPR's *Proceedings* in 1892, but he followed this in 1898 with his conversion to the survival hypothesis.

In 1901 the New York *Herald* carried a story by Mrs. Piper headlined "Mrs. Piper's Plain Statement" and often referred to as her "Confession." Although it is sometimes said she "confessed" to fraud, Piper in fact wrote only that she could not be sure that spirits were controlling her; she tended to believe that she got her information by extrasensory perception (ESP). This, indeed, was the major interpretive question about her mediumship (about all mediumship), and psychical researchers were—and are—to be found on both sides themselves.

With Hodgson's sudden death in 1905, a crisis arose concerning the voluminous Piper records. Because the SPR had sponsored most of the research, they claimed them; but because the records contained so much personal information, American sitters were reluctant to let them go. James H. HYSLOP, who replaced Hodgson at the helm of the ASPR, fought hard to keep the records in the United States, but lost the battle.

In 1906 Piper made a second trip to England, this time to participate in the complex network of mediumistic communications known as the cross correspondences (q.v.). Her contributions, as usual, were outstanding.

Unfortunately, Piper's sittings after she returned to the United States in 1908 were badly managed. The psychologists G. Stanley Hall and Amy Tanner were allowed to experiment with her during this period, which lasted into 1909. (Tanner describes this work in her 1910 book, *Studies in Spiritualism*.) Sittings were devoted largely to personal matters, sitters were left unsupervised, and records were not systematically taken. Piper also was subjected to extremely harsh treatment, evidently in order to test the depth of her trance. Among other results, her daughter Alta stated, was a "badly blistered and swollen tongue which caused Piper considerable pain and inconvenience for several days."

Due to the treatment she received at this time, Piper suffered a temporary suspension of "power" that lasted well into her third and last trip to England, in 1909–1911. When the mediumship resumed, it was in the form of automatic writing rather than trance (her trance was never to return). Piper was once more briefly in her old form, but after she returned to the United States in 1912, she ceased working for more than 10 years. She held a few sittings with Gardner MURPHY in 1924 and agreed to a contract with the BOSTON SOCIETY FOR PSYCHIC RESEARCH in 1926 and 1927, but then retired for good.

Piper died on July 3, 1950, at the age of 91. A medium of the first rank, she had given much of her life unstintingly in service of science, and as a result many who had previously doubted the possibility of survival after death became convinced of its actuality. These included Hyslop in addition to Hodgson. William James also may have been persuaded, although he never said so publicly.

Another part of Piper's legacy is even more important. Prior to her discovery psychical research had concentrated on physical mediums, the vast majority of whom were exposed as frauds; but after Piper the interest shifted to mental mediums, and she had equally important successors (see GARRETT, EILEEN J.; LEONARD, GLADYS OSBORNE).

Further reading:

Gauld, Alan. *The Founders of Psychical Research.* London: Routledge & Kegan Paul, 1968.

———. *Mediumship and Survival: A Century of Investigations.* London: William Heinemann, Ltd., 1982.

Matlock, James G. "Leonora or Leonore? A note on Mrs. Piper's First Name." *Journal of the American Society for Psychical Research* 82 (1989):281–90.

Piper, Alta L. *The Life and Work of Mrs. Piper.* London: Kegan Paul, 1929.

Tanner, Amy, and G. Stanley Hall. *Studies in Spiritualism.* New York: Appleton, 1910.

planchette A device intended to facilitate communication with spirits and spirits of the dead. The planchette consists of a thin heart-shaped wooden platform with three legs. Two of the legs are on wheels and the third is a pencil with the point down. The user places fingertips on the platform and invites spirits to guide movements to write out messages or draw pictures. In this fashion, the discarnate are said to communicate with the living. In some cases, mediums using planchettes have been alleged to reproduce exactly the handwriting of deceased persons.

The term "planchette" means "little board" in French. It is named after a well-known French Spiritualist, M. Planchette, who invented it in 1853. The device became popular among French Spiritualists and in 1868 it was discovered by American toy makers, who mass-produced it and sold it through bookstores. The planchette became a popular fad in America and the United Kingdom, and also was adopted as a tool by many of the physical mediums of Spiritualism.

Although credited to Planchette, the device probably has much older origins. The Greek philosopher Pythagoras was said to hold seances at which a mystic table, mounted on wheels, moved to point to signs inscribed on a stone slab. It has been suggested that Pythagoras discovered similar devices in use in the East during his travels there and adapted them to suit his own purposes.

Use of the planchette has declined along with the decline in physical mediumship and the drop of fad interest in Spiritualism. Most modern mediums prefer to use mental mediumship, in which they allegedly receive impressions of information from discarnate beings and convey them using their own voices. Other mediums allegedly allow spirits to communicate by making use of the mediums' own vocal cords. Automatic writing, using simply a pen or pencil, also has supplanted the planchette.

A variation of the planchette is the OUIJA board.

Further reading:
Fodor, Nandor. *An Encyclopaedia of Psychic Science.* Secaucus, N.J.: Citadel Press, 1966. First published 1933.

Oppenheim, Janet. *The Other World: Spiritualism and Psychical Research in England, 1850–1914.* Cambridge: Cambridge University Press, 1985.

Podmore, Frank (1856–1910) Civil servant and psychical researcher, an early member of the SOCIETY FOR PSYCHICAL RESEARCH (SPR). Podmore is best remembered for his extremely critical stance on the phenomena of Spiritualism and psychical research.

Frank Podmore was born February 5, 1856 in Elstree, Hertfordshire, England. He attended Elstree High School and Haileybury College before receiving a scholarship to Pembroke College, Oxford. As an undergraduate, he became an ardent Spiritualist and contributed many articles to Spiritualist periodicals. He was particularly impressed by the American slate-writing medium Henry SLADE, but when Slade and several of the other mediums in which he believed were exposed as frauds, Podmore turned skeptical. Some have suggested that his aggressive skepticism was a response to his earlier naive belief.

Upon graduation, Podmore went to work for the General Post Office in London. He served on the SPR's first council, and although he never was one of its inner circle, he became one of the society's most active members. After the death of Edmund GURNEY in 1888, Podmore became secretary jointly with Frederic W.H. MYERS; he kept the position until 1896.

Podmore did much of the extensive legwork involved in investigating the 753 cases of telepathy and crisis apparitions included in *Phantasms of the Living* (1886), and he was given credit (along with Gurney and Myers) as one of the book's authors. He was also involved in investigating cases for the subse-

quent "Census of Hallucinations," designed to try to verify the main findings of *Phantasms.*

Podmore had already established himself as a strong critic by the time his own *Apparitions and Thought Transference* appeared in 1892. The book included some original cases, but in organization and theoretical orientation it was reminiscent of *Phantasms.* Podmore reviewed the evidence for telepathy and apparitions and argued that the latter were to be explained as hallucinations by the precipitants in response to information received via telepathy from the agents. He dismissed or discounted the evidence for survival after death, holding that apparitions seen around the time of death (crisis apparitions) were based on impressions conveyed before the agent's demise.

Modern Spiritualism (1902), a two-volume critical survey of 19th-century mediumship, is probably Podmore's best-known work. In it he discusses and discredits the various mediums of the day, sometimes in ways more imaginative than fair. The only medium to pass Podmore's scrutiny was Leonora PIPER, who—significantly—produced mental rather than physical phenomena. Podmore believed, however, that her success was to be explained by an exercise of telepathy (see EXTRASENSORY PERCEPTION) rather than communication with spirits.

In his last book, *The Newer Spiritualism* (1910), Podmore took the position that only telepathy, of the variety of psychic abilities, had been shown to exist. Clairvoyance and precognition he considered chimeras, and he was unalterably opposed to a survival interpretation of apparitions, poltergeists and mediumistic phenomena. He was unable to explain how D.D. HOME operated but concluded that "to say that because we cannot understand some of the feats, therefore they must have been due to spirits or psychic force, is merely an opiate for the uneasiness of suspended judgement, a refuge from the trouble of thinking." Nevertheless, according to Eleanor SIDGWICK, who wrote his obituary, he was genuinely open-minded.

Podmore retired from the Post Office in 1906 and resigned from the SPR council in 1909. He died on August 14, 1910 at the age of 54. His body was found lying face down in the New Pool at Malvern, Worcester, in what may have been a suicide; what exactly occurred in his last hours has never been clear.

Podmore's other books include *Studies in Psychical Research* (1897); *Modern Spiritualism* (1902), reprinted in 1963 under the title *Mediums of the Nineteenth Century; The Naturalisation of the Supernatural* (1908); and *Mesmerism and Christian Science* (1909), reprinted in 1964 under the title *From Mesmer to Christian Science.*

He also published several papers in the SPR *Proceedings*.

Further reading:

Gauld, Alan. *The Founders of Psychical Research*. London: Routledge & Kegan Paul, 1968.

Oppenheim, Janet. *The Other World: Spiritualism and Psychical Research in England, 1850–1914*. Cambridge: Cambridge University Press, 1985.

Pleasants, Helene, ed. *Biographical Dictionary of Parapsychology*. New York: Helix Press, 1964.

Sidgwick, Mrs. Henry. "Frank Podmore and Psychical Research." *Proceedings of the Society for Psychical Research* 25 (1911):5–10.

poltergeist   A mischievous and sometimes malevolent spirit or energy which is characterized by noises, moving objects and general physical disturbances. "Poltergeist" comes from the German terms *poltern*, "to knock," and *geist*, "spirit." Reports of poltergeist disturbances date back to ancient Roman times, appear in the medieval records of Germany, China, and Wales, and continue to be reported from countries around the world. Poltergeists have been studied extensively by psychical researchers and parapsychologists since the 1890s. Various theories have been advanced to explain them.

In earlier times, reports of poltergeist disturbances cite primarily rock- and dirt-throwing, flying objects, loud noises, strange lights and other apparitions, terrible smells, raps, physical and sexual assaults and shrieks. Modern disturbances include those plus high-tech antics such as lightbulbs spinning in their sockets and telephones repeatedly dialing certain numbers. Physical assaults—bitings, spittings, pinchings, punchings and sexual molestations—continue to be reported in a small percentage of cases.

Poltergeist activity usually starts and stops suddenly. It may last from a few hours to years, but rarely lasts longer than a few months. Activity rarely takes place when no one is at home, and usually occurs when a particular individual, or agent, is present. In the late 1970s, English researchers Alan Gauld and A.D. Cornell made a computer analysis of 500 poltergeist cases collected from around the world since later than 1800. They found 63 general characteristics, such as: 24% of poltergeist incidents lasted longer than a year; 58% were most active at night; 48% included rapping sounds; 64% involved the movement of small objects, by far and away the most common phenomenon; 36% involved the movement of large pieces of furniture; and 12% were characterized by the opening and shutting of doors and windows. In those cases where there was an apparent agent—a person who was the focus of the activity—it was most often female and under the age

Illustration of a Victorian English family beset by a poltergeist.

of 20 years; 16% of the cases involved active communication between poltergeist and agent.

Up to about the 19th century, poltergeist activities were routinely blamed on the Devil, demons, witches, and the ghosts of the dead. Beginning in the 19th century, poltergeist activities were associated with the physical mediums of Spiritualism, who allowed themselves, they said, to become temporarily possessed by the spirits of the dead. In more modern times, poltergeists are widely believed to be an involuntary or unconscious type of psychokinesis (PK) on the part of the living, the so-called "agent." The agent is believed to exercise unconscious thought processes that produce the disturbance. Nandor FODOR was among the first to pursue this theory in his investigation in the 1930s; his conclusions were controversial.

Of the 500 cases since 1800 analyzed by Gauld and Cornell, only 7% were blamed on witchcraft and 2% on demons. Demonic cases resemble possessions and are characterized by a seemingly intelligent and malevolent being. Gauld and Cornell noted that in such cases, the supposedly intelligent being does not announce itself as a demon, nor is there any clear evidence to prove a demonic presence. Such cases seem to be a matter of interpretation on the part of the victims, who, believing they are haunted by demons, call in clergy for exorcisms, which reinforces their belief. Beliefs about demon- and witchcraft-caused poltergeists are more common in non-European/American cultures; exorcisms are the typical cures. Nine percent of the Gauld/Cornell cases were attributed to the spirits of the dead. The most common manifestation was a code of raps and scratches, which were common in mediumistic communications with the dead during the heyday of Spiritualism.

Perhaps the first scientist credited with taking poltergeists seriously is Robert Boyle, a 17th-century British physicist and chemist. Boyle met a Protestant minister, Francis Perrault, while on a visit to Geneva. Perrault told him about strange, inexplicable noises and movements of objects that occurred at his home in France. Perrault published his story about "the devil in Mascon" at Boyle's suggestion, and it may be the first detailed account of a poltergeist.

An early investigator was Sir William BARRETT, a 19th-century physicist and one of the founders of the SOCIETY FOR PSYCHICAL RESEARCH (SPR), London. Barrett personally witnessed poltergeist activity during visits to a home in Ireland where a widower and his five children lived. The center of activity appeared to be focused upon the 20-year-old daughter, but Barrett found that the poltergeist would respond to his mental requests for knocks. In four successive trials, Barrett silently asked the entity to knock a certain number of times, and at each time it correctly complied. A contemporary of Barrett's, English psychical researcher Frederic W.H. MYERS, theorized that some poltergeist cases were genuine, and noted that poltergeist phenomena seldom coincided with the phenomena of hauntings.

In the 1920s and 1930s, it was believed among researchers that sexual conflicts, especially during puberty, were the cause of poltergeists. While sexual tension may be a cause or factor in some cases, it cannot explain them all. In the 1940s and 1950s, researchers theorized that poltergeists were the projections of repressed emotions, such as hostility and anger.

One of the most active modern poltergeist researchers has been William G. ROLL, project director of the Psychical Research Foundation in Durham, North Carolina. Roll's research in the 1960s seemed to confirm the psychological dysfunction theory.

Roll studied written reports of 116 cases of poltergeist disturbances, covering four centuries and more than 100 countries on three continents. From these reports and his own personal observations, Roll determined that there were patterns involving "recurrent spontaneous psychokinesis" (RSPK), which are inexplicable, spontaneous physical effects. Since poltergeist activities repeatedly occurred when a particular person was present, the activities appeared to be expressions of unconscious psychokinesis (PK) executed by that individual serving as the agent.

Roll formulated the patterns into a profile. Usually at the center of the activity was a child or teenager who possessed a great deal of internal anger from some type of stressful situation in the household. Psychokinesis was an unconscious way of expressing hostility without fear of punishment. The individual was often completely unaware of the psychic energy causing disturbances. Afterward, he or she experienced feelings of pleasure and happiness without knowing why.

Also, agents are often in a poor state of health, either mentally or physically, and thus can be predisposed to stressful events. Indeed, some psychologists have found that several of their patients with unresolved emotional tensions were associated with, or lived in, houses where poltergeist activity had been reported. Moreover, in studying the personalities of poltergeist agents, psychologists have found anxiety reactions, conversion hysteria, phobias, mania, obsessions, dissociative reactions and schizophrenia. In some cases, psychotherapy eliminates the poltergeist phenomena.

Nonetheless, investigators have found numerous poltergeist cases in which the agent appears to be psychologically stable. Gauld and Cornell have been among those who reject the repressed psychology theory, contending that the psychological tests used were invalid.

Ian STEVENSON, a psychiatrist and parapsychologist, has proposed that the theory that poltergeists are the spirits of the dead has been too often overlooked. In studying a number of cases attributed to living agents and to dead agents, Stevenson noted some significant differences. For example, living agent cases were characterized by meaningless raps; random movement of mostly light objects; short and simple trajectories; much breakage of objects; activities localized around a person, usually under 20 years of age; and relief of symptoms with psychotherapy. On the other hand, discarnate agent cases were characterized by purposeful movement of larger and heavier objects; complicated and long trajectories; little if any breakage; meaningful raps in answer to questions; and relief of symptoms with exorcism, placation or intercession.

Still another theory, proposed by D. Scott ROGO, suggests that a poltergeist is activated by a stressful situation, but the agency is not PK from the living person. Rather, the living person projects some element of his own personality into the apparition-like form that is often witnessed. The form could become autonomous from the agent's physical body and be the cause of the disturbances. Thus, the poltergeist might be some type of independent apparition created or projected by the poltergeist agent.

Further reading:

Fodor, Nandor. *On the Trail of the Poltergeist.* New York: The Citadel Press, 1958.

Gauld, Alan, and A.D. Cornell. *Poltergeists.* London: Routledge & Kegan Paul, 1979.

Myers, Frederic W.H. *Human Personality and Its Survival of Bodily Death Vols. I & II* New ed. New York: Longmans, Green & Co., 1954. First published 1903.

Owen, A.R.G. *Can We Explain the Poltergeist?* New York: Garrett Publications/A Helix Press Book, 1964.

Rogo, D. Scott. *On the Track of the Poltergeist.* Englewood Cliffs, N.J.: Prentice-Hall, 1986.

Roll, William. *The Poltergeist.* Garden City, N.Y.: Nelson Doubleday, Inc., 1972.

Stevenson, Ian. "Are Poltergeists Living or Are They Dead?" *Journal of the American Society for Psychical Research,* 66 (1972):233–52.

Wilson, Colin. *Poltergeist! A Study in Destructive Haunting.* London: New English Library, 1981.

pooka See PUCA.

possession The idea that a person's mind and soul can be possessed by a departed spirit, whether of god, demon or man, has tantalized civilization since antiquity. The ancient Greeks, who worshipped their gods in a very personal manner, believed that the deities interfered in the lives of mortals every day, either by causing them to act in a particular way or by simply taking over their bodies and using them for the gods' own ends. Worshippers of Hinduism and Buddhism attribute all kinds of daily disturbances to both gods and demons. African tribal religions teach that possession by the gods shows favor on man and proof of the gods' powers. The Bible tells how Jesus Christ exorcised the "unclean spirits" during His ministry, and that His disciples were overcome with the Holy Spirit after His death. Stories about the possession of human beings by Devil-inspired entities greatly worried medieval churchmen, and still provide fodder for books and movies today.

Early Christian theologians denied the possibility of spirit possession (the complete takeover by an entity from within) being anything but the Devil's handiwork. Saints suffered torments from the Devil, too, but never succumbed to total possession, only obsession (influence on a person's mind from a spirit without). Claiming possession by the Holy Spirit was of course another matter, but even then the Church suspected the work of the Devil to fool the gullible.

Consequently, anyone found showing signs of unusual behavior or expressing ideas radically different than those currently acceptable was most likely deemed possessed, or *energumenus;* the possessed person is an *energumen.* The Devil claimed his victims in two ways: either by passing directly into a person's mind and soul or by using a witch or wizard to send a demon into the victim through bewitchment. The Church believed that the Devil preferred to employ wicked mankind as his henchmen. Witches transmitted demons to the innocent victim through a charm, potion, amulet or, most likely, food. Apples were especially popular, perhaps because they were readily available, and perhaps because they are symbols of humankind's fall from grace. Formal exorcism in the name of the Lord, sending the Devil and his minions back to Hell, offered the only salvation.

The Catholic Church, which is the only denomination of Christianity to have a formal rite of exorcism, considers four signs proof of demonic possession: clairvoyance, abnormal physical strength, blasphemy and levitation.

Modern occultists, however, view possession or obsession as more of a confusing, disorienting episode than a devilish destruction of the soul. The spirits, perhaps unaware they are dead, become caught in the "net" of mortal beings and need help to pass into their proper realm. In other cases, the entities have purposely returned to contact the living to give a warning or message from beyond. For the victim, such episodes are frightening and debilitating encounters with the supernatural, often causing severe headaches, sleep disorders, strange noises or lights, voices, poltergeist phenomena and maybe even temporary insanity.

Few people besides mediums actively seek spirit possession. The medium, believing the possessed state to be temporary, calls the spirits to speak through him or her during seances. Spirit possession also takes place during the similar phenomenon of channeling (q.v.). The spirits depart on command without formal ritual. Dabbling in automatic writing or Ouija board communications is said by some to risk calling unwanted spirits to the uninitiated novice, often necessitating stronger exorcism practices to expunge the entities.

In his book *Hostage to the Devil,* Jesuit professor Dr. Malachi Martin, a believer in demonic spirits, outlines the stages of possession: the actual entry point; the stage of erroneous judgments by the victim in vital matters, such as making unethical choices; the voluntary yielding of control by the victim to the invading spirit; and finally complete possession. Martin stresses that possession cannot occur without the consent, albeit subliminal, of the victim.

A possessed woman praying to redeem herself from the demons of the Seven Deadly Sins. After a 13th-century English manuscript Bible.

In psychiatry, patients suffering from multiple personalities repress a great deal of hatred, which acts almost like a magnet for evil influences which are sometimes perceived as external spirits or ghosts. Obsession always represents an abnormal condition, and once the patient admits the existence of spirit influence, the idea of spirit obsession cannot be ignored. Severe physical or psychological trauma may so upset the victim that a "window" in the mind opens, allowing spirit influences to enter.

But are spirit obsession and possession tricks of the eager but unbalanced mind? Or, are diseases of the mind—schizophrenia, paranoia, hysteria, compulsion and multiple personality—really the work of spirits controlling their unhappy victims?

SPIRITS AND MULTIPLE PERSONALITY

In some cases of multiple personality, some psychiatrists find that only exorcism—perhaps simply invoking the Lord's name—eliminates one or more of the troubling personalities so that the patient can eventually become one person.

James H. HYSLOP, a former leader of the AMERICAN SOCIETY FOR PSYCHICAL RESEARCH (SPR) and an investigator of spirit obsession, wrote in his book *Contact with the Other World* (1919) that if people believe in telepathy, then invasion of a personality over distance is possible. And if that is true, he said, then it is unlikely that sane and intelligent spirits are the only ones able to exert influence from beyond. Hyslop also stated that persons diagnosed as suffering from hysteria, multiple personality, dementia praecox or other mental disturbances showed, in his view, unmistakable signs of invasion by discarnate entities. He called on the medical establishment to take such situations into account during treatment.

Dr. M. Scott Peck, a self-described "hardheaded scientist," a graduate of Harvard University and a practicing psychiatrist in Connecticut, has claimed that two of his patients suffered from possession by spirits in addition to their other symptoms of multiple personality. In both cases, Peck found the spirits to be evil, actively working to destroy the mind of the host patients.

In his 1983 book *People of the Lie*, Peck describes these patients, their awareness from the beginning of alien presences, and the exorcisms which eventually cleared the way for spiritual healing. When the demonic entities finally revealed themselves, Peck relates, the patient's faces were completely transformed into masks of utter malevolence. One patient became a snake, with writhing body and hooded reptilian eyes, and made darting efforts to bite the exorcism team members. A tremendous weight—an ageless, evil heaviness, or the true Serpent—seemed to be in the room. Peck reported that everyone involved felt such a presence, and it was only relieved when the exorcism succeeded.

Peck's experiences corroborated those of California psychiatrist Dr. Ralph Allison. Although he was conventionally trained in psychiatry at both the UCLA School of Medicine and Stanford Medical Center, Allison has stated that many cases of multiple personality are the result of spirit possession, both nonthreatening and demonic. His controversial 1980 book *Minds in Many Pieces* discusses some of these patients and the inexplicable paranormal occurrences surrounding them. Allison also noted that at least one personality in each patient—sometimes the primary but usually a secondary one—displays striking psychic abilities.

THE INFLUENCE OF SPIRITUALISM

Life everlasting for the spirit—and the ability to contact such spirits through mediums, proving their

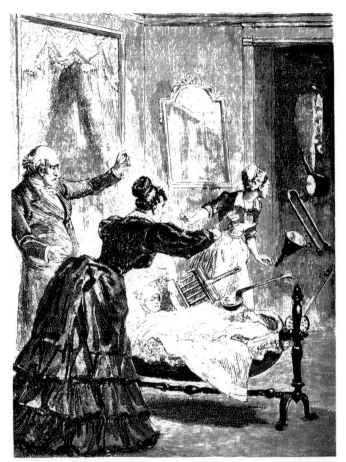

Adolphine Benoit, center, was a French serving girl believed to be possessed because she caused objects to fly about. Most likely, she was a living agent for poltergeist activity. However, an exorcism by a priest banished the offending "spirit."

lives inherited with each new incarnation. Sometimes these subsystems dominate the present life, blocking out reality and controlling the body for extended periods. Successful treatment depended not only on counseling and therapy but on communication with these spirits to understand their presence and get them to depart the victim. Kardec's theories were fashionable in France for a while but did not catch on in the rest of Europe. They found enthusiastic audiences in the Western Hemisphere, however, particularly in Brazil.

Similar views of spirit possession were held by other practitioners of medicine, such as Carl WICK-LAND and his wife, Anna, and Titus BULL, who believed a host of medical ills were caused by confused but benign spirits who needed a gentle exorcism of persuasion.

SPIRIT POSSESSION ELSEWHERE IN THE WORLD

In many non-Western cultures, communication with spirits and deities serves as the centerpiece of religious worship. Possession by a god shows the possessed to be worthy of the god's notice and protection. Even minor accomplishments and setbacks stem directly from the god's active intervention.

Although the followers of Islam worship one god, Allah, they acknowledge the mischief created by minor *djinns* (genies), or *zar* spirits. The *zars*, also called *sars*, possess their victims, usually women, and cause sickness, marital discord and general rebelliousness. The *zars* only depart if they are placated with gifts of clothes, food, liquor, jewelry or other presents for the possessed victim, or perhaps better treatment of the victim by the men in her family (see CULT OF THE ZAR).

In India, spirit possession permeates every facet of daily life. Again the possessed is most often a woman, who attributes her personal problems—menstrual pain, barrenness, the death of children, miscarriage, abuse by husbands or fathers, the husband's infidelities—to the intervention of evil spirits. Exorcism techniques by the shaman include blowing cow-dung smoke, pressing rock salt between the fingers, burning pig excreta, beating the victim or pulling her hair, using copper coins as an offering, reciting prayers or mantras, and offering gifts of candy or other presents. Traditional African worshippers hold similar beliefs about the mischief of the gods, as do the Sinhalese Buddhists of Sri Lanka. Sinhalese exorcist/healers believe certain demons cause particular diseases, usually brought on by discord in the home or workplace.

Besides being female, most of the possessed come from the lower classes: humble laborers or servants.

survival—underlies Spiritualism, a movement that arose in the mid-19th century and became a religion. Although many people claimed to communicate with the dead, the famous rappings of the FOX SISTERS in Hydesville, New York proved the existence of spirits to many nonbelievers and provided the impetus for organized gatherings and seances. The temporary possessions of mediums by alleged spirits of the dead, however, are distinct from demonic and spirit possessions that take over complete control of an individual's personality and life (see MEDIUMSHIP).

A European offshoot of Spiritualism, SPIRITISM, founded by Allan KARDEC, hold that certain illnesses have a spiritual cause and can be treated psychically through communication with spirit guides. Kardec said that persons suffering from epilepsy, schizophrenia and multiple personality showed signs of spirit interference, either from spirits of other dead people or from remnants of the patients' own past lives. Kardec theorized that within each person's personality are what he called "subsystems" of past

Possession gains these people stature, perhaps even resulting in a betterment of their station. At the very least, placation of the gods usually involves showering presents on the victims and promises of better behavior from the victims' families or employers.

In the Caribbean or Latin America, or anywhere tribal Africans were taken to be slaves, worship of the religions of their ancestors—now practiced as Vodoun (voodoo), Santería, candomble or umbanda—involves the possession of the faithful by the gods to obtain true communion and protection. Worshippers, overcome by chanting and the frenzied beating of drums during the ceremonies, are "mounted" by a god, becoming the god's "horse," and take on that god's personal characteristics: a preference for certain foods or colors, perfumes, patterns of speech, use of profanity, even smoking large, smelly cigars. Under possession, the worshipper may endure great extremes of heat and cold, dance unceasingly for hours, suffer from cuts and bruises with no pain, and even tear off the heads of live chickens used for sacrifice with his or her own teeth. Often the possessed issue prophesies and deliver pronouncements about local affairs. The words of the spirits are not always taken seriously, but doubts about the gods' powers are held in check by fear, ridicule by awe. Under possession, the devotee *is* the deity, accorded all rights and honors; however, once possession subsides, the worshipper receives no special treatment.

POSSESSION BY THE HOLY SPIRIT

The idea of possession by the divine presence also appears in Western cultures. The word "enthusiastic" originally meant being filled with the Holy Spirit, or the supreme state of oneness with God. After the crucifixion and resurrection of Jesus Christ, on the first day of Pentecost (the date seven weeks after Passover, in the Jewish calendar), the apostles became possessed with the Holy Spirit. The Book of Acts describes how flames appeared above their heads, and that they spoke in tongues previously unknown to them. Speaking in foreign tongues—glossolalia—and other ecstatic communion with God characterized early Christian worship, but by the Middle Ages the practice had come to signify the work of the Devil instead.

In modern Christian worship, the Pentecostal Movement has revived interest in ecstatic religious practices. The movement began on January 1, 1901 (the first day of the 20th century) when a group of worshippers at Bethel College, in Topeka, Kansas, reportedly received the Holy Spirit. Members of Pentecostal churches may speak in tongues, engage in long prayer revivals, perform faith healing and even roll and writhe on the floor as the spirit fills them.

Further reading:
Ebon, Martin. *The Devil's Bride, Exorcism: Past and Present.* New York: Harper & Row, 1974.

Crabtree, Adam. *Multiple Man: Explorations in Possession and Multiple Personality.* New York: Praeger, 1985.

Rogo, D. Scott. *The Infinite Boundary.* New York: Dodd, Mead & Co., 1987.

Kapferer, Bruce. *A Celebration of Demons.* Bloomington: Indiana University Press, 1983.

Denning, Melita, and Osborne Phillips. *Vodoun Fire: The Living Reality of Mystical Religion.* St. Paul: Llewellyn Publications, 1979.

Martin, Malachi. *Hostage to the Devil.* New York: Harper & Row, 1976.

Playfair, Guy Lyon. *The Unknown Power.* New York: Pocket Books, 1975.

preta In Buddhist and Hindu lore, a type of ghost.

In the Buddhist scheme of reincarnation (q.v.), the realm of the Hungry Ghosts (*pretas*) is a lower segment of the Wheel of Life, the various levels in which one reincarnates according to one's karma. *Pretas* occupy a sort of purgatory between lives of those who have accumulated the bad karma of envy, refusal of alms, greed, etc. They must work off this karma, forgotten by their relatives, in a state of constant hunger and thirst. The torture continues until the karma has been balanced. *Pretas* are said to look like burnt trees, to or have needle-sized throats and mountain-sized bellies. They live in crossroads, which are a favorite congregating place of spirits, ghosts, witches and deities associated with the underworld. They also gather outside houses and at boundaries.

In Hindu belief, the *preta* is the tiny ghost of the dead, about the size of a thumb, that either resides in the corpse or remains near the home of the deceased for one year after the funeral. When the year is up, rites are performed to send the soul to heaven, where it is rewarded for the good deeds performed on earth. Without the rites, the soul could not escape its *preta* condition. Later, the soul enters its final place.

Pretas also are ghosts of a cripple or a child.

Further reading:
Leach, Maria, and Jerome Fried, eds. *Funk & Wagnalls Standard Dictionary of Folklore, Mythology, and Legend.* San Francisco: Harper & Row, 1979.

The Encyclopedia of Eastern Philosophy and Religion. Boston: Shambhala, 1989.

Price, Harry (1881–1948) One of the most colorful figures in the history of psychical research and author of many popular books on psychical phenomena. As much at home in conjuring as in psychical research, Price is suspected of fraud in connection with several of his investigations, including the most famous one, the BORLEY RECTORY haunting. Little that he wrote about himself may be trusted, with the result that the standard story of his life is largely fictitious. The following account owes much to the research of Trevor Hall as documented in his book *Search for Harry Price* (1978).

Harry Price was born on January 17, 1881 in London (not in Shrewsbury, Shropshire as claimed by Price). His father was a grocer and later a traveling salesman for a paper-making firm (not the owner of the establishment, as Price would have us believe). Price was raised and educated in the New Cross area of London (instead of the more upscale Brockley, from which his future wife's family hailed). Although Price claimed that when he finished school he was taken into his father's business, it seems that he spent the decade after his graduation in about 1898 without steady employment, pursuing various odd jobs. In 1908, he married a wealthy heiress, Constance Mary Knight, and became a man of independent means.

In later years, Price often said that his first psychic experience concerned a haunted house he investigated at the age of 15. The story is dubious, and Price's own accounts of it vary; yet something of the sort may really have happened. In his autobiography, *Search for Truth: My Life for Psychical Research* (1942), Price wrote that he and a friend locked themselves into the building one night, equipped with camera and flash, to await the disturbances. At about 11:30 they heard what sounded like someone stamping around in clogs in the room above, then down the main staircase, and up again. Setting up the camera in the hall, they waited for the ghost to descend the stairs once more. After about an hour it came. The boys waited until the footsteps were about halfway on their return trip up the stairs, then triggered the camera. As they did, there was an explosion, and the ghost was heard to stumble—though this sound turned out to have been made by a pan thrown against the stairs because Price had used too much gunpowder in setting up the flash. The photographic plate showed nothing but an over-exposed staircase.

Price claimed that he had begun to be interested in conjuring, and to collect books on conjuring, Spiritualism, and psychical research, in childhood, but it seems clear that only after his marriage would he have had the wherewithal to do this. Still, he must have been interested in these subjects in childhood, very possibly as a result of an experience in a haunted house, or he would not have moved so quickly to gain expertise in them. By the time Price joined the SOCIETY FOR PSYCHICAL RESEARCH (SPR) in 1920, he was already considered an expert on conjuring and fraudulent mediumship. In 1921, he became honorary (i.e., unpaid) librarian for the internationally renowned Magic Circle.

It was partly on the strength of his knowledge of conjuring that the SPR sent him to investigate the claims of the spirit photographer William HOPE. Price sought to ingratiate himself with Hope and others at the BRITISH COLLEGE OF PSYCHIC SCIENCE, and although in his report in the SPR *Proceedings* for February 1922 he claimed to have exposed a fraud, there were charges that Price, not Hope, had tampered with the photographic plates. Hard evidence one way or another was never forthcoming, but subsequent events in Price's life must lead one to wonder whether Hope's defenders were not right in this case.

In May 1922 Price accompanied longtime SPR researcher and fellow conjurer Eric Dingwall to Munich, Germany to observe Willi Schneider in sittings in the laboratory of Baron Albert von SCHRENCK-NOTZING. Schneider was a physical medium (see SCHNEIDER BROTHERS), in whose presence rappings were heard and objects moved without physical contact (see PSYCHOKINESIS). Both Price and Dingwall were impressed and signed a statement to that effect. Price later said that Schneider had made him realize that not all physical phenomena could be explained in terms of deception and self-deception.

Price's next crucial meeting with the psychic came early the following year, when he met a young woman named Dorothy Stella CRANSHAW on the train from London to his home in Pulborough. Cranshaw (or Stella C., as she came to be known) was a nurse who claimed to have psychokinetic abilities. Price arranged for a series of seances with Cranshaw at the London Spiritual Alliance (see COLLEGE OF PSYCHIC STUDIES). Although these sittings apparently were successful, they caused strain between Price and his conjuring friends as well as between him and the SPR—the former because they believed he had sold out, the latter because they distrusted the Spiritualist connection. A second series of sittings was begun at the SPR late in 1923, but after only two sessions Stella declined to continue, giving as her reason the drain on her time and energy the seances represented.

Price had given his collection of books to the SPR on permanent loan in 1922. Some have read this move as a bid for influence. However this may be, Price soon became disgruntled with the SPR's apparent bias against physical mediumship and established his own National Laboratory for Psychical Research. When the laboratory opened its doors at the beginning of 1926, it was in the quarters of the London Spiritualist Alliance (now the College of Psychic Studies), a move not destined to endear him to the conservative SPR. Indeed, in 1927, his collection of books was returned to him. But Price's penchant for exposing fraudulent mediums did not sit well with his landlord either, and the Alliance's president, Sir Arthur Conan DOYLE, was a constant irritant until his death in 1930. When the National Laboratory's lease expired at the end of that year, Price found other quarters for his laboratory.

During this same period (1925–1931), Price was foreign research officer for the AMERICAN SOCIETY FOR PSYCHICAL RESEARCH (ASPR), a position which required him to report on European psychical research for the society's *Journal*. He was one of the British delegates to the Second International Congress on Psychical Research in Warsaw in 1923, where he sat with the Polish physical medium, Jan GUZIK. He did not think much of Guzik, and did not hesitate to say so publicly. He was more impressed with the Romanian "devil girl" Eleanore ZUGUN, whom he studied in his laboratory in 1926. When Doyle died, Price arranged for sittings with Eileen J. GARRETT, in an effort to communicate with him. Messages were received from Doyle, but far more important were a series of communications from the pilot of a dirigible that had gone down around the same time (see R-101 CASE).

When Baron Schrenck-Notzing died late in 1929, Price invited Willi Schneider's brother Rudi, also a physical medium, to visit his laboratory for tests. Rudi accepted, and two series of experiments were conducted in 1929 and 1930; a third was held in 1932. All were successful, as were tests with Rudi elsewhere. But then in 1933, Price dropped a bombshell on the world of a psychical research when he claimed to have photographic proof that Rudi had freed an arm during a 1932 seance, physically moving the handkerchief he was supposed to be affecting psychically. Although most of Price's colleagues in psychical research suspected that Price himself was the guilty party, the unsophisticated public took the "exposure" at face value.

Price's accusation was all the more devastating because he had spent much effort building up Rudi's public image. Price was a master at manipulating the media; a showman at heart, he always saw to it that whatever he did made the headlines. His penchant for being in the news backfired on him in 1932, when he traveled to the Hartz Mountains in Germany to test a 15th-century magic spell that was said to be able to transform a goat into a handsome young man. The test failed, and Price was widely ridiculed for

attempting it. The same year found him undertaking another farcical investigation, of a supposed talking mongoose in Cashen's Gap on the Isle of Man.

At the same time that his public image was suffering, Price's "exposure" of Rudi Schneider made points for him in academia. Having been rebuffed for years in his efforts to affiliate his laboratory with psychical research organizations (he approached the SPR repeatedly, and in 1929 was turned down by the IN-STITUT METAPSYCHIQUE INTERNATIONAL), in 1933 he offered his library to the University of London. The offer was accepted "in principle," and a University Council for Psychical Investigation was set up in 1934. At the end of 1937, the university provided office space for the council and made room for Price's books and laboratory equipment. (Earlier that year, Price had received official notification that Hitler's Third Reich respected psychical research as a science, and he had been offered a position at the University of Bonn.) Price also founded the National Film Library of the British Film Institute, with a donation of rare films in 1935, and was its chairman until 1941.

Price is perhaps best known outside of psychical research for his investigation of the haunted Borley Rectory, which began in 1929 and continued until 1947, when the building was torn down. Price reported his research in two popular books, *The Most Haunted House in England: Ten Years' Investigation of Borley Rectory* (1940) and *The End of Borley Rectory* (1946). Suspicions that not all phenomena were genuine were entertained at least from the early 1930s. However, the scope of the charges—and their substance—was not made public until after Price's death, in a book jointly written by Eric Dingwall, K.M. Goldney and Trevor Hall (1956). The writers take the extreme position that there was nothing at all paranormal about the disturbances; however, given the rest of Price's life, the idea that he helped them out is not at all implausible.

Price suffered a heart attack at home in Pulborough on March 29, 1948, and died almost instantly. He was 67.

Although Price boasted that his library contained some 20,000 volumes, when it was assessed by the University of London after his death, it was found to contain only about half that number. It is now housed at the University of London as the Harry Price Library of Magical Literature.

Price's numerous books include, in addition to the ones previously mentioned, *Revelations of a Spirit Medium* (with Eric Dingwall, 1922), *Cold Light on Spiritualistic Phenomena* (1922), *Stella C.* (1925), *Rudi Schneider* (1930), *Regurgitation and The Duncan Mediumship*

(1931), *An Account of Some Further Experiments with Rudi Schneider* (1933), *Leaves from a Psychist's Case Book* (1933), *A Report on Two Experimental Fire-Walks* (1936), *Confessions of Ghost Hunter* (1936), *The Haunting of Cashen's Gap* (with R.S. Lambert, 1936), *Fifty Years of Psychical Research* (1939) and *Poltergeist Over England* (1945).

In 1945 Price and novelist Upton Sinclair coauthored a screenplay, "Hauntings," based on the Borley disturbances. Also to Price's credit is a motion picture called *Psychical Research* (1941) and a contribution on "Faith and Fire-Walking" to the *Encyclopaedia Britannica* (1936).

Further reading:

Dingwall, Eric, K.M. Goldney, and Trevor Hall. *The Haunting of Borley Rectory.* London: Duckworth, 1956.

Gregory, A. *The Strange Case of Rudi Schneider.* Metuchen, N.J.: Scarecrow Press, 1985.

Hall, Trevor. *Search for Harry Price.* London: Duckworth, 1978.

Inglis, Brian. *Science and Parascience: A History of the Paranormal, 1914–1939.* London: Hodder and Stoughton, 1984.

Price, Harry. *Search for Truth: My Life for Psychical Research.* London: Pall Mall, 1942.

Tabori, Paul. *Harry Price: The Biography of a Ghost Hunter.* London: Atheneum, 1950.

Prince, Walter Franklin (1863–1934)

Episcopal minister and psychical researcher, therapist for an early, celebrated case of multiple personality. Only the last 18 years of his life were devoted to psychical research, but during that time he came to be recognized as a leading figure of his day.

Walter Franklin Prince was born on April 22, 1863 in Detroit, Maine. In 1881 he graduated from Maine Wesleyan Seminary and in 1886 he received a B.D. from Drew Theological Seminary. He also attended Yale, receiving a Ph.D. from that institution in 1899.

Prince married Lelia Madora Colman in 1885. The couple had no children, but they later adopted a young woman who had come to Prince for psychological counseling. Prince, then rector of All Saints Church in Pittsburgh, had some knowledge of abnormal psychology, and he recognized in his parishioner the signs of what was then called "secondary personality." He began what was to become several years of intensive work with the woman, whom he and his wife named Theodosia. She made her greatest improvement after she left her abusive father to live with the Princes, and in 1908 they formally adopted her.

One of Theodosia's personalities—called Sleeping Margaret—claimed to be a discarnate spirit, and this presented a problem of interpretation for which Prince turned for help to James H. HYSLOP at the AMERICAN SOCIETY FOR PSYCHICAL RESEARCH (ASPR). His subsequent correspondence with Hyslop not only helped Prince in his therapy, it also gave him his first direct acquaintance with psychical research. When Prince wrote his account of the case, he gave Theodosia the name "Doris Fischer." It was published in two volumes of the ASPR's *Proceedings* in 1915 and 1916 (see DORIS FISCHER CASE).

In 1916 the Princes moved to New York City, where Prince became director of therapeutics at St. Mark's Church; the following year he resigned from this position and joined the staff of the ASPR as Hyslop's assistant. He quickly established himself as a careful, although often critical, investigator. He had a fair knowledge of conjuring techniques, was on good terms with Harry HOUDINI, and wrote important exposes of slate-writing and spirit photography.

When Hyslop died in 1920, Prince became the ASPR's research officer and the editor of its *Journal* and *Proceedings*. Hyslop had intended that Prince be his successor, but, perhaps because he was showing signs of age (although only 57 he was already going deaf; and not everyone found him easy to get along with), Prince was not named the society's director. Control passed instead to the board of trustees, with fateful consequences for Prince as well as for the ASPR.

A central event of this period was the investigation of the medium "Margery" (see CRANDON, MINA STINSON). Under the influence of one of its editors, J. Malcolm Bird, *Scientific American* magazine had announced a $2,500 prize for a demonstration of physical mediumship deemed genuine by a special committee. Prince was named to this committee, which sat with Crandon throughout 1924.

The *Scientific American* committee eventually decided against Crandon. Bird, however, believed in the mediumship, and when the ASPR hired him to take charge of research on physical phenomena (leaving Prince with mental mediumship and other research) in January 1925, Prince resigned and moved to Boston to take up a new position with the BOSTON SOCIETY FOR PSYCHIC RESEARCH.

Prince received another blow in 1925 with the death of his wife. Nevertheless, his years with the Boston Society were to be productive and important.

In 1927, in Europe for the Third International Congress on Psychical Research (he had also attended the first congress in Copenhagen in 1921), he had sittings with the Austrian medium Rudi SCHNEIDER, reaching negative but controversial conclusions about his abilities.

Prince's enemies, in fact, often accused him of bias against physical phenomena. His supporters considered him to be an especially careful observer whose judgment failed him only when it came to his own adopted daughter—in his book *The Psychic in the House* (1927), he recorded apparently paranormal phenomena surrounding Theodosia that many have considered dubious.

Prince's contribution to the study of other phenomena has been less a matter of debate. He was very interested in everyday psychic experiences and conducted a questionnaire survey of 10,000 persons listed in *Who's Who in America*. He considered the testimony of this elite population especially valuable, because these persons were well known, and their veracity and sincerity were not usually open to question. For the same reason, he collected celebrity accounts for his book *Noted Witnesses for Psychic Occurrences* (1928).

He gathered together all the material he could find relating to Patience WORTH, published as *The Case of Patience Worth* (1928), and when Upton Sinclair published his book *Mental Radio* (1930), describing ESP drawing experiments he had conducted with his wife, Prince obtained the targets and the drawings and wrote an independent evaluation of them for the Boston Society's *Bulletin*. Later editions of Sinclair's book have often included Prince's report as a supplement.

Prince also supported other researchers and published important work by John F. Thomas (awarded the first doctorate in parapsychology given by an American university, Duke, in 1928), psychologist George Estabrooks, and J.B. RHINE (see BOSTON SOCIETY FOR PSYCHIC RESEARCH). The Boston Society was, in fact, the first publisher of Rhine's seminal monograph, *Extra-Sensory Perception* (1934).

The capstone of Prince's relatively brief but distinguished career in psychical research came with his election to the presidency of the London-based SOCIETY FOR PSYCHICAL RESEARCH (SPR) in 1930 and 1931; he was the first American after William JAMES to be so honored.

Prince died on August 7, 1934 at his home in Hingham, Massachusetts.

In addition to the books mentioned, Prince authored *The Enchanted Boundary: A Survey of Negative Reactions to Claims of Psychic Phenomena, 1820–1930* (1930). He also wrote numerous articles and monographs for the ASPR's *Journal* and *Proceedings of the ASPR* and for the Boston Society's *Bulletin*.

Further reading:

Berger, Arthur S. *Lives and Letters in American Parapsychology.* Jefferson, N.C.: McFarland, 1988.
Prince, Walter Franklin (1930). Presidential address. *Proceedings of the Society for Psychical Research*, 1930.

Tietze, T.R. "Ursa Major: An Impressionistic Appreciation of Walter Franklin Prince." *Journal of the American Society for Psychical Research* 70 (1976):1–34.
Walter Franklin Prince: A Tribute to his Memory. Boston: Boston Society for Psychic Research, 1935.

proxy sitting   See PIPER, LEONORA.

pseudopods   Ectoplasmic extrusions from a medium which develop into a sort of hand or arm are called pseudopods, or false limbs. The producing of ectoplasm in a seance can be accomplished by trickery, and various mediums have been exposed.

The first recorded pseudopods were attributed to medium Eusapia PALLADINO in 1894. In seances with Professor Charles Richet, Sir Oliver LODGE, Frederic W.H. MYERS and the Polish professor Julien Ochorowicz at Richet's home on the Ile Roubaud, France, Palladino frequently extruded a third arm and hand which lifted, pushed and clutched objects during the sitting. Everard Feilding, son of the Earl of Denbigh, thought that Palladino's pseudopods looked like long, black knobbly things with cauliflowers at the ends.

But Palladino's knobbly cauliflowers paled in comparison to the ectoplasmic emanations of Marthe BERAUD, alias Eva C. From 1909 to 1913, Eva C. was investigated by Juliette Bisson, who became Beraud's closest friend and colleague, and by Baron Albert von SCHRENCK-NOTZING, a German physician. Schrenck-Notzing set up rigorous test procedures to guard against fraud. He witnessed writhing tentacles of ectoplasm exude from Beraud's mouth, eyes, ears and nose. The tentacles often assumed faces or shapes, some resembling President Wilson, King Ferdinand of Bulgaria and other popular government or historical figures. Schrenck-Notzing called these faces *ideoplasts*, or images reproduced from faces or pictures Beraud may have seen in the past. Critics noted that some of the ideoplasts were identical to magazine photographs.

According to Bisson, Beraud's best pseudopods appeared when they were in seance alone together. In 1911, Eva C., totally naked, produced a pseudopod structure that became an unformed baby in what Bisson called a pseudobirth. Skeptics found such wonderful occurrences more an expression of sexual manifestations than paranormal ones.

Not long after Schrenck-Notzing's experiments, William J. Crawford investigated Irish medium Kathleen Goligher, whose ectoplasmic "psychic rods" lifted tables. In a series of experiments on the origin of these rods, Crawford used powdered carmine to trace the ectoplasm's journey rather than resort to indelicate inspection of Goligher's body. The carmine trail began at her vaginal area.

Mina Stinson CRANDON, alias Margery, claimed many of the manifestations at her seances were done by a pseudopod which also emanated from between her legs. This pseudopod rang bells, threw megaphones and formed hands. Originally invisible, the pseudopod materialized in sessions with Eric J. Dingwall of the SOCIETY FOR PSYCHICAL RESEARCH. Dingwall, at first greatly impressed, described the pseudopod as an umbilical cord connecting the medium with her extra hands. Clasping one of the ectoplasmic hands, Dingwall found it like cold, raw beef or soft, wet rubber.

Dramatic photographs show Crandon extruding a third hand from her navel; the hand is poorly formed and looks like a filled glove. Harvard psychology professor William McDougall noted that the hand only appeared when Crandon's husband was seated at her right. When McDougall showed Dingwall's photographs to his colleagues in the biology department, they surmised that the hand was made of animal lung tissue. Dingwall himself later suspected that Crandon concealed her ectoplasm in the vagina and extruded it through muscular contractions.

Further reading:
Brandon, Ruth. *The Spiritualists.* New York: Alfred A. Knopf, 1983.
Doyle, Sir Arthur Conan. *The History of Spiritualism Vol. I & II.* New York: Arno Press, 1975.
Fodor, Nador. *An Encyclopaedia of Psychic Science.* Secaucus, N.J.: The Citadel Press, 1966. First published 1933.
Mysteries of the Unknown: Spirit Summonings. Alexandria, Va.: Time-Life Books, 1989.

psychography See AUTOMATIC WRITING; SLATE-WRITING.

Psychokinesis (PK) A paranormal phenomenon in which matter can be affected at a distance. Psychokinesis (PK) can occur spontaneously or through an apparent projection of will.

PK has been recorded since ancient times in descriptions of the feats of holy men and wizards, including levitation, miraculous healings, invisibility, luminosities, apports and the movement of objects without visible cause. The evil eye, a widespread folk belief that certain individuals can harm and kill with a glance, is a form of PK.

PK occurs in physical mediumship involving materializations, ectoplasm, levitation, apports and asports, table tipping, rapping and the playing of musical instruments. PK occurs in poltergeist cases, most commonly in the movement of objects. PK also can occur in hauntings and cases involving apparitions. Often these physical feats are attributed to spirits or spirits of the dead. Researchers have found that in many cases, unwitting human agents are creating the PK (see FODOR, NANDOR). Other cases remain unexplained.

Early psychical researchers, such as members of the SOCIETY FOR PSYCHICAL RESEARCH (SPR), studied PK by sitting at seances with mediums. In the 1930s, PK research moved into the laboratory. Research has been hampered by contradictory findings, and even some exposures of fraud.

J.B. RHINE made famous controlled dice tests in which subjects attempted to influence the outcome of tossed dice. Rhine concluded that ESP is a necessary part of the PK process, and one implies the other. In order to influence any matter, ESP must occur at precisely the right point in space and time. Rhine also found that drugs, emotions, attitudes toward the paranormal, and altered states such as hypnosis could affect PK and ESP performance for better or worse.

After Rhine, PK research was divided into two categories. Macro-PK involves observable events, such as influencing dice, coins or the sequences of numbers produced by a random event generator. Micro-PK involves weak or slight effects not visible to the naked eye and requiring statistical evaluation, such as changing temperatures, magnetic fields or the molecular content of water. Modern parapsychologists have devoted more attention to micro-PK.

See also HOME, DANIEL DUNGLAS; SCHNEIDER BROTHERS.

Further reading:
Edge, Hoyt L., Robert L. Morris, John Palmer, and Joseph H. Rush. *Foundations of Parapsychology.* Boston: Routledge & Kegan Paul, 1986.
Rhine, J.B. *The Reach of the Mind.* New York: William Sloane Assoc., 1947.
Rhine, Louisa E. *Mind Over Matter: Psychokinesis.* New York: Collier Books, 1970.
Targ, Russell, and Harold E. Puthoff. *Mind Reach: Scientists Look At Psychic Ability.* New York: Delacorte Press, 1977.
Wolman, Benjamin B., ed. *Handbook of Parapsychology.* New York: Van Nostrand Reinhold, 1977.

psychopomp In mythology, a supernatural being who conducts the soul in safety to the afterworld. Psychopomps are universal in myth and lore. In Greek mythology, the god Hermes is a psychopomp; in Egyptian myth, the job is shared by the deities Thoth and Anubis.

Animals can be psychopomps as well as deities. (See DOLPHIN.) In various shamanic traditions, shamans employ mystical horses as psychopomps to carry them to the underworld, where they commune with spirits and recover the souls of the sick.

See also SHAMANISM.

puca (also **pooka**) In Irish folklore, a spirit that is both helpful and mischievous. The puca has the helpful characteristics of the household brownie and the mischievous characteristics of the bogey and the bucca.

The puca is a shape-shifter and is often seen in the form of a black animal or a black half-animal. When he is so inclined, he favors humans by enabling them to understand animal speech and by protecting them from evil spirits. If treated well, household pucas will clean up the house during the night and also do yard work. Ungrateful people invoke the puca's wrath. He also bedevils grave robbers.

In English folklore the puca is known as puck, a household spirit who in medieval times was viewed as having a particularly malicious nature and was often identified with the Devil. Puck is also known as Robin Goodfellow, described in 16th-century literature as the child of a human girl and a fairy. Robin Goodfellow has the ability to shape-shift into animals and enjoys playing tricks on humans. He also performs household chores in return for milk or cream and bread or cake.

R-101 case Incident involving the famous Irish medium Eileen J. GARRETT, in which spirits of the dead allegedly solved the mystery of a tragic airship disaster, the crash of the British dirigible R-101 on her maiden voyage in 1930. All 46 persons on board were killed. The spirits of the dead crew communicated evidential information through Garrett, thus providing support for survival after death. The case had interesting legal implications.

Garrett had several premonitions of the impending disaster years before it happened. In 1926, Garrett was walking her dog in Hyde Park in London one day when she had a vision of a phantom dirigible in the sky. It appeared normal. In 1928, while walking near Holland Park in London, she saw the airship again, only this time it was partially covered by clouds; it wobbled, gave off smoke, was buffeted about and disappeared. She believed it to be a real disaster and was surprised to find no news of it in the press. Meanwhile, the construction of two dirigibles in England, the R-100 and the R-101, was made public. One was to fly to India on its maiden voyage; Garrett was certain it would be the R-101, and that it would crash. Garrett sent a warning to Sir Sefton Brancker, director of civil aviation; Brancker laughed at her. Also in 1928, during a seance, Garrett gave a message from a deceased Captain Raymond Hinchcliffe warning his friend, Ernest Johnston, the navigator of the R-101, not to go on the maiden voyage because the ship would crash. Johnston did not take the message seriously. In 1929, Garrett saw a third vision of a dirigible in the sky over London, in flames.

The R-101 was declared by Brancker to be "safe as a house, except for the millionth chance." It lifted off on October 4, 1930 and crashed in France on October 5. Garrett knew about it before the news reached the media. Brancker was among the victims.

Three days after the crash, Garrett conducted a seance intended to communicate with Sir Arthur Conan DOYLE, who had died on July 7. Garrett's control, Uvani, began to relay messages from the dead captain of R-101, Flight Lieutenant H. Carmichael Irwin. The specific and technical information about the airship, its testing and flight was of such a confidential nature that Harry PRICE, one of the sitters, worried about espionage. He sent a copy of the transcript to Sir John Simon, chairman of the Court of Inquiry, who was heading an investigation of the disaster. When the seance story appeared in the press, other military officials became interested, including Major Oliver Villiers, a close friend of Brancker.

Irwin allegedly communicated again, joined by several others who had died in the crash, including Brancker, Major G.H. Scott, Wing Commander R.B. Colmore and Ernest Johnston, the navigator. The spirits claimed that the R-101 had had a gas leak that had been ignored by officials who wanted to launch on time. The ship had been too heavy for the engines, which backfired and ignited the escaping gas. Furthermore, the ship had been plagued by other problems: a bad air pump that failed and an improperly functioning fuel pump. The ship had never reached cruising altitude and had scraped treetops as it passed over France. The problems had been known prior to launch, but the decision had been made to proceed. The crew had not wanted to appear "faint of heart," and had figured that if they made it across the English Channel, they could come down in France and claim that bad weather had forced them to land.

Villiers was convinced he had spoken with the spirits of the dead crew, and he gave information from Garrett's seven seances to Simon. Simon said he could do nothing with it, however, as testimony from the dead would never be accepted in a court of law.

Twenty-five years later, Villiers gave another copy of the seance records to author James Leasor, who wrote *The Millionth Chance: The Story of the R-101*.

Villiers believed the dead crew wanted the world to know the truth of what happened.

The information was not considered in the official inquiry of the clash because of the alleged sources, spirits of the dead.

Further reading:

Angoff, Allan. *Eileen Garrett and the World Beyond the Senses.* New York: William Morrow, 1974.

radiant boys The glowing ghosts of boys who have been murdered by their mothers, whose appearance portends ill luck and violent death. Radiant boys appear in the folklore of England and Europe, possibly originating with the *Kindermorderinn* (children murdered by their mothers) of Germanic folklore. There are numerous radiant boys stories in the Cumberland area of England, which was settled by Germanic and Scandinavian peoples in the 9th and 10th centuries.

A radiant boy once haunted the Howard family's Corby Castle in Cumberland, making its most famous appearance in 1803. The castle—really a manor house—stands on a fortification site once used by the Romans. Part of the old house adjoins a Roman-built tower. According to an account written in 1824, the radiant boy haunted a room in part of the old house adjoining the tower. The origin of the ghost is not known, but he plagued many an overnight guest with his appearances and noises. The room had an air of gloom which Howard sought to dispel by changing some of the furniture.

Howard recorded in his journal that an incident took place on September 8, 1803 involving the rector of Greystoke, who, with his wife, was among the guests staying at the castle. The rector and his wife had planned to stay several days, but after their first night they announced at breakfast that they intended to depart. The Howards were stunned.

Some time later, the rector confessed the reason. Howard quoted him as saying:

> Soon after we went to bed we fell asleep. It might be between one and two in the morning when I awoke. I observed that the fire was totally extinguished; but although that was the case, and we had no light, I saw a glimmer in the middle of the room, which suddenly increased to a bright flame. I looked out, apprehending that something had caught fire; when, to my amazement, I beheld a beautiful boy clothed in white, with bright locks resembling gold, standing by my bedside, in which position he remained some minutes, fixing his eyes upon me with a mild and benevolent expression. He then glided gently towards the side of the chimney; where it is obvious there is no possible egress, and entirely

> disappeared. I found myself again in total darkness, and all remained quiet until the usual hour of rising. I declare this to be a true account of what I saw at Corby Castle, upon my word as a clergyman.

It is not known if anything ill befell the rector; some 20 years later, he was still talking about the ghost. The radiant boy no longer haunts the castle. The room, called "the Ghost Room," is a study.

Lord Castlereagh, second Marquis of Londonderry and one of England's most illustrious statesmen in the early 19th century, allegedly saw a radiant boy years before he committed suicide. There are different versions of the story.

According to one, the episode occurred when he was a young man, Captain Robert Stewart. He was posted in Ireland, and one day he went hunting and became lost. With darkness coming on, he sought lodging at the home of a gentleman. There were other guests in the house, and Stewart was invited to stay a few days and join their hunt. He agreed.

When it came time to retire, Stewart was taken to a room with little furniture and a blazing fire. He fell asleep and was awakened suddenly by a bright light in the room. At first he thought it was the fire. The fire, however, had gone out, but the light seemed to emanate from the chimney. Gradually Stewart became aware of the glowing form of a beautiful naked boy, surrounded by a dazzling brilliance. The boy gave him an earnest look and then faded away.

Stewart thought he had been played a joke and was mightily offended. The following morning, he brusquely announced his departure. The host managed to pry the details out of him, and gave the butler a tongue-lashing for putting Stewart in "the Boy's Room." The butler protested that he had lit a fire "to keep him from coming out."

The host explained to Stewart that according to a tradition in his family, whoever saw the radiant boy would first rise to great prosperity and power and then suddenly die a violent death. Stewart, the second heir in line in his family, was unconcerned.

Within a few years, however, his older brother drowned in a boating accident. Stewart left the army and entered politics, rising quickly. He was influential in creating the Act of Union between England and Ireland in 1800. He served as secretary of war in 1805 and 1807, and as foreign secretary from 1812 on. Despite his success, he was not well liked and was even hated by many for his cold demeanor. In 1821, his father died, making him Lord Castlereagh, second Marquis of Londonderry.

In 1822, Lord Castlereagh's fortunes abruptly began to dim. He suffered from gout, and the stresses of his career began to take a heavy personal toll. He became paranoid and suspicious and acted strangely, and was feared to be losing his mind. He was confined to his country house, North Cray Place, and forbidden to have razors, lest he do something foolish. On August 12, 1822 he took a penknife and slashed his throat, killing himself.

Author Edward Bulwer-Lytton later advanced another story as to how Castlereagh came upon a radiant boy. Bulwer-Lytton said that Castlereagh had stayed at Knebworth, the Lytton family seat, at a time prior to his confinement. One morning he appeared at breakfast looking very pale, and said that a strange boy with long yellow hair had appeared in his room, sitting in front of the fire. The boy had drawn his finger across his throat three times and then vanished. The story most likely is one of Bulwer-Lytton's inventions. He often would invite guests to sleep in the "haunted room" and then sneak upstairs and scare them.

See also DEATH OMENS.

Further reading:
Cohen, Daniel. *The Encyclopedia of Ghosts.* New York: Dodd, Mead & Co., 1984.
Harper, Charles G. *Haunted Houses: Tales of the Supernatural With Some Accounts of Hereditary Curses and Family Legends.* Rev. and enlarged ed. London: Cecil Palmer, 1924.

rainbow   See BRIDGE OF SOULS.

rakshasa   In Indian folklore, a demon which appears as a black figure with yellow or flaming hair, and wearing a wreath of entrails. Their name literally means "destroyer," and rakshasas are considered to be evil and hostile to mankind. They can take many shapes, including beautiful men and women and animals or birds, such as dogs, vultures and owls. Generally, however, they are monstrous in appearance, with huge bellies, slits for eyes and matted hair. If not black, they are yellow, green or blue.

Rakshasas are nocturnal creatures and have disgusting habits, such as eating human flesh and drinking human blood from the skull; eating food which has been sneezed upon, walked upon or soiled by insects; and eating corpses. They also roam around forests looking for animals to eat, always trying to satisfy an insatiable hunger. They have the power to reanimate corpses, and will take possession of an unwary man through his food, causing madness or illness. One touched by a rakshasa dies.

Despite their formidable evil powers, rakshasas, like many demonic beings, are reputed to be dimwitted. According to Indian lore, one may banish them simply by saying "Uncle."

Further reading:
Hurwood, Bernhardt J. *Passport to the Supernatural: An Occult Compendium from All Ages and Many Lands.* New York: Taplinger, 1972.
Leach, Maria, and Jerome Fried, eds. *Funk & Wagnalls Standard Dictionary of Folklore, Mythology, and Legend.* San Francisco: Harper & Row, 1979.

rapping   One of the earliest discovered means of alleged spirit communication. Rapping includes any knocking, thumping, bumping or tapping associated with discarnate messages.

The 9th-century chronicle *Rudolf of Fulda* refers to communications from a rapping intelligence. Paracelsus, a 16th-century Swiss physician and alchemist, called raps *pulsatio mortuorum*, or an omen of approaching death. Rapping spirits, or *spiritus percutiens*, were conjured away at the benediction of medieval Catholic churches. In 1520, Melanchthon reported rapping at Oppenheim, Germany. Rappers appeared in 1521 in Lyons, France and in 1610 at Ayr, Scotland. In 1661, Rev. Joseph Glanvil wrote extensively of the rapping at Tedworth, England in *Sadiucismus Triumphatus* (see DRUMMER OF TEDWORTH). Rev. Samuel Wesley, father of John Wesley, the founder of Methodism, and his family heard rapping at Epworth Vicarage in 1716 (see EPWORTH RECTORY).

But not until Maggie and Kate Fox asked "Mr. Splitfoot" to answer questions via rapping at Hydesville, New York in 1848 did so many people begin to believe in the phenomenon of spirit communication (see FOX SISTERS). At first the spirit only rapped twice for yes and not at all for no, but eventually elder brother David Fox worked out an alphabet code, in which the spirit tediously communicated his message.

A short time later, the girls' older sister, Leah Fish, took Kate and their mother to Rochester, but the rappings followed the young girl. By this time, the sensation was spreading, and various people in and around Rochester discovered their mediumship. Rappings were heard everywhere, giving the "Rochester knockings" terrific press coverage. From there, budding Spiritualists all over America were communicating with the discarnate via rapping, and the phenomenon remains a staple of spirit communication.

No doubt much of the rapping was produced fraudulently. Maggie and Kate Fox, both in the beginning and later in Maggie's famous renunciation of Spiritualism in 1888, ascribed the raps to their talented toes, which they were able to crack against the floorboards with very little discernible movement of leg muscles. Kate also confided that if the questioner called out the alphabet code, the medium could easily read changes in facial muscles and reveal the correct answer. The effect of raps coming from all parts of the room was easily suggested to a willing listener.

Famous magicians such as Harry HOUDINI and J.N. Maskelyne, intent on debunking Spiritualism, offered many explanations and techniques for rapping. With the medium's hands outstretched on the table during the seance, rapping could be produced by tightly pressing the thumbnails together and then allowing one nail to slip against the other. A better method was slipping one's knee or shoe against the table leg. Other mediums slightly moistened their fingers and slid them gently along the tabletop.

Still others employed mechanical devices hidden in their clothes or shoes to create the raps. One of the most ingenious consisted of a small, hollow metal tube which contained a long burlap needle that moved up and down like a piston. Heavy black thread attached the needle to a tiny hook in an inconspicuous seam, which the medium carefully worked out of the fabric during the dark seance. Once the needle was exposed, the medium attached a leaded cork to the top of the needle and maneuvered it so that raps were heard throughout the sitting.

Electrical devices operated by wire produced raps from the heels of the medium's shoe. By moving the foot under the table, the medium could make the sitters think the raps were coming from beneath their own hands. Surgeon William Faulkner admitted to the London Dialectical Committee in 1869 that he regularly sold trick magnets to produce rapping sounds.

Nevertheless, thousands of sitters heard the din and believed. Spiritualist Andrew Lang asserted that if someone had wanted to create a method of spirit communication, it would not have been cumbersome rapping. Psychical researcher Professor Charles Richet wrote that if these rappings were true (and he believed they were), they proved the actions of human or nonhuman intelligence upon matter.

Finally, medium D.D. HOME convinced one of his sitters, Lord Adare's father, that spirits just *had* to rap. By remaining in the earth's atmosphere, the spirits get so charged, so full of electricity, he claimed, that they must release the energy to obtain relief.

Rapping is a characteristic of numerous poltergeist cases and occurs in hauntings.

Further reading:

Brandon, Ruth. *The Spiritualists*. New York: Alfred A. Knopf Inc., 1983.
Cannell, J.C. *The Secrets of Houdini*. New York: Bell Publishing Co., 1989.
Doyle, Sir Arthur Conan. *The History of Spiritualism Vol. I & II*. New York: Arno Press, 1975.
Fodor, Nandor. *An Eneyclopaedia of Psychic Science*. Secaucus, N.J.: The Citadel Press, 1966. First published 1933.
Houdini, Harry. *Houdini: A Magician Among the Spirits*. New York: Arno Press, 1972.

Raudive, Konstantin See ELECTRONIC VOICE PHENOMENON.

Raynham Hall Stately English manor house haunted for the last 250 years by the "Brown Lady," who allegedly was once captured on film in one of the most spectacular spirit photographs on record.

Raynham Hall, the seat of the Marquesses of Townshend, is located a few miles southwest of Fakenham in Norfolk. The Townshends became marquesses in 1786, and for generations they lavishly entertained royalty at Raynham Hall.

The identity of the Brown Lady is uncertain; it is believed she is the ghost of Lady Dorothy Townshend, wife of the second and most famous marquess of Townshend, daughter of Robert Walpole, member of Parliament for Houghton, and sister of Sir Robert Walpole, the first prime minister of England.

At age 26, Dorothy married her childhood love, Lord Charles Townshend, who had suffered the loss of his first wife about a year earlier in 1711. According to legend, Dorothy had been the mistress of Lord Wharton, and when Townshend discovered this after their marriage, he kept her locked in her apartment at the hall. It is not known how she died. Different versions of the legend say it was either of a broken heart, a fall down the staircase, or smallpox.

A portrait identified as Lady Dorothy hung in the hall until it was sold in 1904. The woman is dressed in brown brocade trimmed in yellow with a ruff around the throat. Her eyes are large and shining. It was rumored that the portrait looked normal when seen during the day, but if seen by candlelight the face became evil-looking and skull-like with no eyes.

Numerous stories of encounters with the Brown Lady have been recorded over the centuries. One of the most famous occurred in the early 19th century, when George IV, then regent, visited at the hall and was given the State bedroom. He awoke in the middle of the night to see a woman dressed in brown with dishevelled hair and a face of ashy paleness standing beside the bed. He was so frightened that he vowed he would not stay "another hour in this accursed house."

The Brown Lady was seen at Christmastime 1835 by Colonel Loftus, one of the many guests staying at the hall. Loftus saw the ghost twice on succeeding nights. The first time, she was standing outside of Lady Townshend's room. When pursued by Loftus, she went down the corridor and vanished. The second night, he encountered her on the staircase; she was carrying a lamp. He described her as a stately lady in rich brocade with a coif (a tight-fitting cap) on her hair, but only empty, dark hollows for eyes. Loftus made a sketch of her, which he showed to guests at breakfast the following morning.

Not long after that, Captain Frederick Marryat, a novelist, was invited to the hall. Marryat had a weak theory that the ghost was somehow connected to smugglers and poachers who once had been prevalent in the area. One night, he and two of Lord Charles Townshend's nephews came face to face with the Brown Lady in a corridor. She held a lighted lamp and grinned at Marryat in what he termed "a diabolical manner." He was carrying a pistol, which he raised and shot at the ghost point-blank. The ghost disappeared. Marryat later swore the bullet passed right through her. It was found lodged in a door behind where the ghost had stood.

Following that episode, the Brown Lady was not reported again until 1926, when she was encountered by the then Marquis Townshend, who was a boy at the time, and one of his friends.

In 1936 Lady Townshend hired a photographer, Indra Shira, to take photographs of the interior of Raynham Hall. Shira and his assistant, Mr. Provand, were taking flash photographs of the staircase when Shira saw a vaporous form take shape on the stairs. It assumed the form of a woman who appeared to be draped in something white. The ghost began to descend the staircase. Shira excitedly ordered Provand to take a picture. Provand could not see the apparition, but he aimed his camera in the direction indicated by Shira. Provand would not believe that Shira had seen a ghost, and he accepted a five-pound bet that the photograph would show the white form. It did—the Brown Lady appeared as an outline wearing something like a wedding gown and veil. The photograph was published in *Country Life* magazine on December 1, 1936 and caused a sensation. The photograph has been examined by experts, but no evidence of fraud has ever been detected. (See SPIRIT PHOTOGRAPHY.)

The Brown Lady also is said to haunt Houghton Hall, the home her brother built on the site of the old family home, occupied by Walpoles for some 600 years. It is said that Lady Townshend spent some of the happiest years of her life at Houghton. According to legend, her ghost appeared to the prince regent while he was sleeping in the State Bedroom. As a result, he transferred to other, albeit humbler, quarters.

Further reading:
Canning, John, ed. *50 Great Ghost Stories.* New York: Bonanza Books, 1988. First published 1971.
Folklore, Myths and Legends of Britain. London: Reader's Digest Assoc., 1977.
Hole, Christina. *Haunted England.* London: B.T. Batsford Ltd., 1940.

reciprocal apparitions   See APPARITIONS; WILMOT APPARITION.

recurrent spontaneous psychokinesis (RSPK)   See POLTERGEIST; ROLL, WILLIAM GEORGE, JR.

reincarnation   The idea that the soul returns after death to a new body to live another life. Belief in reincarnation is not limited to the higher religions of the East, but is found in tribal societies around the world.

According to a poll taken by the Gallup organization in 1981, almost a quarter of the American population believes in reincarnation. Although the Gallup poll did not go into the details of the belief, it is likely that most Americans' ideas on the subject are derived from Hinduism or Buddhism, perhaps by way of Spiritualism, Spiritism, or Theosophy. What many do not realize is that Hindu ideas (out of which the Buddhist developed) grew out of a set of beliefs characteristic of the indigenous tribal peoples of India. These latter beliefs were part of a set of beliefs about spirits and souls that form the widespread worldview of animism (q.v.), which has been called the world's earliest religion.

Animistic soul beliefs are more complex and varied than Western beliefs. Different tribal societies hold different beliefs, which, however, may be seen to be related to the same general set of ideas or principles. This indicates that probably there was once a universal set of beliefs from which the various beliefs found today have diverged over time.

One common characteristic of animistic beliefs about reincarnation is that the spirit of a deceased person undergoes a division after death, one part of it traveling to the Land of the Dead (see AFTERLIFE) where it becomes an ancestral spirit, while another part of it returns to earth to animate a new body. Some tribal peoples believe that each person has more than one soul, and in this case, one of the souls may reincarnate, while another becomes an ancestral spirit.

A person's name is often believed to have spiritual qualities in tribal societies, to the point that it even becomes a type of soul. Many Eskimo groups have what has been called a "name soul," which means that the soul is an inherent part of a name, and in naming a child, one also gives it a soul. If a child cries incessantly, this is supposed to be because it has been wrongly named, and if the proper name is found and given to the child, it will calm down. Shamans may be called in to divine the identity of the ancestor believed to be crying for its name.

The idea that a child who will not stop crying has been wrongly named has been reported from many other societies in the Americas and in Africa, and the intentional inducement of crying is sometimes used as a way of determining which ancestor has been reincarnated in a newborn baby. A baby is made to cry (perhaps by splashing water on it), and the names of deceased relatives are called out, until it stops its bawling. The Nandi of East Africa blow snuff up a baby's nose to make it cry, and expect it to sneeze when the correct name is called out. The name is then given to the baby, so that it has the same name it had in its previous life.

Crying tests are not the only method used to determine the past life identity of a child. Very often one of the parents has a dream which seems to predict that a certain person will be reborn to them. In many societies, babies are checked for birthmarks or birth defects that might indicate who they were, and sometimes corpses are marked with the intention of providing a way of tracking the deceased into his or her next life. In West Africa, mutilation is especially common with children who die in infancy, particularly if the same family has lost two or more children in a row. This is believed to be the same child returning again and again, but intentionally dying young each time, as a torment to its parents. By marking the body of one of these children, it is believed, their spirits will be rendered unattractive to their fellows, who will therefore allow them to remain living when they are reborn the next time around.

Reincarnation may be facilitated or impeded through burial practices (see FUNERAL RITES AND CUSTOMS). Children are sometimes buried beneath the floor of the home, with the idea that this will make it easier for their souls to return to their mothers. Adults, whose spirits are stronger and thus both more dangerous in their after-death state and better able to find their way back home, are less often buried in the home, but may instead be buried on the outskirts of the village. In Africa, some tribes have been reported to have another means of manipulating the incarnation process: persons who are undesirable for one reason or another are simply thrown into the bush. They are thus discouraged or prevented from taking rebirth in the community.

Human beings may be reborn not only as human children, but, in many societies at least, also as animals. Occasionally one finds the belief that the soul transmigrates through a series of different animal forms before it ceased to exist. However, one also finds the belief that at the end of this series, or perhaps after a single animal life, a person is reborn as a human being, and most probably this was the original belief. In the animistic system, many different animal species are believed to have souls. For Native Americans, animals allow themselves to be hunted and killed by human beings so long as this is done properly and humanely. Proper hunting procedures also ensure the reincarnation of the animals' spirits and the continuation of the species in the following season.

Of the several ways animistic reincarnation beliefs differ from those typical of Hinduism and Buddhism, the most important is the concept of karma. Karma, which has been called a "moral law of cause and effect," refers to the idea that the circumstances of one's present life are molded by one's actions (good and not so good) in previous lives, and, in a complimentary way, that what one does in this life will help to determine the course of one's destiny in future lives. This idea, which for many persons is inextricably associated with the idea of reincarnation, was part of the development of animistic beliefs into the familiar doctrine of Hinduism. The concept of karma is absent from animistic beliefs about reincarnation.

This is very interesting, because good evidence of karma is lacking in the scientific studies of reincarnation made by Ian STEVENSON and others. Stevenson has specialized in the study of children who claim to remember previous lives. Significantly, many of Stevenson's cases include not just verbal claims by the children, but many of the same "signs" of reincarnation recognized by tribal peoples, such as birthmarks and birth defects, announcing dreams, and phobias that relate to some previous life trauma (such as a death). Moreover, some cases of children who claim to remember previous lives have been reported by anthropologists, and these cases closely resemble Stevenson's in form. It may thus be said that scientific investigation supports the animistic type of belief better than the Hindu and Buddhist one.

Further reading:
Bendann, Effie. *Death Customs: An Analytical Study of Burial Rites.* London: Kegan Paul, Trench, and Trubner, 1930.
Gallup, George, Jr. *Adventures in Immortality: A Look Beyond the Threshold of Death.* New York: McGraw-Hill, 1982.

Guiley, Rosemary Ellen. *Tales of Reincarnation*. New York: Pocket Books, 1987.

Head, Joseph, and S.L. Cranston. *Reincarnation: The Phoenix Fire Mystery*. New York: Julian Press, 1977.

Matlock, James G. "Past Life Memory Case Studies." In S. Krippner, ed. *Advances in Parapsychological Research 6*, 184–297. Jefferson, N.C.: McFarland, 1990.

Stevenson, Ian. *Children Who Remember Previous Lives: A Question of Reincarnation*. Charlottesville: University Press of Virginia, 1987.

Tylor, Edward Burnett. *Religion in Primitive Culture*. New York: Harper and Row, 1956.

releasement   A modern term for an exorcism of an earthbound spirit, or a discarnate being attached to a place or person. "Releasement" refers primarily to exorcisms not performed by clergy. It is preferred by some mediums and therapists because it does not carry the same associations with the demonic as the term "exorcism."

In releasement, a medium or psychically attuned person makes mental contact with an earthbound spirit who is haunting a site and causing a disturbance, or is obsessing a person. Often, this spirit supposedly does not know he or she is dead, or is bound to the earth plane by unfinished business. Persons who practice releasement say that simply finding out the earthbound spirit's "story," that is, his or her life and death and perhaps unfinished business, is often sufficient to send the spirit on its way to the next world. This transition is marked by the appearance of white light, and the spirit is urged to move toward the light (persons who have a near-death experience often report that they move toward a brilliant white light, which they interpret variously as God, heaven or the Other Side). Sometimes the earthbound spirit has to be coaxed or convinced to move on. Sometimes it is led away by helping spirits that appear. These helping spirits include angelic beings, other spirits of the dead whom the earthbound one knew in life, or the spirits of animals with whom the person had strong emotional attachments, such as a pet.

Releasement also is called "depossession," a term that applies specifically to an outgrowth of past-life therapy (involving the discovery of alleged past lives). Patients are "depossessed," or exorcised, of discarnate human spirits and nonhuman spirits. The spirits are suspected of causing physical, emotional and mental problems, some of them allegedly karmic in origin. According to therapists, most attached entities are not evil or demonic, though such beings have been encountered.

One authority on depossession is American psychologist and past-life therapist Edith Fiore, whose findings have been supported by other past life therapists. In regressing patients to past-lives, Fiore said she noticed an increasing incidence of spirit possession and interference. Based on her experience with some 30,000 cases, Fiore estimated that 70% of all patients have at least one spirit attached to them. Some individuals have several and some have a great number. Most "possessees," as they are called, are unaware of the invasion. Their typical symptoms include unexplained swings in mood or behavior, chronic pains and illnesses, suicidal urges, personality problems, and abusive behavior with drugs and alcohol. Fiore believes that most cases of substance abuse, as well as most cases of mental illness such as schizophrenia and multiple personality disorder, are due to spirit possession.

Therapists have identified varying degrees of spirit possession: (1) attachment, in which the spirit hovers near the host's aura and the relationship is loose; (2) oppression, in which the spirit invades the host's aura, with intermittent or mild effect; (3) obsession, in which the spirit invades the host's physical body, bringing with it all the personality traits and habits it had while last alive; and (4) full possession, in which the spirit invades the body and displaces the host's psyche, creating another personality. In some cases, victims suffer both obsession and possession.

The majority of possessing spirits are said to be earthbound spirits of the dead. Some attach themselves to a member of their family, while others find hosts who subconsciously invite possession, or make a hospitable environment for it through negative emotions or substance abuse, which are said to weaken the aura. Other victims become possessed during illness, when the aura also is weakened. According to Fiore, even a single drink of alcohol can make one vulnerable to possession.

A theory has been advanced that many Vietnam veterans who suffer from post-traumatic stress syndrome—many of the symptoms of which overlap with multiple personality disorder—are carrying the attached spirits of fellow soldiers who were killed.

When the host is hypnotized and the spirits are invited to "come out" and identify themselves, most confess they are staying on the earth plane because they do not want to be dead, or because they are lost and confused. Some do not realize they are dead. When pointed toward the light and urged to move on, they reportedly leave their hosts. If not depossessed, the spirits may remain attached for the lifetime of the host, or may wander off and find new hosts. Some possessing spirits are said to be elementals of low intelligence, or beings that exhibit demonic and evil natures. Some of these nonhuman entities are identified as thought-forms, while others appear to be supernatural in origin. The nonhuman entities also are dispatched by persuasion. If necessary, therapists call on spirit guides or "Beings of Light" for assistance in difficult depossessions.

Following depossession, patients report feeling lighter and better, and say they experience a cessation of troublesome conditions. The departing spirits do not return, but patients are advised how to protect themselves from future invasions by other spirits.

Fiore has found that many possessions seem to be karmic: the patients had in past after-death states possessed living humans and, in some cases, had possessed the very spirits who were possessing them in the present. Releasing the possessing spirit apparently balances the karma, according to Fiore. Cases also have been reported of patients being possessed by their previous past lives. Some therapists say that past-life recalls themselves may not be the past-lives of the patients, but of the possessing spirits around them.

Forms of releasement are practiced the world over; spirits have long been blamed for causing virtually all ills and back luck, and they are routinely exorcised. In the early days of Spiritualism, people suffering from unusual mental symptoms often attended seances in hopes of having "low" spirits exorcised. The first medically trained person to approach mental illness as due to spirit possession was Dr. Carl A. WICKLAND, an American physician and psychologist who had attended numerous Spiritualist seances. Wickland and his wife, Anna, used electric shock to exorcise unwanted entities from the auras of their patients. A contemporary of the Wicklands was Titus BULL, a New York physician and neurologist who accepted Spiritualist beliefs concerning spirit obsession and possession, and who endorsed treatment by persuasive exorcism in seances. Bull conducted research with James H. HYSLOP, a distinguished psychical researcher who helped organize and preside over the AMERICAN SOCIETY FOR PSYCHICAL RESEARCH.

See CULT OF THE ZAR; EXORCISM; POSSESSION; WYLEY, GRAHAM.

Further reading:
Albertson, Maurice L., Dan S. Ward, & Bill Baldwin, "Post-Traumatic Stress Disorders of Vietnam Veterans: A Proposal for Research and Therapeutic Healing Utilizing Depossession," *The Journal of Regression Therapy*, 3 (Spring 1988):56–61.
Fiore, Edith. *The Unquiet Dead: A Psychologist Treats Spirit Possession.* Garden City, N.Y.: Dolphin/Doubleday & Co., 1987.
Ireland-Frey, Louise. "Clinical Depossession: Releasement of Attachment Entities from Unsuspecting Hosts," *The Journal of Regression Therapy* 1 (Fall 1986):90–101.
Rogo, D. Scott. *The Infinite Boundary.* New York: Dodd, Mead & Co., 1987.
Wickland, Carl A. *Thirty Years Among the Dead.* North Hollywood, Calif.: Newcastle Publishing Co., 1974. First published 1924.

Resurrection Mary   One of Chicago's most famous ghosts, who fits the characteristics of the PHANTOM HITCHHIKER. The ghost, a beautiful blonde, blue-eyed girl dressed in white, has been reported in the Chicago environs since 1934, the year of her alleged death.

Resurrection Mary takes her name from Resurrection Cemetery, located in Justice, a suburb of Chicago, where she is supposed to be buried. Her full name is unknown, and her existence is unproved. The best that can be gleaned from old cemetery records is that a Polish girl near Mary's age is buried in the cemetery.

According to legend, Mary was killed in an automobile accident one night in 1934 after an evening of dancing at the former O. Henry Ballroom, now the Willowbrook Ballroom. Her ghost is said to have begun making appearances in 1939. Motorists reported that a girl dressed in a white ballgown tried to jump on the running boards of their automobiles, or that a girl in white suddenly appeared in the road and hitched a ride to the O. Henry, where she danced the night away with strangers. When the ballroom closed, she would ask someone for a ride home and give vague instructions to drive north on Archer Avenue, the road on which Resurrection Cemetery is located. She reportedly would vanish from the car as it passed the cemetery. On other occasions, she would ask the driver to stop at the cemetery, where she would get out and disappear through the locked gates, or simply vanish from the car. She also has been seen inside the cemetery, staring through the bars of the gate.

Her perplexed escorts and dance partners described Mary as aloof and quiet, with icy cold skin. She appears to have conversed more than the average phantom hitchhiker, who typically offers little more than a destination.

Reports of Resurrection Mary increased following renovations to the cemetery in the mid-1970s. She has been seen and picked up at various suburban locations, and her destination always takes the driver past the cemetery.

Further reading:
Scott, Beth, and Michael Norman. *Haunted Heartland.* New York: Warner Books, 1985.

retrocognition A displacement in time in which one apparently sees into the past, to either experience or review events of which one has no prior knowledge, or to obtain accurate information which is not in one's own memory. Retrocognition seems to occur spontaneously in everyday life, in dreams, and in parapsychology laboratory experiments. Psychics use it in readings for clients. It is sometimes called "postcognition."

When retrocognition happens spontaneously, it can take the form of a vision. One enters a building or looks out a window, and instead of seeing the present surroundings, sees how the site looked in the past, perhaps peopled with individuals who seem either real or ghostly. Sometimes such experiences are fleeting and are passed off as imagination, while other times they seem very real and frightening.

Retrocognition occurs in cases of hauntings and apparitions, in which events from the past are seen and/or heard. It is as though events from the past keep replaying on some cosmic sound and video track, perceived on rare occasions by persons who somehow psychically tune in to them. Perhaps, as psychologist Gardner MURPHY suggested, at certain times people gain access to the Akashic Records, said to be the repository of all sound and action from all time. Murphy also suggested that most apparitions and ghosts are cases of retrocognition, in which an individual becomes momentarily displaced in time. The individual is not actually transported back in time, but remains in the present while hallucinating the scenes from the past.

Perhaps the most famous case of retrocognition occurred shortly after the turn of the 20th century in Versailles, when two Englishwomen thought they saw apparitions from the 1770s just prior to the French Revolution (see VERSAILLES GHOSTS).

A striking case investigated by Murphy occurred in the 1960s to Coleen Buterbaugh. As she entered an office suite in the music building at Nebraska Wesleyan University, she was arrested by a strange and strong odor. Suddenly she saw a tall woman with old-fashioned clothes and hairdo, who was reaching up to the shelves of an old music cabinet. Buterbaugh also sensed a masculine presence sitting at a desk to the side. She looked out a window and saw the campus as it had appeared nearly 50 years earlier. Buterbaugh realized that the vision was not in the present and that she had somehow slipped back in time. Later, it was determined that the apparition of the woman matched a Miss Mills, who had worked at the university as a music teacher from 1912 until her sudden death in 1936 in a room across the hall from the office suite.

Another well-known retrocognition case concerns the Battle of Nechanesmere, which took place on May 20, 685 in Scotland and later was considered one of the major events of the Dark Ages in Britain. The Picts, led by King brude mac Beli, routed the invading Northumbrians, led by King Ecgfrith. Ecgfrith, his entire royal bodyguard and most of his army were killed; those who survived fled.

Almost 1,265 years later, on January 2, 1950, the aftermath of the battle was witnessed by a woman in her fifties, E.F. Smith, who came upon the scene as though it were continuing on in time without beginning or end. Smith had been visiting friends one evening; on the return drive home, snowfall caused her car to slide into a ditch. She was not injured. With her dog, she began walking to the village of Letham, near Nechanesmere, some eight miles away.

About a half-mile from the village, Smith spotted a mass of torches moving through the night. As she continued on, she saw figures, dressed in what later was identified as 7th-century garb, holding the torches and moving through the fields, turning over bodies. Smith heard no sounds and felt no fear; her only concern was her barking dog, which she feared would awaken the villagers of Letham. Investigators surmised that she may have witnessed a haunting of phantom Picts, still searching the battlefield for their dead.

Not all retrocognitive experiences involve visions. One that was consisted only of sound occurred in 1951 at Dieppe, France, when two Englishwomen believed they heard phantom sounds of the famous air raid that had taken place there during World War II (see DIEPPE RAID).

In both the Nechanesmere and Dieppe cases, telepathy, clairvoyance and hallucinations were ruled out as possible causes.

Retrocognition has not been tested much in the laboratory because of the difficulty of ruling out the possibility of clairvoyance of existing historical records, and telepathy. Nonetheless, it is used in applied psi fields such as psychic criminology (solving crimes and finding missing persons) and psychic archaeology (see BOND, FREDERICK BLIGH).

Further reading:

Jahn, Robert G., and Brenda J. Dunne. *Margins of Reality: The Role of Consciousness in the Physical World.* San Diego: Harcourt, Brace, Jovanovich, 1987.

MacKenzie, Andrew. *Hauntings and Apparitions.* London: William Heinemann Ltd., 1982.

Murphy, Gardner. "Direct Contacts with Past and Future: Retrocognition and Precognition." *Journal of the American Society for Psychical Research* 61 (1967):3–23.

Wolman, Benjamin B., ed. *Handbook of Parapsychology.* New York: Van Nostrand Reinhold, 1977.

revenant   The dead who return from the grave. "Revenant," a term common in earlier times, is still sometimes used as a synonym for ghost. Nearly all civilizations have, at least at some time during history, fostered the belief in the ability of the dead to return to the world of the living. Humans and animals can be revenants.

Revenants take various forms, from filmy beings (the modern concept of ghosts) to solid forms that appear to be living, until they abruptly disappear. In Irish lore, revenants include living corpses, bodies that revive in order to briefly partake of their own funerals. Vampires also may be considered revenants.

For a discussion of phenomena, motifs and theories concerning the returning dead, see GHOST.

Rhine, J(oseph) B(anks) (1895–1980)   Founder and director of the Parapsychology Laboratory at Duke University, often called the father of modern parapsychology (experimental psychical research). He believed that the limits of extrasensory perception would have to be established before any meaningful work could be done on the problem of survival after death, but he never lost a personal interest in the latter.

J.B. Rhine was born on September 29, 1895 in a log house in the Pennsylvania mountains. From his childhood he heard many stories of omens, warnings and messages from unseen agencies, although his skeptical father taught him to dismiss them as so much superstitious nonsense. When he was about 12, Rhine had a religious experience and decided on a life in the ministry; he held this determination until he met Louisa Ella Weckesser, his future wife, whose critical attitude to religion gradually brought him to question his faith.

Rhine served in the Marines from 1917 to 1919. He and Louisa Weckesser were married in 1920. Rhine began to study biology and plant physiology, preparing for a career in forestry. He received his Ph.D. in botany from the University of Chicago in 1925; Louisa Rhine had received her Ph.D. in the same

The walking dead frightening soldiers on a moonlit night.

subject from the same institution the previous year. But Rhine did not find botany satisfying; more and more his mind turned to psychic experiences. The Rhines had heard Sir Arthur Conan DOYLE lecture in Chicago in 1922, and his claim to be in touch with his deceased son made Rhine wonder whether psychical research might provide a way of establishing proof of a nonphysical world.

Rhine joined the AMERICAN SOCIETY FOR PSYCHICAL RESEARCH (ASPR) in 1924 and in 1925 began to abstract foreign-language publications for the ASPR's *Journal*. The *Journal* at this time was under the editorship of J. Malcolm Bird and was printing many stories of the Boston medium "Margery" (see CRANDON, MINA STINSON). Rhine was enough impressed by what he read to want to conduct his own research with Crandon. Boston was across the river from Cambridge and Harvard, where William McDougall, a prominent figure in psychical research, then taught. It was partly with the idea of studying under McDougall and partly with the idea of investigating Crandon that the Rhines left Morgantown in June 1926 and moved to Boston.

On July 1 the Rhines had a sitting with Crandon which left Rhine badly disillusioned. He had seen the medium kick a megaphone within reach of her hand in the dark, and when he checked a balance after the seance he found that the weight had been moved so that the "wrong" side would go down. He quickly wrote to the ASPR about what he had seen; later he resigned his membership in the society.

The Rhines had based their decision to leave Morgantown partly on a belief in Bird's presentation of the mediumship, Louisa Rhine wrote in *Something Hidden* (1983), her book on their life together, but now suddenly everything was up in the air. They had reached Cambridge to find McDougall leaving for sabbatical, and the Crandon mediumship had turned out to be a fraud. Fortunately, there was Walter Franklin PRINCE at the BOSTON SOCIETY FOR PSYCHICAL RESEARCH.

Prince had left his position as research officer with the ASPR partly because he, too, was skeptical of the Crandon mediumship. He arranged for the Rhines to have sittings with a mental medium, Minnie Meserve Soule, on behalf of a Detroit school administrator, John F. Thomas, who was working on his doctorate under McDougall. Thomas, in turn, arranged for the Rhines to go to Duke University in the fall of 1927 to assist him in his data analysis. Duke had hired McDougall away from Harvard after his sabbatical.

Rhine at first worked as a research assistant to McDougall as well as Thomas. He stayed on to teach psychology after Thomas received his Ph.D. (the first awarded in parapsychology by an American university), and in the fall of 1930 he and McDougall, along with others in the psychology department, began the ESP experiments that would make the Parapsychology Laboratory world-famous. The association with Prince now had another benefit—Prince edited and the Boston Society published Rhine's monograph *Extra-Sensory Perception* (1934), in which he reported the results of those early experiments.

The Soule sittings they had conducted for Thomas had been interesting, but the Rhines disagreed with Thomas over their interpretation. Thomas believed that these and other of his seance communications were genuine messages from his deceased wife, whereas the Rhines thought they could be explained on the basis of the medium's ESP. The debate was an old one, going back to the beginnings of the SOCIETY FOR PSYCHICAL RESEARCH in London in 1882.

But Rhine had not lost his personal interest in the survival problem. In a series of popular books and lectures, as well as scientific papers and editorials published in the *Journal of Parapsychology*, which he founded at Duke in 1937, he was quick to point out that ESP supported a dualistic separation of body and mind. And if body and mind were separate, then in theory the mind should be able to survive the body's death. Until the limits of ESP were established, however, he believed there was no scientific way of pursuing the survival problem.

The Parapsychology Laboratory continued in operation at Duke until Rhine's retirement in 1965, when he moved it off-campus to the new Foundation for Research on the Nature of Man, where it is still in existence. Rhine died on February 20, 1980 at his home in Hillsborough, North Carolina.

Rhine's popular books, all of them best-sellers, include *New Frontiers of the Mind* (1937), *The Reach of the Mind* (1947) and *New World of the Mind* (1953).

Further reading:

Berger, Arthur S. *Lives and Letters in American Parapsychology.* Jefferson, N.C.: McFarland, 1988.

Matlock, J.G. "Cat's paw: Margery and the Rhines, 1926." *Journal of Parapsychology* 51 (1987):229–47.

Mauskopf, Seymour, and Michael McVaugh. *The Elusive Science.* Baltimore: Johns Hopkins, 1980.

Rhine, Louisa E. *Something Hidden.* Jefferson, N.C.: McFarland, 1983.

Rao, K.R., ed. *J.B. Rhine: On the Frontiers of Science.* Jefferson, N.C.: McFarland, 1982.

Roaring Bull of Bagbury   In English folklore, a bogie-like spirit, or even the Devil, in the form of a ghostly, frightening bull. As a mortal, the bull had been a mean man who had performed only two good deeds in his whole life. As a ghost, he was doomed to haunt a farm with such loud roars and bellows that the farmer called 12 parsons together to "lay" (exorcise) him. The parsons drove the bull to the church where they finally conjured him into a size so small that they could stuff him into a snuff-box. The box was sent to the Red Sea for 1,000 years.

Rodgers, Louis (1901–?) English medium who gained international fame for his apparent ability to project his double.

Louis Rodgers was 30 years old when he moved to Melbourne, Australia and established himself as a medium, holding seances to communicate with the dead. He was a tall, handsome but slightly mournful-looking man with long black hair. His reputed mediumistic ability quickly gained him a large and loyal clientele. His favorite reply, in answer to questions about his ability, was "I am at the mercy of the spirits. Wherever they call me I must go."

Rodgers' ability to bilocate became known in 1935, when two of his Melbourne clients inadvertantly discovered he had been seen simultaneously in Melbourne and Sydney. In Melbourne, he had conducted a seance, while in Sydney, he had met with a woman and conducted a lengthy conversation with her. Rumors about his double began to spread. When asked about it, Rodgers merely would smile and perhaps give his enigmatic answer about being at the mercy of the spirits.

The BILOCATIONS attracted the attention of the Australian law enforcement, which suspected Rodgers of fraud, and also of Dr. Martin Spencer, director of the Victoria Institute for Psychic Research, who specialized in exposing fraud. Spencer asked Rodgers to undergo tests, but the medium demurred, saying he did not want scientific hypotheses to jeopardize his career. Spencer persisted and finally prevailed.

The experiments with Rodgers began in April 1937. Rodgers agreed to remain in Melbourne for three weeks, and to be followed by one of Spencer's investigators. Other investigators were stationed in Sydney and other locations where Rodgers' double had been reported, and were to telephone Spencer immediately upon seeing the double.

On the third day, Rodgers was spotted in Sydney, where he had checked into a hotel. The Sydney investigator knocked on the door of the hotel room and spoke to the occupant, a tall man with long black hair who identified himself as Louis Rodgers. At the same time, however, Rodgers was in Melbourne lunching with Spencer.

Informed by telephone of the Sydney sighting, Spencer dismissed it as a possible hoax done with an impersonator. Rodgers rebutted that four days hence, he would prove his bilocation ability once and for all, and hoped he then would be left alone.

On the appointed day, Rodgers was locked inside Spencer's office with Spencer and three witnesses. He asked Spencer for a password, and was given "Lilac." After about an hour, the Sydney investigator called to report spotting a man who looked like Rodgers on the street in Sydney. Another hour later, Spencer received another phone call which, according to the operator, came from Sydney. This time, Spencer heard not the voice of his investigator, but Rodger's voice, saying, "This is Louis Rodgers. The password is 'Lilac.' "

Spencer never stated whether or not Rodgers' bilocation was genuine or a fraud, but he once admitted privately to a friend that he thought the medium's ability was genuine.

Rodgers was killed during World War II while serving with the Australian Army in Europe.

Further reading:
Knight, David C. *The Moving Coffins: Ghosts and Hauntings Around the World.* Englewood Cliffs, N.J.: Prentice-Hall, 1983.

Rogo, D. Scott (1950–1990) American parapsychologist, prolific author and lecturer. His wide and varied interests included poltergeist and haunting phenomena, out-of-body experiences, psychokinesis, extrasensory perception, anomalies, UFOs and reincarnation. His life ended prematurely in murder by (at press time) an unknown assailant.

D. Scott Rogo was born on February 1, 1950 to Jack and Winifred Rogo of Los Angeles. He earned a bachelor's degree at California State University in Northridge in 1972, and then did graduate work in the psychology of music. He then elected to devote his professional interests to parapsychology. His first book, *NAD: A Study of Some Unusual "Other World" Experiences,* was published in 1970 (NAD is a Sanskrit term for transcendental music). Before his death in 1990, Rogo authored nearly 30 books, most of them on the paranormal and related subjects, and numerous articles.

In 1973 Rogo was a visiting research consultant for the Psychical Research Foundation (then at Durham, N.C.), and in 1975 he served in the same capacity for the Maimonides Medical Center's division of parapsychology in Brooklyn, New York (since defunct). He was director of research for the former Southern California Society of Psychical Research. He also lectured and taught on parapsychology at colleges and universities in California, including the University of California, Whitman College and John

F. Kennedy University. In 1978, Rogo became a consulting editor for *Fate* magazine, a position he still held at the time of his death.

Rogo was stabbed to death in the den of his home in Northridge, California on or about August 15, 1990. On August 16, a neighbor noticed that Rogo's lawn sprinkler had been running for two days, and notified the police. There were no suspects, and the police did not believe the murder was related to Rogo's interest in the paranormal. Burglary apparently was not a motive, for nothing seemed to be missing.

Rogo had never married and had no children.

In the area of apparitions, poltergeists and hauntings, Rogo's best-known works are *An Experience of Phantoms* (1974), *The Poltergeist Experience* (1979) and *On the Track of the Poltergeist* (1986). His research included numerous first-hand investigations of reported phenomena. His examination of the phenomenon known as PHONE CALLS FROM THE DEAD, in which individuals apparently receive calls from or place calls to persons no longer living, was published as *Phone Calls from the Dead* (1979), coauthored with Raymond Bayless.

Rogo took issue with the repressed hostility theory as the leading cause of poltergeist outbreaks. He contended it could be a factor in some, but not all, cases. Rogo believed that different poltergeist cases emerge from different psychological roots, and that some that occur in non-Western cultures could have legitimate causes that Westerners would consider offbeat, such as fear of witchcraft and black magic.

Within the parapsychology establishment, Rogo was often faulted for poor scholarship, which, critics said, led to erroneous conclusions.

Further reading:
Berger, Arthur S. *Lives and Letters in American Parapsychology: A Biographical History, 1850–1987.* Jefferson, N.C.: McFarland & Co., 1988.
Clark, Jerome. "D. Scott Rogo (1950–1990)." *Fate* 43 (December 1990):45–48.

rolang ("The corpse who stands up")   A magical rite performed by Tibetan Buddhist *ngagspas* (sorcerers), intended to animate corpses for the purpose of obtaining from them a magical charm.

There are several types of *rolang*. In one, described by French explorer Alexandra David-Neel during her journeys in Tibet in the early 20th century, the sorcerer shuts himself alone with the corpse in a dark room. He lies on top of it, mouth to mouth, and mentally chants a magical formula. It is crucial that he exclude all other thoughts from his mind. If he does the ritual successfully, the corpse eventually begins to move about, then stands up and tries to escape. No matter how hard the corpse struggles, the sorcerer must cling to it, still mouth to mouth, still mentally chanting the magical spell. Finally, the moment arrives that the sorcerer has waited for: the corpse's tongue protrudes from its mouth. The sorcerer bites it off, and the corpse collapses. The sorcerer takes the tongue and dries it, thus turning it into a magical weapon of great potency.

Failure of the sorcerer to stay in control means certain death at the hands of the berserk corpse. Stories exist of corpses that kill the sorcerer and escape to roam the countryside like evil Frankenstein monsters.

Although the ritual is said to take place in actuality, David-Neel believed that the ritual was acted out in trance and took place only within the altered consciousness of the sorcerer. She was shown at least one alleged dessicated tongue.

Prior to the introduction of Buddhism into Tibet in the 8th century, *rolang* was performed during funeral ceremonies by the shamans of Bön, the early, shamanistic religion of the country.

In another Tibetan sorcery corpse rite, *trong-jug*, the spirit of a living being is made to pass into a corpse and animate it.

Even if not animated by ritual, corpses are believed to be able to come to life without warning and harm the living, according to traditional belief. Upon death, lamas stay continually with a corpse until it is taken to the cemetery. The corpse is bound in a sitting posture, and the lamas recite magical formulae to prevent it from breaking its bonds and murdering others in a rampage.

Further reading:
David-Neel, Alexandra. *Magic and Mystery in Tibet.* New York: Dover Books, 1971. First published 1929.
Foster, Barbara, and Michael Foster. *Forbidden Journey: The Life of Alexandra David-Neel.* San Francisco: Harper & Row, 1987.

Roll, William George, Jr. (1926–)   American parapsychologist who has specialized in the study of poltergeists and phenomena suggesting survival after death.

William G. Roll was born on July 3, 1926 in Bremen, Germany. He graduated from the University of California at Berkeley in 1949. Roll received a B.Litt. from Oxford University in 1960, and a Ph.D. from the University of Lund, Sweden in 1989. In 1950, he married Muriel Gold. The Rolls have a daughter and two sons.

In his teens, during World War II when he was living in Denmark, Roll would sometimes wake up during the night and find himself able to leave his body (see OUT-OF-BODY EXPERIENCE). On one occasion he moved out of the house as far as the garden. He had no doubt that he was not dreaming or hallucinating, and that his "mind" had actually detached itself from his body. Although he has since come to a different conclusion about the meaning of such experiences (he now believes them to be purely psychological), they played a significant role in his choice of parapsychology as a career.

After the close of World War II, Roll moved to California, where his father was then living. Enrolling at Berkeley, he studied philosophy and psychology, the closest fields to psychical research he could find. In 1950 he went to Oxford University to study the philosophical aspects of parapsychology under the British philosopher Henry Habberly Price. With support from Oxford and later from the SOCIETY FOR PSYCHICAL RESEARCH (SPR) and Eileen J. GARRETT of the PARAPSYCHOLOGY FOUNDATION, he set up a small research laboratory. From 1952 to 1957, he headed the Oxford Society for Psychical Research.

While at Oxford, Roll got in touch with J.B. RHINE at Duke University in Durham, North Carolina. In 1957 Rhine invited Roll to Durham, later extending his offer by two years, and Roll temporarily broke off his studies.

In 1958, Roll and fellow parapsychologist J.G. Pratt were sent by Rhine to investigate a poltergeist that had been reported on Seaford, Long Island (see SEAFORD POLTERGEIST). Their report, published in the *Journal of Parapsychology* that same year, concluded that the disturbances were most likely the result of unconscious psychokinesis on the part of a teenage boy in the family. Roll and Pratt coined the term "recurrent spontaneous psychokinesis" (RSPK) to cover cases of recurrent psychokinetic activity. This term has caught on and is in general use in parapsychology today as a synonym for "poltergeist."

In 1959, Rhine hosted a conference on "Incorporeal Personal Agency" at Duke. An important outcome of this conference was the decision by Charles F. Ozanne to fund a new institute dedicated to research on survival. Roll was named director of the Psychical Research Foundation (PRF), which began operation in 1960. In 1962, the PRF left the Parapsychology Laboratory for its own quarters in Durham. Roll was now giving full time to survival research. He investigated several more poltergeists, including one at a souvenir warehouse in Miami (see MIAMI POLTERGEIST). An important series of experiments on out-of-body experiences using a kitten as a detector were conducted at the PRF (see OUT-OF-BODY EXPERIENCES). In 1987, when Roll left Durham to take the position

of William James Professor of Psychology at West Georgia College in Carrollton, Georgia, he took the PRF with him.

Roll is skeptical of the evidence for personal survival. In an important publication in the series *Advances in Parapsychological Research* (vol. 3, 1977), Roll outlined a model of survival that holds that although the body dies, memory impressions live on and are connected to one another in a vast "psi field," through which they are accessible to living persons through a psychometry-like process.

Roll continues to view poltergeists entirely in terms of RSPK, and hypothesizes that they are due to repressed tensions on the part of the subjects, typically teenagers. His work was featured in an article in *Omni* magazine in August 1988, and his investigation of a haunting on the retired cruise ship the *Queen Mary* formed a segment of the popular NBC television show *Unsolved Mysteries* that same year.

Roll served as president of the international professional Parapsychological Association in 1964. His books include *Theory and Experiment in Psychical Research* (1975), his B. Litt. thesis for Oxford; *The Poltergeist* (1972), based largely on his own case investigations; and *This World or That: An Examination of Parapsychological Findings Suggestive of the Survival of Human Personality After Death* (1989), his doctoral dissertation for the University of Lund.

Further reading:

Pleasants, Helene, ed. *Biographical Dictionary of Parapsychology.* New York: Helix Press, 1964.

Roll, William George. *The Poltergeist.* Garden City, N.Y.: Doubleday, 1972.

Rosenheim Poltergeist   Case of paranormal occurrences in a German town that defied natural explanation. Some of the phenomena seemed to be directed by a disembodied "intelligence."

The case began in November 1967 in a law office in the Bavarian town of Rosenheim. Phenomena were primarily electrical and electronic: neon ceiling lights repeatedly went out; fuses blew without apparent cause; developing fluid in a copy machine spilled several times of its own accord; and numerous problems erupted with the telephone equipment. Four telephones rang simultaneously, calls were cut short, and bills rose precipitously. In addition, sharp banging noises were heard.

The case was investigated by Hans Bender of the Institut für Grenzgebiete der Psychologie and others. Electronic monitoring equipment was installed, and large deflections in the power supply were measured in conjunction with the phenomena. Furthermore, these deflections occurred only during office hours.

The phenomena themselves seemed to be associated with a human focal point, a 19-year-old employee, Anna S. Whenever she walked down the hall, light fixtures would begin to swing behind her and light bulbs that were turned off would explode. Phenomena decreased the farther away she was. The investigators recorded the swinging light fixtures and banging noises on a video recorder.

After the investigation began, a new phenomenon arose: the movement and rotation of pictures hanging on the walls. In some cases, the pictures rotated 360 degrees or fell off their hooks. One was videotaped rotating 320 degrees.

A test apparatus attached to the telephone revealed that the time announcement number was dialed four or five times a minute by invisible means; on some days, the number was dialed 40 to 50 times in a row. Employees denied doing the dialing.

More interesting was that at the same time, four dialings of a nine-digit Munich number were registered simultaneously. According to Bender, the psychokinesis (PK) required to do this would involve a mechanical influence upon certain springs at millisecond time intervals, which would require sophisticated technical knowledge.

The investigators concluded that:

- The phenomena defied explanation in terms of theoretical physics;
- The phenomena seemed to be the result of nonperiodic, short duration forces;
- The phenomena, especially the telephone incidents, did not seem to involve pure electrodynamic effects;
- The phenomena included both simple and complex events;
- The movements, especially involving the telephone, seemed to be performed by "intelligently controlled forces that have a tendency to evade investigation."

See also SEAFORD POLTERGEIST.

Further reading:

Bender, Hans. "An Investigation of 'Poltergeist' Occurrences." *Proceedings—Parapsychological Association* 5:31–33. Durham, N.C.: Parapsychological Association, 1968.

Karger, F., and G. Zicha. "Physical Investigation of Psychokinetic Phenomena in Rosenheim, Germany, 1967." *Proceedings—Parapsychological Association* 5:33–35. Durham, N.C.: Parapsychological Association, 1968.

Rugg, Peter   See PHANTOM TRAVELERS.

Runolfur Runolfsson Case   Unusual case of a DROP-IN COMMUNICATOR who professed to be looking for a missing part of his corpse.

The case took place between 1937 and 1940 and involved one of Iceland's most famous trance mediums, Hafsteinn Bjornsson, who at the time was conducting a series of regular seances with a group of persons in Reykjavik. In the autumn of 1937, an unknown entity dropped in and identified himself by saying, "My name is Jon Jonsson or Madur Mansson. What the hell does it matter to you what my name is?" Asked what he wanted, the entity said, "I am looking for my leg. I want to have my leg." Asked where his leg might be, he said, "It is in the sea."

Thereafter, for about one year, the communicator periodically dropped in on Bjornsson, demanding his leg. The personality was crude and pushed other spirits out of the way. He also asked for snuff, rum and coffee, making the medium go through the motions of sniffing, and asking sitters to pour out an extra glass of rum or cup of coffee for him.

It was not until a fish merchant named Ludvik Gudmundsson joined the sittings that progress was made: the entity said Gudmunsson knew about his leg, which was at his house at Sandgerdi. Gudmunsson was perplexed and professed to know nothing.

The entity then gave what he said was his real name and divulged his history. His name was Runolfur Runolfsson, or "Runki" for short, and he had died in October 1879 at the age of 52. He had gone to a friend's home during a storm and had gotten drunk. He attempted to walk home, but stopped on some rocks by the shore to drink more liquor from the bottle he carried. He passed out and the tide carried him out to sea, where he drowned. His body washed back ashore in January 1880, picked and torn at by birds and animals. The corpse was buried with a thigh bone missing. Now, nearly 60 years later, the entity Runki wanted the bone back.

A search of historical records was made, and the life and death of Runki was verified. Gudmunsson asked around the village for information concerning the possible fate of the thigh bone. Eventually, he discovered that a carpenter who had built the inner walls of his house reportedly had placed a leg bone between two walls.

In 1940, one room of Gudmunsson's house was torn open and a thigh bone was discovered. It was extraordinarily long, thus supporting Runki's description of himself as a tall man. Gudmunsson took the bone to his office and kept it for a year in a coffin that he had made for it. The bone was then given a proper religious burial at Utskalar. At a subsequent seance, Runki said he had been present at the burial and reception and expressed his gratitude. He described the activities in great detail, even including cakes that were served.

Instead of disappearing, Runki stayed in contact with Bjornsson and eventually became one of the medium's main controls. Initially, Runki said he liked himself the way he was and did not want to modify his crude ways. Gradually he softened, and helped other communicators contact the medium.

Further reading:

Haraldsson, Erlendur, and Ian Stevenson. "An Experiment with the Icelandic Medium Hafsteinn Bjornsson." *Journal of the American Society for Psychical Research* 68 (1974):192–202.

————. "A Communicator of the 'Drop In' Type in Iceland: The Case of Runolfur Runolfsson." *Journal of the American Society for Psychical Research* 69 (1975):33–59.

rusalka   In Russian folklore, the spirit of a maiden who drowns by accident or by force and becomes a ghost who haunts the spot where she died.

Rusalki, as they are called in plural, are also beautiful, gentle river nymphs said to inhabit the small alluvial islands in the rivers of southern Russia, where they secretly help poor, hard-working fishermen. Although little is known about the *rusalki*, they are believed to bathe in the lakes and rivers and wring out their long green hair on the green meadows of the water's edge. They appear mostly at Pentecost when the people sing and dance, and throw their specially-woven garlands to the nymphs.

Saint-John's-wort (also St. Johnswort) A genus of perennial herbs and shrubs bearing yellow flowers (*hypericum perforatum*), believed to have the power to drive away the Devil, demons, witches, imps, fairies and ghosts.

Saint-John's-wort may have come from Assyria, where it was hung over doors during religious festivals as protection against evil spirits and influences. Because it flowers at about the time of the summer solstice (June 21 or 22), it played an important role in pagan religious rites and sun worship festivals. The Romans burned it in bonfires on Midsummer Day. The Greeks also used it in exorcism, believing that its fragrance would drive away evil spirits.

Under Christianity, the plant was rededicated to St. John the Baptist, whose birthday, St. John's Day, is observed on June 24. Medieval priests continued the customs of the Greeks in using the plant in exorcism, and it acquired the monicker "devil's flight." The Church also continued the pagan custom of gathering the plant at Midsummer Eve, to be draped about windows and doors and hung on the necks of children to protect them against illness for a year. Midsummer is not the only time the plant is effective: one may gather it any Friday and wear it on the neck in order to dispel melancholy and drive away all manner of spirits.

In the 17th century, Saint-John's-wort was often used in the exorcism of demons and ghosts, and it was said to expose witches and protect against bewitchment.

According to folklore on the Isle of Wight, if a person steps on Saint-John's-wort, a fairy horse will appear under him and race off with him for the entire night.

See also CHARMS AGAINST GHOSTS.

Further reading:
Guiley, Rosemary Ellen. *The Encyclopedia of Witches and Witchcraft*. New York: Facts On File, 1989.

Magic and Medicine of Plants. Pleasantville, N.Y.: Reader's Digest Assn., 1986.

São Paulo Stone-thrower A well-witnessed poltergeist disturbance of rains of stones and other objects that plagued the family of Don Cid de Ulhoa Centro of São Paulo, Brazil in 1959.

The disturbances began abruptly on Sunday, April 12, 1959, during preparations for a relaxed Sunday noon meal. Don Cid was reading a newspaper; his wife, Doña Regina, and the maid, Francesca, were working in the kitchen; and the three children were playing in a hallway. Suddenly there sounded two loud thumps. When he went to investigate, Don Cid was told by the children that someone had thrown two stones at them. The culprit had not been seen. Several minutes later, a veritable torrent of stones began falling throughout the entire hacienda, dropping apparently from nowhere into every room save one in which the children took cover. Though stones rained down everywhere, no one was hit. Stones ricocheted off walls, rolled wildly about the floors and bounced into the air as though propelled upward.

Don Cid attempted to discover the origin of the stones by examining their trajectories, but was nonplussed. He called in neighbors, who were equally dumbfounded at what they saw.

During the next 48 hours, the rains of stones came and went. In addition, other objects began flying about the house: crockery, pots, pans, kitchen utensils and food. Finally, Don Cid, exasperated, summoned a priest, Father Henrique de Morais Matos, for an exorcism.

First, Father Matos attempted an experiment. He seized an egg that was floating through the air and placed it in the refrigerator. Shortly afterward, he saw an egg smash against the wall of the butler's pantry. The egg did not break, but floated to the floor. Father Matos picked it up and found that it was cool to the touch. He went to the refrigerator and found that the egg he had placed there was missing.

Father Matos then performed an exorcism, and the disturbances abated, but only temporarily. Two more exorcisms also failed to solve the problem. After 40 days and nights, the haunting ceased, a inexplicably as it had begun.

The chief suspect as perpetrator of the stone-throwing was the maid, Francesca, a teenager. Francesca remained remarkably calm throughout the rains of stones, claiming that she just "knew" she would not be hurt by them. She denied any involvement in the disturbance, but local mediums stated that she unknowingly possessed great latent mediumistic powers that had attracted spirits. Francesca left Don Cid's household soon after the disturbances ended. It is possible that she was indeed a focal point for psychokinetic energy, due to repressed tensions.

See also PSYCHOKINESIS.

Further reading:
Knight, David C. *The Moving Coffins: Ghosts and Hauntings Around the World.* Englewood Cliffs, N.J.: Prentice-Hall, 1983.

Samhain See ALL HALLOWS EVE.

sar See CULT OF THE ZAR.

Saturday The last day of the week, and thus the end of a cycle, is both lucky and unlucky in superstition and folklore; some unlucky beliefs pertain to the supernatural. It is a widespread belief that persons born on a Saturday can see ghosts. In Eastern European lore, such persons are believed to be able to see vampires. In Greek lore as late as the 19th century, Saturday was held to be the proper day for killing vampires, for it was the only time during the week that vampires slept in their graves or tombs. The body would be taken out and burned.

See also GHOST SEERS.

Sauchie Poltergeist A brief poltergeist outbreak that occurred in Sauchie, Scotland in 1960–61, centered around an 11-year-old girl. Various phenomena, witnessed by five persons, were concluded to be paranormal. No discarnate or disembodied being manifested, and the most likely explanation of the cause was a combination of rapid puberty and intense, repressed emotions on the part of the girl.

The child, Virginia Campbell, was the youngest of several children of James and Annie Campbell, who were in their mid-fifties. The family was Irish, and Virginia had been raised in County Donegal. Her father worked a farm near Moville. Virginia, the only remaining child at home, appears to have been a shy child. Her only companions in addition to her parents were her dog, Toby, and another girl, Anna.

Around 1960, the Campbells decided to relocate to Scotland. One of their sons, Thomas, lived near Sauchie and worked in coal mining. In the fall of 1960, Virginia and her mother went to live with Thomas and his family while Mr. Campbell stayed behind in Ireland to dispose of the farm. Thomas's family included his wife, a daughter, Margaret, age nine, and a son, Derek, age six. Virginia was left to live with the family while her mother took a job at a boarding house in Dollar, a community some miles from Sauchie. Virginia was required to share not only a bedroom with Margaret, but also a double bed.

Virginia was enrolled in primary school. The teacher, Margaret Stewart, found her bright, well behaved and shy. She had difficulty making herself understood to the other students, and had difficulty understanding their speech.

At about this time, Virginia began undergoing a rapid pubescence.

The first disturbances began on the night of November 22, 1960 in the Campbell home. A "thunking" noise, like a bouncing ball, was heard in the girls' bedroom. When they came downstairs and into the living room, the noise followed them. It ceased when Virginia went to sleep.

The next day, Virginia was kept home from school. At teatime, the Campbells witnessed a sideboard, untouched by anyone, move out from the wall and back again. More knockings were heard all over the house that night after Virginia went to bed, but not to sleep. Several neighbors also heard the noise.

At midnight, the worried Campbells summoned a local pastor from the Church of Scotland, Reverend T.W. Lund, to the house. Lund heard the knockings and noticed they emanated from the bed head. When he took hold of it, he felt it vibrating in accordance with the knocks. Lund also witnessed a large and heavy linen chest rock, rise and travel about 18 inches. When Margaret was told to get back into bed with Virginia, a burst of violent knocking erupted, as though her presence was unwelcome.

For the next several days, through November 27, knockings and movements of objects occurred in the household. The family doctor, W.H. Nisbet, saw unusual movements and rufflings of Virginia's pillow while her head was on it. In school, Stewart witnessed a desk behind Virginia rise off the floor about an inch and settle down. Stewart immediately checked the desk to make sure it had not been manipulated through trickery and satisfied herself that it had not.

On the night of November 27, Virginia seemed to enter a "trance" in bed and called out for her dog, Toby, and friend, Anna, in Ireland.

More disturbances of noises and movements occurred at the Campbell home and at school through December 1. On that date, Nisbet and Logan set up a movie camera and a tape recorder in the girls' bedroom. Virginia retired at 9 P.M. Beginning at 10:30 P.M., a variety of noises were recorded, as well as another of Virginia's near-hysterical "trances." At 11 P.M., Lund and three other ministers conducted a rite seeking divine intercession (not the same as an exorcism), which seemed to have no effect; in fact, knockings sounded throughout the rite.

Distinctive noises included loud knocks and a rasping sawing noise. Logan attempted to reproduce the sawing noise himself by drawing his fingernails across various materials, but he could not.

Following this episode, Logan and Nisbet thought it best to curtail publicity. They announced that a "cure" had been effected. Apparently, phenomena began to diminish, for few evidential occurrences were reported after December 1. The most remarkable event occurred on January 23, 1961, with the movement of a bowl of bulbs across Stewart's desk at school. The bulbs had been placed on the desk by Virginia.

The case was investigated by A.R.G. Owen, a mathematician and parapsychologist, who interviewed the witnesses. The Campbells appeared to be well-adjusted people, and the atmosphere of their home seemed to be a stable, normal one. The phenomena were determined to be paranormal. Other incidents occurred that seemed less reliable.

Trickery on the part of Virginia, the other children, or adults was ruled out. Also, there were no geophysical conditions, such as earth tremors, tidal action or the movement of underground water, that could account for the phenomena. Finally, the movements of objects were not due to any temporary states of weightlessness, as has been theorized might happen in atmospheric drafts.

Discarnate beings were eliminated as a possible cause, for none had manifested during Virginia's "trances" or had communicated with the knockings. None of the witnesses sensed anything malign present; in fact, the phenomena had been awe-inspiring but not frightening. And, Virginia had never complained about being possessed or harassed by unseen agents.

The most likely cause was Virginia herself. Her rapid pubescence may have generated the energy to create poltergeist forces. These forces also may have been exacerbated by repressed homesickness, shyness and feelings of alienation. She may have been extremely self-conscious about her physical changes, which may explain the violent eruption of knockings on the occasion when Margaret was instructed to get back into bed with her. The "trances," which were not comparable to mediumistic trances, did give evidence of emotional upset. Finally, the entire episode may have been in part an attention-getting device.

Owen found the case similar to other poltergeist cases of record, in particular the DRUMMER OF TEDWORTH, which occurred in the 17th century in England.

See also FODOR, NANDOR.

Further reading:
Owen, A.R.G. *Can We Explain the Poltergeist?* New York: Helix Press/Garrett Publications, 1964.

Sawston Hall   The ghosts of Queen Mary Tudor (Mary I) and a Lady in Grey are said to haunt this 16th-century home in Cambridgeshire, England. The haunting appears to be tied to an incident which happened on July 7–8, 1553.

Mary Tudor (1516–58) was the daughter of Henry VIII and Catherine of Aragon. Because of her parents' divorce, she was forced to declare herself illegitimate and renounce the Catholic Church. She was later absolved by the pope. In 1553 Mary became involved in a struggle for the throne of England. Edward VI, Henry VIII's son by his third wife, Jane Seymour, was dying of tuberculosis, and was persuaded by John Dudley, the Duke of Northumberland, to confer the crown on Dudley's daughter-in-law, Lady Jane Grey, who was Henry VIII's grandniece. The people, however, rallied behind Mary Tudor.

The Duke attempted to imprison Mary. She fled, and on the night of July 7, 1553 she was taken in and hidden at Sawston Hall by the occupants, a family named Huddleston. At dawn on July 8, Northumberland's men approached the house, and Mary escaped disguised as a milkmaid. In revenge, the men burned the house down.

Lady Jane Grey's reign lasted but nine days. Mary Tudor was crowned queen and Lady Jane Grey was imprisoned and then beheaded.

In gratitude to the Huddlestons, Mary—who later was called "Bloody Mary" for her persecution of the Protestants—rebuilt Sawston Hall. A portrait of her still hangs in the Great Hall. Her ghost is seen gliding serenely through the house and moving at great speed through the gardens. The second haunting specter, the Lady in Gray (see GRAY LADIES), appears in the Tapestry Room, where she knocks three times at the door and then floats across the room.

Legend has it that Mary slept in the Tapestry Room; it is unlikely, though the four-poster bed there did survive the fire. However, those who have spent the night in "Mary's Room" report being disturbed by phantoms and sounds of rapping at the door and someone fiddling with the latch. Nocturnal tappings also have been reported in a bedroom nearby. Sounds of a spinet and a girl laughing drift through the house.

Further reading:

Folklore, Myths and Legends of Britain. London: Reader's Digest Assoc., 1977.

Underwood, Peter. *A Gazeteer of British Ghosts.* Rev. ed. London: Pan Books, Ltd., 1973.

Schneider Brothers Austrian physical mediums, Willi (1903–1971) and Rudi (1908–1957). Rudi, the younger, was one of the most celebrated mediums of his day and was studied by most of the important psychical researchers in continental Europe, England and the United States using some of the most sophisticated instruments then available. As is the rule with great mediums, however, his career did not pass without controversy.

Willi and Rudi's father was a printer in Braunau-am-Inn, Austria, where both were born. Two of their other four brothers, Hans and Karl, were also psychically gifted, although to a lesser extent than they themselves were.

It all began one night when the Schneider family was playing with a Ouija board and discovered that whatever requests they made of the board were carried out—even to the displacement of objects on the far side of the room. At one early seance, the tablecloth was slowly raised from the table, even though no one was near enough to touch it. Willi at this time was only 14, but he soon developed into a full-fledged medium, with a female control called "Olga." His seances were characterized by a range of phenomena, particularly the movement of objects without contact (see PSYCHOKINESIS and MATERIALIZATION).

Willi's fame spread until it came to the attention of the German physician and sexologist, Baron Albert von SCHRENCK-NOTZING, who undertook a study of Willi. Schrenck-Notzing had his first series of seances with Willi in 1919, when he was 16. The serious work, however, began in 1921, after the boy had finished high school, when he moved to Munich for a year and placed himself in Schrenck-Notzing's charge. Between December 1921 and July 1922, Willi held 56 seances for Schrenck-Notzing, witnessed by scientists from various fields.

Schrenck-Notzing was an experienced investigator of physical mediumship, and he knew how to limit and detect trickery. The seance room was carefully searched in advance and kept locked during seances. Willi was strip-searched and required to wear special tights, covered with luminous pins and buttons, so that any movement he made would be visible in the dark. The room was lighted with red light bulbs (white light was widely believed to be harmful to the medium) on the table in the center of the circle of sitters. The sitters joined hands, those closest to Willi holding his arms and legs. The objects he was to influence were on the table with the light bulbs, which was separated from him by a wire screen.

Under these conditions, Schrenck-Notzing and the other sitters heard rappings, felt cold breezes, and saw levitations of objects, as well as materializations of various sorts. The materializations started out as amorphous blobs, which quickly developed into various shapes, often resembling hands, arms or legs.

Among those who attended seances in 1922 were Harry PRICE and Eric Dingwall, who signed statements that they had witnessed genuine phenomena. Dingwall's endorsement was particularly important, because he had the reputation of being an inveterate skeptic when it came to physical phenomena. Both Dingwall and Price were familiar with conjuring, and both had previously exposed fraudulent mediums.

But Willi wanted to be a dentist. As he concentrated on his apprenticeship, his mediumship began to weaken. Leaving the Baron, he moved to Vienna, where he lived with a Dr. Holub, who ran a sanatorium. Late in 1924, after Holub's death, he traveled to London by invitation of the SOCIETY FOR PSYCHICAL RESEARCH (SPR), under the auspices of which he had a series of sittings. The results were disappointing. Willi returned to Braunau and continued to work with Schrenck-Notzing, but his powers were much weaker, and he soon ceased to give regular seances. He died in 1971.

Rudi Schneider began to manifest similar talents when he was 11, an even younger age than Willi. At a seance with Willi in the Schneider home, his control, Olga, declared that the "power" was not strong enough, and that she wanted Rudi to assist. Since he was asleep in bed at that hour, his parents objected. Olga said nothing in reply, but a few minutes later, Rudi, deep in trance, opened the door and joined the circle of sitters. After that night, Olga attached herself to Rudi and never spoke through Willi again. Willi's control became "Mina," another female personality.

Rudi's mediumship began to be widely publicized following a visit by Harry Price in the spring of 1926, when he brought with him a reporter from the London *Daily News*. As happened so often with Willi, there were mysterious sounds, object movements, cold breezes and materialized limbs. The reporter was impressed and wrote a series of articles describing what he had seen. But more skeptical commentary was soon to follow. The first major controversy erupted following publication in the metaphysical journal *Psyche* of a hypothesis of fraud that involved a confederate sneaking into the seance room unobserved. The article was written by an American journalist, W.J. Vinton, who had attended 10 seances along with Dingwall. Vinton's hypothesis was supported by Malcolm Bird of the AMERICAN SOCIETY FOR PSYCHICAL RESEARCH (ASPR), who attended only a single seance during which he was supposed to have been guarding the door. Another skeptic was Walter Franklin PRINCE, who attended 10 sittings and saw only some curtains blowing, which he concluded could have been contrived.

Stung by Vinton's suggestions, which of course implied the inadequacy of his experimental methods, Schrenck-Notzing arranged for a series of sittings to be conducted under a newly devised system partly of electrical and partly of tactile control. Unfortunately, before these experiments could be carried out (they were planned for 1929), Schrenck-Notzing died.

Harry Price was quick to invite Rudi to visit his National Laboratory for Psychical Research in London. Two series of experiments were conducted there in 1929 and 1930. These employed the electrical controls planned by Schrenck-Notzing, which Price extended to include the entire circle of sitters. The hands and feet of the medium and all of the sitters were thus joined in a single circuit, so that it would have been impossible for any of them to have helped out the phenomena without all knowing about it.

The experiments were highly successful, with the now familiar Schneider family effects. There were cold breezes, falls in temperature, violent movements of curtains, levitations of a waste paper basket and table, as well as materializations of arms and hands. Price, always quick to capitalize on publicity, offered a 1,000-pound award to any conjurer who could do what Rudi had done, under the same conditions. There were no takers.

Rudi's next major experimental series was arranged by Eugene OSTY at the INSTITUT METAPSYCHIQUE INTERNATIONAL (IMI) in Paris in October and November 1930. This series incorporated an infrared beam which crossed the room between Rudi and a table on which were placed objects that he was to move. At first the beam was connected to a battery of cameras, which went off automatically when the beam was crossed. This occurred quite often, but Rudi was always caught hunched in his chair, deep in trance. The cameras were then replaced by a bell, which would sometimes sound for 30 seconds or longer. Later experiments designed to measure the deflection of the beam found that it was never absorbed as completely as it would have been if it were interrupted by a material object. Whatever was crossing the infrared beam, causing the bells to ring, and at the same time sometimes moving objects on the table, was only quasi-material.

In the spring of 1932, Rudi returned for a third series at Price's lab. He was now 28 and was distracted by his fiancee, Mitzi Mangl, whom he insisted upon bringing with him. Out of 27 seances, little or nothing happened at 18 of them. At the remaining nine, however, the usual phenomena were observed, under conditions similar to those imposed by Osty at the IMI. Rudi's powers seemed to be on the wane, but they were still strong enough to confirm the earlier findings. A series of sittings arranged by the British psychologist Sir Charles Hope were even weaker in terms of observable phenomena, but once again the infrared apparatus recorded occlusions; in 27 sittings, there were a total of 84 movements of objects, but no fewer than 275 partial occlusions of the infrared beam. It was hoped to capture the occlusions on an infrared plate through a process of silhouette photography invented by the physicist John William Strutt (Lord Rayleigh), but this was unsuccessful, possibly for technical reasons. Further experiments with modifications to the apparatus probably would have been carried out, had Price not dropped a bombshell into the proceedings, just as Hope was reporting his results.

Price claimed to have photographic evidence that Rudi had managed to free an arm and move a handkerchief at sittings held at the National Institute for Psychical Research in March 1932. Although the probability that the fraud was not Rudi but Price himself was suspected at the time, a good demonstration of this was not to come for many years. Anita Gregory reviews the sequence of events in detail in her book *The Strange Case of Rudi Schneider* (1985) and shows how Price's vanity and hunger for publicity drove him to sacrifice his own later work with Rudi in order to compromise that of his colleagues. The damage to the public's perception of Rudi was severe, and in Gregory's opinion, Price's "exposure," coming as it did after so much publicity, was the greatest setback psychical research has ever suffered.

Rudi married Mitzi and gave up mediumship. He became a successful automobile mechanic, eventually owning his own garage. He died on April 28, 1957 at Weyer, Austria.

Further reading:

Gregory, Anita. *The Strange Case of Rudi Schneider.* Metuchen, N.J.: Scarecrow Press, 1985.

Inglis, Brian. *Science and Parascience: A History of the Paranormal, 1914–1939.* London: Hodder and Stoughton, 1984.

Osty, Eugene. *Supernormal Aspects of Energy and Matter.* London: Society for Psychical Research, 1933.

Price, Harry. *Rudi Schneider.* London: Methuen, 1930.

Tabori, Paul. *Companions of the Unseen.* New Hyde Park, N.Y.: University Books, 1968.

Schrenck-Notzing, Baron Albert Phillbert Franz, Freiherr von (1862–1929)

Pioneering German psychotherapist and psychical researcher, famous for his studies of physical mediumship, which earned his the nickname Gespensterbaron, or "Ghost Baron."

Baron Albert von Schrenck-Notzing was born on May 18, 1862 in Oldenburg, Germany. His was a noble family which traced its roots back to the 15th century and included civil and military functionaries employed by the grand dukes of Hanover and Oldenburg, hence his hereditary title. He studied the treatment of nervous disorders along with fellow student Sigmund Freud, and received his M.D. in 1888 for a study of the therapeutic use of hypnosis in a Munich hospital.

For a time, Schrenck-Notzing devoted himself to his medical practice, establishing himself as one of the foremost authorities of his day on hypnosis, sexuality and criminal pathology. His study of hypnotism had also introduced him to the psychic, an interest which was heightened by his acquaintance with the French physiologist Charles Richet, whom he met at a conference in Paris in 1889. The Baron translated Richet's reports on telepathy experiments into German in 1891. Through his marriage the following year to Gabrielle Siegle, who came from a wealthy industrial family, he became financially independent, and he gave up his medical career for psychical research.

Schrenck-Notzing's first foray into his new field came in the form of telepathy experiments, modeled on those of Richet. The direction of his research changed sharply, however, when Richet invited him to participate in a series of sittings with Eusapia PALLADINO at his home on the Ile de Ribaud in France in 1894. Palladino was a physical medium who, although she was not above cheating when given the chance, could produce rappings, tilt tables, and move objects without physical contact (see PSYCHOKINESIS). Although according to Spiritualism such effects are accomplished through spirit agency, Richet and his friends at the British SOCIETY FOR PSYCHICAL RESEARCH (SPR), some who were present at these sittings as well, believed them to be produced by Palladino herself, by some paranormal means.

Physical mediumship appealed to Schrenck-Notzing, fascinated as he was with the mind's unconscious workings. He began to travel throughout Europe to work with different mediums, some of whom he was able to expose as fakes. His first major subject was Marthe BERAUD, whom he met in Paris in 1909. She had been studied previously by Richet in Algiers. Unlike Palladino, Beraud did not produce raps or tilt tables, but while in trance she exuded a substance (named ECTOPLASM by Richet) which built itself up into various forms (see MATERIALIZATION). Schrenck-Notzing studied Beraud (to whom he gave the sobriquet "Eva C.") for four years, in Paris and at a laboratory he built in his home in Munich, before publishing his results.

Although *The Phenomena of Materialisation* (1913, English-language edition 1920) provides a detailed account of Schrenck-Notzing's investigations, together with those of Beraud's Paris sponsor, Juliette Bisson, and Richet, it met with immediate criticism from several quarters. The Baron's erstwhile medical colleagues were sure that he had taken leave of his senses. The public disliked the book because they found it disgusting to think that the spirits were as ugly as the ectoplasmic formations they found depicted in the accompanying photographs. And the international psychical research community, which should have been more receptive, had long since concluded that all physical mediumship was hokum, and turned a cold shoulder as well.

Nevertheless, Schrenck-Notzing persevered in his work. When a retired Austrian naval officer, who had read and been impressed by *The Phenomena of Materialisation,* wrote to tell the Baron about two brothers who were physical mediums, he arranged sittings with them. Schrenck-Notzing took up the regular study of Willi Schneider in 1919 and of his brother Rudi in 1925. When this work, too, was criticized from abroad, despite the elaborate precautions against trickery which he had instituted, Schrenck-Notzing and a German friend, Karl Kroll, developed an electrical system to be used for controlling the medium during seances. Unfortunately, before the planned program of experiments could be carried out, both men died, and the method of electric control was left to others to develop further (see SCHNEIDER BROTHERS).

Schrenck-Notzing's death came on February 12, 1929 in Munich, following an operation for acute appendicitis.

Further reading:

Inglis, Brian. *Science and Parascience: A History of the Paranormal, 1914–1939.* London: Hodder and Stoughton, 1984.

Pleasants, Helene. *Biographical Dictionary of Parapsychology.* New York: Helix Press, 1964.

Tabori, Paul. *Pioneers of the Unseen.* New York: Taplinger, 1972.

Walther, Gerda. "Schrenck-Notzing: Pioneer Researcher." *Tomorrow Magazine* (Winter 1958):38–46.

Schwalm, Maurice (1928–) Lay American psychical researcher and investigator of reports of hauntings, ghosts and poltergeists.

Maurice Schwalm was born in 1928 in Kansas City, Missouri. He earned a bachelor of arts degree in history from the University of Missouri at Kansas City in 1951, and went to work in the insurance industry.

His interest in psychical research began in 1970, when he attended seminars on 19th- and 20th-century mediumship given by Robert Ashby, research director of the SPIRITUAL FRONTIERS FELLOWSHIP. Ashby founded a psychical research group in Kansas City. Schwalm assisted Hubert Pearce, formerly a star extrasensory perception (ESP) subject of J.B. RHINE, in the research and programming for the group. Investigation techniques included "meditation circles" (similar to seances, but without a specified medium, and without deep trance); spirit photography; and the capture of paranormal voices on audio tape (see ELECTRONIC VOICE PHENOMENON).

Schwalm's investigations have included the Playhouse of the University of Missouri at Kansas City, which long had a reputation for being haunted. The ghost was said to be that of a friend of the stage manager who had died in the stage manager's arms in the lobby in 1957. The stage manager could hear her distinctive ghostly walk upon the stage, and he desired to contact her spirit. In 1970, Schwalm and a psychic visited the playhouse to conduct a meditation with the stage manager. During the meditation, the man appeared shocked and said that the ghost had slapped him with a cold hand and was laughing at him. No explanation for this behavior was given, and the manager asked to end all efforts to communicate with the ghost. At another meditation session, taped by a local television crew, an image appeared on the videotape that was interpreted as the ghost of the deceased manager standing at the top of the catwalk, where she had often stood in life. Paranormal voices also were recorded on audio tape.

Another major investigation was of Lilac Hill, a historic site in Fayetteville, Missouri that suddenly became haunted in 1977. Phenomena included sounds of chains being dragged down an upstairs hall, dead-bolts being unlocked and an invisible "something" that seemed to climb into the owners' bed at night. During a meditation circle, a spirit communicator appeared and said, "A black widow—a widow in black." It was later identified as "Miss Minnie," the last mistress of the original family that had owned Lilac Hill, and who had died in 1949. According to Schwalm's investigation of the history of the house, Miss Minnie disapproved of her brother, "Jim Bo," for his consorting with descendants of family slaves. He had also married a woman known as "the widow in black" against Miss Minnie's wishes.

Miss Minnie reportedly continues to haunt the house, and seems to have adjusted to technology. In 1987, family members heard a vacuum cleaner running in the living room, and found the equipment had been moved from where it had been left. Miss Minnie was also blamed for sounds of a vacuum cleaner in the living room, and for interfering in family quarrels with distinct odors. Children living in the house say they can see and hear her.

In 1990 Schwalm retired from his position of claims supervisor and devoted himself full time to his interests in parapsychology and the paranormal. He has written numerous articles and columns, and has contributed to anthologies of true accounts of the paranormal. In addition, he is chairman of the Occult Studies Special Interest Group of Mid-America Mensa, and is a fellow of the AMERICAN SOCIETY FOR PSYCHICAL RESEARCH, an academic member of the Academy of Religion and Psychical Research and a member of the GHOST RESEARCH SOCIETY. In 1992, Schwalm was appointed a regional coordinator by the Center for North American Crop Circle Studies. He lives in Kansas City, Missouri.

screaming skulls Ghosts in skulls are said to haunt a number of places, particularly in England. While the skulls might not be physically attached to bodies, they seem to be emotionally attached to houses where they wish to continue to live in spirit. When the skulls are removed from the house, either through burial or some disposal effort, the skulls protest with hauntings and poltergeist activity.

Many so-called screaming skulls belong to victims of religious persecution during the 16th century Reformation incited by King Henry VIII or from Oliver Cromwell's Roundheads during the English Civil War in the mid-17th century. Other skulls are from people who lost their heads in various violent episodes, such as murders.

The victims share a common wish, however, often expressed on their deathbeds, which is to be buried within the walls of the house; otherwise their spirits will not rest in peace. When their wishes are ignored with burials in a grave or vault, they reportedly protest with unexplained happenings and strange noises, such as bangs, crashes and moans. Usually, a house's occupants make the connection between the disturbances and the burial, and disinter the skull for placement within the house, atop a staircase, beam or table. One screaming skull resides in a home encased in glass.

Trouble ensues any time someone tries to rid the house of the skull. People have taken drastic measures, such as throwing the skulls in moats, lakes or rivers. They have tried to break them up, burn them, grind them to dust, or bury them in quicklime or in the walls of mountains. Nothing works.

Sometimes, it is said, the skull will settle for simply terrifying the villain with an inexplicable reappearance in its original place. More often, the skull allegedly will take its revenge by bringing the person some type of bad luck, even death to him or a relative. Violent storms or fires may destroy the property. Or, crops may fail and cattle may dry up or die.

Some of the most famous screaming skulls are:

THE WARDLEY SKULL

This screaming skull belongs to Wardley Hall, located a few miles outside Manchester, England. The skull, which dates from the reign of Edward VI, is associated with both an improbable legend and a likely tale.

The legend involves Roger Downes, a dissolute member of the family who owned the house at the time of the English Civil War. One day while in London drinking and carousing, Downes vowed that he would kill the first man he would meet. A poor, hapless tailor chanced by and Downes thrust his sword through him. Downes was arrested and tried for the murder, but his influence at court enabled him to go free.

Comeuppance was soon at hand, however. Shortly thereafter Downes was crossing London Bridge in a drunken and rowdy state. He attacked a watchman with his rapier. The watchman fought back and was strong enough to successfully sever Downes' head from his body with one blow of his weapon.

The watchman and his friends sent the head to Wardley Hall. Later, the skull was placed in an aperture in the wall above the house's main staircase, but not before several unsuccessful efforts allegedly were made to get rid of it by burning or drowning. Subsequent efforts to move the skull met with violent responses such as destructive storms.

But such a colorful story was discounted because the last Downes of Wardley, oddly enough named

Roger and also a rake, was buried in the family vault with his head intact. Rather, the skull was more likely to be that of Dom Edward Ambrose Barlow, identified in the *History of Wardley Hall, Lancashire* by H.V. Hart-Davis and S. Holme.

It seems that before the English Civil War and its religious persecutions against Catholics, Francis Downes owned Wardley Hall. He and his wife were devout Catholics and they dangerously allowed Mass to be celebrated in the Hall's chapel. Barlow, a Benedictine monk who had successfully eluded authorities for 24 years, met his fate on Easter Sunday 1641 while officiating at neighboring Morleys Hall.

Barlow was seized, arrested, tried and condemned to be hanged, drawn and quartered. His head was impaled either at a Manchester church or Lancaster castle. Downes secretly removed it and took it back to Wardley, where he hid it so well that all trace of it was lost until the mid-18th century.

At that time, Wardley was owned by Matthew Moreton, who found the skull in a box that had accidentally fallen out of a ruined wall. A servant later thought it was the skull of an animal and threw it into the moat. That night, a terrible storm broke out, and Moreton theorized that it was the skull screaming for its place to be restored in the house. Moreton drained the moat and recovered the skull.

THE BETTISCOMBE SKULL

A screaming skull that takes its name from an old farmhouse near Lyme Regis, Dorset, England, and is tied to a local legend. The skull traditionally was thought to belong to a slave from the West Indies brought to Bettiscombe Manor to serve Azariah Pinney in the 17th century.

The slave was either the victim of, or the perpetrator of, a murder. On his deathbed he stated that his spirit would not rest and would haunt Bettiscombe until his body was taken back to his homeland. Contrary to his wish, he was buried on English soil in Bettiscombe churchyard, and he thereafter fulfilled his warning by haunting the place in protest. Screams were heard from the grave, and unexplained noises were heard in the farmhouse. The noises were silenced only when the body was dug up.

Renewed attempts to bury it brought about the same noisy reactions. This procedure was repeated so often that the skeleton was lost and only the head remained. The skull finally came to rest on a winding staircase leading to the roof of the house.

The myth was shattered, however, when Professor Gilbert Causey of the Royal College of Surgeons concluded that the skull belonged to a prehistoric woman in her early twenties, perhaps a sacrificial victim meant to bring prosperity to an earlier dwelling built on the site. In spite of this pronouncement, the skull remains at Bettiscombe Manor as insurance against the professor's possible misdiagnosis.

THE BURTON AGNES SKULL

This screaming skull is associated with the North Yorkshire home built in 1598 by three sisters of the Griffith family. One sister, Ann, had a fateful meeting with robbers on a road near her home. One of the robbers struck her when she refused to part with a ring once belonging to her mother. Hearing her cries, villagers rescued the beaten woman and carried her home, where she died five days later. Ann's dying wish was that her head should be buried in the walls of her home, which was called Burton Agnes.

Instead, the family buried her under the old Norman church on the grounds. Shortly thereafter, strange noises were heard in the house. The sisters suspected that it was Ann pleading to come home. They had her coffin opened. To their astonishment, the body was completely intact while the head had become severed; the skull was grinning.

The parish priest recommended that the head be removed and taken back to the house. This the sisters did, whereupon all noises stopped. The noises did not reoccur until the house passed by inheritance to the Boynton family, who had the skull removed.

Once again, Ann made it clear that she was not to be banished from Burton Agnes. The skull again was subdued only when it came to rest on a table in the hall. Years later, another inheritor bricked the skull up somewhere behind the paneling; it still has not been found. Even though Ann's wish was finally honored, she reportedly makes a ghostly appearance around the anniversary of her death.

TUNSTEAD FARM SKULL

An imperfect skull named "Dickie," probably that of a woman, haunts a farmhouse, Tunstead Farm, near Chapel-en-le-Frith, England. According to one legend, a girl was murdered at some unknown date in the room where the skull is kept. Another legend says that Ned Dixon, an ancestor of the farmhouse's owners, was murdered in the room. The house also is said to be haunted by a woman's ghost, which appeared in the late 19th century to herald the death of the tenant's daughter.

Dickie is said to function as an unworldly guardian of the house. It has been said to sound noises and knockings at the approach of strangers. Some of these disturbances, including the rattling of farm tools in the barn, has been so severe that temporary hired help have complained and even fled the premises. Dickie also has sounded warnings upon the birthing or illness of farm animals, or upon the imminent death of a member of the family.

Like other screaming skulls, Dickie resents relocation. Once it was stolen and taken to Disley. An ensuing racket at both Tunstead Farm and Disley was so unendurable that the thieves gladly returned it. Similar disturbance broke out after the skull was buried in consecrated ground.

Further reading:
Hole, Christina. *Haunted England*. London: B.T. Batsford, 1940.

Maple, Erie. *The Realm of Ghosts*. New York: A.S. Barnes & Co., 1964.

Whitaker, Terence. *Haunted England*. Chicago: Contemporary Books, 1987.

Seaford Poltergeist The first modern investigation by parapsychologists of poltergeist disturbances in a Seaford, Long Island household in 1958. The case might also aptly be called "the bottle-popping poltergeist," as it was characterized by numerous bottles inexplicably popping their tightened screw tops and spilling their contents.

As is typical of most poltergeist cases, the disturbances began without warning, lasted five weeks, and ceased without warning or reason. The case remains unsolved.

The disturbances afflicted the James Herrmann family, whose members included Mr. and Mrs. Herrmann and their 13-year-old daughter, Lucille, and 12-year-old son, Jimmy. A cousin of Mr. Hermann, Marie Murtha, visited during some of the outbreaks.

The incidents began on February 6 and 7, 1958 with the mysterious opening and spilling of bottles in the house when the children were present by themselves. The family were devout Catholics, and Mrs. Hermann placed bottles of holy water in the house. This had no effect; in fact, the incidents escalated.

On February 9, while the entire family was in the dining room at about 10:15 A.M., they suddenly heard distinct popping noises in different parts of the house. They discovered that in the master bedroom a bottle of holy water had once again opened and was spilling its contents, and a new bottle of toilet water had opened and likewise was spilling. In the bathroom, a bottle of shampoo and a bottle of medicine had lost their caps, fallen over and were spilling. In the kitchen, a bottle of starch was spilling, and in the cellar, a can of paint thinner had lost its top and was spilling.

This was too much for the Herrmann family, and Mrs. Herrmann called the police. An officer arrived to investigate, and while he was in the house, more popping noises were heard. In the bathroom, the shampoo bottle, which had been righted and re-capped, was open again and spilling. Nothing could be found to explain the incidents.

A newspaper report came to the attention of para-psychologists J.B. RHINE, William G. ROLL and Gaither Pratt. They obtained permission from the family to investigate. Pratt and Roll spent a total of 10 days off and on with the family and were present when more bottle-poppings occurred. In addition, household objects such as figurines flew about or were upset, sometimes breaking or incurring damage. The Hermanns were so distraught that on several occasions they left the house to stay with friends. They also contacted a bishop to ask for a rite of exorcism to be performed, but they were told that the rite was not used for this kind of disturbance (apparently the haunting did not appear to be demonic in nature).

During the five weeks, 67 individual disturbances occurred, of which 64 were disturbances of objects and three were unexplained thumping sounds. All disturbances were reported to the police. Of the 64 incidents of disturbances to objects, 40 involved the same 16 objects, each of which suffered two to four disturbances. Twenty-three of the 64 object incidents were bottle-poppings.

Some of the disturbances were heard but not witnessed, while others were witnessed. Perhaps most unusual were the overturning of two bottles in the bathroom, witnessed by Mr. Hermann and Jimmy. One moved straight ahead and the other spun to the right at the same time. Both crashed into the sink.

Pratt and Roll interviewed all members of the household and attempted to find natural explanations for the incidents. To determine whether some unknown pressure was causing the bottles to pop their tops, they purchased dry ice and placed it in containers with screw caps. However, the gases that built up escaped beneath the caps without forcing them off. They succeeded in exploding a bottle made of thin glass, but the cap remained screwed to the neck.

Pratt and Roll also investigated and eliminated the following possible causes: high-frequency radio waves, vibrations in the floor, electrical malfunctions, down-drafts from the chimney, changes in the level of underground water (the house had its own well), settling of the foundation of the house, airplane noise from the nearby airport and plumbing problems.

From the outset, Jimmy was suspected as the agent of the disturbances, for they seemed to happen only when he was home, and only when he was awake.

Both Hermann and a police detective accused the boy of playing tricks in an effort to induce him to confess, but Jimmy steadfastly denied any role in the matter. Roll and Pratt concluded that fraud was un-likely, given the logistics involved in producing the effects and the complete lack of evidence that any family members were accomplices.

The poltergeist disturbance ended on March 10 with the top-popping of a bleach bottle in the base-ment. Pratt and Roll were present in the house with family members, but no one was near or witnessed the actual incident. The bottle, only partially filled, had not spilled its contents. But the cap landed right-side up and left a wet spot on the floor.

The poltergeist was not to make another appear-ance, and soon after that Pratt and Roll departed. The Hermanns apparently were not bothered again.

It is possible that Jimmy was an unwitting agent, causing what Roll and Pratt termed "recurrent spon-taneous psychokinesis" (RSPK), the spontaneous and temporary disturbances of objects. Laboratory experi-ments have demonstrated that people can influence the movement of objects in motion, such as rolling dice. It is extremely difficult, however, for test sub-jects to move stationary objects, as was the case with the Seaford Poltergeist.

The Seaford case involved no effort at communica-tion of any sort, as is sometimes the case involving poltergeists that seem to be discarnate agents.

Further reading:

Pratt, J.G., and W.G. Roll. "The Seaford Disturbances." *Journal of the Society for Psychical Research* 22 (June 1958):79–124.
Roll, William G. *The Poltergeist.* Garden City, N.Y.: Nelson Doubleday, 1972.

seance A sitting organized for the purpose of re-ceiving spirit communications or paranormal mani-festations via the services of a medium.

References to seance communications date back as far as the writings of Porphyry in the 3rd century AD. In 1659 Rev. Meric Casaubon wrote *A True and Faithful Relation of What Passed Between Dr. Dee and Some Spirits,* the first recorded seance. Not much else on such spirit meetings appeared until the meteoric rise of the FOX SISTERS in the mid-1800s. Seances were popular during the rise of Spiritualism and continue to be conducted in modern times. Early Spiritualist seances were dramatic and theatrical, taking place in darkened parlors around circular tables and featuring physical mediumistic feats. Most modern seances involve mental mediumship and are more informal.

Seances are most often held in the home of either the medium or one of the sitters, but they can take place anywhere two or more people gather for such

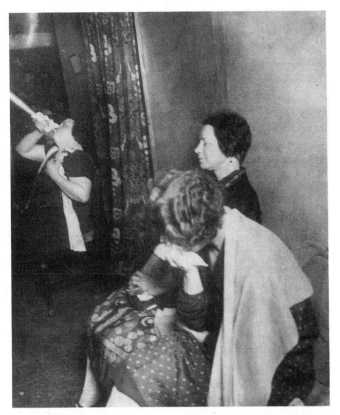

Three women at a seance. Courtesy U.S. Library of Congress.

purpose. General observances are followed to help ensure success. Participants should be nearly equally divided by gender, and younger sitters seem to exude more favorable psychic attraction than older ones. Any sitters who are worried about the proceedings or are overly skeptical should be avoided. A circular arrangement of chairs around a table seems to work best, with no more than eight sitters. Hands are placed flat on the table, fingers touching, or sometimes clasped. Several mediums, most notably the DAVENPORT BROTHERS, conducted seances for audiences numbering over a thousand.

Strangers should be admitted to the seance circle carefully, introduced only after at least six sittings have been held with the same persons. No more than two or three seances should be conducted weekly, and each should last no more than two hours unless the spirits ask for an extension. Mediums must guard against extreme swings of emotion and never take stimulants. Unwritten codes of conduct forbid sitters to grab the medium in case such a sudden jarring could jeopardize the medium's return to consciousness, causing illness or perhaps even death.

Mediums consider music and conversation to be vital to the success of the seance. Most sittings open with hymns and prayers—in many cases, the Lord's Prayer—and include songs and prayers throughout

the seance. William Stainton MOSES found that music harmonizes and soothes the situation; critics, however, believe music covers a multitude of fraudulent noises. Conversation masks noise, too, but also breaks the fear and tension created by spirit manifestations.

The furnishings of the seance room, and its location, set the tone for the sitting. Places steeped in colorful history, such as castles, catacombs, country houses and old churches, make propitious seance locales. The furniture should be simple, preferably wood, and should not be ornamented with cushions or hangings. Physical mediums once included a so-called cabinet, a kind of enclosure to attract spiritual energy. This was a piece of furniture, like an armoire, but most often it was nothing more than a corner of the room hung with black curtains. The medium went inside the cabinet for manifestations or sat outside. Modern-day mediums, most of whom are mental, seldom use such props.

Lighting, or lack of it, characterized most early seances. Mediums needed darkness to initiate spirit manifestation—critics would claim to perpetrate fraud—using either moonlight or red incandescent light. D.D. HOME often worked in full light, however, and many mental mediums do also.

In the days of physical mediumship, sitters often recognized the arrival of spirits by a rush of cool air in the room, following by rapping or strange lights. Mental mediums may enter a trance, begin automatic writing or merely announce a spirit's presence.

Not every seance is successful, and sitters should not expect particular results. First-time sitters may be disappointed, and some participants may see phenomena others miss. Nevertheless, just the anticipation of phenomena grips the imagination and jangles the nerves, raising the hair on the back of the neck. A seance is immediate and powerful, playing upon the sitters' sensibilities with a drama that no other occult reading can match. But to the initiated, the seance can open the doorway to a mysterious other world.

Further reading:
Chaney, Rev. Robert G. *Mediums and the Development of Mediumship.* Freeport, N.Y.: Books for Libraries Press, 1972.
Fodor, Nandor. *An Encyclopaedia of Psychic Science.* Secaucus, N.J.: The Citadel Press, 1966. First published 1933.
Pearsall, Ronald. *The Table-Rappers.* New York: St. Martin's Press, 1973.
Somerlott, Robert. *"Here, Mr. Splitfoot": An Informal Exploration into Modern Occultism.* New York: The Viking Press, 1971.

Seven Whistlers In English folklore, spirits that portend death. Flying together like seven birds, they sing or whistle at night to signal that one or more deaths will take place.

See also DEATH OMENS.

shamanism Spiritualistic systems in various tribal cultures characterized by nonworldly realities in which the priest, a shaman, searches for lost souls of the living, communes with various totem spirits and spirits of the dead and performs various supernatural feats. Shamanism bears many similarities to Western mediumship and seances.

The term "shamanism," from the Tungusic term *saman*, in its purest sense refers to societies in Siberia and Central Asia; it is generally applied to similar practices found elsewhere in the non-Western world. According to archeological evidence, shamanic techniques are at least 20,000 years old.

Traditionally, a person, usually a man, becomes a shaman according to heredity or by election by the "supernaturals." The latter occurs as a serious illness, of which the initiate must heal himself. During the course of the illness, he learns how to access non-ordinary realms, where he meets the spirits and souls of the dead that will assist him in his magical-spiritual work. In some cultures, shamans are called to their profession during vision quests, vigils in the wilderness in which attempts are made to receive one's destiny from the supernaturals.

After receiving the calling, the shaman undergoes rigorous training under an elder shaman. He is initiated in a rite of symbolic dismemberment, death and resurrection; in some cases, he might literally be regarded as a ghost by the villagers.

The shaman's helping spirits take many forms, including animals, birds, insects, fish, plants or spirits of the dead. Each spirit has a specific function and helps him in performing his duties. Shamans also may have a GUARDIAN SPIRIT.

When shamans are called upon to perform their offices—primarily healing and divination—they enter their nonordinary reality through techniques such as drumming, rattling, chanting, dancing, fasting, sexual abstinence, sweat baths, staring into flames, concentrating on imagery, or isolation in darkness. In some societies, the use of psychedelic drugs is employed.

Once entranced, the shaman has clairvoyance to see spirits and souls, and the mediumistic ability to communicate with them. He can travel to the heavens to act as intermediary to the gods, or descend to the underworld to the land of the dead, where lost souls roam. The kidnapping or lost ways of the souls of the living are believed to be responsible for many kinds of illnesses. Only the retrieval of the souls can effect a cure (see SOUL LOSS). Other cures are effected by "sucking" out the disease or illness with the help of the shaman's spirits.

Shamans, like some mediums, resort to sleight-of-hand tricks, particularly in sucking out sicknesses. They produce objects such as stones and pieces of bone, which they say are responsible for the illness, and then palm them to make them "magically" disappear. Some shamans contend that this sleight-of-hand has nothing to do with the real cure, but is done only to provide "evidence" to the patient and witnesses that a cure has taken place.

Like Western mediums, many shamans demonstrate their powers at seances, which take place in darkened quarters such as a tent. They may be bound at the hands and feet to prevent trickery. The seance commences with singing. Phenomena of the spirits include spirit voices, rappings and other noises, poltergeist effects, shaking of the tent, movement of objects without contact, levitations, handling of hot coals without injury, speaking in tongues (glossolalia) and the howling of animals, which are the "voices" of the spirit helpers.

The spirit helpers parallel the Western medium's controls in terms of the assistance they provide the shaman; however, they are much more dictatorial and exert much more influence upon their human being. Spirit helpers dictate to a shaman how he will dress, how he will live and what he will do. If he fails to follow their instructions, they may become unhappy with him and kill him, according to belief.

Another similarity between shamanic and Western seances is the belief that to disturb the shaman/medium before the seance is over—such as by turning on a light or interfering with the spirits—will jeopardize his or her life.

Differences also exist. Some shamans do not enter trance states during a seance. In general, a seance energizes and invigorates a shaman, whereas a seance usually exhausts a Western medium. The path to becoming a shaman is often long and painful, whereas it is seldom so for a medium. Shamans live outside the everyday life of their communities and are regarded as being part of another world. Some male shamans even spiritually change their sex, and take men as their wives; they also have "supernatural husbands" in nonordinary reality. Western mediums generally carry on mainstream lives.

Western researchers who have studied shamanism have attempted to explain its relation to Western mediumship. According to one theory, both possess an essential interconnection that harkens back to a more primitive phase of humankind's existence (see ANIMISM).

Further reading:

Barnouw, Victor. "Siberian Shamanism and Western Spiritualism." *Journal of the Society of Psychical Research* 36 (1942):140–68.

Eliade, Mircea. *Shamanism.* Princeton, N.J.: Princeton University Press, 1964.

Halifax, Joan. *Shaman: The Wounded Healer.* New York: Crossroad, 1982.

Harner, Michael. *The Way of the Shaman.* New York: Bantam, 1986.

Kalweit, Holger. *Dreamtime and Inner Space: The World of the Shaman.* Boston: Shambhala Publications, 1984.

Nicholson, Shirley, comp. *Shamanism.* Wheaton, Ill.: The Theosophical Publishing House, 1987.

Villoldo, Alberto, and Stanley Krippner. *Healing States.* New York: Fireside/Simon & Schuster, 1986.

The catfish kami *that lives at the bottom of the ocean and causes all earthquakes.*

Shinto The indigenous and animistic philosophy/religion of Japan, which provides a bridge between the living and their ancestral spirits, ancient gods and supernatural forces. Shinto is also polytheistic and shamanic in nature. The divine manifests in all natural phenomena.

"Shinto" means "the way of the *kami,*" which in turn approximately means "gods" or "spirits." Kami are not so much beings as they are transcendent, sacred forces or essences that inspire awe and reverence. Every life form possesses its own *kami*-nature, as do the elements.

Shinto has unknown origins; the earliest extant records are from the 8th century. Originally, it was not a religion, but a way of life, a philosophy of the interwoven nature of the world and the cosmos. It has no central authority, no doctrines and no scriptures. Nonetheless, it has had a powerful influence on the Japanese way of life, fostering an understanding of the interconnectedness of all things, and a need for harmony. It has integrated into it elements of Buddhist religion and Confucian philosophy.

The supreme *kami* is Amaterasu Omigami, the Sun Goddess, who is regarded as the protector of the Japanese nation and people. In myth, Amaterasu was born to Izanagi and Izanami, the *kami* who created Japan as the most beautiful place in the world. Their myriad offspring were sent to give *kami*-nature to the earth in its elements, geophysical formations, animals and people. Typically, *kami* have no names but are identified by general characteristics associated with locales, clans, villages and families. They are worshipped at communal shrines. The *kami* are believed to intervene in the affairs of humans for either good or evil, as do demons and angels. Shamanistic mediums communicate with *kami* and seek their favors or exorcise them if they are causing bad luck or illness.

Besides the *kami,* Shinto also worships ancestral spirits of clan chieftains and venerated humans who achieved great spiritual awareness during life, or who exhibited great heroism or even great evil. The remains of such persons are enshrined. Their spirits are petitioned for favors and intercession.

Shinto shrines are usually a thatched roof supported by pillars. They are located near fresh water, which is needed for purification. The gateway to the shrine, called the *tori,* marks the threshhold between the ordinary and sacred worlds. Inside the shrine are rocks or mirrors, which represent the *kami.* Symbolic offerings are short sticks with paper streamers attached.

In Shinto homes, small altars called *kamidama* ("god-shelf") are kept in a living-room closet. Family members pay homage to *kami* with daily offerings of rice, salt, water and food. Household Shinto revolves around domestic affairs and rites of passage.

During the 19th century, Shinto became a state religion in Japan; various sects developed. Alongside Shinto was tennoism, or worship of the emperor, which dates back to 3rd-century Japan. The emperor was regarded as an offspring of the creator *kami,* an *arahito gami* or "living god," and as the intermediary between the Japanese nation and Amaterasu. Following the defeat of Japan in World War II, the emperor was forced to renounce his divinity and State Shinto was abolished. It survived as a sectarian religion. When Emperor Hirohito died in 1989, he was given a Shinto burial, the first state Shinto ceremony to take place since the end of the war.

Sectarian Shinto includes sects that pursue mystical and ecstatic experiences through pilgrimages to Mount Fuji, ecstatic dancing and firewalking. Other sects devote themselves to spiritual healing. Shinto sects have been exported to the Western world and Latin America.

Household Shinto is on the decline in modern Japan, due in part to a decreasing interest on the part of young people.

See also SHAMANISM.

Further reading:
Hori, Ichiro. *Folk Religion in Japan.* Chicago: University of Chicago Press, 1968.
Parrinder, Geoffrey. *Mysticism in the World's Religions.* New York: Oxford University Press, 1976.
Picken, Stuart D.B. *Shinto: Japan's Spiritual Roots.* Tokyo: Kodansha International, 1980.

Ship of the Dead A universal motif in mythology that is a means by which the souls of the dead leave earth for the afterworld. The Ship of the Dead appears either in a cloud, or is enveloped in a driving mist. In order to reach its destination, it soars above mountains and moors and sails at sea no matter what weather and tide conditions prevail. According to one legend, upon the death of a certain pirate the Ship of the Dead appeared in a cloud. As the ship sailed over the roof of the man's house, the pirate's soul entered the ship, and sounds of a stormy sea could be heard in the house.

In Borneo, the ship is known as Tempon-teloris and appears in the shape of a bird, the rhinoceros-hornbill. Traveling along with the person's soul are all the stores which were laid out at the feast of the dead, and all the slaves who were sacrificed for the feast.

See also PHANTOM SHIPS.

Shiwanna (Cloud People) In Pueblo myth, spirits associated with the dead. The Shiwanna live in the four or six regions of the universe, each of which has its own color, or else live in the mountains, below a lake or spring, or in town by the sea. The spirits and the dead are represented by clouds and are impersonated by kachina dolls and masked dancers in kachina ceremonies.

See also KACHINA.

Shrieking Pits Circular pits at Aylmerton in Norfolk, England, said to be haunted by a figure in white that emits shrieks and agonized cries. The pits are thought to be the remains of a prehistoric settlement. The structures were built below the ground and roofed with turf to form hillocks or mounds. Such hillocks are associated with fairies in folklore, and the Aylmerton pits are said to be haunted by them.

Possible natural explanations for the eerie noises and sights are mist and the cries of birds.

Further reading:
Hole, Christina. *Haunted England.* London: B.T. Batsford Ltd., 1940.

Shug Monkey, The See BLACK SHUCK.

Sidgwick, Eleanor Mildred Balfour (1845–1936)
Mathematician and educator, for many years principal of the first women's college in Cambridge, and a leading figure in the SOCIETY FOR PSYCHICAL RESEARCH (SPR). A member of the BALFOUR FAMILY, she was married to the philosopher Henry SIDGWICK, whose intellectual qualities and interests she shared.

Eleanor Balfour Sidgwick was born March 11, 1845 at the Balfour family estate at Wittinghame, East Lothian, Scotland, not far from the border with England. She was the eldest of eight surviving children. Her father died in 1856, when she was nine, and her mother followed him in 1872. Eleanor, who was 27 at the time of her mother's death, inherited the management of Wittinghame.

Eleanor had been educated at home, there then being limited opportunities for the formal education of women in Britain. Both her parents, however, supported education and professional work for women, and she was encouraged in her study of mathematics, for which she showed a special aptitude. In her twenties, she collaborated with her brother-in-law, Lord Rayleigh, in experimental work on electrical standards of measurement, and she published three scientific papers with him.

Like other members of the Balfour family, she was interested in psychical phenomena, and she was part of a group formed in 1874 to investigate Spiritualism claims. It was through this group that she met Henry Sidgwick, whom she married in 1876. The couple were brought together not only by their mutual interest in mediumship, but by their commitment to women's education. Although her husband was elected the SPR's first president when the society was founded in 1882, Sidgwick herself did not become actively involved for two more years.

She was otherwise occupied with Newnham College, the first women's college at Cambridge, established on Henry Sidgwick's initiative in 1871. Eleanor Sidgwick served as treasurer of Newnham from 1876 to 1919, as vice principal from 1880 to 1892, and as principal from 1892 to 1910. Sidgwick's career at Newnham makes her contributions to the SPR even more impressive. She more than made up for her delay in joining the society, becoming active in research and writing and later serving in several official capacities. She edited the SPR *Journal* and *Proceedings* from 1888 to 1897.

Sidgwick reviewed the research of the group to which she had belonged in the 1870s in a paper, "Results of a Personal Investigation into the Physical Phenomena of Spiritualism," published in the SPR *Proceedings* in 1886. She concluded that although work such as that of Sir William CROOKES with D.D. HOME lent support to the possibility of paranormal physical abilities, in her personal experience she had encountered a great deal of trickery, and she judged the majority of published studies of mediumship to be substandard in design and reporting.

Sidgwick helped to compile cases for *Phantasms of the Living* (1885) and several years later, in 1918, published a one-volume abridgment. This was followed in 1922 by a long paper in the SPR *Proceedings* summarizing similar cases received by the society since the original publication of the book.

Among Sidgwick's most noteworthy analytical achievements was her book-length discussion of Leonora PIPER's mediumship, which appeared in the SPR *Proceedings* in 1915. In this influential paper, she marshalled evidence that Piper's controls behaved more like secondary personalities than independent discarnate entities. These same controls, however, often showed paranormal knowledge of events in the lives of the persons with whom they purported to be in contact, which Sidgwick interpreted as exercises of ESP on Piper's part. She discounted a survival interpretation.

Sidgwick was elected to the SPR's governing council in 1901 and served as its secretary from 1907 until her death in 1936. She was president in 1908 and 1909 and again in 1932, on the 50th anniversary of the founding of the society, when she was made president of honor jointly with Sir Oliver LODGE. These various positions allowed Sidgwick to exercise a strong influence over the SPR for much of her life. This was the more true because many of the early leaders of the society had died by the turn of the 20th century: Edmund GURNEY in 1894, Henry Sidgwick in 1900, and Frederic W.H. MYERS in 1901.

Her early experiences investigating physical mediumship proved to be formative in her attitudes toward such claims; many psychical researchers, not to mention Spiritualists, believed that her opposition to reports of such phenomena in SPR publications amounted to prejudice.

For much of her life, Sidgwick was also skeptical about whether there was survival after death, but she seems to have changed her mind in her last years. Her brother Gerald Balfour (see BALFOUR FAMILY) read her acceptance speech for her second SPR

presidency in 1932, at the close of which he said that he had been authorized to state that, while belief did not constitute proof, nevertheless Sidgwick had been brought by her long study of the evidence to a belief in survival.

Sidgwick died February 10, 1936 at her family home in Scotland. She was 91.

Further reading:

Alvarado, Carlos. "The History of Women in Parapsychology." *Journal of Parapsychology* 53 (1989):233–49.

Gauld, Alan. *The Founders of Psychical Research.* London: Routledge & Kegan Paul, 1968.

Haynes, Renee. *The Society for Psychical Research, 1882–1982: A History.* London: William Heinemann Ltd., 1982.

Inglis, Brian. *Science and Parascience.* London: Hodder and Stoughton, 1984.

Sidgwick, Eleanor. *Mrs. Henry Sidgwick: A Memoir by Her Niece.* London: Sidgwick and Jackson, 1938.

Sidgwick, Henry (1838–1900) Cambridge philosopher, founding member and first president of the SOCIETY FOR PSYCHICAL RESEARCH (SPR). Sidgwick's academic stature lent important support to the SPR in its early, formative years.

Henry Sidgwick was born May 31, 1838 in Skipton, Yorkshire, England. His father, the Reverend William Sidgwick, headmaster of the Skipton grammar school, died when Sidgwick was three, and he and three other children were raised by their mother alone. Sidgwick attended preparatory schools in Bristol and in Blackheath before entering Rugby in 1852. In 1855 he went to Trinity College, Cambridge to study classics and mathematics.

Sidgwick received several honors and upon graduation in 1859 was appointed to a teaching fellowship at Trinity. This position, however, required him to declare himself "a bona fide member of the Church of England," and this his gradually developing religious doubts no longer allowed him to do. He resigned in 1869, but the College created a position for him as lecturer in moral sciences. In 1883, Sidgwick was elected Knightbridge professor of moral philosophy, a position he held for the remainder of his life. Among his students were Arthur Balfour (see BALFOUR FAMILY), Edmund GURNEY and Frederic W.H. MYERS.

Sidgwick's interest and involvement in psychical research was longstanding. He joined the Cambridge Ghost Club at Trinity as an undergraduate. In 1860 he attended his first sitting with a professional medium; he considered this person to be "a complete humbug," but it did not dampen his interest in spiritistic phenomena. Myers recounts how on a "starlight walk" in 1869 he asked Sidgwick "whether he thought that when Tradition, Intuition, Metaphysics had failed to solve the riddle of the Universe, there was still a chance that from any actual observable phenomena—ghosts, spirits, whatever they might be—some valid knowledge might be drawn as to the World Unseen.'' Sidgwick replied in the affirmative, and in 1874 Sidgwick and Myers joined with Balfour, Gurney and others in a series of more careful investigations.

This group sat with many of the more important mediums of the day, but with discouraging results. At many sittings nothing happened; at others trickery was detected or strongly suspected. Sidgwick found the whole thing ''dreary and disappointing.'' But the investigations were important in another way; through them he became acquainted with Balfour's sister Eleanor, whom he married in 1876.

Sidgwick and Eleanor Balfour (see SIDGWICK, ELEANOR BALFOUR) shared not only a passion for psychical research, but also a dedication to the education of women. Sidgwick sponsored special courses for women beginning in the early 1870s, and in 1874 he helped to found Newnham College, the first women's college at Cambridge, of which his wife became the principal in 1892.

The disillusioning seances of the later 1870s could easily have led Sidgwick to drop psychical research from a central place in his life, were it not for the work of Sir William BARRETT, the physicist who conducted a successful series of experiments on telepathy. Barrett was instrumental in bringing together scientists and Spiritualists in an organization for the serious investigation of a broad range of psychical phenomena. Sidgwick was invited to become the first president of this new society (the SPR); he hesitated, but eventually agreed, and with his acceptance Myers and Gurney as well as other members of the earlier group also joined.

Sidgwick served as president of the SPR in 1882, 1883, and 1884. He resigned the following year to allow for a change (his place was taken by the eminent physicist Balfour Stewart), but took up the editorship of the society's publications. He then succeeded Stewart for a second period as president, this lasting from 1888 to 1892.

In 1884 Sidgwick proposed the creation of a committee to investigate the mediumistic claims of Madame Helena P. Blavatsky, cofounder of the Theosophical Society. He served on this committee during its deliberations in London, and underwrote the trip of Richard HODGSON to India to look into the case.

Sidgwick played a major role in organizing the Census of Hallucinations, conducted between 1889 and 1894 in an effort to verify the findings of the 1885 case collection, *Phantasms of the Living*, and he

appears as first author of the report, published in the SPR *Proceedings* in 1894.

Sidgwick also took part in investigations of Eusapia PALLADINO, but these only confirmed his earlier distrust of physical mediumship. At the end of his life, he had a few sittings with the mental medium Leonora PIPER; but although he was impressed by the evidence of supernormal knowledge she exhibited with some of his friends and colleagues, his own experience was once again disappointing.

Sidgwick died on August 28, 1900 of cancer, at the home of his wife's brother-in-law, John Strutt (Lord Rayleigh), in Terling, Essex.

Sidgwick's works of philosophy include *The Methods of Ethics* (1874), *Principles of Political Economy* (1883) and *Practical Ethics* (1898).

Further reading:

Berger, Arthur S. *Aristocracy of the Dead*. Jefferson, N.C.: McFarland, 1987.

Broad, C.D. ''Henry Sidgwick and Psychical Research'' *Proceedings of the Society for Psychical Research* 45 (1938):131–61.

Gauld, Alan. *The Founders of Psychical Research*. London: Routledge & Kegan Paul, 1968.

Haynes, Renee. *The Society for Psychical Research, 1882–1892: A History*. London: William Heinemann Ltd., 1982.

Oppenheim, Janet. *The Other World: Spiritualism and Psychical Research in England, 1850–1914*. Cambridge: Cambridge University Press, 1985.

silkies Female spirits, dressed in rustling silk, that inhabit the borderlands between England and Scotland. Silkies perform household chores and are traditionally valued by people living in large houses. But silkies can be perverse, too; a house that is tidy might be left disarranged, and a messy house might be put in order. A silky also can act as the guardian of a house, killing any intruder suspected of being out for harm.

See also CAULD LAD OF HILTON; POLTERGEIST.

silly how See CAUL.

silver In folklore, silver is an effective metal with magical powers for dealing with the supernatural. Silver bullets will bring down vampires, bogies, werewolves, giants, persons who lead charmed lives, sorcerers and witches, and the familiar spirits of sorcerers and witches. When familiars (usually demons in animal shape) are wounded or killed, their masters are wounded or killed in the same fashion. Silver also protects against bewitchment, the evil eye, negative influences and evil spirits. Since ancient times, it has been used in amulets to protect people, homes and buildings. Silver nails in a coffin prevent the spirit of the corpse from escaping. Some occultists believe the metal enhances psychic faculties.

Silver's power against the supernatural may have to do with its associations with the Moon, an abode of the dead in folklore and myth, the silvery glow of which powers the creatures and beings of the night and the Otherworld. The Incas considered silver to be not a metal but a divine quality, and associated it with the luster of moonlight; they called it the tears of the Moon. Alchemists call silver Luna or Diana, after the Roman goddess of the Moon. In Chinese lore, the Moon is called the silver candle.

See also CHARMS AGAINST GHOSTS.

Further reading:
Guiley, Rosemary Ellen. *The Encyclopedia of Witches and Witchcraft*. New York: Facts On File, 1989.

Leach, Maria, and Jerome Fried, eds. *Funk & Wagnalls Standard Dictionary of Folklore, Mythology, and Legend*. San Francisco: Harper & Row, 1979.

Silver Birch   See BARBANELL, MAURICE.

Slade, Dr. Henry   Perhaps the most famous slate-writing medium during the 19th century. Henry Slade (the "Dr." apparently was adopted for effect) was so adept at producing slate phenomena that scientists, journalists, royalty and even magicians came to believe in the truth of Spiritualism.

Slade's birth and early life remain a mystery. But following the epidemic of mediumistic discovery in the 1850s, Slade began holding seances in New York City about 1860–61, working in that city for 15 years. In 1876, the Grand Duke Constantine of Russia asked Theosophists Madame Helena P. Blavatsky and Colonel Henry Steel Olcott to find a suitable medium for psychic investigation by the Imperial University of St. Petersburg. After a series of tests, Blavatsky and Olcott chose Slade, who left for Europe in July.

He arrived in London on July 13 and decided to remain a while to educate the British public about the wonders of slate phenomena. He gave seances in his rooms at Russell Square, amazing sitters with writing on sealed slates, materialized hands and even levitation. A reporter from the London *World* wrote that he felt spirit pinches, saw ghostly hands, heard violent rappings and read various messages on the slates, all in full light.

Various eminent scientists and men of letters sat with Slade, and nearly all were won over. The great naturalist Alfred Russel Wallace believed completely in Slade's powers, as did Rev. William Stainton MOSES. Even a doubter like psychical researcher Frank POD-MORE, a founder of the SOCIETY FOR PSYCHICAL RE-SEARCH (SPR) in London, found the manifestations miraculous.

But not everyone was convinced. In September, E. Ray Lankester, professor of zoology at University College, London, and Dr. Horatio B. Donkin, a physician at Westminster Hospital, determined to unmask Slade. Lankester had been a member of the Selecting Committee of the British Association for the Advancement of Science but had left when the group accepted a paper on Spiritualism written by Sir William BARRETT. Lankester and Donkin each paid a pound for admission to the seance. Before the climax of the sitting, Lankester seized a slate and found writing on it before it was supposed to appear. He submitted the exposure to the London *Times* and brought charges against Slade under the Vagrancy Act for taking money under false pretenses.

The case stirred passionate controversy. Spiritualists, led by Wallace, maintained that the spirits follow no schedule and could have penned the message at any time during the seance. But when the case came to trial at the Bow Street Police Court on October 1, the magistrate, albeit impressed with the volume of Spiritualist support, ruled that he must judge based on the known course of nature. He convicted Slade and sentenced him to three months' imprisonment with hard labor.

Slade was released on bail pending appeal. When the case was reheard, the conviction was overturned on a technicality. Finding his health in decline, Slade hurriedly left England for the Continent before Lankester could issue another summons.

His plans to tour France were blocked by published accounts in Paris of his English exposure, so Slade proceeded to The Hague for a rest. From there he appealed to Lankester for a chance to prove his innocence, but the professor declined. Slade next traveled to Germany, where he mystified the court conjurer, Samuel Bellachini. He appeared in Denmark, then finally sat for the Grand Duke Constantine in St. Petersburg.

In December 1877, Slade submitted to rigorous investigation by Johann Zollner, professor of physics and astronomy at the University of Leipzig. Assisted by three other professors, Zollner became completely convinced of the genuine nature of Slade's manifestations. He published his findings in *Transcendental Physics*, which was translated into English by C.C. Massey and published in 1880. Years later the Seybert Commission, charged with investigating every facet of Spiritualism, discredited Zollner's work.

Slade toured Australia after sitting for Zollner, then returned to America. In 1885, Slade sat for the Seybert Commission in Philadelphia. They found him guilty of fraud. In 1886, Slade and his business manager were arrested for deceiving the public in Weston, West Virginia. They were later released without prosecution.

In 1883, John W. Truesdell published an expose of Slade in his book *Bottom Facts of Spiritualism.* Posing as Sam Johnson of Rome, New York, Truesdell attended a seance with Slade. He purposely left an unsealed letter in his overcoat pocket, knowing it would be searched for clues, and snooped around the seance room before the sitting. Finding a prewritten slate under the sideboard, Truesdell added the message: "Henry, look out for this fellow. He is up to snuff—Alcinda." Alcinda was the name of Slade's deceased wife.

During the seance, a message from "Mary Johnson," purportedly Sam's sister, appeared. Truesdell, alias Johnson, said that was incorrect, and Slade surreptitiously drew the seance table over to the sideboard. He stealthily retrieved the prepared slate, and he became enraged when he saw the additional message. Demanding to know who had done such a thing, Truesdell answered, "Spirits." After a pause, Slade continued as if nothing had happened.

Slade's career deteriorated rapidly after such bad publicity. He died penniless, an alcoholic and mentally unstable, in a Michigan sanatorium in 1905.

Further reading:

Doyle, Sir Arthur Conan. *The History of Spiritualism Vol. I & II.* New York: Arno Press, 1975.

Fodor, Nandor. *An Encyclopaedia of Psychic Science.* Secaucus, N.J.: The Citadel Press, 1966. First published 1933.

Houdini, Harry. *Houdini: A Magician Among the Spirits.* New York: Arno Press, 1972.

Oppenheim, Janet. *The Other World: Spiritualism and Psychical Research in England 1850–1914.* New York: Cambridge University Press, 1985.

Podmore, Frank. *Mediums of the Nineteenth Century.* New Hyde Park, N.Y.: University Books, 1963. First published as *Modern Spiritualism,* London, 1902.

Slain Legionnaires In May 1912, several companies of French Legionnaires in a lonely desert blockhouse in Algeria were witness to the strange sight of ghostly comrades walking through the sand. The case was never formally investigated but was recorded, and it remains as one of the more interesting and unusual collective apparitional sightings.

The recorder of the incident, Rene Dupre, reported that as his company and two others had marched toward the blockhouse, they were ambushed by Arab tribesmen about two miles from their destination, and five Legionnaires had been killed before the tribesmen were sent in retreat. The dead were buried

immediately, and stones were piled on the graves to prevent marauding by animals.

Two weeks after the incident, Dupre was standing guard one night when, after midnight, he spotted the lone figure of a man approaching in a staggering and zigzag fashion. As it grew closer, Dupre, aided by moonlight, was able to see that the figure was dressed in a Legionnaire's uniform. Then he suddenly realized that he could see through the figure.

Dupre summoned others, who gathered to watch the figure stagger about as though searching for something. One of the men recognized it as Leduc, one of the slain soldiers. At that moment, the phantom dissolved.

Leduc's ghost did not appear again until four nights later, at about 1:30 A.M. Again the ghost staggered about and then vanished. One of the soldiers on guard duty claimed he could see blood on the phantom's face; Leduc had been shot in the temple.

Three nights later, Dupre was again on night guard duty when he and several others spotted another lone phantom. This figure, which also zigzagged about, was identified as another one of the ambushed dead, Sergeant Schmidt. The ghost of Schmidt reappeared two nights later.

No one could explain the odd movements of the ghosts, until one of the Legionnaires suggested that Leduc and Schmidt were looking for each other—they had been close friends in life.

On the 15th night from the time that Dupre had first spotted Leduc, he and about 30 other Legionnaires were up watching the sands. At about 2:00 A.M., two ghostly figures were sighted, marching together along the sand. They were too distant to be identified, but of course, everyone assumed them to be Leduc and Schmidt, together at last in spirit. The ghosts were observed for about one minute before they disappeared over a dune, one of them raising an arm as if to signal farewell. The ghosts were never seen again.

Further reading:

Knight, David C. *The Moving Coffins: Ghosts and Hauntings Around the World.* Englewood Cliffs, N.J.: Prentice-Hall, 1983.

slate writing The appearance of writing on a blank slate, allegedly through the intervention of the spirits. Slate writing also is called psychography.

Unlike most other mediumistic phenomena, slate writing seemed to offer many early Spiritualists irrefutable proof of spirit presence. The seances could be held in full light, conditions presented ample opportunity to guard against fraud, and most sittings produced results. Many believers testified that as they watched the medium the entire time, chicanery was impossible. However, trickery was often employed.

Students no longer use slates for schoolwork, but in the 19th century they were a common tool and were available everywhere. Slates came in single or double, hinged models, usually framed; the double slates could be latched. Sitters often brought their own new, clean slates to the seance, locked and sealed, and were amazed to find the blank surfaces covered with writing by the spirits.

A slate-writing seance usually proceeded as follows: After the slates had been thoroughly washed and examined, a sitter would ask a question aloud, or, to be even more secretive, would seal a question in an envelope. The medium would then hold the slate at one end underneath the tabletop with the fingers of his right hand and would keep his thumb above the table. The sitter would hold the other end with one hand and grasp the medium's left hand with his or her other one. In this rather awkward position it was difficult for the sitter to observe the slate or the medium's fingers under the table. Soon, scratchy writing sounds would be heard, followed by two or three raps when the spirits were finished. And there would appear the answer, even to the sealed question.

A variation of slate-writing perfected by Kate Fox (see FOX SISTERS) was called "mirror-writing"; the medium wrote backward on the slate and held it up to a mirror to read. Another manifestation produced pictures on the slates instead of words.

The most famous slate-writer was "Dr." Henry SLADE. He conducted seances in New York for 15 years before receiving the endorsement of Madame Helena Petrovna Blavatsky and her associate, Colonel Henry Steel Olcott, the cofounders of the Theosophical Society. Olcott recommended Slade for study at the University of St. Petersburg in Russia. En route to St. Petersburg in July 1876, he stopped in London to introduce the British to slate-writing. Several scientists and scholars found no indications of trickery and left Slade's seances convinced of supernormal agencies. He was later exposed as a fraud, however, by Prof. E. Ray Lankester and Dr. Horatio B. Donkin and was convicted of taking money under false pretenses. The conviction was overturned on a technicality and Slade rapidly left England.

His career continued for a few years, but he lost his place of supremacy to William Eglinton and Dr. Francis Ward Monck, who also were later suspected of fraud. One member of the SOCIETY FOR PSYCHICAL RESEARCH, S.J. Davey, became so adept at reproducing Slade's effects that he held seances himself. Al-

though he never tried to pass himself off as a medium, even sitters who knew he conjured the writing still believed the spirits had had a hand.

Magicians such as J.N. Maskelyne and Harry HOUDINI showed the public that there were two basic ways of producing the slate-writing phenomena. The first was to attach a tiny bit of slate pencil to a ring on one of the fingers holding the slate under the table and use it to scratch out an answer. Once the answer had been written, the medium would suffer a nervous spasm, or a coughing spell—anything to divert the sitter's attention—and deftly flip the slate over, so that it appeared the writing had formed on the side up under the tabletop. The writing was understandably crude and often illegible. Some mediums even learned how to write with their feet.

The other method involved writing out the answer beforehand and switching the slates while the sitter's attention was again diverted. The substitute could be hidden on the medium's person or in or near the furniture or could even be provided by a confederate from another room. Often the seance would be interrupted by a knock at the door, and the medium would rise to answer a seemingly unrelated question. Slates would be surreptitiously switched before the medium returned. Too often the sitter was so completely bowled over that this interruption was overlooked. Penmanship vastly improved with this technique.

Another method involved writing the message beforehand and concealing it with a flap of silicated gauze, or thin slate. One side of the flap is covered with fabric to match the table covering, and when laid down is not noticed. An even better method was to use newspaper and drop the pre-written slate on another newspaper, where it would be camouflaged.

Trick slates and manipulation of the hinge mechanisms allowed proficient slate-writing mediums to produce writing on the inside surfaces of a locked double slate. If the medium was a good talker, he could switch slates even over a sitter's head without his or her knowledge. Other mediums used confederates to read the questions and provide the answers, then make the switch. A few employed trap panels or trap doors in the seance room for the assistants to use. Especially talented slate-writing mediums prepared their slate pencils with iron filings, then used a magnet to pull the pencil and write backwards. This technique necessitated using a mirror as Kate Fox had done.

To draw pictures on the slates, the medium covered the entire slate with slate pencil or chalk, rubbing lightly until the surface was white. Then pictures cut from magazines or newspapers (it was suggested to leave about a one-inch margin around the lines) were wet and laid on the powdered surface. Taking a pencil, the medium traced the lines of the picture, allowed the paper to dry and then removed it, leaving an excellent impression.

As for the sealed questions and slates provided by the sitters, a talented medium could insert a tiny wire prong in the small unsealed part of an envelope, twirl the wire and pull the message out through the opening, read it and return it. The envelope remained sealed. And since slates were so commonplace, most mediums kept a supply of all the available types, ready to replace in any situation.

Finally, if the slate-writing medium needed more help than he could devise on his own, firms such as the Ralph E. Sylvestre Co. in Chicago offered trick slates of all types through a mail-order catalogue entitled "Gambols With the Ghosts."

Further reading:

Cannell, J.C. *The Secrets of Houdini.* New York: Bell Publishing Co., 1989.

Douglas, Alfred. *Extra-Sensory Powers: A Century of Psychical Research.* Woodstock, N.Y.: The Overlook Press, 1976.

Doyle, Sir Arthur Conan. *The History of Spiritualism Vol. I & II.* New York: Arno Press, 1975.

Fodor, Nandor. *An Encyclopaedia of Psychic Science.* Secaucus, N.J.: The Citadel Press, 1966. First published 1933.

Houdini, Harry. *Houdini: A Magician Among the Spirits.* New York: Arno Press, 1972.

Mysteries of the Unknown: Spirit Summonings. Alexandria, Va.: Time-Life Books, 1989.

Oppenheim, Janet. *The Other World: Spiritualism and Psychical Research in England 1850–1914.* New York: Cambridge University Press, 1985.

Podmore, Frank. *Mediums of the Nineteenth Century.* New Hyde Park, N.Y.: University Books, 1963. First published as *Modern Spiritualism*, London, 1902.

Smurl Haunting The home of Jack and Janet Smurl in West Pittston, Pennsylvania, was the scene of an alleged terrible, terrifying haunting from 1985 to 1987. The case received wide attention in the media. Although the house went through three exorcisms and investigation by demonologists Ed and Lorraine Warren, the demon apparently refused to leave. Skeptics, however, considered the case to be a hoax, or at the least not to be caused by anything paranormal. The alleged hauntings were chronicled in a book and portrayed in a movie.

The house involved is a duplex, built in 1896 on a quiet street in a middle-class neighborhood. After Hurricane Agnes flooded much of northeastern Pennsylvania in 1972, the Smurl family was forced to leave their home in Wilkes-Barre. Jack's parents, John and Mary Smurl, bought the house in West

Pittston in 1973 for $18,000. They lived in the right half, and Jack, Janet and their first two daughters, Dawn and Heather, moved into the left half. The Smurls spent time and money redecorating and remodeling, doing much of the work themselves.

The Smurls say they are a close, loving family. Both Jack and Janet grew up in the area, meeting in 1967 and marrying in 1968. Jack served in the Navy, becoming a neuropsychiatric technician. Both Smurls were brought up in practicing Catholic homes and have strong religious beliefs. They enjoyed living with Jacks' parents and had no trouble sharing the duplex with them. The first 18 months on Chase Street were happy ones.

But strange things began to occur after that, according to the Smurls. In January 1974, a strange stain appeared on new carpet. Jack's television set burst into flame. Water pipes leaked even after repeated soldering. The new sink and bathtub in the remodeled bathroom were found severely scratched, as if a wild animal had clawed at them. Freshly painted woodwork in the bathroom showed scratches as well. In 1975, their oldest daughter Dawn repeatedly saw people floating around in her bedroom.

By 1977, the Smurls realized their house was in some way spooked. Toilets flushed without anyone using them. Footsteps were heard on the stairs; drawers opened and closed when no one was in the room. Radios blared even when unplugged. Empty porch chairs rocked and creaked. Strange sour smells filled the house. Jack felt ghostly caresses. By now there were two more Smurls (twins Shannon and Carin were born in 1977), and the family was tired of the nonsense.

In 1985, what had been annoying disturbances became frightening experiences. The house was often ice cold. John and Mary Smurl heard loud and abusive, obscene language coming from Jack and Janet's side when they were not even arguing. Then in February, Janet heard her name called several times when she was alone in the basement.

Two days later, icy cold announced the arrival of a black human-shaped form, about five feet nine inches tall, with no facial features. First it appeared to Janet in her kitchen, then it dematerialized through the wall and appeared to Mary Smurl.

From that point on, the haunting increased, according to the family's reports. A large ceiling light fixture crashed down on Shannon, nearly killing her, on the night 13-year-old Heather was to be confirmed. Jack levitated. In June, Janet was violently pulled off her bed after making love to her husband, while Jack lay paralyzed, gagging from a foul odor. The family's German shepherd, Simon, was repeatedly picked up, thrown around or whipped. Terrible rapping or scratching noises were heard in the walls. Phantom dogs ran through the duplex. Shannon was tossed out of bed and down the stairs. Invisible snakes hissed, bedspreads were shredded, and heavy footsteps crossed the attic. Even neighbors were not spared; several heard screams and strange noises coming from the house when the Smurls were not there, and other detected the presence in their own homes. Most of the neighbors were sympathetic. The Smurls vowed to fight.

In January 1986, Janet heard about Ed and Lorraine Warren, psychical researchers and demonologists from Monroe, Connecticut. Although skeptical, the Smurls called the Warrens. When the Warrens arrived, accompanied by Rosemary Frueh, a registered nurse and psychic, they began the investigation by quizzing the Smurls carefully about their religious beliefs, the happiness of their family life and whether they had ever practiced Satanism, used a Ouija board or in any way invited the supernatural into their home. Then the Warrens and Frueh walked the house, identifying the bedroom closet as the crossover point between the two sides of the duplex. The team said they detected the presence of four evil spirits. Three were minor, but the fourth was a demon.

Without any evidence of family discord, occult invitation or tragedy, the Warrens could only surmise that the demon must have been dormant, probably for decades, and had risen to draw on the emotional energy generated by the girls' entrance into puberty.

The Warrens tried twice to get the demon to expose itself by playing tapes of religious music and confronting it with prayer. The demon reacted by shaking the mirror and dresser drawers; another time by spelling out "You filthy bastard. Get out of this house." The portable television emitted an eerie, silvery white glow. Only prayer and holy water seemed to stop the manifestations.

Phenomena continued. The eerie glow returned, the pounding in the walls worsened, Jack and Janet were slapped, bitten and viciously tickled. Small items disappeared. One day, Janet tried to talk to the demon, asking it to rap once for yes and twice for no. When she asked the demon if it were there to harm them, it rapped once. Two women dressed in Colonial clothing appeared to Jack.

Even more horrifying, Jack was raped by a scaly succubus posing as an old woman with a young body. Her eyes were red and her gums green. Ed Warren was choked and also suffered terrible flu symptoms. An incubus sexually assaulted Janet, and pig noises (supposedly signs of a serious demonic infestation) could be heard in the walls.

The Smurls said they tried several times to obtain support and action from the Church. The Roman Catholic Diocese of Scranton said it would consult with experts, but official involvement seemed unlikely. At one point, Janet thought she was getting help from a Father O'Leary, but discovered he didn't exist: it was the demon allegedly impersonating a priest.

The Warrens brought in Father (now Bishop) Robert F. McKenna, a traditionalist priest who refused to abide by the changes in ritual mandated by the Second Vatican Council. He said mass in Latin and had performed more than 50 exorcisms for the Warrens. He conducted the ancient rite, infuriating the demon.

The haunting continued. Daughter Carin fell seriously ill from a strange fever and nearly died. Dawn was nearly raped by the presence. Janet and Mary had slash marks and bites on their arms. Everyone was depressed. Ed Warren explained they were in the second demonic stage, oppression, which follows infestation and is followed by possession and death.

McKenna performed a second exorcism in late spring, but to no avail. The demon even accompanied the family on camping trips in the Poconos and harrassed Jack at work. The family could not move to another house since the demon would just follow. After repeated refusals by the Church to help, the Smurls decided to appear on television.

Remaining anonymous behind a screen, the Smurls were interviewed by Richard Bey on a local Philadelphia talk show called "People Are Talking." The demon retaliated. It levitated Janet and then hurled her against the wall. It appeared to Jack as a monstrous creature resembling a pig on two legs. A human hand came up through the mattress and grabbed Janet by the back of the neck. Jack was raped again.

In August 1986, the Smurls felt that the risk of ridicule did not outweigh the need to tell their story to a wider audience and granted an interview to the Wilkes-Barre *Sunday Independent* newspaper. Almost immediately their home became a tourist attraction for the press, curious onlookers and skeptics who wished to investigate. Some skeptics, who included some of the Smurls's neighbors, said they believed the family was concocting a story in order to profit from book and movie contracts.

Paul Kurtz, chairman of the COMMITTEE FOR THE SCIENTIFIC INVESTIGATION OF CLAIMS OF THE PARANORMAL (CSICOP) in Buffalo, New York, sought to investigate but was rebuffed by the family and the Warrens. Kurtz proposed to put up the family for a week in a hotel with a private security guard while a team of investigators examined the house. Kurtz also offered free psychiatric and psychological examinations, which might have provided clues to the alleged activity. The Smurls said the people at CSICOP had already made up their minds that their story was a hoax, and they preferred to work with the Warrens and the Church. Two CSICOP investigators went to the Smurl house but were denied entrance. Kurtz later opined in an article he wrote for *Skeptical Inquirer*, CSICOP's journal, that the case was not paranormal, and the Smurls had denied CSICOP access because they were afraid of what the organization would discover. He cited discrepancies in Dawn Smurl's accounts of her experiences and was critical of the involvement of the Warrens. Kurtz suggested natural explanations for some of the phenomena experienced by the Smurls, including:

- abandoned mine voids in the area settling and creating strange noises;
- delusions by Jack Smurl that he was raped by a ghost;
- a broken sewer pipe causing foul smells;
- pranks by teenagers.

Kurtz also pointed out that there were no police records of complaints of the haunting by Mrs. Smurl, though she said she contacted police. Kurtz also wondered about the motivation to make money on the case, since the Smurls began talking with Hollywood film companies shortly after the story broke in the press. The Smurls denied any interest in money.

Ed Warren raised more doubts among reporters and skeptics during a press conference he called in late August 1986. Warren said they had recorded paranormal sounds—groanings and gruntings—and had videotaped an unclear image of a dark mass moving about the house. Asked by journalists and CSICOP to produce the tapes, he declined. He told one journalist he had given the tapes to a TV company, the name of which he could not remember, and he told Kurtz and other reporters that the tapes were in the exclusive possession of the Church. However, Church authorities later said nothing had been turned over to them.

Warren also declined reporters' requests to stay in the house, saying that no one had paid attention when the Smurls had first begged the media to spend a night to witness phenomena, and that such requests were now out of the question. Warren said the Smurls would no longer deal with the press, and he was in charge of the case.

The Smurls contacted a medium, Mary Alice Rinkman, who examined the house and corroborated the Warrens' finding of four spirits. She identified one as a confused old woman named Abigail and another as a dark mustachioed man named Patrick who had murdered his wife and her lover and had then been hung by a mob. She could not identify the third, but the fourth was a powerful demon.

Press coverage finally pushed the Scranton diocese into action, and they archly offered to take over the investigation. The Warrens, meanwhile, planned a mass exorcism with several priests. Prayer groups came to the house to give comfort. Rev. Alphonsus Travold of St. Bonaventure University, asked by the diocese to investigate, said he believed the Smurls were sincere and disturbed by the events, but he could not say whether demonic presence was the true cause.

McKenna came a third time to exorcise the house in September 1986; this time the ritual seemed to work. There were no disturbances for about three months.

Right before Christmas 1986, Jack again saw the black form, beckoning him to the third stage of possession. He clutched his rosary and prayed, hoping this was an isolated incident. But the banging noises, terrible smells and violence started again.

The Smurls moved to another town shortly before the book about their ordeal, *The Haunted*, went to press in 1988. The Church performed a fourth exorcism in 1989, which finally seemed to give them peace. A movie version of *The Haunted* was released in 1991.

Further reading:

Anzalone, Charles. "Claims That House Is Haunted Touch Off Spirited Debate." *Buffalo News* (August 27, 1986).

Collins, Jim. "Alternatives to Occult Events May Explain Smurl's Claims." *The Scrantonian-Tribune* (November 2, 1986).

Curran, Robert. *The Haunted: One Family's Nightmare.* New York: St. Martin's Press, 1988.

Kurtz, Paul. "A Case Study of the West Pittston 'Haunted' House." *The Skeptical Inquirer* 11 (Winter 1986–87):137–46.

Marusak, Joseph. "Scientists Offer Smurls Free Psychiatric Help." *Wilkes-Barre Times Leader* (August 19, 1986).

O'Connor, John J. "Confronting the Supernatural at Home and in the Past." *The New York Times* (May 6, 1991):B-3.

Rotstein, Gary, "Town Is Divided over 'Haunted' Family." *Pittsburg Post-Gazette* (August 25, 1986).

Society for Psychical Research (SPR) The first major organization for scientific research into the paranormal was founded in 1882 in London. The

Society for Psychical Research (SPR) arose in part out of popular interest in Spiritualism and an interest in bringing science and religion together with scientific validation of Spiritualist phenomena. Early topics of research included hypnosis and multiple personality, extrasensory perception (ESP), poltergeists, apparitions and mediumship.

The SPR had its origins in the interest in Spiritualist phenomena of Henry SIDGWICK, Frederic W.H. MYERS and Edmund GURNEY, all Fellows of Trinity College at Cambridge. In 1873, Myers became intrigued after sitting at a seance conducted by the medium C. Williams, who purportedly materialized the huge and hairy hand of the spirit control John KING. Sidgwick was skeptical but agreed to participate in investigations. Myers then organized an informal group of upper-crust individuals whose members included Gurney, Arthur Balfour and his sister Eleanor (see BALFOUR FAMILY), and others. Eleanor married Sidgwick in 1876. The group became known as the "Sidgwick group." Myers, probably the most enthusiastic member about mediumship, was usually the first to identify a medium and initiate an investigation. Often, however, the investigations exposed fraud.

Meanwhile, other societies were also conducting scientific investigations, including the London Dialectical Society, formed in the late 1860s, and various Spiritualist organizations. Sir William BARRETT advocated a new society in 1882. It was formed from Spiritualists and the Sidgwick group, and called itself the Society for Psychical Research. Sidgwick was elected the first president.

Six research committees were established to pursue thought-transference (later renamed telepathy by Myers); mesmerism, hypnotism, clairvoyance and related phenomena; "sensitives;" apparitions and hauntings; physical phenomena associated with Spiritualistic mediums; and the collection and collation of data on all those subjects.

The Sidgwicks attracted eminent scientists and scholars to the SPR, among them Sir William CROOKES, Sir Oliver LODGE, Sir Arthur Conan DOYLE, William JAMES, and later Sigmund Freud, Carl G. Jung and others. In 1885, the SPR helped found the AMERICAN SOCIETY FOR PSYCHICAL RESEARCH (ASPR).

The SPR's investigations of Spiritualism, which failed to scientifically validate survival after death and exposed many mediums of fraud, contributed to the decline of interest in physical mediumship. By 1887, many Spiritualist members felt the SPR was not serving Spiritualism well, and departed.

By 1900 the SPR had produced 11,000 pages of reports and articles. In addition, substantial works included *Phantasms of the Living* (1886), by Gurney, Myers and Podmore, a comprehensive study of apparitions, and *Human Personality and the Survival of Bodily Death* (1903), by Myers, an examination of evidence for survival after death.

By 1910, the key male members of the Sidgwick group were dead and the Sidgwick era came to an end. However, they reportedly communicated through various mediums and in cross correspondences (q.v.).

In the 1940s, the SPR, like the ASPR, began to devote more attention to laboratory experiments, though to a lesser degree. The SPR is more active than the ASPR in investigation of poltergeists and apparitions.

The SPR defines its current fields of study as:

- The nature of all forms of paranormal cognition, including telepathy, clairvoyance, precognition, retrocognition, remote viewing, psychometry, dowsing and veridical hallucinations of various kinds;
- The reality and nature of all forms of paranormal action, including PK, poltergeist phenomena, teleportation and human levitation;
- Altered states of consciousness in connection with hypnotic trance, dreaming, out-of-body experiences, near-death experiences and sensory deprivation, as well as the paranormal effects that appear to be associated with them;
- Phenomena associated with psychic sensitivity or mediumship, such as automatic writing, alleged spirit communication and physical manifestations;
- Evidence suggesting survival after death and evidence suggesting reincarnation;
- Other relevant phenomena which appear, *prima facie*, to contravene accepted scientific principles;
- Social and psychological aspects of such phenomena, within and across cultural boundaries;
- Development of new conceptual models and new ways of thinking concerning the application of accepted scientific theories to the findings of psychical research. Of particular interest is the subject of time.

Research articles are published in a *Journal* and *Proceedings*, while informal articles appear in the *Newsletter* and *Newsletter Supplement*.

Further reading:

Brown, Slater. *The Heyday of Spiritualism.* New York: Hawthorn Books, 1970.

Douglas, Alfred. *Extrasensory Powers: A Century of Psychical Research.* London: Victor Gollancz Ltd., 1976.

Gauld, Alan. *The Founders of Psychical Research.* London: Routledge & Kegan Paul, 1968.

The weighing of souls in the afterworld court of Osiris. The heart is weighed against the feather of truth. The hearts of good souls are lighter and the hearts of guilty or bad souls are heavier. From an ancient Egyptian papyrus.

Haynes, Renee. *The Society for Psychical Research: 1882–1982: A History*. London: Macdonald & Co., 1982.

soul The concept of "soul" is difficult to define, because it has been used in different ways in different contexts. In essence, it refers to the life-force of an individual, as distinguished from that person's physical body. A tripartite distinction of body, soul and spirit is sometimes made. In this case, "spirit" denotes the life-force, whereas "soul" refers to an individual's core identity. In all religious traditions except classical Buddhism, the soul is held to be immortal, although it may be associated with a series of physical bodies in different lifetimes (see REINCARNATION).

The Buddhist doctrine of *anatta*, or "no soul," teaches that the soul is a figment of the human imagination, from which it follows that it is incapable of survival after death (q.v.). Reincarnation results from karma—the effect of all actions, good and bad—and does not involve the transmission of consciousness or personality between lifetimes.

According to Christianity and the other major religions of the West, an individual's soul is created by God at the beginning of each new life and deposited by Him in that person's body. After the body's demise, the soul is not extinguished, but continues to exist in an afterworld. Christians hold that the individual will eventually have a bodily resurrection.

Tribal cultures such as the Native Americans, Africans or Australian Aborigines, have a more complex system of beliefs about the soul (see ANIMISM). In some societies, one finds the belief that the body is home to more than a single soul at a given time. In some belief systems, different souls are inherited from each parent and are transmitted through members of the appropriate sex to their children. In other cases, different souls are responsible for different bodily functions—one may be associated with the breath, another with the intellect, a third with the bones, and so forth.

Almost always one or the other of these souls is believed to be separable from the body during life, and the wanderings of this soul are believed to be responsible for dreaming and for illness, the permanent departure of the soul resulting in death (see SOUL LOSS). After death, the soul (or spirit) may separate into two or more parts, perhaps becoming a ghost, an ancestral spirit, and a reincarnating spirit—thus, no contradiction is recognized between reincarnation and survival in the afterlife. The soul or spirit is believed to be a body double, and is sometimes equated with a person's shadow.

In Spiritualism, the concept of soul is midway between that found in Western religions and in animism. The soul is conceived as discrete and indivisible, and each person is normally allotted one, and only one. The soul, however, is detachable from the body and may leave it, as during out-of-body experiences and near-death experiences. The astral body is conceived as a "vehicle" for the soul, if not as a reflection of the soul itself. Apparitions, likewise, are considered by many to be appearances of the astral body.

On the assumption that the soul is quasi-physical and has some mass, attempts have been made to weigh the body at death in hopes of finding evidence of the soul. In the most famous experiment of this sort, conducted by Duncan McDougall in 1907, five patients were weighted as they died. In two cases, there was an initial abrupt weight loss of one-half ounce, followed by a second abrupt loss of one ounce, within three minutes of death. In a third case, there was a slight weight loss, followed by a great weight gain, then a weight loss after 15 minutes. However, these results are not scientifically conclusive.

Further reading:
Alvarado, Carlos S. "The Physical Detection of the Astral Body: An Historical Perspective." *Theta* 8 (1980):4–7.
Broad, C.D. *Religion, Philosophy and Psychical Research*. New York: Humanities Press, 1969.
Kung, Hans. *Eternal Life? Life after Death as a Medical, Philosophical and Theological Problem*. Garden City, N.Y.: Doubleday, 1984.
Myers, Frederic W.H. *Human Personality and Its Survival of Bodily Death*. 2 vols. New York: Longmans, Green, 1903.

Radhakrishnan, R. *2500 Years of Buddhism*. New Delhi: Ministry of Information and Broadcasting, 1956.
Tylor, Edward Burnett. *Religion in Primitive Culture*. New York: Harper and Row, 1956.

soul cakes See FEASTS AND FESTIVALS OF THE DEAD.

soul loss Explanation for illness and death among tribal peoples around the world. The temporary departure of the soul from the body may cause illness; its permanent departure results in death.

In the animistic system of beliefs (see ANIMISM), a person's soul or one of his or her souls is believed to be detachable from the body and to wander at night during dreams. Some persons, notably shamans, are believed to be able to will and control such wanderings, which may in fact be out-of-body experiences. Such wanderings are considered normal and are not a cause of concern, except when the soul for one reason or another cannot find its way back to its body.

Soul loss may have a variety of causes, besides the simple inability of the soul to find its way back home. Sometimes it occurs because the ghost of a recently deceased person has managed to draw the soul away (see GHOST SICKNESS). Soul loss may also be due to witchcraft or sorcery or the action of malevolent supernatural beings, or it may result from external injury or physical shocks to the body. One may kill a person by waking him or her suddenly, before the soul has returned from its nocturnal wanderings.

The illnesses that result from soul loss are especially of a psychological nature. Fainting fits, epileptic seizures, comas, and various other losses of consciousness are good indications of soul loss.

Upon its departure from the body, the soul usually heads for the land of the dead, and the closer it approaches this goal, the weaker and more delirious its owner becomes. When soul loss occurs, it is the task of the shaman to search for the soul and to restore it to its body. This is usually possible so long as the soul has not yet reached the land of the dead, although if the illness has been caused by sorcery or through the action of some discarnate entity, the shaman may have to enter into a spiritual tug-of-war with the offending party.

Soul loss may also occur without its owner feeling any ill effects. In these cases, the person does not know that his soul has been away until he is informed by the shaman, who may have become aware of the situation in a dream and have taken steps to correct it.

See also SHAMANISM.

Further reading:
Eliade, Mircea. *Shamanism*. Princeton, N.J.: Princeton University Press, 1964.
Hultkrantz, Ake. *Conceptions of the Soul among North American Indians*. Stockholm: Ethnographic Museum of Sweden, 1953.
Tylor, Edward Burnett. *Religion in Primitive Culture*. New York: Harper, 1956.

Spiricom See ELECTRONIC VOICE PHENOMENON.

spirit A discarnate being, essence or supernatural force of nature. Spirits may also represent places, such as the spirits of mountains, lakes, trees and especially any site considered to be sacred.

Spirits proliferate in the religions and folklore of the world. Generally, they are believed to exist in an invisible realm that can be seen under certain circumstances or by persons with clairvoyance, and they are believed to intervene regularly in the affairs of humanity, for better or worse. Spirits come in a multitude of guises, such as fairies, elves, dwellers of homes and work places (see KNOCKERS; KOBOLDS), monsters, demons and angels. In ANIMISM, spirits personify primal qualities, characteristics and elemental forces, which are recognized, worshipped and propitiated. The stories of spirits and how they came to earth and interact with humanity are told in myth. In various cosmologies, spirits are organized into hierarchies.

In many societies, including animistic ones, the ancestral spirits of the dead are particularly revered and honored. Such spirits typically reside in a household, where they have their special altar or spirit house. They are fed offerings, recognized in ritual and sought for their advice and protection.

A spirit is not accurately a ghost, or a spirit of the dead, though the distinction between the two is often vague. Spiritualism espouses the belief in the immortality of the soul and refers to spirits of the dead who communicate in mediumship.

Nor is a spirit precisely the soul, though the term "spirit" is often used in describing the soul. For example, Frederic W.H. MYERS, a founder of the SOCIETY FOR PSYCHICAL RESEARCH (SPR), stated in his book *Human Personality and Its Survival of Bodily Death* (1903) that the spirit is "that unknown fraction of a man's personality . . . which we discern as operating before or after death in the metetherial environment." Similarly, medium Arthur FORD defined spirit as "nothing more than the stream of consciousness of a personality with which we are familiar in every human being." This, said Ford, is what survives death, not as a spiritual wraith, but as an "oblong blur." Ford drew his views from the writings of St. Paul, who wrote of a spiritual body. Ford's own control, Fletcher, called the spirit the "risen" body which one takes up after death, and which does not age and has no physical defects. After death, the spirit takes a perfect spirit body that is mature: the old grow young and the young mature. The spirit body has no clothes in earthly sense, but is a garment of light and a projection of thought.

See also DAIMON; FESTIVALS OF THE DEAD; HUNGRY GHOST FESTIVAL; GUARDIAN SPIRIT; KACHINAS; SHAMANISM; SHINTO.

Further reading:

Gauld, Alan. *The Founders of Psychical Research*. London: Routledge & Kegan Paul, 1968.

Leach, Maria, and Jerome Fried, eds. *Funk & Wagnalls Standard Dictionary of Folklore, Mythology, and Legend*. San Francisco: Harper & Row, 1979.

Myers, Frederic W.H. *Human Personality and Its Survival of Bodily Death Vols. I & II*. New ed. New York: Longmans, Green & Co., 1954. First published 1903.

Spraggett, Allen. *Arthur Ford: The Man Who Talked with the Dead*. New York: New American Library, 1973.

spirit photography   Photographs alleged to reveal ghosts, spirits or spirits of the dead. Spirit photography has been controversial since its inception in 1861. Most "spirit photographs" can be explained as flaws on the film, flaws in developing or tricks of light; some have been exposed as hoaxes. At best, spirit photographs are inconclusive and are not reliable evidence of a discarnate presence in a haunting or of survival after death.

The first spirit photograph is credited to Boston jewelry engraver William Mumler. In 1861 he took a self-portrait and, after developing the photographic plate, noticed what appeared to be the image of a dead person next to his. Mumler's discovery came during the expansion of Spiritualism and the popularity of mediumship and seances to communicate with the dead. Spirit photography became a fad, seen as proof of survival. Individuals sat for photographers in hopes of seeing the faces of dead loved ones revealed in the print. One photographer, William Hope, said he took more than 2,500 pictures of "extras," as these ghostly images were called, over a period of about 20 years during the early 20th century. Hope was instrumental in the experiments of the Crewe Circle, an English group that attempted to prove the existence of spirits of the dead by capturing their images on film (see HOPE, WILLIAM).

Typically in early spirit photographs, ghostly faces float above or alongside portraits of living subjects. In some photographs, full-form "spirits" appear. In order not to disappoint clients, unscrupulous photographers doctored their work, superimposing ex-

tras or creating ghostly effects through double exposures. Many fraudulent photographs—some obviously so—were accepted as real. Sometimes the extras turned out to be individuals very much alive. Perhaps most outrageous were photographs in which rings of famous faces hovered about the living subjects. Native Americans in feather headdresses (as "spirit guides") also were popular.

The fraud of spirit photography eventually led to its decline, along with fraudulent physical mediumship. Fraud claimed some famous victims, however, including the eminent Sir Arthur Conan DOYLE, who was fooled by amateurish fake photographs of fairies.

Spirit photography, also called psychic photography, continues in use, but in a much different way. Many investigators of hauntings take photographs of sites with infrared film to see if anything unusual registers. In many cases streaks of light and white shapes appear; most of these remain scientifically inconclusive. Some proponents of spirit photography examine prints for spirit faces that seem to appear in

Fake spirit photograph. Courtesy U.S. Library of Congress.

An unexplained luminosity appears on photo taken of a young girl on a porch . Courtesy Ghost Research Society.

backgrounds. Most likely, these are created by random patterns such as those made by ground cover, foliage, shadows, grains in panelling and building facades. These false effects are called "simulacra," a term coined by English author John Michell, who wrote about them in a book by the same name, *Simulacra* (1979).

The most famous spirit photograph to be examined by scientists and declared "real," that is, free of fraud and without natural explanations, is of the Brown Lady of RAYNHAM HALL.

The GHOST RESEARCH SOCIETY of Oak Lawn, Illinois, collects spirit photographs from around the world. According to president Dale KACZMAREK, about 90 percent can be explained naturally, either as flaws in the film or developing or as simulacra. The remaining 10 percent include photographs of shadows, streak and blotches of light that have no apparent explanation. These photographs are considered paranormal, though not necessarily of a ghost or spirit. They show cloudy patches of light that Kaczmarek calls "paranormal fog," because of their mysterious blue-gray color that seems to defy efforts to duplicate. Since about 1984, Kaczmarek has tried to produce similar effects by shooting through steam, smoke and

vapor with various lens filters and at various light levels, but without success.

The GRS has about five photographs that seem to show actual spirits; that is, they show semitransparent but recognizable human forms with distinct facial features.

The GRS analyzes spirit photographs by scanning them into a computer and digitizing them, which produces images with a higher resolution than those appear on television. Minute details can thus be scrutinized. The photographs are printed out on a laser printer.

It is possible that spirit photographs may be created unwittingly by psychokinesis (PK) on the part of the photographer or subjects, who, by thought and intent, imprint an image on film. This phenomenon is called by parapsychologists "thoughtography," a term coined in the early 1900s by Tomokichi Fukarai, then president of the Psychical Institute of Japan. Fukarai discovered thoughtography in experiments with a medium to test her clairvoyance. In the 1960s, the thoughtography of Ted Serios of Kansas City, Missouri, was studied by parapsychologists. Serios purportedly created images on film by staring into the lens of a Polaroid camera.

According to Kaczmarek, some of the GRS spirit photographs may be examples of thoughtography.

Images of extras that appear on film that has not been exposed are called scotographs. "Psychography," a term that medium William Stainton MOSES used to describe direct spirit writing, also has been alleged to occur on film, in the form of messages written in the handwriting of deceased persons.

The GRS has used a video camera in its investigations of ghosts and poltergeists, but has not captured any inexplicable images on videotape.

Further reading:

Carrington, Hereward. "Experiences in Psychic Photography." *Journal of the American Society for Psychical Research,* 19 (1925):258–267.

Eisenbud, Jule. *The World of Ted Serios.* New York: Pocket Books, 1968.

Fukurai, T. *Clairvoyance & Thoughtography.* New York: Arno Press, 1975. First published in 1931.

Holzer, Hans. *Psychic Photography: Threshold of a New Science?* New York: McGraw-Hill, 1970.

Perlmutt, Cyril. *Photographing the Spirit World: Images from Beyond the Spectrum.* Willingborough, Northamptonshire, England: The Aquarian Press, 1988.

Rickard, Robert and Richard Kelly. *Photographs of the Unknown.* London: New English Library, 1980.

Warrick, F.W. *Experiments in Psychics.* New York: E.P. Dutton & Co., 1939.

spirit writing See AUTOMATIC WRITING; SLATEWRITING.

Spiritism The philosophy of Allan KARDEC, also known as Kardecism (Kardecismo in Brazil) in his honor, stems directly from the Spiritualist movement that swept Europe in the 1850s.

Intrigued by the rapping and table-turning associated with spirit communication, French writer and physician Hippolyte Leon Denizard Rivail (1804–1869) began joining seance circles about 1850. Through the medium Celina Japhet, Rivail learned that in earlier incarnations he had been known as Allan and Kardec, names he later assumed as his pseudonym.

Writing under Kardec, Rivail transcribed many of Japhet's communications while in trance into *Le Livre des Espirits (The Spirits' Book)* in 1856. In it, he expanded traditional Spiritualist philosophy by saying that spiritual progress is possible only by compulsory reincarnation to correct past mistakes. These incarnations occur only as humans, not as animals. He also maintained that certain illnesses have spiritual causes—especially epilepsy, schizophrenia and multiple personality—and can be treated psychically through communication with spirit guides. Such ideas were common within the Spiritualist community, wherein mediums appealed to the spirit world to help rid sufferers of obsessing tormentors.

But Kardec's insistence on the necessity of reincarnation took Spiritualist doctrines beyond proof of survival after death. In fact he was so convinced of the rightness of his beliefs that he actively discouraged investigation of any physical manifestations, except automatic writing, which he thought was less influenced by preconceived ideas. True Spiritists view table rapping, levitation and materializations as just so many parlor games, although ironically, Spiritualists often use "spiritism" to mean the production of physical phenomena. Consequently, psychical research in France lagged behind the rest of Europe by about 20 years.

Within the Spiritualist community in England and the United States, critics of Spiritism asserted that if reincarnation were true, then the spirits with whom mediums were in communication would have discussed the subject; apparently they did not. Medium D.D. HOME commented that he had met at least 12 reincarnationists who claimed to be Marie Antoinette, 6 or 7 who were Mary Queen of Scots and about 20 who were Alexander the Great, but not one plain John Smith. Anna Blackwell, Kardec's translator and principal British supporter, countered that the Continental mind was more receptive to new ideas than the English one.

Spiritist teaching maintains that suffering and illness in this life are the result of spirit influence compounded by remnants of turmoil endured by the individual in past lives. Each time a soul is reborn, wrote Kardec, it brings with it "subsystems" of past lives that may even block out the reality of the current life. Each rebirth, however painful, according to Kardec, enables the soul to improve and eventually attain a higher plane of existence.

Kardec taught that a person is composed of three parts: an incarnate soul, a body and a *perispirit*, or what Kardec described as a semi-material substance that unites soul and body and surrounds the soul like an envelope. All souls are created equal, ignorant and untested, and continue coming back to life until they have nothing more to learn.

At the death of the flesh, the perispirit holds the soul and separates from the body. This process takes longer if the deceased were particularly attached to his or her material existence. Spiritually advanced souls, wrote Kardec, receive death with joy as it signifies release and the promise of future enlightenment. On the other hand, the spirits of those unfortunates who died suddenly or violently cling desperately to their bodies, confused and certain they are not dead. Suicides, especially, try to remain with their material existences, and may reincarnate only to commit suicide again. Only when the perispirit has left the flesh, taught Kardec, does the soul realize it is no longer part of the human world.

Once the perispirit has left the body, the soul returns to the spirit world, where Spiritists believe the soul reviews its past lives and its progress to enlightenment and decides which life-path to pursue next. Each soul has wide latitude in choosing its next life, and often returns to its earthly family. In cases in which two spirits desire to occupy the same body, God, described by Kardec as the Supreme Intelligence and First Cause of All Things, makes the choice.

Spirits who suffered greatly on earth and choose to devote their energies to persecution of the living practice "spirit vampirism," according to Spiritist author Andre Luiz. Kardec did not consider all obsession intentional, however. "Spirit induction" occurs when a confused, recently deceased soul invades a living human on the presumption that death did not happen. Kardec denied the possibility of exorcism by outsiders, whether in the name of the Lord or not. Instead he maintained that exorcism must originate from the obsessed through conviction and prayer, noting proverbially that "God helps those who help themselves."

Kardec's theories enjoyed brief popularity in Europe and then gave way to the next intellectual craze. Spiritist belief in reincarnation, stressing the moral improvement of the soul, led naturally into the reincarnation theories of Theosophy.

But in Brazil, exposed for centuries to African spirits and superstition, Kardecismo took root and remains a powerful religious force in contemporary society, with Kardecist centers all over the country. The movement provides the elite with a metaphysical explanation for life they could not relate to in the magical rites of the poor, and the uneducated receive formal proof of their magical beliefs. Most Brazilians profess Catholicism yet call themselves *espiritas.* In fact, Brazilian Kardecists claim the movement restores Christianity to its foundation, basing the faith on the immortality of the soul. Kardecism also flourishes in the Philippines.

Kardecist healing encompasses prayer, counseling, exploration of past lives through a medium and perhaps psychic surgery. Practitioners of this technique allegedly open the body without anesthetic or surgical instruments and manipulate vital organs and use laying-on of hands to heal all kinds of disease and deformity. The mediums may be uneducated and unskilled, but they claim to be guided by the spirits of past physicians. While some claims of psychic surgery remain unexplained, others have been found to involve fraud and stage magic sleight of hand.

The Kardecist psychiatric hospitals, staffed by highly trained doctors, operate comfortably alongside their more traditional counterparts in Brazil and have won the admiration of many non-Spiritist physicians. As early as 1912, psychiatrist Dr. Oscar Pittham, saddened with his profession's inability to treat many sufferers successfully, began collecting funds to establish a so-called "spirit hospital." Finally, in 1934, Pittham's dreams were realized in a new hospital in Porto Allegre. The facility, which doubled in size in 1951, supports more than 600 beds and a staff of more than 200. Other major Kardecist institutions are in Itapira and São Paulo.

Perhaps the hospitals' most remarkable features are their rigorous denial of profit and acceptance of all patients, regardless of race, creed or ability to pay. Hospital directors do not receive salaries.

In fact, all dedicated Spiritist mediums firmly insist that theirs is a God-given talent, not to be used for personal gain. Once a medium begins charging for paranormal services, the gift will disappear. One of Brazil's most famous mediums, Chico Xavier, has transcribed well over a hundred books on science, literature, history, Kardecist philosophy and children stories, yet lives in poverty. He modestly claims that his spirit guides are the true authors.

Kardec acknowledged that such humility does not characterize every medium. His *Medium's Book* (1861) outlined in detail the function of a medium, and any charlatan who wished to learn the tricks of the trade only had to study Kardec's work. Little research has been done on Spiritist phenomena, since believers consider Kardecismo a religion, not a science. The only major organization collecting and studying Spiritist work is the Instituto Brasileiro de Pesquisas Psicobiofisicas (IBPP), or the Brazilian Institute for Psycho-Biophysical Research, founded by Hernani Andrade in 1963.

Further reading:
Doyle, Sir Arthur Conan. *The History of Spiritualism, Vol. I and II.* New York: Arno Press, 1975.
Fodor, Nandor. *An Encyclopaedia of Psychic Science.* Secaucus, N.J.: The Citadel Press, 1966. First published 1933.
Guiley, Rosemary Ellen. *Harper's Encyclopedia of Mystical & Paranormal Experience.* San Francisco: HarperSanFrancisco, 1991.
Playfair, Guy Lyon. *The Unknown Power.* New York: Pocket Books, 1975.
Rogo, D. Scott. *The Infinite Boundary.* New York: Dodd, Mead & Co., 1987.
Villoldo, Alberto, and Stanley Krippner. *Healing States.* New York: Fireside/Simon & Schuster, 1987.

spirits of the living   See ARRIVAL CASES.

Spiritual Frontiers Fellowship   Non-profit organization founded in 1956 by medium Arthur FORD and others to focus the attention of Christian churches on the insights and significance of psychic phenomena. Other key founders were Albin Bro, a missionary and educator, and Paul Higgins, a Methodist pastor. The organization was modeled after the Churches' Fellowship for Psychical Study of Great Britain, founded several years earlier.

The stated purpose of the Spiritual Frontiers Fellowship (SFF) is "to sponsor, explore and interpret the growing interest in psychic phenomena and mystical experience within the church, wherever these experiences relate to effective prayer, spiritual healing and personal survival." Mainstream Christianity, however, has remained disinterested in psychical phenomena.

The SFF headquarters and a library of about 5,000 volumes are in Philadelphia.

An affiliate organization, The Academy of Religion and Psychical Research, based in Bloomfield, Connecticut, is devoted to an exchange of ideas and dialogue to "areas in which religion and psychical research interface."

Spiritualism   Movement that arose in the mid-19th century that derived its appeal from spirit communications and evidence in support of SURVIVAL AFTER

DEATH. Spiritualism did not begin as a religion, but became one, appearing at a time of interest in bringing science and religion together. Fraudulent mediums and the inability of science to validate the claims of Spiritualism soon led to its decline. It remains a vigorous religion around the world, however, especially in Britain, and in the United States and Latin America; many Latin Americans follow an offshoot of Spiritualism called SPIRITISM.

The official birth of Spiritualism is considered to be 1848 when the FOX SISTERS of Hydesville, New York, became famous for their rappings with alleged spirits. The popular interest that made their fame possible had earlier been primed by the psychism-based movements of Swedenborgianism and mesmerism. The former, based on the writings of Emanuel SWEDENBORG's visionary trance visits to the spirit world, and the latter, based on paranormal phenomena exhibited by mesmerized (hypnotized) subjects, began in Europe in the late 18th century and were imported to America. Both movements carried direct contact with the spirit world to the masses.

Of the two earlier movements, mesmerism was by far the more popular in America. Audiences would gather to witness "somnambules," as mesmerized subjects were called, report their visions of the spirit world, and demonstrated "higher phenomena" such as telepathy, clairvoyance, automatic writing, mediumship, precognition, xenoglossy (speaking in an unlearned foreign language), psychometry and psychic healing. Their mediumship of communication with the dead was especially fascinating to the public at large. The lecture circuits became filled with various prophets of the new age, among them Andrew Jackson DAVIS, who delivered lectures in trance on his "Harmonial Philosophy," concerning the fate of the soul after death.

Following the sensation of the Fox sisters, mediums and mystics and Spiritualist journals proliferated. The public eagerly devoured almost any daydream as "visions of the spirit world," and virtually anyone could become a medium and communicate with the dead. Seances became the rage. Early seances were mostly rappings and a few spirit mutterings, but the sessions became more entertaining in order to attract steady and larger audiences. To demonstrate the verity of the spirit world, mediums performed paranormal physical feats, such as levitation, apports and materialization. Trickery was not uncommon, but exposure of fraud did little to dampen early public enthusiasm.

By 1855, Spiritualism claimed two million followers and was a nascent religion on both sides of the Atlantic. It was held that the soul, in a vehicle that was a duplicate of the physical body, survived death and made an immediate transition to the spirit world. Communication with these souls became possible through mediumship. Generally, Spiritualism rejected the doctrine of reincarnation (some adherents of reincarnation joined the Spiritist camp). Today, Spiritualists are divided on the question of reincarnation, with some believing in it and others not.

From the beginning as a religion, Spiritualism had an uncomfortable relationship with Christianity. Some Christians denounced it as satanic, openly harassed Spiritualists, and attempted to have it banned by law. Some Spiritualists believed in breaking away completely from Christianity, while others sought the endorsement of the Christian Church by advocating beliefs in Christian tenets. Mediums (most of whom were women) often were shunned by family and friends.

When scientists began investigating Spiritualist phenomena—specifically mediumistic communications and feats—it was hoped that Spiritualist tenets would be proven. Even many of the investigators, who were among the leading scientists of the day, hoped to find scientific proof for the existence of the soul and its immortality. Scientific proof was—and remains—elusive. What scientists did uncover was a great deal of trickery on the part of many mediums, especially those who claimed to materialize spirits.

Systematic investigations began as early as the 1850s but did not become well organized until 1882, when the SOCIETY FOR PSYCHICAL RESEARCH (SPR) was founded in London. Although the SPR was soon followed by an American branch (which eventually became independent), the AMERICAN SOCIETY FOR PSYCHICAL RESEARCH (ASPR), the more extensive research went on in England rather than in the American birthplace of Spiritualism. Psychical researchers encountered some of the same prejudices as did mediums, and many saw their academic and scientific careers suffer because of criticism and ostracism from their peers.

By the turn of the 20th century, Spiritualism was virtually finished as a widespread, cohesive movement. It never became sufficiently organized to coalesce; dissension, internal politics and the exposes of fraud took their toll. Public interest also began to wane when science was not quickly forthcoming with proof of Spiritualist tenets. World War I brought thousands of bereaved back into seances. However, the heyday of the physical medium was at an end by 1920.

Interest in Spiritualism continued on a smaller and more quiet scale on both sides of the Atlantic and elsewhere in the world. Fraud declined. In the 1930s, psychical research departed from the seance circle and went into the laboratory (see J.B. RHINE).

Although scientists were unable to prove the existence and survival of the soul, the early psychical researchers did much to establish that paranormal phenomena do occur, and also made great contributions to an understanding of consciousness.

Modern Spiritualist churches thrive in Britain, America, Brazil and other countries. Many are modeled on Protestant churches, but without an organized ministry. Emphasis is given to spiritual healing (laying on of hands, energy transfers and prayer) and mental mediumship; some mediums still perform physical mediumship.

Mental mediumship can include trance messages relayed from spirits to the congregation, and trance delivering of sermons. Some Spiritualists work with spirits of the dead, while others espouse contact with highly evolved discarnate beings that is more characteristic of channeling (q.v.).

Spiritualists consider their religion to be also a science; many say that Spiritualism has scientifically proved spiritual phenomena.

The two largest Spiritualist organizations in the world are in Britain: the SPIRITUALIST ASSOCIATION OF GREAT BRITAIN and the SPIRITUALIST'S NATIONAL UNION. The religion had no legal status prior to 1951 due to an old law, the Witchcraft Act of 1735, which enabled the prosecution of mediums as witches. That act was repealed and replaced by a Fraudulent Mediums' Act.

The largest organization in the United States is the National Spiritualist Association of Churches, founded in 1893 and based in Cassadaga, Florida.

Further reading:

Anderson, Roger I. "Spiritualism Before the Fox Sisters." *Parapsychology Review* 18 (1987):9–13.

Brown, Slater. *The Heyday of Spiritualism.* New York: Hawthorn Books, 1970.

Douglas, Alfred. *Extrasensory Powers: A Century of Psychical Research.* London: Victor Gollancz Ltd., 1976.

Gauld, Alan. *The Founders of Psychical Research.* London: Routledge & Kegan Paul, 1968.

Jackson, Herbert G., Jr. *The Spirit Rappers.* Garden City, N.Y.: Doubleday, 1972.

Moore, R. Laurence. *In Search of White Crows.* New York: Oxford University Press, 1977.

Oppenheim, Janet. *The Other World: Spiritualism and Psychical Research in England, 1850–1914.* Cambridge: Cambridge University Press, 1985.

Ortzen, Tony. "Spiritualism in England and America." In *The New Age Catalogue.* New York: Doubleday/Dolphin, 1988.

Pearsall, Ronald. *The Table-Rappers.* New York: St. Martin's Press, 1972.

Spiritualist Association of Great Britain

One of the oldest and largest Spiritualist organizations in the world. The organization was founded in 1872 as the Marylebone Spiritualist Association, Limited, and its purpose was to study psychic phenomena and disseminate evidence obtained through mediumship and "to propagate spiritual truth in the Marylebone area of London."

Despite the popularity of SPIRITUALISM, there was sufficient opposition to the movement, coupled with the threat of prosecution under an outdated Witchcraft Act of 1735, that the Marylebone Spiritualist Association had difficulty obtaining halls for meetings and seances. To counteract some of the opposition, it changed its name to the Spiritual Evidence Society.

The organization was one of the few early British Spiritualist organizations to survive, and by 1960 it had greatly expanded its scope and activities. The name of the organization was changed to the Spiritualist Association of Great Britain (SAGB).

Nearly 200,000 visitors are attracted each year to the headquarters of the SAGB in Belgrave Square, London, especially for its services in spiritual healing. The organization maintains meditation rooms, prayer rooms, a library, a chapel and a meeting hall.

Spiritualists' National Union

One of two of the largest SPIRITUALISM organizations in the world. The Spiritualists' National Union (SNU) was founded in Manchester, England in July 1890 under the original name of Spiritualists' National Federation. The purpose of the organization was to bring Britain's Spiritualists together in a national organization. The key figure in the effort to organization was medium Emma Hardinge Britten, who had founded a Spiritualist journal, *Two Worlds*, in 1887. Britten was an unflagging advocate of both Spiritualism and a national organization of Spiritualists.

In 1901 Spiritualists' National Union Ltd. was formed, and in 1902 it assumed the responsibilities and rights of the Federation. Among the many notable figures active in the SNU were J. Arthur Findlay, a Scottish businessman who willed his family home, Stansted Hall, to be used as a college for psychic studies; Hannen Swaffer, a journalist known as "the Pope of Fleet Street," who helped bring Spiritualism to the masses; Sir Arthur Conan DOYLE, named Honorary President in Spirit; and medium Maurice BARBANELL, a founder of *Psychic News*.

In 1948 the SNU merged with the British Lyceum Union, which had been founded in 1890 for the Spiritualist education of children and youth. In 1970, the SNU launched the SNU Guild of Spiritualist Healers as a branch of the organization. The Guild is a member of the Confederation of Healing Organizations, which establishes guidelines for alternative healing practitioners.

The presidency of the SNU has been held by medium Gordon Higginson since 1970.

The SNU espouses seven principles originally shaped by Britten: (1) the fatherhood of God; (2) the brotherhood of Man; (3) the communion of spirits and the ministry of angels; (4) the continuous existence of the human soul; (5) personal responsibility; (6) compensation and retribution hereafter, for all good or evil done on earth; and (7) eternal progress open to every human soul.

Further reading:
Bassett, Jean. *100 Years of National Spiritualism*. London: The Spiritualists' National Union, 1990.

spittle and spitting   In folklore, spitting averts evil and protects one against ghosts, witches and evil spirits. When one encounters a ghost, the wisdom goes, one must spit on the ground in front of it and demand, "In the name of the Lord, what do you want?" The spittle supposedly prevents the ghost from harming the individual.

spook lights   See GHOST LIGHTS.

spunkie   In Scottish lore, a goblin or trickster ghost similar to the kelpie. The spunkie, which resides in the Scottish Lowlands, is a solitary spirit evil in nature. Commonly believed to be the Devil's agent, he takes special pleasure in tricking travelers who have lost their way. He uses a light to lure his victims, intending to make them think it is a light in a window to which they might go for help. The hapless traveler follows the light, which appears to be nearby. However, the light actually recedes until the spunkie has succeeded in making the traveler fall over a precipice or into a morass.

See also IGNIS FATUUS; JACK-O'-LANTERN.

Staus Poltergeist   A 19th-century poltergeist named for the village of Staus on the shores of Lake Lucerne, Switzerland. The strange, never-explained activities took place from 1860 to 1862, victimizing members of the Joller family. Joller was a distinguished lawyer and member of the Swiss national council.

The hauntings began with a servant girl hearing knocks on her bedstead, which she took to be a prediction of her death. Joller believed the girl imagined them and forbade her to talk about the incident. But a short time later, Joller's wife and one of his three daughters heard raps. Within a few days a friend died, an event they imagined was linked to the raps foretelling death.

Several months later, one of Joller's four sons saw an apparition of a white, indistinct figure, causing him to faint. Several of the other children reported strange happenings. The servant girl said that the spirit followed her to her room and also that it could be heard sobbing all night in the lumber room.

The servant girl was soon replaced in the hope that such reports would stop. But the family's hopes were shattered when the knocks, louder than ever, frightened the children into fleeing from the house, and even began to haunt Joller himself. Knocks were now accompanied by invisible hands locking doors and throwing open locked windows, as well as strange music and voices, and the humming of spinning wheels.

Joller now was forced to overcome his reticence in letting the public know about the strange doings in his house. He sought help from the authorities, clergy and scientists, all of whom were unable to identify the cause of the disturbances, which continued unabated. For six days, the Joller family left the house with the police in occupancy for further investigation. The police withdrew, having heard nor seen any sign of the poltergeist, and the family returned only to be victims of renewed poltergeist activity.

Now the public flocked to the site of the house and Joller became the object of ridicule. He was forced to leave his ancestral home and put in a tenant, who heard nothing from the poltergeist. Witnesses and readers of the Joller story believe that it provides strong support for the theory of discarnate intelligence at work in poltergeist cases.

The case was never solved. In light of modern theories about poltergeists, it is possible that a member of the Joller household was the agent for the activities. The servant girl is the most likely suspect, but since the activities continued after her departure, the agent may have been one of the children.

Further reading:
Spence, Lewis. *The Encyclopedia of the Occult*. London: Bracken Books, 1988. Reprint.

Stone-throwing Devil, The   Unusual poltergeist case that occurred at Great Island, New Hampshire in the late 17th century, characterized by lithoboly, or a mysterious hail of stones that pelted the victims.

Many poltergeist cases include stone throwings and hail. In the 17th century, such incidents were suspected of being caused by witchcraft or demonic possession.

The Stone-throwing Devil case occurred in 1682. Some details were recorded and published by an eyewitness, Richard Chamberlain, who was secretary of what was then the Province of New Hampshire.

Chamberlain witnessed disturbances while a guest at the home of the victim, George Walton, a wealthy landowner. Chamberlain wrote a pamphlet, *Lithobolia, or the Stone-throwing Devil, etc.*, published under his initials, R.C. Esq., in London in 1698. An earlier secondhand account was published in 1684 by the American Puritan minister, Increase Mather, in his book *An Essay for the Recording of Illustrious Providences*. Neither account is very specific or clear.

The exact start of the stone attacks is unknown, but numerous incidents were recorded between May and August of 1682. According to Chamberlain, one Sunday night in May at about 10:00, Walton and his family, servants and guests were surprised by a great pounding of stones upon the roof and all sides of the house. Walton and several persons ran outside, but they could see nothing despite the bright moonlight. Walton found his fence gate torn off its hinges. He and the others were pelted by stones that rained down from the sky.

They returned to the house, where everyone was in a panic; stones apparently were coming through the front door and dropping through the ceiling. Some of them were as large as fists. The occupants immediately suspected a preternatural cause. Though they withdrew from the outer rooms, stones continued to attack them. Stones also battered the windows from the inside, striking them so hard that holes were punched in the leaded glass and bars covering the windows were bent. The stones bounced back into the rooms. Some of the stones seemed to fly out of the fire, and were hot. More stones sent brass and pewter pots and candlesticks flying.

For four hours, stones flew about the house and rained down the chimney. Despite this furious attack, no one in the house was seriously injured.

The next day, servants discovered that household objects were missing. Some were found outside in the yard and in other odd places, while others mysteriously reappeared by falling down the chimney or into rooms as though dropped through the ceiling. Walton's fields were littered with stones. Suspicions about witchcraft were raised when employees spotted a black cat in the orchard. They shot at it, but it escaped unharmed.

A veritable avalanche of stones flew about inside the house that evening. In addition, a hand was seen thrusting out from a hall window (no one was in the hall at the time), tossing more stones upon the porch.

The rains of stones and disturbances of household objects continued for weeks. Occasionally there would be a break of a day or two, and then the stone attacks would resume with greater force and with larger stones. Two stones weighing more than 30 pounds apiece struck the door of a guest room. Walton's field hands also continued to be attacked by stones that rained down from the sky and then disappeared from the ground, only to fall on them again.

One of the severest stone attacks occurred on Monday, June 28, when stones fell on members of the household as they ate supper in the kitchen; the table was broken into pieces. Chamberlain wrote:

> . . . many Stones (some great ones) came thick and threefold among us, and an old howing Iron, from a Room hard by, where such Utensils lay. Then, as if I had been the designed Object for that time, most of the Stones that came (the smaller I mean) hit me, (sometimes pretty hard), to the number of above 20, near 30 . . . and whether I moved, sit, or walk'd, I had them, and great ones sometimes lighting gently on me . . . Then was a Room over the Kitchen infested, that had not been so before, and many Stones greater than usual lumbering there over our Heads, not only to ours, but to the great Disturbance and Affrightment of some Children that lay there.

Walton continued to work the fields with his men despite the stone attacks. On one day Walton claimed to have been struck by more than 40 of them. His injuries left him suffering chronic pain for the rest of his life. In addition, he found corn mysteriously cut off at the roots or uprooted. No agent of the damage was ever seen by anyone; the men said they heard a strange "snorting and whistling" while they worked.

In other incidents, a maid was struck on the head by a falling porringer, and hay baled one day was found the next day strewn about the ground and tossed into the trees. One night, stones and brickbats crashed through a window, toppled books off a case, and tore a foot-long hole in a picture.

No single member of the household seemed to be the focal point of the attacks—all were attacked on occasion—yet most incidents seemed to occur when Walton himself was present. The governor of West Jersey and seven other individuals signed statements attesting to their witnessing some of the disturbances.

Chamberlain, who most probably was a skeptic about witchcraft and the supernatural, seemed convinced otherwise by these terrifying events. He wrote that the incident "has confirmed myself and others in the opinion that there are such things as witches and the effects of witchcraft, or at least the mischievous actions of evil spirits, which some of us do little give credit to, as in the case of witches, utterly rejecting both their operations and their beings." Mather also took the case as an example of the formidable and diabolical powers of witches.

The suspect in this case was a neighbor of Walton's, an elderly woman believed to be a witch. She and Walton were involved in a dispute over a piece of land. They both claimed ownership, and Walton succeeded in securing it. The angry woman was overheard to remark that Walton would "never quietly enjoy that piece of Ground." When the stone attacks started, Walton believed himself to cursed by her.

In August 1682, Walton decided to fight witchcraft with witchcraft. With the help of someone knowledgeable about witchcraft, he attempted to cast a spell to undo the curse and punish his neighbor. This effort consisted of boiling a pot of urine and crooked pins on the fire. But before the urine could boil, a stone fell into it and spilled it. The Waltons refilled the pot with more urine and crooked pins. Another stone fell in the pot and spilled the contents again. Then the handles fell off the pot, and the pot split into pieces. The Waltons gave up.

Meanwhile, the hail of stones continued, destroying Walton's fences and smashing his farm tools. He lodged a complaint with the council in Portsmouth, which summoned both him and the neighbor for interrogation. En route to his appointment, Walton was struck by three fist-sized stones. He showed a head wound to the president of the council.

The outcome of the affair is not recorded. At some point after the council became involved, the lithoboly apparently stopped. The fate of the disputed land is not known; however, Walton's health was ruined.

It is difficult to speculate what may have been the cause of the Stone-throwing Devil due to the limited descriptions extant. Fraud on the part of Walton is unlikely, due to the great amount of suffering and personal injury inflicted upon him and members of his family. Walton may have been an unwitting agent, perhaps due in part to the stress of his dispute with his neighbor, though he does not fit the profile of living agents that has been established by modern researchers. Typically, such agents are adolescents. Witchcraft cannot be ruled out, but it is virtually impossible to prove.

In *The Encyclopedia of Witchcraft and Demonology* (1959), author Rossell Hope Robbins opined that the stones were thrown by persons who opposed Chamberlain, whose administration was unpopular after two years in office. This, too, is unlikely. In his account, Chamberlain repeatedly stated that nosources of the attacks were visible. Furthermore, it is not likely that Chamberlain would have remained a guest in a house under attack by his own critics.

Further reading:

Mather, Increase. *An Essay for the Recording of Illustrious Providences.* 1684. Delmar, N.Y.: Scholars' Facsimiles and Reprints, with introduction by James A. Levernier.

Owen, A.R.G. *Can We Explain the Poltergeist?* New York: HelixPress/Garrett Publications, 1964.

R.C. Esq. (Richard Chamberlain). *Lithobolia: or, the Stone-throwing Devil, etc.* London: 1698.

Robbins, Rossell Hope. *The Encyclopedia of Witchcraft and Demonology.* New York: Bonanza Books, 1981. First published 1959.

Stead, William T. (1849–1912)

One of the greatest crusading journalists of the late 19th century, and also one of the most vocal supporters of Spiritualism. W.T. Stead promoted spirit photography, championed the causes of various mediums and established the "Julia Bureau" for communications between the bereaved and their loved ones.

Stead was a very religious man. Born in 1849 to a Methodist minister and his wife, he took his faith quite personally, usually referring to God as the Senior Partner. Once he embraced Spiritualism, he accepted it totally on faith as well.

Supremely self-confident and imbued with the 19th-century British conviction of mission, Stead envisioned himself as a crusader for God fighting the devil. He first grabbed public attention in 1880 as the editor of *Northern Echo* in Darlington, England, speaking out against Turkey's atrocities against the Bulgarians.

While he was in Darlington, Stead had the first of several premonitions that led him to believe he stood in the Senior Partner's favor. On New Year's Day 1880, he prophesied that before the year was out he would be working on a newspaper in London, although he knew of no newspaper looking to hire him. By midsummer, the *Pall Mall Gazette* changed editors to one more sympathetic to Stead's positions (it had been pro-Turkey), and the new editor, John Morley, offered Stead the post of assistant editor.

Three years later, Stead had his second premonition. While on vacation with his wife on the Isle of Wight, he heard a voice tell him that by March 16, 1894 editor John Morley would leave the paper and Stead would be the *Gazette*'s new editor. Stead understood the prophecy to mean Morley would enter Parliament. By February 24, Morley became an MP when his local representative died suddenly, and Stead assumed the editorship.

In 1885, Stead wrote a sensational exposé of child prostitution and white slavery in England. In an article entitled "The Maiden Tribute of Modern Babylon," Stead reported how he had purchased a 13-year-old girl from her mother and taken her to Paris.

Crowds stormed the paper's offices to buy every copy of the issue. Clergymen denounced Stead as obscene. Members of Parliament debated the question and finally passed legislation outlawing the practice, which had been Stead's aim all along.

But opponents of the legislation, many of whom were sometime users of child prostitutes, pounced upon Stead's failure to get a receipt for the five pounds paid for the girl. Her father, truthfully, claimed no knowledge of the transaction. Stead was arrested and convicted of abduction and sentenced to two months in Holloway Gaol. While there, he maintained a constant correspondence with his well-wishers, maintaining that whatever the future brought, all would be right if man humbly followed God's will. To Stead, every venture was a crusade; he also claimed responsibility for sending the ill-fated General Gordon to Khartoum and for supporting Prime Minister William Gladstone's plans to strengthen the British army.

Stead attended his first seance in 1881 and dabbled in Spiritualism without committing himself. In 1888, he met Madame Helena Petrovna Blavatsky, the Russian mystic and cofounder of the Theosophical Society, through a joint friend, Madame Olga Novikoff, the unofficial envoy for Russia in London. Stead wrote that Blavatsky both attracted and repelled him, but he was fascinated by Theosophy.

When her book *The Secret Doctrine* came out, Blavatsky sent a copy to Stead for review. A great feminist, Stead passed the task to Annie Besant, who occasionally wrote book reviews for the *Gazette*. She begged Stead to meet Blavatsky; subsequently she became a major figure in the development of the Theosophical Society, and a successor to Blavatsky.

Stead loved women and ardently supported their rights and causes. They adored him. He was devoted to his wife and six children, but she detested his flamboyant, free-spending ways and grew less interested in sex as time went on. He turned to Madame Novikoff, whom he met in 1877, and had a passionate affair for two years. He broke it off and returned to his wife, but he remained close friends with Novikoff. Some of his friends attributed his phenomenal energy to frustrated sexual urge; many sexual metaphors color his writing. In any case, Stead pursued nothing halfway.

By 1890, Stead had left the *Pall Mall Gazette* and now edited his own paper, the monthly *Review of Reviews*. During that year he met a young American journalist named Julia Ames, editor of *The Woman's Union Signal* in Chicago. They spent time at his office and in the garden of his Wimbledon home discussing many things, principally religion. She died the next year.

But their talks seemed to tip Stead's faith to Spiritualism. The Christmas 1891 issue of the *Review* was *Real Ghost Stories*, followed by *More Ghost Stories* the next year. Stead warned his readers to be careful of dabbling in the supernatural or occult arts, lest those not level-headed or reverential be exposed to the threat of possession. He put the case for ghosts in terms of personal testimony, saying that as many people had seen apparitions as scientists had seen microbes. Ghosts, then, could be assimilated into modern thought, and Stead was all for practical modernity.

He told of conversations with a woman who claimed to travel in her "Thought Body" (astral form) and his ideas about photographing her in this form. In 1892 he developed a talent for automatic writing, or, as he called it, letting others use his hand. Stead immediately saw the potential for this faculty in obtaining interviews, a journalism technique he pioneered, either with the living or the dead. He claimed to receive letters from various persons that way, although some, like the Countess of Warwick, Stead's friend and the Prince of Wales' mistress, disliked his communicating with her in that manner.

His interviews with the dead were a sensation. He talked to Empress Catherine the Great about the Russian situation and heard from the late prime minister Gladstone regarding the British budget of 1909. All these efforts were attributed to the intercession of Julia Ames, the American journalist, who had come through to Stead in 1892 and organized his spiritualist affairs.

Julia was Stead's principal control and the most frequent user of his hand. She helped him establish his telepathic interviews and was the principal contributor to his latest publishing venture, the quarterly review of psychic literature called *Borderland* begun in 1893. Stead used *Borderland* to publish his "Letters from Julia," in which Julia communicated with Stead about a variety of subjects. Among other things, Julia chastised non-believers for failing to see how the spirits could show the living the way to communion with God. *Borderland* lasted until 1897.

In 1907, Stead's oldest son, Willie, died, bringing the urgency of contact home to Stead in a personal way. For years, since 1894, Julia had been urging him to set up a bureau wherein the bereaved could reach their loved ones on the Other Side. Stead needed at least one thousand pounds to start such a project and as usual was out of money. By Christmas 1908, Julia predicted Stead would get the money from America, and she was right. William Randolph Hearst hired him as a special correspondent at one thousand pounds a year, and Julia's Bureau opened on April 24, 1909.

The Bureau operated quite systematically. Every petitioner first filled out an application, giving name, address, the name of the deceased, the relationship while on earth, and certification that the deceased wanted to speak to the living as much as the living wanted to speak to the deceased. The applicant also had to certify that he or she had read the pamphlet "Julia's Bureau and Borderland Library" and the "Letters from Julia." The completed form was then submitted to the director, Stead's daughter Estelle, who decided if the applicant could proceed first to a psychometrist and then to Julia's secretaries No. 1 and No. 2, both automatists. If, as occasionally happened, the psychometrist and the automatists differed on an applicant, petition was made to Julia herself in council, and her decision was final.

After passing these preliminaries, the applicant filled in Form H, which outlined the tests which would be considered satisfactory evidence for communication, including personal details such as age, sex, description of death, names of relatives, pet names, places names, incidental details and figures of speech. This form was sealed in an envelope. Then the applicant filled in Form D, which informed the Bureau that the applicant had filled in Form H. The applicant had to agree to mail in the sealed Form H along with annotated reports of the messages received from the three sensitives.

Once the paperwork was complete, the psychometrist and the two automatists began. Each sitter was accompanied by a stenographer. No payment was paid to the mediums, as all wages were paid by the Bureau. At the end of the first three months, the Bureau had processed more than 100 cases, confirming Stead's belief in the possibilities of spirit communication. The Bureau was perpetually short of funds and finally closed in 1912. If it had lasted just a little longer, the thousands of bereaved from World War I would probably have made it a successful endeavor.

Stead accepted the concept of the "other side" without question. He detested the SOCIETY FOR PSYCHICAL RESEARCH (SPR) for its niggling of what he considered spiritual truths, and he denied the possibility of fraud. He once said that he would rather die in a workhouse than believe anyone would intentionally deceive him.

Like Sir Arthur Conan DOYLE, Stead was ready to support any psychic phenomena, including spirit photography, a manifestation that could easily be rigged. One of his proudest possessions was a photograph taken by Richard Boursnell in 1902 showing

Stead seated in front of a figure later identified as the Boer commander Piet Botha, who had died in 1899. Stead, a staunch supporter of the Boers in South Africa, claimed no one in England knew of that particular Boer general, even though a report of Botha's death appeared in the *Daily Graphic* of October 24, 1899.

Throughout his life, Stead's premonitions and stories often involved great disasters at sea. In 1893, Stead wrote a story entitled "From the Old World to the New" in which a large ocean liner sinks in the North Atlantic after hitting an iceberg. In a 1909 address to the Cosmos Club, in which he bitterly attacked the SPR, Stead compared their methods to rescuers who instead of throwing a drowning man a life preserver would demand proof of his identity before saving him. In his story, the drowning man was Stead himself. As early as 1886 Stead wrote an editorial in the *Pall Mall Gazette* predicting disaster if oceanliners crossed the ocean without enough lifeboats.

In 1912, Stead was invited to speak at Carnegie Hall on April 21 about world peace. Before sailing for America, he felt that something would happen, he believed for good, as a result of the trip. But that good would not happen in his lifetime. Fulfilling his earlier sea visions, Stead's was one of 1,600 lives lost in the sinking of the *Titanic* on April 14.

But that was not the last of W.T. Stead. Three weeks after his death he appeared in his office at Mowbray House to his daughter, his secretary and some other women. They claimed his face shown radiantly as he called out, "All I told you is true!" Through the medium Mrs. Foster Turner, Stead predicted the horrors of World War I in February 1914, six months before hostilities began. Doyle also heard from Stead, who called Doyle's Spiritualist writings the "Review of Divine Reviews," a play on his earlier journal. Stead told Doyle that he and Cecil Rhodes, their colleague and fellow Empire-builder, had looked into Christ's eyes and that Christ had told Stead to tell Arthur his work was holy—that Doyle's message was His.

Further reading:
Brandon, Ruth. *The Spiritualists*. New York: Alfred A. Knopf, 1983.
Doyle, Sir Arthur Conan. *The History of Spiritualism Vol. I & II*. New York: Arno Press, 1975.
Fodor, Nandor. *An Encyclopaedia of Psychic Science*. Secaucus, N.J.: The Citadel Press, 1966. First published 1933.
Oppenheim, Janet. *The Other World: Spiritualism and Psychical Research in England 1850–1914*. New York: Cambridge University Press, 1985.

Stevenson, Ian (1918–   ) Physician, psychiatrist and psychical researcher, best known for his studies of children who remember previous lives (see REINCARNATION). His lesser-known interests include mediumship, apparitions and poltergeists, in all of which areas he has made methodological and theoretical contributions. As one of the most academically respected psychical researchers in the modern world, he has done much to advance the scientific study of survival after death.

Ian Stevenson was born October 31, 1918 in Montreal, Canada. He was educated at the University of St. Andrews in Scotland and at McGill University in Montreal, from which he received an M.D. in 1943. He trained in psychosomatic medicine and psychiatry in the United States and then taught psychiatry at the Louisiana State University Medical School.

Stevenson became actively involved in psychical research only after taking a position as professor of psychiatry at the University of Virginia in 1957. He became interested in extrasensory perception (ESP) and survival, and began collecting cases of past-life memory. In 1960 he published a two-part article, "The Evidence for Survival from Claimed Memories of Former Incarnations," in the *Journal of the American Society for Psychical Research*. It was named the winning essay in a contest in honor of William JAMES.

Prior to Stevenson's article, reincarnation had not received much attention in psychical research, which looked largely to mediumship and apparitions for evidence for survival. Stevenson, however, reported having found 44 published cases in which a person claimed to have been someone who could be shown to have existed, and the following year he began his own search for cases. By the early 1990s there were some 2,500 cases in his files. Thanks largely to his many books and articles, reincarnation is no longer an outlandish idea.

Stevenson was chairman of the Department of Psychiatry at the University of Virginia in 1967 when Chester Carlson, inventor of the Xerox photocopying process, provided the endowment for a faculty chair. As Carlson Professor of Psychiatry, Stevenson was freed from teaching and administrative duties and was able to devote his full time to research and writing.

In 1968, Stevenson proposed a novel way of investigating the survival of death. He began a program in which people could send him a closed combination lock, the solution to which was known only to themselves, but which they would try to communicate through a medium after their deaths. The idea for the combination lock test came from the sealed letter tests common in the earlier years of psychical research (see SURVIVAL TESTS). The disadvantage of sealed letters is that they can only be opened once, and if description of their contents is wrong, the test has failed. Combination locks, on the other hand, can be tried any number of times, which gives researchers the chance to separate the pretenders from the real communicators. Stevenson received so many locks in the first few months of his project that he had to restrict entrants to the elderly or others who expected their deaths soon. As of 1990, he had not reported any successes.

Much of Stevenson's work with mediumship has concerned drop-in communicators (q.v.), a term he coined to represent those communicators who are unknown to either the medium or the sitters but who simply "drop in" at a seance. Drop-in communicators are thought to provide especially good evidence for survival because the facts about their lives are unknown to everyone present, ruling out telepathy between medium and sitters as a possible explanation for accurate readings.

Some modern psychical researchers try to explain apparitions and poltergeists as the results of actions of living agents, but for Stevenson deceased agents may also be responsible for them, at least in some cases. In a 1975 paper entitled "Are Poltergeists Living or Are They Dead?" he described certain features that seem typical of cases with each type of agent. For instance, in cases with a deceased agent, the phenomena—such as noises and movement of objects—occurred further away from the living person around whom they seemed to center than in cases in which the living "focus person" was also the agent.

A 1982 paper, "The Contribution of Apparitions to the Evidence for Survival," argued that apparitions were produced by a deceased agent and the living subject together, each contributing varying amounts to the experience. This position is in contrast to that of Edmund GURNEY and G.N.M. TYRRELL, who believed that apparitions were hallucinations of the subjects, based on information received via ESP from the agents.

In both of these papers, Stevenson used examples from his research with reincarnation cases. Apparitions of persons about to be reincarnated sometimes appear to the mothers who will bear them. In one poltergeist case, the deceased agent claimed that in a previous life she had been married to, and deserted by, the boy she was plaguing.

Although Stevenson's life's work has been with reincarnation cases, he has tried to place these in perspective by demonstrating the links between them and other types of survival phenomena. In Stevenson's view, the personality after death may communicate with the living through mediums, interact with the world as a poltergeist, or manifest as an apparition, before it reincarnates.

Stevenson has been more successful than many psychical researchers in getting his work accepted by professional journals in other fields, including medicine, psychiatry and anthropology. When his article "Research into the Evidence for Man's Survival After Death" was published in the prestigious *Journal of Nervous and Mental Disease* in 1977, the editors received requests for reprints.

Stevenson was elected president of the international Parapsychological Association in 1968 and 1980 and president of the SOCIETY FOR PSYCHICAL RESEARCH for the 1988–89 term.

His books include *Telepathic Impressions* (1970), *Twenty Cases Suggestive of Reincarnation* (2nd edition 1974), a series of four volumes under the general title *Cases of the Reincarnation Type* (1975–1983), and a summary of his work called *Children Who Remember Previous Lives: A Question of Reincarnation* (1987).

Further reading:

Berger, Arthur S. *Lives and Letters in American Parapsychology: A Biographical History, 1850–1987.* Jefferson, N.C.: McFarland, 1988.

Pleasants, Helene, ed. *Biographical Dictionary of Parapsychology.* New York: Helix Press, 1964.

Stevenson, Ian. "The Combination Lock Test for Survival." *Journal of the American Society for Psychical Research* 62 (1968):246–54.

——. *Twenty Cases Suggestive of Reincarnation.* 2nd ed. Charlottesville: University Press of Virginia, 1974. First published in 1966 as *Proceedings of the American Society for Psychical Research* 26.

——. *Cases of the Reincarnation Type.* Vols. 1–4. Charlottesville: University Press of Virginia, 1975–83.

——. "Are Poltergeists Living or Are They Dead?" *Journal of the American Society for Psychical Research* 366 (1966):233–52.

succubus See DEMONS.

super-ESP Theory that explains that apparitions of the living and mediumship are produced by extraordinary extrasensory perception (ESP) of the living. If super-ESP is true, then it negates survival after death.

The term "super-ESP" was coined in the late 1950s by Hornell HART, an American sociologist and psychical researcher, but the concept was considered by the earliest psychical researchers, including French physiologist Charles Richet and the founders of the SOCIETY FOR PSYCHICAL RESEARCH (SPR).

In investigating mediums, researchers found evidence that clairvoyance and telepathy could account for information unknown to the medium but allegedly produced by spirits of the dead. Similarly, apparitions could be explained as a projection of telepathy among the living.

Support for super-ESP came in the famous Soal case of 1925. Dr. S.G. Soal participated in sittings with Blanche Cooper, a London medium, who claimed to have contacted Gordon Davis, a friend of Soal's whom Soal believed had been killed in World War I. Davis chatted about personal subjects, his wife and child, and he used idiosyncratic speech that Soal identified with his friend. Later, Soal discovered that Davis was alive and living in London. He theorized that clairvoyance, perhaps unwitting, had enabled Cooper to pick up "evidential" material from either Soal or Davis.

Psychologist Gardner MURPHY elaborated on the theory of super-ESP, suggesting that it might create pseudo-spirit personalities, as well as apparitions of the dead, that seem real.

Skeptics of super-ESP, contend that while it might explain some episodes, it cannot explain all. Mediums who have provided personal information to dozens of sitters would have to perform seemingly phenomenal feats of clairvoyance and telepathy. Nor does super-ESP adequately explain drop-in communicators, who are unknown to medium and sitters, or apparitions of the dead, who would be nothing more than projections from the thoughts of a living person. If seen simultaneously by more than one person, such an apparition would have to be created and passed on through telepathy.

Nonethelesss, it is virtually impossible to rule out super-ESP as an explanation. Too little is known about the nature and operation of extrasensory perception, and of the bounds and functions of human consciousness.

Further reading:

Gauld, Alan. "The 'Super-ESP' Hypothesis." *Proceedings of the Society for Psychical Research* 53 (1961):226–46.

——. *Mediumship and Survival.* London: William Heinemann Ltd., 1982.

Hart, Hornell. *The Enigma of Survival.* Springfield, Ill.: Charles C. Thomas, 1959.

Murphy, Gardner. "Difficulties Confronting the Survival Problem." *Journal of the American Society for Psychical Research* 39 (1945):67–94.

survival after death The belief that a spiritual aspect of the human being survives the destruction of the physical body is a feature of all religious traditions, with the exception of classical Buddhism, which denies the existence of the soul. For Spiritualists, belief in survival rests not on faith, but on manifestations of discarnate spirits, such as in mediumship. An unquiet relationship exists between Spiritualism and psychical research, the scientific field under the purview of which the "survival question" falls. Many psychical researchers do not accept survival as proven, but hold that the evidence can be explained more satisfactorily in terms of ESP among living persons. In addition to mediumistic communications, out-of-body experiences and near-death experiences, as well as apparitions, hauntings and poltergeists, bear on the problem of survival.

Belief in survival is found not only in the great religious traditions; it is also a tenet of the animism characteristic of tribal societies in the Americas, Africa, Asia and Australia. According to anthropologist E.B. Tylor, belief in the persistence of the human spirit indefinitely after death once existed alongside beliefs in reincarnation. Animistic ideas about reincarnation evolved into those of Hinduism, Buddhism, and their offshoots and may have been the basis of the Christian idea of resurrection. Tylor portrayed animistic soul beliefs as being grounded in experiences such as apparitions, mediumistic trances, and dreams in which one seemed to travel out of one's body and meet other human figures, much in the manner of the modern Spiritualist. Indeed, Tylor recognized a direct link between animism and Spiritualism.

Thus, belief in survival after death in one form or another is found among almost all of the world's peoples, and seems to stretch far back in time. The tendency to disbelieve in survival on the ground that it cannot be scientifically "proven" may be traced to the European Enlightenment of the 18th century. Nineteenth-century Spiritualism, with its appeal to "scientific" demonstrations, was a direct reaction to this way of thinking and an attempt to counter it in its own terms.

By the end of the 19th century, Spiritualism claimed millions of adherents, on both sides of the Atlantic, and had led to attempts to verify its claims (the SOCIETY FOR PSYCHICAL RESEARCH, or SPR, was founded in 1882, the AMERICAN SOCIETY FOR PSYCHICAL RESEARCH, or ASPR, three years later). Early psychical researchers, however, encountered much trickery and concluded that there was little substance in the Spiritualist claims. Moreover, apparitions seemed to many to be explicable as telepathically-inspired hallucinations. The psychical research societies were not founded to study the survival problem, as is commonly believed, but to determine what basis there might be for ESP.

Interest soon shifted to survival, however, with the discovery of Leonora PIPER. Piper was a different sort of medium than that usually encountered in the Spiritualism of the day; rather than producing physical phenomena, such as table levitations and materializations of objects, she went into trance and seemed to deliver verbal messages from deceased persons.

Piper worked closely with the SPR and ASPR throughout her career, and her mediumship was responsible for converting several (e.g., Richard HODGSON, James H. HYSLOP, Sir Oliver LODGE) to a belief in survival. After Piper, similar "mental mediums" were found and studied, among them Eileen J. GARRETT and Gladys Osborne LEONARD.

The importance of trance communications from mediums such as Piper, Leonard and Garrett was that they provided information that could be checked against the written sources and the memories of living persons. Establishing the paranormal basis of their knowledge then depended on showing that they had not, or could not, have received their information normally (if fraudulently), such as by reading up on their sitters ahead of time. Even when a paranormal source was indicated, however, it was possible that a medium's information had come not from discarnate spirits, but from living minds or physical sources through ESP.

Various attempts were made to control mediumistic ESP, including the use of "proxy sitters," stand-ins for persons seeking to communicate with deceased persons, who knew as little as possible about the object of the sittings. Special attention was given to drop-in communicators (q.v.), about whom neither the medium nor the sitters knew anything. Particular value is attached to cross correspondences (q.v.), the meaning of which was apparent only by taking in conjunction messages received through two or more different mediums, and which therefore implied some directing intelligence behind them. Nevertheless, ESP could in theory be stretched to cover the evidence from even these special classes (see SUPER-ESP), and increasing awareness of this gradually led to a decline in survival research, in favor of experiments to establish the limits of ESP. This movement, which continues today, received its greatest impetus from the work of J.B. RHINE.

Better evidence for physical mediumship began to appear around the turn of the century as well. The medium most responsible for the change of opinion was Eusapia PALLADINO. Palladino's mediumship was similar to that of D.D. HOME, the only famous 19th-century medium of whom no good reason for fraud was ever alleged. Careful studies in laboratory settings were later conducted with the SCHNEIDER BROTHERS. Materialization phenomena were reported in association with the Schneiders and with Marthe BERAUD ("Eva C.") and by William Jackson CRAWFORD and Thomas HAMILTON. Although Crawford and Hamilton accepted the Spiritualist hypothesis that discarnate spirits were responsible for these phenomena, most other researchers believed that they were produced by the mediums themselves, unconsciously, via psychokinesis. The latter explanation is the one favored by most psychical researchers today. Psychokinesis has also been suggested to explain many poltergeist outbreaks, in which objects move or fly about without contact. Poltergeists often center around a particular person, whom many researchers consider to be the "agent" responsible for their production. Many poltergeist agents are pre-adolescent children, a circumstance that has led skeptics to suspect trickery—as has indeed been demonstrated in some cases. In those cases involving paranormal activity, hormonal changes around the time of puberty are often implicated. In the case of Eleanore ZUGUN, a series of striking phenomena ceased almost overnight when menstruation began. The agents in a few poltergeist cases appear to be deceased persons, but these are relatively rare. Such cases may also be cases of haunting.

The evidence for survival from out-of-body and near-death experiences is more tenuous, and the most that can be said about these is that they are not incompatible with the survival hypothesis. If conscious awareness can exist apart from the body during life, then it could in principle survive death as well.

Although mediumship, apparitions, poltergeists, and out-of-body and near-death experiences typically are discussed separately, many actual cases cannot be so simply classified. In reciprocal apparitions, for instance, the agent has an apparent out-of-body experience during which he or she seems to travel to a distant place, where he or she is perceived as an apparition. The WILMOT APPARITION is an especially complex case of this type, involving also a dream vision of the agent. Mediumship and apparitions are less commonly associated, unless materialization phenomena are to be understood in this way. Nonetheless, there are cases of mediumistic communicators who appear as apparitions. Psychokinetic or poltergeist effects (e.g., rappings) are typical of physical mediumship. In the case of "Stella C." (see CRANSHAW, DOROTHY STELLA) poltergeist phenomena turned out to be associated with an unsuspected mediumistic capability.

Cases that involve more than one mode of experience strengthen the argument that can be made for survival on the basis of each type taken separately. It is much easier to conceive of a discarnate spirit that appears as an apparition, acts upon the world as a poltergeist, and communicates through a medium, than it is to imagine how all these things could be produced simultaneously through ESP and psy-

chokinesis by living persons. Good evidence for survival also comes from those cases in which the agent seems to have a special reason, or intention, to communicate, or in which the agent conveys information unknown to the sitter (in a case of mediumship) or the percipient (in an apparition case). In the CHAFFIN WILL CASE, an apparition indicates the place where a second will is hidden.

Informed skeptics of the survival hypothesis point to many inconsistencies in the data, and to problem cases such as those of fictitious or living communicators. One communicator through Piper identified herself as the author George Eliot but claimed she had met Adam Bede, actually a character in one of her novels, in the afterworld. In another famous case, a communicator who presented himself as deceased turned out to be very much alive. Cases in which it seems probable that the information came from the sitter via ESP are not uncommon, and there are a few cases in which the apparent ESP link was not with the sitter, but with someone the sitter knew. In one such case, a medium described in great detail images that were in the mind of a person the sitter had visited on the way to the seance, but which had not been communicated verbally.

If survival of death is a fact, it is clear that the process of mediumistic communication and the perception of apparitions, for instance, are complex activities. At a minimum, the data seem to call for an interaction between the agent and the medium or percipient that would allow the information to be filtered and modified by the latter at an unconscious level before coming to conscious awareness. Ideas along these lines have been suggested by several researchers, including Frederic W.H. MYERS, James H. HYSLOP and Hornell HART. Such ideas presume the survival of personality in its entirety, and although philosophers have questioned whether the idea is coherent, it is at least theoretically possible that survival occurs only in a fragmentary way, as William G. ROLL has suggested. Other theorists, such as Frederick Bligh BOND, believe that survival occurs only in the form of some type of celestial data bank. Animistic ideas are again different and involve such conceptions as multiple souls and spirits which undergo differentiation and division after death.

Spiritualism as a religious movement peaked during the late 19th century in both the United States and Europe, but Spiritualist organizations and publications continue to this day. Spiritualism is particularly strong in Britain, where the COLLEGE OF PSYCHIC STUDIES attracts many new members each year. In the United States, the popularity of CHANNELING suggests a belief in survival as well. Indeed, a Gallup poll taken in the early 1980s found that two-thirds of Americans believed in survival after death. There was little or no variation by sex, age, level of education, or religious affiliation. The tendency to doubt whether there is survival after death not only is modern, it is found among a minority of persons even in today's society.

Further reading:

Ducasse, C.J. *A Critical Examination of the Belief in a Life After Death.* Springfield, Ill.: Charles C Thomas, 1961.

Gauld, Alan. *Mediumship and Survival: A Century of Investigations.* London: William Heinemann Ltd., 1982.

Gallup, George. *Adventures in Immortality: A Look Beyond the Threshhold of Death.* New York: McGraw-Hill, 1982.

Kung, Hans. *Eternal Life? Life After Death as a Medical Philosophical and Theological Problem.* Garden City, N.Y.: Doubleday, 1984.

Murphy, Gardner. *Three Papers on the Survival Problem.* New York: American Society for Psychical Research, 1945.

Penelhum, Terence. *Survival and Disembodied Existence.* London: Routledge and Kegan Paul, 1970.

Roll, William G. "The Changing Perspective on Life After Death." In *Advances in Parapsychological Research 3*: 147–291. New York: Plenum, 1982.

Stevenson, Ian. "Research Into the Evidence of Man's Survival After Death." *Journal of Nervous and Mental Disease* 165 (1977):152–70.

Tylor, Edward Burnett. *Religion in Primitive Culture.* New York: Harper and Row, 1956.

survival tests Tests created by living persons with the idea that they will attempt to communicate their solutions through mediums after death, intended to provide evidence for their survival after death. The most popular form of such tests was once the "sealed envelope," but this has lately given way to combination locks and texts enciphered using special codes.

Frederic W.H. MYERS described some apparently successful survival tests in his *Human Personality and Its Survival of Bodily Death* (1903). In one case, a brother left with his sister one piece of a brick marked with a streak of ink, telling her that he would hide the other part in a place that only he would know. After his death, his sister and their mother began trying to communicate with him through mediums, without success until they tried sitting at home. After some period of trying, their table began to tilt, and, by calling out the alphabet and recording the letter at which the tilt came, they were able to receive a message from the deceased brother, telling them where he had hidden his part of the brick. They discovered the brick in the place indicated, and it was found to match the piece left with the sister.

The same brother left a sealed envelope, the contents of which he communicated in the same way.

Sealed letter tests were for a time very fashionable, but the interpretation of the results was not always straightforward. For one thing, even apparently successful results, such as those above, could be interpreted as examples of clairvoyance rather than spirit communication. The sister could have determined clairvoyantly where the piece of brick was hidden, and through her own psychokinesis could have caused the table to tip out the message. The same is true of the sealed letter; the sister could have read the contents clairvoyantly. In this instance, the message was read accurately, but if the communication is not a verbatim representation of the message in the envelope, but only refers to it obliquely, other questions arise. Such is the case with the sealed envelope left by Myers himself.

Another crucial problem with such tests is that the envelope can only be opened once. If the communication is wrong, there is no second chance. In order to get around this limitation, the British mathematician and psychical researcher Robert Thouless devised what he called the "cipher test." He invented a code and encoded two passages, with the idea that after death he would communicate not the message, but a key to the code that would allow the message to be read. The cipher test had the advantage that it could be tried any number of times, and it also provided the opportunity for psychics and mediums to get the solution from Thouless through ESP before his death. If mediums provided the solution only after Thouless's death, this strengthened the likelihood that they had received it from Thouless's spirit.

Thouless's cipher test required some ingenuity, and not all persons who wished to leave such tests for themselves felt themselves up to it. It was in view of providing a simpler test that Ian STEVENSON introduced the "combination lock test." This required a person to buy a particular kind of combination lock and to set it, committing the solution to memory, but not writing it down anywhere. As with the cipher test, the idea was for the person to communicate a key word that would allow the lock to be opened. Stevenson described the test publicly, and invited everyone who was interested to deposit such locks with him. The response was so tremendous that he soon had to limit the depositors to the elderly or others who faced imminent death.

Neither the cipher nor combination lock tests have been very successful. Thouless died in 1984, and sittings aimed at allowing him to communicate his code were begun soon thereafter. However, as of

1989, no successful communications had been received from him. J.G. Pratt, an experimental parapsychologist with an interest in psychical research and survival, set one of Stevenson's combination locks before he died in 1979, but no successful communications have been received from him.

Further reading:

Gauld, Alan. *Mediumship and Survival: A Century of Investigations.* London: Heinemann, 1982.

Myers, Frederic W.H. *Human Personality and Its Survival of Bodily Death Vols. I & II.* New ed. New York: Longmans, Green & Co., 1954. First published 1903.

Stevenson, Ian. "The Combination Lock Test for Survival." *Journal of the American Society for Psychical Research* 62 (1968):246–54.

Stevenson, Ian, Arthur T. Oram, and Betty Markwick. "Two Tests of Survival After Death: Report on Negative Results." *Journal of the Society for Psychical Research* 55 (1989):329–36.

Thouless, Robert H. *From Anecdote to Experiment in Psychical Research.* London: Routledge and Kegan Paul, 1972.

Swaffer, Hannen See SPIRITUALISTS' NATIONAL UNION.

Swedenborg, Emanuel (1688–1772) Swedish mystic and medium who became renowned for his visions of and travels to the spiritual planes, where he saw the afterlife of souls of the dead.

Swedenborg's mystical experiences came late in life. Professionally, he was a scientist and a scholar. He worked as the special assessor to the Royal College of Mines under Charles XII. Other than holding a belief in the existence of the soul, Swedenborg gave little thought to spiritual matters. He was 56 in 1743 when he had his first vision of the spiritual world in a dream. He then began having a series of dreams, ecstatic visions, trances and illuminations in which he visited heaven and hell, talked with Jesus and God, communicated with the spirits of the dead (he called them "angels"), and was shown the order and nature of the universe. These revelations were radically different from the teachings of the Christian Church. Swedenborg also began experiencing clairvoyance of events on earth, perhaps in out-of-body experiences, including a famous incident in 1759 in which he "saw" a great fire in Stockholm some 300 miles away.

Swedenborg believed himself to be a divine messenger and began to disseminate his revelations to others. He quit his job and became a recluse and semi-vegetarian so that he could devote himself exclusively to his visions. He became an instrument of automatic writing for the angels. Sometimes his trances would go on for days, and his catatonic state would alarm his housekeeper. He learned how to induce trances rather than wait for them to happen spontaneously. In his otherworldly visits, he claimed to converse with some of the great figures of history, including Plato, Aristotle and Napoleon and other historical luminaries.

Many of Swedenborg's peers believed he suddenly went insane. The Church actively opposed him. For most, his writings were too advanced, and it was not until after his death that a Swedenborgian movement took hold. He died in 1772 at age 84 in London, where he spent many of his later years. Swedenborgianism along with mesmerism paved the way for the advent of Spiritualism in the mid-19th century.

Swedenborg said that God created man to exist simultaneously in the physical and spiritual worlds. The spiritual world is an inner domain that influences humankind, though most persons have lost their awareness of it. The inner world survives death with its own eternal memory of every thought, emotion and action accumulated over a lifetime. The memory influences the souls' fate of heaven or hell.

Swedenborg said that after death, souls enter an earth-like transition plane where they are met by dead relatives and friends. After a period of self-evaluation, they choose their heaven or hell. The afterworlds are products of the mind created during life on earth; Swedenborg did not believe that Jesus's crucifixion absolved the sins of humankind. Generally, hell is frightening, with souls with monstrous faces (called "demons"), but has no Satan. Heaven is a replication of earth with souls who are "angels." In both spheres, souls carry on life with work, leisure, marriage, war and crime. Both spheres have societal structures and governments. It is possible for souls to advance in the afterlife, but never to leave heaven or hell, which are permanent states. Swedenborg did not believe in reincarnation.

Spiritualists adopted many of Swedenborg's views but rejected his concept of hell and divided his heaven into seven spheres through which the soul passes after death.

Swedenborgianism became a religion and is still practiced by a small number of followers around the world. The first churches were established in England in 1778 and in America in 1792. The Swedenborg Society was established in 1810 to publish and disseminate Swedenborg's prolific works. His most widely read work is *Heaven and Hell*, which describes the afterlife.

Further reading:

Brown, Slater. *The Heyday of Spiritualism.* New York: Hawthorn Books, 1970.

Douglas, Alfred. *Extrasensory Powers: A Century of Psychical Research.* London: Victor Gollancz Ltd., 1976.

Swedenborg, Emanuel. *Divine Providence.* New York: The Swedenborg Foundation, 1972. First published 1764.

———. *Divine Love and Wisdom.* New York: American Swedenborg Printing and Publishing Society, 1904. First published 1763.

———. *The Four Doctrines.* New York: The Swedenborg Foundation, 1976. First published 1763.

Wilson, Colin. *The Occult.* New York: Vintage Books, 1973.

Swooning Shadow   See BLACK SHUCK.

T

telephone communication with the dead See PHONE CALLS FROM THE DEAD.

teleportation See APPORT.

Theatre Royal Venerable theater on Drury Lane in London claimed to be home to an assortment of theater-loving ghosts. The present structure is actually the fourth theater constructed at the site during a 300-year history.

The theater's most famous ghost is the Man in Gray, a non-threatening spirit that has haunted it for more than a century. Unlike most ghosts, which are regarded as ill omens, the Man in Gray is thought to bring good luck to actors and plays alike. The ghost is so highly regarded that an offer to exorcise him was once flatly refused by the theater management.

The Man in Gray is so named because he invariably appears dressed in a long gray cloak, knee breeches and buckle shoes apparently dating to the 18th century. Observers say he is handsome, wears a powdered wig and carries a three-cornered hat. The hilt of a sword can be seen beneath the cloak. His identity is unknown, but it is believed that he may once have been a young man who was stabbed to death and walled up inside the theater. In the 19th century, workmen repairing the balcony found a hidden room behind a wall. Inside was a skeleton of a young man, whose ribs still held a dagger. Fragments of clothing were dated to the 18th century. There is no record of a murder occurring at the theater. Various suggestions have been put forward, including one that holds the victim was a Georgian dandy who was killed in a fight over a beautiful actress.

Only the very psychically sensitive are believed to be able to see the Man in Gray: often only one or two people in a group will spot him while the others do not. Many who have glimpsed the phantom believe him to be a flesh-and-blood actor dressed in costume, and thus do not report seeing a ghost.

The Man in Gray is most curiously a daytime ghost, and is seen between the hours of 9 A.M. and 6 P.M., never later. He appears mostly at rehearsals, when there are few people in the theater, but sometimes shows up for matinee performances. Only once has he been spotted backstage. He walks slowly from one end of the balcony to the other and disappears into the wall. Sometimes he takes a seat in the upper section, then disappears into the wall after a performance. He also vanishes if someone tries to move too close to him. At least one monarch, King George VI, made a trip to the theater specifically to catch a glimpse of the ghost, but the phantom declined to appear.

The ghost has exhibited a fine critical eye and ear for the catchy tune. Since he usually is seen at rehearsals of plays and musicals destined to be hits, his appearance is considered a lucky omen. Among the winners picked by the phantom are the musicals *Oklahoma, Carousel, South Pacific* and *The King and I.*

Oklahoma, in fact, seemed to be highly popular with ghosts; several other apparitions in addition to the Man in Gray were reported seen in the audience and backstage. The ghost of Charles II, a theater-lover during his life, and the ghosts of his attendants were seen at a performance of *Oklahoma* in 1948.

Also during the run of *Oklahoma,* one American actress, Betty Jo Jones, reported that her performance was not going well until she felt a ghost gently push her into a different position and guide her around the stage on two successive nights. Her performances improved and so satisfied the ghost that he patted her on the back.

Another ghostly pat on the back was felt by Doreen Duke, an inexperienced young actress who auditioned for *The King and I.* Duke felt unseen hands help her around the stage. She landed the part, but the hands still guided her during rehearsal and through her anxiety-ridden opening night.

It is thought that the helpful ghost may be that of Joe Grimaldi, a comic and singer who liked to help up-and-coming young performers when he was alive. The Theatre Royal was his favorite theater. Before Grimaldi died in 1837, he specified that his head was to be severed from his body and that he was to be buried in the shade of St. James Church, Islington, which is near the Theatre Royal.

The Theatre Royal also houses at least one unpleasant ghost, believed to be Charles Macklin, a mean actor who killed a colleague, Thomas Hallam, during a brawl. Macklin was never brought to justice and reputedly lived to age 107. His ghost is said to prowl the backstage corridors.

Other ghost residents are said to be Charles Keene, a noted 19th century actor, and Dan Leno, a pantomime comic who went insane and died at the age of 43. Keene's ghost, dressed quaintly, has been seen sitting among the audience watching performances. Leno's ghost has been seen backstage in a certain dressing room.

See also ADELPHI THEATRE.

Further reading:
Cohen, Daniel. *The Encyclopedia of Ghosts.* New York: Dodd, Mead & Co., 1984.
Folklore, Myths and Legends of Britain. London: Reader's Digest Assoc., 1977.
Underwood, Peter. *Haunted London.* London: George G. Harrup & Co., 1973.
Whitaker, Terence. *Haunted England.* Chicago: Contemporary Books, 1987.

Thompson-Gifford Case   A case of apparent spirit obsession, and the most famous case investigated by James H. HYSLOP, psychical researcher and an early president of the AMERICAN SOCIETY FOR PSYCHICAL RESEARCH (ASPR). Hyslop considered the case proof of the reality of spirit obsession.

Frederic L. Thompson, then a 39-year-old metalworker and weekend artist, first visited Hyslop in January 1907. Thompson claimed he was under the influence of the late R. Swain Gifford, a noted landscape painter in the late 1800s, experiencing tremendous urges to paint and sketch trees and rocky coasts that he had never seen before. Although Thompson had met Gifford one summer in New Bedford, Massachusetts, and had contacted him in 1898 to ask for a recommendation to the Tiffany Glass Company, the two men were hardly acquaintances, much less friends. Thompson moved to New York in 1900, where he was employed in metal and jewelry work. He did not know that Gifford died on January 15, 1905.

By the late summer and fall of that year, Thompson was overcome with strong impulses to paint. He did not understand these urges, but he began to visualize pictures he knew Gifford had painted on the New Bedford coast. He referred to his artist alter ego as "Mr. Gifford," a fact confirmed to Hyslop by Thompson's wife, Carrie.

But in January 1906, Thompson saw an exhibition of the works of "the late R. Swain Gifford" and realized for the first time that Gifford was dead. Fascinated by the similarities between Gifford's paintings and his own recent efforts, he could almost feel the fresh sea breezes. Then a voice came to him, saying "You see what I have done. Go on with the work," and he blacked out.

Thompson continued painting, as his private life and finances deteriorated under the ever-increasing compulsions. He believed he was going insane—two physicians diagnosed him as a paranoid—and finally visited Hyslop after hearing of the doctor's work in psychical research. Hyslop was intrigued, but at first believed Thompson was suffering from personality disintegration. But if there were any truth to Thompson's claims, Hyslop believed consulting a medium would shed light on the situation. So he and Thompson met with Margaret Gaule on January 18, 1907.

Gaule immediately sensed the presence of an artist, although Hyslop had given her no information about Thompson, even introducing him as "Mr. Smith." She described landscape scenes, much as Thompson had detailed them to Hyslop two days earlier. On March 16, Hyslop took Thompson to Boston, to sit with Minnie M. Soule (referred to in Hyslop's papers as "Mrs. Chenoweth"), who was judged the most talented medium of her day. Her spirit communicator, Sunbeam, gave her information about Gifford's personal habits, even his clothing and rugs—items later confirmed by Gifford's widow—and vividly described a certain scene of gnarled trees overlooking the water that had haunted Thompson for days. Such communications convinced Thompson he was not going insane, and he left for the New England coast to try to find the pictures in his mind.

Throughout the summer and autumn of 1907, Thompson traveled over Gifford's favorite island haunts, recognizing scenes he had been compelled to paint, hearing music and even the voice he had heard at the Gifford exhibition. On one of the trees Thompson sought, Gifford had carved his initials, "R.S.G., 1902." By early 1908, Thompson was completing large paintings and selling them. Prominent art critics who viewed the works agreed they bore uncanny resemblances to Gifford's works. Hyslop still harbored suspicions that Thompson was merely cultivating long-harbored desires to be an artist, and that his association with Gifford had influenced him more than he realized.

To prove whether Thompson was obsessed with the spirit of Gifford or had merely incorporated the memory of Gifford into his work, Hyslop decided to establish contact with the dead artist. After an initial sitting with Gaule, Hyslop brought Soule down to New York from Boston so that he and Thompson could meet with her regularly. During the seance of June 4, 1908, Soule appeared to be receiving communications from Gifford, and she finally revealed that the artist was elated over his power to return and finish his work through Thompson. Later seances revealed hundreds of evidential communications about scenes and colors that indicated Gifford's influence.

Back in Boston, Soule met with Hyslop alone on July 15. During the seance, the supposed spirit of Gifford revealed he had sent a dream of the angel of death to Thompson. When Hyslop returned to New York, Mrs. Thompson visited Hyslop, worried about a dream of death her husband had recently experienced and then sketched. Hyslop felt he was close to establishing real contact with Gifford's spirit, which had yet to positively identify himself. Hyslop attended no more seances on the Thompson case until December 1908, and this time he consulted Mrs. Willis M. Cleaveland as the medium. Cleaveland's first sessions were disappointing, but on the morning of December 9, she sat with Thompson alone. Her communicator addressed Thompson, telling him that he had given his work to him and not to neglect it. Through automatic writing, Cleaveland first tried to write initials, then began sketching scenes of the Massachusetts coast that Thompson had visited the summer before. The spirit reminisced about his childhood and early paintings, then admonished Thompson to continue with the work, and not to forget him. Finally, the spirit told Thompson he had to go, and scrawled "R.S.G." using Cleaveland's hand.

Hyslop firmly believed that he had found a true case of spirit obsession in Frederic Thompson/R. Swain Gifford. Later investigations, some alleging fraud or super-telepathy, never quite refuted Hyslop's earlier conclusions. Gifford's spirit reportedly never bothered Thompson again, but he left his metalworking career and became a full-time painter, joining the then-prestigious Salmagundi Club for professional painters in 1912. He worked out of New York for a few years, then moved to Martha's Vineyard off the coast of New Bedford. Returning to New York in the 1920s, Thompson continued to paint and sculpt, showing his works in various exhibitions and ap-

parently making a good living. He worked out of Miami in the late 1920s, and probably died about 1927.

Further reading:

Hyslop, James H. *Contact with the Other World*. New York: The Century Co., 1919.

Rogo, D. Scott. *The Infinite Boundary*. New York: Dodd, Mead & Co., 1987.

Thornton Heath Poltergeist   A case involving a house in London haunted by a most unusual poltergeist in 1938. The poltergeist activity was centered on Mrs. Forbes, the mistress of Thornton Heath, who was described by an investigator, Nandor FODOR, as suffering from "poltergeist psychosis." Fodor asserted that the psychosis was an episodic mental disturbance of schizophrenic character, and that Mrs. Forbes' unconscious mind was responsible for the activities finally determined to be fraudulent. Fodor eventually identified the cause as sexual trauma that had occurred in Mrs. Forbes's childhood, and had been repressed.

The full story, however, was not told until 1945 when Fodor, director of research of the International Institute for Psychical Research, gave a lecture at the Association for the Advancement of Psychotherapy and published it in the *Journal of Clinical Psychopathology*.

The delay was the result of public and professional criticism directed at Fodor as a result of his emphasis on the psychological aspects of the case. Matters became so intolerable to Fodor that he successfully sued some of his critics for libel. Eventually, however, Fodor was vindicated by winning recognition for his theory.

Mrs. Forbes, a woman of 35 years, lived at Thornton Heath with her husband and son. From his very first day of observation, Fodor entertained the notion that Mrs. Forbes could be causing the activities by normal means, despite her visible signs of distress in reaction to the activities, and his lack of proof.

At first, Fodor was the sole eyewitness to the many poltergeist incidents taking place in the house. He suggested that Mrs. Forbes should be studied at the Institute where he and his colleagues would keep an eye on her. Precautions included having her undress for a body check and having her wear special clothes for easy viewing of any sleight-of-hand tricks.

But the perplexing incidents continued at the Institute. Dishes floated and crashed to the floor, glasses flew out of Mrs. Forbes' hand, objects from Thornton Heath mysteriously appeared in the Institute (10 miles away) and clattered to the floor. Objects suddenly appeared in Mrs. Forbes' hand or inside a box.

At the same time as he was gathering evidence of the poltergeist activities, Fodor was investigating Mrs. Forbes' psychological background. He found enough material to conclude that she was a neurotic with a disorganized psyche. Her past was replete with incidents of hysterical reactions and a dissociated personality which included hearing voices, having visions and signs of lapsing unconsciousness.

Mrs. Forbes was even believed to be bent on self-punishment, and she revealed physical signs of her self-destructive attempts. One alleged experience with an apparition at Thornton Heath that tried to strangle her with a necklace left her with burn-like marks on her neck. Another time she reportedly was clawed by a phantom tiger which left five long weals on her arms. Still another time she claimed that a vampire had visited her during the night, bit her, and left two puncture marks on her neck.

Fodor and other eyewitnesses at the Institute watched Mrs. Forbes as she appeared to be choked by some unseen hand which also left marks on her neck. Fodor explained this phenomenon as Mrs. Forbes intensely wishing the death of a man she saw in a vision. In her imagination she identified so strongly with him that she had him hanged in her own body.

But Fodor was certain that Mrs. Forbes was using trickery, hiding objects in her clothing that she would quickly retrieve while seeking to distract her observers with another activity. Once Fodor requested that she be stripped in daylight so that she could be examined for secreting these small objects that seemingly appeared from nowhere and fell to the floor.

Nothing was revealed, but Fodor knew that no proper conclusions could be made without either a medical or X-ray examination. Initially objecting and then agreeing, Mrs. Forbes had the X-ray and thereby proved Fodor to be correct. Two small objects were seen to be held under Mrs. Forbes' left breast. They later appeared in her hands after she had allegedly collapsed.

This event convinced Fodor that Mrs. Forbes was fabricating the hauntings. At the same time, she demonstrated hysterical reactions, such as abdominal swelling, to being prevented from revealing the objects from their secret places under her clothing. Fodor further became convinced that Mrs. Forbes knew what she was doing and took a great deal of delight in fooling her observers.

Yet, he believed that such a case demonstrated the need for a new departure in psychical research, one that sought to understand the mental processes that go before, or along with, such practices, no matter how fraudulent. In Fodor's opinion, Mrs. Forbes' choice of objects, her obvious signs of distress before she revealed them, and many of her monitory hallucinations, all pointed to the unconscious nature of her behavior.

Further reading:
Fodor, Nandor. *On the Trail of the Poltergeist.* New York: The Citadel Press, 1958.

toad In occult lore, the toad is said to be psychically sensitive and can detect the presence of a ghost. Its presence in a house or garden is considered to be protective against the supernatural.

Folklore also holds that toads are favorite familiars (demons in animal shape) of witches, and that witches shape-shift into toads. In certain areas, toads are death omens of sorts. In part of England, it was once a practice to capture a toad, break its hind legs, sew it up in a bag live and tie the bag around the neck of a patient. The toad's survival or death would foretell the fate of the patient.

See also CHARMS AGAINST GHOSTS.

Thouless, Robert See SURVIVAL TESTS.

tommyknocker See KNOCKER.

totemism That part of animism that relates to a mystical connection believed to occur between human beings and certain features of the world in which they live, especially wild animals. Totemism has sometimes been thought to be a coherent system in its own right, but it has been shown to refer only to a loose set of practices, which do not always or of necessity appear together.

The word "totem" entered the English language in the published journal of John Long (1791), an English trader who spent several years among the Ojibwa as an interpreter. Long equated the totem with the Ojibwa guardian spirit, which some later writers have held to be an error.

The concept of "totemism" received a major boost when it was presented by Emile Durkheim in *The Elementary Forms of the Religious Life* (1912) as the world's most primitive religion, based on its appearance among certain groups of Australian Aborigines. The Aranda of Central Australia claimed descent through reincarnation from their totem animal, which led Durkheim to suggest that the idea of the totem had led to the idea of the soul. A depiction of the totem might be used to mark ritual objects, suggesting to Durkheim that the essence of the totem's meaning lay in its evocation of a primal magical or spiritual force, called mana. The association of the totem and mana also explained why people were prohibited from eating their totem animals, Durkheim believed.

Even by the time Durkheim wrote, questions had been raised about totemism as a coherent system, identifiable as such. In *Totemism* (1963), anthropologist Claude Levi-Strauss reviewed what had been written about the subject and showed just how varied were the beliefs and practices that might be classified as totemic. Social groups named after animals, taboos on eating the animal to which one "belonged," and descent from the animal, were found widely, though not always together. Moreover, a totem was not necessarily an animal—it might be a natural phenomenon, a physical feature, even a man-made object. Totemism emerges from Levi-Strauss' study as a heterogeneous collection of beliefs related to some fundamental animistic ideas, that were classed together by anthropologists because they seemed to relate to the same type of things. For members of tribal societies, however, "totemism" has no recognizable meaning.

The American anthropologist Ralph Linton has written about a situation he encountered during World War I, when he belonged to the 42nd or "Rainbow" Division of the American Expeditionary Force, which shows how natural and easy it is for such practices to develop, even in modern society. Linton's division was given its name by a staff officer because the division was composed of units from so many states that their regimental colors were as varied as those of the rainbow. It started as a nickname, but as soon as the division arrived in France, the name came into common use. When asked what division they were from, men would answer: "I am a Rainbow."

Some five or six months after the division had got its name, it was generally agreed that a rainbow was an appropriate symbol for it—a rainbow was said to appear every time the division went into action, no matter what the weather was like at the time. Then the Rainbow Division found itself stationed alongside the 77th Division, which had its own symbol, the Statue of Liberty. Men of the Rainbow Division imitated those of the Statue of Liberty Division by beginning to wear rainbow insignia. These practices caught on, so that by the end of the war, the entire American Expeditionary Force was composed of various well-defined groups, each with its own special set of insignia, ideas and observances.

Linton identified several ways in which the behavior of the American troops was similar to that of tribal peoples: (1) segmentation into groups conscious of their identity; (2) the identification of each group with an animal, thing, or natural phenomenon; (3)

the use of this term as a form of address, or in conversation with strangers; (4) the use of an emblem to signify personal or group ownership of articles; (5) respect for the "patron" represented by the emblem; and (6) a vague belief in the power of this patron to look out for their interests.

Further reading:

Durkheim, Emile. *The Elementary Forms of the Religious Life.* Glencoe, Ill.: Free Press, 1965.

Levi-Strauss, Claude. *Totemism.* Boston: Beacon Press, 1963.

Linton, Ralph. "Totemism and the A.E.F." *American Anthropologist* 26 (1924):296–300.

Radin, Paul. *Primitive Religion: Its Nature and Origin.* New York: Dover Publications, 1957.

Tylor, Edward Burnett. *Religion in Primitive Culture.* New York: Harper and Row, 1956.

Tower of London This blood-soaked site once served as a prison and execution site, and it is said to be filled with the ghosts of victims who lost their heads on its scaffold. Many ghosts have been sighted by sentries who see them either standing at various tower windows, walking on the grounds or passing through walls and doors. Ghosts most often are headless, and include men, women and children—and a bear that presumably dates from the Tower's days as a menagerie. Most ghosts travel alone, but apparitions moving in processions have also been seen.

One of the first sightings ever recorded was the ghost of Thomas à Becket, first seen in 1241, 71 years after his murder in Canterbury Cathedral when he was its archbishop. Although the presence of Becket's ghost is unusual because he was not killed at the Tower, it was fitting that he returned to haunt it, because he was a Londoner who once had been constable of the Tower.

More unusual was Becket's probable reason for haunting the Tower. It seems that the Tower's neighbors were being disturbed by alterations made at the site and Becket's ghost appeared to protest them. A priest reportedly saw the apparition striking the walls with his cross, whereupon they immediately crumbled.

The ghost most frequently seen is that of Anne Boleyn, second wife of King Henry VIII, whom he had beheaded in 1536. Boleyn's ghost appears either just below the room where she spent her last night, walking in front of the Tower chapel, or walking toward the Thames River which runs alongside the Tower.

Three other ghosts are of beheaded women, one of whom was Catherine Howard, another hapless wife of King Henry VIII. The others were Margaret, Countess of Salisbury, and Lady Jane Grey.

The Countess met a particularly horrendous end in 1541 when her executioner's ax failed to hit her neck on his first three attempts, hit it only halfway on his fourth try, and succeeded only with his fifth blow. The Countess screamed and struggled between each attempt, and it is these cries of terror that reportedly are heard from her ghost about the time of the anniversary of her death.

Lady Jane Grey was little more than a child of 17 when she was executed after reigning as a queen for nine days in 1553. Her apparition was seen a few times in the 1950s, around the time of the anniversary of her death.

The ghost of King Henry VIII has been said to float in mid-air past a sentry. Other spirits sighted belong to notables in English history, such as the Duke of Northumberland, whose ghost was such a familiar figure to sentries that they nicknamed the path between the Martin and Constable Towers, Northumberland's Walk.

Other hauntings include Sir Walter Raleigh, executed in 1618 on orders of King James I, and the ghosts of King Edward V and Prince Richard, brothers who died as children in 1483 when their uncle wanted them out of his way to claim the throne as King Richard III.

Further reading:

Folklore, Myths and Legends of Britain. London: Reader's Digest Assoc., 1977.

Hole, Christina. *Haunted England*. London: B.T. Batsford Ltd., 1940.

Whitaker, Terence. *Haunted England*. Chicago: Contemporary Books, 1987.

tree ghosts   Trees are widely believed to be favorite dwelling places for ghosts of the dead. In northern India, for example, many local shrines are built under trees for the propitiation of the resident ghosts. The Bira is a tree that is home to the Bagheswar, a tiger godling which is one of the most dreaded deities for the jungle tribes of Mirzapur. In the Dakkim, it is thought that the spirit of the pregnant woman of Churel lives in a tree.

The Abor and Padam peoples of East Bengal believe that ghosts in trees kidnap children. In the Konkan, the medium, called a Bhagat, who becomes possessed is called Jhad, or tree. In Indian lore, Devadatta worshipped a tree which suddenly broke in two one day. A nymph appeared and lured Devadatta inside, where he found a palace full of jewels and saw the maiden daughter of the King of the Yakshas, Vidyatprabha, lying on a couch.

See also CHUREL; KAN HOTIDAN.

Tregeagle, Jan (also **Tregagle, Jan**)   The ghost of a 17th-century sinner from Cornwall, England who was summoned from the grave and set to eternal and fruitless tasks.

A historical Jan Tregeagle existed; he was a local magistrate, stern and unpopular, who used his position to amass a fortune. According to legend, he accomplished this by forgery, fraud, seizing the estates of orphans and selling his soul to the Devil. He is also alleged to have murdered his wife and children, but no historical proof of this exists.

Worried about his after-death fate, Tregeagle is said to have bribed local clergy so that he could be buried on consecrated ground in St. Breock's churchyard. However, several years after his death he was summoned from the grave, and his eternal travail began.

Legends differ as to the fate of Tregeagle. According to one story, a legal dispute arose between two families over ownership of a piece of land near Bodmin. Tregeagle had served as lawyer to one of the parties in the dispute and had fraudulently obtained title to the land himself. The dispute was taken to the Bodmin assizes. There, the defendant produced Tregeagle's ghost as a witness, which he had called up from the grave. The ghost testified that the defendant had been defrauded, and the jury found in the man's favor.

But the defendant refused to return Tregeagle's ghost to the grave, claiming that calling him up had been so difficult and dreadful, he wanted nothing further to do with the matter. The clergy was consulted, and decided that in order to save Tregeagle's soul from the clutches of the Devil, they would have to keep the ghost busy for eternity.

Tregeagle was bound by spells and dispatched to Dozmary Pool, a supposedly bottomless lake (it now often dries out during hot and dry summers). He was to empty the lake with a leaky limpet shell. A pack of whisht hounds (q.v.) kept him at his task. One night, terrified by a storm, Tregeagle ran away. He was pursued by the baying, headless hounds all across Bodmin Moor. Tregeagle reached a chapel at Roche Rock, but only managed to stick his head in the window. When the hellhounds reached him, his screams could be heard for miles.

After several days of torment, he was rescued by the priest of the Rock, who, with two saints, led him to Padstow beach. There, Tregeagle was set to weaving ropes from sand. The incoming tide always destroyed his efforts, and his howling could be heard far and wide.

He became such a nuisance that St. Petroc, Padstow's patron saint, forced him to move on to Berepper, near Helston. There Tregeagle was assigned to empty Berepper beach of sand, carrying it sack by sack across the estuary of the Loe and dumping it at Porthleven. The tide once again destroyed his efforts. While he was crossing the estuary, a demon tripped him and he spilled his sand. It formed a ridge, now known as Loe Bar, that blocked the harbor.

The residents of Helston were angry to lose their harbor, and they shackled Tregeagle and packed him off to Land's End at the very tip of Cornwall. He was told to sweep the sand from Porthcurno Cave into Mill Bay, an impossible task due to the tides. Tregeagle's howls of protest are still heard whenever a gale rages and throws sand back on the beach.

In another version of the tale, the court dispute concerned a loan between two men witnessed by Tregeagle while alive. The debtor denied receiving the loan and declared in court that if Tregeagle had indeed witnessed the deal, he should come and declare it. To the court's astonishment, Tregeagle's ghost suddenly appeared and set the record straight. He told the debtor it would not be so easy to send him back to the grave.

Tregeagle then followed the man everywhere. Finally the harried man sought the help of clergy and exorcists. They drew a magic circle around the man, and the spirit of Tregeagle appeared in the form of a black bull and tried to get at him, but was prevented by the circle. While a parson read holy words, Tregeagle became increasingly gentle. Finally he allowed himself to be bound with hempen cord and led away to Gwenvor Cove. There the exorcists assigned him to making a truss of sand, to be bound with ropes of sand and then carried to Carn Olva.

This was an impossible task, but Tregeagle labored at it until one cold winter when he got an idea. He poured water from Velan Dreath brook over the truss. It froze, and he was able to carry it to Carn Olva.

Freed from his bondage, Tregeagle flew at once back to the man who had summoned him from the grave, and would have attacked him had not the man had the fortune to have an innocent child in his arms. The man sent for the clergy, who once again succeeded in binding Tregeagle. They returned him to Gwenvor Cove and assigned him the same task, but prohibited him from going near fresh water. Tregeagle still labors away on the shores of Whitsand Bay. Whenever a northern storm rolls in and destroys his work, his howls are heard throughout the countryside.

Today in Cornwall, the term "Tregeagle" is applied to anyone who blusters and protests, and to children who squall.

Further reading:

Brooks, J.A., ed. *Cornish Ghosts and Legends*. Norwich, England: Jarrold Colour Publications, 1981.

Folklore, Myths and Legends of Britain. London: Reader's Digest Assn. Ltd., 1973.

trumpet   Cardboard and aluminum trumpets once were popular in Spiritualist seances to help amplify the voices of spirits, so that they could communicate in direct voice mediumship. The use of trumpets appears to have been started by Jonathan Koons in the mid-19th century at the behest of spirit control John KING. Trumpets also reportedly levitated and floated in the air during some mediums' seances. Communication through trumpets declined along with physical mediumship in general.

TUNSTEAD FARM SKULL   See SCREAMING SKULLS.

Turpin, Dick   One of Britain's most infamous highwaymen, whose ghost is said to still haunt Hounslow Heath and large stretches of highway between London and the Scotland border.

Dick Turpin, from Essex, was a butcher who became a cattle thief, murderer and robber. Most of his criminal activities were carried out in the early 18th century in Essex, North London and Yorkshire. He was one of the many "Knights of the High Toby," the highwaymen who waylaid travelers along the dangerous country lanes and the major highways such as the Great North Road. He is said to have hidden in numerous pubs and inns, some of which bear his name today.

Turpin was somewhat of a popular hero in his day, because the highwaymen's robbing of the rich delighted poorer folk. Unlike the legendary Robin Hood, however, they did not give to the poor, but kept their loot themselves. In reality, Turpin and his ilk were anything but heroes. They brutalized people and committed heinous crimes to increase their own wealth. A newspaper story of 1735 tells of how Turpin and his band raided a farm at Edgware. When the farmer protested that he had no money, they took his breeches down and set his rear end on fire.

Turpin was in his early thirties when he was hanged in 1739 at York for stealing cattle. He bowed gallantly to the women present and then threw himself off the ladder. The crowd was so taken with this spectacular performance that they stole his body and buried it in quicklime to prevent it from being sold to anatomists, as was often the custom of the day. Turpin's tomb is in the churchyard of St. Denys and St. George. The leg irons that held him in prison are on display at York Castle Museum.

Ghost stories about Dick Turpin invariably surround his exploits as a highwayman. He is reported at so many locations that almost any spectral horseman, especially on the Al highway, has been called Dick Turpin. In the Midlands, he is reported to haunt the A5 (Watling Street) between Hinckley and Nuneaton, wearing a large black tricorn hat and a coat with brilliant red sleeves. Some ghost hunters, however, believe this specter is that of another, unknown highwayman.

Turpin is said to haunt the area near Woughton-on-the-Green, on B488. The figure is cloaked and hazy, and moves restlessly about as though waiting for something to happen. He is also seen astride his spectral black horse, riding through the area at night. Turpin did in fact use this village as a hideaway following crimes committed in the Watling Street area, which is about three miles away. At the Old Swan Inn, he forced a blacksmith to reverse the shoes on his horse in order to confuse his pursuers. He escaped when his pursuers rode off in the opposite direction.

Turpin's ghost also is said to haunt the A11 between London and Norwich, especially the stretch north of Loughton through Epping Forest. The ghost, mounted on his black horse, gallops down Traps Hill with a thin woman clutching at his waist, her feet dragging on the ground. She shrieks piteously. According to legend, this haunting is the result of Turpin's brutal act toward an old and wealthy widow who lived near Loughton. He waylaid her one evening and tortured her until she revealed the hiding place of her jewelry. Then he tied her to his horse and dragged her to her death.

Turpin's ghost also is said to be among those haunting Heathrow Airport. The airport is located in Hounslow Heath, an area about 25 square miles in size to the west of London once said to be plagued by highwaymen. Turpin's invisible form reportedly creeps up behind airline staff, breathes down their necks and pants like a dog.

Turpin's galloping spectral black horse is often incorrectly identified as the famous Black Bess. That horse was ridden by another highwayman, William Nevison. In 1678, Nevison rode from London to York in a mere 15 hours and 35 minutes in order to establish an alibi. King Charles II was so amused by this that he christened Nevison "Swift Nicks" and

granted him a pardon. Nevison, like Turpin, still met his fate on the gallows, in 1685.

Further reading:

Brooks, J.A. *Ghosts of London: The East End, City and North.* Norwich, England: Jarrold Colour Publications, 1982.

Folklore, Myths and Legends of Britain. London: Reader's Digest Assoc., 1977.

Harries, John. *The Ghost Hunter's Road Book.* Rev. ed. London: Charles Letts & Co., Ltd., 1974.

Hole, Christina. *Haunted England.* London: B.T. Batsford Ltd., 1940.

Twigg, Ena (1914–   )

One of the most famous British mediums in the latter part of the 20th century, Twigg promoted Spiritualism through radio and television broadcasts. Her uncanny successes and plain housewifely ways caused thousands of people from all walks of life to seek her services, either in private seances or through letters and telephone calls.

Twigg was born shortly before the outbreak of World War I in Gillingham, Kent, England to Harry and Frances Baker, the second of four children. She described her childhood as happy and ordinary but admits she was psychic from a very early age, remembering out-of-body experiences as early as two years, when she "flew" about the house after being tucked into bed. She often saw spirits, whom she called "the misty people"; they foretold her beloved father's untimely death when Ena was 14. All of the Bakers were psychic, but most of them denied their talents.

After her father's death and her mother's remarriage 18 months later, Twigg drew closer to her childhood friend, Harry Twigg, and they married when Ena was 17. Harry joined the Royal Navy, and most of their working lives were spent on the move in different ports throughout the world. The Twiggs had no children.

Twigg's paranormal experiences increased after her marriage, much to her chagrin. She had visions of Harry, wherever he was in the world, and received visitations from her deceased father. When she fell seriously ill with heart disease, spirit doctors healed her, asking that she help others in return. At that point Twigg relented, vowing to develop her talents as clairvoyant, clairaudient and trance medium for society's greater good. Twigg also performed psychometry and direct voice mediumship.

The spirits showed her all of World War II before it occurred and helped her track Harry on board ship when his whereabouts were unknown. She helped many bereaved widows and families reach their loved ones. She became increasingly active in the fight to have Spiritualism recognized in Britain as a religion, and gave sittings both in private and in public. Twigg also worked as a healer.

In 1957, Twigg appeared on BBC-TV's "Press Conference," the first time an avowed Spiritualist had appeared on television. With the repeal of the Witchcraft Act of 1754 in 1951, and its replacement by the Fraudulent Mediums Act, Spiritualism gained wider acceptance as a legitimate faith, and Twigg often spoke for Spiritualism at Anglican church conferences. She gained the support of Rev. Canon Mervyn Stockwood, Bishop of Southwark Cathedral, and Canon John D. Pearce-Higgins, vice-provost of Southwark. In March 1967, Twigg sat on a panel discussing survival for "Meeting Point," a religious program on the BBC, thereby breaking the 30-year ban on Spiritualist participation in religious broadcasting. Her television and radio appearances increased, gaining her more requests for sittings than she could accommodate.

The Twiggs traveled all over Europe and to the United States, gaining more converts. Exhausted, Twigg eliminated her public clairvoyant performances, moved with Harry to a small house in East Acton Lane, London, and devoted her time to private seances.

Perhaps her most famous series of communications began in March 1966, when she sat with American Episcopal bishop James A. PIKE. The bishop's flat in Cambridge, England had been host to poltergeist phenomena for the past two weeks when he called Canon Pearce-Higgins for help, and Pearce-Higgins suggested a seance with Twigg. During the sitting, the bishop's son James Jr., who had recently died of an overdose of pills in New York City, came through strongly, as did the young man's godfather, liberal theologian Paul Tillich. Both Tillich and Jim Jr. encouraged the bishop to continue the fight against charges of heresy by conservative church officials.

In another sitting with Twigg, and later through mediums George Daisley and Arthur FORD, Jim Jr. came through often. During a televised seance with Ford and Bishop Pike, Ford spoke in trance on Jim's behalf for about two hours. Because of her earlier contact, this event gave Twigg even more television exposure.

Tragically, Twigg served as medium for the bishop three years later, when he died in the Judaean wilderness. Before searchers had found the body, Bishop Pike came through Twigg while in trance in a sitting with her husband Harry and Canon Pearce-Higgins. The session was long and tortured as the bishop struggled with his transition to the Other Side.

Throughout her life and work, Twigg taught that Spiritualism was not about death but life. If people could believe that death was not the end, that the spirit survives, then their lives—their living—would be richer.

Further reading:
Twigg, Ena, with Ruth Hagy Brod. *Ena Twigg: Medium.* London: W.H. Allen, 1973.

Tyrone, Admiral Sir George A crisis apparition of the distinguished British naval officer, Admiral Sir George Tyrone, appeared on the night of his drowning, astonishing guests who were enjoying a party at his London home.

On June 22, 1893, Admiral Tyrone was in command of the HMS *Victoria*, part of the Mediterranean Fleet. For unknown reasons, he gave a command that led to the collision of the *Victoria* with another ship, the *Camperdown*. The two ships were leading columns of the fleet when Tyrone gave the order for the columns to turn inward, even though it would result in a head-on collision between the lead ships. At the last moment, he ordered full steam astern to try to avert the crash, but it was too late, and the *Camperdown* struck the *Victoria*. Tyrone's ship went down, and he drowned.

At the approximate time of the accident, Lady Tyrone was hosting an elegant party at their Easton Place home in London. The guests were stunned when Admiral Tyrone, in full uniform, suddenly appeared, walked across the room and disappeared.

It is possible that the emotional distress of the accident, and Tyrone's knowledge of his imminent demise as his ship went down, enabled a projection of himself to appear to his wife and others (see APPARITIONS).

Further reading:
Cohen, Daniel. *The Encyclopedia of Ghosts.* New York: Dodd, Mead & Co., 1984.

Tyrrell, George Nugent Merle (1879–1952) Mathematician, engineer and psychical researcher, a leading member of the SOCIETY FOR PSYCHICAL RESEARCH (SPR). Best known for his theoretical work on apparitions, he also made experimental studies of extrasensory perception (ESP) and was the author of several books that, although now largely forgotten, were well regarded in his day.

G.N.M. Tyrrell studied physics and mathematics at the University of London. He was an early student of Guglielmo Marconi, and helped to develop the radio. When he joined the SPR in 1908, he was in Mexico demonstrating Marconi's wireless to the government. During World War I he served as a signals officer in the British Army.

After the war, Tyrrell turned to psychical research; it was to become the consuming interest of his life. He devised an experiment the task of which was to pick out boxes (rather than to guess the designs on cards) and he was among the first to apply statistics to the analysis of results. His experiments met with much success, but after his equipment was destroyed in an air raid during World War II, he turned his full efforts to writing instead.

For Tyrrell, psychical research meant "the exploration of the human personality," especially of its unconscious levels. In all of his books, he was concerned with the relationship between ESP and the unconscious. In *Science and Psychical Phenomena* (1938), he suggested that the human personality underwent varying amounts of disintegration after death, and it was these fragments with which the medium came into touch, recreating out of them a personality more or less like the original.

Tyrrell's most lasting achievement was his theory of apparitions, first given as the SPR's Myers Memorial Lecture (see MYERS, FREDERIC W.H.) in 1942. The lecture was later revised and published posthumously as a book in 1953. Although by no means universally accepted (see APPARITIONS), the theory has been influential and continues to receive attention today.

Tyrrell followed Edmund GURNEY in believing that apparitions were hallucinations of the precipient based on information received via ESP from the agent, but he proposed that a two-stage process was involved. In the first stage a part of the unconscious he called the "Producer" became aware of the agent's situation via ESP, and in the second stage the "Stage Carpenter" produced the "apparitional drama," using such familiar psychological processes as dreams, visions and impressions.

By this means Tyrrell accounted not only for the veridical (evidential) aspects of apparition cases, but also for such troublesome features as apparitions' clothing and the fact that they were sometimes seen riding in carriages; these were props ordered by the Stage Carpenter to create a realistic scene.

Tyrrell was a member of the SPR Council from 1940 until his death and its president for 1945–46. He died on October 29, 1952.

His other books include *Grades of Significance* (1930), *The Personality of Man* (1946), *Homo Faber* (1951) and *Apparitions* (1953).

Further reading:

MacKenzie, Andrew. *Hauntings and Apparitions*. London: William Heinemann Ltd., 1982.

Salter, W.H., G.W. Fisk, and Harry H. Price. "G.N.M. Tyrrell and his Contributions to Psychical Research." *Journal of the American Society for Psychical Research* 37 (1953):63–71.

Tyrrell, G.N.M. *Science and Psychical Phenomena*. London: Methuen, 1938.

———. *Apparitions*. London: Duckworth, 1953.

U

Underwood, Peter (1923–) English lay investigator of the paranormal, including cases of apparitions, hauntings and poltergeists; president and chief investigator of the GHOST CLUB since 1960.

Peter Underwood was born on May 16, 1923 in Letchworth Garden City, Hertsfordshire, to a deeply religious family; his father was an elder in the Plymouth Brethren. The first of many encounters with the paranormal took place at age nine, when Underwood saw an apparition of his father hours after his father's death. He awoke his mother, who acknowledged the next morning that she also had seen the ghost, but she always refused to talk about it.

From an early age, Underwood was fascinated by stories about ghosts and hauntings, and pursued occasional investigations on his own and with friends. These investigations increased in frequency over the years, establishing Underwood as an objective authority on the subject.

Following a private education, Underwood began office work at the printing and binding works of J.M. Dent and Sons publishers. After three years he joined the firm's publishing office. In 1942, he was called to join the Suffolk Regiment (Infantry), but was later discharged for health reasons. In 1944, he married Joyce Elizabeth Davey. They had two children: Chris (b. 1946), a bank manager, and Pamela (b. 1949), the wife of a publisher.

Underwood's interest in hauntings led him to join the SOCIETY FOR PSYCHICAL RESEARCH in 1946, as well as other scientifically oriented organizations. He was primarily interested in spontaneous phenomena, but became interested in all aspects of psychic activity, including the induced phenomena of mediumship after witnessing flying trumpets and other apparently supernormal phenomena at a seance at the COLLEGE OF PSYCHIC STUDIES. In 1947, he first visited BORLEY RECTORY, where he encountered nothing paranormal, but did hear "distinct" footsteps in the direction of the Nun's Walk, said to be haunted by the ghost of a nun.

The same year, Harry PRICE, who made the Borley Rectory case famous, invited Underwood to join the Ghost Club. Thirteen years later, in 1960, Underwood became president of the organization, a post he still holds. He joined the prestigious Savage Club in 1966, and was made a Fellow of the Royal Society of Arts in 1987.

In 1971, he left Dent's and turned to writing, lecturing and media projects on the paranormal. By this time, he had become known as "Britain's Number One Ghost Hunter," and had had first-hand experience not only of hauntings, but also of experimental seances and experiments into precognition, clairvoyance, hypnotism and ESP.

As a psychical researcher, he has sought to represent the middle ground between skepticism and uncritical belief. Underwood has investigated hundreds of reported hauntings, and has found that the overwhelming majority of them have natural explanations. However, he does believe that there are different types of ghosts, and that some people do see them. He defines some of the major types of ghosts as:

- Elemental, or primitive or racial-memory manifestations, which occur primarily in rural areas and are attached to particular sites. Elemental ghosts are rare, but when they do appear they often are terrifying and malevolent; encounters with them are frightening. They have symbolic or magical attributes. Exorcisms do not always work.
- Poltergeists or psycho-activated phenomena, such as deathbed visions and crisis apparitions, that are perhaps triggered by the intense emotions and trauma surrounding death and dying.
- Traditional or historical ghosts, which are associated with old and historic houses. These ghosts

typically glide about in period clothing, following floorplans that existed in earlier times. They do not speak and seem to be oblivious to the presence of the living. Those that are identified usually suffered during their life on earth.

- Mental imprint manifestations and atmospheric "photograph" ghosts, which seem to be a kind of psychic energy imprinted on the atmosphere of a place, and which can be accessed by certain psychically sensitive individuals. The imprint seems to be a recording of the past that never alters. These ghosts usually must be seen from certain angles and at certain times, otherwise they disappear. Visual apparitions may be accompanied by apparitional sounds. Imprint ghosts usually disappear gradually over time, although Underwood hypothesizes that repeated sighting by the living can revive the psychic energy that keeps them going.
- Time distortion and cyclic ghosts, which are replays of events from the past. Underwood calls them "a kind of hiccup in time" and cities the VERSAILLES GHOSTS as a possible example. When these scenes replay periodically, they become cyclical or recurring ghosts (see HAMPTON COURT).
- Ghosts of the living, which may be projections of a DOUBLE as in cases of BILOCATION. These may be products of telepathy and CLAIRVOYANCE, or perhaps nothing more than errors in judgment. Interestingly, Underwood himself may have been the subject of projection in the 1950s, which he describes in his autobiography, *No Common Task*

(1983). He was in the habit of stopping at a coffee house in Goodwin's Court in London in the morning. The proprietor would bring him a cup of black coffee after he sat down. One morning Underwood went there with poet/author James Turner. The proprietor told Underwood that he had already come to the shop about a half-hour earlier, alone and wearing a different suit. "Underwood" had smiled and nodded at the proprietor, but when the man came out with the coffee, "Underwood" was gone.

- Haunted objects, which are associated with poltergeist phenomena (see SCREAMING SKULLS).

Underwood lectures widely, consults to the media, and is the author of more than three dozen books on haunted sites in Britain, the paranormal, ghost-hunting and other subjects. Among the best-known titles are *A Gazetteer of British Ghosts* (his first, 1971); *Into the Occult* (1972); *Haunted London* (1973); *A Gazetteer of Scottish and Irish Ghosts* (1973); *The Vampire's Bedside Companion* (1975); *No Common Task: The Autobiography of a Ghost-hunter* (1983); *The Ghost-Hunter's Guide* (1986); *Dictionary of the Supernatural* (1978); *Queen Victoria's Other World* (1986); and *Exorcism!* (1990).

Further reading:

Underwood, Peter. *No Common Task: The Autobiography of a Ghost-hunter*. London: Harrup Ltd., 1983.

———. *The Ghost Hunter's Guide*. Poole, Dorset, England: Blandford Press, 1986.

———. *The Ghost Hunters*. London: Robert Hale, 1985.

———. *This Haunted Isle*. London: Harrup, 1984.

V

vampire   In folklore, the undead. There are many types of vampires in beliefs found all over the world. A vampire is either the living dead—a resurrected corpse—or the spirit of a corpse that leaves its grave at night and walks the world of the living to feed off of them to survive. Some vampires, particularly in Eastern, Middle Eastern and tribal mythologies, are demons that attack at night, and are associated with night terrors.

The term "vampire" came into English usage in 1732, handed down from German and French accountes of vampire superstitions discovered in Eastern Europe. The Slavic vampire cult contains many words for "vampire" with different shades of meaning that refer to werewolves, reverants, demons that eat the sun and moon, humans who can shape-shift, certain kinds of witches, and monstrous sucking animals, as well as living corpses.

In the Balkans, where a vampire cult flourished in the late Middle Ages, a vampire was suspected of infesting a graveyard when people reported seeing apparitions of the dead that pestered them and bit them, or sat on their chests and suffocated them at night. Such symptoms are similar to cases of biting poltergeists and to the OLD HAG. Vampires also were blamed for plagues, invisible terrors that bothered people at night and wasting diseases that brought death. A search of graves was made, and if a body was found seemingly incorrupt with signs of fresh blood on it, it was decreed a vampire and was dispatched by being dismembered, burned or staked through the heart. Such measures are universally employed to keep ghosts of the dead from leaving their graves and wandering about.

Modern researchers have suggested premature burial as a natural explanation for the incorrupt corpse. It is more likely that normal decomposition conditions perhaps medically unknown in earlier times explain the vampire corpse. For example, it is normal for corpses to shift; this might give the appearance of life and movement when a coffin was opened. A corpse that is staked may emit noises interpreted as "shrieks" simply from air in the lungs being forced past the glottis. The "fresh blood" probably is the corpse's own blood, which often leaks from orifices. The shiny nailbeds that earlier peoples took to be fresh fingernail growth probably are the underbeds that are exposed when the outer finger nails slough off.

Western fiction and film have popularized the vampire as an entirely different creature, a glamorous and seductive living dead person who bites people (usually on the neck) to drink their blood.

Further reading:
Barber, Paul. *Vampires, Burial and Death: Folklore and Reality.* New Haven: Conn.: Yale University Press, 1988.
Guiley, Rosemary Ellen. *Vampires Among Us.* New York: Pocket Books, 1991.

Vanishing Hitchhiker   See PHANTOM HITCHHIKER.

vardøger   See ARRIVAL CASES.

Versailles Ghosts   One of the most famous ghost cases of the 20th century, involving apparitions of people and buildings in the Petit Trianon at Versailles dating to the 1770s prior to the French Revolution. Reports of apparitions in the Petit Trianon were recorded as early as 1870, but Versailles became an important and controversial case for psychical researchers beginning in the summer of 1901.

Some background history of the Petit Trianon is helpful in order to understand the hauntings. The Petit Trianon was commissioned by Louis XV for his mistress, the Marquise de Pompadour. The house was designed by Gabriel, the royal architect, and work on it began in 1762. In 1764, the Marquise died, and she was succeeded as royal mistress by Madame Dubarry. The house was finished in 1770, and Madame Dubarry lived in it occasionally. A carriageway led to the Allee de la Menagerie, the King's small farm on the grounds. Almost immediately upon completion, changes and additions were made. A chapel was added to the house by 1773, and room for it was made from part of the kitchen and service premises. Steps leading to the kitchen door were replaced with new steps that served both the chapel and service doors. Construction of the chapel necessitated the closing of the carriageway, the southern end of which was obliterated by 1771. Louis XV died in 1774, and his grandson, King Louis XVI, gave the Petit Trianon to Queen Marie Antoinette, who quickly made plans for changes in the garden.

On August 10, 1901, two English academics, Eleanor Jourdain, the daughter of a Derbyshire vicar, and Annie Moberly, the daughter of a bishop of Salisbury, visited Versailles. Neither was familiar with the layout of the area. They left the Grand Trianon and walked a long route toward the Petit Trianon, and seemed to lose their way for awhile. Upon finding the garden and entering it, Moberly suddenly felt what she later described as "an extraordinary depression." Both felt as though they were walking in a dream. The atmosphere was very still, eerie and oppressed. The surroundings looked unpleasant, unnatural and flat, almost two-dimensional. They saw two men whom they took for gardeners, dressed in period costumes of gray-green coats and small, tricornered hats. They asked the men for directions, and were told to continue straight ahead. They saw a bridge and a kiosk. Near the kiosk sat a man in a slouched hat and cloak; for some reason, they disliked his appearance. A man with a "curious smile" and odd accent ran up behind them and gave them further directions to the house; they thought he was one of the' gardeners they had encountered at the entrance. He disappeared abruptly. Near the house, in the English garden in front of the Petit Trianon, Moberly saw a woman, wearing a pale green fichu, sitting on a seat in the grass. Jourdain did not notice her. The attention of both women was drawn by a young man who came out a door of the house, banging it behind him. He looked amused, like the running man. They saw the carriageway to the house.

Later, in discussing their experiences on that day, Moberly and Jourdain concluded the Petit Trianon was haunted. They recalled that though a breeze had been blowing as they had departed the grounds of the Grand Trianon, the air had been "intensely still" upon their arrival at the Petit Trianon, and there had been no effects of light or shade. After encountering the two men in green, Moberly said, "I began to feel as if I were walking in my sleep; the heavy dreami-

ness was oppressive." The strange experience lasted about half an hour.

During the next 10 years, Moberly and Jourdain revisited the Petit Trianon in an attempt to unravel the mystery. On her second visit, on January 2, 1902, Jourdain once again encountered the heavy, eerie feeling, this time after crossing a bridge to the Hameau, Marie-Antionette's hamlet. She saw two laborers, dressed in tunics and capes with pointed hoods, loading sticks in a cart. She turned aside for a moment, and when she looked back, she saw that the men and cart were a great distance away. She also heard faint band music playing.

Moberly did not return a second time until July 4, 1904, accompanied by Jourdain and a French woman. They could not find the paths they had taken on their roundabout route in 1901, nor did they see the kiosk or bridge. Where they had seen the lady on the grass, they found instead an enormous rhododendron bush many years old. People were everywhere, whereas in 1901, the grounds had seemed strangely empty, save for the few persons they had seen.

After conducting historical research, Moberly and Jourdain believed they had seen visions of the Petit Trianon during the days of Marie Antionette in 1789, and that the lady on the grass was the queen herself, who reputedly liked to sit at that spot. Moberly theorized they had somehow entered into the queen's memory when she had been alive. The clothing they had seen was not worn by any of the grounds staff in 1901; the door of the house, which the young man had banged, was in fact in a ruined and disused part of the chapel. The kiosk and bridge they had seen no longer existed. They identified the two gardeners as the Bersey brothers, who were attendants to Marie Antoinette.

Moberly and Jourdain wrote their experiences in a book, *An Adventure*, published in 1911. They were derided by skeptics in the psychical research community, who criticized their research as unreliable and amateurish. They had not written down any recollections until November 1901, far too long a passage of time for memory to be certain, critics argued. The music heard in 1902 could have been one of the many military units which practiced maneuvers in the nearby area. The banging door could have been a sound nearby which they mistook for a banging door. In reviewing the book, Eleanor SIDGWICK, secretary of the SOCIETY FOR PSYCHICAL RESEARCH (SPR), stated that there did not seem to be sufficient grounds to prove a paranormal experience. Sidgwick proposed that Moberly and Jourdain had seen real persons and real things, the details of which became altered by tricks of memory after they decided they had seen ghosts.

Despite such criticism, *An Adventure* received wide publicity. Others began reporting similar experiences in the Trianons to the SPR. John Crooke, his wife and son, of England, reported that in July 1908 they had visited the Grand Trianon and had twice seen "the sketching lady." The fair-haired woman was dressed in clothing of another century, a cream-colored skirt, white fichu, and white, untrimmed, flapping hat. She sat on a low stool on the grass and appeared to be sketching on a piece of paper. She paid no attention to them until Crooke, who was an artist, tried to see what she was drawing, and then she turned her paper away with a quick flick of her wrist. She seemed to be annoyed. The Crookes believed at the time that she was a ghost, they said later, because the lady seemed to grow out of, and vanish into, the scenery "with a slight quiver of adjustment." The Crookes also reported seeing a man and another woman in old-fashioned dress, and hearing faint band music. The visions seemed to be accompanied by a vibration in the air.

Although the Crookes' experiences took place three years before *An Adventure* was published, critics were quick to point out that the family had said nothing until reading the book, and that therefore, their accounts were likely to have been influenced by what they had read.

Still other ghostly reports surfaced. In October 1928 two Englishwoman, Clare M. Burrow and Ann Lambert (later Lady Hay), visited Versailles. Neither had read *An Adventure*. They left the Grand Trianon and walked toward the Petit Trianon. Burrow felt a strange depression. They saw an old man dressed in a green and silver uniform, and asked him for directions. He shouted at them in hurried, hoarse and unintelligible French. He suddenly seemed sinister, and the women hurried on. Looking back, they were astonished to see that he had vanished. They also saw other persons, men and women, dressed in period clothing. When they spied the Petit Trianon through the trees, they were relieved. Later, Burrow read *An Adventure* and felt she had also experienced a haunting.

In September 1938, Elizabeth Hatton walked alone through the grounds of the Petit Trianon, heading toward Marie Antoinette's village. Suddenly, a man and a woman in period peasant dress appeared about six feet in front of her, drawing a wooden trundle cart bearing logs. They passed by silently. Hatton turned to watch them, and they gradually vanished. Hatton had not read *An Adventure* before her visit.

On October 10, 1949, Jack and Clara Wilkinson took their four-year-old son to Versailles. All three saw a woman in period dress, with a parasol, standing on the steps of the Grand Trianon. She did not seem ghostly, but when they looked away and then looked back moments later, she had vanished.

On May 21, 1955, a London solicitor and his wife walked through the grounds. As they left the Grand Trianon and headed toward the Petit Trianon, the grounds seemed strangely deserted. There had been a thunderstorm, and the air was heavy and oppressive. The wife felt depressed. Then the sun came out, and the couple saw coming toward them two men and a woman, who were about 100 yards off. They were dressed in period costumes. The woman wore a long, full dress of brilliant yellow, while the men wore black breeches, black shoes with silver buckles, black hats and knee-length, open coats. The husband and wife conversed as they walked. Suddenly, they noticed the three persons had vanished—and there was nowhere for them to go that was out of sight.

These and other reports were investigated by members of the SPR. Opinions as to the validity of the Versailles ghosts remained divided. Among the skeptics was W.H. Salter, who wrote in 1950 that faults of memory could not be excluded from the accounts. Salter observed that a public park is "about the worst setting for a ghost-story" from the standpoint of evidence, for it is impossible to ascertain later exactly who was in a park, and where, at a given moment. He suggested that the period costumes seen were the dress of living persons, for Versailles attracted a colorful range of persons from various occupations and countries.

G.W. Lambert was more inclined to believe that paranormal events had taken place. He discovered that in 1775 the royal gardeners, Claude Richard, 65, and his son Antoine, 35, wore green livery. Lambert proposed that the two men in gray-green seen by Moberly and Jourdain were apparitions of the Richards. Burrow, who had also seen a man in green, told Lambert that she estimated the man's age was around 60. Lambert found eight significant consistencies with what Moberly and Jourdain had seen. However, the conditions they described had existed at Versailles in the summer of 1770 during the reign of Louis XV—not during the days of Marie Antoinette, as the women had believed. Lambert's findings were published in a series of articles between 1953 and 1962.

In 1965, the Versailles "Adventure," as it was called in the media, was given a natural explanation by Philippe Jullian in his book *Un Prince 1900—Robert de Montesquiou*. Jullian said that Montesquiou, a poet, and his admirers were in the habit of spending days in the Trianon park at the turn of the century. Some apparently came in period costume, judging from existing photographs. Therefore, Moberly and Jourdain simply had witnessed Montesquiou and his friends rehearsing a *tableau-vivant* for an outdoor party.

Jullian's book had a great impact upon Dr. Joan Evans, who had inherited the copyright to *An Adventure*, which was in its fifth printing by 1955. Evans decided to put the matter to rest by prohibiting more English editions of the book.

The matter, however, did not end. In subsequent years, more hauntings have been reported and examined by both English and French investigators. In 1982, Andrew MacKenzie, a member of the SPR, theorized that all the experiences fit a pattern of an "aimless haunting," which does not seem to be linked to traumatic or violent events. Life at Versailles was fairly tranquil during 1770–71. MacKenzie suggested that the area acquired emotional power because its inhabitants of the time somehow sensed that their era was nearing an end.

The controversy over the validity of the Versailles hauntings remains unresolved.

See also RETROCOGNITION.

Further reading:
Coleman, Michael, ed. *The Ghosts of the Trianon: The Complete An Adventure by C.A.E. Moberly and E.F. Jourdain.* Wellingborough, Northamptonshire, England: The Aquarian Press, 1988.
Lambert, G.W. "Antoine Richard's Garden: A Postscript to *An Adventure.*" Parts 1 and 2, *Journal of the Society for Psychical Research* 37 (1953):117–54. Part 3, *Journal of the Society for Psychical Research* 37 (1954):266–79.
———. "Antoine Richard's Garden Revisited" *JSPR* 41 (1962):279–92.
MacKenzie, Andrew. *Apparitions and Ghosts.* New York: Popular Library, 1971.

vetala An evil spirit in Indian folklore who haunts cemeteries and reanimates corpses. The *vetala* is demonic in appearance, with a human body the hands and feet of which are turned backward. *Vetalas* are said to live in stones scattered about the hills; in Decca, they are guardians of villages and live in red-painted stones. When not reanimating corpses, *vetalas* love to play tricks on the living.

W

wandering ghosts See FLYING DUTCHMAN; PHANTOM HITCHHIKER; PHANTOM TRAVELERS.

Wardley Skull See SCREAMING SKULLS.

weeping woman See LA LLORONA.

Weir, Thomas (c. 1600–1670) At age 69 or 70, Major Thomas Weir, one of the most respected citizens of Edinburgh, suddenly announced of his own volition that he had long practiced witchcraft, black magic and unspeakable sexual crimes. His fellow citizens at first did not believe him, but were nonetheless scandalized. Weir and his sister, Jean, whom he implicated in his confession, were executed for their alleged crimes, and they left behind one of the most famous haunted houses in Scottish legend.

For his entire life, Weir had been a model citizen. As a soldier, he had served Parliament in the Civil War, and in 1649 he had been appointed commander of the City Guard. He was considered a most pious Presbyterian. No one could explain what possessed him to confess to crimes which surely he knew would doom him. In fact, his confession was so absurd in light of his outward conduct that initially others believed him to have gone mad.

Weir, however, persisted in his claims. He said he had long practiced black magic and necromancy, and was a servant of the Devil. He had committed incest with Jean from the time she was a teenager until she was about 50. Then, disgusted with her wrinkles, he had turned to other young girls: Margaret Bourdon, the daughter of his dead wife, and Bessie Weems, a servant. He had also committed sodomy with various animals, including sheep, cows and his mare.

Finally, an investigation was made of his claims, and at Weir's insistence, he and Jean were arrested and brought to trial. Jean told the arresting guards to seize the Major's staff, which she said was a gift from the Devil and the source of Weir's power. She said the staff would go shopping for Weir, run before him in the streets to clear the way, and answer the door at home.

The Weirs were charged with sexual crimes and were brought to trial on April 29, 1670. Doctors and clergy tried to help Weir, but he cursed them and said his damnation was already sealed in Heaven. "I find nothing within me but blackness and darkness, brimstone and burning to the bottom of Hell," he said. Doctors believed him to be of sound mind, but thought Jean to be demented.

Jean voluntarily confessed to incest, which she blamed on her brother's witchcraft. On September 7, 1648, they had traveled in a coach drawn by six horses to Musselburgh to meet with the Devil, and had signed a pact with him. She also confessed to consorting with witches, fairies and necromancers, and to having a familiar who spun huge quantities of wool for her and helped her carry out various evil acts.

Weir was convicted of adultery, incest, one count of fornication and one count of bestiality. On Monday, April 11, 1670, his death sentence was carried out, and he was strangled at a stake between Edinburgh and Leith. His body was burned to ashes, and his staff along with it. One witness said that the staff "gave rare turnings and was long a-burning as also himself." Jean was hanged on April 12 in the Grassmarket in Edinburgh. To the end, she was contemptuous of everyone.

After their deaths, reports circulated that Weir's cloaked ghost, clutching the magical staff, flitted about the city at night. Weir's house, Bow Head, was said to be haunted. A spectral coach was reportedly seen driving to the door to take Weir and his sister away to hell. The house remained vacant for about 100 years, until the low rent lured in a poor, elderly couple. On their first night, a calf gazed at them through the window while they were in bed, so they claimed. This event, interpreted as a sign of the

Devil, caused them to move out the next day. No one else ever lived there again.

Bow Head became a celebrated haunted house. As late as 1825, it was said to be full of lights and the sounds of spinning, dancing and howling. Weir's ghost was reported to emerge from the alley at midnight, mount a headless black horse and gallop off in a whirlwind of flame. His enchanted staff was said to parade through the rooms.

The house, in ruins from neglect, was demolished in 1830. Its site is not now known, but it is said that the Major's staff has still been heard tapping in the Grassmarket, and visions have still been seen of Jean's fire-blackened face.

Further reading:
Guiley, Rosemary Ellen. *The Encyclopedia of Witches and Witchcraft.* New York: Facts On File, 1989.
Harper, Charles G. *Haunted Houses: Tales of the Supernatural With Some Accounts of Hereditary Curses and Family Legends.* Rev. and enlarged ed. London: Cecil Palmer, 1924.

Whaley House Mansion in San Diego, California allegedly haunted by the ghosts of numerous people and animals. The central phantom is "Yankee Jim" Robinson, who was executed in 1852 for attempting to steal the only pilot boat in the San Diego harbor.

Robinson was sentenced to be hanged on the property where the Whaley House was to be built. According to legend, the hanging scaffold was not properly constructed. Robinson dropped only 5 feet instead of 15, and thus did not die immediately of a broken neck. Instead, it took about 15 minutes for him to be strangled, an agonizing death in which he kicked and struggled while dangling from the rope. Two of his accomplices were later caught, but they received light sentences.

The Whaley House, commissioned by businessman Thomas Whaley for his bride, Anna Eloise deLaunay, was completed in 1957. The Whaleys made it a social center. Family members, however, long believed that Robinson's ghost stalked the mansion, still upset over his brutal death. The children of the Whaleys heard heavy footsteps upstairs. The last of the children, Lillian Whaley, lived in the house until her death in 1953 at age 89.

After her death, the house fell into disrepair and eventually was scheduled for demolition. A citizens' committee saved it, and the Whaley House is now an historic home furnished with period pieces and open to the public.

In the 1960s, San Diego City College students staged an original play, *Yankee Jim,* in the courtroom of the Whaley House. Ghostly footsteps were heard upstairs after the play was over.

Various psychics and mediums who have visited the house claim that it is home to a menagerie of ghosts of men, women, children and animals. Only one other seems to have an identity: Anna Eloise Whaley, seen walking about the rooms carrying a candle and checking windows and locks. Poltergeist phenomena reported include burglar alarms being set off, windows opening and closing, a rotating chandelier, a baby cradle that rocks by itself, and a windmill that runs on a mysterious icy wind.

Further reading:
Riccio, Dolores, and Joan Bingham. *Haunted Houses USA.* New York: Pocket Books, 1989.

Wharton, Edith See MOUNT, THE.

whirlwinds In Native North American lore, whirlwinds are associated with spirits of the dead and with evil. The Shoshoni of Wyoming, Montana, Idaho and Colorado believe that whirlwinds are apparitions of dead people and that they can be dangerous. According to legend, a company of Shoshoni women went out walking one day, and a whirlwind arose. One of the women cursed it. The whirlwind attacked her and broke her leg, and destroyed her tent. The Gros Ventre also believe whirlwinds are spirits of the dead, and observe that whirlwinds often are seen in cemeteries when there is no wind anywhere else. In the myths and folktakes of the Mandan-Hidatsa, whirlwinds are the vehicles by which the spirits of the dead travel about. The winds swirl up out of the graves.

Among tribes in California and other parts of the West, whirlwinds are said to be evil spirits; a dead shaman's dust; or a shaman's "pain." The latter refers to animated objects, such as crystals and stones, which are believed to be both the source of a shaman's power and the cause of illness. Various beliefs hold that whirlwinds can poison, will cause miscarriages or will carry off children.

Further reading:
Eliade, Mircea. *Shamanism.* Princeton, N.J.: Princeton University Press, 1964.
Hultkrantz, Ake. *Native Religions of North America.* San Francisco: Harper & Row, 1987.

Whisht hounds (also Wish hounds, Wisht hounds, Wist hounds) Spectral hellhounds which haunt Wistman's Wood and vicinity in Dartmoor in Devon, England. *Whisht* is an old west-country term for "spooky" and is derived from *Wisc,* a name for the Norse god of wisdom and war, Odin (Woden). The hounds are also called Yell-hounds and Yeth-hounds in some parts of Devon.

The Whisht hounds are headless and glowing black. They roam the moors with their master, Odin, who carries a hunting horn or hunting pole. Sometimes their master is said to be the Devil or Sir Francis DRAKE; he is either astride a horse or on foot. The hounds are said to chase the souls of unbaptized children. Another story holds that the hounds themselves are the souls of unbaptized children who return to hunt down their parents.

Persons unfortunate enough to meet the hounds supposedly die within a year, if they do not perish that very night. It is particularly dangerous to meet them head-on. Anyone who sees the hounds must immediately lie face down with arms and legs crossed and repeat the Lord's Prayer until they have passed. Dogs who hear the Whisht hounds baying are certain to die.

The Whisht hounds most frequently are about late on Sunday nights. Baying and breathing fire and smoke, they sweep across the moors and end their run by vanishing over a crag. According to lore, anyone who pursues them goes over the cliff to his death.

Writing in the *Quarterly Review* in July 1873, R.J. King gave this description of the Whisht hounds:

> The cry of the whish or whished hounds is heard occasionally in the loneliest recesses of the hills whilst neither dogs nor huntsmen are anywhere visible. At other times (generally on Sundays) they show themselves—jetblack, breathing flames and followed by a swarthy figure who carries a hunting pole. Wise or Wish, according to Kemble, was the name of Woden, the lord of "wish" who is probably represented by the master of these dogs of darkness.

The hounds' haunt is suitably spooky: the moors are quiet, save for a nearly constant, low, moaning wind. Wistman's Wood is filled with eerie-looking, moss-covered oak trees, half-buried boulders, and an occasional pile of sheep bones, the remains of some predator's attack. Nearby are the ruins of a haunted prehistoric village. The hounds are said to emerge from the wood every St. John's Eve (Midsummer Eve).

The Whisht hounds have been seen since 1677 in the area of Buckfastleigh. In that year, legend has it, an evil man named Sir Richard Cabell was swept off to hell on the night he died. His body was interred in a pagoda in the local churchyard. Whoever pokes a finger through the keyhole of the structure will have the end of it chewed by a ghost.

The hounds also have been seen at Buckfastleigh Abbey near Yelverton, along Abbot's Way, led by the ghost of Sir Francis Drake.

Reports of the hounds have dwindled in the late 20th century, perhaps because of a decline in belief in folklore and the supernatural.

Both the Whisht hounds and BLACK SHUCK, a spectral black dog, have been credited with inspiring Sir Arthur Conan Doyle in his writing of *The Hound of the Baskervilles*.

See also DEATH OMENS; TREGEAGLE, JAN; WILD HUNT.

Further reading:

Briggs, Katherine. *An Encyclopedia of Fairies: Hobgoblins, Brownies, Bogies, and Other Supernatural Creatures.* New York: Pantheon Books, 1976.

Brown, Theo. *Devon Ghosts.* Norwich, England: Jarrold Colour Publications, 1982.

Folklore, Myths and Legends of Britain. London: Reader's Digest Assn. Ltd., 1973.

Wickland, Dr. Carl A. (1861–1945) Dr. Carl A. Wickland, a physician, and his wife, Anna, a medium, were practitioners of persuasive exorcism of discarnate entities. Using mild electronic current, Wickland said he could force a possessing spirit to leave its victim, enter Anna's body, and then finally depart forever.

A native of Sweden, Wickland emigrated to the United States in 1881. He married Anna in 1896 and moved to Chicago to study medicine at Durham Medical College. Following his graduation in 1900, he worked in private practice before turning to psychiatry. He soon came to believe that spirits played an unrecognized role in psychiatric problems and illness, and began research into this uncharted area.

According to Wickland, the offending spirit often did not realize that its earthly form was dead. Wickland "enlightened" the spirit and sent it on its way. If the spirit resisted, Wickland called on "helper spirits" to keep the possessing spirit in a so-called "dungeon," out of the aura (energy field) of the victim or Anna, until the spirit gave up its selfish attitude and departed.

To facilitate the spirit's entrance into Anna and its eventual departure, Wickland invented a static electricity machine which transmitted low-voltage electric shock to the patient, causing the possessing spirit great discomfort. Although resembling Dr. Frankenstein-style electric machines in movies, the device was a forerunner of low-voltage electric shock treatment currently used in psychotherapy today.

Wickland was not concerned with proving the identities of the possessing spirits. Rather, he believed that they seldom would provide evidential information because of their allegedly confused states of mind. Some, he said, spoke only in foreign tongues through his wife.

In 1918, the Wicklands moved to Los Angeles, where Wickland founded the National Psychological Institute for the treatment of obsession. The building is still standing and is occupied by seamstresses in the garment industry.

Wickland wrote of his experiences in *Thirty Years Among the Dead* (1924) and *The Gateway of Understanding* (1934). Anna Wickland died in 1937, the same year as medium Minnie M. Soule, prompting Wickland to go to England looking for another medium. He approached Bertha Harris, a celebrated platform clairvoyant and trance psychic, but she refused. Wickland's work was overlooked by the psychical research establishment, in part because of he did not document information that could help prove the identities of the possessing spirits.

See also DEPOSSESSION.

Further reading:

Rogo, D. Scott. *The Infinite Boundary*. New York: Dodd, Mead & Co., 1987.
Wickland, Carl. *Thirty Years Among the Dead*. N. Hollywood, Calif.: Newcastle Publishing Co., 1974. First published 1924.

Wild Edric Medieval fighter of England said to haunt the mines of the borderlands near Wales with his fairy wife and band of warriors.

Wild Edric rose to fame during the Norman Conquest of Britain in the 11th-century. Within a century of his death, his life and exploits were legend.

According to the Domesday Book, Wild Edric was a landowner in Shropshire and Herefordshire. He was a nephew of Edric of Streona, Ealdorman of Mercia, who betrayed King Edmund at the Battle of Ashingdon. King Canute ordered that his corpse be thrown over the London Wall as a result.

In the summer of 1067, Wild Edric led an uprising against the Norman invaders in the Welsh Marches. He overran Herefordshire and threatened the Norman garrison in Hereford. For two years, he and his men rebelled against the conquerors, ravaging the countryside. In 1069, they sacked Shrewsbury in Shropshire. Wild Edric was never beaten nor captured, yet for reasons unknown, he gave up his fight in 1070.

He made his peace with William the Conqueror, who received him with honors at court, according to legend. And in 1072, Wild Edric joined the Normans in a fight against the Scottish. No surviving records tell of his fate after that, or when, where and how he died.

In legend, Wild Edric was not permitted to die because he joined the Normans; instead, he was condemned to haunt the lead lines of his native lands

forever. He lives below the earth with Lady Godda, his fairy wife, and a band of followers. Miners call them the "Old Men" and say that the sounds of their tapping are clues to the locations of rich lodes (see KNOCKER).

The story of how Wild Edric met his fairy wife was legend by the 12th century and is the earliest fairy bride tale on record. According to the story, Wild Edric was out hunting in the forest of Clun one day. He lost his way and wandered about until nightfall, accompanied only by a young page. Finally he saw the lights of a large house, and went to it.

Inside, a group of noble ladies were dancing in a circle. They were taller and fairer than human women, and they were dressed in elegant linen clothes. As they danced gracefully, they sang a song, the words of which Wild Edric could not understand.

One of the women was a maid so beautiful that Wild Edric instantly fell in love with her. He rushed in and snatched her up. The other women fought with teeth and nails, but he and his page held them off and escaped with their prize.

For three days, the maid refused to speak. On the fourth day, she admonished him never to reproach her on account of her sisters, lest he lose both his bride and his good fortune, and pine away and die an early death. Wild Edric pledged he would not, and he would remain forever faithful and constant to her.

They were married in the presence of all the nobles far and wide. King William the Conqueror, hearing of the fairy bride, Lady Godda, invited them to court in London. And though others accompanied the newlyweds to attest to her superhuman origin, her great beauty was enough to convince the king.

For many years, Wild Edric and Lady Godda lived happily at his estates in the West Shropshire hills. One evening he returned late from hunting and could not find his wife. When she at last appeared, he snapped at her and wondered that her sisters had detained her. Instantly Lady Godda vanished, for Wild Edric had broken his pledge. He was overcome with grief, and searched for her where he had first found her in the forest of Clun, to no avail. He cried and wailed for her day and night, but she never answered and never appeared. Soon he pined away and died.

This version, however, is supplanted by the prevailing legend that Wild Edric lives on in the Shropshire lead mines, where he has been restored to his wife and a band of warriors, who share his fate. Whenever England is threatened with war, Wild Edric and his troop are said to ride out from the lead mines and gallop over the hills to battle the enemy.

They ride in the direction of the enemy's country. Their very appearance means that the war will be serious. The band was spotted at the start of the Napoleonic Wars in the late 18th century. Just before the start of the Crimean War (1853–56), Wild Edric was again reported riding out on his white horse, blasting his horn, dressed in green with a white feather in his cap and a short sword hanging from a golden belt. He had short, dark and curly hair and bright black eyes. He was accompanied by Lady Godda, who had waist-long, wavy blonde hair and also was dressed in green. Around her forehead was a white band of linen with a gold ornament. She carried a dagger at her waist.

Similar legends about the rescue of England in times of dire need center on other famous figures, such as Sir Francis Drake and King Arthur.

Compare to DRAKE, SIR FRANCIS.

Further reading:

Briggs, Katherine. *An Encyclopedia of Fairies: Hobgoblins, Brownies, Bogies, and Other Supernatural Creatures.* New York: Pantheon Books, 1976.

Folklore, Myths and Legends of Britain. London: Reader's Digest Assoc., 1977.

Hole, Christian. *Haunted England.* London: B.T. Batsford, 1940.

Wild Hunt   Spectral nocturnal procession of huntsmen, ghosts of the dead, horses and hounds. The Wild Hunt has it origins in Norse and Teutonic mythologies. On stormy nights, the god Odin (Woden), in the guise of a mounted huntsman, races across the sky with a pack of baying spectral hounds. The retinue roams about the countryside, reveling and laying waste. Anyone who is unlucky enough to see the procession is immediately transported to a foreign land. And anyone foolish enough to speak to the Huntsman is doomed to die.

The Wild Hunt has numerous leaders, both male and female. In the lore of northern Germany, it is often led by Holda (also Holde, Hulda, Holle and Holte), goddess of the hearth and motherhood. In southern Germany, she traditionally was called Bertha (also Berhta, Berta and Perchta), the name by which the Norse goddess Frigga was known. Bertha means "bright." She is associated with the moon, and watches over the souls of unbaptized children. Bertha's lunar aspect led to her association with Diana, the Roman goddess of the moon; thus, Diana came to lead the Wild Hunt as well. Her night train punished the lazy and wicked, but if food was left out for them, they ate it and magically replenished it before they moved on.

After the Reformation and the abolishment of the concept of purgatory among the Protestants, the Wild

The Wild Hunt.

Hunt became the fate of the unbaptized dead, especially infants. Such persons could not be buried on consecrated ground, and so were placed on the north side of the churchyard (an unhallowed spot), where, it was believed, they remained earthbound. They became fair game for the hounds of the Wild Hunt, which chased them to hell.

The Wild Hunt appears in British lore, where the procession is sometimes led by HERNE THE HUNTER or simply the Devil. In the spread of Christianity, pagan deities were degraded to the level of demons and the Devil. During the witch hunts of the late Middle Ages and Renaissance, the Wild Hunt retinue was said to include witches as well as spirits of the dead, and to be led sometimes by Hecate, Greek goddess of witchcraft and the dark of the moon. The Wild Hunt also is led by national British heroes such as Sir Francis DRAKE, who rides not on horseback but in a phantom coach or hearse that tears across the countryside from Tavistock to Plymouth in Devon, accompanied by demons and headless dogs.

A Cornish version of the Wild Hunt, Devil's Dandy Dogs, is a pack of spectral hounds that runs along the ground or just above it, hunting for human souls. A 12th-century account describes the hunters as 20 to 30 in number, and astride black horses and black bucks. Their pitch-black hounds had staring, hideous eyes. Monks between Peterborough and Stamford, England heard the hunt all night long, hounds baying and horns blowing (see WHISHT HOUNDS).

The Wild Hunt has been reported as recently as the 1940s, flying over the land on Samhain, ALL HALLOWS EVE. Unlucky observers are advised to fall to the ground and recite the Lord's Prayer in order to prevent their souls from being snatched up by the hellhounds.

See also DEATH OMENS.

Further reading:

Folklore, Myths and Legends of Britain. London: Reader's Digest Assoc., 1977.

Guiley, Rosemary Ellen. *The Encyclopedia of Witches and Witchcraft.* New York: Facts On File, 1989.

Hole, Christina. *Haunted England.* London: B.T. Batsford Ltd., 1940.

Maple, Eric. *The Realm of Ghosts.* New York: A.S. Barnes & Co., 1964.

Russell, Jeffrey B. *A History of Witchcraft.* London: Thames and Hudson, 1980.

Will-o'-the-Wisp   See IGNIS FATUUS.

Willington Mill   A strange haunting of a large house in Willington Mill, England, which involved noises, levitation and movement of objects, mysterious rains of objects and apparitions of people and animals. The phenomena plagued various residents for the better part of the 19th century, but no reason could ever be found for them. One of the residents, Joseph Procter, a Quaker, kept a diary of the disturbance, which was published in the *Journal of the Society for Psychical Research*, along with comments from Procter's son, Edmund, in 1892. A detailed account of the haunting also was published in the *Newcastle Weekly Leader* at about the same time.

Prior to the occupancy of the Procters, who were owners of the adjacent flour mill, the 10- to 12-room house was occupied by cousins of the family, the Unthanks. The Unthanks had heard that the house was haunted, but during their 25-year tenancy beginning in 1806, they had not been disturbed once.

For the Procters, the nuisance began at the end of 1834. After some months, the nursemaid confessed to being frightened at night by sounds of thumping and pacing in an unoccupied room on the second floor. Following this confession, other members of the household began to hear the noises, but searches of the room yielded nothing. The nursemaid left and another was hired, but was not told of the haunting. She, too, heard noises in the empty room.

The sounds began to manifest during the day; witnesses thought a man in heavy boots was running about upstairs. The invisible perpetrator seemed to have a mischievous sense of humor, for if the Procters or their friends slept in the room, sat up in it all night, or otherwise waited to hear the noises, nothing happened. As soon as they left, however, the thumping and running sounds would commence, according to the servants.

As time went on, other phenomena occurred, in daytime as well as at night. A white figure of a woman was seen in a second-story window; later, in the same window, a luminous and transparent figure that looked like a priest in a white surplice appeared. Other noises occurred, including sounds of a clock winding, a bullet striking wood, whistling and whizzing, sticks breaking and drumming. (See also DRUMMER OF CORTACHY and DRUMMER OF TEDWORTH.) Beds shook, moved and raised up on one side, and the floor vibrated. There were moans, cries and voices that seemed to say "Chuck," "Never mind" and "Come and get it." There were sensations of presences by the beds at night, accompanied by icy coldness and heavy, invisible pressure upon parts of bodies. The family took to sleeping with a candle burning all through the night; occasionally, the candle was mysteriously extinguished.

In December 1840, the phenomena inexplicably abated, and the Procters thought they were at last at peace. In May 1841, however, the disturbances started anew. In addition to noises, Edmund, who was then under the age of two, claimed to see a monkey that pulled his bootstrap and tickled his foot. The apparition was seen disappearing beneath a bed by other family members. On another occasion, a white face was glimpsed staring down from the stairs leading to the garret. Another child saw a man enter his bedroom, walk to the window, fling it open, shut it, and walk out of the room.

Procter's diary ended in 1841, but the disturbances did not. In 1847, the family admitted defeat and, for that and other reasons, left the house, after enduring nearly 13 years of haunting. On their last night in the house, they were tormented by continuous noises—thuds, nonhuman-like steps and furniture being moved about—as though the spirits were moving out as well. Mercifully, nothing followed the Procters to their new home at Camp Villa, North Shields.

The house was divided into two apartments and occupied by the foreman and chief clerk of the flour mill. These families were occasionally disturbed by strange noises and at least one apparition, but they did not seem to be plagued as badly as the Procters. In 1867, the house was rented to a firm of millers. The new occupants suffered greatly in the house, and at least one family refused to stay under any terms.

Joseph Procter then put the entire property up for sale, and the house was vacant for a time. During the vacancy, son Edmund and others spent a night in the house, hoping to hear noises, but nothing happened. Edmund also participated in a seance at the house conducted by an unnamed but reputedly well-known medium from Newcastle-on-Tyne. Apparently some phenomena were produced—Edmund gave no details in his account—but no communication was established with any spirits who might be responsible.

The house and mill were sold to a firm of guano merchants. One of their machinists reportedly was troubled by disturbances but could find no source or explanation.

Eventually, the mill was closed and turned into a warehouse, and the house was divided into small tenements. Around 1889–90, Edmund Procter interviewed several tenants and was told there had been no disturbances. The mystery of Willington Mill ends there.

Further reading:

Sitwell, Sacheverell. *Poltergeists: Fact or Fancy.* New York: Dorset Press, 1988. First published 1959.

Stead, W.T. *Borderland: A Casebook of True Supernatural Stories.* New Hyde Park, N.Y.: University Books, 1970. Previously published as *Real Ghost Stories*, 1897.

Wilmot Apparition   An apparition of the living, both collective and reciprocal, that occurred on board a steamship in 1863. The case has a number of unusual features that make it a classic in the history of psychical research.

S.R. Wilmot, a manufacturer who lived in Bridgeport, Connecticut, set sail from Liverpool, England to New York on the steamer *City of Limerick* on October 3, 1863. His sister, Eliza, accompanied him. Wilmot shared a stern berth with an Englishman, William J. Tait.

On the second day out, a severe storm arose at sea, lasting for nine days. The ship sustained some damage. Wilmot experienced seasickness and remained in his berth for several days.

On the night following the eighth day of the storm, the winds and sea abated a little, and Wilmot was at last able to fall into a much-needed sleep. Toward morning, he dreamed he saw his wife come to the door of the stateroom, clad in her white nightdress. At the door, she noticed that Wilmot was not alone in the room, and hesitated. Then she entered, came to Wilmot's side, bent down and kissed and caressed him, and then quietly left.

When Wilmot awoke, he was startled to see Tait staring down at him from his upper berth, which was off to one side and not directly above Wilmot. "You're a pretty fellow to have a lady come and visit you in this way," said Tait. Wilmot had no idea what the man was talking about. Tait explained that he had been awake when he saw a woman in a white nightdress enter the stateroom and kiss and caress the sleeping Wilmot. His description exactly matched Wilmot's dream.

Tait later asked Wilmot's sister if she had been the one to steal up to the stateroom, but Eliza denied it. Wilmot then told her about his dream and how it matched what Tait had seen.

The incident seemed so bizarre to Wilmot that he questioned Tait about it repeatedly, and on three separate occasions Tait related the same account. When the ship reached New York on October 22, Tait and Wilmot went their separate ways and never saw each other again.

On October 23, Wilmot went by rail to Watertown, Connecticut, where his wife and children were staying with Mrs. Wilmot's parents. His wife immediately asked if Wilmot had received a visit from her on the night he had had the dream.

She then told him that the reports of storms at sea had caused her great worry about his safety at sea. She had been further stressed by the news that another ship, the *Africa*, had run aground in the same storm and had been forced to shore at St. John's Newfoundland, with serious damage.

On the night that the storm began to abate, Mrs. Wilmot lay awake in bed for a long time thinking about her husband. At about four o'clock in the morning, it seemed to her that she actually went out to search for him. She crossed the stormy sea until she came to a long, black steamship. She went up the side, descended into the cabin, passed through to the stern and proceeded until she found Wilmot's stateroom. She described the room accurately to Wilmot, and said that when she came to the doorway, she saw a man in the upper berth intently watching her. For a moment she was frightened to go in. She decided to enter, and went to Wilmot's side, where she kissed and caressed him, and then went away.

When she awoke in the morning, Mrs. Wilmot told her mother about the experience, which seemed to have been a dream, yet was so vivid that Mrs. Wilmot could not shake the feeling that she had physically visited her husband aboard the ship.

The case was examined in 1889 and 1890 by members of the SOCIETY FOR PSYCHICAL RESEARCH, which had been informed of details by a friend of Wilmot's. Richard HODGSON, Edmund GURNEY and Eleanor SIDGWICK took testimony from Wilmot, his wife and sister; Tait was deceased. The researchers considered the case a remarkable one, despite the fact that more than 20 years had elapsed between the incident and the recording of its details. Even allowing for inevitable lapses of memory and the lack of Tait's account, the case differed from other collective and reciprocal apparitions. The researchers considered various explanations; however, none of them is satisfactory.

Collective apparitions, in which an apparition is perceived by more than one person, are unusual. Even more unusual are reciprocal apparitions, in which the agent and percipient see each other, as did Mrs. Wilmot and Tait. The Wilmot case is further complicated by the fact that one of the percipients saw the apparition in a dream, and another saw the apparition in a waking state as though it had material reality. (Wilmot said that as a child he had experienced clairvoyant dreams, but nothing similar to this incident.) The agent, Mrs. Wilmot, felt she was present on the ship, but the experience had a dream-like quality.

Gurney and Sidgwick throught the incident was most likely due to telepathy and clairvoyance. Mrs. Wilmot's intense anxiety and thoughts concerning her husband, and her desire to see him and comfort him, were communicated telepathically to Wilmot. Because he was sleeping at the time, they took the form of a dream. Sidgwick felt the dream strengthened the telepathic hypothesis. In addition, Mrs. Wilmot's desire to see her husband enabled her to see the stateroom clairvoyantly.

To explain the presence of the apparition seen by Tait, the researchers theorized that Tait in turn had received telepathic impressions from Wilmot, which took visual form.

Another possibility, which was dismissed by the researchers, was that an objective presence had appeared in the stateroom—a "phantasmogenetic efficacy," as they called it, located in space and within a range of Tait's senses. In other words, perhaps Mrs. Wilmot actually projected herself spontaneously out-of-body to appear on board the ship, and what Tait saw was her double.

From a modern perspective, the telepathy explanation seems cumbersome at best and does not adequately account for the apparition seen by Tait. An out-of-body projection seems more likely. However, modern researchers do not agree on what constitutes an out-of-body experience. The Wilmot case remains a puzzle.

Further reading:

Gurney, Edmund, Frederic W.H. Myers, and Frank Podmore. *Phantasms of the Living.* London: Kegan Paul, Trench, Trubner & Co., Ltd., 1918.

Myers, Frederic W.H. *Human Personality and Its Survival of Bodily Death Vols. I & II.* 1903. New York: Longmans, Green & Co., 1954.

Sidgwick, Eleanor. "On the Evidence for Clairvoyance." *Proceedings of the Society for Psychical Research* 8 (1891):30–99.

Winchester House   A sprawling mansion south of San Francisco built in the 19-century for the pleasure

Oliver Fisher Winchester.

of ghosts by Sarah Winchester, the heir to the Winchester rifle fortune. The legend of how this house came to be, and what took place within its rooms, is a bizarre one.

In New Haven, Connecticut, Sarah married William Winchester, the son and heir to the Winchester fortune. Her happiness was short-lived, for she soon lost both her husband and their only child, a daughter. Her grief may have been too much for her, for Sarah's behavior changed radically. She became a house-bound recluse. Her inheritance, a fortune of about $20 million and an income of about $1,000 a day, offered her no solace.

For comfort, she turned to the hope offered by Spiritualism that she could communicate with the spirit of her husband. To that end, she invited mediums to the house to conduct seances. None was successful in contacting William. Then Sarah found Adam Coons, a gifted medium in Boston. Coons said he could see William, and he delivered a message from him warning Sarah that she would be haunted forever by the ghosts of Winchester rifle victims unless she made amends to them.

Sarah was instructed to sell her New Haven house and move to the West, where William would help her select a new home for herself and the ghosts. According to legend, when Sarah found an eight-room house on 44 acres in the Santa Clara Valley, she heard a voice say, "This is it."

Sarah bought the house and embarked on a strange remodeling program that lasted for 36 years. She hired construction workers to enlarge the house. The crew worked seven days a week, following her instructions, which often had them destroying their work and doing it over again.

Eventually, the house spread over six acres. It was an architectural nightmare, with odd-angled rooms and wings, stairways to nowhere, secret passageways and doors that opened onto blank walls. In all, the house had 160 rooms, 47 fireplaces, 2,000 doors, 40 staircases and dozens of secret rooms and corridors.

During the construction, Sarah became obsessed with the number 13, and required rooms to have 13 windows, 13 chandeliers, and 13 lights and stairways to have 13 steps, etc.

Two special rooms for the ghosts were a windowless seance room and a secret chamber called the Blue Room. It was said that every night at midnight, Sarah donned special robes and went to the Blue Room to entertain her ghostly guests, who were summoned by a tolling bell. She also threw them dinner parties, always setting 13 places, one for herself and 12 for ghosts. She served them four- and five-course meals cooked by master chefs from Paris and Vienna.

Sarah died in September 1922, bequeathing her house to a niece with instructions that the ghosts continue to be welcome and cared for. Winchester House has remained a ghostly haven and now is a tourist attraction. Most of the rooms are sealed.

Further reading:

Cohen, Daniel. *The Encyclopedia of Ghosts*. New York: Dodd, Mead & Co., 1984.

Riccio, Dolores, and Joan Bingham. *Haunted Houses USA*. New York: Pocket Books, 1989.

windigo (also **wendigo, wiendigo**) In North American Indian beliefs, a dangerous, cannibalistic being. The Algonquian say it roams about forests, devouring hapless human beings. Hunters who become lost and are forced to eat human flesh become windigos. The Objibwa consider it to be an ice monster who can possess individuals and cause them to eat their own family members. The windigo sickness is the worst type of psychic sickness that can befall a shaman, and can be brought on by egotistical abuse of shamanic powers or loss of control in spirit possession.

White settlers in Minnesota regarded the windigo of the Ojibwa as a death omen ghost; the superstition was prevalent in some parts of the state as late as the early 20th century. The windigo was described as a 15-foot-tall being in dazzling white, with a star in the middle of its forehead. It roamed the forests, swamps and prairies. Its appearance, in either day or night, was inevitably followed by a death in the family.

See also BANSHEE; DEATH OMENS.

Further reading:

Grim, John A. *The Shaman: Patterns of Religious Healing Among the Ojibway Indians*. Norman, Okla.: University of Oklahoma Press, 1983.

Windsor Castle Twelfth-century castle built by William the Conqueror said to be haunted by four of the British sovereigns who are buried there. The royal ghosts of King Henry VIII, his daughter Queen Elizabeth I, King Charles I and King George III have been seen throughout the years by sentries. Other ghosts belong to people who had served the sovereigns in their households or armies.

Two other apparitions are those of a very old ghost and a very young one. The ghost of Richard II's forester, HERNE THE HUNTER, has been a frequent spirit for centuries since he hung himself from a tree on the castle grounds. Even King Henry VIII claimed to have seen him. In 1863, the tree was cut down and Queen Victoria used the wood in her own fire, hoping to "kill the ghost." Nevertheless, Herne's spirit is said to still make visits. Much more recently, a young royal guardsman who committed suicide in 1927 reportedly returned as an apparition.

Sentries have reported seeing the ghost of King Henry VIII walking along the castle battlements, but he has also appeared in the cloisters, which are said to be his favorite haunt. Henry's spirit is said to be accompanied by groans and the sound of him dragging his ulcerated leg.

One favorite room for ghostly appearances has been the royal library. The ghost of Queen Elizabeth I, the last Tudor monarch, appeared there before Her Royal Highness Princess Margaret. Elizabeth's spirit is said to have haunted the site since her death in 1603. Other visitations to the book-lined room were witnessed by Empress Frederick of Germany and a Grenadier Guard.

Two other spirits visiting the library are King George III, whose madness caused him to be confined to the castle during the last years of his life in the 1820s, and King Charles I, who was beheaded in 1649 after the English Civil War.

Further reading:

Underwood, Peter. *A Gazeteer of British Ghosts.* Rev. ed. London: Pan Books, Ltd., 1973.

Whitaker, Terence. *Haunted England.* Chicago: Contemporary Books, 1987.

witching hour   According to superstition, the time of night when ghosts, fairies and other supernatural beings are about on earth and are most likely to be encountered. By the strictest definition, the witching hour is the hour of midnight on the night of a full moon, the apex of the powers of witches, who are said to draw their magical strength from the MOON. The term is often used to mean the hour of midnight in general. Haunting phenomena occur often at night, especially between the hours of midnight and three A.M. According to popular occult belief, these are the hours when "psychic vibrations" are at their strongest, or the "veil between the worlds" is the thinnest.

Worth, Patience   Famous automatism case involving a drop-in communication with a literary bent.

Patience Worth, as the spirit identified herself, began communicating to a St. Louis housewife, Pearl Curran, through a Ouija board on July 8, 1913. The pointer spelled out the message, "Many moons ago I lived. Again I come. Patience Worth my name."

Worth said little about herself, acknowledging only that she had been born in 1649 in Dorsetshire, England to a poor family. She had never married, but had gone to the American colonies, where she was killed in an Indian massacre.

Through Curran, Worth began to dictate various literary works that consumed years of effort. For five years, Curran relied on the Ouija, and then she began to recite letters while the pointer circled the board. By 1920, she dictated in automatic speech.

The works were published and found an enthusiastic popular and critical audience. In the first five years, Worth's *oeuvre* totaled four million words in 29 volumes: 2,500 poems, plays, short stories, allegories, epigrams, and six full-length historical novels set in different periods. The most popular novels were *The Sorry Tale*, a 300,000-word epic about the life of Jesus that took more than two years to dictate, and *Hope Trueblood*, set in Victorian England. Other novels were *Telka, The Pot Upon the Wheel, Samuel Wheaton* and *The Merry Tale.* Worth also dictated poetry on demand.

The mediumship began to deteriorate in 1922, possibly due to emotional changes in Curran's life with her first pregnancy (at age 39) and the deaths of her husband and mother. Public interest also waned, and Worth made fewer appearances. Curran died in 1937.

Scholars have analyzed the Worth works and found them to be authentic in historical detail. Plots and characters are well developed. However, the Old English used by Worth does not appear much in writings later than the 13th century. It is possible that Curran (who left school at age 14) was reaching into her own unconscious to obtain the material, though it seems unlikely that an uneducated person would have such knowledge of historical periods and such literary skill. The case remains inconclusive.

Further reading:

Litvag, Irving. *Singer in the Shadows: The Strange Story of Patience Worth.* New York: Macmillan, 1972.

Prince, Walter Franklin. *The Case of Patience Worth.* Boston: Boston Society for Psychic Research, 1927.

wraith   See DOUBLE.

Wyley, Graham (1936–   )   One of England's leading contemporary investigators of hauntings, ghosts, poltergeists and related paranormal phenomena. Graham Wyley has investigated more than 500 cases throughout the United Kingdom. He has been called by the media "Britain's Number One Ghostbuster," and is consulted by numerous celebrities and members of the British aristocracy.

Wyley was born on February 24, 1936 in Harrow, Middlesex, to a middle-class family. He had a private school education at Harrow. He graduated in 1951 and then worked in finance in the City of London. In 1955, he joined the National Aeronautics and Space Administration (NASA) as a salesman and engineer. After 17 years, he left to become self-employed as a precision engineer. Health reasons required him to give up that line of work after eight years, and he turned to running a florist and greengrocer shop in Lynton. In the mid-1980s, he sold that business and devoted himself full time to investigating the paranormal. Wyley lives in Brixham, Devon with his wife, Thelma, who assists him in investigations.

From an early age, Wyley was interested in the paranormal. During his employment with NASA, he became interested in UFOs because of astronauts' accounts of encounters with strange vehicles. This interest eventually shifted to poltergeists and ghosts, and Wyley began to investigate reports of hauntings.

Graham Wyley. Courtesy Graham Wyley.

His investigations initially involved ghost-hunting techniques popularized by Harry PRICE, Peter UNDERWOOD and others. He soon discovered he had a natural clairsentience for detecting unseen presences, and began to rely upon his own psychic sense in assessing a situation. He takes photographs, using regular film, if he feels there is a presence at a site. The photographs and negatives often show unusual or unexplainable phenomena.

Wyley believes ghosts are earthbound spirits, the lowest form of the spirit world. They belong to persons who do not live out their intended lifespan, but die prematurely of accident, illness, murder or suicide. For various reasons, some of these spirits remain earthbound because of unfinished business. They usually haunt the place where they were happiest in life, or the place where they died. When their unfinished business is discovered, the ghosts are released from their earthly imprisonment and move on to the next higher spiritual plane. Successful exorcisms require the projection of loving thoughts and energy toward the trapped spirits. (See DEPOSSESSION.)

Wyley says that ghosts retain a low-level intelligence that enables them to make their presence known and to communicate with a psychically receptive individual. About one in 12 persons is able to sense a nonphysical presence, he says. Psychic investigation itself can lead to releasement of the earthbound spirits: as soon as their unfinished business is discovered, they seem to be liberated. Wyley says he can communicate with ghosts mentally, but does not consider himself a medium, because he does not access the higher planes where the ghosts go after the releasement.

Poltergeists, he says, are created under the same circumstances of premature death as ghosts; however, the individuals concerned suffered great abuse during childhood, which, post mortem, creates a negative emotional content to the haunting. Wyley has encountered no poltergeists that seem to be non-human entities.

Wyley's investigations have led him to conclude that poltergeists manifest according to a three-year cycle. During the first year, they make their presence known. In the second year, they cause violent movement of objects. In the third year, they make physical contact with their victims, causing accidents, marks and bruises, and perpetrating sexual assaults. Their purpose, according to Wyley, is to force humans to vacate spaces they feel belong to them. He exorcises them in the same manner as ghosts, by attempting to discover their unfinished business and by projecting loving energy to them.

Wyley also believes that some hauntings are not due to earthbound spirits, but are merely the psychic vibrations of events, which linger in a spot. These "recordings" have no intelligence and are not threatening in nature; thus no exorcisms are effective. Some of these recordings inexplicably fade with time.

According to Wyley, ghosts and poltergeists take energy from three primary sources in order to manifest phenomena. One source is leys, which are believed to be invisible lines of earth energy. Many haunted sites sit on top of intersecting leys, he says. A second source is static electricity. A third is bio-electric energy, the body's own force field. Poltergeists in particular draw bioelectric energy from children.

After years of investigating and exorcising spirits, Wyley found that his own psychic healing powers developed, including the ability to perform absent spiritual healings. He uses these powers to help individuals who seek his assistance.

One of Wyley's more interesting possessions is a miniature skeleton purported to be that of an adult man. The shrunken form, 10 inches tall, is called "William" and "The Little Man." It was found in 1974, walled up in an old sea chest in a Brixham cottage. Reportedly, whoever has owned or touched the skeleton has fallen into bad luck and disaster. Wyley came into possession of William in 1990. He keeps the skeleton in a box with a glass lid. Apparently he and Thelma are impervious to its alleged curse, for they have been able to keep and touch the bones without ill effect. The skeleton has been examined by a Home Office pathologist, who pronounced it genuine.

According to mediums consulted, the skeleton is that of William Young, an 18th-century slave trader from Brixham. Young had been five feet, eleven inches in height. In Gambia, Africa, he was cursed by a witch doctor and began to shrink. He died of illness at age 48 in 1747, only 10 inches tall. Local church records document that a small casket was paid for by the church at about the same date. The sum was six pence.

Wyley is the author of *Strange West Country Hauntings* (1989) and *Ghosts of Brixham* (1990), as well as books on the entertainment industry and celebrities. He also researches and writes on curses, voodoo and black magic.

Wyley has appeared on a television series, *True Ghosts,* for which he investigated reports of paranormal happenings, and interviewed celebrities about their experiences.

Further reading:

Wyley, Graham. *Strange West Country Hauntings.* Brixham, Devon, England. G. & T. Books, 1989.

———. *Ghosts of Brixham.* Exeter, Devon, England. Obelisk Publications, 1990.

Z

Zar See CULT OF THE ZAR.

zombie In Vodoun (Voodoo), a dead person allegedly restored to life by a sorcerer called a *bokor*. The zombie has no will of its own, but acts as a robot-like slave to the *bokor*. Meanwhile, others believe the person to be dead.

The word "zombie" probably comes from the Congo word *nzambi*, which means "the spirit of a dead person." Zombies may in fact be real, but not as the resurrected dead; they most likely are poisoned and severely brain-damaged individuals who give the appearance of being dead, according to investigations by such individuals as ethnobiologist Wade Davis, author of *The Serpent and the Rainbow* (1985).

Davis said he interviewed real zombies in Haiti, who told him how they had "died." They had been administered powerful poisons through food or open wounds that made them sink into a death-like coma. After being buried alive, they were "resurrected" by the *bokor* with another chemical mixture. The *bokor* beat them and starved them into submission; damage from the poisons left them physically and mentally impaired.

The poison, usually a powder, contains various toxic plants and animals and often human remains—the latter added more for grisly detail than deadly results. In the first stage, the *bokor* and his assistants bury a bouga toad and a sea snake together in a jar until they "die from rage," or exude more poisonous venom in their desperate state. The bouga toad, or *bufo marinus*, is a native of the New World that conquered the Old World of black magic as well. The toad's glands secrete *bufogenin* and *bufotoxin*, compounds 50 to 100 times more potent than digitalis, and cause death by rapid heartbeat and eventual heart failure. The toad also contains *bufotenine*, a hallucinogen.

Next the *bokor* adds ground millipedes and tarantulas to four plant products. The first is *tcha-tcha* seeds from the *albizzia lebbeck* tree, a poisonous plant that causes pulmonary edema, added to *consigne seeds* from a type of mahogany tree with no known toxic properties. Next the *bokor* adds leaves from the *pomme cajou*, or common cashew (*Anacardium occidentale*), and leaves from the *bresillet* tree (*Comocladia glabra*). The last two plants are related to poison ivy and cause severe skin irritations. All of these ingredients are ground into powder and buried for two days.

After disinterment, the *bokor* adds ground *tremblador* and *desmembre* plants, which Davis was not able to identify botanically. Next come four more plants: the *maman guepes* (*Urera baccifera*), *mashasa* (*Dalechampia scandens*), *Dieffenbachia sequine* and *bwa pine* (*Zanthoxylum matinicense*). The first two belong to the stinging nettle family, with tiny hairs that act like syringes, injecting a chemical similar to formic acid into the skiin. Dieffenbachia, also known as "dumbcane," contains oxalate needles that act like ground glass when swallowed. The name "dumbcane" comes from the 19th-century practice of forcing slaves to eat the plant's leaves, causing the larnyx to swell and making breathing difficult, speaking impossible. The last one, bwa pine, has sharp spines.

Next come the poisonous animals. Skins of white tree frogs (*Osteopilus dominicencis*) are ground with two species of tarantulas, then added to another bouga toad and four species of puffer fish, all of the genus *Fugu*: *Sphoeroides testudineus*, *Sphoeroides spengleri*, *Diodon hystrix* and *Diodon holacanthus*. Ground human remains can be added for effect.

The puffer fish get their name from their habit of puffing up their ugly spiny bodies into balls to ward off attackers. But such efforts are unnecessary, as the fish contain *tetrodotoxin*, one of the most poisonous substances in the world—500 times more toxic than cyanide, 150,000 times more potent than cocaine. One tiny drop on the head of a pin is fatal to a grown man. Nevertheless, many Asian people, especially the Japanese, love eating the fish, since only some parts contain the toxin. Specially trained chefs are licensed by the government to prepare the delicacy, but at least 100 gourmets lose at this culinary Russian roulette each year.

The poison's effects are horrific. Beginning with symptoms of malaise, pallor, dizziness and a tickling or tingling sensation in the lips, the prickly feeling extends to the fingers, toes, arms and legs, eventually leading to complete numbness. The victim salivates profusely, then sweats, suffering extreme weakness, headache and subnormal body temperatures, followed by decreased blood pressure and rapid, weak pulse. The victim then suffers nausea, vomiting, diarrhea and gastric pain. The eye pupils constrict, then dilate, then lose all corneal and pupillary reflexes. The lungs suffer severe respiratory distress, then the lips, extremities and finally the entire body turn blue. First the body twitches crazily, then it becomes completely paralyzed. The eyes become glassy, the body cannot move, and the victim may fall into a coma. Most terrible, however, is that the victim remains completely conscious throughout the ordeal—which takes about 30 to 45 minutes—and can watch and hear his friends and physician pronounce him dead, and perhaps witness his own funeral and burial before finally dying of suffocation.

Not all victim of tetrodotoxin die, but there is no antidote. Those who have survived described the early tingling sensations as feeling like flying, and tell of their terror as they watch the doctor work on them without being able to say or do anything. Knowing they could be buried alive was described by one survivor as true hell. Even doctors cannot tell whether the victim has crossed the border between life and death.

The *bokor*, experienced in administering just the right dosage of his concoction (although not every zombie comes back), raises the victim from his tomb in a day or two and then gives him a hallucinogenic mixture of sweet potato, cane sugar and *Datura stramonium*, commonly called the "zombie's cucumber."

Zombies supposedly are made to work in the fields and in bakeries. Stories tell of some working as bookkeepers and shop clerks. They are said to require little food, but cannot be given salt, which will return their power of speech and sense of taste, and will send the zombie back to his grave to escape the *bokor*.

Although zombification depends on the poison, making a zombie requires belief in magic and the faith that zombies are real. In Vodoun, sorcerers, not poison, make zombies, who have captured the soul—the *ti bon ange* ("little good angel") of the deceased. If the *bokor* takes the *ti bon ange* and not the body, he can make a "zombie astral," or a ghost who wanders

at the command of the *bokor*. To prevent this from happening, the deceased's relatives "kill" the body twice, stabbing it in the heart or decapitating it. Without the soul, the body is empty, matter without morality. Haitians do not fear being harmed by a zombie as much as becoming one.

Zombification apparently is very selective capital punishment. Dating back to the days of slavery and even earlier to Africa, blacks had always established their own judicial tribunals for keeping the community under control. By means of poisons, magic and extreme secrecy, these organizations maintained a cloak of fear about their neighbors, administering swift justice to any who broke the codes. Stories of people who banded together to eat human flesh, to dance in cemeteries and to raise the dead inspired enough dread to cause any lawbreaker to think twice.

Such legends served a purpose, but were not entirely true. Followers of the secret societies pray to Baron Samedi, god of the graveyard, dance in red or no clothing in moonlit ceremonies, carry coffins and sacrifice animals. Such performances make great theater. But they do not eat human flesh, and they do not make zombies for sport.

The societies were—and are—a well-organized system of local justice, in which no member or a member of his family suffers a hurt or wrong without redress. The Vodoun secret societies act quickly, thoroughly and clandestinely to punish wrongdoers and those who talk about the societies' actions.

Further reading:

Begley, Sharon. "Zombies and Other Mysteries." *Newsweek* (February 22, 1988).

Davis, Wade. *The Serpent and the Rainbow*. New York: Simon and Schuster/Warner Books, 1985.

Eliade, Mircea, ed. in chief. *The Encyclopedia of Religion*. New York: Macmillan, 1987.

Guiley, Rosemary Ellen. *The Encyclopedia of Witches and Witchcraft*. New York: Facts On File, 1989.

Zugun, Eleanore (1913–?) Romanian poltergeist child who was studied by several psychical researchers, including Harry PRICE. The most striking feature of Zugun's case is the scars and bite marks she suffered, as she believed, at the hands of the Devil.

Eleanore Zugun was born on May 24, 1913 in the Romanian village of Talpa. Her mother died when she was young, but otherwise she seems to have had an ordinary childhood until the outbreak of the poltergeist phenomena, when she was 12.

One day in February 1925, it is said, Eleanore set off on a walk to her grandmother's home, in the village of Budhai a few miles away. On the way, she found some money by the roadside. This she spent on candy, all of which she ate herself, causing an argument with one of her cousins. Overhearing the argument, her grandmother—a woman of 105 who was reputed to be a witch—told Eleanore that the money had been left by the Devil, and that by converting the money into candy, then eating it, she had ingested the Devil. Furthermore, she said, Eleanore would never again be free of him.

Eleanore stayed overnight with her grandmother, and the next day, stones pounded the house from outside, breaking windows. Small objects close to Eleanore jumped and flew about. The grandmother took this as proof of diabolic possession, a diagnosis in which the other villagers were quick to concur. Eleanore was sent home to Talpa, where, three days later, the phenomena broke out again.

The Zuguns were having dinner in the kitchen when a stone came crashing through the window. It was round and wet, like the stones in the river which ran close by their cottage. Eleanore's father hurried to get a priest, who marked the stone with a cross and threw it back in the river. A little later, the same stone—identifiable by the priest's mark—flew back in through the broken window. The family took this to mean that the Devil was so powerful that he could defy the mark of the cross. They decided to send Eleanore away for a while, and got a neighbor to take her in, but soon the phenomena started up there. Eleanore was beaten, and threats were made to send her to a lunatic asylum.

The girl ran home in terror. Her father arranged for an exorcism, but this only resulted in another series of incidents: an iron pot burst and windows shattered, flinging glass onto Eleanore's family and other villagers. A special mass was said, and a pilgrimage made, but nothing helped—the strange and destructive events not only continued, they became worse. Eleanore was sent to a convent, where other bizarre events occurred. A heavy table levitated, and nuns' habits were aported from one cell to another, through thick walls and locked doors. More masses were said; more exorcisms were conducted; Eleanore was examined by psychologists; she was hypnotized. But it was all for nothing; the phenomena continued unabated. Finally, she was declared insane and was sent to the local asylum.

Fortunately for Eleanore, the case had begun to attract press attention, and this in turn led to the involvement of psychical researchers. The first to arrive was a German, Fritz Grunewald, who visited Talpa and talked to everyone he could find with knowledge of the case. Grunewald persuaded Eleanore's father to take her from the asylum, and he witnessed some of the phenomena himself. Early in 1925, he returned to Germany to find friends for Eleanore to stay with; since he was a bachelor and lived alone, he could not take her in himself. Unfortunately—as if Eleanore's life were not already tragic enough—before he was able to make the necessary arrangements, Grunewald suffered a heart attack and died.

Luckily, a new benefactor was soon to appear. This was the Countess Zoe Wassilko-Serecki, a Romanian woman who lived in Vienna. She formally adopted Eleanore and took her to Vienna in September 1925. The Countess was much interested in psychical research, and part of her design was to be able to observe the phenomena at close hand. In this she was not to be disappointed: Over the next year, she recorded more than 900 events, most of which directly affected Eleanore. Bottles of ink were spilled over her or in her bed, her shoes became filled with water, her toys were destroyed, her books were mutilated, her sewing would vanish without trace. In many instances, the Countess or one of the several observers she invited to her apartment for an afternoon would be watching Eleanore at the time these things happened. Often they would hear sounds of objects landing, and occasionally they saw them materialize out of the air.

Two months after Eleanore's arrival in Vienna, a different sort of phenomenon began. This was the sudden appearance on her arms, hands, chest, or face of scratches, pin-pricks or bite marks. The first of these occurred when the Countess and an acquaintance were attempting to hold a mediumistic seance with Eleanore. Both her hands were being held when suddenly she cried out, drew back, and announced that she had been stabbed by something sharp, like a needle. This happened several times, and on each occasion there appeared at the spot she indicated a round, red, inflamed spot, with a darker red puncture mark in the center. For days after this, colored marks, such as might be made by colored pencils, appeared on her cheek.

These marks soon gave way to the bite marks, the manifestation of which would make the girl cry out even louder than usual. Observers would immediately begin to see thick, white welts arise on her skin. The bite marks matched those which Eleanore would have made herself, and they and the other marks were always on parts of her body that she could have reached, but they occurred so frequently when her hands were held or she was being closely watched that most researchers had no doubt that she was not deliberately inflicting them on herself. Eleanore was convinced that all these phenomena were the work of the Devil, which she called by the Romanian word, "Dracu."

Harry Price met Eleanore at the Countess's apartment in Vienna in April 1926 and was impressed enough with what he saw to invite Eleanore and her patron to visit his National Laboratory for Psychical Research in London. They made the trip at the end of September. The mysterious disturbances continued in this new setting, where they were witnessed by reporters and several prominent scientists. Price noticed that Eleanore would do her best to propitiate Dracu, leaving choice morsels—large nuts, pieces of cake or chocolate—around the room for him. She believed these peace offerings kept Dracu from hurting her still more. Price, however, monitored the girl's pulse rate and found that immediately after each event, it rose from 75 to about 95 beats per minute. This was a clear indication that Eleanore was in some way physiologically connected with the phenomena, and suggested that she, and not Dracu, was responsible for their production. Evidently she had taken her grandmother's statement about her possession so much to heart that she was causing herself to be hurt.

The Countess wrote about Eleanore in several sources and published a small book on the case (*Der Spuk von Talpa*, 1926). Not surprisingly, her reports met the same resistance from skeptics as do all reports of striking psychic phenomena. The Countess was accused of fraud, a charge she challenged in court. The magistrate found against her on technical grounds; the form of the article in question was said to show no intention of libel. Price and several continental European researchers who had seen Eleanore in person came to the Countess's defense, while other skeptics joined in on the other side. The Countess appealed the magistrate's verdict to a higher court, which again found for the critic, on the ground that his was "justified criticism."

Eleanore was 12 when the poltergeist phenomena began, and she was 13 when she was studied in Price's laboratory. She had not yet reached puberty. Poltergeist phenomena are often associated with children during this pre-adolescent period, and there was great interest in psychical research circles about how puberty would affect Eleanore's case. In fact, as soon as she began to menstruate, early in 1928, all the phenomena ceased. At the same time, Eleanore underwent a rapid mental and physical development.

Besides providing Eleanore shelter and studying her poltergeist phenomena, the Countess had nursed and nurtured her, in the space of a few months turning her from an ignorant and suspicious peasant child into a charming and responsive young lady. When the poltergeist activity ended, the Countess helped her adopted daughter become apprenticed to a Viennese ladies' hairdresser. Eleanore did extremely well at this work, gained a diploma, and returned to Romania, where she set herself up in business in the town of Czernowitz. So far as is known, Dracu never again interfered in her life.

Further reading:

Gauld, Alan, and Tony Cornell. *Poltergeist.* London: Routledge and Kegan Paul, 1979.

Price, Harry. *Poltergeist Over England.* London: Country Life Limited, 1945.

Tabori, Paul. *Companions of the Unseen.* New Hyde Park, N.Y.: University Books, 1968.

Wassilko-Serecki, Zoe, Countess. "Observations on Eleanore Zugun." *Journal of the American Society for Psychical Research* 20 (1926):513–22, 593–603.

INDEX

Boldface locators indicate extensive treatment of a topic